PEARSON   ALWAYS LEARNING

MSU Reader: Selections for EN 1113—Comp II

Ann Spurlock, Director of Composition
LaToya Bogard • Daniel J. White
Brad Campbell • Becky McLauchlin Whitten

Custom Edition for Mississippi State University

Excerpts taken from:
Literature and Society: An Introduction to Fiction, Poetry, Drama, Nonfiction, Fourth Edition
by Pamela J. Annas and Robert C. Rosen

ISBN 10: 1-256-27470-4
ISBN 13: 978-1-256-27470-4

Copyright Acknowledgments

Detailed Contents

Money and Work   373

Peace and War   437

Nonfiction

Nonfiction

PLATO

Plato (c. 428–347 b.c.), one of the most influential philosophers in history, was born into a wealthy, aristocratic family, presumably in Athens. A pupil of Socrates (and teacher of Aristotle), Plato left Athens for nearly 20 years after his mentor's death in 399 b.c. Upon his return in 380 b.c., he established the Academy and taught there for the remainder of his life. Much of Plato's philosophy appears in his "dialogues"—conversations between Socrates and his students. Three of these "dialogues," the *Apology*, the *Crito*, and the *Phaedo*, immortalized Socrates' trial and final days. Other well-known works of Plato include the *Republic* and *Laws*. Plato's belief in the separate existence of the body and soul and the existence of an eternal order of Forms (the Theory of Forms) have influenced Western thought for more than 2,000 years. In "The Allegory of the Cave" (from the *Republic*), Plato argues the need to differentiate between the world of the senses and physical phenomena and the world of knowledge.

The Allegory of the Cave

Socrates: And now, I said, let me show in a figure how far our nature is enlightened or unenlightened:—Behold! human beings living in an underground den, which has a mouth open towards the light and reaching all along the den; here they have been from their childhood, and have their legs and necks chained so that they cannot move, and can only see before them, being prevented by the chains from turning round their heads. Above and behind them a fire is blazing at a distance, and between the fire and the prisoners there is a raised way; and you will see, if you look, a low wall built along the way, like the screen which marionette players have in front of them, over which they show the puppets.

The den, the prisoners: the light at a distance;   1

Glaucon: I see.

And do you see, I said, men passing along the wall carrying all sorts of vessels, and statues and figures of animals made of wood and stone and various materials, which appear over the wall? Some of them are talking, others silent.

You have shown me a strange image, and they are strange prisoners.

Like ourselves, I replied; and they see only their own shadows, or the shadows of one another, which the fire throws on the opposite wall of the cave?

The low wall, and the moving figures of which the shadows are seen on the opposite wall of the den. 5

True, he said; how could they see anything but the shadows if they were never allowed to move their heads?

And of the objects which are being carried in like manner they would only see the shadows?

Yes, he said.

And if they were able to converse with one another, would they not suppose that they were naming what was actually before them?

Very true. 10

And suppose further that the prison had an echo which came from the other side, would they not be sure to fancy when one of the passersby spoke that the voice which they heard came from the passing shadow?

The prisoners would mistake the shadows for realities.

No question, he replied.

To them, I said, the truth would be literally nothing but the shadows of the images.

That is certain.

And now look again, and see what will naturally follow if the prisoners are released and disabused of their error. At first, when any of them is liberated and compelled suddenly to stand up and turn his neck round and walk and look towards the light, he will suffer sharp pains; the glare will distress him, and he will be unable to see the realities of which in his former state he had seen the shadows; and then conceive some one saying to him, that what he saw before was an illusion, but that now, when he is approaching nearer to being and his eye is turned towards more real existence, he has a clearer vision— what will be his reply? And you may further imagine that his instructor is pointing to the objects as they pass and requiring him to name them—will he not be perplexed? Will he not fancy that the shadows which he formerly saw are truer than the objects which are now shown to him?

And when released, they would still persist in maintaining the superior truth of the shadows. 15

Far truer.

And if he is compelled to look straight at the light, will he not have a pain in his eyes which will make him turn away to take refuge in the objects of vision which he can see, and which he will conceive to be in reality clearer than the things which are now being shown to him?

True, he said.

And suppose once more, that he is reluctantly dragged up a steep and rugged ascent, and held fast until he is forced into the presence of the sun himself, is he not likely to be pained and irritated? When he approaches the light his eyes will be

When dragged upwards, they would be dazzled by excess of light.

dazzled, and he will not be able to see anything at all of what are now called realities.

Not all in a moment, he said.

20

He will require to grow accustomed to the sight of the upper world. And first he will see the shadows best, next the reflections of men and other objects in the water, and then the objects themselves; then he will gaze upon the light of the moon and the stars and the spangled heaven; and he will see the sky and the stars by night better than the sun or the light of the sun by day?

Certainly.

Last of all he will be able to see the sun, and not mere reflections of him in the water, but he will see him in his own proper place, and not in another; and he will contemplate him as he is.

At length they will see the sun and understand his nature.

Certainly.

He will then proceed to argue that this is he who gives the season and the years, and is the guardian of all that is in the visible world, and in a certain way the cause of all things which he and his fellows have been accustomed to behold?

25

Clearly, he said, he would first see the sun and then reason about him.

And when he remembered his old habitation, and the wisdom of the den and his fellow-prisoners, do you not suppose that he would felicitate himself on the change, and pity them?

They would then pity their old companions of the den.

Certainly, he would.

And if they were in the habit of conferring honours among themselves on those who were quickest to observe the passing shadows and to remark which of them went before, and which followed after, and which were together; and who were therefore best able to draw conclusions as to the future, do you think that he would care for such honors and glories, or envy the possessors of them? Would he not say with Homer, "Better to be the poor servant of a poor master," and to endure anything, rather than think as they do and live after their manner?

Yes, he said, I think that he would rather suffer anything than entertain those false notions and live in this miserable manner.

30

Imagine once more, I said, such as one coming suddenly out of the sun to be replaced in his old situation; would he not be certain to have his eyes full of darkness?

To be sure, he said.

And if there were a contest, and he had to compete in measuring the shadows with the prisoners who had never moved out of the den, while his sight was still weak, and before his eyes had become steady (and the time which would be needed to acquire this new habit of sight might be very considerable) would he not be ridiculous? Men would say of him that up he went and down he came without his eyes; and that it was better not even to think of ascending; and if any one tried to loose another and lead him up to the light, let them only catch the offender, and they would put him to death.

But when they returned to the den they would see much worse than those who had never left it.

No question, he said.

This entire allegory, I said, you may now append, dear Glaucon, to the previous argument; the prison-house is the world of sight, the light of the fire is the sun, and you will not misapprehend me if you interpret the journey upwards to be the ascent of the soul into the intellectual world according to my poor belief, which, at your desire, I have expressed—whether rightly or wrongly God knows. But, whether true or false, my opinion is that in the world of knowledge the idea of good appears last of all, and is seen only with an effort; and when seen, is also inferred to be the universal author of all things beautiful and right, parent of light and of the lord of light in this visible world, and the immediate source of reason and truth in the intellectual; and that this is the power upon which he who would act rationally either in public or private life must have his eye fixed.

35

The prison is the world of sight, the light of the fire is the sun.

I agree, he said, as far as I am able to understand you.

Questions on Meaning

1. What do the prisoners believe they are seeing as they watch the shadows on the wall? How do the echoes of the voices of the men who cast the shadows reinforce this belief?
2. What happens when a prisoner is released from the den and is "compelled to look straight at the light"? What will he see at first; what will he see as his eyes adjust? Why will he initially not accept that what he is seeing outside the cave is real? What does the prisoner see when he is returned to the cave? What does he then feel about reality? Why would the other prisoners distrust him and want to "put him to death"?

Questions on Rhetorical Strategy and Style

1. What is the thesis of Plato's allegory? How would you summarize its application to life in general?
2. The dialogue presented here is built around a narration. Find where Plato also uses description and cause and effect within his story of the prisoners.

3. What do the den (the prison), the prisoners, the shadow, the sun, and the journey out of the cave and into sunlight symbolize in Plato's allegory? Why would Plato choose to use an allegory to present his ideas?

Writing Assignments

1. Write an allegory to argue against the philosophy of a person or group with whom you disagree—such as white supremacists (race), monarchists (politics), or monopolists (business). Chose your symbolism to clarify the argument. As Plato learned from Socrates, ask rhetorical questions as you make each of your points to confirm that your reader follows—and does not disagree with—your arguments.
2. How might you apply Plato's teaching to your life? Write an essay about a time when your concept of reality was altered because of some knowledge you gained—it could be learning the truth about a friend or becoming aware of the facts about an event or situation. How did your "ascent into the intellectual world" change you? How did others respond to you once they realized that you no longer saw things as they did?

HENRY DAVID THOREAU (1817–1862)

"I went to the woods to live life to the fullest . . ." And so begins Henry David Thoreau's germinal work *Walden, or Life in the Woods*. The book itself embodies many of the fundamental precepts of American Transcendentalism—a school of thought, led by Ralph Waldo Emerson, that stressed the human's intuitive ability to "transcend" the rational world of science and society in order to discover higher truths about life. Centered in Concord, Massachusetts, Thoreau's birthplace and home for most of his life, the Transcendentalists would have a large impact on Thoreau's world-view. In 1833, Thoreau was accepted to Harvard after barely passing the entrance exams. He went on to study math, the classics, and the natural sciences, graduating with honors in 1837. At about the same time, Thoreau met and developed a friendship with Emerson, who encouraged Thoreau to keep a daily journal and to write. Emerson employed Thoreau for some time writing for the Transcendentalist journal *The Dial*, giving him an opportunity to publish his own writings as well as cultivate his own developing thought. In 1845, Thoreau "left for the woods" and built a small cabin on the shore of Walden Pond (2 miles from any neighbor), where he lived for "2 years, 2 months and 2 days" writing and sustaining himself by fishing and growing his own food. It was here that Thoreau began to find his voice, writing about nature and speculating about the individual's relation to society. *Walden, or Life in the Woods* was finally published in 1854, after several years of crafting and revision. It is a difficult work to classify, incorporating naturalist essays, philosophical tracts, and social criticism—but Thoreau brings these disparate elements under the broad umbrella of transcendental thought, exploring such themes as humanity's relationship to nature, the individual's duty to self and fellow humans, and the importance of following one's desired path in life as dictated by the individual and not societal norms. Indeed, these themes run throughout Thoreau's writing. In recent years, scholars have focused more on Thoreau's style in relation to his philosophy—his use of hyperbole and puns; his construction of proverb-like arguments, enhanced by irony; and his candid, often humorous, precision of language. In addition to his massive 40-volume journal, his other works include *A Week on the Concord and Merrimack Rivers* (1849) and *A Yankee in Canada, with Anti-Slavery and Reform Papers* (1866). Though much of his work has been published posthumously, "Civil Disobedience" (published in 1849) is an essay written by Thoreau after being jailed for refusing to pay taxes to a Massachusetts state legislature that supported slavery. Like *Walden*, "Civil Disobedience" has continually roused successive generations to utilize nonviolent means for cultural change, influencing such leaders as Mahatma Gandhi in India and Martin Luther King, Jr. in the United States.

Civil Disobedience (1849)

I heartily accept the motto,—"That government is best which governs least;"[1] and I should like to see it acted up to more rapidly and systematically. Carried out, it finally amounts to this, which also I believe,—"That government is best which governs not at all;" and when men are prepared for it, that will be the kind of government which they will have. Government is at best but an expedient; but most governments are usually, and all governments are sometimes, inexpedient. The objections which have been brought against a standing army, and they are many and weighty, and deserve to prevail, may also at last be brought against a standing government. The standing army is only an arm of the standing government. The government itself, which is only the mode which the people have chosen to execute their will, is equally liable to be abused and perverted before the people can act through it. Witness the present Mexican war,[2] the work of comparatively a few individuals using the standing government as their tool; for, in the outset, the people would not have consented to this measure.

This American government,—what is it but a tradition, though a recent one, endeavoring to transmit itself unimpaired to posterity, but each instant losing some of its integrity? It has not the vitality and force of a single living man; for

---

[1] On the masthead of the *United States Magazine and Democratic Review*.
[2] 1846–1848; begun with the annexation of Texas by the United States; seen by many critics as an attempt to extend slavery to the West.

a single man can bend it to his will. It is a sort of wooden gun to the people themselves; and, if ever they should use it in earnest as a real one against each other, it will surely split. But it is not the less necessary for this; for the people must have some complicated machinery or other, and hear its din, to satisfy that idea of government which they have. Governments show thus how successfully men can be imposed on, even impose on themselves, for their own advantage. It is excellent, we must all allow; yet this government never of itself furthered any enterprise, but by the alacrity with which it got out of its way. *It* does not keep the country free. *It* does not settle the West. *It* does not educate. The character inherent in the American people has done all that has been accomplished; and it would have done somewhat more, if the government had not sometimes got in its way. For government is an expedient by which men would fain succeed in letting one another alone; and, as has been said, when it is most expedient, the governed are most let alone by it. Trade and commerce, if they were not made of India rubber, would never manage to bounce over the obstacles which legislators are continually putting in their way; and, if one were to judge these men wholly by the effects of their actions, and not partly by their intentions, they would deserve to be classed and punished with those mischievous persons who put obstructions on the railroads.

But, to speak practically and as a citizen, unlike those who call themselves no-government men, I ask for, not at once no government, but *at once* a better government. Let every man make known what kind of government would command his respect, and that will be one step toward obtaining it.

After all, the practical reason why, when the power is once in the hands of the people, a majority are permitted, and for a long period continue, to rule, is not because they are most likely to be in the right, nor because this seems fairest to the minority, but because they are physically the strongest. But a government in which the majority rule in all cases cannot be based on justice, even as far as men understand it. Can there not be a government in which majorities do not virtually decide right and wrong, but conscience?—in which majorities decide only those questions to which the rule of expediency is applicable? Must the citizen ever for a moment, or in the least degree, resign his conscience to the legislator? Why has every man a conscience, then? I think that we should be men first, and subjects afterward. It is not desirable to cultivate a respect for the law, so much as for the right. The only obligation which I have a right to assume, is to do at any time what I think right. It is truly enough said, that a corporation has no conscience; but a corporation of conscientious men is a corporation *with* a conscience. Law never made men a whit more just; and, by means of their respect for it, even the well-disposed are daily made the agents of injustice. A common and natural result of an undue respect for law is, that you may see a file of soldiers, colonel, captain, corporal, privates, powder-monkeys and all, marching in admirable order over hill and dale to the wars, against their wills, aye, against their common sense and consciences, which makes it very steep marching indeed, and produces a palpitation of the heart. They have no doubt that it is a damnable business in which they are concerned; they are all peaceably inclined. Now, what are they? Men at all? or small moveable forts and magazines, at the service of some unscrupulous man in power? Visit the Navy Yard, and behold a marine, such a man as an American government can make, or such as it can make a man with its black arts, a mere shadow and reminiscence of humanity, a man laid out alive and standing, and already, as one may say, buried under arms with funeral accompaniments, though it may be

> "Not a drum was heard, nor a funeral note,
> As his corse to the ramparts we hurried;
> Not a soldier discharged his farewell shot
> O'er the grave where our hero we buried."[3]

The mass of men serve the State thus, not as men mainly, but as machines, with their bodies. They are the standing army, and the militia, jailers, constables, *posse comitatus,* &c. In most cases there is no free exercise whatever of the judgment or of the moral sense; but they put themselves or a level with wood and earth and stones; and wooden men can perhaps be manufactured that will serve the purpose as well. Such command no more respect than men of straw, or a lump of dirt. They have the same sort of worth only as horses and dogs. Yet such as these even are commonly esteemed good citizens. Others, as most legislators, politicians, lawyers, ministers, and office-holders, serve the State chiefly with their heads; and, as they rarely make any moral distinctions, they are as likely to serve the devil, without intending it, as God. A very few, as heroes, patriots, martyrs, reformers in the great sense, and *men,* serve the State with their consciences also, and so necessarily resist it for the most part; and they are commonly treated by it as enemies. A wise man will only be useful as a man, and will not submit to be "clay," and "stop a hole to keep the wind away,"[4] but leave that office to his dust at least:—

> "I am too high-born to be propertied,
> To be a secondary at control,
> Or useful serving-man and instrument
> To any sovereign state throughout the world."[5]

He who gives himself entirely to his fellow-men appears to them useless and selfish; but he who gives himself partially to them is pronounced a benefactor and philanthropist.

How does it become a man to behave toward this American government to-day? I answer that he cannot without disgrace be associated with it. I cannot for an instant recognize that political organization as *my* government which is the *slave's* government also.

---

[3]From "The Burial of Sir John Moore at Corunna," by Charles Wolfe.
[4]From William Shakespeare, *Hamlet,* V, i, 236–37.
[5]From William Shakespeare, *King John,* V, ii, 79–82.

All men recognize the right of revolution; that is, the right to refuse allegiance to and to resist the government, when its tyranny or its inefficiency are great and unendurable. But almost all say that such is not the case now. But such was the case, they think, in the Revolution of '75. If one were to tell me that this was a bad government because it taxed certain foreign commodities brought to its ports, it is most probable that I should not make an ado about it, for I can do without them: all machines have their friction; and possibly this does enough good to counterbalance the evil. At any rate, it is a great evil to make a stir about it. But when the friction comes to have its machine, and oppression and robbery are organized, I say, let us not have such a machine any longer. In other words, when a sixth of the population of a nation which has undertaken to be the refuge of liberty are slaves, and a whole country is unjustly overrun and conquered by a foreign army, and subjected to military law, I think that it is not too soon for honest men to rebel and revolutionize. What makes this duty the more urgent is the fact, that the country so overrun is not our own, but ours is the invading army.

Paley,[6] a common authority with many on moral questions, in his chapter on the "Duty of Submission to Civil Government," resolves all civil obligation into expediency; and he proceeds to say, "that so long as the interest of the whole society requires it, that is, so long as the established government cannot be resisted or changed without public inconveniency, it is the will of God that the established government be obeyed, and no longer."—"This principle being admitted, the justice of every particular case of resistance is reduced to a computation of the quantity of the danger and grievance on the one side, and of the probability and expense of redressing it on the other." Of this, he says, every man shall judge for himself. But Paley appears never to have contemplated those cases to which the rule of expediency does not apply, in which a people, as well as an individual, must do justice, cost what it may. If I have unjustly wrested a plank from a drowning man, I must restore it to him though I drown myself. This, according to Paley, would be inconvenient. But he that would save his life, in such a case, shall lose it. This people must cease to hold slaves, and to make war on Mexico, though it cost them their existence as a people.

In their practice, nations agree with Paley; but does any one think that Massachusetts does exactly what is right at the present crisis?

"A drab of state, a cloth-o'-silver slut,
To have her train borne up, and her soul trail in the dirt."[7]

Practically speaking, the opponents to a reform in Massachusetts are not a hundred thousand politicians at the South, but a hundred thousand merchants and farmers here, who are more interested in commerce and agriculture than they

---

[6]William Paley (1743–1805), British philosopher.
[7]From Cyril Tourneur, *The Revenger's Tragedie* (1607), IV, iv, 71–72.

are in humanity, and are not prepared to do justice to the slave and to Mexico, *cost what it may.* I quarrel not with far-off foes, but with those who, near at home, co-operate with, and do the bidding of those far away, and without whom the latter would be harmless. We are accustomed to say, that the mass of men are unprepared; but improvement is slow, because the few are not materially wiser or better than the many. It is not so important that many should be as good as you, as that there be some absolute goodness somewhere; for that will leaven the whole lump. There are thousands who are *in opinion* opposed to slavery and to the war, who yet in effect do nothing to put an end to them; who, esteeming themselves children of Washington and Franklin, sit down with their hands in their pockets, and say that they know not what to do, and do nothing; who even postpone the question of freedom to the question of free-trade, and quietly read the prices-current along with the latest advices from Mexico, after dinner, and, it may be, fall asleep over them both. What is the price-current of an honest man and patriot to-day? They hesitate, and they regret, and sometimes they petition; but they do nothing in earnest and with effect. They will wait, well disposed, for others to remedy the evil, that they may no longer have it to regret. At most, they give only a cheap vote, and a feeble countenance and God-speed, to the right, as it goes by them. There are nine hundred and ninety-nine patrons of virtue to one virtuous man; but it is easier to deal with the real possessor of a thing than with the temporary guardian of it.

All voting is a sort of gaming, like chequers or backgammon, with a slight moral tinge to it, a playing with right and wrong, with moral questions; and betting naturally accompanies it. The character of the voters is not staked. I cast my vote, perchance, as I think right; but I am not vitally concerned that that right should prevail. I am willing to leave it to the majority. Its obligation, therefore, never exceeds that of expediency. Even voting *for the right* is *doing* nothing for it. It is only expressing to men feebly your desire that it should prevail. A wise man will not leave the right to the mercy of chance, nor wish it to prevail through the power of the majority. There is but little virtue in the action of masses of men. When the majority shall at length vote for the abolition of slavery, it will be because they are indifferent to slavery, or because there is but little slavery left to be abolished by their vote. *They* will then be the only slaves. Only *his* vote can hasten the abolition of slavery who asserts his own freedom by his vote.

I hear of a convention to be held at Baltimore, or elsewhere, for the selection of a candidate for the Presidency, made up chiefly of editors, and men who are politicians by profession; but I think, what is it to any independent, intelligent, and respectable man what decision they may come to, shall we not have the advantage of his wisdom and honesty, nevertheless? Can we not count upon some independent votes? Are there not many individuals in the country who do not attend conventions? But no: I find that the respectable man, so called, has immediately drifted from his position, and despairs of his country, when his country has more reason to despair of him. He forthwith adopts one of the candidates thus selected as the only *available* one, thus proving that he is himself *available* for any purposes of the demagogue. His vote is of no more worth than that of any unprincipled foreigner or hireling native, who may have been bought. Oh for a man who is a *man,* and, as my neighbor says, has a bone in his back which you cannot pass your hand through! Our statistics are at fault: the population has been returned too large. How many *men* are there to a square thousand miles in this country? Hardly one. Does not America offer any inducement for men to settle here? The American has dwindled into an Odd Fellow,—one who may be known by the development of his organ of gregariousness, and a manifest lack of intellect and cheerful self-reliance; whose first and chief concern, on coming into the world, is to see that the alms-houses are in good repair; and, before yet he has lawfully donned the virile garb, to collect a fund for the support of the widows and orphans that may be; who, in short, ventures to live only by the aid of the mutual insurance company, which has promised to bury him decently.

It is not a man's duty, as a matter of course, to devote himself to the eradication of any, even the most enormous wrong; he may still properly have other concerns to engage him; but it is his duty, at least, to wash his hands of it, and, if he gives it no thought longer, not to give it practically his support. If I devote myself to other pursuits and contemplations, I must first see, at least, that I do not pursue them sitting upon another man's shoulders. I must get off him first, that he may pursue his contemplations too. See what gross inconsistency is tolerated. I have heard some of my townsmen say, "I should like to have them order me out to help put down an insurrection of the slaves, or to march to Mexico,—see if I would go;" and yet these very men have each, directly by their allegiance, and so indirectly, at least, by their money, furnished a substitute. The soldier is applauded who refuses to serve in an unjust war by those who do not refuse to sustain the unjust government which makes the war; is applauded by those whose own act and authority he disregards and sets at nought; as if the State were penitent to that degree that it hired one to scourge it while it sinned, but not to that degree that it left off sinning for a moment. Thus, under the name of order and civil government, we are all made at last to pay homage to and support our own meanness. After the first blush of sin, comes its indifference; and from immoral it becomes, as it were, *un*moral, and not quite unnecessary to that life which we have made.

The broadest and most prevalent error requires the most disinterested virtue to sustain it. The slight reproach to which the virtue of patriotism is commonly liable, the noble are most likely to incur. Those who, while they disapprove of the character and measures of a government, yield to it their allegiance and support, are undoubtedly its most conscientious supporters, and so frequently the most serious obstacles to reform. Some are petitioning the State to dissolve the Union, to disregard the requisitions of the President. Why do they not dissolve it themselves,—the union between themselves and the State,—and refuse to pay their quota into its treasury? Do not they stand in the same relation to the State, that the State does to the Union? And have not the same reasons prevented the State from resisting the Union, which have prevented them from resisting the State?

How can a man be satisfied to entertain an opinion merely, and enjoy *it?* Is there any enjoyment in it, if his opinion is that he is aggrieved? If you are cheated out of a single dollar by your neighbor, you do not rest satisfied with knowing that you are cheated, or with saying that you are cheated, or even with petitioning him to pay you your due; but you take effectual steps at once to obtain the full amount, and see that you are never cheated again. Action from principle,—the perception and the performance of right,—changes things and relations; it is essentially revolutionary, and does not consist wholly with any thing which was. It not only divides states and churches, it divides families; aye, it divides the *individual,* separating the diabolical in him from the divine.

Unjust laws exist: shall we be content to obey them, or shall we endeavor to amend them, and obey them until we have succeeded, or shall we transgress them at once? Men generally, under such a government as this, think that they ought to wait until they have persuaded the majority to alter them. They think that, if they should resist, the remedy would be worse than the evil. But it is the fault of the government itself that the remedy *is* worse than the evil. *It* makes it worse. Why is it not more apt to anticipate and provide for reform? Why does it not cherish its wise minority? Why does it cry and resist before it is hurt? Why does it not encourage its citizens to be on the alert to point out its faults, and *do* better than it would have them? Why does it always crucify Christ, and excommunicate Copernicus and Luther, and pronounce Washington and Franklin rebels?

One would think, that a deliberate and practical denial of its authority was the only offense never contemplated by government; else, why has it not assigned its definite, its suitable and proportionate penalty? If a man who has no property refuses but once to earn nine shillings for the State, he is put in prison for a period unlimited by any law that I know, and determined only by the discretion of those who placed him there; but if he should steal ninety times nine shillings from the State, he is soon permitted to go at large again.

If the injustice is part of the necessary friction of the machine of government, let it go, let it go: perchance it will wear smooth,—certainly the machine will wear out. If the injustice has a spring, or a pulley, or a rope, or a crank, exclusively for itself, then perhaps you may consider whether the remedy will not be worse than the evil; but if it is of such a nature that it requires you to be the agent of injustice to another, then, I say, break the law. Let your life be a counter friction to stop the machine. What I have to do is to see, at any rate, that I do not lend myself to the wrong which I condemn.

As for adopting the ways which the State has provided for remedying the evil, I know not of such ways. They take too much time, and a man's life will be gone. I have other affairs to attend to. I came into this world, not chiefly to make this a good place to live in, but to live in it, be it good or bad. A man has not every thing to do, but something; and because he cannot do *every thing,* it is not necessary that he should do *something* wrong. It is not my business to be petitioning the governor or the legislature any more than it is theirs to petition me; and, if they should not hear my petition, what should I do then? But in this case the State has provided no way; its very Constitution is the evil. This may seem to be harsh and stubborn and unconciliatory; but it is to treat with the utmost kindness and consideration the only spirit that can appreciate or deserves it. So is all change for the better, like birth and death which convulse the body.

I do not hesitate to say, that those who call themselves abolitionists should at once effectually withdraw their support, both in person and property, from the government of Massachusetts, and not wait till they constitute a majority of one, before they suffer the right to prevail through them. I think that it is enough if they have God on their side, without waiting for that other one. Moreover, any man more right than his neighbors, constitutes a majority of one already.

I meet this American government, or its representative the State government, directly, and face to face, once a year, no more, in the person of its tax-gatherer; this is the only mode in which a man situated as I am necessarily meets it; and it then says distinctly, Recognize me; and the simplest, the most effectual, and, in the present posture of affairs, the indispensablest mode of treating with it on this head, of expressing your little satisfaction with and love for it, is to deny it then. My civil neighbor, the tax-gatherer, is the very man I have to deal with,—for it is, after all, with men and not with parchment that I quarrel,—and he has voluntarily chosen to be an agent of the government. How shall he ever know well what he is and does as an officer of the government, or as a man, until he is obliged to consider whether he shall treat me, his neighbor, for whom he has respect, as a neighbor and well-disposed man, or as a maniac and disturber of the peace, and see if he can get over this obstruction to his neighborliness without a ruder and more impetuous thought or speech corresponding with his action? I know this well, that if one thousand, if one hundred, if ten men whom I could name,—if ten *honest* men only,–aye, if *one* HONEST man, in this State of Massachusetts, *ceasing to hold slaves,* were actually to withdraw from this copartnership, and be locked up in the county jail therefor, it would be the abolition of slavery in America. For it matters not how small the beginning may seem to be: what is once well done is done for ever. But we love better to talk about it: that we say is our mission. Reform keeps many scores of newspapers in its service, but not one man. If my esteemed neighbor, the State's ambassador,[8] who will devote his days to the settlement of the question of human rights in the Council Chamber, instead of being threatened with the prisons of Carolina, were to sit down the prisoner of Massachusetts, that State which is so anxious to foist the sin of slavery upon her sister,—though at present she can discover only an act of inhospitality to be the ground of a quarrel with her,—the Legislature would not wholly waive the subject the following winter.

Under a government which imprisons any unjustly, the true place for a just man is also a prison. The proper place to-day, the only place which Massachusetts has provided for her freer and less desponding spirits, is in her prisons, to

---

[8]Samuel Hoar (1778–1856), sent by the state of Massachusetts to South Carolina to help black sailors from Massachusetts who were taken from their ships there, was evicted from Charleston by the South Carolina legislature.

be put out and locked out of the State by her own act, as they have already put themselves out by their principles. It is there that the fugitive slave, and the Mexican prisoner on parole, and the Indian come to plead the wrongs of his race, should find them; on that separate, but more free and honorable ground, where the State places those who are not *with* her but *against* her,—the only house in a slave-state in which a free man can abide with honor. If any think that their influence would be lost there, and their voices no longer afflict the ear of the State, that they would not be as an enemy within its walls, they do not know by how much truth is stronger than error, nor how much more eloquently and effectively he can combat injustice who has experienced a little in his own person. Cast your whole vote, not a strip of paper merely, but your whole influence. A minority is powerless while it conforms to the majority; it is not even a minority then; but it is irresistible when it clogs by its whole weight. If the alternative is to keep all just men in prison, or give up war and slavery, the State will not hesitate which to choose. If a thousand men were not to pay their tax-bills this year, that would not be a violent and bloody measure, as it would be to pay them, and enable the State to commit violence and shed innocent blood. This is, in fact, the definition of a peaceable revolution, if any such is possible. If the tax-gatherer, or any other public officer, asks me, as one has done, "But what shall I do?" my answer is, "If you really wish to do any thing, resign your office." When the subject has refused allegiance, and the officer has resigned his office, then the revolution is accomplished. But even suppose blood should flow. Is there not a sort of blood shed when the conscience is wounded? Through this wound a man's real manhood and immortality flow out, and he bleeds to an everlasting death. I see this blood flowing now.

I have contemplated the imprisonment of the offender, rather than the seizure of his goods,—though both will serve the same purpose,—because they who assert the purest right, and consequently are most dangerous to a corrupt State, commonly have not spent much time in accumulating property. To such the State renders comparatively small service, and a slight tax is wont to appear exorbitant, particularly if they are obliged to earn it by special labor with their hands. If there were one who lived wholly without the use of money, the State itself would hesitate to demand it of him. But the rich man—not to make any invidious comparison—is always sold to the institution which makes him rich. Absolutely speaking, the more money, the less virtue; for money comes between a man and his objects, and obtains them for him; and it was certainly no great virtue to obtain it. It puts to rest many questions which he would otherwise be taxed to answer; while the only new question which it puts is the hard but superfluous one, how to spend it. Thus his moral ground is taken from under his feet. The opportunities of living are diminished in proportion as what are called the "means" are increased. The best thing a man can do for his culture when he is rich is to endeavour to carry out those schemes which he entertained when he was poor. Christ answered the Herodians according to their condition. "Show me the tribute-money," said he;—and one took a penny out of his pocket;—If you use money which has the image of Caesar on it, and which he has made current and valuable, that is, *if you are men of the State,* and gladly enjoy the advantages of Caesar's government, then pay him back some of his own when he demands it; "Render therefore to Caesar that which is Caesar's, and to God those things which are God's,"—leaving them no wiser than before as to which was which; for they did not wish to know.

When I converse with the freest of my neighbors, I perceive that, whatever they may say about the magnitude and seriousness of the question, and their regard for the public tranquility, the long and the short of the matter is, that they cannot spare the protection of the existing government, and they dread the consequences of disobedience to it to their property and families. For my own part, I should not like to think that I ever rely on the protection of the State. But, if I deny the authority of the State when it presents its tax-bill, it will soon take and waste all my property, and so harass me and my children without end. This is hard. This makes it impossible for a man to live honestly and at the same time comfortably in outward respects. It will not be worth the while to accumulate property; that would be sure to go again. You must hire or squat somewhere, and raise but a small crop, and eat that soon. You must live within yourself, and depend upon yourself, always tucked up and ready for a start, and not have many affairs. A man may grow rich in Turkey even, if he will be in all respects a good subject of the Turkish government. Confucius said,—"If a State is governed by the principles of reason, poverty and misery are subjects of shame; if a State is not governed by the principles of reason, riches and honors are the subjects of shame." No: until I want the protection of Massachusetts to be extended to me in some distant southern port, where my liberty is endangered, or until I am bent solely on building up an estate at home by peaceful enterprise, I can afford to refuse allegiance to Massachusetts, and her right to my property and life. It costs me less in every sense to incur the penalty of disobedience to the State, than it would to obey. I should feel as if I were worth less in that case.

Some years ago, the State met me in behalf of the church, and commanded me to pay a certain sum toward the support of a clergyman whose preaching my father attended, but never I myself. "Pay it," it said, "or be locked up in the jail." I declined to pay. But, unfortunately, another man saw fit to pay it. I did not see why the schoolmaster should be taxed to support the priest, and not the priest the schoolmaster; for I was not the State's schoolmaster, but I supported myself by voluntary subscription. I did not see why the lyceum should not present its tax-bill, and have the State to back its demand, as well as the church. However, at the request of the selectmen, I condescended to make some such statement as this in writing:—"Know all men by these presents, that I, Henry Thoreau, do not wish to be regarded as a member of any incorporated society which I have not joined." This I gave to the town-clerk; and he has it. The State, having thus learned that I did not wish to be regarded as a member of that church, has never made a like demand on me since; though it said that it must adhere to its original presumption that time. If I had known how to name them, I should then have signed off in detail from all the societies which I never signed on to; but I did not know where to find a complete list.

I have paid no poll-tax for six years. I was put into a jail once on this account, for one night; and, as I stood considering the walls of solid stone, two or three feet thick, the door of wood and iron, a foot thick, and the iron grating which strained the light, I could not help being struck with the foolishness of that institution which treated me as if I were mere flesh and blood and bones, to be locked up. I wondered that it should have concluded at length that this was the best use it could put me to, and had never thought to avail itself of my services in some way. I saw that, if there was a wall of stone between me and my townsmen, there was a still more difficult one to climb or break through, before they could get to be as free as I was. I did not for a moment feel confined, and the walls seemed a great waste of stone and mortar. I felt as if I alone of all my townsmen had paid my tax. They plainly did not know how to treat me, but behaved like persons who are underbred. In every threat and in every compliment there was a blunder; for they thought that my chief desire was to stand the other side of that stone wall. I could not but smile to see how industriously they locked the door on my meditations, which followed them out again without let or hinderance, and *they* were really all that was dangerous. As they could not reach me, they had resolved to punish my body; just as boys, if they cannot come at some person against whom they have a spite, will abuse his dog. I saw that the State was half-witted, that it was timid as a lone woman with her silver spoons, and that it did not know its friends from its foes, and I lost all my remaining respect for it, and pitied it.

Thus the State never intentionally confronts a man's sense, intellectual or moral, but only his body, his senses. It is not armed with superior wit or honesty, but with superior physical strength. I was not born to be forced. I will breathe after my own fashion. Let us see who is the strongest. What force has a multitude? They only can force me who obey a higher law than I. They force me to become like themselves. I do not hear of *men* being *forced* to live this way or that by masses of men. What sort of life were that to live? When I meet a government which says to me, "Your money or your life," why should I be in haste to give it my money? It may be in a great strait, and not know what to do: I cannot help that. It must help itself, do as I do. It is not worth the while to snivel about it. I am not responsible for the successful working of the machinery of society. I am not the son of the engineer. I perceive that, when an acorn and a chestnut fall side by side, the one does not remain inert to make way for the other, but both obey their own laws, and spring and grow and flourish as best they can, till one, perchance, overshadows and destroys the other. If a plant cannot live according to its nature, it dies; and so a man.

The night in prison was novel and interesting enough. The prisoners in their shirt-sleeves were enjoying a chat and the evening air in the door-way, when I entered. But the jailer said, "Come, boys, it is time to lock up;" and so they dispersed, and I heard the sound of their steps returning into the hollow apartments. My room-mate was introduced to me by the jailer, as "a first-rate fellow and a clever man." When the door was locked, he showed me where to hang my hat, and how he managed matters there. The rooms were whitewashed once a month; and this one, at least, was the whitest, most simply furnished, and probably the neatest apartment in the town. He naturally wanted to know where I came from, and what brought me there; and, when I had told him, I asked him in my turn how he came there, presuming him to be an honest man, of course; and, as the world goes, I believe he was. "Why," said he, "they accuse me of burning a barn; but I never did it." As near as I could discover, he had probably gone to bed in a barn when drunk, and smoked his pipe there; and so a barn was burnt. He had the reputation of being a clever man, had been there some three months waiting for his trial to come on, and would have to wait as much longer; but he was quite domesticated and contented, since he got his board for nothing, and thought that he was well treated.

He occupied one window, and I the other; and I saw, that if one stayed there long, his principal business would be to look out the window. I had soon read all the tracts that were left there, and examined where former prisoners had broken out, and where a grate had been sawed off, and heard the history of the various occupants of that room; for I found that even here there was a history and a gossip which never circulated beyond the walls of the jail. Probably this is the only house in the town where verses are composed, which are afterward printed in a circular form, but not published. I was shown quite a long list of verses which were composed by some young men who had been detected in an attempt to escape, who avenged themselves by singing them.

I pumped my fellow-prisoner as dry as I could, for fear I should never see him again; but at length he showed me which was my bed, and left me to blow out the lamp.

It was like travelling into a far country, such as I had never expected to behold, to lie there for one night. It seemed to me that I never had heard the town-clock strike before, nor the evening sounds of the village; for we slept with the windows open, which were inside the grating. It was to see my native village in the light of the middle ages, and our Concord was turned into a Rhine stream, and visions of knights and castles passed before me. They were the voices of old burghers that I heard in the streets. I was an involuntary spectator and auditor of whatever was done and said in the kitchen of the adjacent village-inn,—a wholly new and rare experience to me. It was a closer view of my native town. I was fairly inside of it. I never had seen its institutions before. This is one of its peculiar institutions; for it is a shire town. I began to comprehend what its inhabitants were about.

In the morning, our breakfasts were put through the hole in the door, in small oblong-square tin pans, made to fit, and holding a pint of chocolate, with brown bread, and an iron spoon. When they called for the vessels again, I was green enough to return what bread I had left; but my comrade seized it, and said that I should lay that up for lunch or dinner. Soon after, he was let out to work at haying in a neighboring field, whither he went every day, and would not be back till noon; so he bade me good-day, saying that he doubted if he should see me again.

When I came out of prison,—for some one interfered, and paid the tax,—I did not perceive that great changes had taken place on the common, such as he observed who went in a youth, and emerged a tottering and gray-headed man; and yet a change had to my eyes come over the scene,—the town, and State, and country,—greater than any that mere time could effect. I saw yet more distinctly the State in which I lived. I saw to what extent the people among whom I lived could be trusted as good neighbors and friends; that their friendship was for summer weather only; that they did not greatly purpose to do right; that they were a distinct race from me by their prejudices and superstitions, as the Chinamen and Malays are; that, in their sacrifices to humanity, they ran no risks, not even to their property; that, after all, they were not so noble but they treated the thief as he had treated them, and hoped, by a certain outward observance and a few prayers, and by walking in a particular straight though useless path from time to time, to save their souls. This may be to judge my neighbors harshly; for I believe that most of them are not aware that they have such an institution as the jail in their village.

It was formerly the custom in our village, when a poor debtor came out of jail, for his acquaintances to salute him, looking through their fingers, which were crossed to represent the grating of a jail window, "How do ye do?" My neighbors did not thus salute me, but first looked at me, and then at one another, as if I had returned from a long journey. I was put into jail as I was going to the shoemaker's to get a shoe which was mended. When I was let out the next morning, I proceeded to finish my errand, and, having put on my mended shoe, joined a huckleberry party, who were impatient to put themselves under my conduct; and in half an hour,—for the horse was soon tackled,—was in the midst of a huckleberry field, on one of our highest hills, two miles off; and then the State was nowhere to be seen.

This is the whole history of "My Prisons."[9]

I have never declined paying the highway tax, because I am as desirous of being a good neighbor as I am of being a bad subject; and, as for supporting schools, I am doing my part to educate my fellow-countrymen now. It is for no particular item in the tax-bill that I refuse to pay it. I simply wish to refuse allegiance to the State, to withdraw and stand aloof from it effectually. I do not care to trace the course of my dollar, if I could, till it buys a man, or a musket to shoot one with,—the dollar is innocent,—but I am concerned to trace the effects of my allegiance. In fact, I quietly declare war with the State, after my fashion, though I will still make what use and get what advantage of her I can, as is usual in such cases.

If others pay the tax which is demanded of me, from a sympathy with the State, they do but what they have already done in their own case, or rather they abet injustice to a greater extent than the State requires. If they pay the tax from a mistaken interest in the individual taxed, to save his property or prevent his

---

[9]Reference to *Le Mie Prigioni* (1832), prison memoirs of Silvio Pellico.

going to jail, it is because they have not considered wisely how far they let their private feelings interfere with the public good.

This, then, is my position at present. But one cannot be too much on his guard in such a case, lest his action be biassed by obstinacy, or an undue regard for the opinions of men. Let him see that he does only what belongs to himself and to the hour.

I think sometimes, Why, this people mean well; they are only ignorant; they would do better if they knew how: why give your neighbors this pain to treat you as they are not inclined to? But I think, again, this is no reason why I should do as they do, or permit others to suffer much greater pain of a different kind. Again, I sometimes say to myself, When many millions of men, without heat, without ill-will, without personal feeling of any kind, demand of you a few shillings only, without the possibility, such is their constitution, of retracting or altering their present demand, and without the possibility, on your side, of appeal to any other millions, why expose yourself to this overwhelming brute force? You do not resist cold and hunger, the winds and the waves, thus obstinately; you quietly submit to a thousand similar necessities. You do not put your head into the fire. But just in proportion as I regard this as not wholly a brute force, but partly a human force, and consider that I have relations to those millions as to so many millions of men, and not of mere brute or inanimate things, I see that appeal is possible, first and instantaneously, from them to the Maker of them, and, secondly, from them to themselves. But, if I put my head deliberately into the fire, there is no appeal to fire or to the Maker of fire, and I have only myself to blame. If I could convince myself that I have any right to be satisfied with men as they are, and to treat them accordingly, and not according, in some respects, to my requisitions and expectations of what they and I ought to be, then, like a good Mussulman and fatalist, I should endeavor to be satisfied with things as they are, and say it is the will of God. And, above all, there is this difference between resisting this and a purely brute or natural force, that I can resist this with some effect; but I cannot expect, like Orpheus, to change the nature of the rocks and trees and beasts.

I do not wish to quarrel with any man or nation. I do not wish to split hairs, to make fine distinctions, or set myself up as better than my neighbors. I seek rather, I may say, even an excuse for conforming to the laws of the land. I am but too ready to conform to them. Indeed I have reason to suspect myself on this head; and each year, as the tax-gatherer comes round, I find myself disposed to review the acts and position of the general and state governments, and the spirit of the people, to discover a pretext for conformity. I believe that the State will soon be able to take all my work of this sort out of my hands, and then I shall be no better a patriot than my fellow-countrymen. Seen from a lower point of view, the Constitution, with all its faults, is very good; the law and the courts are very respectable; even this State and this American government are, in many respects, very admirable and rare things, to be thankful for, such as a great many have described them; but seen from a point of view a little higher, they are what I have described them; seen from a higher still, and the highest, who shall say what they are, or that they are worth looking at or thinking of at all?

However, the government does not concern me much, and I shall bestow the fewest possible thoughts on it. It is not many moments that I live under a government, even in this world. If a man is thought-free, fancy-free, imagination-free, that which is *not* never for a long time appearing *to be* to him, unwise rulers or reformers cannot fatally interrupt him.

I know that most men think differently from myself; but those whose lives are by profession devoted to the study of these or kindred subjects, content me as little as any. Statesmen and legislators, standing so completely within the institution, never distinctly and nakedly behold it. They speak of moving society, but have no resting-place without it. They may be men of a certain experience and discrimination, and have no doubt invented ingenious and even useful systems, for which we sincerely thank them; but all their wit and usefulness lie within certain not very wide limits. They are wont to forget that the world is not governed by policy and expediency. Webster never goes behind government, and so cannot speak with authority about it. His words are wisdom to those legislators who contemplate no essential reform in the existing government; but for thinkers, and those who legislate for all time, he never once glances at the subject. I know of those whose serene and wise speculations on this theme would soon reveal the limits of his mind's range and hospitality. Yet, compared with the cheap professions of most reformers, and the still cheaper wisdom and eloquence of politicians in general, his are almost the only sensible and valuable words, and we thank Heaven for him. Comparatively, he is always strong, original, and, above all, practical. Still his quality is not wisdom, but prudence. The lawyer's truth is not Truth, but consistency, or a consistent expediency. Truth is always in harmony with herself, and is not concerned chiefly to reveal the justice that may consist with wrong-doing. He well deserves to be called, as he has been called, the Defender of the Constitution. There are really no blows to be given by him but defensive ones. He is not a leader, but a follower. His leaders are the men of '87.[10] "I have never made an effort," he says, "and never propose to make an effort; I have never countenanced an effort, and never mean to countenance an effort, to disturb the arrangement as originally made, by which the various States came into the Union." Still thinking of the sanction which the Constitution gives to slavery, he says, "Because it was a part of the original compact,—let it stand." Notwithstanding his special acuteness and ability, he is unable to take a fact out of its merely political relations, and behold it as it lies absolutely to be disposed of by the intellect,—what, for instance, it behoves a man to do here in America to-day with regard to slavery, but ventures, or is driven, to make some such desperate answer as the following, while professing to

---

[10]Those who wrote the Constitution.

speak absolutely, and as a private man,—from which what new and singular code of social duties might be inferred?—"The manner," says he, "in which the government of those States where slavery exists are to regulate it, is for their own consideration, under their responsibility to their constituents, to the general laws of propriety, humanity, and justice, and to God. Associations formed elsewhere, springing from a feeling of humanity, or any other cause, have nothing whatever to do with it. They have never received any encouragement from me, and they never will."

They who know of no purer sources of truth, who have traced up its stream no higher, stand, and wisely stand, by the Bible and the Constitution, and drink at it there with reverence and humility; but they who behold where it comes trickling into this lake or that pool, gird up their loins once more, and continue their pilgrimage toward its fountain-head.

No man with a genius for legislation has appeared in America. They are rare in the history of the world. There are orators, politicians, and eloquent men, by the thousand; but the speaker has not yet opened his mouth to speak, who is capable of settling the much-vexed questions of the day. We love eloquence for its own sake, and not for any truth which it may utter, or any heroism it may inspire. Our legislators have not yet learned the comparative value of free-trade and of freedom, of union, and of rectitude, to a nation. They have no genius or talent for comparatively humble questions of taxation and finance, commerce and manufactures and agriculture. If we were left solely to the wordy wit of legislators in Congress for our guidance, uncorrected by the seasonable experience and the effectual complaints of the people, America would not long retain her rank among the nations. For eighteen hundred years, though perchance I have no right to say it, the New Testament has been written; yet where is the legislator who has wisdom and practical talent enough to avail himself of the light which it sheds on the science of legislation?

The authority of government, even such as I am willing to submit to,—for I will cheerfully obey those who know and can do better than I, and in many things even those who neither know nor can do so well,—is still an impure one: to be strictly just, it must have the sanction and consent of the governed. It can have no pure right over my person and property but what I concede to it. The progress from an absolute to a limited monarchy, from a limited monarchy to a democracy, is a progress toward a true respect for the individual. Is a democracy, such as we know it, the last improvement possible in government? Is it not possible to take a step further towards recognizing and organizing the rights of man? There will never be a really free and enlightened State, until the State comes to recognize the individual as a higher and independent power, from which all its own power and authority are derived, and treats him accordingly. I please myself with imagining a State at last which can afford to be just to all men, and to treat the individual with respect as a neighbor; which even would not think it inconsistent with its own repose, if a few were to live aloof from it, not meddling with it, nor embraced by it, who fulfilled all the duties of neighbors and fellow-men. A State which bore this kind of fruit, and suffered it to drop off as fast as it ripened, would prepare the way for a still more perfect and glorious State, which also I have imagined, but not yet anywhere seen.

Study and Discussion Questions

1. What is wrong, according to Thoreau, with the very concept of government?
2. How does Thoreau characterize and what is his objection to a standing army?
3. Define *expediency*. Define *justice*.
4. What two injustices supported by the U.S. government is Thoreau protesting?
5. What is Thoreau's opinion of majority rule?
6. How do we support and help maintain government policies, according to Thoreau?
7. In Thoreau's philosophy, where does responsibility reside?
8. How does Thoreau tell us he personally protests injustice?
9. What does Thoreau say about his night in jail?
10. How does Thoreau feel about his home town after spending a night in its jail?
11. Someone else pays Thoreau's tax and he is let out of jail; a couple of hours later he is picking berries in a field. Does this undermine his argument, or is this irrelevant?
12. How is Thoreau "free"? Give some examples from the essay.
13. What are the lower, higher, and highest points of view to which Thoreau refers?
14. Where, according to Thoreau, ought power ultimately be located?

Suggestions for Writing

1. List some ways in which Thoreau's position in "Civil Disobedience" is idealistic and ways in which it is practical. Would you say he is more idealistic or more practical? Why?
2. Early in "Civil Disobedience," Thoreau says, "The only obligation which I have a right to assume is to do at any time what I think right." Do you agree with him or not? Take an example from your own experience to support your argument.
3. Take Thoreau's position and apply it to a current issue of conscience, expediency, and justice.
4. "Under a government which imprisons any unjustly, the true place for a just man is also a prison," writes Thoreau. What rights would *you* be willing to go to prison to defend?

❀ ❀ ❀

SOJOURNER TRUTH (1797?–1883)

Isabella (later Isabella Van Wagener) was born a slave in upstate New York, escaped in 1827, and in 1829 moved to New York City, where she worked as a servant. She developed her speaking talent working with an evangelical preacher. In 1843, she had visions and heard voices that led her to take the name Sojourner Truth, and she began touring the country, preaching religion and the abolition of slavery. Near the end of the Civil War, she helped recruit black troops for the Union army. She was a powerful and a popular speaker, and, at an 1851 women's rights convention in Akron, Ohio, she turned the tide in an angry debate between feminists and conservative ministers with the following speech, recorded by a convention participant. In the sermon-like *"Ain't I a Woman?"* Truth convincingly exposes the blatant contradictions of white, male, and middle-class hegemony.

Ain't I a Woman? (1851)

Well, children, where there is so much racket there must be something out of kilter. I think that 'twixt the negroes of the South and the women at the North, all talking about rights, the white men will be in a fix pretty soon. But what's all this here talking about?

That man over there says that women need to be helped into carriages, and lifted over ditches, and to have the best place everywhere. Nobody ever helps me into carriages, or over mud-puddles, or gives me any best place! And ain't I a woman? Look at me! Look at my arm! I have ploughed and planted, and gathered into barns, and no man could head me! And ain't I a woman? I could work as much and eat as much as a man—when I could get it—and bear the lash as well! And ain't I a woman? I have borne thirteen children, and seen them most all sold off to slavery, and when I cried out with my mother's grief, none but Jesus heard me! And ain't I a woman?

Then they talk about this thing in the head; what's this they call it? [Intellect, someone whispers.] That's it, honey. What's that got to do with women's rights or negro's rights? If my cup won't hold but a pint, and yours holds a quart, wouldn't you be mean not to let me have my little half-measure full?

Then that little man in black there, he says women can't have as much rights as men, 'cause Christ wasn't a woman! Where did your Christ come from? Where did your Christ come from? From God and a woman! Man had nothing to do with Him.

If the first woman God ever made was strong enough to turn the world upside down all alone, these women together ought to be able to turn it back, and get it right side up again! And now they is asking to do it, the men better let them.

Obliged to you for hearing me, and now old Sojourner ain't got nothing more to say.

Study and Discussion Questions

1. How does Sojourner Truth use the Bible to argue for women's rights?
2. What is ironic about her argument concerning intellect?
3. List Truth's metaphors and images.
4. Locate some of her rhetorical devices (e.g., repetition). What other effective argumentative strategies does she use?
5. How does she overturn both race and gender stereotypes to make her argument?
6. This is a speech, so read it out loud.

Suggestions for Writing

1. Look at "Ain't I a Woman" as part of a political speech, not to win an election but to promote a cause. Compare this to a political speech in the twenty-first century. How is it similar? How is it different?
2. Compare/contrast Sojourner Truth's "Ain't I a Woman" to another famous speech by an African American, Martin Luther King's "I Have a Dream" (Protest).

HARRIET JACOBS (1813–1897)

Harriet Ann Jacobs was born into slavery. Her mother died when Jacobs was six years old, and Jacobs was taken in by her owner, Margaret Horniblow, who taught her how to read and write. Horniblow died six years later, and Jacobs was put in the custody of Dr. James Norcom (Dr. Flint in the narrative). After resisting years of sexual harassment from Norcom, she was sent to his plantation as punishment. Knowing that her children might suffer for her defiance, she escaped and hid in a secret cubby-hole in the roof of her grandmother's (a freed slave) house for the next seven years. When the opportunity finally arrived, Jacobs escaped to New York, where she met the abolitionist Lydia Maria Child, who would help her publish *Incidents in the Life of a Slave Girl* under the pseudonym Linda Brent. As Jacobs wrote in the preface to the first edition, she wanted "to arouse the women of the North to a realizing sense of the condition of women in the South, still in bondage, suffering what I suffered, and most of them far worse." At the time, most slave narratives were written from the male perspective (e.g., Frederick Douglass's *Narrative of the Life of Frederick Douglass: An American Slave*); Jacobs's account exposed to the world the plight of female slaves (the selling of their children as punishment, the sexual abuse by slave owners). The genre of the slave narrative served as an important catalyst for the beginning of the Civil War.

FROM *Incidents in the Life of a Slave Girl*   (1861)

V

THE TRIALS OF GIRLHOOD

During the first years of my service in Dr. Flint's family, I was accustomed to share some indulgences with the children of my mistress. Though this seemed to me no more than right, I was grateful for it, and tried to merit the kindness by the faithful discharge of my duties. But I now entered on my fifteenth year— a sad epoch in the life of a slave girl. My master began to whisper foul words in my ear. Young as I was, I could not remain ignorant of their import. I tried to treat them with indifference or contempt. The master's age, my extreme youth, and the fear that his conduct would be reported to my grandmother, made him bear this treatment for many months. He was a crafty man, and resorted to many means to accomplish his purposes. Sometimes he had stormy, terrific ways, that made his victims tremble; sometimes he assumed a gentleness that he thought must surely subdue. Of the two, I preferred his stormy moods, although they left me trembling. He tried his utmost to corrupt the pure principles my grandmother had instilled. He peopled my young mind with unclean images, such as only a vile monster could think of. I turned from him with disgust and hatred. But he was my master. I was compelled to live under the same roof with him—where I saw a man forty years my senior daily violat-ing the most sacred commandments of nature. He told me I was his property; that I must be subject to his will in all things. My soul revolted against the mean tyranny. But where could I turn for protection? No matter whether the slave girl be as black as ebony or as fair as her mistress. In either case, there is no shadow of law to protect her from insult, from violence, or even from death; all these are inflicted by fiends who bear the shape of men. The mistress, who ought to protect the helpless victim, has no other feelings towards her but those of jealousy and rage. The degradation, the wrongs, the vices, that grow out of slav-ery, are more than I can describe. They are greater than you would willingly believe. Surely, if you credited one half the truths that are told you concerning the helpless millions suffering in this cruel bondage, you at the north would not help to tighten the yoke. You surely would refuse to do for the master, on your own soil, the mean and cruel work which trained bloodhounds and the lowest class of whites do for him at the south.

Every where the years bring to all enough of sin and sorrow; but in slavery the very dawn of life is darkened by these shadows. Even the little child, who is accustomed to wait on her mistress and her children, will learn, before she is twelve years old, why it is that her mistress hates such and such a one among the slaves. Perhaps the child's own mother is among those hated ones. She lis-tens to violent outbreaks of jealous passion, and cannot help understanding what is the cause. She will become prematurely knowing in evil things. Soon she will learn to tremble when she hears her master's footfall. She will be compelled to realize that she is no longer a child. If God has bestowed beauty upon her, it will prove her greatest curse. That which commands admiration in the white woman only hastens the degradation of the female slave. I know that some are too much brutalized by slavery to feel the humiliation of their position; but many slaves feel it most acutely, and shrink from the memory of it. I cannot tell how much I suffered in the presence of these wrongs, nor how I am still pained by the retrospect. My master met me at every turn, reminding me that I belonged to him, and swearing by heaven and earth that he would compel me to submit to him. If I went out for a breath of fresh air, after a day of unwearied toil, his footsteps dogged me. If I knelt by my mother's grave, his dark shadow fell on me even there. The light heart which nature had given me became heavy with sad forebodings. The other slaves in my master's house noticed the change. Many of them pitied me; but none dared to ask the cause. They had no need to inquire. They knew too well the guilty practices under that roof; and they were aware that to speak of them was an offence that never went unpunished.

I longed for some one to confide in. I would have given the world to have laid my head on my grandmother's faithful bosom, and told her all my troubles. But Dr. Flint swore he would kill me, if I was not as silent as the grave. Then, although my grandmother was all in all to me, I feared her as well as loved her. I had been accustomed to look up to her with a respect bordering upon awe. I was very young, and felt shamefaced about telling her such impure things, especially as I knew her to be very strict on such subjects. Moreover, she was a woman of a high spirit. She was usually very quiet in her demeanor, but if her indignation was once roused, it was not very easily quelled. I had been told that she once chased a white gentleman with a loaded pistol, because he insulted one of her daughters. I dreaded the consequences of a violent outbreak; and both pride and fear kept me silent. But though I did not confide in my grandmother, and even evaded her vigilant watchfulness and inquiry, her presence in the neighborhood was some protection to me. Though she had been a slave, Dr. Flint was afraid of her. He dreaded her scorching rebukes. Moreover, she was known and patronized by many people; and he did not wish to have his villainy made public. It was lucky for me that I did not live on a distant plantation, but in a town not so large that the inhabitants were ignorant of each other's affairs. Bad as are the laws and customs in a slaveholding community, the doctor, as a professional man, deemed it prudent to keep up some outward show of decency.

O, what days and nights of fear and sorrow that man caused me! Reader, it is not to awaken sympathy for myself that I am telling you truthfully what I suffered in slavery. I do it to kindle a flame of compassion in your hearts for my sisters who are still in bondage, suffering as I once suffered.

I once saw two beautiful children playing together. One was a fair white child; the other was her slave, and also her sister. When I saw them embracing each other, and heard their joyous laughter, I turned sadly away from the lovely sight. I foresaw the inevitable blight that would fall on the little slave's heart. I knew how soon her laughter would be changed to sighs. The fair child grew up to be a still fairer woman. From childhood to womanhood her pathway was blooming with flowers, and overarched by a sunny sky. Scarcely one day of her life had been clouded when the sun rose on her happy bridal morning.

How had those years dealt with her slave sister, the little playmate of her childhood? She, also, was very beautiful; but the flowers and sunshine of love were not for her. She drank the cup of sin, and shame, and misery, whereof her persecuted race are compelled to drink.

In view of these things, why are ye silent, ye free men and women of the north? Why do your tongues falter in maintenance of the right? Would that I had more ability! But my heart is so full, and my pen is so weak! There are noble men and women who plead for us, striving to help those who cannot help themselves. God bless them! God give them strength and courage to go on! God bless those, every where, who are laboring to advance the cause of humanity!

XVII

THE FLIGHT

"$300 REWARD! Ran away from the subscriber, an intelligent, bright, mulatto girl, named Linda, 21 years of age. Five feet four inches high. Dark eyes, and black hair inclined to curl; but it can be made straight. Has a decayed spot on a front tooth. She can read and write, and in all probability will try to get to the Free States. All persons are forbidden, under penalty of the law, to harbor or employ said slave. $150 will be given to whoever takes her in the state, and $300 if taken out of the state and delivered to me, or lodged in jail.

DR. FLINT"

XXI

THE LOOPHOLE OF RETREAT

A small shed had been added to my grandmother's house years ago. Some boards were laid across the joists at the top, and between these boards and the roof was a very small garret, never occupied by any thing but rats and mice. It was a pent roof, covered with nothing but shingles, according to the southern custom for such buildings. The garret was only nine feet long and seven wide. The highest part was three feet high, and sloped down abruptly to the loose board floor. There was no admission for either light or air. My uncle Phillip, who was a carpenter, had very skilfully made a concealed trap-door, which communicated with the storeroom. He had been doing this while I was waiting in the swamp. The storeroom opened upon a piazza. To this hole I was conveyed as soon as I entered the house. The air was stifling; the darkness total. A bed had been spread on the floor. I could sleep quite comfortably on one side; but the slope was so sudden that I could not turn on the other without hitting the roof. The rats and mice ran over my bed; but I was weary, and I slept such sleep as the wretched may, when a tempest has passed over them. Morning came. I knew it only by the noises I heard; for in my small den day and night were all the same. I suffered for air even more than for light. But I was not comfortless. I heard the voices of my children. There was joy and there was sadness in the sound. It made my tears flow. How I longed to speak to them! I was eager to look on their faces; but there was no hole, no crack, through which I could peep. This continued darkness was oppressive. It seemed horrible to sit or lie in a cramped position day after day, without one gleam of light. Yet I would have chosen this, rather than my lot as a slave, though white people considered it an easy one; and it was so compared with the fate of others. I was never cruelly overworked; I was never lacerated with the whip from head to foot; I was never so beaten and bruised that I could not turn from one side to the other; I never had my heel-strings cut to prevent my running away; I was never chained to a log and forced to drag it about, while I toiled in the fields from morning till night; I was never branded with hot iron, or torn by bloodhounds. On the contrary, I had always been kindly treated, and tenderly cared for, until I came into the hands of Dr. Flint. I had never wished for freedom till then. But though my life in slavery was comparatively devoid of hardships, God pity the woman who is compelled to lead such a life!

My food was passed up to me through the trap-door my uncle had contrived; and my grandmother, my uncle Phillip, and aunt Nancy would seize such opportunities as they could, to mount up there and chat with me at the opening. But of course this was not safe in the daytime. It must all be done in darkness. It was impossible for me to move in an erect position, but I crawled about my den for exercise. One day I hit my head against something, and found it was a gimlet. My uncle had left it sticking there when he made the trap-door. I was as rejoiced as Robinson Crusoe could have been at finding such a treasure. It put a lucky thought into my head. I said to myself, "Now I will have some light. Now I will see my children." I did not dare to begin my work during the daytime, for fear of attracting attention. But I groped round; and having found the side next the street, where I could frequently see my children, I stuck the gimlet in and waited for evening. I bored three rows of holes, one above another; then I bored out the interstices between. I thus succeeded in making one hole about an inch long and an inch broad. I sat by it till late into the night, to enjoy the little whiff of air that floated in. In the morning I watched for my children. The first person I saw in the street was Dr. Flint. I had a shuddering, superstitious feeling that it was a bad omen. Several familiar faces passed by. At last I heard the merry laugh of children, and presently two sweet little faces were looking up at me, as though they knew I was there, and were conscious of the joy they imparted. How I longed to *tell* them I was there!

My condition was now a little improved. But for weeks I was tormented by hundreds of little red insects, fine as a needle's point, that pierced through my skin, and produced an intolerable burning. The good grandmother gave me herb teas and cooling medicines, and finally I got rid of them. The heat of my den was intense, for nothing but thin shingles protected me from the scorching summer's sun. But I had my consolations. Through my peeping-hole I could watch the children, and when they were near enough, I could hear their talk. Aunt Nancy brought me all the news she could hear at Dr. Flint's. From her I learned that the doctor had written to New York to a colored woman, who had been born and raised in our neighborhood, and had breathed his contaminating atmosphere. He offered her a reward if she could find out any thing about me. I know not what was the nature of her reply; but he soon after started for New York in haste, saying to his family that he had business of importance to transact. I peeped at him as he passed on his way to the steamboat. It was a satisfaction to have miles of land and water between us, even for a little while; and it was a still greater satisfaction to know that he believed me to be in the Free States. My little den seemed less dreary than it had done. He returned, as he did from his former journey to New York, without obtaining any satisfactory information. When he passed our house next morning, Benny[1] was standing at the gate. He had heard them say that he had gone to find me, and he called out, "Dr. Flint, did you bring my mother home? I want to see her." The doctor stamped his foot at him in a rage, and exclaimed, "Get out of the way, you little damned rascal! If you don't, I'll cut off your head."

Benny ran terrified into the house, saying, "You can't put me in jail again. I don't belong to you now." It was well that the wind carried the words away from the doctor's ear. I told my grandmother of it, when we had our next conference at the trap-door; and begged of her not to allow the children to be impertinent to the irascible old man.

Autumn came, with a pleasant abatement of heat. My eyes had become accustomed to the dim light, and by holding my book or work in a certain position near the aperture I contrived to read and sew. That was a great relief to the tedious monotony of my life. But when winter came, the cold penetrated through the thin shingle roof, and I was dreadfully chilled.

---

[1]Her son, whose father, Mr. Sands, is white.

The winters there are not so long, or so severe, as in northern latitudes; but the houses are not built to shelter from cold, and my little den was peculiarly comfortless. The kind grandmother brought me bed-clothes and warm drinks. Often I was obliged to lie in bed all day to keep comfortable; but with all my precautions, my shoulders and feet were frostbitten. O, those long, gloomy days, with no object for my eye to rest upon, and no thoughts to occupy my mind, except the dreary past and the uncertain future! I was thankful when there came a day sufficiently mild for me to wrap myself up and sit at the loophole to watch the passers by. Southerners have the habit of stopping and talking in the streets, and I heard many conversations not intended to meet my ears. I heard slave-hunters planning how to catch some poor fugitive. Several times I heard allusions to Dr. Flint, myself, and the history of my children, who, perhaps, were playing near the gate. One would say, "I wouldn't move my little finger to catch her, as old Flint's property," Another would say, "I'll catch *any* nigger for the reward. A man ought to have what belongs to him, if he *is* a damned brute." The opinion was often expressed that I was in the Free States. Very rarely did any one suggest that I might be in the vicinity. Had the least suspicion rested on my grandmother's house, it would have been burned to the ground. But it was the last place they thought of. Yet there was no place, where slavery existed, that could have afforded me so good a place of concealment.

Dr. Flint and his family repeatedly tried to coax and bribe my children to tell something they had heard said about me. One day the doctor took them into a shop, and offered them some bright little silver pieces and gay handkerchiefs if they would tell where their mother was. Ellen[2] shrank away from him, and would not speak; but Benny spoke up, and said, "Dr. Flint, I don't know where my mother is. I guess she's in New York; and when you go there again, I wish you'd ask her to come home, for I want to see her; but if you put her in jail, or tell her you'll cut her head off, I'll tell her to go right back."

XXIX

PREPARATIONS FOR ESCAPE

I hardly expect that the reader will credit me, when I affirm that I lived in that little dismal hole, almost deprived of light and air, and with no space to move my limbs, for nearly seven years. But it is a fact; and to me a sad one, even now; for my body still suffers from the effects of that long imprisonment, to say

---

[2]Her daughter.

nothing of my soul. Members of my family, now living in New York and Boston, can testify to the truth of what I say.

Countless were the nights that I sat late at the little loophole scarcely large enough to give me a glimpse of one twinkling star. There, I heard the patrols and slave-hunters conferring together about the capture of runaways, well knowing how rejoiced they would be to catch me.

Season after season, year after year, I peeped at my children's faces, and heard their sweet voices, with a heart yearning all the while to say, "Your mother is here." Sometimes it appeared to me as if ages had rolled away since I entered upon that gloomy, monotonous existence. At times, I was stupefied and listless; at other times I became very impatient to know when these dark years would end, and I should again be allowed to feel the sunshine, and breathe the pure air.

After Ellen left us, this feeling increased. Mr. Sands had agreed that Benny might go to the north whenever his uncle Phillip could go with him; and I was anxious to be there also, to watch over my children, and protect them so far as I was able. Moreover, I was likely to be drowned out of my den, if I remained much longer; for the slight roof was getting badly out of repair, and uncle Phillip was afraid to remove the shingles, lest some one should get a glimpse of me. When storms occurred in the night, they spread mats and bits of carpet, which in the morning appeared to have been laid out to dry; but to cover the roof in the daytime might have attracted attention. Consequently, my clothes and bedding were often drenched; a process by which the pains and aches in my cramped and stiffened limbs were greatly increased. I revolved various plans of escape in my mind, which I sometimes imparted to my grandmother, when she came to whisper with me at the trap-door. The kind-hearted old woman had an intense sympathy for runaways. She had known too much of the cruelties inflicted on those who were captured. Her memory always flew back at once to the sufferings of her bright and handsome son, Benjamin, the youngest and dearest of her flock. So, whenever I alluded to the subject, she would groan out, "O, don't think of it, child. You'll break my heart." I had no good old aunt Nancy now to encourage me; but my brother William and my children were continually beckoning me to the north.

And now I must go back a few months in my story. I have stated that the first of January was the time for selling slaves, or leasing them out to new masters. If time were counted by heart-throbs, the poor slaves might reckon years of suffering during that festival so joyous to the free. On the New Year's day preceding my aunt's death, one of my friends, named Fanny, was to be sold at auction, to pay her master's debts. My thoughts were with her during all the day, and at night I anxiously inquired what had been her fate. I was told that she had been sold to one master, and her four little girls to another master, far distant; that she had escaped from her purchaser, and was not to be found. Her mother was the old Aggie I have spoken of. She lived in a small tenement belonging to my grandmother, and built on the same lot with her own house. Her dwelling was searched and watched, and that brought the patrols so near me that I was obliged to keep very close in my den. The hunters were somehow eluded; and not long afterwards Benny accidentally caught sight of Fanny in her mother's hut. He told his grandmother, who charged him never to speak of it, explaining to him the frightful consequences; and he never betrayed the trust. Aggie little dreamed that my grandmother knew where her daughter was concealed, and that the stooping form of her old neighbor was bending under a similar burden of anxiety and fear; but these dangerous secrets deepened the sympathy between the two old persecuted mothers.

My friend Fanny and I remained many weeks hidden within call of each other; but she was unconscious of the fact. I longed to have her share my den, which seemed a more secure retreat than her own; but I had brought so much trouble on my grandmother, that it seemed wrong to ask her to incur greater risks. My restlessness increased. I had lived too long in bodily pain and anguish of spirit. Always I was in dread that by some accident, or some contrivance, slavery would succeed in snatching my children from me. This thought drove me nearly frantic, and I determined to steer for the North Star at all hazards. At this crisis, Providence opened an unexpected way for me to escape. My friend Peter came one evening, and asked to speak with me. "Your day has come, Linda," said he. "I have found a chance for you to go to the Free States. You have a fortnight to decide." The news seemed too good to be true; but Peter explained his arrangements, and told me all that was necessary was for me to say I would go. I was going to answer him with a joyful yes, when the thought of Benny came to my mind. I told him the temptation was exceedingly strong, but I was terribly afraid of Dr. Flint's alleged power over my child, and that I could not go and leave him behind. Peter remonstrated earnestly. He said such a good chance might never occur again; that Benny was free, and could be sent to me; and that for the sake of my children's welfare I ought not to hesitate a moment. I told him I would consult with uncle Phillip. My uncle rejoiced in the plan, and bade me go by all means. He promised, if his life was spared, that he would either bring or send my son to me as soon as I reached a place of safety. I resolved to go, but thought nothing had better be said to my grandmother till very near the time of departure. But my uncle thought she would feel it more keenly if I left her so suddenly. "I will reason with her," said he, "and convince her how necessary it is, not only for your sake, but for hers also. You cannot be blind to the fact that she is sinking under her burdens." I was not blind to it. I knew that my concealment was an ever-present source of anxiety, and that the older she grew the more nervously fearful she was of discovery. My uncle talked with her, and finally succeeded in persuading her that it was absolutely necessary for me to seize the chance so unexpectedly offered.

The anticipation of being a free woman proved almost too much for my weak frame. The excitement stimulated me, and at the same time bewildered me. I made busy preparations for my journey, and for my son to follow me. I resolved to have an interview with him before I went, that I might give him cautions and advice, and tell him how anxiously I should be waiting for him at the north. Grandmother stole up to me as often as possible to whisper words of counsel. She insisted upon my writing to Dr. Flint, as soon as I arrived in the Free States, and asking him to sell me to her. She said she would sacrifice her house, and all she had in the world, for the sake of having me safe with my children in any part of the world. If she could only live to know *that* she could die in peace. I promised the dear old faithful friend that I would write to her as soon as I arrived, and put the letter in a safe way to reach her; but in my own mind I resolved that not another cent of her hard earnings should be spent to pay rapacious slaveholders for what they called their property. And even if I had not been unwilling to buy what I had already a right to possess, common humanity would have prevented me from accepting the generous offer, at the expense of turning my aged relative out of house and home, when she was trembling on the brink of the grave.

I was to escape in a vessel; but I forbear to mention any further particulars. I was in readiness, but the vessel was unexpectedly detained several days. Meantime, news came to town of a most horrible murder committed on a fugitive slave, named James. Charity, the mother of this unfortunate young man, had been an old acquaintance of ours. I have told the shocking particulars of his death, in my description of some of the neighboring slaveholders. My grandmother, always nervously sensitive about runaways, was terribly frightened. She felt sure that a similar fate awaited me, if I did not desist from my enterprise. She sobbed, and groaned, and entreated me not to go. Her excessive fear was somewhat contagious, and my heart was not proof against her extreme agony. I was grievously disappointed, but I promised to relinquish my project.

When my friend Peter was apprised of this, he was both disappointed and vexed. He said, that judging from our past experience, it would be a long time before I had such another chance to throw away. I told him it need not be thrown away; that I had a friend concealed near by, who would be glad enough to take the place that had been provided for me. I told him about poor Fanny, and the kind-hearted, noble fellow, who never turned his back upon any body in distress, white or black, expressed his readiness to help her. Aggie was much surprised when she found that we knew her secret. She was rejoiced to hear of such a chance for Fanny, and arrangements were made for her to go on board the vessel the next night. They both supposed that I had long been at the north, therefore my name was not mentioned in the transaction. Fanny was carried on board at the appointed time, and stowed away in a very small cabin. This accommodation had been purchased at a price that would pay for a voyage to England. But when one proposes to go to fine old England, they stop to calculate whether they can afford the cost of the pleasure; while in making a bargain to escape from slavery, the trembling victim is ready to say, "Take all I have, only don't betray me!"

The next morning I peeped through my loophole, and saw that it was dark and cloudy. At night I received news that the wind was ahead, and the vessel had not sailed. I was exceedingly anxious about Fanny, and Peter too, who was running a tremendous risk at my instigation. Next day the wind and weather remained the same. Poor Fanny had been half dead with fright when they carried her on board, and I could readily imagine how she must be suffering now. Grandmother came often to my den, to say how thankful she was I did not go. On the third morning she rapped for me to come down to the storeroom. The poor old sufferer was breaking down under her weight of trouble. She was easily flurried now. I found her in a nervous, excited state, but I was not aware that she had forgotten to lock the door behind her, as usual. She was exceedingly worried about the detention of the vessel. She was afraid all would be discovered, and then Fanny, and Peter, and I, would all be tortured to death, and Phillip would be utterly ruined, and her house would be torn down. Poor Peter! If he should die such a horrible death as the poor slave James had lately done, and all for his kindness in trying to help me, how dreadful it would be for us all! Alas, the thought was familiar to me, and had sent many a sharp pang through my heart. I tried to suppress my own anxiety, and speak soothingly to her. She brought in some allusion to aunt Nancy, the dear daughter she had recently buried, and then she lost all control of herself. As she stood there, trembling and sobbing, a voice from the piazza called out, "Whar is you, aunt Marthy?" Grandmother was startled, and in her agitation opened the door, without thinking of me. In stepped Jenny, the mischievous housemaid, who had tried to enter my room, when I was concealed in the house of my white benefactress. "I's bin huntin ebery whar for you, aunt Marthy," said she. "My missis wants you to send her some crackers." I had slunk down behind a barrel, which entirely screened me, but I imagined that Jenny was looking directly at the spot, and my heart beat violently. My grandmother immediately thought what she had done, and went out quickly with Jenny to count the crackers locking the door after her. She returned to me, in a few minutes, the perfect picture of despair. "Poor child!" she exclaimed, "my carelessness has ruined you. The boat ain't gone yet. Get ready immediately, and go with Fanny. I ain't got another word to say against it now; for there's no telling what may happen this day."

Uncle Phillip was sent for, and he agreed with his mother in thinking that Jenny would inform Dr. Flint in less than twenty-four hours. He advised getting me on board the boat, if possible; if not, I had better keep very still in my den, where they could not find me without tearing the house down. He said it would not do for him to move in the matter, because suspicion would be immediately excited; but he promised to communicate with Peter. I felt reluctant to apply to him again, having implicated him too much already; but there seemed to be no alternative. Vexed as Peter had been by my indecision, he was true to his generous nature, and said at once that he would do his best to help me, trusting I should show myself a stronger woman this time.

He immediately proceeded to the wharf, and found that the wind had shifted, and the vessel was slowly beating down stream. On some pretext of urgent necessity, he offered two boatmen a dollar apiece to catch up with her.

He was of lighter complexion than the boatmen he hired, and when the captain saw them coming so rapidly, he thought officers were pursuing his vessel in search of the runaway slave he had on board. They hoisted sails, but the boat gained upon them, and the indefatigable Peter sprang on board.

The captain at once recognized him. Peter asked him to go below, to speak about a bad bill he had given him. When he told his errand, the captain replied, "Why, the woman's here already; and I've put her where you or the devil would have a tough job to find her."

"But it is another woman I want to bring," said Peter. "*She* is in great distress, too, and you shall be paid any thing within reason, if you'll stop and take her."

"What's her name?" inquired the captain.

"Linda," he replied.

"That's the name of the woman already here," rejoined the captain. "By George! I believe you mean to betray me."

"O!" exclaimed Peter, "God knows I wouldn't harm a hair of your head. I am too grateful to you. But there really *is* another woman in great danger. Do have the humanity to stop and take her!"

After a while they came to an understanding. Fanny, not dreaming I was any where about in that region, had assumed my name, though she called herself Johnson. "Linda is a common name," said Peter, "and the woman I want to bring is Linda Brent."

The captain agreed to wait at a certain place till evening, being handsomely paid for his detention.

Of course, the day was an anxious one for us all. But we concluded that if Jenny had seen me, she would be too wise to let her mistress know of it; and that she probably would not get a chance to see Dr. Flint's family till evening, for I knew very well what were the rules in that household. I afterwards believed that she did not see me; for nothing ever came of it, and she was one of those base characters that would have jumped to betray a suffering fellow being for the sake of thirty pieces of silver.

I made all my arrangements to go on board as soon as it was dusk. The intervening time I resolved to spend with my son. I had not spoken to him for seven years, though I had been under the same roof, and seen him every day, when I was well enough to sit at the loophole. I did not dare to venture beyond the storeroom; so they brought him there, and locked us up together, in a place concealed from the piazza door. It was an agitating interview for both of us. After we had talked and wept together for a little while, he said, "Mother, I'm glad you're going away. I wish I could go with you. I knew you was here; and I have been *so* afraid they would come and catch you!"

I was greatly surprised, and asked him how he had found it out.

He replied, "I was standing under the eaves, one day, before Ellen went away, and I heard somebody cough up over the wood shed. I don't know what made me think it was you, but I did think so. I missed Ellen, the night before she went away; and grandmother brought her back into the room in the night; and I thought maybe she'd been to see *you,* before she went, for I heard grandmother whisper to her, 'Now go to sleep; and remember never to tell.' "

I asked him if he ever mentioned his suspicions to his sister. He said he never did; but after he heard the cough, if he saw her playing with other children on that side of the house, he always tried to coax her round to the other side, for fear they would hear me cough, too. He said he had kept a close lookout for Dr. Flint, and if he saw him speak to a constable, or a patrol, he always told grandmother. I now recollected that I had seen him manifest uneasiness, when people were on that side of the house, and I had at the time been puzzled to conjecture a motive for his actions. Such prudence may seem extraordinary in a boy of twelve years, but slaves, being surrounded by mysteries, deceptions, and dangers, early learn to be suspicious and watchful, and prematurely cautious and cunning. He had never asked a question of grandmother, or uncle Phillip, and I had often heard him chime in with other children, when they spoke of my being at the north.

I told him I was now really going to the Free States, and if he was a good, honest boy, and a loving child to his dear old grandmother, the Lord would bless him, and bring him to me, and we and Ellen would live together. He began to tell me that grandmother had not eaten any thing all day. While he was speaking, the door was unlocked, and she came in with a small bag of money, which she wanted me to take. I begged her to keep a part of it, at least, to pay for Benny's being sent to the north; but she insisted, while her tears were falling fast, that I should take the whole. "You may be sick among strangers," she said, "and they would send you to the poorhouse to die." Ah, that good grandmother!

For the last time I went up to my nook. Its desolate appearance no longer chilled me, for the light of hope had risen in my soul. Yet, even with the blessed prospect of freedom before me, I felt very sad at leaving forever that old homestead, where I had been sheltered so long by the dear old grandmother; where I had dreamed my first young dream of love; and where, after that had faded away, my children came to twine themselves so closely round my desolate heart. As the hour approached for me to leave, I again descended to the storeroom. My grandmother and Benny were there. She took me by the hand, and said, "Linda, let us pray." We knelt down together, with my child pressed to my heart, and my other arm round the faithful, loving old friend I was about to leave forever. On no other occasion has it ever been my lot to listen to so fervent a supplication for mercy and protection. It thrilled through my heart, and inspired me with trust in God.

Peter was waiting for me in the street. I was soon by his side, faint in body, but strong of purpose. I did not look back upon the old place, though I felt that I should never see it again.

Study and Discussion Questions

1. What are some of the effects of living as a slave that Jacobs describes in this excerpt from her narrative?
2. Jacobs relates feelings common to people who are abused—shame, fear, anger, confusion. How does the social structure that Jacobs was in have a particular impact on her sense of self in this situation?
3. Why does Jacobs beg her grandmother not to "allow the children to be impertinent" to Dr. Flint?
4. To whom, and for what purpose, is Jacobs writing? How do her audience and her purpose shape the language she uses? Jacobs wrote her narrative under a pen name, Linda Brent. Why do you think she chose to do this?
5. How might the excerpt here be different if it were written for other former slaves?
6. Of her seven years hiding in the garret, Jacobs writes, "My body still suffers from the effects of that long imprisonment, to say nothing of my soul." In what way do you think her "soul" still suffers?

Suggestions for Writing

1. Write a journal entry Jacobs might have written one day while hiding in the garret. Write a journal entry Jacobs might have written on the boat heading north.
2. Research Harriet Jacobs's role in the abolitionist movement and write a paper about her life once she went north.
3. Compare/contrast Jacobs's narrative with a slave narrative written by a man, for example Frederick Douglass's. How did gender create different circumstances for slaves?

VIRGINIA WOOLF (1882–1941)

Virginia Woolf was born in London and grew up in an environment of wealth and culture, meeting many of the most distinguished intellectuals of the time. Unlike her brothers, Virginia and her sister were not sent to school or the university, but educated at home. From her mother's death in 1895 to the death of her father, writer Leslie Stephen, in 1904, she was responsible for running the household; after that, she moved to London and became the center of the intellectual and artistic Bloomsbury Group. In 1912, she married Leonard Woolf; a decade later she began a long relationship with the writer Vita Sackville-West. Woolf's experimental fiction helped to define modernism as a literary movement and earned her a reputation as a major English novelist.

Her continuing attacks of depression and her fear of a Nazi invasion of England led to her suicide in 1941. Among her works are the novels *Mrs. Dalloway* (1925), *To the Lighthouse* (1927), *The Waves* (1931), and *Three Guineas* (1938). In "Shakespeare's Sister," excerpted from the nonfiction *A Room of One's Own* (1929), Woolf asks the rhetorical question, ". . . what would have happened had Shakespeare had a wonderfully gifted sister . . ." as a way to set up a critique of patriarchal notions of genius and the lack of opportunity for talented women.

Shakespeare's Sister   (1929)

It would have been impossible, completely and entirely, for any woman to have written the plays of Shakespeare in the age of Shakespeare. Let me imagine, since facts are so hard to come by, what would have happened had Shakespeare had a wonderfully gifted sister, called Judith, let us say. Shakespeare himself went, very probably—his mother was an heiress—to the grammar school, where he may have learnt Latin—Ovid, Virgil and Horace—and the elements of grammar and logic. He was, it is well known, a wild boy who poached rabbits, perhaps shot a deer, and had, rather sooner than he should have done, to marry a woman in the neighbourhood, who bore him a child rather quicker than was right. That escapade sent him to seek his fortune in London. He had, it seemed, a taste for the theatre; he began by holding horses at the stage door. Very soon he got work in the theatre, became a successful actor, and lived at the hub of the universe, meeting everybody, knowing everybody, practising his art on the boards, exercising his wits in the streets, and even getting access to the palace of the queen. Meanwhile his extraordinarily gifted sister, let us suppose, remained at home. She was as adventurous, as imaginative, as agog to see the world as he was. But she was not sent to school. She had no chance of learning grammar and logic, let alone of reading Horace and Virgil. She picked up a book now and then, one of her brother's perhaps, and read a few pages. But then her parents came in and told her to mend the stockings or mind the stew and not moon about with books and papers. They would have spoken sharply but kindly, for they were substantial people who knew the conditions of life for a woman and loved their daughter—indeed, more likely than not she was the apple of her father's eye. Perhaps she scribbled some pages up in an apple loft on the sly, but was careful to hide them or set fire to them. Soon, however, before she was out of her teens, she was to be betrothed to the son of a neighbouring woolstapler. She cried out that marriage was hateful to her, and for that she was severely beaten by her father. Then he ceased to scold her. He begged her instead not to hurt him, not to shame him in this matter of her marriage. He would give her a chain of beads or a fine petticoat, he said; and there were tears in his eyes. How could she disobey him? How could she break his heart? The force of her own gift alone drove her to it. She made up a small parcel of her belongings, let herself down by a rope one summer's night and took the road to London. She was not seventeen. The birds that sang in the hedge were not more musical than she was. She had the quickest fancy, a gift like her brother's, for the tune of words. Like him, she had a taste for the theatre. She stood at the stage door; she wanted to act, she said. Men laughed in her face. The manager—a fat, loose-lipped man—guffawed. He bellowed something about poodles dancing and women acting—no woman, he said, could possibly be an actress. He hinted—you can imagine what. She could get no training in her craft. Could she even seek her dinner in a tavern or roam the streets at midnight? Yet her genius was for fiction and lusted to feed abundantly upon the lives of men and women and the study of their ways. At last—for she was very young, oddly like Shakespeare the poet in her face, with the same grey eyes and rounded brows—at last Nick Greene the actor-manager took pity on her; she found herself with child by that gentleman and so—who shall measure the heat and violence of the poet's heart when caught and tangled in a woman's body?—killed herself one winter's night and lies buried at some cross-roads where the omnibuses now stop outside the Elephant and Castle.[1]

That, more or less, is how the story would run, I think, if a woman in Shakespeare's day had had Shakespeare's genius. But for my part, I agree with the deceased bishop, if such he was—it is unthinkable that any woman in Shakespeare's day should have had Shakespeare's genius. For genius like Shakespeare's is not born among labouring, uneducated, servile people. It was not born in England among the Saxons and the Britons. It is not born today among the working classes. How, then, could it have been born among women whose work began, according to Professor Trevelyan, almost before they were out of the nursery, who were forced to it by their parents and held to it by all the power of law and custom? Yet genius of a sort must have existed among women as it must have existed among the working classes. Now and again an Emily Brontë or a Robert Burns[2] blazes out and proves its presence. But certainly it never got itself on to paper. When, however, one reads of a witch being ducked, of a woman possessed by devils, of a wise woman selling herbs, or even of a very remarkable man who had a mother, then I think we are on the track of a lost novelist, a suppressed poet, of some mute and inglorious Jane Austen, some Emily Brontë who dashed her brains out on the moor or mopped and mowed about the highways crazed with the torture that her gift had put her to. Indeed, I would venture to guess that Anon, who wrote so many poems without signing them, was often a woman.

---

[1]A tavern.
[2]Brontë (1818–1848), English novelist; Burns (1759–1796), Scottish poet.

Study and Discussion Questions

1. What kind of education does Woolf say Shakespeare received? What kind would Judith receive?
2. How do Judith's parents demonstrate their love for her?
3. How does Judith's father try to get her to marry?
4. How do theater people respond to her desire to act and to write?
5. Woolf writes that Judith's "genius was for fiction and lusted to feed abundantly upon the lives of men and women and the study of their ways." What kept her from doing this?

Suggestions for Writing

1. What are the dangers of challenging the limits of what you are allowed to do—in this sketch? in your own life?
2. Write a paragraph stating Woolf's thesis. Why is creating Judith as a character an effective way of making this argument?
3. Are there any ways in which women today who want to write are barred from certain kinds of experience?

MERIDEL LE SUEUR (1899–1996)

Meridel Le Sueur was born in Iowa and attended high school in Kansas but did not finish. She lived in an anarchist commune in New York City, worked briefly as an actress in Hollywood, and in the late 1920s began publishing journalism and fiction. Her political activism led in the 1950s to her blacklisting, and the FBI intimidated publishers into rejecting her work. She was rediscovered by feminists in the 1970s and a number of her earlier works were reprinted. Much of Le Sueur's writing is set in the American Midwest, from frontier times to urban life in the twentieth century yet rather than reproducing typical stereotypes, Le Sueur sought to dismantle any simple notions about Midwestern life. Permeated with working-class experience, Le Sueur's vision of this landscape and its democratic possibilities is less about romanticized individualism and more about the contradictions inherent in social and class struggle. Among her writings are a novel, *The Girl* (1939; first published in 1978) and the collections *Annunciation* (1935), *Salute to Spring* (1940), *Harvest: Collected Stories* (1977), *I Hear Men Talking and Other Stories* (1984), and *Ripening: Selected Work 1927–1980* (1986). In "Women on the Breadlines," originally published in 1932, Le Sueur meditates on the neglect of unemployed and sometimes homeless women during the pre–New Deal years of the Great Depression.

Women on the Breadlines

(1932)

I am sitting in the city free employment bureau. It's the women's section. We have been sitting here now for four hours. We sit here every day, waiting for a job. There are no jobs. Most of us have had no breakfast. Some have had scant rations for over a year. Hunger makes a human being lapse into a state of lethargy, especially city hunger. Is there any place else in the world where a human being is supposed to go hungry amidst plenty without an outcry, without protest, where only the boldest steal or kill for bread, and the timid crawl the streets, hunger like the beak of a terrible bird at the vitals?

We sit looking at the floor. No one dares think of the coming winter. There are only a few more days of summer. Everyone is anxious to get work to lay up something for that long siege of bitter cold. But there is no work. Sitting in the room we all know it. That is why we don't talk much. We look at the floor dreading to see that knowledge in each other's eyes. There is a kind of humiliation in it. We look away from each other. We look at the floor. It's too terrible to see this animal terror in each other's eyes.

So we sit hour after hour, day after day, waiting for a job to come in. There are many women for a single job. A thin sharp woman sits inside a wire cage looking at a book. For four hours we have watched her looking at that book. She has a hard little eye. In the small bare room there are half a dozen women sitting on the benches waiting. Many come and go. Our faces are all familiar to each other, for we wait here every day.

This is a domestic employment bureau. Most of the women who come here are middle-aged, some have families, some have raised their families and are now alone, some have men who are out of work. Hard times and the man leaves to hunt for work. He doesn't find it. He drifts on. The woman probably doesn't hear from him for a long time. She expects it. She isn't surprised. She struggles alone to feed the many mouths. Sometimes she gets help from the charities. If she's clever she can get herself a good living from the charities, if she's naturally a lick spittle, naturally a little docile and cunning. If she's proud then she starves silently, leaving her children to find work, coming home after a day's searching to wrestle with her house, her children.

Some such story is written on the faces of all these women. There are young girls too, fresh from the country. Some are made brazen too soon by the city. There is a great exodus of girls from the farms into the city now. Thousands of farms have been vacated completely in Minnesota. The girls are trying to get work. The prettier ones can get jobs in the stores when there are any, or waiting on table, but these jobs are only for the attractive and the adroit. The others, the real peasants, have a more difficult time.

Bernice sits next to me. She is a Polish woman of thirty-five. She has been working in people's kitchens for fifteen years or more. She is large, her great body in mounds, her face brightly scrubbed. She has a peasant mind and finds it hard even yet to understand the maze of the city where trickery is worth more than brawn. Her blue eyes are not clever but slow and trusting. She suffers from loneliness and lack of talk. When you speak to her, her face lifts and brightens as if you had spoken through a great darkness, and she talks magically of little things as if the weather were magic, or tells some crazy tale of her adventures on the city streets, embellishing them in bright colors until they hang heavy and thick like embroidery. She loves the city anyhow. It's exciting to her, like a bazaar. She loves to go shopping and get a bargain, hunting out the places where stale bread and cakes can be had for a few cents. She likes walking the streets looking for men to take her to a picture show. Sometimes she goes to five picture shows in one day, or she sits through one the entire day until she knows all the dialog by heart.

She came to the city a young girl from a Wisconsin farm. The first thing that happened to her, a charlatan dentist took out all her good shining teeth and the fifty dollars she had saved working in a canning factory. After that she met men in the park who told her how to look out for herself, corrupting her peasant mind, teaching her to mistrust everyone. Sometimes now she forgets to mistrust everyone and gets taken in. They taught her to get what she could for nothing, to count her change, to go back if she found herself cheated, to demand her rights.

She lives alone in little rooms. She bought seven dollars' worth of second-hand furniture eight years ago. She rents a room for perhaps three dollars a month in an attic, sometimes in a cold house. Once the house where she stayed was condemned and everyone else moved out and she lived there all winter alone on the top floor. She spent only twenty-five dollars all winter.

She wants to get married but she sees what happens to her married friends, left with children to support, worn out before their time. So she stays single. She is virtuous. She is slightly deaf from hanging out clothes in winter. She had done people's washing and cooking for fifteen years and in that time saved thirty dollars. Now she hasn't worked steady for a year and she has spent the thirty dollars. She had dreamed of having a little house or a houseboat perhaps with a spot of ground for a few chickens. This dream she will never realize.

She has lost all her furniture now along with the dream. A married friend whose husband is gone gives her a bed for which she pays by doing a great deal of work for the woman. She comes here every day now sitting bewildered, her pudgy hands folded in her lap. She is hungry. Her great flesh has begun to hang in folds. She has been living on crackers. Sometimes a box of crackers lasts a week. She has a friend who's a baker and he sometimes steals the stale loaves and brings them to her.

A girl we have seen every day all summer went crazy yesterday at the YW. She went into hysterics, stamping her feet and screaming.

She hadn't had work for eight months. "You've got to give me something," she kept saying. The woman in charge flew into a rage that probably came from days and days of suffering on her part, because she is unable to give jobs, having none. She flew into a rage at the girl and there they were facing each other in a rage both helpless, helpless. This woman told me once that she could hardly bear the suffering she saw, hardly hear it, that she couldn't eat sometimes and had nightmares at night.

So they stood there, the two women, in a rage, the girl weeping and the woman shouting at her. In the eight months of unemployment she had gotten ragged, and the woman was shouting that she would not send her out like that. "Why don't you shine your shoes?" she kept scolding the girl, and the girl kept sobbing and sobbing because she was starving.

"We can't recommend you like that," the harassed YWCA woman said, knowing she was starving, unable to do anything. And the girls and the women sat docilely, their eyes on the ground, ashamed to look at each other, ashamed of something.

Sitting here waiting for a job, the women have been talking in low voices about the girl Ellen. They talk in low voices with not too much pity for her, unable to see through the mist of their own torment. "What happened to Ellen?" one of them asks. She knows the answer already. We all know it.

A young girl who went around with Ellen tells about seeing her last evening back of a cafe downtown, outside the kitchen door, kicking, showing her legs so that the cook came out and gave her some food and some men gathered in the alley and threw small coin on the ground for a look at her legs. And the girl says enviously that Ellen had a swell breakfast and treated her to one too, that cost two dollars.

A scrub woman whose hips are bent forward from stooping with hands gnarled like watersoaked branches clicks her tongue in disgust. No one saves their money, she says, a little money and these foolish young things buy a hat, a dollar for breakfast, a bright scarf. And they do. If you've ever been without money, or food, something very strange happens when you get a bit of money, a kind of madness. You don't care. You can't remember that you had no money before, that the money will be gone. You can remember nothing but that there is the money for which you have been suffering. Now here it is. A lust takes hold of you. You see food in the windows. In imagination you eat hugely; you taste a thousand meals. You look in windows. Colors are brighter; you buy something to dress up in. An excitement takes hold of you. You know it is suicide but you can't help it. You must have food, dainty, splendid food, and a bright hat so once again you feel blithe, rid of that ratty gnawing shame.

"I guess she'll go on the street now," a thin woman says faintly, and no one takes the trouble to comment further. Like every commodity now the body is difficult to sell and the girls say you're lucky if you get fifty cents.

It's very difficult and humiliating to sell one's body.

Perhaps it would make it clear if one were to imagine having to go out on the street to sell, say, one's overcoat. Suppose you have to sell your coat so you can have breakfast and a place to sleep, say, for fifty cents. You decide to sell your only coat. You take it off and put it on your arm. The street, that has before been just a street, now becomes a mart, something entirely different. You must approach someone now and admit you are destitute and are now selling your clothes, your most intimate possessions. Everyone will watch you talking to the stranger showing him your overcoat, what a good coat it is. People will stop and watch curiously. You will be quite naked on the street. It is even harder to try to sell one's self, more humiliating. It is even humiliating to try to sell one's labor. When there is no buyer.

The thin woman opens the wire cage. There's a job for a nursemaid, she says. The old gnarled women, like old horses, know that no one will have them walk the streets with the young so they don't move. Ellen's friend gets up and goes to the window. She is unbelievably jaunty. I know she hasn't had work since last January. But she has a flare of life in her that glows like a tiny red flame and some tenacious thing, perhaps only youth, keeps it burning bright. Her legs are thin but the runs in her old stockings are neatly mended clear down her flat shank. Two bright spots of rouge conceal her pallor. A narrow belt is drawn tightly around her thin waist, her long shoulders stoop and the blades show. She runs wild as a colt hunting pleasure, hunting sustenance.

It's one of the great mysteries of the city where women go when they are out of work and hungry. There are not many women in the bread line. There are no flop houses for women as there are for men, where a bed can be had for a quarter or less. You don't see women lying on the floor at the mission in the free flops. They obviously don't sleep in the jungle or under newspapers in the park. There is no law I suppose against their being in these places but the fact is they rarely are.

Yet there must be as many women out of jobs in cities and suffering extreme poverty as there are men. What happens to them? Where do they go? Try to get into the YW without any money or looking down at heel. Charities take care of very few and only those that are called "deserving." The lone girl is under suspicion by the virgin women who dispense charity.

I've lived in cities for many months broke, without help, too timid to get in bread lines. I've known many women to live like this until they simply faint on the street from privations, without saying a word to anyone. A woman will shut herself up in a room until it is taken away from her, and eat a cracker a day and be as quiet as a mouse so there are no social statistics concerning her.

I don't know why it is, but a woman will do this unless she has dependents, will go for weeks verging on starvation, crawling in some hole, going through the streets ashamed, sitting in libraries, parks, going for days without speaking to a living soul like some exiled beast, keeping the runs mended in her stockings, shut up in terror in her own misery, until she becomes too super-sensitive and timid to even ask for a job.

Bernice says even strange men she has met in the park have sometimes, that is in better days, given her a loan to pay her room rent. She has always paid them back.

In the afternoon the young girls, to forget the hunger and the deathly torture and fear of being jobless, try to pick up a man to take them to a ten-cent show. They never go to more expensive ones, but they can always find a man willing to spend a dime to have the company of a girl for the afternoon.

Sometimes a girl facing the night without shelter will approach a man for lodging. A woman always asks a man for help. Rarely another woman. I have known girls to sleep in men's rooms for the night on a pallet without molestation and be given breakfast in the morning.

It's no wonder these young girls refuse to marry, refuse to rear children. They are like certain savage tribes, who, when they have been conquered, refuse to breed.

Not one of them but looks forward to starvation for the coming winter. We are in a jungle and know it. We are beaten, entrapped. There is no way out. Even if there were a job, even if that thin acrid woman came and gave everyone in the room a job for a few days, a few hours, at thirty cents an hour, this would all be repeated tomorrow, the next day and the next.

Not one of these women but knows that despite years of labor there is only starvation, humiliation in front of them.

Mrs. Gray, sitting across from me, is a living spokesman for the futility of labor. She is a warning. Her hands are scarred with labor. Her body is a great puckered scar. She has given birth to six children, buried three, supported them all alive and dead, bearing them, burying them, feeding them. Bred in hunger they have been spare, susceptible to disease. For seven years she tried to save her boy's arm from amputation, diseased from tuberculosis of the bone. It is almost too suffocating to think of that long close horror of years of child-bearing, child-feeding, rearing, with the bare suffering of providing a meal and shelter.

Now she is fifty. Her children, economically insecure, are drifters. She never hears of them. She doesn't know if they are alive. She doesn't know if she is alive. Such subtleties of suffering are not for her. For her the brutality of hunger and cold. Not until these are done away with can those subtle feelings that make a human being be indulged.

She is lucky to have five dollars ahead of her. That is her security. She has a tumor that she will die of. She is thin as a worn dime with her tumor sticking out of her side. She is brittle and bitter. Her face is not the face of a human being. She has borne more than it is possible for a human being to bear. She is reduced to the least possible denominator of human feelings.

It is terrible to see her little bloodshot eyes like a beaten hound's fearful in terror.

We cannot meet her eyes. When she looks at any of us we look away. She is like a woman drowning and we turn away. We must ignore those eyes that are surely the eyes of a person drowning, doomed. She doesn't cry out. She goes down decently. And we all look away.

The young ones know though. I don't want to marry. I don't want any children. So they all say. No children. No marriage. They arm themselves alone, keep up alone. The man is helpless now. He cannot provide. If he propagates he cannot take care of his young. The means are not in his hands. So they live alone. Get what fun they can. The life risk is too horrible now. Defeat is too clearly written on it.

So we sit in this room like cattle, waiting for a nonexistent job, willing to work to the farthest atom of energy, unable to work, unable to get food and lodging, unable to bear children—here we must sit in this shame looking at the floor, worse than beasts at a slaughter.

It is appalling to think that these women sitting so listless in the room may work as hard as it is possible for a human being to work, may labor night and day, like Mrs. Gray wash streetcars from midnight to dawn and offices in the early evening, scrub for fourteen and fifteen hours a day, sleep only five hours or so, do this their whole lives, and never earn one day of security, having always before them the pit of the future. The endless labor, the bending back, the water-soaked hands, earning never more than a week's wages, never having in their hands more life than that.

It's not the suffering of birth, death, love that the young reject, but the suffering of endless labor without dream, eating the spare bread in bitterness, being a slave without the security of a slave.

Study and Discussion Questions

1. What does Le Sueur suggest is specific to *women's* experience during the Great Depression?
2. What is the narrator's relation to the scene she describes?
3. List the characteristics of each of the following women: Bernice, Ellen, Mrs. Gray.
4. List examples of metaphor and simile in this essay. How do they contribute to the mood and the argument Le Sueur is creating?
5. What is Le Sueur's thesis in this essay?
6. Where are the men?
7. Characterize the relation of these women to each other.

Suggestions for Writing

1. Analyze the passage that begins "It is very difficult and humiliating to sell one's body" and ends "When there is no buyer." What series of analogies is Le Sueur making in this passage?
2. To what extent has the situation of unemployed and poor women changed or not changed in the United States since Le Sueur published this essay in 1932? What factors can you advance to account for this?
3. What emotional response did you have to "Women on the Breadlines"? What in particular evoked that response?

❀ ❀ ❀

GEORGE ORWELL

George Orwell is the pen name used by the British author Eric Blair (1903–1950). Orwell was born in the Indian village of Motihari, near Nepal, where his father was stationed in the Civil Service. India was then part of the British Empire; Orwell's grandfather too had served the Empire in the Indian Army. From 1907 to 1922 Orwell lived in England, returning to India and Burma and a position in the Imperial Police, which he held until 1927. This is the period about which he writes in "Shooting an Elephant." Thereafter he lived in England, Paris, Spain, and elsewhere, writing on a wide range of topics. He fought in the Spanish Civil War and was actively engaged in several political movements, always against totalitarianism of any kind. He is best known today for two novels of political satire: *Animal Farm* (1945) and *1984* (1949). He was also a prolific journalist and essayist, with his essays collected in five volumes. "Shooting an Elephant" was first published in 1936 and later collected in a book of the same name in 1950. Note that Orwell is writing as an older, wiser man about events that took place when he was in his early twenties some two decades previously. This combined perspective of the young man experiencing the incident and the older man looking back on it is part of the rich reading experience.

Shooting an Elephant

In Moulmein, in Lower Burma, I was hated by large numbers of people— the only time in my life that I have been important enough for this to happen to me. I was sub-divisional police officer of the town, and in an aimless, petty, kind of way anti-European feeling was very bitter. No one had the guts to raise a riot, but if a European woman went through the bazaars alone somebody would probably spit betel juice over her dress. As a police officer I was an obvious target and was baited whenever it seemed safe to do so. When a nimble Burman tripped me up on the football field and the referee (another Burman) looked the other way, the crowd yelled with hideous laughter. This happened more than once. In the end the sneering yellow faces of young men that met me everywhere, the insults hooted after me when I was at a safe distance, got badly on my nerves. The young Buddhist priests were the worst of all. There were several thousand of them in the town and none of them seemed to have anything to do except stand on street corners and jeer at Europeans.

1

From *Shooting an Elephant and Other Essays* by George Orwell. Published by Harcourt Brace and Company. Harcourt Brace and Company and Heath & Co., Ltd.

All this was perplexing and upsetting. For at that time I had already made up my mind that imperialism was an evil thing and the sooner I chucked up my job and got out of it the better. Theoretically—and secretly, of course—I was all for the Burmese and all against their oppressors, the British. As for the job I was doing, I hated it more bitterly than I can perhaps make clear. In a job like that you see the dirty work of Empire at close quarters. The wretched prisoners huddling in the stinking cages of the lock-ups, the grey, cowed faces of the long-term convicts, the scarred buttocks of the men who had been flogged with bamboos—all these oppressed me with an intolerable sense of guilt. But I could get nothing into perspective. I was young and ill-educated and I had had to think out my problems in the utter silence that is imposed on every Englishman in the East. I did not even know that the British Empire is dying, still less did I know that it is a great deal better than the younger empires that are going to supplant it. All I knew was that I was stuck between my hatred of the empire I served and my rage against the evil-spirited little beasts who tried to make my job impossible. With one part of my mind I thought of the British Raj as an unbreakable tyranny, as something clamped down, in *saecula saeculorum,* upon the will of prostrate peoples; with another part I thought that the greatest joy in the world would be to drive a bayonet into a Buddhist priest's guts. Feelings like these are the normal by-products of imperialism; ask any Anglo-Indian official, if you can catch him off duty.

One day something happened which in a roundabout way was enlightening. It was a tiny incident in itself, but it gave me a better glimpse than I had had before of the real nature of imperialism—the real motives for which despotic governments act. Early one morning the sub-inspector at a police station the other end of the town rang me up on the 'phone and said that an elephant was ravaging the bazaar. Would I please come and do something about it? I did not know what I could do, but I wanted to see what was happening and I got on to a pony and started out. I took my rifle, an old .44 Winchester and much too small to kill an elephant, but I thought the noise might be useful *in terrorem.* Various Burmans stopped me on the way and told me about the elephant's doings. It was not, of course, a wild elephant, but a tame one which had gone "must." It had been chained up, as tame elephants always are when their attack of "must" is due, but on the previous night it had broken its chain and escaped. Its mahout, the only person who could manage it when it was in that state, had set out in pursuit, but had taken the wrong direction and was now twelve hours' journey away, and in the morning the elephant had suddenly reappeared in the town. The Burmese population had no weapons and were quite helpless against it. It had already destroyed somebody's bamboo hut, killed a cow and raided some fruit-stalls and devoured the stock; also it had met the municipal rubbish van and, when the driver jumped out and took to his heels, had turned the van over and inflicted violence upon it.

The Burmese sub-inspector and some Indian constables were waiting for me in the quarter where the elephant had been seen. It was a very poor quarter, a labyrinth of squalid bamboo huts, thatched with palm-leaf, winding all over a steep hillside. I remember that it was a cloudy, stuffy, morning at the beginning of the rains. We began questioning the people as to where the elephant had gone and, as usual, failed to get any definite information. That is invariably the case in the East; a story always sounds clear enough at a distance, but the nearer you get to the scene of events the vaguer it becomes. Some of the people said that the elephant had gone in one direction, some said that he had gone in another, some professed not even to have heard of any elephant. I had almost made up my mind that the whole story was a pack of lies, when we heard yells a little distance away. There was a loud, scandalized cry of "Go away, child! Go away this instant!" and an old woman with a switch in her hand came round the corner of a hut, violently shooing away a crowd of naked children. Some more women followed, clicking their tongues and exclaiming; evidently there was something that the children ought not to have seen. I rounded the hut and saw a man's dead body sprawling in the mud. He was an Indian, a black Dravidian coolie, almost naked, and he could not have been dead many minutes. The people said that the elephant had come suddenly upon him round the corner of the hut, caught him with its trunk, put its foot on his back and ground him into the earth. This was the rainy season and the ground was soft, and his face had scored a trench a foot deep and a couple of yards long. He was lying on his belly with arms crucified and head sharply twisted to one side. His face was coated with mud, the eyes wide open, the teeth bared and grinning with an expression of unendurable agony. (Never tell me, by the way, that the dead look peaceful. Most of the corpses I have seen looked devilish.) The friction of the great beast's foot had stripped the skin from his back as neatly as one skins a rabbit. As soon as I saw the dead man I sent an orderly to a friend's house nearby to borrow an elephant rifle. I had already sent back the pony, not wanting it to go mad with fright and throw me if it smelt the elephant.

The orderly came back in a few minutes with a rifle and five cartridges, and meanwhile some Burmans had arrived and told us that the elephant was in the paddy fields below, only a few hundred yards away. As I started forward practically the whole population of the quarter flocked out of the houses and followed me. They had seen the rifle and were all shouting excitedly that I was going to shoot the elephant. They had not shown much interest in the elephant when he was merely ravaging their homes, but it was different now that he was going to be shot. It was a bit of fun to them, as it would be to an English crowd; besides they wanted the meat. It made me vaguely uneasy. I had no intention of shooting the elephant—I had merely sent for the rifle to defend myself if necessary—and it is always unnerving to have a crowd following you. I marched down the hill, looking and feeling a fool, with the rifle over my shoulder and an evergrowing army of people jostling at my heels. At the bottom, when you got away from the huts, there was a metalled road and beyond that a miry waste of paddy fields a thousand yards across, not yet ploughed but soggy from the first rains and dotted with coarse grass. The elephant was standing eight yards from the road, his left side towards us. He took not the slightest notice of the crowd's

5

approach. He was tearing up bunches of grass, beating them against his knees to clean them and stuffing them into his mouth.

I had halted on the road. As soon as I saw the elephant I knew with perfect certainty that I ought not to shoot him. It is a serious matter to shoot a working elephant—it is comparable to destroying a huge and costly piece of machinery—and obviously one ought not to do it if it can possibly be avoided. And at that distance, peacefully eating, the elephant looked no more dangerous than a cow. I thought then and I think now that his attack of "must" was already passing off; in which case he would merely wander harmlessly about until the mahout came back and caught him. Moreover, I did not in the least want to shoot him. I decided that I would watch him for a little while to make sure that he did not turn savage again, and then go home.

But at that moment I glanced round at the crowd that had followed me. It was an immense crowd, two thousand at the least and growing every minute. It blocked the road for a long distance on either side. I looked at the sea of yellow faces above the garish clothes—faces all happy and excited over this bit of fun, all certain that the elephant was going to be shot. They were watching me as they would watch a conjurer about to perform a trick. They did not like me, but with the magical rifle in my hands I was momentarily worth watching. And suddenly I realized that I should have to shoot the elephant after all. The people expected it of me and I had got to do it; I could feel their two thousand wills pressing me forward, irresistibly. And it was at this moment, as I stood there with the rifle in my hands, that I first grasped the hollowness, the futility of the white man's dominion in the East. Here was I, the white man with his gun, standing in front of the unarmed native crowd— seemingly the leading actor of the piece; but in reality I was only an absurd puppet pushed to and fro by the will of those yellow faces behind. I perceived in this moment that when the white man turns tyrant it is his own freedom that he destroys. He becomes a sort of hollow, posing dummy, the conventionalized figure of a sahib. For it is the condition of his rule that he shall spend his life in trying to impress the "natives," and so in every crisis he has got to do what the "natives" expect of him. He wears a mask, and his face grows to fit it. I had got to shoot the elephant. I had committed myself to doing it when I sent for the rifle. A sahib has got to act like a sahib; he has got to appear resolute, to know his own mind and do definite things. To come all that way, rifle in hand, with a thousand people marching at my heels, and then to trail feebly away, having done nothing—no, that was impossible. The crowd would laugh at me. And my whole life, every white man's life in the East, was one long struggle not to be laughed at.

But I did not want to shoot the elephant. I watched him beating his bunch of grass against his knees, with that preoccupied grandmotherly air that elephants have. It seemed to me that it would be murder to shoot him. At that age I was not squeamish about killing animals, but I had never shot an elephant and never wanted to. (Somehow it always seems worse to kill a *large* animal.)

Besides, there was the beast's owner to be considered. Alive, the elephant was worth at least a hundred pounds; dead, he would only be worth the value of his tusks, five pounds, possibly. But I had got to act quickly. I turned to some experienced-looking Burmans who had been there when we arrived, and asked them how the elephant had been behaving. They all said the same thing: he took no notice of you if you left him alone, but he might charge if you went too close to him.

It was perfectly clear to me what I ought to do. I ought to walk up to within, say, twenty-five yards of the elephant and test his behavior. If he charged, I could shoot; if he took no notice of me, it would be safe to leave him until the mahout came back. But also I knew that I was going to do no such thing. I was a poor shot with a rifle and the ground was soft mud into which one would sink at every step. If the elephant charged and I missed him, I should have about as much chance as a toad under a steam-roller. But even then I was not thinking particularly of my own skin, only of the watchful yellow faces behind. For at that moment, with the crowd watching me, I was not afraid in the ordinary sense, as I would have been if I had been alone. A white man mustn't be frightened in front of "natives"; and so, in general, he isn't frightened. The sole thought in my mind was that if anything went wrong those two thousand Burmans would see me pursued, caught, trampled on and reduced to a grinning corpse like that Indian up the hill. And if that happened it was quite probable that some of them would laugh. That would never do. There was only one alternative. I shoved the cartridges into the magazine and lay down on the road to get a better aim.

The crowd grew very still, and a deep, low, happy sigh, as of people who see 10
the theatre curtain go up at last, breathed from innumerable throats. They were going to have their bit of fun after all. The rifle was a beautiful German thing with cross-hair sights. I did not then know that in shooting an elephant one would shoot to cut an imaginary bar running from ear-hole to ear-hole. I ought, therefore, as the elephant was sideways on, to have aimed straight at his ear-hole; actually I aimed several inches in front of this, thinking the brain would be further forward.

When I pulled the trigger I did not hear the bang or feel the kick—one never does when a shot goes home—but I heard the devilish roar of glee that went up from the crowd. In that instant, in too short a time, one would have thought, even for the bullet to get there, a mysterious, terrible change had come over the elephant. He neither stirred nor fell, but every line of his body had altered. He looked suddenly stricken, shrunken, immensely old, as though the frightful impact of the bullet had paralysed him without knocking him down. At last, after what seemed a long time—it might have been five seconds, I dare say—he sagged flabbily to his knees. His mouth slobbered. An enormous senility seemed to have settled upon him. One could have imagined him thousands of years old. I fired again into the same spot. At the second shot he did not collapse but climbed with desperate slowness to his feet and stood weakly upright, with legs sagging and head drooping. I fired a third time. That was the shot that did for him. You could see the agony of it jolt his whole body and knock the last remnant of strength from his legs. But in falling he seemed for a moment to rise, for as his hind legs collapsed beneath him he seemed to tower upward like a huge rock toppling, his trunk reaching skywards like a tree. He trumpeted, for the first and only time. And then down he came, his belly towards me, with a crash that seemed to shake the ground even where I lay.

I got up. The Burmans were already racing past me across the mud. It was obvious that the elephant would never rise again, but he was not dead. He was breathing very rhythmically with long rattling gasps, his great mound of a side painfully rising and falling. His mouth was wide open—I could see far down into caverns of pale pink throat. I waited a long time for him to die, but his breathing did not weaken. Finally I fired my two remaining shots into the spot where I thought his heart must be. The thick blood welled out of him like red velvet, but still he did not die. His body did not even jerk when the shots hit him, the tortured breathing continued without a pause. He was dying, very slowly and in great agony, but in some world remote from me where not even a bullet could damage him further. I felt that I had got to put an end to that dreadful noise. It seemed dreadful to see the great beast lying there, powerless to move and yet powerless to die, and not even to be able to finish him. I sent back for my small rifle and poured shot after shot into his heart and down his throat. They seemed to make no impression. The tortured gasps continued as steadily as the ticking of a clock.

In the end I could not stand it any longer and went away. I heard later that it took him half an hour to die. Burmans were bringing dahs and baskets even before I left, and I was told they had stripped his body almost to the bones by the afternoon.

Afterwards, of course, there were endless discussions about the shooting of the elephant. The owner was furious, but he was only an Indian and could do nothing. Besides, legally I had done the right thing, for a mad elephant has to be killed, like a mad dog, if its owner fails to control it. Among the Europeans opinion was divided. The older men said I was right, the younger men said it was a damn shame to shoot an elephant for killing a coolie, because an elephant was worth more than any damn Coringhee coolie. And afterwards I was very glad that the coolie had been killed; it put me legally in the right and it gave me a sufficient pretext for shooting the elephant. I often wondered whether any of the others grasped that I had done it solely to avoid looking a fool.

Questions on Meaning

1. Orwell confesses to many strong emotions about the Burmese people, such as his comment "I thought that the greatest joy in the world would be to drive a bayonet into a Buddhist priest's guts." Does he actually hate these people? Explain your answer with examples from the essay.

2. At the beginning of the third paragraph Orwell introduces the "tiny incident" that will for him reveal the "real motives for which despotic governments act." What are those motives, as revealed by the incident and Orwell's later comments?
3. Even before the incident with the elephant, Orwell tells us he had discovered that "imperialism was an evil thing." How many different kinds of "evil" are shown through the course of the essay?

Questions on Rhetorical Strategy and Style

1. The primary rhetorical strategy used in this essay is narration—telling the story of shooting the elephant. In addition to the story itself, Orwell keeps up a sort of running commentary on the meaning of the story, helping us understand it as he analyzes the events of the story. Reread the essay and chart how Orwell moves back and forth between narration and analysis.
2. Orwell is particularly vivid in his descriptive language, often achieving a larger meaning through descriptive details and figurative language. Reread the section of the essay that describes the elephant's slow death as he seems "thousands of years old" (paragraph 11) What meanings are suggested by the language Orwell uses in this descriptive passage?

Writing Assignments

1. Fear of embarrassment before others can be a powerful motivating force, as the young Orwell discovers in this incident. Search your memory for a time when you yourself took some action simply to avoid embarrassment. How did it feel at the time? Did you feel foolish afterwards? Would you do the same again now in the same circumstances? Try to be as honest in your self-evaluation as Orwell was in his.
2. Have you ever been among a large group of people very different from yourself, either in another country or in a different cultural group in the United States? Did your concerns lead to fears or negative feelings about these others? Some social scientists have said that people naturally fear things or other people that are very different from themselves, that negative reactions are "normal" even if not healthy or fair to the others. Do you think there is such a natural impulse in people? What are the good and bad effects of this impulse? Present your thoughts in an essay exploring the topic.
3. We all have a "public self" and a "private self." Your public self may be the self you show to others in the academic world or on the job. It may be similar to your private self, what you really are like inside, or it may be very different. The two selves may be harmonious or in conflict, as they were for Orwell. Write an essay defining the difference between these two selves and exploring both the constructive and problematic aspects of this duality.

❀ ❀ ❀

MOHANDAS K. GANDHI

Mohandas Karamchand Gandhi (1869–1948), called the Mahatma ("Great Soul"), is widely considered one of the great leaders of the twentieth century. Not only did he successfully lead the nonviolent struggle to end Britain's imperial rule of his native India, but he also developed a philosophy of nonviolent resistance and civil disobedience campaigns that continues to be used to protest and change the unjust exercise of authority throughout the world. In addition, the example of his own life of devotion to his people and country, to truth, to nonviolence, and to self-sacrifice in these causes made him millions of admirers.

An English-trained lawyer, Gandhi moved to Natal, South Africa, early in his career. To protest the country's policies of racial discrimination, he founded the Natal Indian Congress in 1894 and then began to develop his concept of *satyagraha*: nonviolent, but sometimes illegal, resistance to illegitimate authority. *Satyagraha* was first put into practice in mass civil disobedience in South Africa, and Gandhi brought it back to India when he returned there in 1914. In 1915 he founded his first religious community, called the Satyagraha Ashram, in his native district of Gujarat. After World War I ended, Gandhi began organizing mass nonviolent demonstrations and other acts of civil disobedience aimed at repressive colonial laws and, ultimately, at forcing the British to grant Indian Home Rule. Gandhi was arrested, convicted, and imprisoned for seditious conspiracy in 1922. He continued to speak, write, and lead the movement for Home Rule in the 1920s, 1930s, and 1940s. In the 1947 Partition, India and Pakistan were created as independent states, dividing the Hindu and Muslim majority populations. During the violence that broke out between the two populations at Partition, Gandhi, who had opposed the two-state model, began a fast to protest the bloodshed and to work for peace and understanding. During this fast, a Hindu fanatic, enraged by Gandhi's words of brotherhood, assassinated him on January 30, 1948.

THIRD CLASS IN INDIAN RAILWAYS
BY
M. K. GANDHI

GANDHI PUBLICATIONS LEAGUE
BHADARKALI-LAHORE

It was not without great diffidence that I undertook to speak to you at all. And I was hard put to it in the selection of my subject. I have chosen a very delicate and difficult subject. It is delicate because of the peculiar views I hold upon Swadeshi, and it is difficult because I have not that command of language which is necessary for giving adequate expression to my thoughts. I know that I may rely upon your indulgence for the many shortcomings you will no doubt find in my address, the more so when I tell you that there is nothing in what I am about to say that I am not either already practising or am not preparing to practise to the best of my ability. It encourages me to observe that last month you devoted a week to prayer in the place of an address. I have earnestly prayed that what I am about to say may bear fruit and I know that you will bless my word with a similar prayer.

After much thinking I have arrived at a definition of Swadeshi that, perhaps, best illustrates my meaning. Swadeshi is that spirit in us which restricts us to the use and service of our immediate surroundings to the exclusion of the more remote. Thus, as for religion, in order to satisfy the requirements of the definition, I must restrict myself to my ancestral religion. That is the use of my immediate religious surrounding. If I find it defective, I should serve it by purging it of its defects. In the domain of politics I should make use of the indigenous institutions and serve them by curing them of their proved defects. In that of economics I should use only things that are produced by my immediate neighbours and serve those industries by making them efficient and complete where they might be found wanting. It is suggested that such Swadeshi, if reduced to practice, will lead to the millennium. And, as we do not abandon our pursuit after the millennium, because we do not expect quite to reach it within our times, so may we not abandon Swadeshi even though it may not be fully attained for generations to come.

Let us briefly examine the three branches of Swadeshi as sketched above. Hinduism has become a conservative religion and, therefore, a mighty force because of the Swadeshi spirit underlying it. It is the most tolerant because it is non-proselytising, and it is as capable of expansion today as it has been found to be in the past. It has succeeded not in driving out, as I think it has been erroneously held, but in absorbing Buddhism. By reason of the Swadeshi spirit, a Hindu refuses to change his religion, not necessarily because he considers it to be the best, but because he knows that he can complement it by introducing reforms. And what I have said about Hinduism is, I suppose, true of the other great faiths of the world, only it is held that it is specially so in the case of Hinduism. But here comes the point I am labouring to reach. If there is any substance in what I have said, will not the great missionary bodies of India, to whom she owes a deep debt of gratitude for what they have done and are doing, do still better and serve the spirit of Christianity better by dropping the goal of proselytising while continuing their philanthropic work? I hope you will not consider this to be an impertinence on my part. I make the suggestion in all sincerity and with due humility. Moreover I have some claim upon your attention. I have endeavoured to study the Bible. I consider it as part of my scriptures. The spirit of the Sermon on the Mount competes almost on equal terms with the Bhagavad Gita for the domination of my heart. I yield to no Christian in the strength of devotion with which I sing "Lead kindly light" and several other inspired hymns of a similar nature. I have come under the influence of noted Christian missionaries belonging to different denominations. And enjoy to this day the privilege of friendship with some of them. You will perhaps, therefore, allow that I have offered the above suggestion not as a biased Hindu, but as a humble and impartial student of religion with great leanings towards Christianity. May it not be that "Go ye unto all the world" message has been somewhat narrowly interpreted and the spirit of it missed? It will not be denied, I speak from experience, that many of the conversions are only so-called. In some cases the appeal has gone not to the heart but to the stomach. And in every case a conversion leaves a sore behind it which, I venture to think, is avoidable. Quoting again from experience, a new birth, a change of heart, is perfectly possible in every one of the great faiths. I know I am now treading upon thin ice. But I do not apologise in closing this part of my subject, for saying that the frightful outrage that is just going on in Europe, perhaps shows that the message of Jesus of Nazareth, the Son of Peace, had been little understood in Europe, and that light upon it may have to be thrown from the East.

I have sought your help in religious matters, which it is yours to give in a special sense. But I make bold to seek it even in political matters. I do not believe that religion has nothing to do with politics. The latter divorced from religion is like a corpse only fit to be buried. As a matter of fact, in your own silent manner, you influence politics not a little. And I feel that, if the attempt to separate politics from religion had not been made as it is even now made, they would not have degenerated as they often appear to have done. No one considers that the political life of the country is in a happy state. Following out the Swadeshi spirit, I observe the indigenous institutions and the village panchayats hold me. India is really a republican country, and it is because it is that, that it has survived every shock hitherto delivered. Princes and potentates, whether they were Indian born or foreigners, have hardly touched the vast masses except for collecting revenue. The latter in their turn seem to have rendered unto Caesar what was Caesar's and for the rest have done much as they have liked. The vast organisation of caste answered not only the religious wants of the community, but it answered to its political needs. The villagers managed their internal affairs through the caste system, and through it they dealt with any oppression from the ruling power or powers. It is not possible to deny of a nation that was capable of producing the caste system its wonderful power of organisation. One had but to attend the great Kumbha Mela at Hardwar last year to know how skilful that organisation must have been, which without any seeming effort was able effectively to cater for more than a million pilgrims. Yet it is the fashion to say that we lack organising ability. This is true, I fear, to a certain extent, of those who have been nurtured in the new traditions. We have laboured under a terrible handicap owing to an almost fatal departure from the Swadeshi spirit. We, the educated classes, have received our education through a foreign tongue. We have therefore not reacted upon the masses. We want to represent the masses, but we fail. They recognise us not much more than they recognise the English officers. Their hearts are an open book to neither. Their aspirations are not ours. Hence there is a break. And you witness not in reality failure to organise but want of correspondence between the representatives and the represented. If during the last fifty years we had been educated through the vernaculars, our elders and our servants and our neighbours would have partaken of our knowledge; the discoveries of a Bose or a Ray would have been household treasures as are the Ramayan and the Mahabharat. As it is, so far as the masses are concerned, those great discoveries might as well have been made by foreigners. Had instruction in all the branches of learning been given through the vernaculars, I make bold to say that they would have been enriched wonderfully. The question of village sanitation, etc., would have been solved long ago. The village panchayats would be now a living force in a special way, and India would almost be enjoying self-government suited to its requirements and would have been spared the humiliating spectacle of organised assassination on its sacred soil. It is not too late to mend. And you can help if you will, as no other body or bodies can.

And now for the last division of Swadeshi, much of the deep poverty of the masses is due to the ruinous departure from Swadeshi in the economic and industrial life. If not an article of commerce had been brought from outside India, she would be today a land flowing with milk and honey. But that was not to be. We were greedy and so was England. The connection between England and India was based clearly upon an error. But she does not remain in India in error. It is her declared policy that India is to be held in trust for her people. If this be true, Lancashire must stand aside. And if the Swadeshi doctrine is a sound doctrine, Lancashire can stand aside without hurt, though it may sustain a shock for the time being. I think of Swadeshi not as a boycott movement undertaken by way of revenge. I conceive it as religious principle to be followed by all. I am no economist, but I have read some treatises which show that England could easily become a self-sustained country, growing all the produce she needs. This may be an utterly ridiculous proposition, and perhaps the best proof that it cannot be true, is that England is one of the largest importers in the world. But India cannot live for Lancashire or any other country before she is able to live for herself. And she can live for herself only if she produces and is helped to produce everything for her requirements within her own borders. She need not be, she ought not to be, drawn into the vertex of mad and ruinous competition which breeds fratricide, jealousy and many other evils. But who is to stop her great millionaires from entering into the world competition? Certainly not legislation. Force of public opinion, proper education, however, can do a great deal in the desired direction. The hand-loom industry is in a dying condition. I took special care during my wanderings last year to see as many weavers as possible, and my heart ached to find how they had lost, how families had retired from this once flourishing and honourable occupation. If we follow the Swadeshi doctrine, it would be your duty and mine to find out neighbours who can supply our wants and to teach them to supply them where they do not know how to proceed, assuming that there are neighbours who are in want of healthy occupation. Then every village of India will almost be a self-supporting and self-contained unit, exchanging only such necessary commodities with other villages where they are not locally producible. This may all sound nonsensical. Well, India is a country of nonsense. It is nonsensical to parch one's throat with thirst when a kindly Mahomedan is ready to offer pure water to drink. And yet thousands of Hindus would rather die of thirst than drink water from a Mahomedan household. These nonsensical men can also, once they are convinced that their religion demands that they should wear garments manufactured in India only and eat food only grown in India, decline to wear any other clothing or eat any other food. Lord Curzon set the fashion for tea-drinking. And that pernicious drug now bids fair to overwhelm the nation. It has already undermined the digestive apparatus of hundreds of thousands of men and women and constitutes an additional tax upon their slender purses. Lord Hardinge can set the fashion for Swadeshi, and almost the whole of India forswear foreign goods. There is a verse in the Bhagavad Gita, which, freely rendered, means, masses follow the classes. It is easy to undo the evil if the thinking portion of the community were to take the Swadeshi vow even though it may, for a time, cause considerable inconvenience. I hate legislative interference, in any department of life. At best it is the lesser evil. But I would tolerate, welcome, indeed, plead for a stiff protective duty upon foreign goods. Natal, a British colony, protected its sugar by taxing the sugar that came from another British colony, Mauritius. England has sinned against India by forcing free trade upon her. It may have been food for her, but it has been poison for this country.

It has often been urged that India cannot adopt Swadeshi in the economic life at any rate. Those who advance this objection do not look upon Swadeshi as a rule of life. With them it is a mere patriotic effort not to be made if it involved any self-denial. Swadeshi, as defined here, is a religious discipline to be undergone in utter disregard of the physical discomfort it may cause to individuals. Under its spell the deprivation of a pin or a needle, because these are not manufactured in India, need cause no terror. A Swadeshist will learn to do without hundreds of things which today he considers necessary. Moreover, those who dismiss Swadeshi from their minds by arguing the impossible, forget that Swadeshi, after all, is a goal to be reached by steady effort. And we would be making for the goal even if we confined Swadeshi to a given set of articles allowing ourselves as a temporary measure to use such things as might not be procurable in the country.

There now remains for me to consider one more objection that has been raised against Swadeshi. The objectors consider it to be a most selfish doctrine without any warrant in the civilised code of morality. With them to practise Swadeshi is to revert to barbarism. I cannot enter into a detailed analysis of the position. But I would urge that Swadeshi is the only doctrine consistent with the law of humility and love. It is arrogance to think of launching out to serve the whole of India when I am hardly able to serve even my own family. It were better to concentrate my effort upon the family and consider that through them I was serving the whole nation and, if you will, the whole of humanity. This is humility and it is love. The motive will determine the quality of the act. I may serve my family regardless of the sufferings I may cause to others. As for instance, I may accept an employment which enables me to extort money from people, I enrich myself thereby and then satisfy many unlawful demands of the family. Here I am neither serving the family nor the State. Or I may recognise that God has given me hands and feet only to work with for my sustenance and for that of those who may be dependent upon me. I would then at once simplify my life and that of those whom I can directly reach. In this instance I would have served the family without causing injury to anyone else. Supposing that everyone followed this mode of life, we should have at once an ideal state. All will not reach that state at the same time. But those of us who, realising its truth, enforce it in practice will clearly anticipate and accelerate the coming of that happy day. Under this plan of life, in seeming to serve India to the exclusion of every other country I do not harm any other country. My patriotism is both exclusive and inclusive. It is exclusive in the sense that in all humility I confine my attention to the land of my birth, but it is inclusive in the sense that my service is not of a competitive or antagonistic nature. Sic utere tuo ut alienum non la is not merely a legal maxim, but it is a grand doctrine of life. It is the key to a proper practice of Ahimsa or love. It is for you, the custodians of a great faith, to set the fashion and show, by your preaching, sanctified by practice, that patriotism based on hatred "killeth" and that patriotism based on love "giveth life."

Questions on Meaning

1. Swadeshi is probably a new word for most readers. Look at Gandhi's definition in the second paragraph and look up the word in a dictionary. Putting aside both definitions, how would you define the term?
2. To whom is Gandhi speaking? What is the occasion of the address?
3. How does Gandhi feel free trade has impacted his country and Britain?
4. Imperialistic nations often explain their need to stay in a country by claiming that the native inhabitants are incapable of managing their own affairs. How does Gandhi respond to this reasoning?
5. What is the "hand-loom" industry, and why is it so important to Gandhi?

Questions on Rhetorical Strategy and Style

1. In what ways does Gandhi establish ethos early in the speech?
2. Gandhi's speech is inherently persuasive. Identify a few moments where he uses persuasive language and explain the intended effect on his audience.
3. The speech is organized into five primary sections. Examine his three primary claims and discuss the relative merits of organizing his speech in this manner.
4. How does Gandhi refute objections to his plan? In what ways is he successful? Unsuccessful?

Writing Assignments

1. In the section where Gandhi discusses politics, he claims there is a separation between "the representatives and the represented." What reasons does Gandhi offer for this separation? Considering your government, what specific factors may contribute to a similar separation? Write a long paragraph or brief essay exploring this separation.
2. Gandhi claims that "[politics] divorced from religion is like a corpse only fit to be buried." Considering this passage, write a long paragraph or brief essay defending the United States' separation of church and state or offer support for Gandhi's position in the United States.
3. How does Gandhi interpret the Sermon on the Mount and what does he say about proselytizing? Examine his methods and strategies for inoffensively presenting his ideas.
4. According to Gandhi, what responsibilities do he and his audience have if they are going to follow Swadeshi? Reflecting on these responsibilities, what will result from following the Swadeshi doctrine?
5. Write a long paragraph or brief essay describing the impact of implementing Swadeshi in the United States.

❀ ❀ ❀

MOHANDAS K. GANDHI AND JUDAH L. MAGNES

In 1938, Gandhi responded to requests from friends and supporters to speak out about the rise of Hitler and anti-Semitism in Germany. Gandhi condemned the racism of the Nazis, which he believed was similar to the racial and religious discrimination and oppression he had experienced and fought throughout his life. In his *Harijan* article of November 26, 1938, published only a few weeks after the state-sponsored German pogrom against the Jews known as *Kristalnacht*, he recommends that the Jews adopt *satyagraha* to combat persecution.

In response to this letter, several prominent Jewish leaders wrote public letters to Gandhi. Martin Buber, the Austrian-born religious philosopher (1878–1965), replied at length. Buber wrote from Palestine, where he had recently fled from Nazi Germany. He criticized the analogy Gandhi drew between the Jews of Germany and the Indians of South Africa. Another response came from Judah L. Magnes (1877–1948), the president of Hebrew University in Jerusalem. Magnes was born in San Francisco and became a prominent Reform Jewish rabbi and social activist. He embraced pacifism during World War I and spoke at antiwar rallies in 1917. When he moved to Palestine after the war, he worked for Arab-Jewish reconciliation and eventually advocated a binational state. Magnes writes to Gandhi on February 26, 1939, with admiration for his ideas and work but with reservations and questions about his understanding of the Jews' plight in Nazi Germany.

How Should the German Jews Respond to Nazi Persecution?

M. K. Gandhi, "The Jews"

Several letters have been received by me asking me to declare my views about the persecution of the Jews in Germany. It is not without hesitation that I venture to offer my views on this very difficult question. 1

My sympathies are all with the Jews. I have known them intimately in South Africa. Some of them became lifelong companions. Through these friends I came to learn much of their age-long persecution. They have been the untouchables of Christianity. The parallel between their treatment by Christians and the treatment of untouchables by Hindus is very close. Religious sanction has been invoked in both cases for the justification of the inhuman treatment meted out to them. Apart from the friendships, therefore, there is the more common universal reason for my sympathy for the Jews.

The German persecution of the Jews seems to have no parallel in history. The tyrants of old never went so mad as Hitler seems to have gone. And he is doing it with religious zeal. For, he is propounding a new religion of exclusive and militant nationalism in the name of which any inhumanity becomes an act of humanity to he rewarded here and hereafter. The crime of an obviously mad but intrepid youth is being visited upon his whole race with unbelievable ferocity. If there ever could be a justifiable war in the name of and for humanity, a war against Germany, to prevent the wanton persecution of a whole race, would be completely justified. But I do not believe in any war. A discussion of the pros and cons of such a war is, therefore, outside my horizon or province.

But if there can be no war against Germany, even for such a crime as is being committed against the Jews, surely there can be no alliance with Germany. How can there be alliance between a nation which claims to stand for justice and democracy and one which is the declared enemy of both? Or is England drifting towards armed dictatorship and all it means?

Germany is showing to the world how efficiently violence can be worked when it is not hampered by any hypocrisy or weakness masquerading as humanitarianism. It is also showing how hideous, terrible and terrifying it looks in its nakedness. 5

Can the Jews resist this organized and shameless persecution? Is there a way to preserve their self-respect, and not to feel helpless, neglected and forlorn? I submit there is. No person who has faith in a living God need feel helpless or forlorn. Jehovah of the Jews is a God more personal than the God of the Christians, the Mussalmans or the Hindus, though as a matter of fact, in essence, He is common to all and one without a second and beyond description. But as the Jews attribute personality to God and believe that He rules every action of theirs, they ought not to feel helpless. If I were a Jew and were born in Germany and earned my livelihood there, I would claim Germany as my home even as the tallest gentile German might, and challenge him to shoot me or cast me in the dungeon; I would refuse to be expelled or to submit to discriminating treatment. And for doing this I should not wait for the fellow Jews to join me in civil resistance, but would have confidence that in the end the rest were bound to follow my example. If one Jew or all the Jews were to accept the prescription here offered, he or they cannot be worse off than now. And suffering voluntarily undergone will bring them an inner strength and joy which no number of resolutions of sympathy passed in the world outside Germany can. Indeed, even if Britain, France and America were to declare hostilities against Germany, they can bring no inner joy, no inner strength. The calculated violence of Hitler may even result in a general massacre of the Jews by way of his first answer to the declaration of such hostilities. But if the Jewish mind could be prepared for voluntary suffering, even the massacre I have imaged could be turned into a day of thanksgiving and joy that Jehovah had wrought deliverance of the race even at the hands of the tyrant. For to the God-fearing, death has no terror. It is a joyful sleep to be followed by a waking that would be all the more refreshing for the long sleep.

It is hardly necessary for me to point out that it is easier for the Jews than for the Czechs to follow my prescription. And they have in the Indian Satyagraha campaign in South Africa an exact parallel. There the Indians occupied precisely the same place that the Jews occupy in Germany. The persecutions had also a religious tinge. President Kruger used to say that the white Christians were the chosen of God and Indians were inferior beings created to serve the whites. A fundamental clause in the Transvaal constitution was that there should be no equality between the whites and colored races including Asiatics. There too the Indians were consigned to ghettos described as locations. The other disabilities were almost of the same type as those of the Jews in Germany. The Indians, a mere handful, resorted to Satyagraha without any backing from the world outside or the Indian Government. Indeed the British officials tried to dissuade the satyagrahis from their contemplated step. World opinion and the Indian Government came to their aid after eight years of fighting. And that too was by way of diplomatic pressure, not of a threat of war.

But the Jews of Germany can offer Satyagraha under infinitely better auspices than the Indians of South Africa. The Jews are a compact, homogeneous community in Germany. They are far more gifted than the Indians of South Africa. And they have organized world opinion behind them. I am convinced that, if someone with courage and vision can arise among them to lead them in non-violent action, the winter of their despair can in the twinkling of an eye be turned into the summer of hope. And what has today become a degrading man-hunt can he turned into a calm and determined stand offered by unarmed men and women possessing the strength of suffering given to them by Jehovah. It will be then a truly religious resistance offered against the godless fury of a dehumanized man. The German Jews will score a lasting victory over the German gentiles in the sense that they will have converted the latter to an appreciation of human dignity. They will have rendered service to fellow-Germans and proved their title to be the real Germans as against those who are today dragging, however unknowingly, the German name into the mire. . . .

Judah L. Magnes, "A Letter to Gandhi"

What you have said recently about the Jews is the one statement I have yet seen which needs to be grappled with fundamentally. Your statement is a challenge, particularly to those of us who had imagined ourselves your disciples.

I am sure you must be right in asserting the Jews of Germany can offer Satyagraha to the "godless fury of their dehumanized oppressors."

But how and when? You do not give the answer. You may say that you are not sufficiently acquainted with the German persecution to outline the practical technique of Satyagraha for use by the German Jews. But one of the great things about you and your doctrine has been that you have always emphasized the chance of practical success, if Satyagraha be offered. Yet to the German Jews you have not given the practical advice which only your unique experience could provide, and I wonder if it is helpful merely in general terms to call upon the Jews of Germany to offer Satyagraha. I have heard that many a Jew of Germany has asked himself how and when Satyagraha must be offered without finding the answer. Conditions in Germany are radically different from those that have prevailed in South Africa and in India. Those of us who are outside Germany must, I submit, think through most carefully the advice we proffer the unfortunates who are caught in the claws of the Hitler beast. . . .

If ever a people was a people of nonviolence through century after century, it was the Jews. I think they need learn but little from anyone in faithfulness to their God and in their readiness to suffer while they sanctify His Name.

What is new and great about you has seemed to me this, that you have 5 exalted nonviolence into the dominant principle of all of life, both religious, social and political; and that you have made it into a practical technique both of communing with the divine and of battling for a newer world, which would respect the human personality of even the most insignificant outcast. You exhort the German Jew to add "the surpassing contribution of non-violent action" to the precious contribution he has already made to mankind. But you could be of much greater help by showing how the technique of Satyagraha could be of practical use to the German Jews.

You would have the right to say that some Jew should point this technique out. But we have no one comparable to you as religious and political leader.

There are, as I am aware, other elements besides nonviolence in Satyagraha. There is non-cooperation, and the renunciation of property, and the disdain of death.

The Jews are a people who exalt life, and they can hardly be said to disdain death. Leviticus 18:5 reads: "My Judgments, which if a man do he shall live in them," and the interpretation adds, as a principle of Jewish life, "and not die through them." For this reason I have often wondered if we Jews are fit subjects for Satyagraha. As to property, it is but natural that Jews should want to take along with them a minimum of their property from Germany or elsewhere, so as not to fall a burden upon others. It would, I am sure, give you satisfaction to see how large numbers of refugees, who in Germany were used to wealth, comfort, culture, have, without too much complaint and very often cheerfully, buckled down to a new life in Palestine, many of them in the fields or in menial employment in the cities.

It is in the matter of non-cooperation that I have a question of importance to put to you.

A plan is being worked out between the Evian Refugee Committee and the German Government which appears to me to be nothing short of devilish. The details are not yet known. But it seems to amount to this: The German Government is to confiscate all German Jewish property, and in exchange for increased foreign trade and foreign currency which Jews are to bring them, they will permit a limited number of Jews to leave Germany annually for the next several years. The scheme involves the sale of millions of pounds of debentures to be issued by a Refugee or Emigration Bank to be created. Whether Governments are to subscribe to these debentures, I do not know. But certainly the whole Jewish world will be called upon to do so.

Here is the dilemma: If one does not subscribe, no Jews will be able to escape from this prison of torture called Germany. If one does subscribe, one will be cooperating with that Government, and be dealing in Jewish flesh and blood in a most modern and up-to-date slave market. I see before me here in Jerusalem a child who is happy, now that he is away from the torment there; and his brother, or parent, or grandparent. One of the oldest of Jewish sayings is: "Who saves a single soul in Israel is as if he had saved a whole world." Not to save a living soul? And yet to cooperate with the powers of evil and darkness? Have you an answer?

You touch upon a vital phase of the whole subject when you say that, "if there ever could be a justifiable war in the name of and for humanity, a war against Germany, to prevent the wanton persecution of a whole race, would be completely justified. But I do not believe in any war. A discussion of the pros and cons of such a war is therefore outside my horizon and province."

But it is on "the pros and cons of such a war" that I would ask your guidance. The question gives me no rest, and I am sure there are many like myself. Like you, I do not believe in any war. I have pledged myself never to take part in a war. I spoke up for pacifism in America during the World War [I], alongside of many whose names are known to you. That war brought the "peace" of Versailles and the Hitlerism of today. But my pacifism, as I imagine the pacifism of many others, is passing through a pitiless crisis. I ask myself: Suppose America, England, France are dragged into a war with the Hitler bestiality, what am I to do and what am I to teach? This war may destroy the life of a large part of the youth of the world, and force those who remain alive to lead the lives of savages. Yet I know I would pray with all my heart for the defeat of the Hitler inhumanity; and am I then to stand aside and let others do the fighting? During the last war I prayed for a peace without defeat or victory.

The answer given by Romain Rolland in his little book, *Par la révolution la paix* (1935), seems to be that while he himself as an individual continues to refuse to bear arms, he will do everything he can to help his side (at that time, Russia) to win the war. That is hardly a satisfying answer.

I ask myself how I might feel if I were not a Jew. Is the Hitler iniquity really   15 as profound as I imagine? I recall that during the last war the arguments against Germany were much the same as those of today. I took no stock in those arguments then. Perhaps it is the torture of my own people that enrages me unduly? Yet it is my conviction that, being a Jew, my sense of outrage at injustice may, perhaps, be a bit more alive than the average, and therefore more aware of the evils which the Hitler frenzy is bringing upon all mankind. The Jew, scattered as he is, is an outpost, bearing the brunt earlier of an action against mankind, and bearing it longest. For a dozen reasons, he is a convenient scapegoat. I say this in order to make the point that if the Jew is thoroughly aroused about an evil such as the Hitler madness, his excitement and indignation are apt to be based not only on personal hurt, but on a more or less authentic appraisal of the evil that must be met.

If you will take the trouble of looking at the little pamphlet I am sending, *Fellowship in War* (1936), you will see that I have an ineradicable belief that no war whatsoever can be a righteous war. The war tomorrow for the "democracies" or for some other noble slogan will be just as unrighteous or as fatuous as was the "war to save democracy" yesterday. Moreover, to carry on the war, the democracies will perforce become totalitarian. Not even a war against the ghastly Hitler savagery can be called righteous, for we all of us have sinned, conquerors and conquered alike, and it is because of our sins, because of our lack of generosity and of the spirit of conciliation and renunciation, that the Hitler beast has been enabled to raise its head. Even on the pages of the Nuremberg *Memorbuch* we find the words "Because of our many sins" this and that massacre took place. There can be no war for something good. That is a contradiction in terms. The good is to be achieved through totally different means.

But a war against something evil? If the Hitler cruelty launches a war against you, what would you do, what will you do? Can you refrain from making a choice? It is a choice of evils—a choice between the capitalisms, the imperialisms, the militarisms of the western democracies, and between the Hitler religion. Can one hesitate as to which is the lesser of these two evils? Is not a choice therefore imperative? I am all too painfully conscious that I am beginning to admit that if Hitler hurls his war upon us, we must resist. For us it would thus become not a righteous war, nor, to use your term, a justifiable war, but a necessary war, not for something good, but, because no other choice is left us, against the greater evil. Or do you know of some other choice? ...

1939

Questions about the Passages

1. Why might Gandhi begin with his sympathy for the Jews and his comparison of them to the untouchables within Hinduism?
2. Gandhi implicitly criticizes England in paragraph 4 for the Munich Agreement of October 1938, which Neville Chamberlain had just negotiated a few months before. What is the basis of Gandhi's objection to England's "alliance" with Germany?
3. What is the connection, according to Gandhi, between belief in God and nonviolent resistance or *satyagraha*? What advantages does Gandhi believe the Jews have over the Czechs, who had been forced to cede the Sudetenland to Germany in September 1938?
4. Magnes finds Gandhi's view not fully convincing. In what ways?
5. What aspect of Jewish belief does Magnes think might make Jews poor practitioners of *satyagraha*?
6. Why does Magnes ask Gandhi's guidance about a possible war with Nazi Germany? What case does Magnes make to fight Hitler?

Question about the Argument

1. Gandhi asserts several assumptions, notably in paragraphs 2, 3, 6, 7, and 8. What are they? Does he provide any evidence to support these assumptions? How does he use them in his argument?

THOMAS S. WHITECLOUD (1914–1972)

Thomas S. Whitecloud was born in New York City. His mother was of European descent and his father a Chippewa Indian who graduated from Yale Law School. As a young boy, Whitecloud's father decided to leave his family and return to the Lac du Flambeau Reservation in Wisconsin, where he grew up. Though Whitecloud continued to live with his mother, he spent periods of time living on the reservation. He attended a number of different public and federal Indian schools and worked miscellaneous jobs, including truck driving, farm work, and boxing, until he finally found his milieu at the University of Redlands. Although Whitecloud considered writing and studying literature, he instead opted to study medicine. He received his M.D. in the early 1940s, then served as a surgeon in Europe during World War II. After the war, he worked as an Indian Service doctor in various states until establishing a private practice in Texas. At the time of his death, Whitecloud had several works (essays and poetry) in manuscript form. "Blue Winds Dancing," published his senior year in college, is considered Whitecloud's most notable work.

Blue Winds Dancing   (1938)

There is a moon out tonight. Moon and stars and clouds tipped with moonlight. And there is a fall wind blowing in my heart. Ever since this evening, when against a fading sky I saw geese wedge southward. They were going home.... Now I try to study, but against the pages I see them again, driving southward. Going home.

Across the valley there are heavy mountains holding up the night sky, and beyond the mountains there is home. Home, and peace, and the beat of drums, and blue winds dancing over snow fields. The Indian lodge will fill with my people, and our gods will come and sit among them. I should be there then. I should be at home.

But home is beyond the mountains, and I am here. Here where fall hides in the valleys, and winter never comes down from the mountains. Here where all the trees grow in rows; the palms stand stiffly by the roadsides, and in the groves the orange trees line in military rows, and endlessly bear fruit. Beautiful, yes; there is always beauty in order, in rows of growing things! But it is the beauty of captivity. A pine fighting for existence on a windy knoll is much more beautiful.

In my Wisconsin, the leaves change before the snows come. In the air there is the smell of wild rice and venison cooking; and when the winds come whispering through the forests, they carry the smell of rotting leaves. In the evenings, the loon calls, lonely; and birds sing their last songs before leaving. Bears dig roots and eat late fall berries, fattening for their long winter sleep. Later, when the first snows fall, one awakens in the morning to find the world white and beautiful and clean. Then one can look back over his trail and see the tracks following. In the woods there are tracks of deer and snowshoe rabbits, and long streaks where partridges slide to alight. Chipmunks make tiny footprints on the limbs; and one can hear squirrels busy in hollow trees, sorting acorns. Soft lake waves wash the shores, and sunsets burst each evening over the lakes, and make them look as if they were afire.

That land which is my home! Beautiful, calm—where there is no hurry to get anywhere, no driving to keep up in a race that knows no ending and no goal. No classes where men talk and talk, and then stop now and then to hear their own words come back to them from the students. No constant peering into the maelstrom of one's mind; no worries about grades and honors; no hysterical preparing for life until that life is half over; no anxiety about one's place in the thing they call Society.

I hear again the ring of axes in deep woods, the crunch of snow beneath my feet. I feel again the smooth velvet of ghost-birch bark. I hear the rhythm of the drums.... I am tired. I am weary of trying to keep up this bluff of being civilized. Being civilized means trying to do everything you don't want to, never doing anything you want to. It means dancing to the strings of custom and tradition; it means living in houses and never knowing or caring who is next door. These civilized white men want us to be like them—always dissatisfied, getting a hill and wanting a mountain.

Then again, maybe I am not tired. Maybe I'm licked. Maybe I am just not smart enough to grasp these things that go to make up civilization. Maybe I am just too lazy to think hard enough to keep up.

Still, I know my people have many things that civilization has taken from the whites. They know how to give; how to tear one's piece of meat in two and share it with one's brother. They know how to sing—how to make each man his own songs and sing them; for their music they do not have to listen to other men singing over a radio. They know how to make things with their hands, how to shape beads into design and make a thing of beauty from a piece of birch bark.

But we are inferior. It is terrible to have to feel inferior; to have to read reports of intelligence tests, and learn that one's race is behind. It is terrible to sit in classes and hear men tell you that your people worship sticks of wood— that your gods are all false, that the Manitou forgot your people and did not write them a book.

I am tired. I want to walk again among the ghost-birches. I want to see the leaves turn in autumn, the smoke rise from the lodgehouses, and to feel the blue winds. I want to hear the drums; I want to hear the drums and feel the blue whispering winds.

There is a train wailing into the night. The trains go across the mountains. It would be easy to catch a freight. They will say he has gone back to the blanket; I don't care. The dance at Christmas. . . .

A bunch of bums warming at a tiny fire talk politics and women and joke about the Relief and the WPA[1] and smoke cigarettes. These men in caps and overcoats and dirty overalls living on the outskirts of civilization are free, but they pay the price of being free in civilization. They are outcasts. I remember a sociology professor lecturing on adjustment to society; hobos and prostitutes and criminals are individuals who never adjusted, he said. He could learn a lot if he came and listened to a bunch of bums talk. He would learn that work and a woman and a place to hang his hat are all the ordinary man wants. These are all he wants, but other men are not content to let him want only these. He must be taught to want radios and automobiles and a new suit every spring. Progress would stop if he did not want these things. I listen to hear if there is any talk of communism or socialism in the hobo jungles. There is none. At best there is a sort of disgusted philosophy about life. They seem to think there should be a better distribution of wealth, or more work, or something. But they are not rabid about it. The radicals live in the cities.

I find a fellow headed for Albuquerque, and talk road-talk with him. "It is hard to ride fruit cars. Bums break in. Better to wait for a cattle car going back to the Middle West, and ride that." We catch the next east-bound and walk the tops until we find a cattle car. Inside, we crouch near the forward wall, huddle, and try to sleep. I feel peaceful and content at last. I am going home. The cattle car rocks. I sleep.

---

[1]Works Progress Administration, Federal government agency established in 1935 to create jobs for the unemployed.

Morning and the desert. Noon and the Salton Sea, lying more lifeless than a mirage under a somber sun in a pale sky. Skeleton mountains rearing on the skyline, thrusting out of the desert floor, all rock and shadow and edges. Desert. Good country for an Indian reservation. . . .

Yuma and the muddy Colorado. Night again, and I wait shivering for the dawn.

Phoenix. Pima country. Mountains that look like cardboard sets on a forgotten stage. Tucson. Papago country. Giant cacti that look like petrified hitchhikers along the highways. Apache country. At El Paso my road-buddy decides to go on to Houston. I leave him, and head north to the mesa country. Las Cruces and the terrible Organ Mountains, jagged peaks that instill fear and wondering. Albuquerque. Pueblos along the Rio Grande. On the boardwalk there are some Indian women in colored sashes selling bits of pottery. The stone age offering its art to the twentieth century. They hold up a piece and fix the tourists with black eyes until, embarrassed, he buys or turns away. I feel suddenly angry that my people should have to do such things for a living. . . .

Santa Fe trains are fast, and they keep them pretty clean of bums. I decide to hurry and ride passenger coaltenders. Hide in the dark, judge the speed of the train as it leaves, and then dash out, and catch it. I hug the cold steel wall of the tender and think of the roaring fire in the engine ahead, and of the passengers back in the dining car reading their papers over hot coffee. Beneath me there is blur of rails. Death would come quick if my hands should freeze and I fall. Up over the Sangre De Cristo range, around cliffs and through canyons to Denver. Bitter cold here, and I must watch out for Denver Bob. He is a railroad bull who has thrown bums from fast freights. I miss him. It is too cold, I suppose. On north to the Sioux country.

Small towns lit for the coming Christmas. On the streets of one I see a beam-shouldered young farmer gazing into a window filled with shining silver toasters. He is tall and wears a blue shirt buttoned, with no tie. His young wife by his side looks at him hopefully. He wants decorations for his place to hang his hat to please his woman. . . .

Northward again. Minnesota, and great white fields of snow; frozen lakes, and dawn running in dusk without noon. Long forests wearing white. Bitter cold, and one night the northern lights. I am nearing home.

I reach Woodruff at midnight. Suddenly I am afraid, now that I am but twenty miles from home. Afraid of what my father will say, afraid of being looked on as a stranger by my own people. I sit by a fire and think about myself and all the other young Indians. We just don't seem to fit in anywhere— certainly not among the whites, and not among the older people. I think again about the learned sociology professor and his professing. So many things seem to be clear now that I am away from school and do not have to worry about some man's opinion of my ideas. It is easy to think while looking at dancing flames.

Morning. I spend the day cleaning up, and buying some presents for my family with what is left of my money. Nothing much, but a gift is a gift, if a man buys it with his last quarter. I wait until evening, then start up the track toward home.

Christmas Eve comes in on a north wind. Snow clouds hang over the pines, and the night comes early. Walking along the railroad bed, I feel the calm peace of snowbound forests on either side of me. I take my time; I am back in a world where time does not mean so much now. I am alone; alone but not nearly so lonely as I was back on the campus at school. Those are never lonely who love the snow and the pines; never lonely when the pines are wearing white shawls and snow crunches coldly underfoot. In the woods I know there are the tracks of deer and rabbit; I know that if I leave the rails and go into the woods I shall find them. I walk along feeling glad because my legs are light and my feet seem to know that they are home. A deer comes out of the woods just ahead of me, and stands silhouetted on the rails. The North, I feel, has welcomed me home. I watch him and am glad that I do not wish for a gun. He goes into the woods quietly, leaving only the design of his tracks in the snow. I walk on. Now and then I pass a field, white under the night sky, with houses at the far end. Snow comes from the chimneys of the houses, and I try to tell what sort of wood each is burning by the smoke; some burn pine, others aspen, others tamarack. There is one from which comes black coal smoke that rises lazily and drifts out over the tops of the trees. I like to watch houses and try to imagine what might be happening in them.

Just as a light snow begins to fall, I cross the reservation boundary; somehow it seems as though I have stepped into another world. Deep woods in a white-and-black winter night. A faint trail leading to the village.

The railroad on which I stand comes from a city sprawled by a lake—a city with a million people who walk around without seeing one another; a city sucking the life from all the country around; a city with stores and police and intellectuals and criminals and movies and apartment houses; a city with its politics and libraries and zoos.

Laughing, I go into the woods. As I cross a frozen lake I begin to hear the drums. Soft in the night the drums beat. It is like the pulse beat of the world. The white line of the lake ends at a black forest, and above the trees the blue winds are dancing.

I come to the outlying houses of the village. Simple box houses, etched black in the night. From one or two windows soft lamp light falls on the snow. Christmas here, too, but it does not mean much; not much in the way of parties and presents. Joe Sky will get drunk. Alex Bodidash will buy his children red mittens and a new sled. Alex is a Carlisle man, and tries to keep his home up to white standards. White standards. Funny that my people should be ever falling farther behind. The more they try to imitate whites the more tragic the result. Yet they want us to be imitation white men. About all we imitate well are their vices.

The village is not a sight to instill pride, yet I am not ashamed; one can never be ashamed of his own people when he knows they have dreams as beautiful as white snow on a tall pine.

Father and my brother and sister are seated around the table as I walk in. Father stares at me for a moment, then I am in his arms, crying on his shoulder. I give them the presents I have brought, and my throat tightens as I watch my sister save carefully bits of red string from the packages. I hide my feelings by wrestling with my brother when he strikes my shoulder in token of affection. Father looks at me, and I know he has many questions, but he seems to know why I have come. He tells me to go on alone to the lodge, and he will follow.

I walk along the trail to the lodge, watching the northern lights forming in the heavens. White waving ribbons that seem to pulsate with the rhythm of the drums. Clean snow creaks beneath my feet, and a soft wind sighs through the trees, singing to me. Everything seems to say "Be happy! You are home now—you are free. You are among friends—we are your friends; we, the trees, and the snow, and the lights." I followed the trail to the lodge. My feet are light, my heart seems to sing to the music, and I hold my head high. Across white snow fields blue winds are dancing.

Before the lodge door I stop, afraid. I wonder if my people will remember me. I wonder—"Am I Indian, or am I white?" I stand before the door a long time. I hear the ice groan on the lake, and remember the story of the old woman who is under the ice, trying to get out, so she can punish some runaway lovers. I think to myself, "If I am white I will not believe that story; if I am Indian, I will know that there is an old woman under the ice." I listen for a while, and I know that there is an old woman under the ice. I look again at the lights, and go in.

Inside the lodge there are many Indians. Some sit on benches around the walls, others dance in the center of the floor around a drum. Nobody seems to notice me. It seems as though I were among a people I have never seen before. Heavy women with long black hair. Women with children on their knees— small children that watch with intent black eyes the movements of the dancers, whose small faces are solemn and serene. The faces of the old people are serene, too, and their eyes are merry and bright. I look at the old men. Straight, dressed in dark trousers and beaded velvet vests, wearing soft moccasins. Dark, lined faces intent on the music. I wonder if I am at all like them. They dance on, lifting their feet to the rhythm of the drums, swaying lightly, looking upward. I look at their eyes, and am startled at the rapt attention to the rhythm of the music.

The dance stops. The men walk back to the walls, and talk in low tones or with their hands. There is little conversation, yet everyone seems to be shar- ing some secret. A woman looks at a small boy wandering away, and he comes back to her.

Strange, I think, and then remember. These people are not sharing words— they are sharing a mood. Everyone is happy. I am so used to white people that it seems strange so many people could be together without someone talking. These Indians are happy because they are together, and because the night is beautiful outside, and the music is beautiful. I try hard to forget school and white people, and be one of these—my people. I try to forget everything but the night, and it is a part of me; that I am one with my people and we are all a part of something universal. I watch eyes, and see now that the old people are speaking to me. They nod slightly, imperceptibly, and their eyes laugh into mine. I look around the room. All the eyes are friendly; they all laugh. No one questions my being here. The drums begin to beat again, and I catch the invitation in the eyes of the old men. My feet begin to lift to the rhythm, and I look out beyond the walls into the night and see the lights. I am happy. It is beautiful. I am home.

Study and Discussion Questions

1. What are some of the things that draw Whitecloud back home?
2. What are his major criticisms of "civilization"?
3. Depression-era social criticism often focuses on poverty, on unequal distribution of material wealth. How does Whitecloud's social criticism go further?
4. What does Whitecloud find to admire, and to connect with, among the "bums"?
5. What are some of the signs that Whitecloud is not fully at one with the people of his village?
6. Why is the essay titled "Blue Winds Dancing"? Why "blue"? Why "dancing"?

Suggestions for Writing

1. Explain, using evidence from the essay, why you think Whitecloud will, or will not, return to school after Christmas. Will his protest remain merely verbal?
2. Have you experienced anything at all like what Whitecloud describes? Has going to college alienated you in any way from your family or community? If so, discuss how your experience is similar to and different from his.
3. Does Whitecloud idealize life on the reservation? Are there any hints in the essay that all is not well there?

RICHARD WRIGHT (1908–1960)

Richard Wright was born in Natchez, Mississippi. Despite a tumultuous childhood of poverty, Wright managed to graduate from his high school as valedictorian. Afterward, he moved to Memphis and, working odd jobs to support himself, began reading and writing prolifically. In 1927 he moved to Chicago and joined the Federal Writer's Project a few years later. Like many writers and intellectuals disillusioned with the breakdown of capitalism during the Great Depression, Wright joined the Communist Party during the 1930s in response to social inequities. Although Wright left the party years later, Marxist thought would inevitably influence his writing. The publication of *Native Son* (1940) brought Wright national recognition, selling 200,000 copies within 30 days. *Native Son*, like much of Wright's early work, is written in the naturalistic mode, exploring the pathology of racism and its determining effects on both the individual and society. A prolific writer of novels, essays, poetry, and short stories, selected works include the story collections *Uncle Tom's Children* (1938) and *Eight Men* (1945); the novels *Native Son* (1940), the autobiographical *Black Boy* (1945), *The Outsider* (1953), and *The Long Dream* (1958). Several of his works have been published posthumously, including *American Hunger* (1977). "The Man Who Went to Chicago" is included in *Eight Men*. A larger version of the essay was included as part of *American Hunger*.

The Man Who Went to Chicago   (1945)

When I rose in the morning the temperature had dropped below zero. The house was as cold to me as the Southern streets had been in winter. I dressed, doubling my clothing. I ate in a restaurant, caught a streetcar, and rode south, rode until I could see no more black faces on the sidewalks. I had now crossed the boundary line of the Black Belt and had entered the territory where jobs were perhaps to be had from white folks. I walked the streets and looked into shop windows until I saw a sign in a delicatessen: PORTER WANTED.

I went in and a stout white woman came to me.

"Vat do you vant?" she asked.

The voice jarred me. She's Jewish, I thought, remembering with shame the obscenities I used to shout at Jewish storekeepers in Arkansas.

"I thought maybe you needed a porter," I said.

"Meester 'Offman, he eesn't here yet," she said. "Vill you vait?"

"Yes, ma'am."

"Seet down."

"No, ma'am, I'll wait outside."

"But eet's cold out zhere," she said.

"That's all right," I said.

She shrugged. I went to the sidewalk. I waited for half an hour in the bitter cold, regretting that I had not remained in the warm store, but unable to go back inside. A bald, stoutish white man went into the store and pulled off his coat. Yes, he was the boss man . . .

"Zo you vant a job?" he asked.

"Yes, sir," I answered, guessing at the meaning of his words.

"Vhere you vork before?"

"In Memphis, Tennessee."

"My brudder-in-law vorked in Tennessee vonce," he said.

I was hired. The work was easy, but I found to my dismay that I could not understand a third of what was said to me. My slow Southern ears were baffled by their clouded, thick accents. One morning Mrs. Hoffman asked me to go to a neighboring store—it was owned by a cousin of hers—and get a can of chicken *à la* king. I had never heard the phrase before and I asked her to repeat it.

"Don't you know nosing?" she demanded of me.

"If you would write it down for me, I'd know what to get," I ventured timidly.

"I can't vite!" she shouted in a sudden fury. "Vat kinda boy iss you?"

I memorized the separate sounds that she had uttered and went to the neighboring store.

"Mrs. Hoffman wants a can Cheek Keeng Awr Lar Keeng," I said slowly, hoping he would not think I was being offensive.

"All vite," he said, after staring at me a moment.

He put a can into a paper bag and gave it to me; outside in the street I opened the bag and read the label: Chicken *à la* King. I cursed, disgusted with myself. I knew those words. It had been her thick accent that had thrown me off. Yet I was not angry with her for speaking broken English; my English, too, was broken. But why could she not have taken more patience? Only one answer came to my mind. I was black and she did not care. Or so I thought . . . I was persisting in reading my present environment in the light of my old one. I reasoned thus: though English was my native tongue and America my native land, she, an alien, could operate a store and earn a living in a neighborhood where I could not even live. I reasoned further that she was aware of this and was trying to protect her position against me.

It was not until I had left the delicatessen job that I saw how grossly I had misread the motives and attitudes of Mr. Hoffman and his wife. I had not yet learned anything that would have helped me to thread my way through these perplexing racial relations. Accepting my environment at its face value, trapped by my own emotions, I kept asking myself what had black people done to bring this crazy world upon them?

The fact of the separation of white and black was clear to me; it was its effect upon the personalities of people that stumped and dismayed me. I did not feel that I was a threat to anybody; yet, as soon as I had grown old enough to think, I had learned that my entire personality, my aspirations, had long ago been discounted; that, in a measure, the very meaning of the words I spoke could not be fully understood.

And when I contemplated the area of No Man's Land into which the Negro mind in America had been shunted I wondered if there had ever been in all human history a more corroding and devastating attack upon the personalities of men than the idea of racial discrimination. In order to escape the racial attack that went to the roots of my life, I would have gladly accepted any way of life but the one in which I found myself. I would have agreed to live under a system of feudal oppression, not because I preferred feudalism but because I felt that feudalism made use of a limited part of a man, defined man, his rank, his function in society. I would have consented to live under the most rigid type of dictatorship, for I felt that dictatorships, too, defined the use of men, however degrading that use might be.

While working as a porter in Memphis I had often stood aghast as a friend of mine had offered himself to be kicked by the white men; but now, while working in Chicago, I was learning that perhaps even a kick was better than uncertainty . . . I had elected, in my fevered search for honorable adjustment to the American scene, not to submit and in doing so I had embraced the daily horror of anxiety, of tension, of eternal disquiet. I could now sympathize with—though I could never bring myself to approve—those tortured blacks who had given up and had gone to their white tormentors and had said: "Kick me, if that's all there is for me; kick me and let me feel at home, let me have peace!"

Color-hate defined the place of black life as below that of white life; and the black man, responding to the same dreams as the white man, strove to bury within his heart his awareness of this difference because it made him lonely and afraid. Hated by whites and being an organic part of the culture that hated him, the black man grew in turn to hate in himself that which others hated in him. But pride would make him hate his self-hate, for he would not want whites to know that he was so thoroughly conquered by them that his total life was conditioned by their attitude; but in the act of hiding his self-hate, he could not help but hate those who evoked his self-hate in him. So each part of his day would be consumed in a war with himself, a good part of his energy would be spent in keeping control of his unruly emotions, emotions which he had not wished to have, but could not help having. Held at bay by the hate of others, preoccupied with his own feelings, he was continuously at war with reality. He became inefficient, less able to see and judge the objective world. And when he reached that state, the white people looked at him and laughed and said:

"Look, didn't I tell you niggers were that way?"

To solve this tangle of balked emotion, I loaded the empty part of the ship of my personality with fantasies of ambition to keep it from toppling over into the sea of senselessness. Like any other American, I dreamed of going into business and making money; I dreamed of working for a firm that would allow me to advance until I reached an important position; I even dreamed of organizing secret groups of blacks to fight all whites . . . And if the blacks would not agree to organize, then they would have to be fought. I would end up again with self-hate, but it was now a self-hate that was projected outward upon other blacks. Yet I knew—with that part of my mind that the whites had given me—that none of my dreams were possible. Then I would hate myself for allowing my mind to dwell upon the unattainable. Thus the circle would complete itself.

Slowly I began to forge in the depths of my mind a mechanism that repressed all the dreams and desires that the Chicago streets, the newspapers, the movies were evoking in me. I was going through a second childhood; a new sense of the limit of the possible was being born in me. What could I dream of that had the barest possibility of coming true? I could think of nothing. And, slowly, it was upon exactly that nothingness that my mind began to dwell, that constant sense of wanting without having, of being hated without reason. A dim notion of what life meant to a Negro in America was coming to consciousness in me, not in terms of external events, lynchings, Jim Crowism, and the endless brutalities, but in terms of crossed-up feeling, of emotional tension. I sensed that Negro life was a sprawling land of unconscious suffering, and there were but few Negroes who knew the meaning of their lives, who could tell their story.

Word reached me that an examination for postal clerk was impending and at once I filed an application and waited. As the date for the examination drew near, I was faced with another problem. How could I get a free day without losing my job? In the South it would have been an unwise policy for a Negro to have gone to his white boss and asked for time to take an examination for another job. It would have implied that the Negro did not like to work for the white boss, that he felt he was not receiving just consideration and, inasmuch as most jobs that Negroes held in the South involved a personal, paternalistic relationship, he would have been risking an argument that might have led to violence.

I now began to speculate about what kind of man Mr. Hoffman was, and I found that I did not know him; that is, I did not know his basic attitude toward Negroes. If I asked him, would he be sympathetic enough to allow me time off with pay? I needed the money. Perhaps he would say: "Go home and stay home if you don't like this job!" I was not sure of him. I decided, therefore, that I had better not risk it. I would forfeit the money and stay away without telling him.

The examination was scheduled to take place on a Monday; I had been working steadily and I would be too tired to do my best if I took the examination without benefit of rest. I decided to stay away from the shop Saturday, Sunday, and Monday. But what could I tell Mr. Hoffman? Yes, I would tell him that I had been ill. No, that was too thin. I would tell him that my mother had died in Memphis and that I had gone down to bury her. That lie might work.

I took the examination and when I came to the store on Tuesday, Mr. Hoffman was astonished, of course.

"I didn't sink you vould ever come back," he said.

"I'm awfully sorry, Mr. Hoffman."

"Vat happened?"

"My mother died in Memphis and I had to go down and bury her," I lied.

He looked at me, then shook his head.

"Rich, you lie," he said.

"I'm not lying," I lied stoutly.

"You vanted to do somesink, zo you zayed ervay," he said shrugging.

"No, sir. I'm telling you the truth," I piled another lie upon the first one.

"No. You lie. You disappoint me," he said.

"Well, all I can do is tell you the truth," I lied indignantly.

"Vy didn't you use the phone?"

"I didn't think of it," I told a fresh lie.

"Rich, if your mudder die, you vould tell me," he said.

"I didn't have time. Had to catch the train," I lied yet again.

"Vhere did you get the money?"

"My aunt gave to me," I said, disgusted that I had to lie and lie again.

"I don't vant a boy vat tells lies," he said.

"I don't lie," I lied passionately to protect my lies.

Mrs. Hoffman joined in and both of them hammered at me.

"Ve know. You come from ze Zouth. You feel you can't tell us ze truth. But ve don't bother you. Ve don't feel like people in ze Zouth. Ve treat you nice, don't ve?" they asked.

"Yes, ma'am," I mumbled.

"Zen vy lie?"

"I'm not lying," I lied with all my strength.

I became angry because I knew that they knew that I was lying. I had lied to protect myself, and then I had to lie to protect my lie. I had met so many white faces that would have violently disapproved of my taking the examination that I could not have risked telling Mr. Hoffman the truth. But how could I tell him that I had lied because I was so unsure of myself? Lying was bad, but revealing my own sense of insecurity would have been worse. It would have been shameful, and I did not like to feel ashamed.

Their attitudes had proved utterly amazing. They were taking time out from their duties in the store to talk to me, and I had never encountered anything like that from whites before. A Southern white man would have said: "Get to hell out of here!" or "All right, nigger. Get to work." But no white people had ever stood their ground and probed at me, questioned me at such length. It dawned upon me that they were trying to treat me as an equal, which made it even more impossible for me ever to tell them that I had lied, why I had lied. I felt that if I confessed I would be giving them a moral advantage over me that would have been unbearable.

"All vight, zay and vork," Mr. Hoffman said. "I know you're lying, but I don't care, Rich."

I wanted to quit. He had insulted me. But I liked him in spite of myself. Yes, I had done wrong; but how on earth could I have known the kind of people I was working for? Perhaps Mr. Hoffman would have gladly consented for me to take the examination; but my hopes had been far weaker than my powerful fears.

Working with them from day to day and knowing that they knew I had lied from fear crushed me. I knew that they pitied me and pitied the fear in me. I resolved to quit and risk hunger rather than stay with them. I left the job that following Saturday, not telling them that I would not be back, not possessing the heart to say good-by. I just wanted to go quickly and have them forget that I had ever worked for them.

After an idle week, I got a job as a dishwasher in a North Side café that had just opened. My boss, a white woman, directed me in unpacking barrels of dishes, setting up new tables, painting, and so on. I had charge of serving breakfast; in the late afternoon I carted trays of food to patrons in the hotel who did not want to come down to eat. My wages were fifteen dollars a week; the hours were long, but I ate my meals on the job.

The cook was an elderly Finnish woman with a sharp, bony face. There were several white waitresses. I was the only Negro in the café. The waitresses were a hard, brisk lot, and I was keenly aware of how their attitudes contrasted with those of Southern white girls. They had not been taught to keep a gulf between me and themselves; they were relatively free of the heritage of racial hate.

One morning as I was making coffee, Cora came forward with a tray loaded with food and squeezed against me to draw a cup of coffee.

"Pardon me, Richard," she said.

"Oh, that's all right," I said in an even tone.

But I was aware that she was a white girl and that her body was pressed closely against mine, an incident that had never happened to me before in my life, an incident charged with the memory of dread. But she was not conscious of my blackness or of what her actions would have meant in the South. And had I not been born in the South, her trivial act would have been as unnoticed by me as it was by her. As she stood close to me, I could not help thinking that if a Southern white girl had wanted to draw a cup of coffee, she would have commanded me to step aside so that she might not come in contact with me. The work of the hot and busy kitchen would have had to cease for the moment so that I could have taken my tainted body far enough away to allow the Southern white girl a chance to get a cup of coffee. There lay a deep, emotional safety in knowing that the white girl who was now leaning carelessly against me was not thinking of me, had no deep, vague, irrational fright that made her feel that I was a creature to be avoided at all costs.

One summer morning a white girl came late to work and rushed into the pantry where I was busy. She went into the women's room and changed her clothes; I heard the door open and a second later I was surprised to hear her voice:

"Richard, quick! Tie my apron!"

She was standing with her back to me and the strings of her apron dangled loose. There was a moment of indecision on my part, then I took the two loose strings and carried them around her body and brought them again to her back and tied them in a clumsy knot.

"Thanks a million," she said, grasping my hand for a split second, and was gone.

I continued my work, filled with all the possible meanings that the tiny, simple, human event could have meant to any Negro in the South where I had spent most of my hungry days.

I did not feel any admiration or any hate for the girls. My attitude was one of abiding and friendly wonder. For the most part I was silent with them, though I knew that I had a firmer grasp of life than most of them. As I worked I listened to their talk and perceived its puzzled, wandering, superficial fumbling with the problems and facts of life. There were many things they wondered about that I could have explained to them, but I never dared.

During my lunch hour, which I spent on a bench in a near-by park, the waitresses would come and sit beside me, talking at random, laughing, joking, smoking cigarettes. I learned about their tawdry dreams, their simple hopes, their home lives, their fear of feeling anything deeply, their sex problems, their husbands. They were an eager, restless, talkative, ignorant bunch, but casually kind and impersonal for all that. They knew nothing of hate and fear, and strove instinctively to avoid all passion.

I often wondered what they were trying to get out of life, but I never stumbled upon a clue, and I doubt if they themselves had any notion. They lived on the surface of their days; their smiles were surface smiles, and their tears were surface tears. Negroes lived a truer and deeper life than they, but I wished that Negroes, too, could live as thoughtlessly, serenely, as they. The girls never talked of their feelings; none of them possessed the insight or the emotional equipment to understand themselves or others. How far apart in culture we stood! All my life I had done nothing but feel and cultivate my feelings; all their lives they had done nothing but strive for petty goals, the trivial material prizes of American life. We shared a common tongue, but my language was a different language from theirs.

It was in the psychological distance that separated the races that the deepest meaning of the problem of the Negro lay for me. For these poor, ignorant white girls to have understood my life would have meant nothing short of a vast revolution in theirs. And I was convinced that what they needed to make them complete and grown-up in their living was the inclusion in their personalities of a knowledge of lives such as I lived and suffered containedly.

As I, in memory, think back now upon those girls and their lives I feel that for white America to understand the significance of the problem of the Negro will take a bigger and tougher America than any we have yet known. I feel that America's past is too shallow, her national character too superficially optimistic, her very morality too suffused with color hate for her to accomplish so vast and complex a task. Culturally the Negro represents a paradox: Though he is an organic part of the nation, he is excluded by the entire tide and direction of American culture. Frankly, it is felt to be right to exclude him, and it is felt to be wrong to admit him freely. Therefore if, within the confines of its present culture, the nation ever seeks to purge itself of its color hate, it will find itself at war with itself, convulsed by a spasm of emotional and moral confusion. If the nation ever finds itself examining its real relation to the Negro, it will find itself doing infinitely more than that; for the anti-Negro attitude of whites represents but a tiny part—though a symbolically significant one—of the moral attitude of the nation. Our too-young and too-new America, lusty because it is lonely, aggressive because it is afraid, insists upon seeing the world in terms of good and bad, the holy and the evil, the high and the low, the white and the black; our America is frightened by fact, by history, by processes, by necessity. It hugs the easy way of damning those whom it cannot understand, of excluding those who look different; and it salves its conscience with a self-draped cloak of righteousness. Am I damning my native land? No; for I, too, share these faults of character! And I really do not think that America, adolescent and cocksure, a stranger to suffering and travail, an enemy of passion and sacrifice, is ready to probe into its most fundamental beliefs.

I knew that not race alone, not color alone, but the daily values that gave meaning to life stood between me and those white girls with whom I worked. Their constant outwardlooking, their mania for radios, cars, and a thousand other trinkets, made them dream and fix their eyes upon the trash of life, made it impossible for them to learn a language that could have taught them to speak of what was in theirs or others' hearts. The words of their souls were the syllables of popular songs.

The essence of the irony of the plight of the Negro in America, to me, is that he is doomed to live in isolation, while those who condemn him seek the basest goals of any people on the face of the earth. Perhaps it would be possible for the Negro to become reconciled to his plight if he could be made to believe that his sufferings were for some remote, high, sacrificial end; but sharing the culture that condemns him, and seeing that a lust for trash is what blinds the nation to his claims, is what sets storms to rolling in his soul.

Though I had fled the pressure of the South, my outward conduct had not changed. I had been schooled to present an unalteringly smiling face and I continued to do so despite the fact that my environment allowed more open expression. I hid my feelings and avoided all relationships with whites that might cause me to reveal them.

Tillie, the Finnish cook, was a tall, ageless, red-faced, raw-boned woman with long snow-white hair, which she balled in a knot at the nape of her neck. She cooked expertly and was superbly efficient. One morning as I passed the sizzling stove, I thought I heard Tillie cough and spit, but I saw nothing; her face, obscured by steam, was bent over a big pot. My senses told me that Tillie had coughed and spat into that pot, but my heart told me that no human being could possibly be so filthy. I decided to watch her. An hour or so later I heard Tillie clear her throat with a grunt, saw her cough and spit into the boiling soup. I held my breath; I did not want to believe what I had seen.

Should I tell the boss lady? Would she believe me? I watched Tillie for another day to make sure that she was spitting into the food. She was; there was no doubt of it. But who would believe me if I told them what was happening?

I was the only black person in the café. Perhaps they would think that I hated the cook. I stopped eating my meals there and bided my time.

The business of the café was growing rapidly and a Negro girl was hired to make salads. I went to her at once.

"Look, can I trust you?" I asked.

"What are you talking about?" she asked.

"I want you to say nothing, but watch that cook."

"For what?"

"Now, don't get scared. Just watch the cook."

She looked at me as though she thought I was crazy; and frankly, I felt that perhaps I ought not say anything to anybody.

"What do you mean?" she demanded.

"All right," I said. "I'll tell you. That cook spits in the food."

"What are you saying?" she asked aloud.

"Keep quiet," I said.

"Spitting?" she asked me in a whisper. "Why would she do that?"

"I don't know. But watch her."

She walked away from me with a funny look in her eyes. But half a hour later she came rushing to me, looking ill, sinking into a chair.

"Oh, God, I feel awful!"

"Did you see it?"

"She *is* spitting in the food!"

"What ought we do?" I asked.

"Tell the lady," she said.

"She wouldn't believe me," I said.

She widened her eyes as she understood. We were black and the cook was white.

"But I can't work here if she's going to do that," she said.

"Then you tell her," I said.

"She wouldn't believe me either," she said.

She rose and ran to the women's room. When she returned she stared at me. We were two Negroes and we were silently asking ourselves if the white boss lady would believe us if we told her that her expert white cook was spitting in the food all day long as it cooked on the stove.

"I don't know," she wailed, in a whisper, and walked away.

I thought of telling the waitresses about the cook, but I could not get up enough nerve. Many of the girls were friendly with Tillie. Yet I could not let the cook spit in the food all day. That was wrong by any human standard of conduct. I washed dishes, thinking, wondering; I served breakfast, thinking, wondering; I served meals in the apartments of patrons upstairs, thinking, wondering. Each time I picked up a tray of food I felt like retching. Finally the Negro salad girl came to me and handed me her purse and hat.

"I'm going to tell her and quit, goddamn," she said.

"I'll quit too, if she doesn't fire her," I said.

"Oh, she won't believe me," she wailed, in agony.

"You tell her. You're a woman. She might believe you."

Her eyes welled with tears and she sat for a long time; then she rose and went abruptly into the dining room. I went to the door and peered. Yes, she was at the desk, talking to the boss lady. She returned to the kitchen and went into the pantry; I followed her.

"Did you tell her?" I asked.

"Yes."

"What did she say?"

"She said I was crazy."

"Oh, God!" I said.

"She just looked at me with those gray eyes of hers," the girl said. "Why would Tillie do that?"

"I don't know," I said.

The boss lady came to the door and called the girl; both of them went into the dining room. Tillie came over to me; a hard cold look was in her eyes.

"What's happening here?" she asked.

"I don't know," I said, wanting to slap her across the mouth.

She muttered something and went back to the stove, coughed, and spat into a bubbling pot. I left the kitchen and went into the back areaway to breathe. The boss lady came out.

"Richard," she said.

Her face was pale. I was smoking a cigarette and I did not look at her.

"Is this true?"

"Yes, ma'am."

"It couldn't be. Do you know what you're saying?"

"Just watch her," I said.

"I don't know," she moaned.

She looked crushed. She went back into the dining room, but I saw her watching the cook through the doors. I watched both of them, the boss lady and the cook, praying that the cook would spit again. She did. The boss lady came into the kitchen and stared at Tillie, but she did not utter a word. She burst into tears and ran back into the dining room.

"What's happening here?" Tillie demanded.

No one answered. The boss lady came out and tossed Tillie her hat, coat, and money.

"Now, get out of here, you dirty dog!" she said.

Tillie stared, then slowly picked up her hat, coat, and the money; she stood a moment, wiped sweat from her forehead with her hand, then spat—this time on the floor. She left.

Nobody was ever able to fathom why Tillie liked to spit into the food.

Brooding over Tillie, I recalled the time when the boss man in Mississippi had come to me and had tossed my wages to me and said:

"Get out, nigger! I don't like your looks."

And I wondered if a Negro who did not smile and grin was as morally loathsome to whites as a cook who spat into the food.

The following summer I was called for temporary duty in the post office, and the work lasted into the winter. Aunt Cleo succumbed to a severe cardiac condition and, hard on the heels of her illness, my brother developed stomach ulcers. To rush my worries to a climax, my mother also became ill. I felt that I was maintaining a private hospital. Finally, the postoffice work ceased altogether and I haunted the city for jobs. But when I went into the streets in the morning I saw sights that killed my hope for the rest of the day. Unemployed men loitered in doorways with blank looks in their eyes, sat dejectedly on front steps in shabby clothing, congregated in sullen groups on street corners, and filled all the empty benches in the parks of Chicago's South Side.

Luck of a sort came when a distant cousin of mine, who was a superintendent for a Negro burial society, offered me a position on his staff as an agent. The thought of selling insurance policies to ignorant Negroes disgusted me.

"Well, if you don't sell them, somebody else will," my cousin told me "You've got to eat, haven't you?"

During that year I worked for several burial and insurance societies that operated among Negroes, and I received a new kind of education. I found that the burial societies, with some exceptions, were mostly "rackets." Some of them conducted their business legitimately, but there were many that exploited the ignorance of their black customers.

I was paid under a system that netted me fifteen dollars for every dollar's worth of new premiums that I placed upon the company's books, and for every dollar's worth of old premiums that lapsed I was penalized fifteen dollars. In addition, I was paid a commission of ten per cent on total premiums collected, but during the Depression it was extremely difficult to persuade a black family to buy a policy carrying even a dime premium. I considered myself lucky if, after subtracting lapses from new business, there remained fifteen dollars that I could call my own.

This "gambling" method of remuneration was practiced by some of the burial companies because of the tremendous "turnover" in policyholders, and the companies had to have a constant stream of new business to keep afloat. Whenever a black family moved or suffered a slight reverse in fortune, it usually let its policy lapse and later bought another policy from some other company.

Each day now I saw how the Negro in Chicago lived, for I visited hundreds of dingy flats filled with rickety furniture and ill-clad children. Most of the policyholders were illiterate and did not know that their policies carried clauses severely restricting their benefit payments, and, as an insurance agent, it was not my duty to tell them.

After tramping the streets and pounding on doors to collect premiums, I was dry, strained, too tired to read or write. I hungered for relief and, as a salesman of insurance to many young black girls, I found it. There were many comely black housewives who, trying desperately to keep up their insurance payments, were willing to make bargains to escape paying a ten-cent premium. I had a long, tortured affair with one girl by paying her ten-cent premium each week. She was an illiterate black child with a baby whose father she did not know. During the entire period of my relationship with her, she had but one demand to make of me: she wanted me to take her to a circus. Just what significance circuses had for her, I was never able to learn.

After I had been with her one morning—in exchange for the dime premium—I sat on the sofa in the front room and began to read a book I had with me. She came over shyly.

"Lemme see that," she said.

"What?" I asked.

"That book," she said.

I gave her the book; she looked at it intently. I saw that she was holding it upside down.

"What's in here you keep reading?" she asked.

"Can't you really read?" I asked.

"Naw," she giggled. "You know I can't read."

"You can read *some*," I said.

"Naw," she said.

I stared at her and wondered just what a life like hers meant in the scheme of things, and I came to the conclusion that it meant absolutely nothing. And neither did my life mean anything.

"How come you looking at me that way for?"

"Nothing."

"You don't talk much."

"There isn't much to say."

"I wished Jim was here," she sighed.

"Who's Jim?" I asked, jealous. I knew that she had other men, but I resented her mentioning them in my presence.

"Just a friend," she said.

I hated her then, then hated myself for coming to her.

"Do you like Jim better than you like me?" I asked.

"Naw. Jim just likes to talk."

"Then why do you be with me, if you like Jim better?" I asked, trying to make an issue and feeling a wave of disgust because I wanted to.

"You all right," she said, giggling. "I like you."

"I could kill you," I said.

"What?" she exclaimed.

"Nothing," I said, ashamed.

"Kill me, you said? You crazy, man," she said.

"Maybe I am," I muttered, angry that I was sitting beside a human being to whom I could not talk, angry with myself for coming to her, hating my wild and restless loneliness.

"You oughta go home and sleep," she said. "You tired."

"What do you ever think about?" I demanded harshly.

"Lotta things."

"What, for example?"

"You," she said, smiling.

"You know I mean just one dime to you each week," I said.

"Naw, I thinka lotta you."

"Then what do you think?"

"Bout how you talk when you talk. I wished I could talk like you," she said seriously.

"Why?" I taunted her.

"When you gonna take me to a circus?" she demanded suddenly.

"You ought to be in a circus," I said.

"I'd like it," she said, her eyes shining.

I wanted to laugh, but her words sounded so sincere that I could not.

"There's no circus in town," I said.

"I bet there is and you won't tell me 'cause you don't wanna take me," she said, pouting.

"But there's no circus in town, I tell you!"

"When will one come?"

"I don't know."

"Can't you read it in the papers?" she asked.

"There's nothing in the papers about a circus."

"There is," she said. "If I could read, I'd find it."

I laughed, and she was hurt.

"There *is* a circus in town," she said stoutly.

"There's no circus in town," I said. "But if you want to learn to read, then I'll teach you."

She nestled at my side, giggling.

"See that word?" I said, pointing.

"Yeah."

"That's an 'and,'" I said.

She doubled, giggling.

"What's the matter?" I asked.

She rolled on the floor, giggling.

"What's so funny?" I demanded.

"You," she giggled. "You so funny."

I rose.

"The hell with you," I said.

"Don't you go and cuss me now," she said. "I don't cuss you."

"I'm sorry," I said.

I got my hat and went to the door.

"I'll see you next week?" she asked.

"Maybe," I said.

When I was on the sidewalk, she called to me from a window.

"You promised to take me to a circus, remember?"

"Yes." I walked close to the window. "What is it you like about a circus?"

"The animals," she said simply.

I felt that there was a hidden meaning, perhaps, in what she had said, but I could not find it. She laughed and slammed the window shut.

Each time I left her I resolved not to visit her again. I could not talk to her, I merely listened to her passionate desire to see a circus. She was not calculating; if she liked a man, she just liked him. Sex relations were the only relations she had ever had; no others were possible with her, so limited was her intelligence.

Most of the other agents also had their bought girls and they were extremely anxious to keep other agents from tampering with them. One day a new section of the South Side was given to me as a part of my collection area, and the agent from whom the territory had been taken suddenly became very friendly with me.

"Say, Wright," he asked, "did you collect from Ewing on Champlain Avenue yet?"

"Yes," I answered, after consulting my book.

"How did you like her?" he asked, staring at me.

"She's a good-looking number," I said.

"You had anything to do with her yet?" he asked.

"No, but I'd like to," I said laughing.

"Look," he said. "I'm a friend of yours."

"Since when?" I countered.

"No, I'm really a friend," he said.

"What's on your mind?"

"Listen, that gal's sick," he said seriously.

"What do you mean?"

"She's got the clap," he said. "Keep away from her. She'll lay with anybody."

"Gee, I'm glad you told me," I said.

"You had your eye on her, didn't you?" he asked.

"Yes, I did," I said.

"Leave her alone," he said. "She'll get you down."

That night I told my cousin what the agent had said about Miss Ewing. My cousin laughed.

"That gal's all right," he said. "That agent's been fooling around with her. He told you she had a disease so that you'd be scared to bother her. He was protecting her from you."

That was the way the black women were regarded by the black agents. Some of the agents were vicious; if they had claims to pay to a sick black woman and if the woman was able to have sex relations with them, they would insist upon it, using the claims money as a bribe. If the woman refused, they would report to the office that the woman was a malingerer. The average black woman would submit because she needed the money badly.

As an insurance agent it was necessary for me to take part in one swindle. It appears that the burial society had originally issued a policy that was—from their point of view—too liberal in its provisions, and the officials decided to exchange the policies then in the hands of their clients for other policies carrying stricter clauses. Of course, this had to be done in a manner that would not allow the policyholder to know that his policy was being switched—that he was being swindled. I did not like it, but there was only one thing I could do to keep from being a party to it: I could quit and starve. But I did not feel that being honest was worth the price of starvation.

The swindle worked in this way. In my visits to the homes of the policyholders to collect premiums, I was accompanied by the superintendent who claimed to the policyholder that he was making a routine inspection. The policyholder, usually an illiterate black woman, would dig up her policy from the bottom of a trunk or chest and hand it to the superintendent. Meanwhile I would be marking the woman's premium book, an act which would distract her from what the superintendent was doing. The superintendent would exchange the old policy for a new one which was identical in color, serial number, and beneficiary, but which carried smaller payments. It was dirty work and I wondered how I could stop it. And when I could think of no safe way I would curse myself and the victims and forget about it. (The black owners of the burial societies were leaders in the Negro communities and were respected by whites.)

When I reached the relief station, I felt that I was making a public confession of my hunger. I sat waiting for hours, resentful of the mass of hungry people about me. My turn finally came and I was questioned by a middle-class Negro woman who asked me for a short history of my life. As I waited, I became aware of something happening in the room. The black men and women were mumbling quietly among themselves; they had not known one another before they had come here, but now their timidity and shame were wearing off and they were exchanging experiences. Before this they had lived as individuals, each somewhat afraid of the other, each seeking his own pleasure, each stanch in that degree of Americanism that had been allowed him. But now life had tossed them together, and they were learning to know the sentiments of their neighbors for the first time; their talking was enabling them to sense the collectivity of their lives, and some of their fear was passing.

Did the relief officials realize what was happening? No. If they had, they would have stopped it. But they saw their "clients" through the eyes of their profession, saw only what their "science" allowed them to see. As I listened to the talk, I could see black minds shedding many illusions. These people now knew that the past had betrayed them, had cast them out; but they did not know what the future would be like, did not know what they wanted. Yes, some of the things that the Communists said were true; they maintained that there came times in history when a ruling class could no longer rule. And now I sat looking at the beginnings of anarchy. To permit the birth of this new consciousness in these people was proof that those who ruled did not quite know what they were doing, assuming that they were trying to save themselves and their class. Had they understood what was happening, they would never have allowed millions of perplexed and defeated people to sit together for long hours and talk, for out of their talk was rising a new realization of life. And once this new conception of themselves had formed, no power on earth could alter it.

I left the relief station with the promise that food would be sent to me, but I also left with a knowledge that the relief officials had not wanted to give to me. I had felt the possibility of creating a new understanding of life in the minds of people rejected by the society in which they lived, people to whom the Chicago *Tribune* referred contemptuously as the "idle" ones, as though these people had deliberately sought their present state of helplessness.

Who would give these people a meaningful way of life? Communist theory defined these people as the molders of the future of mankind, but the Communist speeches I had heard in the park had mocked that definition. These people, of course, were not ready for a revolution; they had not abandoned their past lives by choice, but because they simply could not live the old way any longer. Now, what new faith would they embrace? The day I begged bread from the city officials was the day that showed me I was not alone in my loneliness; society had cast millions of others with me. But how could I be with them? How many understood what was happening? My mind swam with questions that I could not answer.

I was slowly beginning to comprehend the meaning of my environment; a sense of direction was beginning to emerge from the conditions of my life. I began to feel something more powerful than I could express. My speech and manner changed. My cynicism slid from me. I grew open and questioning. I wanted to know.

If I were a member of the class that rules, I would post men in all the neighborhoods of the nation, not to spy upon or club rebellious workers, not to break strikes or disrupt unions, but to ferret out those who no longer respond to the system under which they live. I would make it known that the real danger does not stem from those who seek to grab their share of wealth through force, or from those who try to defend their property through violence, for both of these groups, by their affirmative acts, support the values of the system under which they live. The millions that I would fear are those who do not dream of the prizes that the nation holds forth, for it is in them, though they may not know it, that a revolution has taken place and is biding its time to translate itself into a new and strange way of life.

I feel that the Negroes' relation to America is symbolically peculiar, and from the Negroes' ultimate reactions to their trapped state a lesson can be learned about America's future. Negroes are told in a language they cannot possibly misunderstand that their native land is not their own; and when, acting upon impulses which they share with whites, they try to assert a claim to their birthright, whites retaliate with terror, never pausing to consider the consequences should the Negroes give up completely. The whites never dream that they would face a situation far more terrifying if they were confronted by Negroes who made no claims at all than by those who are buoyed up by social aggressiveness. My knowledge of how Negroes react to their plight makes me declare that no man can possibly be individually guilty of treason, that an insurgent act is but a man's desperate answer to those who twist his environment so that he cannot fully share the spirit of his native land. Treason is a crime of the State.

Christmas came and I was once more called to the post office for temporary work. This time I met many young white men and we discussed world happenings, the vast armies of unemployed, the rising tide of radical action. I now detected a change in the attitudes of the whites I met; their privations were making them regard Negroes with new eyes, and, for the first time, I was invited to their homes.

When the work in the post office ended, I was assigned by the relief system as an orderly to a medical research institute in one of the largest and wealthiest hospitals in Chicago. I cleaned operating rooms, dog, rat, mice, cat, and rabbit pans, and fed guinea pigs. Four of us Negroes worked there and we occupied an underworld position, remembering that we must restrict ourselves—when not engaged upon some task—to the basement corridors, so that we would not mingle with white nurses, doctors, or visitors.

The sharp line of racial division drawn by the hospital authorities came to me the first morning when I walked along an underground corridor and saw two long lines of women coming toward me. A line of white girls marched past, clad in starched uniforms that gleamed white; their faces were alert, their step quick, their bodies lean and shapely, their shoulders erect, their faces lit with the light of purpose. And after them came a line of black girls, old, fat, dressed in ragged gingham, walking loosely, carrying tin cans of soap powder, rags, mops, brooms . . . I wondered what law of the universe kept them from being mixed? The sun would not have stopped shining had there been a few black girls in the first line, and the earth would not have stopped whirling on its axis had there been a few white girls in the second line. But the two lines I saw graded social status in purely racial terms.

Of the three Negroes who worked with me, one was a boy about my own age, Bill, who was either sleepy or drunk most of the time. Bill straightened his hair and I suspected that he kept a bottle hidden somewhere in the piles of hay which we fed to the guinea pigs. He did not like me and I did not like him, though I tried harder than he to conceal my dislike. We had nothing in common except that we were both black and lost. While I contained my frustration, he drank to drown his. Often I tried to talk to him, tried in simple words to convey to him some of my ideas, and he would listen in sullen silence. Then one day he came to me with an angry look on his face.

"I got it," he said.

"You've got what?" I asked.

"This old race problem you keep talking about," he said.

"What about it?"

"Well, it's this way," he explained seriously. "Let the government give every man a gun and five bullets, then let us all start over again. Make it like it was in the beginning. The ones who come out on top, white or black, let them rule."

His simplicity terrified me. I had never met a Negro who was so irredeemably brutalized. I stopped pumping my ideas into Bill's brain for fear that the fumes of alcohol might send him reeling toward some fantastic fate.

The two other Negroes were elderly and had been employed in the institute for fifteen years or more. One was Brand, a short, black, morose bachelor; the other was Cooke, a tall, yellow, spectacled fellow who spent his spare time keeping track of world events through the Chicago *Tribune*. Brand and Cooke hated each other for a reason that I was never able to determine, and they spent a good part of each day quarreling.

When I began working at the institute, I recalled my adolescent dream of wanting to be a medical research worker. Daily I saw young Jewish boys and girls receiving instruction in chemistry and medicine that the average black boy or girl could never receive. When I was alone, I wandered and poked my fingers into strange chemicals, watched intricate machines trace red and black lines on ruled paper. At times I paused and stared at the walls of the rooms, at the floors, at the wide desks at which the white doctors sat; and I realized—with a feeling that I could never quite get used to—that I was looking at the world of another race.

My interest in what was happening in the institute amused the three other Negroes with whom I worked. They had no curiosity about "white folks' things," while I wanted to know if the dogs being treated for diabetes were getting well; if the rats and mice in which cancer had been induced showed any signs of responding to treatment. I wanted to know the principle that lay behind the Aschheim-Zondek tests that were made with rabbits, the Wassermann tests that were made with guinea pigs. But when I asked a timid question I found that even Jewish doctors had learned to imitate the sadistic method of humbling a Negro that the others had cultivated.

"If you know too much, boy, your brains might explode," a doctor said one day.

Each Saturday morning I assisted a young Jewish doctor in slitting the vocal cords of a fresh batch of dogs from the city pound. The object was to devocalize the dogs so that their howls would not disturb the patients in the other parts of the hospital. I held each dog as the doctor injected Nembutal into its veins to make it unconscious; then I held the dog's jaws open as the doctor inserted the scalpel and severed the vocal cords. Later, when the dogs came to, they would lift their heads to the ceiling and gape in a soundless wail. The sight became lodged in my imagination as a symbol of silent suffering.

To me Nembutal was a powerful and mysterious liquid, but when I asked questions about its properties I could not obtain a single intelligent answer. The doctor simply ignored me with:

"Come on. Bring me the next dog. I haven't got all day."

One Saturday morning, after I had held the dogs for their vocal cords to be slit, the doctor left the Nembutal on a bench. I picked it up, uncorked it, and smelled it. It was odorless. Suddenly Brand ran to me with a stricken face.

"What're you doing?" he asked.

"I was smelling this stuff to see if it had any odor," I said.

"Did you really smell it?" he asked me.

"Yes."

"Oh, God!" he exclaimed.

"What's the matter?" I asked.

"You shouldn't've done that!" he shouted.

"Why?"

He grabbed my arm and jerked me across the room.

"Come on!" he yelled, snatching open the door.

"What's the matter?" I asked.

"I gotta get you to a doctor 'fore it's too late," he gasped.

Had my foolish curiosity made me inhale something dangerous?

"But—Is it poisonous?"

"Run, boy!" he said, pulling me. "You'll fall dead."

Filled with fear, with Brand pulling my arm, I rushed out of the room, raced across a rear areaway, into another room, then down a long corridor. I wanted to ask Brand what symptoms I must expect, but we were running too fast. Brand finally stopped, gasping for breath. My heart beat wildly and my blood pounded in my head. Brand then dropped to the concrete floor, stretched out on his back, and yelled with laughter, shaking all over. He beat his fists against the concrete; he moaned, giggled, he kicked.

I tried to master my outrage, wondering if some of the white doctors had told him to play the joke. He rose and wiped tears from his eyes, still laughing. I walked away from him. He knew that I was angry and he followed me.

"Don't get mad," he gasped through his laughter.

"Go to hell," I said.

"I couldn't help it," he giggled. "You looked at me like you'd believe anything I said. Man, you was scared."

He leaned against the wall, laughing again, stomping his feet. I was angry, for I felt that he would spread the story. I knew that Bill and Cooke never ventured beyond the safe bounds of Negro living, and they would never blunder into anything like this. And if they heard about this, they would laugh for months.

"Brand, if you mention this, I'll kill you," I swore.

"You ain't mad?" he asked, laughing, staring at me through tears.

Sniffing, Brand walked ahead of me. I followed him back into the room that housed the dogs. All day, while at some task, he would pause and giggle, then smother the giggling with his hand, looking at me out of the corner of his eyes, shaking his head. He laughed at me for a week. I kept my temper and let him amuse himself. I finally found out the properties of Nembutal by consulting medical books; but I never told Brand.

One summer morning, just as I began work, a young Jewish boy came to me with a stop watch in his hand.

"Dr.———wants me to time you when you clean a room," he said. "We're trying to make the institute more efficient."

"I'm doing my work, and getting through on time," I said.

"This is the boss's order," he said.

"Why don't you work for a change?" I blurted, angry.

"Now, look," he said. "*This* is my work. Now *you* work."

I got a mop and pail, sprayed a room with disinfectant, and scrubbed at coagulated blood and hardened dog, rat, and rabbit feces. The normal temperature of a room was ninety, but, as the sun beat down upon the skylights, the temperature rose above a hundred. Stripped to my waist, I slung the mop, moving steadily like a machine, hearing the boy press the button on the stop watch as I finished cleaning a room.

"Well, how is it?" I asked.

"It took you seventeen minutes to clean that last room," he said. "That ought to be the time for each room."

"But that room was not very dirty," I said.

"You have seventeen rooms to clean," he went on as though I had not spoken. "Seventeen times seventeen make four hours and forty-nine minutes." He wrote upon a little pad. "After lunch, clean the five flights of stone stairs. I timed a boy who scrubbed one step and multiplied that time by the number of steps. You ought to be through by six."

"Suppose I want relief?" I asked.

"You'll manage," he said and left.

Never had I felt so much the slave as when I scoured those stone steps each afternoon. Working against time, I would wet five steps, sprinkle soap powder, and then a white doctor or a nurse would come along and, instead of avoiding the soapy steps, would walk on them and track the dirty water onto the steps that I had already cleaned. To obviate this, I cleaned but two steps at a time, a distance over which a ten-year-old child could step. But it did no good. The white people still plopped their feet down into the dirty water and muddied the other clean steps. If I ever really hotly hated unthinking whites, it was then. Not once during my entire stay at the institute did a single white person show enough courtesy to avoid a wet step. I would be on my knees, scrubbing, sweating, pouring out what limited energy my body could wring from my meager diet, and I would hear feet approaching. I would pause and curse with tense lips:

"These sonofabitches are going to dirty these steps again, goddamn their souls to hell!"

Sometimes a sadistically observant white man would notice that he had tracked dirty water up the steps, and he would look back down at me and smile and say:

"Boy, we sure keep you busy, don't we?"

And I would not be able to answer.

The feud that went on between Brand and Cooke continued. Although they were working daily in a building where scientific history was being made, the light of curiosity was never in their eyes. They were conditioned to their racial "place," had learned to see only a part of the whites and the white world; and the whites, too, had learned to see only a part of the lives of the blacks and their world.

Perhaps Brand and Cooke, lacking interests that could absorb them, fuming like children over trifles, simply invented their hate of each other in order to have something to feel deeply about. Or perhaps there was in them a vague tension stemming from their chronically frustrating way of life, a pain whose cause they did not know; and, like those devocalized dogs, they would whirl and snap at the air when their old pain struck them. Anyway, they argued about the weather, sports, sex, war, race, politics, and religion; neither of them knew much about the subjects they debated, but it seemed that the less they knew the better they could argue.

The tug of war between the two elderly men reached a climax one winter day at noon. It was incredibly cold and an icy gale swept up and down the Chicago streets with blizzard force. The door of the animal-filled room was locked, for we always insisted that we be allowed one hour in which to eat and rest. Bill and I were sitting on wooden boxes, eating our lunches out of paper bags. Brand was washing his hands at the sink. Cooke was sitting on a rickety stool, munching an apple and reading the Chicago *Tribune*.

Now and then a devocalized dog lifted his nose to the ceiling and howled soundlessly. The room was filled with many rows of high steel tiers. Perched upon each of these tiers were layers of steel cages containing the dogs, rats, mice, rabbits, and guinea pigs. Each cage was labeled in some indecipherable scientific jargon. Along the walls of the room were long charts with zigzagging red and black lines that traced the success or failure of some experiment. The lonely piping of guinea pigs floated unheeded about us. Hay rustled as a rabbit leaped restlessly about in its pen. A rat scampered around in its steel prison. Cooke tapped the newspaper for attention.

"It says here," Cooke mumbled through a mouthful of apple, "that this is the coldest day since 1888."

Bill and I sat unconcerned. Brand chuckled softly.

"What in hell you laughing about?" Cooke demanded of Brand.

"You can't believe what that damn *Tribune* says," Brand said.

"How come I can't?" Cooke demanded. "It's the world's greatest newspaper."

Brand did not reply; he shook his head pityingly and chuckled again.

"Stop that damn laughing at me!" Cooke said angrily.

"I laugh as much as I wanna," Brand said. "You don't know what you talking about. The *Herald-Examiner* says it's the coldest day since 1873."

"But the *Trib* oughta know," Cooke countered. "It's older'n that *Examiner.*"

"That damn *Trib* don't know nothing!" Brand drowned out Cooke's voice.

"How in hell you know?" Cooke asked with rising anger.

The argument waxed until Cooke shouted that if Brand did not shut up he was going to "cut his black throat."

Brand whirled from the sink, his hands dripping soapy water, his eye blazing.

"Take that back," Brand said.

"I take nothing back! What you wanna do about it?" Cooke taunted.

The two elderly Negroes glared at each other. I wondered if the quarrel was really serious, or if it would turn out harmlessly as so many others had done.

Suddenly Cooke dropped the Chicago *Tribune* and pulled a long knife from his pocket; his thumb pressed a button and a gleaming steel blade leaped out. Brand stepped back quickly and seized an ice pick that was stuck in a wooden board above the sink.

"Put that knife down," Brand said.

"Stay 'way from me, or I'll cut your throat," Cooke warned.

Brand lunged with the ice pick. Cooke dodged out of range. They circled each other like fighters in a prize ring. The cancerous and tubercular rats and mice leaped about in their cages. The guinea pigs whistled in fright. The diabetic dogs bared their teeth and barked soundlessly in our direction. The Aschheim-Zondek rabbits flopped their ears and tried to hide in the corners of their pens. Cooke now crouched and sprang forward with the knife. Bill and I jumped to our feet, speechless with surprise. Brand retreated. The eyes of both men were hard and unblinking; they were breathing deeply.

"Say, cut it out!" I called in alarm.

"Them damn fools is really fighting," Bill said in amazement.

Slashing at each other, Brand and Cooke surged up and down the aisles of steel tiers. Suddenly Brand uttered a bellow and charged into Cooke and swept him violently backward. Cooke grasped Brand's hand to keep the ice pick from sinking into his chest. Brand broke free and charged Cooke again, sweeping him into an animal-filled steel tier. The tier balanced itself on its edge for an indecisive moment, then toppled.

Like kingpins, one steel tier lammed into another, then they all crashed to the floor with a sound as of the roof falling. The whole aspect of the room altered quicker than the eye could follow. Brand and Cooke stood stock-still, their eyes fastened upon each other, their pointed weapons raised; but they were dimly aware of the havoc that churned about them.

The steel tiers lay jumbled; the doors of the cages swung open. Rats and mice and dogs and rabbits moved over the floor in wild panic. The Wassermann guinea pigs were squealing as though judgment day had come. Here and there an animal had been crushed beneath a cage.

All four of us looked at one another. We knew what this meant. We might lose our jobs. We were already regarded as black dunces; and if the doctors saw this mess they would take it as final proof. Bill rushed to the door to make sure that it was locked. I glanced at the clock and saw that it was 12:30. We had one half-hour of grace.

"Come on," Bill said uneasily. "We got to get this place cleaned."

Brand and Cooke stared at each other, both doubting.

"Give me your knife, Cooke," I said.

"Naw! Take Brand's ice pick *first*," Cooke said.

"The hell you say!" Brand said. "Take his knife *first!*"

A knock sounded at the door.

"Sssssh," Bill said.

We waited. We heard footsteps going away. We'll all lose our jobs, I thought.

Persuading the fighters to surrender their weapons was a difficult task, but at last it was done and we could begin to set things right. Slowly Brand stooped and tugged at one end of a steel tier. Cooke stooped to help him. Both men seemed to be acting in a dream. Soon, however, all four of us were working frantically, watching the clock.

As we labored we conspired to keep the fight a secret; we agreed to tell the doctors—if any should ask—that we had not been in the room during our lunch hour; we felt that that lie would explain why no one had unlocked the door when the knock had come.

We righted the tiers and replaced the cages; then we were faced with the impossible task of sorting the cancerous rats and mice, the diabetic dogs, the Aschheim-Zondek rabbits, and the Wassermann guinea pigs. Whether we kept our jobs or not depended upon how shrewdly we could cover up all evidence of the fight. It was pure guesswork, but we had to try to put the animals back into the correct cages. We knew that certain rats or mice went into certain cages, but we did not know *what* rat or mouse went into *what* cage. We did not know a tubercular mouse from a cancerous mouse—the white doctors had made sure that we would not know. They had never taken time to answer a single question; though we worked in the institute, we were as remote from the meaning of the experiments as if we lived in the moon. The doctors had laughed at what they felt was our childlike interest in the fate of the animals.

First we sorted the dogs; that was fairly easy, for we could remember the size and color of most of them. But the rats and mice and guinea pigs baffled us completely.

We put our heads together and pondered, down in the underworld of the great scientific institute. It was a strange scientific conference; the fate of the entire medical research institute rested in our ignorant, black hands.

We remembered the number of rats, mice, or guinea pigs—we had to handle them several times a day—that went into a given cage, and we supplied the number helter-skelter from those animals that we could catch running loose on the floor. We discovered that many rats, mice, and guinea pigs were missing—they had been killed in the scuffle. We solved that problem by taking healthy stock from other cages and putting them into cages with sick animals. We repeated this process until we were certain that, numerically at least, all the animals with which the doctors were experimenting were accounted for.

The rabbits came last. We broke the rabbits down into two general groups; those that had fur on their bellies and those that did not. We knew that all those rabbits that had shaven bellies—our scientific knowledge adequately covered this point because it was our job to shave the rabbits—were undergoing the Aschheim-Zondek tests. But in what pen did a given rabbit belong? We did not know. I solved the problem very simply. I counted the shaven rabbits; they numbered seventeen. I counted the pens labeled "Aschheim-Zondek," then proceeded to drop a shaven rabbit into each pen at random. And again we were numerically successful. At least white America had taught us how to count. . . .

Lastly we carefully wrapped all the dead animals in newspapers and hid their bodies in a garbage can.

At a few minutes to one the room was in order; that is, the kind of order that we four Negroes could figure out. I unlocked the door and we sat waiting, whispering, vowing secrecy, wondering what the reaction of the doctors would be.

Finally a doctor came, gray-haired, white-coated, spectacled, efficient, serious, taciturn, bearing a tray upon which sat a bottle of mysterious fluid and a hypodermic needle.

"My rats, please."

Cooke shuffled forward to serve him. We held our breath. Cooke got the cage which he knew the doctor always called for at that hour and brought it forward. One by one, Cooke took out the rats and held them as the doctor solemnly injected the mysterious fluid under their skins.

"Thank you, Cooke," the doctor murmured.

"Not at all, sir," Cooke mumbled with a suppressed gasp.

When the doctor had gone we looked at one another, hardly daring to believe that our secret would be kept. We were so anxious that we did not know whether to curse or laugh. Another doctor came.

"Give me A-Z rabbit number 14."

"Yes, sir," I said.

I brought him the rabbit and he took it upstairs to the operating room. We waited for repercussions. None came.

All that afternoon the doctors came and went. I would run into the room—stealing a few seconds from my step-scrubbing—and ask what progress was being made and would learn that the doctors had detected nothing. At quitting time we felt triumphant.

"They won't ever know," Cooke boasted in a whisper.

I saw Brand stiffen. I knew that he was aching to dispute Cooke's optimism, but the memory of the fight he had just had was so fresh in his mind that he could not speak.

Another day went by and nothing happened. Then another day. The doctors examined the animals and wrote in their little black books, in their big black books, and continued to trace red and black lines upon the charts.

A week passed and we felt out of danger. Not one question had been asked.

Of course, we four black men were much too modest to make our contribution known, but we often wondered what went on in the laboratories after that secret disaster. Was some scientific hypothesis, well on its way to validation and ultimate public use, discarded because of unexpected findings on that cold winter day? Was some tested principle given a new and strange refinement because of fresh, remarkable evidence? Did some brooding research worker—those who held stop watches and slopped their feet carelessly in the water of the steps I tried so hard to keep clean—get a wild, if brief, glimpse of a new scientific truth? Well, we never heard. . . .

I brooded upon whether I should have gone to the director's office and told him what had happened, but each time I thought of it I remembered that the director had been the man who had ordered the boy to stand over me while I was working and time my movements with a stop watch. He did not regard me as a human being. I did not share his world. I earned thirteen dollars a week and I had to support four people with it, and should I risk that thirteen dollars by acting idealistically? Brand and Cooke would have hated me and would have eventually driven me from the job had I "told" on them. The hospital kept us four Negroes as though we were close kin to the animals we tended, huddled together down in the underworld corridors of the hospital, separated by a vast psychological distance from the significant processes of the rest of the hospital—just as America had kept us locked in the dark underworld of American life for three hundred years—and we had made our own code of ethics, values, loyalty.

Study and Discussion Questions

1. How many jobs does the narrator tell us about in "The Man Who Went to Chicago"? List and briefly describe each one.
2. What does the narrator learn (a) about himself and (b) about the world he lives in from each job experience?
3. One of the more insidious consequences of oppression is the way it affects the behavior and self-image of those who are oppressed. List examples Wright gives us of this phenomenon in "The Man Who Went To Chicago."
4. What insight does the narrator come to in the relief station?
5. What motivates the narrator in each case to (a) quit Hoffman's, (b) work as an insurance agent, and (c) keep quiet about the laboratory mishap?
6. What do the dogs without vocal cords symbolize?
7. Wright moves between narration and argument in this essay. Note in the text where he is musing/philosophizing/making an argument and where he is narrating/telling a story.

8. Is this combination of narration and reflection/argument effective? What would he gain or lose by only telling the story? What would he gain or lose by only writing the argument?

Suggestions for Writing

1. How do you think a white person's work experiences would have been similar to and different from those of Wright's narrator?
2. List at least three aspects of Wright's criticism of white Americans' treatment of black Americans. Find evidence from "The Man Who Went To Chicago" to support each of your points.
3. Write about a job experience of your own in which you felt exploited, frustrated, and/or misunderstood.

DOROTHY ALLISON (b. 1949)

Dorothy Allison was born in Greenville, South Carolina, and was the first person from her family to finish high school. She studied at Florida Presbyterian College (now Eckerd College) and the New School for Social Research in New York City. Working in the tradition of other Southern writers such as Flannery O'Connor and William Faulkner, Allison's writings offer a more contemporary and complex picture of southern, working-class culture. In both her poetry and fiction, Allison's working class, female characters struggle to find understanding as they grapple with issues of class, gender and sexuality. Her work includes *The Women Who Hate Me: Poetry 1980–1990* (1991); the novels *Bastard Out of Carolina* (1992) and *Cavedweller* (1998); a collection of short stories, *Trash* (1988); an essay collection, *Skin: Talking About Sex, Class and Literature* (1993); and the memoir, *One or Two Things I Know for Sure* (1995). "Gun Crazy", first printed in *Skin*, tells the story of one girl's experience learning to shoot a real gun. In her eloquent personal essay, "A Question of Class," Allison tells the story of her working-class/poor/white trash background and of her development as a writer, while at the same time debunking American myths about social class.

A Question of Class   (1993)

The first time I heard, "They're different than us, don't value human life the way we do," I was in high school in Central Florida. The man speaking was an army recruiter talking to a bunch of boys, telling them what the army was really like, what they could expect overseas. A cold angry feeling swept over me. I had heard the word *they* pronounced in that same callous tone before. *They,* those people over there, those people who are not us, they die so easily, kill each other so casually. They are different. *We,* I thought. *Me.*

When I was six or eight back in Greenville, South Carolina, I had heard that same matter-of-fact tone of dismissal applied to me. "Don't you play with her. I don't want you talking to them." Me and my family, we had always been *they.* Who am I? I wondered, listening to that recruiter. Who are my people? We die so easily, disappear so completely—we/they, the poor and the queer. I pressed my bony white trash fists to my stubborn lesbian mouth. The rage was a good feeling, stronger and purer than the shame that followed it, the fear and the sudden urge to run and hide, to deny, to pretend I did not know who I was and what the world would do to me.

My people were not remarkable. We were ordinary, but even so we were mythical. We were the *they* everyone talks about—the ungrateful poor. I grew up trying to run away from the fate that destroyed so many of the people I loved, and having learned the habit of hiding, I found I had also learned to hide from myself. I did not know who I was, only that I did not want to be *they,* the ones who are destroyed or dismissed to make the "real" people, the important people, feel safer. By the time I understood that I was queer, that habit of hiding was deeply set in me, so deeply that it was not a choice but an instinct. Hide, hide to survive, I thought, knowing that if I told the truth about my life, my family, my sexual desire, my history, I would move over into that unknown territory, the land of they, would never have the chance to name my own life, to understand it or claim it.

Why are you so afraid? my lovers and friends have asked me the many times I have suddenly seemed a stranger, someone who would not speak to them, would not do the things they believed I should do, simple things like applying for a job, or a grant, or some award they were sure I could acquire easily. Entitlement, I have told them, is a matter of feeling like we rather than they. You think you have a right to things, a place in the world, and it is so intrinsically a part of you that you cannot imagine people like me, people who seem to live in your world, who don't have it. I have explained what I know over and over, in every way I can, but I have never been able to make clear the degree of my fear, the extent to which I feel myself denied: not only that I am queer in a world that hates queers, but that I was born poor into a world that despises the poor. The need to make my world believable to people who have never experienced it is part of why I write fiction. I know that some things must be felt to be understood, that despair, for example, can never be adequately analyzed; it must be lived. But if I can write a story that so draws the reader in that she imagines herself like my characters, feels their sense of fear and uncertainty, their hopes and terrors, then I have come closer to knowing myself as real, important as the very people I have always watched with awe.

I have known I was a lesbian since I was a teenager, and I have spent a good twenty years making peace with the effects of incest and physical abuse. But what may be the central fact of my life is that I was born in 1949 in Greenville, South Carolina, the bastard daughter of a white woman from a desperately poor family, a girl who had left the seventh grade the year before, worked as a waitress, and was just a month past fifteen when she had me. That fact, the inescapable impact of being born in a condition of poverty that this society finds shameful, contemptible, and somehow deserved, has had dominion over me to such an extent that I have spent my life trying to overcome or deny it. I have learned with great difficulty that the vast majority of people believe that poverty is a voluntary condition.

I have loved my family so stubbornly that every impulse to hold them in contempt has sparked in me a countersurge of pride—complicated and undercut by an urge to fit us into the acceptable myths and theories of both mainstream society and a lesbian-feminist reinterpretation. The choice becomes Steven Spielberg movies or Erskine Caldwell[1] novels, the one valorizing and the other caricaturing, or the patriarchy as villain, trivializing the choices the men and women of my family have made. I have had to fight broad generalizations from every theoretical viewpoint.

Traditional feminist theory has had a limited understanding of class differences and of how sexuality and self are shaped by both desire and denial. The ideology implies that we are all sisters who should only turn our anger and suspicion on the world outside the lesbian community. It is easy to say that the patriarchy did it, that poverty and social contempt are products of the world of the fathers, and often I felt a need to collapse my sexual history into what I was willing to share of my class background, to pretend that my life both as a lesbian and as a working-class escapee was constructed by the patriarchy. Or conversely, to ignore how much my life was shaped by growing up poor and talk only about what incest did to my identity as a woman and as a lesbian. The difficulty is that I can't ascribe everything that has been problematic about my life simply and easily to the patriarchy, or to incest, or even to the invisible and much-denied class structure of our society.

In my lesbian-feminist collective we had long conversations about the mind/body split, the way we compartmentalize our lives to survive. For years I thought that that concept referred to the way I had separated my activist life from the passionate secret life in which I acted on my sexual desires. I was convinced that the fracture was fairly simple, that it would be healed when there was time and clarity to do so—at about the same point when I might begin to understand sex. I never imagined that it was not a split but a splintering, and I passed whole portions of my life—days, months, years—in pure directed progress, getting up every morning and setting to work, working so hard and so continually that I avoided examining in any way what I knew about my life. Busywork became a trance state. I ignored who I really was and how I became that person, continued in that daily progress, became an automaton who was what she did.

I tried to become one with the lesbian-feminist community so as to feel real and valuable. I did not know that I was hiding, blending in for safety just as I had done in high school, in college. I did not recognize the impulse to forget.

---

[1]American novelist (1903–1987).

I believed that all those things I did not talk about, or even let myself think too much about, were not important, that none of them defined me. I had constructed a life, an identity in which I took pride, an alternative lesbian family in which I felt safe, and I did not realize that the fundamental me had almost disappeared.

It is surprising how easy it was to live that life. Everyone and everything cooperated with the process. Everything in our culture—books, television, movies, school, fashion—is presented as if it is being seen by one pair of eyes, shaped by one set of hands, heard by one pair of ears. Even if you know you are not part of that imaginary creature—if you like country music not symphonies, read books cynically, listen to the news unbelievingly, are lesbian not hetero-sexual, and surround yourself with your own small deviant community—you are still shaped by that hegemony, or your resistance to it. The only way I found to resist that homogenized view of the world was to make myself part of some-thing larger than myself. As a feminist and a radical lesbian organizer, and later as a sex radical (which eventually became the term, along with pro-sex feminist, for those who were not anti-pornography but anti-censorship, those of us argu-ing for sexual diversity), the need to belong, to feel safe, was just as important for me as for any heterosexual, nonpolitical citizen, and sometimes even more important because the rest of my life was so embattled.

The first time I read the Jewish lesbian Irena Klepfisz's poems,[2] I experienced a frisson of recognition. It was not that my people had been "burned off the map" or murdered as hers had. No, we had been encouraged to destroy ourselves, made invisible because we did not fit the myths of the noble poor generated by the mid-dle class. Even now, past forty and stubbornly proud of my family, I feel the draw of that mythology, that romanticized, edited version of the poor. I find myself looking back and wondering what was real, what was true. Within my family, so much was lied about, joked about, denied, or told with deliberate indirection, an undercurrent of humiliation or a brief pursed grimace that belied everything that had been said. What was real? The poverty depicted in books and movies was romantic, a backdrop for the story of how it was escaped.

The poverty portrayed by left-wing intellectuals was just as romantic, a platform for assailing the upper and middle classes, and from their perspective, the working-class hero was invariably male, righteously indignant, and inhumanly noble. The reality of self-hatred and violence was either absent or caricatured. The poverty I knew was dreary, deadening, shameful, the women powerful in ways not generally seen as heroic by the world outside the family.

My family's lives were not on television, not in books, not even comic books. There was a myth of the poor in this country, but it did not include us, no matter how hard I tried to squeeze us in. There was an idea of the good poor—hard-working, ragged but clean, and intrinsically honorable. I understood that we were the bad poor: men who drank and couldn't keep a job; women, invariably

---

[2]*A Few Words in the Mother Tongue: Poems, Selected and New* (Eighth Mountain Press: Portland, Oregon, 1990) [Allison's note].

pregnant before marriage, who quickly became worn, fat, and old from working too many hours and bearing too many children; and children with runny noses, watery eyes, and the wrong attitudes. My cousins quit school, stole cars, used drugs, and took dead-end jobs pumping gas or waiting tables. We were not noble, not grateful, not even hopeful. We knew ourselves despised. My family was ashamed of being poor, of feeling hopeless. What was there to work for, to save money for, to fight for or struggle against? We had generations before us to teach us that nothing ever changed, and that those who did try to escape failed.

My mama had eleven brothers and sisters, of whom I can name only six. No one is left alive to tell me the names of the others. It was my grandmother who told me about my real daddy, a shiftless pretty man who was supposed to have married, had six children, and sold cut-rate life insurance to poor Black people. My mama married when I was a year old, but her husband died just after my little sister was born a year later.

When I was five, Mama married the man she lived with until she died. Within the first year of their marriage Mama miscarried, and while we waited out in the hospital parking lot, my stepfather molested me for the first time, something he continued to do until I was past thirteen. When I was eight or so, Mama took us away to a motel after my stepfather beat me so badly it caused a family scandal, but we returned after two weeks. Mama told me that she really had no choice: she could not support us alone. When I was eleven I told one of my cousins that my stepfather was molesting me. Mama packed up my sisters and me and took us away for a few days, but again, my stepfather swore he would stop, and again we went back after a few weeks. I stopped talking for a while, and I have only vague memories of the next two years.

My stepfather worked as a route salesman, my mama as a waitress, laundry worker, cook, or fruit packer. I could never understand, since they both worked so hard and such long hours, how we never had enough money, but it was also true of my mama's brothers and sisters who worked hard in the mills or the furnace industry. In fact, my parents did better than anyone else in the family. But eventually my stepfather was fired and we hit bottom—nightmarish months of marshals at the door, repossessed furniture, and rubber checks. My parents worked out a scheme so that it appeared my stepfather had abandoned us, but instead he went down to Florida, got a new job, and rented us a house. He returned with a U-Haul trailer in the dead of night, packed us up, and moved us south.

The night we left South Carolina for Florida, my mama leaned over the backseat of her old Pontiac and promised us girls, "It'll be better there." I don't know if we believed her, but I remember crossing Georgia in the early morning, watching the red clay hills and swaying grey blankets of moss recede through the back window. I kept looking at the trailer behind us, ridiculously small to contain everything we owned. Mama had packed nothing that wasn't fully paid off, which meant she had only two things of worth: her washing and sewing machines, both of them tied securely to the trailer walls. Throughout the trip I fantasized an accident that would burst that trailer, scattering old clothes and cracked dishes on the tarmac.

I was only thirteen. I wanted us to start over completely, to begin again as new people with nothing of the past left over. I wanted to run away from who we had been seen to be, who we had been. That desire is one I have seen in other members of my family. It is the first thing I think of when trouble comes—the geographic solution. Change your name, leave town, disappear, make yourself over. What hides behind that impulse is the conviction that the life you have lived, the person you are, is valueless, better off abandoned, that running away is easier than trying to change things, that change itself is not possible. Sometimes I think it is this conviction—more seductive than alcohol or violence, more subtle than sexual hatred or gender injustice—that has dominated my life and made real change so painful and difficult.

Moving to Central Florida did not fix our lives. It did not stop my stepfather's violence, heal my shame, or make my mother happy. Once there, our lives became controlled by my mother's illness and medical bills. She had a hysterectomy when I was about eight and endured a series of hospitalizations for ulcers and a chronic back problem. Through most of my adolescence she superstitiously refused to allow anyone to mention the word *cancer.* When she was not sick, Mama and my stepfather went on working, struggling to pay off what seemed an insurmountable load of debts.

By the time I was fourteen, my sisters and I had found ways to discourage most of our stepfather's sexual advances. We were not close, but we united against him. Our efforts were helped along when he was referred to a psychotherapist after he lost his temper at work, and was prescribed drugs that made him sullen but less violent. We were growing up quickly, my sisters moving toward dropping out of school while I got good grades and took every scholarship exam I could find. I was the first person in my family to graduate from high school, and the fact that I went on to college was nothing short of astonishing.

We all imagine our lives are normal, and I did not know my life was not everyone's. It was in Central Florida that I began to realize just how different we were. The people we met there had not been shaped by the rigid class structure that dominated the South Carolina Piedmont. The first time I looked around my junior high classroom and realized I did not know who those people were—not only as individuals but as categories, who their people were and how they saw themselves—I also realized that they did not know me. In Greenville, everyone knew my family, knew we were trash, and that meant we were supposed to be poor, supposed to have grim low-paid jobs, have babies in our teens, and never finish school. But Central Florida in the 1960s was full of runaways and immigrants, and our mostly white working-class suburban school sorted us out not by income and family background but by intelligence and aptitude tests. Suddenly I was boosted into the college-bound track, and while there was plenty of contempt for my inept social skills, pitiful wardrobe, and slow drawling accent, there was also something I had never experienced before: a protective anonymity, and a kind of grudging respect and curiosity about who I might become. Because they did not see poverty and hopelessness as a foregone conclusion for my life, I could begin to imagine other futures for myself.

In that new country, we were unknown. The myth of the poor settled over us and glamorized us. I saw it in the eyes of my teachers, the Lion's Club representative who paid for my new glasses, and the lady from the Junior League[3] who told me about the scholarship I had won. Better, far better, to be one of the mythical poor than to be part of the *they* I had known before. I also experienced a new level of fear, a fear of losing what had never before been imaginable. Don't let me lose this chance, I prayed, and lived in terror that I might suddenly be seen again as what I knew myself to be.

As an adolescent I thought that my family's escape from South Carolina played like a bad movie. We fled the way runaway serfs might have done, with the sheriff who would have arrested my stepfather the imagined border guard. I am certain that if we had remained in South Carolina, I would have been trapped by my family's heritage of poverty, jail, and illegitimate children—that even being smart, stubborn, and a lesbian would have made no difference.

My grandmother died when I was twenty, and after Mama went home for the funeral, I had a series of dreams in which we still lived up in Greenville, just down the road from where Granny died. In the dreams I had two children and only one eye, lived in a trailer, and worked at the textile mill. Most of my time was taken up with deciding when I would finally kill my children and myself. The dreams were so vivid, I became convinced they were about the life I was meant to have had, and I began to work even harder to put as much distance as I could between my family and me. I copied the dress, mannerisms, attitudes, and ambitions of the girls I met in college, changing or hiding my own tastes, interests, and desires. I kept my lesbianism a secret, forming a relationship with an effeminate male friend that served to shelter and disguise us both. I explained to friends that I went home so rarely because my stepfather and I fought too much for me to be comfortable in his house. But that was only part of the reason I avoided home, the easiest reason. The truth was that I feared the person I might become in my mama's house, the woman of my dreams—hateful, violent, and hopeless.

It is hard to explain how deliberately and thoroughly I ran away from my own life. I did not forget where I came from, but I gritted my teeth and hid it. When I could not get enough scholarship money to pay for graduate school, I spent a year of rage working as a salad girl, substitute teacher, and maid. I finally managed to find a job by agreeing to take any city assignment where the Social Security Administration needed a clerk. Once I had a job and my own place far away from anyone in my family, I became sexually and politically active, joining the

---

[3]Lion's Club, a social organization for businesspeople; Junior League, an upper-class women's organization that does charitable and volunteer work.

Women's Center support staff and falling in love with a series of middle-class women who thought my accent and stories thoroughly charming. The stories I told about my family, about South Carolina, about being poor itself, were all lies, carefully edited to seem droll or funny. I knew damn well that no one would want to hear the truth about poverty, the hopelessness and fear, the feeling that nothing I did would ever make any difference and the raging resentment that burned beneath my jokes. Even when my lovers and I formed an alternative lesbian family, sharing what we could of our resources, I kept the truth about my background and who I knew myself to be a carefully obscured mystery. I worked as hard as I could to make myself a new person, an emotionally healthy radical lesbian activist, and I believed completely that by remaking myself I was helping to remake the world.

For a decade, I did not go home for more than a few days at a time.

When in the 1980s I ran into the concept of feminist sexuality, I genuinely did not know what it meant. Though I was, and am, a feminist, and committed to claiming the right to act on my sexual desires without tailoring my lust to a sex-fearing society, demands that I explain or justify my sexual fantasies have left me at a loss. How does anyone explain sexual need?

The Sex Wars are over, I've been told, and it always makes me want to ask who won. But my sense of humor may be a little obscure to women who have never felt threatened by the way most lesbians use and mean the words *pervert* and *queer*. I use the word queer to mean more than lesbian. Since I first used it in 1980 I have always meant it to imply that I am not only a lesbian but a transgressive lesbian—femme, masochistic, as sexually aggressive as the women I seek out, and as pornographic in my imagination and sexual activities as the heterosexual hegemony has ever believed.

My aunt Dot used to joke, "There are two or three things I know for sure, but never the same things and I'm never as sure as I'd like." What I know for sure is that class, gender, sexual preference, and prejudice—racial, ethnic, and religious—form an intricate lattice that restricts and shapes our lives, and that resistance to hatred is not a simple act. Claiming your identity in the cauldron of hatred and resistance to hatred is infinitely complicated, and worse, almost unexplainable.

I know that I have been hated as a lesbian both by "society" and by the intimate world of my extended family, but I have also been hated or held in contempt (which is in some ways more debilitating and slippery than hatred) by lesbians for behavior and sexual practices shaped in large part by class. My sexual identity is intimately constructed by my class and regional background, and much of the hatred directed at my sexual preferences is class hatred—however much people, feminists in particular, like to pretend this is not a factor. The kind of woman I am attracted to is invariably the kind of woman who embarrasses respectably middle-class, politically aware lesbian feminists. My sexual ideal is butch, exhibitionistic, physically aggressive, smarter than she wants you to know, and proud of being called a pervert. Most often she is working class, with an aura of danger and an ironic sense of humor. There is a lot of contemporary lip service paid to sexual tolerance, but the fact that my sexuality is constructed within, and by, a butch/femme and leather fetishism is widely viewed with distaste or outright hatred.

For most of my life I have been presumed to be misguided, damaged by incest and childhood physical abuse, or deliberately indulging in hateful and retrograde sexual practices out of a selfish concentration on my own sexual satisfaction. I have been expected to abandon my desires, to become the normalized woman who flirts with fetishization, who plays with gender roles and treats the historical categories of deviant desire with humor or gentle contempt but never takes any of it so seriously as to claim a sexual identity based on these categories. It was hard enough for me to shake off demands when they were made by straight society. It was appalling when I found the same demands made by other lesbians.

One of the strengths I derive from my class background is that I am accustomed to contempt. I know that I have no chance of becoming what my detractors expect of me, and I believe that even the attempt to please them will only further engage their contempt, and my own self-contempt as well. Nonetheless, the relationship between the life I have lived and the way that life is seen by strangers has constantly invited a kind of self-mythologizing fantasy. It has always been tempting for me to play off of the stereotypes and misconceptions of mainstream culture, rather than describe a difficult and sometimes painful reality.

I am trying to understand how we internalize the myths of our society even as we resist them. I have felt a powerful temptation to write about my family as a kind of morality tale, with us as the heroes and middle and upper classes as the villains. It would be within the romantic myth, for example, to pretend that we were the kind of noble Southern whites portrayed in the movies, mill workers for generations until driven out by alcoholism and a family propensity for rebellion and union talk. But that would be a lie. The truth is that no one in my family ever joined a union.

Taken to its limits, the myth of the poor would make my family over into union organizers or people broken by the failure of the unions. As far as my family was concerned union organizers, like preachers, were of a different class, suspect and hated however much they might be admired for what they were supposed to be trying to achieve. Nominally Southern Baptist, no one in my family actually paid much attention to preachers, and only little children went to Sunday school. Serious belief in anything—any political ideology, any religious system, or any theory of life's meaning and purpose—was seen as unrealistic. It was an attitude that bothered me a lot when I started reading the socially conscious novels I found in the paperback racks when I was eleven or so. I particularly loved Sinclair Lewis's[4] novels and wanted to imagine my own family as part of the working man's struggle.

---

[4]American novelist (1885–1951).

"We were not joiners," my aunt Dot told me with a grin when I asked her about the union. My cousin Butch laughed at that, told me the union charged dues, and said, "Hell, we can't even be persuaded to toss money in the collection plate. An't gonna give it to no union man." It shamed me that the only thing my family wholeheartedly believed in was luck and the waywardness of fate. They held the dogged conviction that the admirable and wise thing to do was keep a sense of humor, never whine or cower, and trust that luck might someday turn as good as it had been bad—and with just as much reason. Becoming a political activist with an almost religious fervor was the thing I did that most outraged my family and the Southern working-class community they were part of.

Similarly, it was not my sexuality, my lesbianism, that my family saw as most rebellious; for most of my life, no one but my mama took my sexual preference very seriously. It was the way I thought about work, ambition, and self-respect. They were waitresses, laundry workers, counter girls. I was the one who went to work as a maid, something I never told any of them. They would have been angry if they had known. Work was just work for them, necessary. You did what you had to do to survive. They did not so much believe in taking pride in doing your job as in stubbornly enduring hard work and hard times. At the same time, they held that there were some forms of work, including maid's work, that were only for Black people, not white, and while I did not share that belief, I knew how intrinsic it was to the way my family saw the world. Sometimes I felt as if I straddled cultures and belonged on neither side. I would grind my teeth at what I knew was my family's unquestioning racism while continuing to respect their pragmatic endurance. But more and more as I grew older, what I felt was a deep estrangement from their view of the world, and gradually a sense of shame that would have been completely incomprehensible to them.

"Long as there's lunch counters, you can always find work," I was told by my mother and my aunts. Then they'd add, "I can get me a little extra with a smile." It was obvious there was supposed to be nothing shameful about it, that needy smile across a lunch counter, that rueful grin when you didn't have rent, or the half-provocative, half-pleading way my mama could cajole the man at the store to give her a little credit. But I hated it, hated the need for it and the shame that would follow every time I did it myself. It was begging, as far as I was concerned, a quasi-prostitution that I despised even while I continued to rely on it. After all, I needed the money.

"Just use that smile," my girl cousins used to joke, and I hated what I knew they meant. After college, when I began to support myself and study feminist theory, I became more contemptuous rather than more understanding of the women in my family. I told myself that prostitution is a skilled profession and my cousins were never more than amateurs. There was a certain truth in this, though like all cruel judgments rendered from the outside, it ignored the conditions that made it true. The women in my family, my mother included, had sugar daddies, not johns, men who slipped them money because they needed it so badly. From their point of view they were nice to those men because the men were nice to them, and it was never so direct or crass an arrangement that they would set a price on their favors. Nor would they have described what they did as prostitution. Nothing made them angrier than the suggestion that the men who helped them out did it just for their favors. They worked for a living, they swore, but this was different.

I always wondered if my mother hated her sugar daddy, or if not him then her need for what he offered her, but it did not seem to me in memory that she had. He was an old man, half-crippled, hesitant and needy, and he treated my mama with enormous consideration and, yes, respect. The relationship between them was painful, and since she and my stepfather could not earn enough to support the family, Mama could not refuse her sugar daddy's money. At the same time the man made no assumptions about that money buying anything Mama was not already offering. The truth was, I think, that she genuinely liked him, and only partly because he treated her so well.

Even now, I am not sure whether there was a sexual exchange between them. Mama was a pretty woman, and she was kind to him, a kindness he obviously did not get from anyone else in his life. Moreover, he took extreme care not to cause her any problems with my stepfather. As a teenager, with a teenager's contempt for moral failings and sexual complexity of any kind, I had been convinced that Mama's relationship with that old man was contemptible. Also, that I would never do such a thing. But the first time a lover of mine gave me money and I took it, everything in my head shifted. The amount was not much to her, but it was a lot to me and I needed it. While I could not refuse it, I hated myself for taking it and I hated her for giving it. Worse, she had much less grace about my need than my mama's sugar daddy had displayed toward her. All that bitter contempt I felt for my needy cousins and aunts raged through me and burned out the love. I ended the relationship quickly, unable to forgive myself for selling what I believed should only be offered freely—not sex but love itself.

When the women in my family talked about how hard they worked, the men would spit to the side and shake their heads. Men took real jobs—harsh, dangerous, physically daunting work. They went to jail, not just the cold-eyed, careless boys who scared me with their brutal hands, but their gentler, softer brothers. It was another family thing, what people expected of my mama's people, mine. "His daddy's that one was sent off to jail in Georgia, and his uncle's another. Like as not, he's just the same," you'd hear people say of boys so young they still had their milk teeth. We were always driving down to the county farm to see somebody, some uncle, cousin, or nameless male relation. Shaven-headed, sullen, and stunned, they wept on Mama's shoulder or begged my aunts to help. "I didn't do nothing, Mama," they'd say, and it might have been true, but if even we didn't believe them, who would? No one told the truth, not even about how their lives were destroyed.

One of my favorite cousins went to jail when I was eight years old, for breaking into pay phones with another boy. The other boy was returned to the custody of his parents. My cousin was sent to the boys' facility at the county farm.

After three months, my mama took us down there to visit, carrying a big basket of fried chicken, cold cornbread, and potato salad. Along with a hundred others we sat out on the lawn with my cousin and watched him eat like he hadn't had a full meal in the whole three months. I stared at his near-bald head and his ears marked with fine blue scars from the carelessly handled razor. People were laughing, music was playing, and a tall, lazy, uniformed man walked past us chewing on toothpicks and watching us all closely. My cousin kept his head down, his face hard with hatred, only looking back at the guard when he turned away.

"Sons-a-bitches," he whispered, and my mama shushed him. We all sat still when the guard turned back to us. There was a long moment of quiet, and then that man let his face relax into a big wide grin.

"Uh-huh," he said. That was all he said. Then he turned and walked away. None of us spoke. None of us ate. He went back inside soon after, and we left. When we got back to the car, my mama sat there for a while crying quietly. The next week my cousin was reported for fighting and had his stay extended by six months.

My cousin was fifteen. He never went back to school, and after jail he couldn't join the army. When he finally did come home we never talked, never had to. I knew without asking that the guard had had his little revenge, knew too that my cousin would break into another phone booth as soon as he could, but do it sober and not get caught. I knew without asking the source of his rage, the way he felt about clean, well-dressed, contemptuous people who looked at him like his life wasn't as important as a dog's. I knew because I felt it too. That guard had looked at me and Mama with the same expression he used on my cousin. We were trash. We were the ones they built the county farm to house and break. The boy who was sent home was the son of a deacon in the church, the man who managed the hardware store.

As much as I hated that man, and his boy, there was a way in which I also hated my cousin. He should have known better, I told myself, should have known the risk he ran. He should have been more careful. As I grew older and started living on my own, it was a litany I used against myself even more angrily than I used it against my cousin. I knew who I was, knew that the most important thing I had to do was protect myself and hide my despised identity, blend into the myth of both the good poor and the reasonable lesbian. When I became a feminist activist, that litany went on reverberating in my head, but by then it had become a groundnote, something so deep and omnipresent I no longer heard it, even when everything I did was set to its cadence.

By 1975 I was earning a meager living as a photographer's assistant in Tallahassee, Florida. But the real work of my life was my lesbian-feminist activism, the work I did with the local women's center and the committee to found a women's studies program at Florida State University. Part of my role, as I saw it, was to be a kind of evangelical lesbian feminist, and to help develop a political analysis of this woman-hating society. I did not talk about class, except to give lip service to how we all needed to think about it, the same way I thought we all needed to think about racism. I was a determined person, living in a lesbian collective—all of us young and white and serious—studying each new book that purported to address feminist issues, driven by what I saw as a need to revolutionize the world.

Years later it's difficult to convey just how reasonable my life seemed to me at that time. I was not flippant, not consciously condescending, not casual about how tough a struggle remaking social relations would be, but like so many women of my generation, I believed absolutely that I could make a difference with my life, and I was willing to give my life for the chance to make that difference. I expected hard times, long slow periods of self-sacrifice and grinding work, expected to be hated and attacked in public, to have to set aside personal desire, lovers, and family in order to be part of something greater and more important than my individual concerns. At the same time, I was working ferociously to take my desires, my sexuality, my needs as a woman and a lesbian more seriously. I believed I was making the personal political revolution with my life every moment, whether I was scrubbing the floor of the childcare center, setting up a new budget for the women's lecture series at the university, editing the local feminist magazine, or starting a women's bookstore. That I was constantly exhausted and had no health insurance, did hours of dreary unpaid work and still sneaked out of the collective to date butch women my housemates thought retrograde and sexist never interfered with my sense of total commitment to the feminist revolution. I was not living in a closet: I had compartmentalized my own mind to such an extent that I never questioned why I did what I did. And I never admitted what lay behind all my feminist convictions—a class-constructed distrust of change, a secret fear that someday I would be found out for who I really was, found out and thrown out. If I had not been raised to give my life away, would I have made such an effective, self-sacrificing revolutionary?

The narrowly focused concentration of a revolutionary shifted only when I began to write again. The idea of writing stories seemed frivolous when there was so much work to be done, but everything changed when I found myself confronting emotions and ideas that could not be explained away or postponed until after the revolution. The way it happened was simple and unexpected. One week I was asked to speak to two completely different groups: an Episcopalian Sunday school class and a juvenile detention center. The Episcopalians were all white, well-dressed, highly articulate, nominally polite, and obsessed with getting me to tell them (without their having to ask directly) just what it was that two women did together in bed. The delinquents were all women, 80 percent Black and Hispanic, wearing green uniform dresses or blue jeans and workshirts, profane, rude, fearless, witty, and just as determined to get me to talk about what it was that two women did together in bed.

I tried to have fun with the Episcopalians, teasing them about their fears and insecurities, and being as bluntly honest as I could about my sexual practices. The Sunday school teacher, a man who had assured me of his liberal inclinations, kept blushing and stammering as the questions about my growing up and coming out became more detailed. I stepped out into the sunshine when the meeting was over, angry at the contemptuous attitude implied by all their questioning, and though I did not know why, so deeply depressed I couldn't even cry.

The delinquents were another story. Shameless, they had me blushing within the first few minutes, yelling out questions that were part curiosity and partly a way of boasting about what they already knew. "You butch or femme?" "You ever fuck boys?" "You ever want to?" "You want to have children?" "What's your girlfriend like?" I finally broke up when one very tall, confident girl leaned way over and called out, "Hey, girlfriend! I'm getting out of here next weekend. What you doing that night?" I laughed so hard I almost choked. I laughed until we were all howling and giggling together. Even getting frisked as I left didn't ruin my mood. I was still grinning when I climbed into the waterbed with my lover that night, grinning right up to the moment when she wrapped her arms around me and I burst into tears.

That night I understood, suddenly, everything that had happened to my cousins and me, understood it from a wholly new and agonizing perspective, one that made clear how brutal I had been to both my family and myself. I grasped all over again how we had been robbed and dismissed, and why I had worked so hard not to think about it. I had learned as a child that what could not be changed had to go unspoken, and worse, that those who cannot change their own lives have every reason to be ashamed of that fact and to hide it. I had accepted that shame and believed in it, but why? What had I or my cousins done to deserve the contempt directed at us? Why had I always believed us contemptible by nature? I wanted to talk to someone about all the things I was thinking that night, but I could not. Among the women I knew there was no one who would have understood what I was thinking, no other working-class woman in the women's collective where I was living. I began to suspect that we shared no common language to speak those bitter truths.

In the days that followed I found myself remembering that afternoon long ago at the county farm, that feeling of being the animal in the zoo, the thing looked at and laughed at and used by the real people who watched us. For all his liberal convictions, that Sunday school teacher had looked at me with the eyes of my cousin's long-ago guard. I felt thrown back into my childhood, into all the fears I had tried to escape. Once again I felt myself at the mercy of the important people who knew how to dress and talk, and would always be given the benefit of the doubt, while my family and I would not.

I experienced an outrage so old I could not have traced all the ways it shaped my life. I realized again that some are given no quarter, no chance, that all their courage, humor, and love for each other is just a joke to the ones who make the rules, and I hated the rule-makers. Finally, I recognized that part of my grief came from the fact that I no longer knew who I was or where I belonged. I had run away from my family, refused to go home to visit, and tried in every way to make myself a new person. How could I be working class with a college degree? As a lesbian activist? I thought about the guards at the detention center.

They had not stared at me with the same picture-window emptiness they turned on the girls who came to hear me, girls who were closer to the life I had been meant to live than I could bear to examine. The contempt in their eyes was contempt for me as a lesbian, different and the same, but still contempt.

While I raged, my girlfriend held me and comforted me and tried to get me to explain what was hurting me so bad, but I could not. She had told me so often about her awkward relationship with her own family, the father who ran his own business and still sent her checks every other month. She knew almost nothing about my family, only the jokes and careful stories I had given her. I felt so alone and at risk lying in her arms that I could not have explained anything at all. I thought about those girls in the detention center and the stories they told in brutal shorthand about their sisters, brothers, cousins, and lovers. I thought about their one-note references to those they had lost, never mentioning the loss of their own hopes, their own futures, the bent and painful shape of their lives when they would finally get free. Cried-out and dry-eyed, I lay watching my sleeping girlfriend and thinking about what I had not been able to say to her. After a few hours I got up and made some notes for a poem I wanted to write, a bare, painful litany of loss shaped as a conversation between two women, one who cannot understand the other, and one who cannot tell all she knows.

It took me a long time to take that poem from a raw lyric of outrage and grief to a piece of fiction that explained to me something I had never let myself see up close before—the whole process of running away, of closing up inside yourself, of hiding. It has taken me most of my life to understand that, to see how and why those of us who are born poor and different are so driven to give ourselves away or lose ourselves, but most of all, simply to disappear as the people we really are. By the time that poem became the story "River of Names,"[5] I had made the decision to reverse that process: to claim my family, my true history, and to tell the truth not only about who I was but about the temptation to lie.

By the time I taught myself the basics of storytelling on the page, I knew there was only one story that would haunt me until I understood how to tell it—the complicated, painful story of how my mama had, and had not, saved me as a girl. Writing *Bastard Out of Carolina*[6] became, ultimately, the way to claim my family's pride and tragedy, and the embattled sexuality I had fashioned on a base of violence and abuse.

The compartmentalized life I had created burst open in the late 1970s after I began to write what I really thought about my family. I lost patience with my fear of what the women I worked with, mostly lesbians, thought of who I slept with and what we did together. When schisms developed within my community; when I was no longer able to hide within the regular dyke network; when

---

[5]*Trash* (Firebrand Books: Ithaca, New York, 1988) [Allison's note].
[6]Dutton: New York, 1992 [Allison's note].

I could not continue to justify my life by constant political activism or distract myself by sleeping around; when my sexual promiscuity, butch/femme orientation, and exploration of sadomasochistic sex became part of what was driving me out of my community of choice—I went home again. I went home to my mother and my sisters, to visit, talk, argue, and begin to understand.

Once home I saw that as far as my family was concerned, lesbians were lesbians whether they wore suitcoats or leather jackets. Moreover, in all that time when I had not made peace with myself, my family had managed to make a kind of peace with me. My girlfriends were treated like slightly odd versions of my sisters' husbands, while I was simply the daughter who had always been difficult but was still a part of their lives. The result was that I started trying to confront what had made me unable really to talk to my sisters for so many years. I discovered that they no longer knew who I was either, and it took time and lots of listening to each other to rediscover my sense of family, and my love for them.

It is only as the child of my class and my unique family background that I have been able to put together what is for me a meaningful politics, to regain a sense of why I believe in activism, why self-revelation is so important for lesbians. There is no all-purpose feminist analysis that explains the complicated ways our sexuality and core identity are shaped, the way we see ourselves as parts of both our birth families and the extended family of friends and lovers we invariably create within the lesbian community. For me, the bottom line has simply become the need to resist that omnipresent fear, that urge to hide and disappear, to disguise my life, my desires, and the truth about how little any of us understand—even as we try to make the world a more just and human place. Most of all, I have tried to understand the politics of *they,* why human beings fear and stigmatize the different while secretly dreading that they might be one of the different themselves. Class, race, sexuality, gender—and all the other categories by which we categorize and dismiss each other—need to be excavated from the inside.

The horror of class stratification, racism, and prejudice is that some people begin to believe that the security of their families and communities depends on the oppression of others, that for some to have good lives there must be others whose lives are truncated and brutal. It is a belief that dominates this culture. It is what makes the poor whites of the South so determinedly racist and the middle class so contemptuous of the poor. It is a myth that allows some to imagine that they build their lives on the ruin of others, a secret core of shame for the middle class, a goad and a spur to the marginal working class, and cause enough for the homeless and poor to feel no constraints on hatred or violence. The power of the myth is made even more apparent when we examine how, within the lesbian and feminist communities where we have addressed considerable attention to the politics of marginalization, there is still so much exclusion and fear, so many of us who do not feel safe.

I grew up poor, hated, the victim of physical, emotional, and sexual violence, and I know that suffering does not ennoble. It destroys. To resist destruction, self-hatred, or lifelong hopelessness, we have to throw off the conditioning of being despised, the fear of becoming the *they* that is talked about so dismissively, to refuse lying myths and easy moralities, to see ourselves as human, flawed, and extraordinary. All of us—extraordinary.

Study and Discussion Questions

1. "Entitlement . . . is a matter of feeling like we rather than they," writes Allison in the beginning paragraphs of this essay. What does Allison mean here by "we" and "they"? Give examples of when you have felt either like "we" or like "they."
2. Look up and write definitions for: entitlement, hegemony, frisson, patriarchy, lesbian-feminist, ideology, trash.
3. What is the myth of the poor in the United States: the good noble poor? the bad poor? What does Allison's essay suggest is limiting about both of these categories?
4. Find places in "A Question of Class" where Allison discusses or gives examples of "shame." What does the experience of shame have to do with her arguments about the effects of social class?
5. What does Allison say about anger and related emotions? Find examples in the essay.
6. Discuss "the geographic solution." What does Allison mean by it? Have you ever been tempted by or had experience with this phenomenon? What are its benefits and its limitations?
7. How does Allison say she denied or distorted her background as she moved away from it, went to college on scholarship, moved into middle-class circles and into political activism? Give examples.
8. Discuss the relation to work and to money of (a) the women and (b) the men in Allison's family.
9. Discuss the mixture of grief and outrage that started Allison writing poetry and fiction. What incidents precipitated this reaction? How and why was this an important transition for her? Why is writing, in particular, important for Allison?
10. Discuss the incident when Allison visits her fifteen-year-old cousin in jail. How does this episode become symbolic?
11. Allison talks about her years as a lesbian feminist. How did her social class background affect the way she felt among (and perhaps the way she was seen by) her comrades—other activists, housemates, lovers?

Suggestions for Writing

1. What are the costs for individuals personally and for our society of going along with (a) the myths and (b) the silences and denials around social class in the United States? What does Allison say in this essay? What do you think?

2. Write an account of your own social class background incorporating four or five factors that you believe identify your social class and providing examples from your life to illustrate each factor. How do you think your social class has influenced who you are today?

3. Read another piece of writing by Allison. See "Gun Crazy" in the Growing Up and Growing Older section or read one of Allison's short stories, novels, poems, or essays. Discuss how the two works illuminate each other.

4. What do hopes and expectations (our own, our family's, our society's) have to do with who we become?

❋ ❋ ❋

CHARLES MERRILL PROUDFOOT

Charles Merrill Proudfoot (1923–1998) was a Presbyterian clergyman, scholar, teacher, and social justice activist. He received a B.A. from Austin College, his M. Div. from Austin Presbyterian Theological Seminary, and an M.A. and Ph.D. in Religion from Yale University. Later in life, he earned another M.A. and Ph.D. in philosophy from the University of Kansas and an M.A. in counseling from the University of Missouri, Kansas City. Ordained in Texas in 1950, Proudfoot worked for three years as a pastor there before beginning his long teaching career. He taught philosophy and religion at the predominantly black Knoxville College from 1957 to 1965, when the events recorded in his diary took place. Proudfoot then taught at Park College, in Parkville, Missouri, for thirty-two years, retiring in 1994. His publications include *Diary of a Sit-In* (1962), *Suffering: A Christian Understanding* (1964), and a number of essays on race relations and South Africa. Proudfoot was also one of the authors of the Presbyterian. Church's policy statement on conscientious objectors and, after he accepted his homosexuality at the age of 54, a contributor of an autobiographical essay to *Called Out: The Voices and Gifts of Lesbian, Gay, Bisexual and Transgendered Presbyterians* (1995). In addition, Proudfoot visited prisoners and advocated for their welfare, making monthly visits for seventeen years to the U.S. Disciplinary Barracks at Ft. Leavenworth. He also served on the board of the Western Missouri Coalition for the Abolition of the Death Penalty.

The lunch counter sit-ins began in Greensboro, North Carolina, in February 1960. Sit-ins spread quickly among young people across the South. John Lewis and other college students started similar sit-ins in Nashville, and the students in Knoxville, Tennessee, including some at Proudfoot's college, were moved to sit in to protest segregation. Few professors, and even fewer white professors, participated in these sit-ins, but Proudfoot was one of them; he had promised Robert Booker, the president of Knoxville College's student body, he would. On the first day of the sit-in, June 9, 1960, Proudfoot wrote, "I found myself—a white, bespectacled college professor at the usually conservative age of thirty-six—advancing to my baptism by fire as a sit-in demonstrator!" His diary covers about six weeks, until the downtown merchants of Knoxville agreed to desegregate their counters. The passage below came midway through the protest. It is followed by a brief reflection on civil disobedience from the book's original Afterword.

Diary of a Sit-In

Wednesday, June 29

Today our movement is in crisis and all of us know it. Open violence flared 1
again, and one store has made a countermove we didn't expect.

Spurred by the rising excitement, between sixty and seventy came to sit-in today, enough to hit nearly all the stores whose counters remain open. Miller's was excluded because we hear they have at last completely closed theirs. I chose to go to Walgreen's because I hadn't yet experienced what it is like there. (I found out!) A tall brawny young Negro man named Logan was our leader. I asked him what his work was. He said, "I was working for a cab company until last week, but when I heard about the sit-ins I quit my job so I could help with them. I was only making fifteen or twenty dollars a week, and by working in the sit-ins maybe I can do some real good." What a spirit! Logan is not very well educated, but has a deep sense of justice and seems to know Christian love as more than a theory. He kept tight control of the group. One boy of twelve was with us; Logan called him "Junior" and kept reminding him sharply to sit back on his stool until I pointed out that when Junior sat back, his feet didn't touch the floor! The kids want to do their part, but we shouldn't involve them in some of the things that may happen.

Walgreen's is the only place we go that has booths; Logan and I occupy one together. A man in a white jacket who seems to be in charge of the counter manifests his hostility from the beginning. As he passes by our booth, he conspicuously spits on the floor. The next time he tosses a lighted cigarette on me; it rests in a fold of my coat. I would prefer to ignore it, but must pluck it off before it burns a hole in my good suit. I want to examine the coat to see if it is damaged, but I must not do anything here that will indicate anxiety. A young white fellow stops at our booth, inquires about Robert Booker, whom he says he knows. Now I see him bring coffee which he has ordered to one of our Negro boys and a coke to another. I wish he had not done that. The demonstrators do not touch the drinks. Logan suggests that the drinks may be drugged; I had not thought of that! The man in the white coat comes to pick up the drinks. He deliberately spills the coke over the demonstrator, and now the coffee, exclaiming with mock apology, "Oh, excuse me!"

A woman customer brushes close to our booth and mutters to me, "Take   5
your niggers and get out of here!"

A group of white boys who appear to be high school age come up to our
booth and begin to tantalize me. I do not recognize the fellow who heckled me
before; these boys have a younger appearance, but their line is the same: "Come
on with us, fellow; we're going to show you where you belong!" I am apprehensive, but somehow actual danger is never so fearful as dreaded danger.

As they continue their heckling, I look straight ahead at Logan. Suddenly I
feel myself drenched with what seems a terrific lot of liquid. My glasses are
filmed over; I take them off and hold them in my clenched hands. My eyes
smart—what was the stuff? The liquid has gone down all over my "preachin'
suit." I notice crushed ice too, and realize it must have been a coke—a tall coke,
not poured or spilled, but the contents thrown over me by one of these boys
from a distance of two feet. Logan utters quiet words of encouragement; he is
a great strength to me. I can sense as though I had eyes all over my head that
everyone in the establishment is looking at me; I feel I have the sympathy of
most of them. Nevertheless, it is a mortifying experience to be attacked in public by another person and not be able to do anything in your own defense.

I breathe a bit easier, for the boys have left us now, but I see one go into the
kitchen and speak to some employee—the man in the white coat?—and I fear
he is up to no good. Now they are back, heckling me again. I look straight forward, pretending to pay no attention. Suddenly I am jolted by a severe blow on
the left side of my face. My first thought is of being hit by a batted tennis ball
when I was six years old—it stings like that. It did not feel like the blow of a
clenched fist; it must have been done with the open hand.

Logan reminds me I am not to strike back, but I hardly need that advice. I
do not feel like striking back physically, but does one just sit here and let a
young punk use him for a punching bag? Suddenly the blow comes again, again
hard. Failing to get any response, one or two of the boys grab me and start
pulling me from the booth. I slide my glasses to Logan as we have prearranged,
and hold on.

At precisely this moment a young white man who has been eating in a booth
near ours rises and takes the situation in hand. He is impressively large and
young enough to be damaging. Sternly he says to the boys, "You fellows have
gone far enough and now you'd better get out of here! Look, I'm neutral in this,
but this fellow was just sitting here. You could be arrested for what you've done.
You'd better get out of here before you get into real trouble!"

I wish I could see the boys' faces! They meekly leave and the man leaves too.   10
I will never know his identity and therefore can never thank him, but I have a
feeling he would not wish to be thanked by me. What he did, he did not do for
me, but for his sense of decency and order. What a travesty of both it is that a
customer should have to restore order! I cannot imagine why any hard-headed
business man would allow his store to become a scene of riot.

Nevertheless, here is a clear example of the effectiveness of the non-violent
approach. It has caused this "neutral" to declare himself for decency and order.

A more crucial test will be what he now says about serving Negroes in Walgreen's, and this I will never know. About the effect of non-violence on the agitators themselves, I have some reservations. I believe now that if I had at any time risen from my seat and said "Boo!" to those boys, they would have left me alone. Declared non-resistance brings out the bully in those who are inclined to be bullies.

Logan asks me, "What did the man mean when he said 'impure?'" It takes me some time to realize Logan means the word "neutral." I explain to him what a "neutral" is and am even more impressed with the boy's educated heart. I suppose any one of the white gang could have defined "neutral," but their knowledge hasn't made them good citizens or given them a fair attitude toward their fellow-man.

Half an hour has passed. At exactly 1:00 P.M., the counter lights are turned off. The man who I assume to be the counter manager comes to our booth and says in a decent way, "We've closed now; wouldn't you like to leave?" Logan asks me for advice (since this is his first day as a leader), and I tell him, "I think we could leave as soon as all the others are gone," meaning the customers. This seems to satisfy the manager. Shortly after this, a man stops at our booth and says, "Hey, preacher." I turn, thinking he has a serious purpose. The man is of medium stocky build, black hair slicked back, and appears to be about thirty. He jeers, "Was your mother one?" Surprised, I treat it as a joke and turn forward again. The man proceeds to sit down in a booth along the rear wall with another man; a waitress comes, seems to be conversing with them. Suddenly the man rises from the booth, winds up like a baseball pitcher, and throws something with power down the row of booths at some target behind and to the right of me, I see a white object whiz by in the air.

A woman behind me screams, "Who threw that salt shaker? You've hit my baby! If I had hold of the dirty sonofabitch that hit my baby, I'd tear him in pieces!" The whole place is thrown into turmoil. A crowd collects, some coming in off the street. I can only think of one thing—supposing they charge that one of the Negroes did it! I get the impression the baby is badly injured.

A man who seems to be the manager of the entire store comes to our booth 15 and advises, "You'd better go now." We are definitely ready, but the question now is, "Will we be allowed to go?" For by now the police have arrived and are talking to the woman. Logan goes over to ask the police if it is all right for us to leave. The police are not getting anywhere; nobody is admitting that he knows who threw the shaker. I keep an eye on the culprit who sits innocently in his booth. I am determined not to leave the store until I have told what I know; even if it were not for honesty's sake, it would be to protect our group. Perhaps the police will get around to questioning us. At last the manager comes to me and asks if I know who did the throwing. I tell him without pointing to where the man is sitting. "The waitress must have seen it, because she was standing right beside his booth," I add.

"The waitress says she didn't see anything." That figures; I thought she was flirting with them.

A siren wails, a man in a white uniform enters the store—apparently a police officer on ambulance duty. They talk with the woman some more. Logan finally gets through to the police and they give us permission to leave. The policemen now move back to the booth where the guilty party is sitting. The eight or nine Negroes encircle me to give me protection as we move through the crowd, but I tell them I will have to stay because I witnessed the offense; I ask for one Negro youth to stay with me. Just at this point the police officers escort the culprit and his companion from the store. They have apparently made an arrest. Greatly relieved that no one has accused us—for the opportunity must have made it a temptation—I give my name and address to the store manager and leave with our whole crew.

A crowd which includes a great many white youths is gathered on the sidewalk outside the store. Our danger is so real we can almost smell it, like dogs whiffing the wind. My only safety is in my Negro friends. How topsy-turvy my world has become, when I feel apprehensive among white strangers and perfectly safe only when Negroes are around! I have learned a lot since I came to the college three years ago; my attitude then was not unlike that of the department head at the University who avows that he always rolls up his car windows and locks his doors when he drives through a Negro neighborhood! The white South has always depended on the Negro population for its security and comfort, but in subtle ways that are easy to overlook. It would be good for every white person to have this experience I am having of knowing that my physical safety is completely in the hands of Negro friends.

A few steps from Walgreen's I run across a friend from Norris, Tennessee, who, not knowing our danger, expects me to stop and chat with him for a moment. I ask him to walk along with us, quietly explaining why I cannot stop. The Negro youths stay with me all the way to the parking garage and, despite my protests, wait outside until I drive off.

As I drive home, I am in a state of agitation. In my mind the pieces of evidence become exaggerated into a certainty that the baby is dead or dying. I suffer an agony of conscience: "If we had left immediately when we were first asked, none of this would have happened—Does this not make me a murderer? During those first calm days, it seemed impossible that it could ever come to this! How thin is the line between peace and violence, between life and death, between hope and desperation." 20

Because in my emotional excitement I do not wish to be alone, I stop at the Reese's and share my experiences with them. From there I call Crutcher, who gives as his opinion, "The papers ought to know about this!" Hardly any time elapses before reporters from both the *News-Sentinel* and United Press International call. I am almost afraid to ask about the baby, but one of the reporters mercifully tells me that he doesn't think there has been any serious injury. The salt shaker hit the mother and fell down against the baby. But the baby was only fourteen days old! The object was thrown with great force and obviously went far wide of its intended mark, whatever that may have been. Supposing it had hit just a few inches lower against the infant's head! The *News-Sentinel* reporter rings back, saying that his boss wants to know what kind of doctor I am—a medical doctor? "No, a doctor of philosophy—from Yale University." I sense his disappointment. I can appreciate that if he could tie in the American Medical Association with the sit-ins, it would make quite a sensational story! The word has spread quickly and friends are beginning to call to express their concern. I am basking in the glow of attention, to the point that I am almost hurt that the Associated Press has not yet called!

Questions about the Passage

1. What are the rules that Proudfoot and Logan must follow in their sit-in at the segregated store's lunch counter?
2. What case for civil disobedience does Proudfoot make?

Questions about the Argument

1. Does Proudfoot create sympathy for the difficulty of his task? If so, how? How does the first-person narration shape our attitude to him?
2. What sense of Proudfoot's ethos do you have? How does the fact that this is a day-by-day diary affect his readers' perception of him?
3. Who is Proudfoot's audience? What clues do you have to who his intended audience is?
4. Compare Proudfoot's case for disobeying unjust laws to King's. Do they agree?

MALCOLM X

The remarkable life of **Malcolm X** is well known because of Alex Haley's *The Autobiography of Malcolm X* and Spike Lee's adoring film *Malcolm X*. Born in 1925 into challenging circumstances, the victim of a tortured childhood that created a seething alienation, and drawn first to a life of petty crime. Malcolm X was converted in prison to Islam and thereafter became a leader in the Black Muslims and the black nationalist movement of the early 1960s. A charismatic speaker who was assassinated in 1965 (only months after returning from a pilgrimage to Africa and the Near East and renouncing his separatist agenda). Malcolm X was a foil to his contemporary, Martin Luther King. Jr. The following speech was delivered on November 10, 1963 (six months after King wrote his "Letter from Birmingham Jail," two weeks before President Kennedy was assassinated, and fifteen months before Malcolm X's own death), to an all-black audience gathered in Detroit for a Northern Negro

Leadership Conference; it was also broadcast over the radio. The speech reveals the terms of Malcolm X's differences with King: at the time the two disagreed about the wisdom of segregation versus integration and about whether nonviolent resistance or violent revenge is the better means of countering racism.

Message to the Grassroots

We want to have just an off-the-cuff chat between you and me, us. We want   1 to talk right down to earth in a language that everybody here can easily understand. We all agree tonight, all of the speakers have agreed, that America has a very serious problem. Not only does America have a very serious problem, but our people have a very serious problem. America's problem is us. We're her problem. The only reason she has a problem is she doesn't want us here. And every time you look at yourself, be you black, brown, red or yellow, a so-called Negro, you represent a person who poses such a serious problem for America because you're not wanted. Once you face this as a fact, then you can start plotting a course that will make you appear intelligent, instead of unintelligent.

What you and I need to do is learn to forget our differences. When we come together, we don't come together as Baptists or Methodists. You don't catch hell because you're a Baptist, and you don't catch hell because you're a Methodist. You don't catch hell because you're a Methodist or Baptist, you don't catch hell because you're a Democrat or a Republican, you don't catch hell because you're a Mason or an Elk, and you sure don't catch hell because you're an American; because if you were an American, you wouldn't catch hell. You catch hell because you're a black man. You catch hell, all of us catch hell, for the same reason.

So we're all black people, so-called Negroes, second-class citizens, ex-slaves. You're nothing but an ex-slave. You don't like to be told that. But what else are you? You are ex-slaves. You didn't come here on the "Mayflower." You came here on a slave ship. In chains, like a horse, or a cow, or a chicken. And you were brought here by the people who came here on the "Mayflower," you were brought here by the so-called Pilgrims, or Founding Fathers. They were the ones who brought you here.

We have a common enemy. We have this in common: We have a common oppressor, a common exploiter, and a common discriminator. But once we all realize that we have a common enemy, then we unite—on the basis of what we have in common. And what we have foremost in common is that enemy—the white man. He's an enemy to all of us. I know some of you all think that some of them aren't enemies. Time will tell.

In Bandung back in, I think, 1954, was the first unity meeting in centuries of   5 black people. And once you study what happened at the Bandung conference, and the results of the Bandung conference, it actually serves as a model for the same procedure you and I can use to get our problems solved. At Bandung all the nations came together, the dark nations from Africa and Asia. Some of them were Buddhists, some of them were Muslims, some of them were Christians, some were Confucianists, some were atheists. Despite their religious differences, they came together. Some were communists, some were socialists, some were capitalists—despite their economic and political differences, they came together. All of them were black, brown, red or yellow.

The number-one thing that was not allowed to attend the Bandung conference was the white man. He couldn't come. Once they excluded the white man, they found that they could get together. Once they kept him out, everybody else fell right in and fell in line. This is the thing that you and I have to understand. And these people who came together didn't have nuclear weapons, they didn't have jet planes, they didn't have all of the heavy armaments that the white man has. But they had unity.

They were able to submerge their little petty differences and agree on one thing: That there one African came from Kenya and was being colonized by the Englishman, and another African came from the Congo and was being colonized by the Belgian, and another African came from Guinea and was being colonized by the French, and another came from Angola and was being colonized by the Portuguese. When they came to the Bandung conference, they looked at the Portuguese, and at the Frenchman, and at the Englishman, and at the Dutchman, and learned or realized the one thing that all of them had in common—they were all from Europe, they were all Europeans, blond, blue-eyed and white skins. They began to recognize who their enemy was. The same man that was colonizing our people in Kenya was colonizing our people in the Congo. The same one in the Congo was colonizing our people in South Africa, and in Southern Rhodesia, and in Burma, and in India, and in Afghanistan, and in Pakistan. They realized all over the world where the dark man was being oppressed, he was being oppressed by the white man: where the dark man was being exploited, he was being exploited by the white man. So they got together on this basis—that they had a common enemy.

And when you and I here in Detroit and in Michigan and in America who have been awakened today look around us, we too realize here in America we all have a common enemy, whether he's in Georgia or Michigan, whether he's in California or New York. He's the same man—blue eyes and blond hair and pale skin—the same man. So what we have to do is what they did. They agreed to stop quarreling among themselves. Any little spat that they had, they'd settle it among themselves, go into a huddle—don't let the enemy know that you've got a disagreement.

Instead of airing our differences in public, we have to realize we're all the same family. And when you have a family squabble, you don't get out on the sidewalk. If you do, everybody calls you uncouth, unrefined, uncivilized, savage. If you don't make it at home, you settle it at home: you get in the closet, argue it out behind closed doors, and then when you come out on the street, you pose a common front, a united front. And this is what we need to do in the community, and in the city, and in the state. We need to stop airing our differences in front of the white man, put the white man out of our meetings, and then sit down and talk shop with each other. That's what we've got to do.

I would like to make a few comments concerning the difference between the   10 black revolution and the Negro revolution. Are they both the same? And if they're not, what is the difference? What is the difference between a black revolution and a Negro revolution? First, what is a revolution? Sometimes I'm inclined to believe that many of our people are using this word "revolution" loosely, without taking careful consideration of what this word actually means, and what its historic characteristics are. When you study the historic nature of revolutions, the motive of a revolution, the objective of a revolution, the result of a revolution, and the methods used in a revolution, you may change words. You may devise another program, you may change your goal and you may change your mind.

Look at the American Revolution in 1776. That revolution was for what? For land. Why did they want land? Independence. How was it carried out? Bloodshed. Number one, it was based on land, the basis of independence. And the only way they could get it was bloodshed. The French Revolution—what was it based on? The landless against the landlord. What was it for? Land. How did they get it? Bloodshed. Was no love lost, was no compromise, was no negotiation. I'm telling you—you don't know what a revolution is. Because when you find out what it is, you'll get back in the alley, you'll get out of the way.

The Russian Revolution—what was it based on? Land: the landless against the landlord. How did they bring it about? Bloodshed. You haven't got a revolution that doesn't involve bloodshed. And you're afraid to bleed. I said, you're afraid to bleed.

As long as the white man sent you to Korea, you bled. He sent you to Germany, you bled. He sent you to the South Pacific to fight the Japanese, you bled. You bleed for white people, but when it comes to seeing your own churches being bombed and little black girls murdered, you haven't got any blood. You bleed when the white man says bleed: you bite when the white man says bite: and you bark when the white man says bark. I hate to say this about us, but it's true. How are you going to be nonviolent in Mississippi, as violent as you were in Korea? How can you justify being nonviolent in Mississippi and Alabama, when your churches are being bombed, and your little girls are being murdered, and at the same time you are going to get violent with Hitler, and Tojo, and somebody else you don't even know?

If violence is wrong in America, violence is wrong abroad. If it is wrong to be violent defending black women and black children and black babies and black men, then it is wrong for America to draft us and make us violent abroad in defense of her. And if it is right for America to draft us, and teach us how to be violent in defense of her, then it is right for you and me to do whatever is necessary to defend our own people right here in this country.

The Chinese Revolution—they wanted land. They threw the British out, along   15 with the Uncle Tom Chinese. Yes, they did. They set a good example. When I was in prison, I read an article—don't be shocked when I say that I was in prison. You're still in prison. That's what America means: prison. When I was in prison, I read an article in *Life* magazine showing a little Chinese girl, nine years old: her father was on his hands and knees and she was pulling the trigger because he was an Uncle Tom Chinaman. When they had the revolution over there, they took a whole generation of Uncle Toms and just wiped them out. And within ten years that little girl became a full-grown woman. No more Toms in China. And today it's one of the toughest, roughest, most feared countries on this earth—by the white man. Because there are no Uncle Toms over there.

Of all our studies, history is best qualified to reward our research. And when you see that you've got problems, all you have to do is examine the historic method used all over the world by others who have problems similar to yours. Once you see how they got theirs straight, then you know how you can get yours straight. There's been a revolution, a black revolution, going on in Africa. In Kenya, the Mau Mau were revolutionary: they were the ones who brought the word "Uhuru" to the fore. The Mau Mau, they were revolutionary, they believed in scorched earth, they knocked everything aside that got in their way, and their revolution also was based on land, a desire for land. In Algeria, the northern part of Africa, a revolution took place. The Algerians were revolutionists, they wanted land. France offered to let them be integrated into France. They told France, to hell with France, they wanted some land, not some France. And they engaged in a bloody battle.

So I cite these various revolutions, brothers and sisters, to show you that you don't have a peaceful revolution. You don't have a turn-the-other-cheek revolution. There's no such thing as a nonviolent revolution. The only kind of revolution that is nonviolent is the Negro revolution. The only revolution in which the goal is loving your enemy is the Negro revolution. It's the only revolution in which the goal is a desegregated lunch counter, a desegregated theater, a desegregated park, and a desegregated public toilet: you can sit down next to white folks—on the toilet. That's no revolution. Revolution is based on land. Land is the basis of all independence. Land is the basis of freedom, justice, and equality.

The white man knows what a revolution is. He knows that the black revolution is world-wide in scope and in nature. The black revolution is sweeping Asia, is sweeping Africa, is rearing its head in Latin America. The Cuban Revolution—that's a revolution. They overturned the system. Revolution is in Asia, revolution is in Africa, and the white man is screaming because he sees revolution in Latin America. How do you think he'll react to you when you learn what a real revolution is? You don't know what a revolution is. If you did, you wouldn't use that word.

Revolution is bloody, revolution is hostile, revolution knows no compromise, revolution overturns and destroys everything that gets in its way. And you, sitting around here like a knot on the wall, saying. "I'm going to love these folks no matter how much they hate me." No. you need a revolution. Whoever heard of a revolution where they look arms, as Rev. Cleage was pointing out beautifully, singing "We Shall Overcome"? You don't do that in a revolution. You don't do any singing, you're too busy swinging. It's based on land. A revolutionary wants land so he can set up his own nation, an independent nation. These Negroes aren't asking for any nation—they're trying to crawl back on the plantation.

When you want a nation, that's called nationalism. When the white man became involved in a revolution in this country against England, what was it for? he wanted this land so he could set up another white nation. That's white nationalism. The American Revolution was white nationalism. The French Revolution was white nationalism. The Russian Revolution too—yes, it was—white nationalism. You don't think so? Why do you think Khrushehev and Mao can't get their heads together? White nationalism. All the revolutions that are going on in Asia and Africa today are based on what?—black nationalism. A revolutionary is a black nationalist. He wants a nation. I was reading some beautiful words by Rev. Cleage, pointing out why he couldn't get together with someone else in the city because all of them were afraid of being identified with black nationalism. If you're afraid of black nationalism, you're afraid of revolution. And if you love revolution, you love black nationalism.

To understand this, you have to go back to what the young brother here referred to as the house Negro and the field Negro back during slavery. There were two kinds of slaves, the house Negro and the field Negro. The house Negroes—they lived in the house with master, they dressed pretty good, they ate good because they ate his food—what he left. They lived in the attie or the basement, but still they lived near the master: and they loved the master more than the master loved himself. They would give their life to save the master's house—quicker than the master would. If the master said. "We got a good house here," the house Negro would say. "Yeah, we got a good house here." Whenever the master said "we," he said "we." That's how you can tell a house Negro.

If the master's house caught on fire, the house Negro would fight harder to put the blaze out than the master would. If the master got sick, the house Negro would say, "What's the matter, boss, *we* sick?" *We* sick! He identified himself with his master, more than his master identified with himself. And if you came to the house Negro and said. "Let's run away, let's escape, let's separate," the house Negro would look at you and say. "Man, you crazy. What you mean, separate? Where is there a better house than this? Where can I wear better clothes than this? Where can I eat better food than this?" That was that house Negro. In those days he was called a "house nigger." And that's what we call them today, because we've still got some house niggers running around here.

This modern house Negro loves his master. He wants to live near him. He'll pay three times as much as the house is worth just to live near his master, and then brag about "I'm the only Negro out here." "I'm the only one on my job." "I'm the only one in this school." You're nothing but a house Negro. And if someone comes to you right now and says. "Let's separate," you say the same

20

thing that the house Negro said on the plantation. "What you mean, separate? From America, this good white man? Where you going to get a better job than you get here?" I mean, this is what you say "I ain't left nothing in Africa," that's what you say. Why, you left your mind in Africa.

On that same plantation, there was the field Negro. The field Negroes—those were the masses. There were always more Negroes in the field than there were Negroes in the house. The Negro in the field caught hell. He ate leftovers. In the house they ate high up on the hog. The Negro in the field didn't get anything but what was left of the insides of the hog. They call it "chitt lings" nowadays. In those days they called them what they were—guts. That's what you were—gut-eaters. And some of you are still gut-eaters.

The field Negro was beaten from morning to night; he lived in a shack, in a 25 but; he wore old, castoff clothes. He hated his master. I say he hated his master. He was intelligent. That house Negro loved his master, but that field Negro—remember, they were in the majority, and they hated the master. When the house caught on fire, he didn't try to put it out; that field Negro prayed for a wind, for a breeze. When the master got sick, the field Negro prayed that he'd die. If someone came to the field Negro and said. "Let's separate, let's run," he didn't say. "Where we going?" He'd say, "Any place is better than here." You've got field Negroes in America today. I'm a field Negro. The masses are the field Negroes. When they see this man's house on fire, you don't hear the little Negroes talking about "*our* government is in trouble." They say. "*The* government is in trouble." Imagine a Negro; "*Our* government"! I even heard one say "*our* astronauts." They won't even let him near the plant—and "*our* astronauts"! "*Our* Navy"— that's a Negro that is out of his mind, a Negro that is out of his mind.

Just as the slavemaster of that day used Tom, the house Negro, to keep the field Negroes in check, the same old slavemaster today has Negroes who are nothing but modern Uncle Toms, twentieth-century Uncle Toms, to keep you and me in check, to keep us under control, keep us passive and peaceful and nonviolent. That's Tom making you nonviolent. It's like when you go to the dentist, and the man's going to take your tooth. You're going to fight him when he starts pulling. So he squirts some stuff in your jaw called novocaine, to make you think they're not doing anything to you. So you sit there and because you've got all of that novocaine in your jaw, you suffer—peacefully. Blood running all down your jaw, and you don't know what's happening. Because someone has taught you to suffer—peacefully.

The white man does the same thing to you in the street, when he wants to put knots on your head and take advantage of you and not have to be afraid of your fighting back. To keep you from fighting back, he gets these old religious Uncle Toms to teach you and me just like novocaine, to suffer peacefully. Don't stop suffering—just suffer peacefully. As Rev. Cleage pointed out, they say you should let your blood flow in the streets. This is a shame. You know he's a Christian preacher. If it's a shame to him, you know what it is to me.

There is nothing in our book, the Koran, that teaches us to suffer peacefully. Our religion teaches us to be intelligent. Be peaceful, be courteous, obey the law, respect everyone: but if someone puts his hand on you, send him to the cemetery. That's a good religion. In fact, that's that old-time religion. That's the one that Ma and Pa used to talk about: an eye for an eye, and a tooth for a tooth, and a head for a head, and a life for a life. That's a good religion. And nobody resents that kind of religion being taught but a wolf, who intends to make you his meal.

This is the way it is with the white man in America. He's a wolf—and you're sheep. Any time a shepherd, a pastor, teaches you and me not to run from the white man and, at the same time, teaches us not to fight the white man, he's a traitor to you and me. Don't lay down a life all by itself. No, preserve your life, it's the best thing you've got. And if you've got to give it up, let it be even-steven.

The slavemaster took Tom and dressed him well, fed him well and even gave 30 him a little education—a *little* education: gave him a long coat and a top hat and made all the other slaves look up to him. Then he used Tom to control them. The same strategy that was used in those days is used today, by the same white man. He takes a Negro, a so-called Negro, and makes him prominent, builds him up, publicizes him, makes him a celebrity. And then he becomes a spokesman for Negroes—and a Negro leader.

I would like to mention just one other thing quickly, and that is the method that the white man uses, how the white man uses the "big guns," or Negro leaders, against the Negro revolution. They are not a part of the Negro revolution. They are used against the Negro revolution.

When Martin Luther King failed to desegregate Albany. Georgia, the civil-rights struggle in America reached its low point. King became bankrupt almost, as a leader. The Southern Christian Leadership Conference was in financial trouble: and it was in trouble, period, with the people when they failed to desegregate Albany, Georgia. Other Negro civil-rights leaders of so-called national stature became fallen idols. As they became fallen idols, began to lose their prestige and influence, local Negro leaders began to stir up the masses. In Cambridge, Maryland. Gloria Richardson: in Danville, Virginia, and other parts of the country, local leaders began to stir up our people at the grass-roots level. This was never done by these Negroes of national stature. They control you, but they have never incited you or excited you. They control you, they contain you, they have kept you on the plantation.

As soon as King failed in Birmingham. Negroes took to the streets. King went out to California to a big rally and raised I don't know how many thousands of dollars. He came to Detroit and had a march and raised some more thousands of dollars. And recall, right after that Roy Wilkins attacked King. He accused King and CORE [Congress Of Racial Equality] of starting trouble everywhere and then making the NAACP [National Association for the Advancement of Colored People] get them out of jail and spend a lot of money: they accused King and CORE of raising all the money and not paying it back. This happened: I've got it in documented evidence in the newspaper.

Roy started attacking King, and King started attacking Roy, and Farmer started attacking both of them. And as these Negroes of national stature began to attack each other, they began to lose their control of the Negro masses.

The Negroes were out there in the streets. They were talking about how they were going to march on Washington. Right at that time Birmingham had exploded, and the Negroes in Birmingham—remember, they also exploded. They began to stab the crackers in the back and bust them up side their head—yes, they did. That's when Kennedy sent in the troops, down in Birmingham. After that, Kennedy got on the television and said "this is a moral issue." That's when he said he was going to put out a civil-rights bill. And when he mentioned civil-rights bill and the Southern crackers started talking about how they were going to boycott or filibuster it, then the Negroes started talking—about what? That they were going to march on Washington, march on the Senate, march on the White House, march on the Congress, and tie it up, bring it to a halt, not let the government proceed. They even said they were going out to the airport and lay down on the runway and not let any airplanes land. I'm telling you what they said. That was revolution. That was revolution. That was the black revolution.

It was the grass roots out there in the street. It scared the white man to death, 35 scared the white power structure in Washington. D.C., to death; I was there. When they found out that this black steamroller was going to come down on the capital, they called in Wilkins, they called in Randolph, they called in these national Negro leaders that you respect and told them. "Call it off." Kennedy said. "Look, you all are letting this thing go too far." And Old Tom said. "Boss, I can't stop it, because I didn't start it." I'm telling you what they said. They said. "I'm not even in it, much less at the head of it." They said. "These Negroes are doing things on their own. They're running ahead of us." And that old shrewd fox, he said. "If you all aren't in it. I'll put you in it. I'll put you at the head of it. I'll endorse it. I'll welcome it. I'll help it. I'll join it."

A matter of hours went by. They had a meeting at the Carlyle Hotel in New York City. The Carlyle Hotel is owned by the Kennedy family: that's the hotel Kennedy spent the night at, two nights ago: it belongs to his family. A philanthropic society headed by a white man named Stephen Currier called all the top civil-rights leaders together at the Carlyle Hotel. And he told them. "By you all fighting each other, you are destroying the civil-rights movement. And since you're fighting over money from white liberals, let us set up what is known as the Council for United Civil Rights Leadership. Let's form this council, and all the civil-rights organizations will belong to it, and we'll use it for fund-raising purposes." Let me show you how tricky the white man is. As soon as they got it formed, they elected Whitney Young as its chairman, and who do you think became the co-chairman? Stephen Currier, the white man, a millionaire. Powell was talking about it down at Cobo Hall today. This is what he was talking about. Powell knows it happened. Randolph knows it happened. Wilkins knows it happened. King knows it happened. Every one of that Big Six—they know it happened.

Once they formed it, with the white man over it, he promised them and gave them $800,000 to split up among the Big Six: and told them that after the march was over they'd give them $700,000 more. A million and a half dollars—split up between leaders that you have been following, going to jail for, crying crocodile tears for. And they're nothing but Frank James and Jesse James and the what-do-you-call-em brothers.

As soon as they got the setup organized, the white man made available to them top public-relations experts: opened the news media across the country at their disposal, which then began to project these Big Six as the leaders of the march. Originally they weren't even in the march. You were talking this march talk on Hastings Street, you were talking march talk on Lenox Avenue, and on Fillmore Street, and on Central Avenue, and 32nd Street and 63rd Street. That's where the march talk was being talked. But the white man put the Big Six at the head of it: made them the march. They became the march. They took it over. And the first move they made after they took it over, they invited Walter Reuther, a white man: they invited a priest, a rabbi, and an old white preacher, yes, an old white preacher. The same white element that put Kennedy into power—labor, the Catholics, the Jews, and liberal Protestants: the same clique that put Kennedy in power, joined the march on Washington.

It's just like when you've got some coffee that's too black, which means it's too strong. What do you do? You integrate it with cream, you make it weak. But if you pour too much cream in it, you won't even know you ever had coffee. It used to be hot, it becomes cool. It used to be strong, it becomes weak. It used to wake you up, now it puts you to sleep. This is what they did with the march on Washington. They joined it. They didn't integrate it, they infiltrated it. They joined it, became a part of it, took it over. And as they took it over, it lost its militancy. It ceased to be angry, it ceased to be hot, it ceased to be uncompromising. Why, it even ceased to be a march. It became a picnic, a circus. Nothing but a circus, with clowns and all. You had one right here in Detroit—I saw it on television—with clowns leading it, white clowns and black clowns. I know you don't like what I'm saying, but I'm going to tell you anyway. Because I can prove what I'm saying. If you think I'm telling you wrong, you bring me Martin Luther King and A. Philip Randolph and James Farmer and those other three, and see if they'll deny it over a microphone.

No, it was a sellout. It was a takeover. When James Baldwin came in from   40
Paris, they wouldn't let him talk, because they couldn't make him go by the script. Burt Lancaster read the speech that Baldwin was supposed to make; they wouldn't let Baldwin get up there, because they know Baldwin is liable to say anything. They controlled it so tight, they told those Negroes what time to hit town, how to come, where to stop, what signs to carry, what song to sing, what speech they could make, and what speech they couldn't make; and then told them to get out of town by sundown. And every one of those Toms was out of town by sundown. Now I know you don't like my saying this. But I can back it up. It was a circus, a performance that beat anything Hollywood could ever do, the performance of the year. Reuther and those other three devils should get an Academy Award for the best actors because they acted like they really loved

Negroes and fooled a whole lot of Negroes. And the six Negro leaders should get an award too, for the best supporting cast.

Questions for Discussion

1. To what extent would you say that Malcolm X's "message" is a direct response to King's "Letter from Birmingham Jail"?
2. Does Malcolm X's use of history and historical episodes help his case?

❀ ❀ ❀

MARTIN LUTHER KING, JR. (1929–1968)

Martin Luther King, Jr. was born in Atlanta, Georgia, attended segregated schools, and enrolled at Morehouse College at age fifteen. Despite his religious upbringing (his father was a Baptist minister), King questioned the over-zealous Christianity of his father and developed his own brand of Christian belief and earned a Ph.D. in theology at Boston University. In 1954, King was appointed pastor of a church in Montgomery, Alabama, and the next year, spurred by Rosa Parks's refusal to give up her bus seat to a white man, he led a boycott by African Americans of segregated buses. Two years later he became president of the new civil rights organization, the Southern Christian Leadership Conference, which would be instrumental in the Civil Rights Movement of the 1960s and the end of legal segregation. In 1963, he led a massive march (250,000 people) on Washington, D.C., where he delivered this speech, "I Have a Dream." The following year, at the age of 35, he was awarded the Nobel Prize for Peace for his commitment to nonviolent protest. In both his passionate speeches and his writing, King's style appealed to the conscience of various classes of people through the crafting of rational arguments supported by potent metaphors. King was assassinated in Memphis, Tennessee, in 1968 after giving a speech in support of striking sanitation workers. His books include *Stride Toward Freedom* (1958), *Why We Can't Wait* (1964), and *Trumpet of Conscience* (1968).

I Have a Dream (1963)

I am happy to join with you today[1] in what will go down in history as the greatest demonstration for freedom in the history of our nation.

Fivescore years ago, a great American, in whose symbolic shadow we stand today, signed the Emancipation Proclamation. This momentous decree came as a great beacon light of hope to millions of Negro slaves who had been seared

---

[1]August 28, 1963, at a civil rights demonstration in Washington, D.C.

in the flames of withering injustice. It came as a joyous daybreak to end the long night of their captivity.

But one hundred years later, the Negro still is not free; one hundred years later, the life of the Negro is still sadly crippled by the manacles of segregation and the chains of discrimination; one hundred years later, the Negro lives on a lonely island of poverty in the midst of a vast ocean of material prosperity; one hundred years later, the Negro is still languished in the corners of American society and finds himself in exile in his own land.

So we've come here today to dramatize a shameful condition. In a sense we've come to our nation's capital to cash a check. When the architects of our republic wrote the magnificent words of the Constitution and the Declaration of Independence, they were signing a promissory note to which every American was to fall heir. This note was the promise that all men, yes, black men as well as white men, would be guaranteed the unalienable rights of life, liberty, and the pursuit of happiness.

It is obvious today that America has defaulted on this promissory note in so far as her citizens of color are concerned. Instead of honoring this sacred obligation, America has given the Negro people a bad check; a check which has come back marked "insufficient funds." We refuse to believe that there are insufficient funds in the great vaults of opportunity of this nation. And so we've come to cash this check, a check that will give us upon demand the riches of freedom and the security of justice.

We have also come to this hallowed spot to remind America of the fierce urgency of now. This is no time to engage in the luxury of cooling off or to take the tranquilizing drug of gradualism. Now is the time to make real the promises of democracy; now is the time to rise from the dark and desolate valley of segregation to the sunlit path of racial justice; now is the time to lift our nation from the quicksands of racial injustice to the solid rock of brotherhood; now is the time to make justice a reality for all God's children. It would be fatal for the nation to overlook the urgency of the moment. This sweltering summer of the Negro's legitimate discontent will not pass until there is an invigorating autumn of freedom and equality.

Nineteen sixty-three is not an end, but a beginning. And those who hope that the Negro needed to blow off steam and will now be content, will have a rude awakening if the nation returns to business as usual.

There will be neither rest nor tranquility in America until the Negro is granted his citizenship rights. The whirlwinds of revolt will continue to shake the foundations of our nation until the bright day of justice emerges.

But there is something that I must say to my people who stand on the warm threshold which leads into the palace of justice. In the process of gaining our rightful place we must not be guilty of wrongful deeds.

Let us not seek to satisfy our thirst for freedom by drinking from the cup of bitterness and hatred. We must forever conduct our struggle on the high plane of dignity and discipline. We must not allow our creative protest to degenerate into physical violence. Again and again we must rise to the majestic heights of meeting physical force with soul force.

The marvelous new militancy which has engulfed the Negro community must not lead us to a distrust of all white people, for many of our white brothers, as evidenced by their presence here today, have come to realize that their destiny is tied up with our destiny and they have come to realize that their freedom is inextricably bound to our freedom. This offense we share mounted to storm the battlements of injustice must be carried forth by a biracial army. We cannot walk alone.

And as we walk, we must make the pledge that we shall always march ahead. We cannot turn back. There are those who are asking the devotees of civil rights, "When will you be satisfied?" We can never be satisfied as long as the Negro is the victim of the unspeakable horrors of police brutality.

We can never be satisfied as long as our bodies, heavy with fatigue of travel, cannot gain lodging in the motels of the highways and the hotels of the cities. We cannot be satisfied as long as the Negro's basic mobility is from a smaller ghetto to a larger one.

We can never be satisfied as long as our children are stripped of their selfhood and robbed of their dignity by signs stating "for whites only." We cannot be satisfied as long as a Negro in Mississippi cannot vote and a Negro in New York believes he has nothing for which to vote. No, we are not satisfied, and we will not be satisfied until justice rolls down like waters and righteousness like a mighty stream.

I am not unmindful that some of you have come here out of excessive trials and tribulation. Some of you have come fresh from narrow jail cells. Some of you have come from areas where your quest for freedom left you battered by the storms of persecution and staggered by the winds of police brutality. You have been the veterans of creative suffering. Continue to work with the faith that unearned suffering is redemptive.

Go back to Mississippi; go back to Alabama; go back to South Carolina; go back to Georgia; go back to Louisiana; go back to the slums and ghettos of the northern cities, knowing that somehow this situation can, and will be changed. Let us not wallow in the valley of despair.

So I say to you, my friends, that even though we must face the difficulties of today and tomorrow, I still have a dream. It is a dream deeply rooted in the American dream that one day this nation will rise up and live out the true meaning of its creed—we hold these truths to be self-evident, that all men are created equal.

I have a dream that one day on the red hills of Georgia, sons of former slaves and sons of former slave-owners will be able to sit down together at the table of brotherhood.

I have a dream that one day, even the state of Mississippi, a state sweltering with the heat of injustice, sweltering with the heat of oppression, will be transformed into an oasis of freedom and justice.

I have a dream my four little children will one day live in a nation where they will not be judged by the color of their skin but by content of their character. I have a dream today!

I have a dream that one day, down in Alabama, with its vicious racists, with its governor having his lips dripping with the words of interposition and nullification, that one day, right there in Alabama, little black boys and black girls will be able to join hands with little white boys and white girls as sisters and brothers. I have a dream today!

I have a dream that one day every valley shall be exalted, every hill and mountain shall be made low, the rough places shall be made plain, and the crooked places shall be made straight and the glory of the Lord will be revealed and all flesh shall see it together.

This is our hope. This is the faith that I go back to the South with.

With this faith we will be able to hew out of the mountain of despair a stone of hope. With this faith we will be able to transform the jangling discords of our nation into a beautiful symphony of brotherhood.

With this faith we will be able to work together, to pray together, to struggle together, to go to jail together, to stand up for freedom together, knowing that we will be free one day. This will be the day when all of God's children will be able to sing with new meaning—"my country 'tis of thee; sweet land of liberty; of thee I sing; land where my fathers died, land of the pilgrim's pride; from every mountain side, let freedom ring"—and if America is to be a great nation, this must become true.

So let freedom ring from the prodigious hilltops of New Hampshire.

Let freedom ring from the mighty mountains of New York.

Let freedom ring from the heightening Alleghenies of Pennsylvania.

Let freedom ring from the snow-capped Rockies of Colorado.

Let freedom ring from the curvaceous slopes of California.

But not only that.

Let freedom ring from Stone Mountain of Georgia.

Let freedom ring from Lookout Mountain of Tennessee.

Let freedom ring from every hill and molehill of Mississippi, from every mountainside, let freedom ring.

And when we allow freedom to ring, when we let it ring from every village and hamlet, from every state and city, we will be able to speed up that day when all of God's children—black men and white men, Jews and Gentiles, Catholics and Protestants—will be able to join hands and to sing in the words of the old Negro spiritual, "Free at last, free at last; thank God Almighty, we are free at last."

Study and Discussion Questions

1. What does King mean by the metaphor of the promissory note and the "bad check"?
2. King has two audiences, white Americans and black Americans. What is he saying to each audience and what is directed to both?

3. How does King define the American Dream in this speech?
4. List the parts of *King's* dream.
5. How is the last of the paragraphs that begin "I have a dream" different from the preceding ones?

Suggestions for Writing

1. Gather some examples of the way King uses repetition in this speech. What effect does the repetition have? Read the speech aloud.
2. How much civil rights progress has been made in the years since King made this speech? Give examples of what has changed and what has not.
3. Should ministers and other religious leaders be politically active? Argue for or against.
4. Write a paper comparing/contrasting "I Have a Dream" with King's 1967 speech, "A Time to Break Silence" in the "Peace and War" section.

MARTIN LUTHER KING, JR. (1929–1968)

Martin Luther King, Jr. was born in Atlanta, Georgia, attended segregated schools, and enrolled at Morehouse College at age fifteen. Despite his religious upbringing (his father was a Baptist minister), King questioned the over-zealous Christianity of his father, developed his own brand of Christian belief and earned a Ph.D. in theology at Boston University. In 1954, King was appointed pastor of a church in Montgomery, Alabama and the next year, spurred by Rosa Parks's refusal to give up her bus seat to a white man, he led a boycott by African Americans of segregated buses. Two years later he became president of the new civil rights organization, the Southern Christian Leadership Conference, which would be instrumental in the Civil Rights Movement of the 1960s and the end of legal segregation. In 1963 he led a massive march (250,000 people) on Washington, D.C., where he delivered his speech, "I Have a Dream." The following year, at the age of 35, he was awarded the Nobel Prize for Peace for his commitment to nonviolent protest. In both his passionate speeches and his writing, King's style appealed to the conscience of various classes of people through the crafting of rational arguments supported by potent metaphors: "If America's soul becomes totally poisoned, part of the autopsy must read Vietnam." King was assassinated in Memphis, Tennessee, in 1968 after giving a speech in support of striking sanitation workers. His books include *Stride Toward Freedom* (1958), *Why We Can't Wait* (1964), and *Trumpet of Conscience* (1968). The preceding quote was taken from *A Time to Break Silence* (1967), in which King explains the connection between war and poverty.

FROM ***A Time to Break Silence***[1] (1967)

IMPORTANCE OF VIETNAM

Since I am a preacher by trade, I suppose it is not surprising that I have seven major reasons for bringing Vietnam into the field of my moral vision. There is at the outset a very obvious and almost facile connection between the war in Vietnam and the struggle I, and others, have been waging in America. A few years ago there was a shining moment in that struggle. It seemed as if there was a real promise of hope for the poor—both black and white—through the poverty program. There were experiments, hopes, new beginnings. Then came the buildup in Vietnam and I watched the program broken and eviscerated as if it were some idle political plaything of a society gone mad on war, and I knew that America would never invest the necessary funds or energies in rehabilitation of its poor so long as adventures like Vietnam continued to draw men and skills and money like some demonic destructive suction tube. So I was increasingly compelled to see the war as an enemy of the poor and to attack it as such.

Perhaps the more tragic recognition of reality took place when it became clear to me that the war was doing far more than devastating the hopes of the poor at home. It was sending their sons and their brothers and their husbands to fight and to die in extraordinarily high proportions relative to the rest of the population. We were taking the black young men who had been crippled by our society and sending them eight thousand miles away to guarantee liberties in Southeast Asia which they had not found in southwest Georgia and East Harlem. So we have been repeatedly faced with the cruel irony of watching Negro and white boys on TV screens as they kill and die together for a nation that has been unable to seat them together in the same schools. So we watch them in brutal solidarity burning the huts of a poor village, but we realize that they would never live on the same block in Detroit. I could not be silent in the face of such cruel manipulation of the poor.

My third reason moves to an even deeper level of awareness, for it grows out of my experience in the ghettos of the North over the last three years— especially the last three summers. As I have walked among the desperate, rejected and angry young men I have told them that Molotov cocktails and rifles would not solve their problems. I have tried to offer them my deepest compassion while maintaining my conviction that social change comes most meaningfully through nonviolent action. But they asked—and rightly so—what about Vietnam? They asked if our own nation wasn't using massive doses of

---

[1]Speech delivered April 4, 1967, at the Riverside Church in New York City to Clergy and Laity Concerned, a group opposing the war in Vietnam.

violence to solve its problems, to bring about the changes it wanted. Their questions hit home, and I knew that I could never again raise my voice against the violence of the oppressed in the ghettos without having first spoken clearly to the greatest purveyor of violence in the world today—my own government. For the sake of those boys, for the sake of this government, for the sake of the hundreds of thousands trembling under our violence, I cannot be silent.

For those who ask the question, "Aren't you a civil rights leader?" and thereby mean to exclude me from the movement for peace, I have this further answer. In 1957 when a group of us formed the Southern Christian Leadership Conference, we chose as our motto: "To save the soul of America." We were convinced that we could not limit our vision to certain rights for black people, but instead affirmed the conviction that America would never be free or saved from itself unless the descendants of its slaves were loosed completely from the shackles they still wear. In a way we were agreeing with Langston Hughes,[2] that black bard of Harlem, who had written earlier:

> O, yes,
> I say it plain,
> America never was America to me,
> And yet I swear this oath—
> America will be!

Now, it should be incandescently clear that no one who has any concern for the integrity and life of America today can ignore the present war. If America's soul becomes totally poisoned, part of the autopsy must read Vietnam. It can never be saved so long as it destroys the deepest hopes of men the world over. So it is that those of us who are yet determined that America *will* be are led down the path of protest and dissent, working for the health of our land.

As if the weight of such a commitment to the life and health of America were not enough, another burden of responsibility was placed upon me in 1964; and I cannot forget that the Nobel Prize for Peace was also a commission—a commission to work harder than I had ever worked before for "the brotherhood of man." This is a calling that takes me beyond national allegiances, but even if it were not present I would yet have to live with the meaning of my commitment to the ministry of Jesus Christ. To me the relationship of this ministry to the making of peace is so obvious that I sometimes marvel at those who ask me why I am speaking against the war. Could it be that they do not know that the good news was meant for all men—for Communist and capitalist, for their children and ours, for black and for white, for revolutionary and conservative? Have they forgotten that my ministry is in obedience to the one who loved his enemies so fully that he died for them? What then can I say to the "Vietcong" or to Castro or to Mao as a faithful minister of this one? Can I threaten them with death or must I not share with them my life?

---

[2]American writer (1902–1967).

Finally, as I try to delineate for you and for myself the road that leads from Montgomery[3] to this place I would have offered all that was most valid if I simply said that I must be true to my conviction that I share with all men the calling to be a son of the living God. Beyond the calling of race or nation or creed is this vocation of sonship and brotherhood, and because I believe that the Father is deeply concerned especially for his suffering and helpless and outcast children, I come tonight to speak for them.

This I believe to be the privilege and the burden of all of us who deem ourselves bound by allegiances and loyalties which are broader and deeper than nationalism and which go beyond our nation's self-defined goals and positions. We are called to speak for the weak, for the voiceless, for victims of our nation and for those it calls enemy, for no document from human hands can make these humans any less our brothers.

STRANGE LIBERATORS

And as I ponder the madness of Vietnam and search within myself for ways to understand and respond to compassion my mind goes constantly to the people of that peninsula. I speak now not of the soldiers of each side, not of the junta in Saigon, but simply of the people who have been living under the curse of war for almost three continuous decades now. I think of them too because it is clear to me that there will be no meaningful solution there until some attempt is made to know them and hear their broken cries.

They must see Americans as strange liberators. The Vietnamese people proclaimed their own independence in 1945 after a combined French and Japanese occupation, and before the Communist revolution in China. They were led by Ho Chi Minh. Even though they quoted the American Declaration of Independence in their own document of freedom, we refused to recognize them. Instead, we decided to support France in its reconquest of her former colony.

Our government felt then that the Vietnamese people were not "ready" for independence, and we again fell victim to the deadly Western arrogance that has poisoned the international atmosphere for so long. With that tragic decision we rejected a revolutionary government seeking self-determination, and a government that had been established not by China (for whom the Vietnamese have no great love) but by clearly indigenous forces that included some Communists. For the peasants this new government meant real land reform, one of the most important needs in their lives.

---

[3]Alabama city where King led 1955 boycott to integrate city buses.

For nine years following 1945 we denied the people of Vietnam the right of independence. For nine years we vigorously supported the French in their abortive effort to recolonize Vietnam.

Before the end of the war we were meeting eighty per cent of the French war costs. Even before the French were defeated at Dien Bien Phu, they began to despair of the reckless action, but we did not. We encouraged them with our huge financial and military supplies to continue the war even after they had lost the will. Soon we would be paying almost the full costs of this tragic attempt at recolonization.

After the French were defeated it looked as if independence and land reform would come again through the Geneva agreements. But instead there came the United States, determined that Ho should not unify the temporarily divided nation, and the peasants watched again as we supported one of the most vicious modern dictators—our chosen man, Premier Diem. The peasants watched and cringed as Diem ruthlessly routed out all opposition, supported their extortionist landlords and refused even to discuss reunification with the north. The peasants watched as all this was presided over by U.S. influence and then by increasing numbers of U.S. troops who came to help quell the insurgency that Diem's methods had aroused. When Diem was overthrown they may have been happy, but the long line of military dictatorships seemed to offer no real change—especially in terms of their need for land and peace.

The only change came from America as we increased our troop commitments in support of governments which were singularly corrupt, inept and without popular support. All the while the people read our leaflets and received regular promises of peace and democracy—and land reform. Now they languish under our bombs and consider us—not their fellow Vietnamese—the real enemy. They move sadly and apathetically as we herd them off the land of their fathers into concentration camps where minimal social needs are rarely met. They know they must move or be destroyed by our bombs. So they go—primarily women and children and the aged.

They watch as we poison their water, as we kill a million acres of their crops. They must weep as the bulldozers roar through their areas preparing to destroy the precious trees. They wander into the hospitals, with at least twenty casualties from American firepower for one "Vietcong"-inflicted injury. So far we may have killed a million of them—mostly children. They wander into the towns and see thousands of the children, homeless, without clothes, running in packs on the streets like animals. They see the children degraded by our soldiers as they beg for food. They see the children selling their sisters to our soldiers, soliciting for their mothers.

What do the peasants think as we ally ourselves with the landlords and as we refuse to put any action into our many words concerning land reform? What do they think as we test out our latest weapons on them, just as the Germans tested out new medicine and new tortures in the concentration camps of Europe? Where are the roots of the independent Vietnam we claim to be building? Is it among these voiceless ones?

We have destroyed their two most cherished institutions: the family and the village. We have destroyed their land and their crops. We have cooperated in the crushing of the nation's only non-Communist revolutionary political force—the unified Buddhist church. We have supported the enemies of the peasants of Saigon. We have corrupted their women and children and killed their men. What liberators!

Now there is little left to build on—save bitterness. Soon the only solid physical foundations remaining will be found at our military bases and in the concrete of the concentration camps we call fortified hamlets. The peasants may well wonder if we plan to build our new Vietnam on such grounds as these? Could we blame them for such thoughts? We must speak for them and raise the questions they cannot raise. These too are our brothers.

Perhaps the more difficult but no less necessary task is to speak for those who have been designated as our enemies. What of the National Liberation Front—that strangely anonymous group we call VC or Communists? What must they think of us in America when they realize that we permitted the repression and cruelty of Diem which helped to bring them into being as a resistance group in the south? What do they think of our condoning the violence which led to their own taking up of arms? How can they believe in our integrity when now we speak of "aggression from the north" as if there were nothing more essential to the war? How can they trust us when now we charge them with violence after the murderous reign of Diem and charge them with violence while we pour every new weapon of death into their land? Surely we must understand their feelings even if we do not condone their actions. Surely we must see that the men we supported pressed them to their violence. Surely we must see that our own computerized plans of destruction simply dwarf their greatest acts.

How do they judge us when our officials know that their membership is less than twenty-five percent Communist and yet insist on giving them the blanket name? What must they be thinking when they know that we are aware of their control of major sections of Vietnam and yet we appear ready to allow national elections in which this highly organized political parallel government will have no part? They ask how we can speak of free elections when the Saigon press is censored and controlled by the military junta. And they are surely right to wonder what kind of new government we plan to help form without them—the only party in real touch with the peasants. They question our political goals and they deny the reality of a peace settlement from which they will be excluded. Their questions are frighteningly relevant. Is our nation planning to build on political myth again and then shore it up with the power of new violence?

Here is the true meaning and value of compassion and nonviolence when it helps us to see the enemy's point of view, to hear his questions, to know his assessment of ourselves. For from his view we may indeed see the basic weaknesses of our own condition, and if we are mature, we may learn and grow and profit from the wisdom of the brothers who are called the opposition.

So, too, with Hanoi. In the north, where our bombs now pummel the land, and our mines endanger the waterways, we are met by a deep but understandable mistrust. To speak for them is to explain this lack of confidence in Western words, and especially their distrust of American intentions now. In Hanoi are the men who led the nation to independence against the Japanese and the French, the men who sought membership in the French commonwealth and were betrayed by the weakness of Paris and the willfulness of the colonial armies. It was they who led a second struggle against French domination at tremendous costs, and then were persuaded to give up the land they controlled between the thirteenth and seventeenth parallels as a temporary measure at Geneva. After 1954 they watched us conspire with Diem to prevent elections which would have surely brought Ho Chi Minh to power over a united Vietnam, and they realized they had been betrayed again.

When we ask why they do not leap to negotiate, these things must be remembered. Also it must be clear that the leaders of Hanoi considered the presence of American troops in support of the Diem regime to have been the initial military breach of the Geneva agreements concerning foreign troops, and they remind us that they did not begin to send in any large number of supplies or men until American forces had moved into the tens of thousands.

Hanoi remembers how our leaders refused to tell us the truth about the earlier North Vietnamese overtures for peace, how the president claimed that none existed when they had clearly been made. Ho Chi Minh has watched as America has spoken of peace and built up its forces, and now he has surely heard of the increasing international rumors of American plans for an invasion of the north. He knows the bombing and shelling and mining we are doing are part of traditional pre-invasion strategy. Perhaps only his sense of humor and of irony can save him when he hears the most powerful nation of the world speaking of aggression as it drops thousands of bombs on a poor weak nation more than eight thousand miles away from its shores.

At this point I should make it clear that while I have tried in these last few minutes to give a voice to the voiceless on Vietnam and to understand the arguments of those who are called enemy, I am as deeply concerned about our troops there as anything else. For it occurs to me that what we are submitting them to in Vietnam is not simply the brutalizing process that goes on in any war where armies face each other and seek to destroy. We are adding to the process of death, for they must know after a short period there that none of the things we claim to be fighting for are really involved. Before long they must know that their government has sent them into a struggle among Vietnamese, and the more sophisticated surely realize that we are on the side of the wealthy and the secure while we create a hell for the poor.

Somehow this madness must cease. We must stop now. I speak as a child of God and brother to the suffering poor of Vietnam. I speak for those whose land is being laid waste, whose homes are being destroyed, whose culture is being subverted. I speak for the poor of America who are paying the double price of

*smashed hopes at home and death and corruption in Vietnam. I speak as a citizen
of the world, for the world as it stands aghast at the path we have taken. I speak
as an American to the leaders of my own nation. The great initiative in this war
is ours. The initiative to stop it must be ours.*

Study and Discussion Questions

1. What are King's "seven major reasons for bringing Vietnam into the field
   of [his] moral vision"?
2. What does he mean when he calls Americans the "strange liberators"?
3. Why does King have a number of paragraphs composed entirely or
   mostly of questions? From whose perspective are these questions asked?
   Is there an ethical or moral purpose behind this rhetorical device? Is it
   effective?
4. What are the assumptions underlying his argument that the United
   States must stop military involvement in Vietnam?

Suggestions for Writing

1. Select one paragraph in this speech and analyze it in detail. What is the
   main point or thesis of the paragraph? What are the supporting evidence
   and secondary points?
2. Choose a contemporary war or armed conflict the United States is
   engaged in and apply King's argument to it.
3. If you were to construct an argument against King's position in "A Time
   to Break Silence," what would your major points be? Come up with at
   least five.

JUDY BRADY (b. 1931)

Judy Syfers Brady grew up in the Midwest and studied at the University of
Iowa. In the late 1960s she was an ardent activist for women's rights. In 1971,
her article "I Want A Wife" appeared in the first edition of *Ms.* magazine at a
time when the promise of equality for women had lagged in an American culture still holding tight to traditional roles for women. The article has become a
key document of that era and is now read in university courses throughout the
country. In the piece, Brady deftly uses rhetorical devices (sarcasm, irony,
hyperbole) to create a penetrating social satire. Brady currently lives in San
Francisco, where she continues her activism, working on environmental issues
and with the Women's Cancer Research Center.

I Want a Wife (1971)

I belong to that classification of people known as wives. I am A Wife. And, not altogether incidentally. I am a mother.

Not too long ago a male friend of mine appeared on the scene fresh from a recent divorce. He had one child, who is, of course, with his ex-wife. He is obviously looking for another wife. As I thought about him while I was ironing one evening, it suddenly occurred to me that I, too, would like to have a wife. Why do I want a wife?

I would like to go back to school so that I can become economically independent, support myself, and, if need be, support those dependent upon me. I want a wife who will work and send me to school. And while I am going to school I want a wife to take care of my children. I want a wife to keep track of the children's doctor and dentist appointments. And to keep track of mine, too. I want a wife to make sure my children eat properly and are kept clean. I want a wife who will wash the children's clothes and keep them mended. I want a wife who is a good nurturant attendant to my children, who arranges for their schooling, makes sure that they have an adequate social life with their peers, takes them to the park, the zoo, etc. I want a wife who takes care of the children when they are sick, a wife who arranges to be around when the children need special care, because, of course, I cannot miss classes at school. My wife must arrange to lose time at work and not lose the job. It may mean a small cut in my wife's income from time to time, but I guess I can tolerate that. Needless to say, my wife will arrange and pay for the care of the children while my wife is working.

I want a wife who will take care of *my* physical needs. I want a wife who will keep my house clean. A wife who will pick up after me. I want a wife who will keep my clothes clean, ironed, mended, replaced when need be, and who will see to it that my personal things are kept in their proper place so that I can find what I need the minute I need it. I want a wife who cooks the meals, a wife who is a *good* cook. I want a wife who will plan the menus, do the necessary grocery shopping, prepare the meals, serve them pleasantly, and then do the cleaning up while I do my studying. I want a wife who will care for me when I am sick and sympathize with my pain and loss of time from school. I want a wife to go along when our family takes a vacation so that someone can continue to care for me and my children when I need a rest and change of scene.

I want a wife who will not bother me with rambling complaints about a wife's duties. But I want a wife who will listen to me when I feel the need to explain a rather difficult point I have come across in my course of studies. And I want a wife who will type my papers for me when I have written them.

I want a wife who will take care of the details of my social life. When my wife and I are invited out by my friends, I want a wife who will take care of the babysitting arrangements. When I meet people at school that I like and want to entertain, I want a wife who will have the house clean, will prepare a special meal, serve it to me and my friends, and not interrupt when I talk about the things that interest me and my friends. I want a wife who will have arranged that the children are fed and ready for bed before my guests arrive so that the children do not bother us.

And I want a wife who knows that sometimes I need a night out by myself.

I want a wife who is sensitive to my sexual needs, a wife who makes love passionately and eagerly when I feel like it, a wife who makes sure that I am satisfied. And, of course, I want a wife who will not demand sexual attention when I am not in the mood for it. I want a wife who assumes the complete responsibility for birth control, because I do not want more children. I want a wife who will remain sexually faithful to me so that I do not have to clutter up my intellectual life with jealousies. And I want a wife who understands that *my* sexual needs may entail more than strict adherence to monogamy. I must, after all, be able to relate to people as fully as possible.

If, by chance, I find another person more suitable as a wife than the wife I already have, I want the liberty to replace my present wife with another one. Naturally, I will expect a fresh, new life; my wife will take the children and be solely responsible for them so that I am left free.

When I am through with school and have a job, I want my wife to quit working and remain at home so that my wife can more fully and completely take care of a wife's duties.

My god, who *wouldn't* want a wife?

Study and Discussion Questions

1. What is the point of this essay? Is Brady simply trying to explain how hard a wife works?
2. What does Brady achieve by making her point indirectly? Why doesn't she simply *tell* us how she feels about being a wife? How does the choice of form—satire—serve the writer's purposes?
3. How does repetition function in the essay? Why do so many sentences begin with "I want ..."—in fact with "I want a wife who ..."? What effect does this have on the reader?
4. Brady names a great many things she wants a wife for. How does she organize them? Is the ordering of the paragraphs in which she lists her wants significant?
5. How does the mention, in the second paragraph, of Brady's divorced male friend serve her purpose in the essay?

Suggestions for Writing

1. Would a parallel essay, "I Want a Husband," have equal force? Explain. Try writing one.

2. Try writing an essay modeled on this one, but protesting some other social role you think unfair, one that you might be or imagine yourself in—"I Want a Secretary," for example.
3. Study a number of television or magazine advertisements that depict housewives. How closely do they correspond to the role of wife as Brady describes it? What attitudes do they express towards the role or roles they depict?

STUDS TERKEL (1912–2008)

Louis "Studs" Terkel was born in New York City, the son of Russian-Jewish immigrants. At the age of ten, his family moved to Chicago and opened a rooming house for immigrants. After graduating from high school in 1928, Terkel went on to obtain his law degree from the University of Chicago. Instead of pursuing a career in law though, Terkel found his way into the television industry. Like other politically left-minded entertainers, Terkel was "black-listed" in the late 1940s by the House of Un-American Activities Committee, which forced producers to cancel his show "Studs' Place." Terkel would eventually end up in radio and the host of "The Studs Terkel Program," which aired from 1952 to 1997. One of the main features of the show was Terkel's interviews with people, common and famous alike. Terkel's penchant for interviewing would become the material for his award-winning collections of oral history. Referring to himself as a "guerilla journalist with a tape recorder," Terkel's work takes on issues of race, poverty, labor, and war, as seen from a broad spectrum of personal narratives across America. His books include *Hard Times: An Oral History of the Great Depression* (1970), *Working: People Talk About What They Do All Day and How They Feel About It What They Do* (1974), *American Dreams: Lost and Found* (1980), *The Good War: An Oral History of World War II* (1988, Pulitzer Prize), *Race: How Blacks and Whites Think and Feel About the American Obsession* (1992), and his latest work *Hope Dies Last: Keeping the Faith in Difficult Times* (2003). "Who Built the Pyramids?", the preface to *Working*, is the oral history of Mike Lefevre, a Chicago steelworker.

MIKE LEFEVRE: Who Built the Pyramids?   (1974)

Who built the seven towers of Thebes?
The books are filled with the names of kings.
Was it kings, who hauled the craggy blocks of stone? . . .
In the evening when the Chinese wall was finished
Where did the masons go? . . .
                    —*Bertolt Brecht*

It is a two-flat dwelling, somewhere in Cicero, on the outskirts of Chicago. He is thirty-seven. He works in a steel mill. On occasion, his wife Carol works as a waitress in a neighborhood restaurant; otherwise, she is at home, caring for their two small children, a girl and a boy.

At the time of my first visit, a sculpted statuette of Mother and Child was on the floor, head severed from body. He laughed softly as he indicated his three-year-old daughter: "She Doctor Spock'd it."

I'm a dying breed. A laborer. Strictly muscle work . . . pick it up, put it down, pick it up, put it down. We handle between forty and fifty thousand pounds of steel a day. (Laughs) I know this is hard to believe—from four hundred pounds to three- and four-pound pieces. It's dying.

You can't take pride any more. You remember when a guy could point to a house he built, how many logs he stacked. He built it and he was proud of it. I don't really think I could be proud if a contractor built a home for me. I would be tempted to get in there and kick the carpenter in the ass (laughs), and take the saw away from him. 'Cause I would have to be part of it, you know.

It's hard to take pride in a bridge you're never gonna cross, in a door you're never gonna open. You're mass-producing things and you never see the end result of it. (Muses) I worked for a trucker one time. And I got this tiny satisfaction when I loaded a truck. At least I could see the truck depart loaded. In a steel mill, forget it. You don't see where nothing goes.

I got chewed out by my foreman once. He said, "Mike, you're a good worker but you have a bad attitude." My attitude is that I don't get excited about my job. I do my work but I don't say whoopee-doo. The day I get excited about my job is the day I go to a head shrinker. How are you gonna get excited about pullin' steel? How are you gonna get excited when you're tired and want to sit down?

It's not just the work. Somebody built the pyramids. Somebody's going to build something. Pyramids, Empire State Building—these things just don't happen. There's hard work behind it. I would like to see a building, say, the Empire State, I would like to see on one side of it a foot-wide strip from top to bottom with the name of every bricklayer, the name of every electrician, with all the names. So when a guy walked by, he could take his son and say, "See, that's me over there on the forty-fifth floor. I put the steel beam in." Picasso can point to a painting. What can I point to? A writer can point to a book. Everybody should have something to point to.

It's the not-recognition by other people. To say a woman is *just* a housewife is degrading, right? Okay. *Just* a housewife. It's also degrading to say *just* a laborer. The difference is that a man goes out and maybe gets smashed.

When I was single, I could quit, just split. I wandered all over the country. You worked just enough to get a poke, money in your pocket. Now I'm married and I got two kids . . . (trails off). I worked on a truck dock one time and I was single. The foreman came over and he grabbed my shoulder, kind of gave me a shove. I punched him and knocked him off the dock. I said, "Leave me alone. I'm doing my work, just stay away from me, just don't give me the with-the-hands business."

Hell, if you whip a damn mule he might kick you. Stay out of my way, that's all. Working is bad enough, don't bug me. I would rather work my ass off for eight hours a day with nobody watching me than five minutes with a guy watching me. Who you gonna sock? You can't sock General Motors, you can't sock anybody in Washington, you can't sock a system.

A mule, an old mule, that's the way I feel. Oh yeah. See, (Shows black and blue marks on arms and legs, burns.) You know what I heard from more than one guy at work? "If my kid wants to work in a factory, I am going to kick the hell out of him." I want my kid to be an effete snob. Yeah, mm-hmm. (Laughs.) I want him to be able to quote Walt Whitman, to be proud of it.

If you can't improve yourself, you improve your posterity. Otherwise life isn't worth nothing. You might as well go back to the cave and stay there. I'm sure the first caveman who went over the hill to see what was on the other side—I don't think he went there wholly out of curiosity. He went there because he wanted to get his son out of the cave. Just the same way I want to send my kid to college.

I work so damn hard and want to come home and sit down and lay around. *But I gotta get it out.* I want to be able to turn around to somebody and say, "Hey fuck you." You know? (Laughs.) The guy sitting next to me on the bus too. 'Cause all day I wanted to tell my foreman to go fuck himself, but I can't.

So I find a guy in a tavern. To tell him that. And he tells me too. I've been in brawls. He's punching me and I'm punching him, because we actually want to punch somebody else. The most that'll happen is the bartender will bar us from the tavern. But at work, you lose your job.

This one foreman I've got, he's a kid. He's a college graduate. He thinks he's better than everybody else. He was chewing me out and I was saying, "Yeah, yeah, yeah." He said, "What do you mean, yeah, yeah, yeah. Yes, *sir.*" I told him, "Who the hell are you, Hitler? What is this "*Yes, sir*" bullshit? I came here to work, I didn't come here to crawl. There's a fuckin' difference." One word led to another and I lost.

I got broke down to a lower grade and lost twenty-five cents an hour, which is a hell of a lot. It amounts to about ten dollars a week. He came over—after breaking me down. The guy comes over and smiles at me. I blew up. He didn't know it, but he was about two seconds and two feet away from a hospital. I said, "Stay the fuck away from me." He was just about to say something and was pointing his finger. I just reached my hand up and just grabbed his finger and I just put it back in his pocket. He walked away. I grabbed his finger because I'm married. If I'd a been single, I'd a grabbed his head. That's the difference.

You're doing this manual labor and you know that technology can do it. (Laughs.) Let's face it, a machine can do the work of a man; otherwise they wouldn't have space probes. Why can we send a rocket ship that's unmanned and yet send a man in a steel mill to do a mule's work?

Automation? Depends how it's applied. It frightens me if it puts me out on the street. It doesn't frighten me if it shortens my work week. You read that little thing: what are you going to do when this computer replaces you? Blow up computers. (Laughs.) Really. Blow up computers. I'll be goddamned if a computer is gonna eat before I do! I want milk for my kids and beer for me. Machines can either liberate man or enslave 'im, because they're pretty neutral. It's man who has the bias to put the thing one place or another.

If I had a twenty-hour workweek, I'd get to know my kids better, my wife better. Some kid invited me to go on a college campus. On a Saturday. It was summertime. Hell, if I have a choice of taking my wife and kids to a picnic or going to a college campus, it's gonna be the picnic. But if I worked a twenty-hour week, I could go do both. Don't you think with that extra twenty hours people could really expand? Who's to say? There are some people in factories just by force of circumstance. I'm just like the colored people. Potential Einsteins don't have to be white. They could be in cotton fields, they could be in factories.

The twenty-hour week is a possibility today. The intellectuals, they always say there are potential Lord Byrons, Walt Whitmans, Roosevelts, Picassos working in construction or steel mills or factories. But I don't think they believe it. I think what they're afraid of is the potential Hitlers and Stalins that are there too. The people in power fear the leisure man. Not just the United States. Russia's the same way.

What do you think would happen in this country if, for one year, they experimented and gave everybody a twenty-hour week? How do they know that the guy who digs Wallace[1] today doesn't try to resurrect Hitler tomorrow? Or the guy who is mildly disturbed at pollution doesn't decide to go to General Motors and shit on the guy's desk? You can become a fanatic if you had the time. The whole thing is time. That is, I think, one reason rich kids tend to be fanatic about politics: they have time. Time, that's the important thing.

It isn't that the average working guy is dumb. He's tired, that's all. I picked up a book on chess one time. That thing laid in the drawer for two or three weeks, you're too tired. During the weekends you want to take your kids out. You don't want to sit there and the kid comes up: "Daddy, can I go to the park?" You got your nose in a book? Forget it.

I know a guy fifty-seven years old. Know what he tells me? "Mike, I'm old and tired *all* the time." The first thing happens at work: when the arms start moving, the brain stops. I punch in about ten minutes to seven in the morning. I say hello to a couple of guys I like, I kid around with them. One guy says good morning to you and you say good morning. To another guy you say fuck you. The guy you say fuck you to is your friend.

---

[1]George Wallace, militantly segregationist governor of Alabama.

I put on my hard hat, change into my safety shoes, put on my safety glasses, go to the bonderizer. It's the thing I work on. They rake the metal, they wash it, they dip it in a paint solution, and we take if off. Put it on, take it off, put it on, take it off, put it on, take it off . . .

I say hello to everybody but my boss. At seven it starts. My arms get tired about the first half-hour. After that, they don't get tired any more until maybe the last half-hour at the end of the day. I work from seven to three thirty. My arms are tired at seven thirty and they're tired at three o'clock. I hope to God I never get broke in, because I always want my arms to be tired at seven thirty and three o'clock. (Laughs.) 'Cause that's when I know that there's a beginning and there's an end. That I'm not brainwashed. In between, I don't even try to think.

If I were to put you in front of a dock and I pulled up a skid in front of you with fifty hundred-pound sacks of potatoes and there are fifty more skids just like it, and this is what you're gonna do all day, what would you think about—potatoes? Unless a guy's a nut, he never thinks about work or talks about it. Maybe about baseball or about getting drunk the other night or he got laid or he didn't get laid. I'd say one out of a hundred will actually get excited about work.

Why is it that the communists always say they're for the workingman, and as soon as they set up a country, you got guys singing to tractors? They're singing about how they love the factory. That's where I couldn't buy communism. It's the intellectuals' utopia, not mine. I cannot picture myself singing to a tractor, I just can't. (Laughs.) Or singing to steel. (Singsongs.) Oh whoop-dee-doo, I'm at the bonderizer, oh how I love this heavy steel. No thanks. Never happen.

Oh yeah, I daydeam. I fantasize about a sexy blonde in Miami who's got my union dues. (Laughs.) I think of the head of the union the way I think of the head of my company. Living it up. I think of February in Miami. Warm weather, a place to lay in. When I hear a college kid say, "I'm oppressed," I don't believe him. You know what I'd like to do for one year? Live like a college kid. Just for one year. I'd love to. Wow! (Whispers) Wow! Sports car! Marijuana! (Laughs.) Wild, sexy broads. I'd love that, hell yes, I would.

Somebody has to do this work. If my kid ever goes to college, I just want him to have a little respect, to realize that his dad is one of those somebodies. This is why even on—(muses) yeah, I guess, sure—on the black thing . . . (Sighs heavily.) I can't really hate the colored fella that's working with me all day. The black intellectual I got no respect for. The white intellectual I got no use for. I got no use for the black militant who's gonna scream three hundred years of slavery to me while I'm busting my ass. You know what I mean? (Laughs.) I have one answer for that guy: go see Rockefeller. See Harriman.[2] Don't bother me. We're in the same cotton field. So just don't bug me. (Laughs.)

After work I usually stop off at a tavern. Cold beer. Cold beer right away. When I was single, I used to go into hillbilly bars, get in a lot of brawls. Just

---

[2]Nelson Rockefeller, governor of New York and then vice president of the United States; Averill Harriman, diplomat and U.S. Undersecretary of State.

to explode. I got a thing on my arm here (indicates scar). I got slapped with a bicycle chain. Oh, wow! (Softly) Mmm. I'm getting older. (Laughs.) I don't explode as much. You might say I'm broken in. (Quickly) No, I'll never be broken in. (Sighs.) When you get a little older, you exchange the words. When you're younger, you exchange the blows.

When I get home, I argue with my wife a little bit. Turn on TV, get mad at the news. (Laughs.) I don't even watch the news that much. I watch Jackie Gleason.[3] I look for any alternative to the ten o'clock news. I don't want to go to bed angry. Don't hit a man with anything heavy at five o'clock. He just can't be bothered. This is his time to relax. The heaviest thing he wants is what his wife has to tell him.

When I come home, know what I do for the first twenty minutes? Fake it. I put on a smile. I got a kid three years old. Sometimes she says, "Daddy, where've you been?" I say, "Work." I could have told her I'd been in Disneyland. What's work to a three-year-old kid? If I feel bad, I can't take it out on the kids. Kids are born innocent of everything but birth. You can't take it out on your wife either. This is why you go to a tavern. You want to release it there rather than do it at home. What does an actor do when he's got a bad movie? I got a bad movie every day.

I don't even need the alarm clock to get up in the morning. I can go out drinking all night, fall asleep at four, and bam! I'm up at six—no matter what I do. (Laughs.) It's a pseudo-death, more or less. Your whole system is paralyzed and you give all the appearance of death. It's an in-grown clock. It's a thing you just get used to. The hours differ. It depends. Sometimes my wife wants to do something crazy like play five hundred rummy or put a puzzle together. It could be midnight, could be ten o'clock, could be nine thirty.

What do you do weekends?

Drink beer, read a book. See that one? *Violence in America.* It's one of them studies from Washington. One of them committees they're always appointing. A thing like that I read on a weekend. But during the weekdays, gee . . . I just thought about it. I don't do that much reading from Monday through Friday. Unless it's a horny book. I'll read it at work and go home and do my homework. (Laughs.) That's what the guys at the plant call it— homework. (Laughs.) Sometimes my wife works on Saturday and I drink beer at the tavern.

I went out drinking with one guy, oh, a long time ago. A college boy. He was working where I work now. Always preaching to me about how you need violence to change the system and all that garbage. We went into a hillbilly joint.

---

[3]Comedian and actor, best known for the long running comedy TV series *The Honeymooners.*

Some guy there, I didn't know him from Adam, he said, "You think you're smart." I said, "What's your pleasure?" (Laughs.) He said, "My pleasure's to kick your ass." I told him I really can't be bothered. He said, "What're you, chicken?" I said, "No, I just don't want to be bothered." He came over and said something to me again. I said, "I don't beat women, drunks, or fools. Now leave me alone."

The guy called his brother over. This college boy that was with me, he came nudging my arm, "Mike, let's get out of here." I said, "What are you worried about?" (Laughs.) This isn't unusual. People will bug you. You fend it off as much as you can with your mouth and when you can't, you punch the guy out.

It was close to closing time and we stayed. We could have left, but when you go into a place to have a beer and a guy challenges you—if you expect to go in that place again, you don't leave. If you have to fight the guy, you fight.

I got just outside the door and one of these guys jumped on me and grabbed me around the neck. I grabbed his arm and flung him against the wall. I grabbed him here (indicates throat), and jiggled his head against the wall quite a few times. He kind of slid down a little bit. This guy who said he was his brother took a swing at me with a garrison belt. He just missed and hit the wall. I'm looking around for my junior Stalin (laughs), who loves violence and everything. He's gone. Split. (Laughs.) Next day I see him at work. I couldn't get mad at him, he's a baby.

He saw a book in my back pocket one time and he was amazed. He walked up to me and he said, "You read?" I said, "What do you mean, I read?" He said, "All these dummies read the sports pages around here. What are you doing with a book?" I got pissed off at the kid right away. I said, "What do you mean, all these dummies? Don't knock a man who's paying somebody else's way through college." He was a nineteen-year-old effete snob.

Yet you want your kid to be an effete snob?

Yes. I want my kid to look at me and say, "Dad you're a nice guy, but you're a fuckin' dummy." Hell yes, I want my kid to tell me that he's not gonna be like me . . .

If I were hiring people to work, I'd try naturally to pay them a decent wage. I'd try to find out their first names, their last names, keep the company as small as possible, so I could personalize the whole thing. All I would ask a man is a handshake, see you in the morning. No applications, nothing. I wouldn't be interested in the guy's past. Nobody ever checks on the pedigree on a mule, do they? But they do on a man. Can you picture walking up to a mule and saying, "I'd like to know who his granddaddy was?"

I'd like to run a combination bookstore and tavern. (Laughs.) I would like to have a place where college kids came and a steelworker could sit down and talk. Where a workingman could not be ashamed of Walt Whitman and where a college professor could not be ashamed that he painted his house over the weekend.

If a carpenter built a cabin for poets, I think the least the poets owe the carpenter is just three or four one-liners on the wall. A little plaque: Though we labor with our minds, this place we can relax in was built by someone who can work with his hands. And his work is as noble as ours. I think the poet owes something to the guy who builds the cabin for him.

I don't think of Monday. You know what I'm thinking about on Sunday night? Next Sunday. If you work real hard, you think of a perpetual vacation. Not perpetual sleep . . . What do I think of on a Sunday night? Lord, I wish the fuck I could do something else for a living.

I don't know who the guy is who said there is nothing sweeter than an unfinished symphony. Like an unfinished painting and an unfinished poem. If he creates this thing one day—let's say, Michelangelo's Sistine Chapel. It took him a long time to do this, this beautiful work of art. But what if he had to create this Sistine Chapel a thousand times a year? Don't you think that would even dull Michelangelo's mind? Or if da Vinci had to draw his anatomical charts thirty, forty, fifty, sixty, eighty, ninety, a hundred times a day? Don't you think that would even bore da Vinci?

Way back, you spoke of the guys who built the pyramids, not the pharaohs, the unknowns. You put yourself in their category?

Yes. I want my signature on 'em, too. Sometimes, out of pure meanness, when I make something, I put a little dent in it. I like to do something to make it really unique. Hit it with a hammer. I deliberately fuck it up to see if it'll get by, just so I can say I did it. It could be anything. Let me put it this way: I think God invented the dodo bird so when we get up there we could tell Him, "Don't you ever make mistakes?" and He'd say, "Sure, look." (Laughs.) I'd like to make my imprint. My dodo bird. A mistake, *mine.* Let's say the whole building is nothing but red bricks. I'd like to have just the black one or the white one or the purple one. Deliberately fuck up.

This is gonna sound square, but my kid is my imprint. He's my freedom. There's a line in one of Hemingway's books. I think it's from *For Whom the Bell Tolls.* They're behind the enemy lines, somewhere in Spain, and she's pregnant. She wants to stay with him. He tells her no. He says, "if you die, I die," knowing he's gonna die. But if you go, I go. Know what I mean? The mystics call it the brass bowl. Continuum. You know what I mean? This is why I work. Every time I see a young guy walk by with a shirt and tie and dressed up real sharp, I'm lookin' at my kid, you know? That's it.

Study and Discussion Questions

1. What are some of LeFevre's main complaints about his job?
2. What is the impact of reading the words of the worker himself? Does it surprise you that LeFevre alludes to Whitman and Hemingway?

3. What are LeFevre's feelings about the value of education? What does he want for his children? (And, by the way, does he have the same educational goals in mind for his daughter and for his son?)
4. What's the difference between being a single worker and a married worker, according to LeFevre?
5. What's LeFevre's attitude toward race and social class?
6. Describe a typical work day for LeFevre, from the time he wakes up until the time he goes to bed that night.
7. What are some of LeFevre's hopes and fantasies: (1) about work and (2) about himself and his family?
8. What is the tone of LeFevre's piece? Point to specific words, phrases, images, incidents that support your assessment.

Suggestions for Writing

1. "What's work to a three year old kid"? LeFevre asks this question half jokingly, but consider it seriously as the beginning of a definition of "work."
2. LeFevre has had the experience of being underestimated because of the work he does. Have you ever had this experience? Have you ever been on the other side and judged someone because of what they do for a living? Describe and discuss.
3. What would happen if there were a twenty-hour work week as LeFevre suggests? If they had the time, would people try to change society as LeFevre imagines, or would they just go to bars and start fights more often? What would you do with the time?

❋ ❋ ❋

GLORIA STEINEM

Gloria Steinem (1934–) was born in Toledo, Ohio, and after graduating from Smith College went on to further studies at the University of Delhi and the University of Calcutta. She began a career in political journalism with her column for *New York* magazine in the late 1960s. In 1971 she cofounded Ms. magazine and became its editor, a position she held until 1987. Steinem has been a key figure in the feminist movement and has worked with the National Women's Political Caucus and the Women's Action Alliance. She published her first collection of essays and columns, *Outrageous Acts and Everyday Rebellions*, in 1983, in which the following essay was published, followed by *Revolution from Within* (1992) and *Moving Beyond Words* (1994). "The Importance of Work" explores not only women's right to work but the larger meaningfulness of work for women.

The Importance of Work

Toward the end of the 1970s, the *Wall Street Journal* devoted an eight-part   1
front-page series to "the working woman"—that is, the influx of women into the
paid-labor force—as the greatest change in American life since the Industrial
Revolution.

Many women readers greeted both the news and the definition with cynicism. After all, women have always worked. If all the productive work of human
maintenance that women do in the home were valued at its replacement cost,
the gross national product of the United States would go up by 26 percent. It's
just that we are now more likely than ever before to leave our poorly rewarded,
low-security, high-risk job of homemaking (though we're still trying to explain
that it's a perfectly good one and that the problem is male society's refusal both
to do it and to give it an economic value) for more secure, independent and bet-
ter-paid jobs outside the home.

Obviously, the real work revolution won't come until all productive work is
rewarded—including child rearing and other jobs done in the home—and men
are integrated into so-called women's work as well as vice versa. But the radical change being touted by the *Journal* and other media is one part of that long
integration process: the unprecedented flood of women into salaried jobs, that
is, into the labor force as it has been male-defined and previously occupied by
men. We are already more than 41 percent of it—the highest proportion in history. Given the fact that women also make up a whopping 69 percent of the "discouraged labor force" (that is, people who need jobs but don't get counted in
the unemployment statistics because they've given up looking), plus an official
female unemployment rate that is substantially higher than men's, it's clear that
we could expand to become fully half of the national work force by 1990.

Faced with this determination of women to find a little independence and to
be paid and honored for our work, experts have rushed to ask: "Why?" It's a question rarely directed at male workers. Their basic motivations of survival and personal satisfaction are taken for granted. Indeed, men are regarded as "odd" and
therefore subjects for sociological study and journalistic reports only when they
don't have work, even if they are rich and don't need jobs or are poor and can't
find them. Nonetheless, pollsters and sociologists have gone to great expense to
prove that women work outside the home because of dire financial need, or if we
persist despite the presence of a wage-earning male, out of some desire to buy
"little extras" for our families, or even out of good old-fashioned penis envy.

Job interviewers and even our own families may still ask salaried women the 5
big "Why?" If we have small children at home or are in some job regarded as
"men's work," the incidence of such questions increases. Condescending or
accusatory versions of "What's a nice girl like you doing in a place like this?" have
not disappeared from the workplace.

How do we answer these assumptions that we are "working" out of some
pressing or peculiar need? Do we feel okay about arguing that it's as natural
for us to have salaried jobs as for our husbands whether or not we have young
children at home? Can we enjoy strong career ambitions without worrying
about being thought "unfeminine"? When we confront men's growing resentment of women competing in the work force (often in the form of such guilt-
producing accusations as "You're taking men's jobs away" or "You're damaging
your children"), do we simply state that a decent job is a basic human right for
everybody?

I'm afraid the answer is often no. As individuals and as a movement, we tend
to retreat into some version of a tactically questionable defense: "Womenworkbecausewehaveto." The phrase has become one word, one key on the type-
writer—an economic form of the socially "feminine" stance of passivity and
self-sacrifice. Under attack, we still tend to present ourselves as creatures of
economic necessity and familial devotion. "Womenworkbecausewehaveto" has
become the easiest thing to say.

Like most truisms, this one is easy to prove with statistics. Economic need
is the most consistent work motive—for women as well as men. In 1976, for
instance, 43 percent of all women in the paid-labor force were single, wid-
owed, separated, or divorced, and working to support themselves and their
dependents. An additional 21 percent were married to men who had earned
less than ten thousand dollars in the previous year, the minimum then
required to support a family of four. In fact, if you take men's pensions, stocks,
real estate, and various forms of accumulated wealth into account, a good statistical case can be made that there are more women who "have" to work
(that is, who have neither the accumulated wealth, nor husbands whose work
or wealth can support them for the rest of their lives) than there are men with
the same need. If we were going to ask one group "Do you really need this
job?" we should ask men.

But the first weakness of the whole "have to work" defense is its deceptive-
ness. Anyone who has ever experienced dehumanized life on welfare or any
other confidence-shaking dependency knows that a paid job may be preferable
to the dole, even when the handout is coming from a family member. Yet the
will and self-confidence to work on one's own can diminish as dependency and
fear increase. That may explain why—contrary to the "have to" rationale—
wives of men who earn less than three thousand dollars a year are actually *less*
likely to be employed than wives whose husbands make ten thousand dollars a
year or more.

Furthermore, the greatest proportion of employed wives is found among 10
families with a total household income of twenty-five to fifty thousand dollars a year. This is the statistical underpinning used by some sociologists to
prove that women's work is mainly important for boosting families into the
middle or upper middle class. Thus, women's incomes are largely used for buying "luxuries" and "little extras": a neat double-whammy that renders us secondary within our families, and makes our jobs expendable in hard times. We
may even go along with this interpretation (at least, up to the point of getting
fired so a male can have our job). It preserves a husbandly ego-need to be
seen as the primary breadwinner, and still allows us a safe "feminine" excuse
for working.

But there are often rewards that we're not confessing. As noted in *The
Two-Career Couple,* by Francine and Douglas Hall: "Women who hold jobs by
choice, even blue-collar routine jobs, are more satisfied with their lives than are
the full-time housewives."

In addition to personal satisfaction, there is also society's need for all its
members' talents. Suppose that jobs were given out on only a "have to work"
basis to both women and men—one job per household. It would be unthinkable to lose the unique abilities of, for instance, Eleanor Holmes Norton, the
distinguished chair of the Equal Employment Opportunity Commission. But
would we then be forced to question the important work of her husband,
Edward Norton, who is also a distinguished lawyer? Since men earn more than
twice as much as women on the average, the wife in most households would be
more likely to give up her job. Does that mean the nation could do as well without millions of its nurses, teachers, and secretaries? Or that the rare man who
earns less than his wife should give up his job?

It was this kind of waste of human talents on a society-wide scale that trau-
matized millions of unemployed or underemployed Americans during the
Depression. Then, a one-job-per-household rule seemed somewhat justified,
yet the concept was used to displace women workers only, create intolerable
dependencies, and waste female talent that the country needed. That Depression experience, plus the energy and example of women who were finally
allowed to work during the manpower shortage created by World War II, led
Congress to reinterpret the meaning of the country's full-employment goal in
its Economic Act of 1946. Full employment was officially defined as "the
employment of those who want to work, without regard to whether their
employment is, by some definition, necessary. This goal applies equally to men
and women." Since bad economic times are again creating a resentment of
employed women—as well as creating more need for women to be
employed—we need such a goal more than ever. Women are again being
caught in a tragic double bind: We are required to be strong and then punished
for our strength.

Clearly, anything less than government and popular commitment to this 1946
definition of full employment will leave the less powerful groups, whoever they

may be, in danger. Almost as important as the financial penalty paid by the powerless is the suffering that comes from being shut out of paid and recognized work. Without it, we lose much of our self-respect and our ability to prove that we are alive by making some difference in the world. That's just as true for the suburban woman as it is for the unemployed steel worker.

But it won't be easy to give up the passive defense of "weworkbecausewe-   15 haveto."

When a woman who is struggling to support her children and grandchildren on welfare sees her neighbor working as a waitress, even though that neighbor's husband has a job, she may feel resentful; and the waitress (of course, not the waitress's husband) may feel guilty. Yet unless we establish the obligation to provide a job for everyone who is willing and able to work, that welfare woman may herself be penalized by policies that give out only one public-service job per household. She and her daughter will have to make a painful and divisive decision about which of them gets that precious job, and the whole household will have to survive on only one salary.

A job as a human right is a principle that applies to men as well as women. But women have more cause to fight for it. The phenomenon of the "working woman" has been held responsible for everything from an increase in male impotence (which turned out, incidentally, to be attributable to medication for high blood pressure) to the rising cost of steak (which was due to high energy costs and beef import restrictions, not women's refusal to prepare the cheaper, slower-cooking cuts). Unless we see a job as part of every citizen's right to autonomy and personal fulfillment, we will continue to be vulnerable to someone else's idea of what "need" is, and whose "need" counts the most.

In many ways, women who do not have to work for simple survival, but who choose to do so nonetheless, are on the frontier of asserting this right for all women. Those with well-to-do husbands are dangerously easy for us to resent and put down. It's easier still to resent women from families of inherited wealth, even though men generally control and benefit from that wealth. (There is no Rockefeller Sisters Fund, no J. P. Morgan & Daughters, and sons-in-law may be the ones who really sleep their way to power.) But to prevent a woman whose husband or father is wealthy from earning her own living, and from gaining the self-confidence that comes with that ability, is to keep her needful of that   20 unearned power and less willing to disperse it. Moreover, it is to lose forever her unique talents.

Perhaps modern feminists have been guilty of a kind of reverse snobbism that keeps us from reaching out to the wives and daughters of wealthy men; yet it was exactly such women who refused the restrictions of class and financed the first wave of feminist revolution.

For most of us, however, "womenworkbecausewehaveto" is just true enough to be seductive as a personal defense.

If we use it without also staking out the larger human right to a job, however, we will never achieve that right. And we will always be subject to the false argument that independence for women is a luxury affordable only in good economic times. Alternatives to layoffs will not be explored, acceptable unemployment will always be used to frighten those with jobs into accepting low wages, and we will never remedy the real cost, both to families and to the country, of dependent women and a massive loss of talent.

Worst of all, we may never learn to find productive, honored work as a natural part of ourselves and as one of life's basic pleasures.

Questions on Meaning

1. What's wrong with the explanation "Women work because we have to"? Why does Steinem say this explanation—even when true—is counterproductive for women?
2. Is there naturally a "right" to a job? Does the essay explicitly argue for this right, or simply assume that it exists?
3. Is Steinem arguing for some specific actions to be taken, such as some legislation or new policies for the workplace? If so, what specifically does she want as solutions for the present problem? If not, what exactly is she arguing for?

Questions on Rhetorical Strategy and Style

1. What kinds of evidence does Steinem bring into the essay to strengthen her argument? Identify several examples of these in the essay.
2. Steinem uses the rhetorical strategy of comparison and contrast to explore similarities and differences in men and women working. Go through the essay and mark each such comparison. How does this strategy develop the key ideas of the essay?
3. Is Steinem writing only to women? When she uses the pronoun "we" apparently to refer to both women in general and the reader, does that help solidify her argument or alienate her male readers? Examine the "we" throughout the essay and comment on the effects of specific examples.

Writing Assignments

1. Have society and the working world changed since 1983 when this was first printed? Do you still see the same resentment toward women working that Steinem describes? If so, how is it manifested today, when an even higher percentage of women are working and are working higher level jobs? If not, what has changed since that time to account for present differences?
2. Consider your own experience with work, regardless of whether you are a man or a woman. Have all the jobs you have held given you a sense of fulfillment? Imagine for a moment that you just won the lottery and never needed to work again. Would you? Why or why not? Is this kind of not working any different from not working because your spouse makes plenty of money? Explore the difference in an essay in which you formulate your own thesis about the value of work.

3. Steinem cites one study that shows women who work by choice are more satisfied with their lives than full-time housewives, but she does not go on to argue or explain this in any detail. Think about the concept of satisfaction. Why are women who do not work less satisfied with their lives, since presumably they have more time to engage in a variety of fulfilling activities? What is it about work that provides an important sense of satisfaction for both men and women? Write an essay that presents your thoughts on this phenomenon.

RICHARD RODRIGUEZ (b. 1944)

Richard Rodriguez grew up in San Francisco, one of four children in a Mexican working-class family. In his autobiographical Hunger for Memory (1981), Rodriguez writes in depth about his experiences as a young Mexican American male—his assimilation into American culture and the tensions it produced. Rodriguez obtained his B.A. in English from Stanford in 1974, his M.A. at Columbia, and was then granted a Fulbright fellowship to do Ph.D. work in England. On track for a life in academia, Rodriguez surprised many by declining teaching positions; he instead decided to write full time. Noted for his synthesis of journalism and personal narrative, Rodriguez's subsequent publications include *Days of Obligation: An Argument with My Mexican American Father* (1992) and *Brown: The Last Discovery of America* (2002). "Huck Finn, Dan Quayle, and The Value of Acceptance" originally appeared in the *Los Angeles Times Magazine* in 1992 and concerns sexual and cultural identity.

Huck Finn, Dan Quayle and the Value of Acceptance   (1992)

I am sitting alone in my car, in front of my parents' house—a middle-aged man with a boy's secret to tell. What words will I use to tell them? I hate the word *gay,* find its little affirming sparkle more pathetic than assertive. I am happier with the less polite *queer.* But to my parents I would say *homosexual,* avoid the Mexican slang *joto* (I had always heard it said in our house with hints of condescension), though *joto* is less mocking than the sissy-boy *maricón.*

The buzz on everyone's lips now: Family values. The other night on TV, the vice president of the United States, his arm around his wife, smiled into the camera and described homosexuality as "mostly a choice." But how would he know? Homosexuality never felt like a choice to me.

A few minutes ago Rush Limbaugh, the radio guy with a voice that reminds me, for some reason, of a butcher's arms, was banging his console and booming a near-reasonable polemic about family values. Limbaugh was not very clear about which values exactly he considers to be family values. A divorced man who lives alone in New York?

My parents live on a gray, treeless street in San Francisco not far from the ocean. Probably more than half of the neighborhood is immigrant. India lives next door to Greece, who lives next door to Russia. I wonder what the Chinese lady next door to my parents makes of the politicians' phrase *family values.*

What immigrants know, what my parents certainly know, is that when you come to this country, you risk losing your children. The assurance of family—continuity, inevitability—is precisely what America encourages its children to overturn. *Become your own man.* We who are native to this country know this too, of course, though we are likely to deny it. Only a society so guilty about its betrayal of family would tolerate the pieties of politicians regarding family values.

On the same summer day that Republicans were swarming in Houston[1] (buzzing about family values), a friend of mine who escaped family values awhile back and who now wears earrings resembling intrauterine devices, was complaining to me over coffee about the Chinese. The Chinese will never take over San Francisco, my friend said, because the Chinese do not want to take over San Francisco. The Chinese do not even *see* San Francisco! All they care about is their damn families. All they care about is double-parking smack in front of the restaurant on Clement Street and pulling granny out of the car—and damn anyone who happens to be in the car behind them or the next or the next.

Politicians would be horrified by such an American opinion, of course. But then, what do politicians, Republicans or Democrats, really know of our family life? Or what are they willing to admit? Even in that area where they could reasonably be expected to have something to say—regarding the relationship of family life to our economic system—the politicians say nothing. Republicans celebrate American economic freedom, but Republicans don't seem to connect that economic freedom to the social breakdown they find appalling. Democrats, on the other hand, if more tolerant of the drift from familial tradition, are suspicious of the very capitalism that creates social freedom.

How you become free in America: Consider the immigrant. He gets a job. Soon he is earning more money than his father ever made (his father's authority is thereby subtly undermined). The immigrant begins living a life his father never knew. The immigrant moves from one job to another, changes houses. His economic choices determine his home address—not the other way around. The immigrant is on his way to becoming his own man.

---

[1]Site of 1992 Republican National Convention.

When I was broke a few years ago and trying to finish a book, I lived with my parents. What a thing to do! A major theme of America is leaving home. We trust the child who forsakes family connections to make it on his own. We call that the making of a man.

Let's talk about this man stuff for a minute. America's ethos is anti-domestic. We may be intrigued by blood that runs through wealth—the Kennedys or the Rockefellers—but they seem European to us. Which is to say, they are movies. They are Corleones.[2] Our real pledge of allegiance: We say in America that nothing about your family—your class, your race, your pedigree—should be as important as what you yourself achieve. We end up in 1992 introducing ourselves by first names.

What authority can Papa have in a country that formed its identity in an act of Oedipal rebellion against a mad British king? Papa is a joke in America, a stock sitcom figure—Archie Bunker or Homer Simpson. But my Mexican father went to work every morning, and he stood in a white smock, making false teeth, oblivious of the shelves of grinning false teeth mocking his devotion.

The nuns in grammar school—my wonderful Irish nuns—used to push Mark Twain on me. I distrusted Huck Finn,[3] he seemed like a gringo kid I would steer clear of in the schoolyard. (He was too confident.) I realize now, of course, that Huck is the closest we have to a national hero. We trust the story of a boy who has no home and is restless for the river. (Huck's Pap is drunk.) Americans are more forgiving of Huck's wildness than of the sweetness of the Chinese boy who walks to school with his mama or grandma. (There is no worse thing in America than to be a mama's boy, nothing better than to be a real boy—all boy—like Huck, who eludes Aunt Sally, and is eager for the world of men.)

There's a bent old woman coming up the street. She glances nervously as she passes my car. What would you tell us, old lady, of family values in America?

America is an immigrant country, we say. Motherhood—parenthood—is less our point than adoption. If I had to assign gender to America, I would note the consensus of the rest of the world. When America is burned in effigy, a male is burned. Americans themselves speak of Uncle Sam.

Like the Goddess of Liberty, Uncle Sam has no children of his own. He steals children to make men of them, mocks all reticence, all modesty, all memory. Uncle Sam is a hectoring Yankee, a skinflint uncle, gaunt, uncouth, unloved. He is the American Savonarola—hater of moonshine, destroyer of stills, burner of cocaine. Sam has no patience with mamas' boys.

You betray Uncle Sam by favoring private over public life, by seeking to exempt yourself, by cheating on your income taxes, by avoiding jury duty, by trying to keep your boy on the farm.

---

[2] Italian crime family in *The Godfather*, novel by Mario Puzo and film by Francis Ford Coppola.
[3] Hero of Mark Twain's novel, *The Adventures of Huckleberry Finn*.

Mothers are traditionally the guardians of the family—against America—though even Mom may side with America against queers and deserters, at least when the Old Man is around. Premature gray hair. Arthritis in her shoulders. Bowlegged with time, red hands. In their fiercely flowered housedresses, mothers are always smarter than fathers in America. But in reality they are betrayed by their children who leave. In a thousand ways. They end up alone.

We kind of like the daughter who was a tomboy. Remember her? It was always easier to be a tomboy in America than a sissy. Americans admired Annie Oakley more than they admired Liberace[4] (who, nevertheless, always remembered his mother). But today we do not admire Annie Oakley when we see Mom becoming Annie Oakley.

The American household now needs two incomes, everyone says. Meaning: Mom is *forced* to leave home out of economic necessity. But lots of us know lots of moms who are sick and tired of being mom, or only mom. It's like the nuns getting fed up, teaching kids for all those years and having those kids grow up telling stories of how awful Catholic school was! Not every woman in America wants her life's work to be forgiveness. Today there are moms who don't want their husbands' names. And the most disturbing possibility: What happens when Mom doesn't want to be Mom at all? Refuses pregnancy?

Mom is only becoming an American like the rest of us. Certainly, people all over the world are going to describe the influence of feminism on women (all over the world) as their "Americanization." And rightly so.

Nothing of this, of course, will the politician's wife tell you. The politician's wife is careful to follow her husband's sentimental reassurances that nothing has changed about America except perhaps for the sinister influence of deviants. Like myself.

I contain within myself an anomaly at least as interesting as the Republican Party's version of family values. I am a homosexual Catholic, a communicant in a tradition that rejects even as it upholds me.

I do not count myself among those Christians who proclaim themselves protectors of family values. They regard me as no less an enemy of the family than the "radical feminists." But the joke about families that all homosexuals know is that we are the ones who stick around and make families possible. Call on us. I can think of 20 or 30 examples. A gay son or daughter is the only one who is "free" (married brothers and sisters are too busy). And, indeed, because we have admitted the inadmissible about ourselves (that we are queer)—we are adepts at imagination—we can even imagine those who refuse to imagine us. We can imagine Mom's loneliness, for example. If Mom needs to be taken to church or to the doctor or ferried between Christmas dinners, depend on the gay son or lesbian daughter.

---

[4]Annie Oakley, sharpshooter; Liberace, pianist and entertainer.

I won't deny that the so-called gay liberation movement, along with feminism, undermined the heterosexual household, if that's what politicians mean when they say family values. Against churchly reminders that sex was for procreation, the gay bar as much as the birth-control pill taught Americans not to fear sexual pleasure. In the past two decades—and, not co-incidentally, parallel to the feminist movement—the gay liberation movement moved a generation of Americans toward the idea of a childless adulthood. If the women's movement was ultimately more concerned about getting out of the house and into the workplace, the gay movement was in its way more subversive to Puritan America because it stressed the importance of play.

Several months ago, the society editor of the morning paper in San Francisco suggested (on a list of "must haves") that every society dame must have at least one gay male friend. A ballet companion. A lunch date. The remark was glib and incorrect enough to beg complaints from homosexual readers, but there was a truth about it as well. Homosexual men have provided women with an alternate model of masculinity. And the truth: The Old Man, God bless him, is a bore. Thus are we seen as preserving marriages? Even Republican marriages?

For myself, homosexuality is a deep brotherhood but does not involve domestic life. Which is why, my married sisters will tell you, I can afford the time to be a writer. And why are so many homosexuals such wonderful teachers and priests and favorite aunts, if not because we are freed from the house? On the other hand, I know lots of homosexual couples (male and female) who model their lives on the traditional heterosexual version of domesticity and marriage. Republican politicians mock the notion of a homosexual marriage, but ironically such marriages honor the heterosexual marriage by imitating it.

"The only loving couples I know," a friend of mine recently remarked, "are all gay couples."

This woman was not saying that she does not love her children or that she is planning a divorce. But she was saying something about the sadness of American domestic life: the fact that there is so little joy in family intimacy. Which is perhaps why gossip (public intrusion into the private) has become a national industry. All day long, in forlorn houses, the television lights up a freakish parade of husbands and mothers-in-law and children upon the stage of Sally or Oprah or Phil.[5] They tell on each other. The audience ooohhhs. Then a psychiatrist-shaman appears at the end to dispense prescriptions—the importance of family members granting one another more "space."

The question I desperately need to ask you is whether we Americans have ever truly valued the family. We are famous, or our immigrant ancestors were

---

[5]Sally Jessy Raphael, Oprah Winfrey, and Phil Donahue, television talk show hosts.

famous, for the willingness to leave home. And it is ironic that a crusade under the banner of family values has been taken up by those who would otherwise pass themselves off as patriots. For they seem not to understand America, nor do I think they love the freedoms America grants. Do they understand why, in a country that prizes individuality and is suspicious of authority, children are disinclined to submit to their parents? You cannot celebrate American values in the public realm without expecting them to touch our private lives. As Barbara Bush remarked recently, family values are also neighborhood values. It may be harmless enough for Barbara Bush to recall a sweeter America—Midland, Texas, in the 1950s. But the question left begging is why we chose to leave Midland, Texas. Americans like to say that we can't go home again. The truth is that we don't want to go home again, don't want to be known, recognized. Don't want to respond in the same old ways. (And you know you will if you go back there.)

Little 10-year-old girls know that there are reasons for getting away from the family. They learn to keep their secrets—under lock and key—addressed to Dear Diary. Growing up queer, you learn to keep secrets as well. In no place are those secrets more firmly held than within the family house. You learn to live in closets. I know a Chinese man who arrived in America about 10 years ago. He got a job and made some money. And during that time he came to confront his homosexuality. And then his family arrived. I do not yet know the end of this story.

The genius of America is that it permits children to leave home, it permits us to become different from our parents. But the sadness, the loneliness of America, is clear too.

Listen to the way Americans talk about immigrants. If, on the one hand, there is impatience when today's immigrants do not seem to give up their family, there is also a fascination with this reluctance. In Los Angeles, Hispanics are considered people of family. Hispanic women are hired to be at the center of the American family—to babysit and diaper, to cook and to clean and to ease the dying. Hispanic attachment to family is seen by many Americans, I think, as the reason why Hispanics don't get ahead. But if Asians privately annoy us for being so family oriented, they are also stereotypically celebrated as the new "whiz kids" in school. Don't Asians go to college, after all, to honor their parents?

More important still is the technological and economic ascendancy of Asia, particularly Japan, on the American imagination. Americans are starting to wonder whether perhaps the family values of Asia put the United States at a disadvantage. The old platitude had it that ours is a vibrant, robust society for being a society of individuals. Now we look to Asia and see team effort paying off.

In this time of national homesickness, of nostalgia, for how we imagine America used to be, there are obvious dangers. We are going to start blaming each other for the loss. Since we are inclined, as Americans, to think of ourselves individually, we are disinclined to think of ourselves as creating one another or influencing one another.

But it is not the politician or any political debate about family values that has brought me here on a gray morning to my parents' house. It is some payment I owe to my youth and to my parents' youth. I imagine us sitting in the living room, amid my mother's sentimental doilies and the family photographs, trying to take the measure of the people we have turned out to be in America.

A San Francisco poet, when he was in the hospital and dying, called a priest to his bedside. The old poet wanted to make his peace with Mother Church. He wanted baptism. The priest asked why. "Because the Catholic Church has to accept me," said the poet. "Because I am a sinner."

Isn't willy-nilly inclusiveness the point, the only possible point to be derived from the concept of family? Curiously, both President Bush and Vice President Quayle got in trouble with their constituents recently for expressing a real family value. Both men said that they would try to dissuade a daughter or granddaughter from having an abortion. But, finally, they said they would support her decision, continue to love her, never abandon her.

There are families that do not accept. There are children who are forced to leave home because of abortions or homosexuality. There are family secrets that Papa never hears. Which is to say there are families that never learn the point of families.

But there she is at the window. My mother has seen me and she waves me in. Her face asks: Why am I sitting outside? (Have they, after all, known my secret for years and kept it, out of embarrassment, not knowing what to say?) Families accept, often by silence. My father opens the door to welcome me in.

Study and Discussion Questions:

1. Why does Rodriguez open his personal essay with him sitting by himself in his car outside his parents' house? Why does he end it with his father opening the door for him to come in?
2. Discuss Rodriguez's pondering of the names/labels/designations for his sexual identity. What are the connotations for each of these names? Why is finding the right *name* important—not only in this essay: think about instances in your own experience?
3. In his second paragraph, Rodriguez challenges Dan Quayle's assertion that homosexuality is a choice. (Dan Quayle was the first President Bush's choice for vice-presidential running mate in the 1992 election, an election which they lost.) Rodriguez brings up the political buzz phrase "family values", which is still a hotly debated issue. How do various groups in this country define "family values"? What do *you* think constitute family values you would live by? How does Richard Rodriguez define family values?

4. Rodriguez discusses what seem like two very different issues: American attitudes toward (a) immigrants and (b) gays. What connections is he making?
5. "It was always easier to be a tomboy in America than a sissy." Why might that be? Do you find that to be true in your own experience?
6. Why does Rodriguez want to tell his parents that he is gay?

Suggestions for Writing:

1. Narrate the conversation you imagine Rodriguez will have with his parents about his sexual orientation.

DOROTHY ALLISON (b. 1949)

Dorothy Allison was born in Greenville, South Carolina, and was the first person from her family to finish high school. She studied at Florida Presbyterian College (now Eckerd College) and the New School for Social Research in New York City. Working in the tradition of other southern writers such as Flannery O'Connor and William Faulkner, Allison's writings offer a more contemporary and complex picture of southern, working-class culture. In both her poetry and fiction, Allison's working-class, female characters struggle to find understanding as they grapple with issues of class, gender and sexuality. Her work includes *The Women Who Hate Me: Poetry* 1980–1990 (1991); the novels *Bastard* Out of *Carolina* (1992), and *Cavedweller* (1998); a collection of short stories, *Trash* (1988); an essay collection, *Skin: Talking About Sex, Class and Literature* (1993); and the memoir, *One or Two Things I Know for Sure* (1995). "Gun Crazy," first printed in *Skin*, tells the story of one girl's experience learning to shoot a real gun.

Gun Crazy (1993)

When we were little, my sister and I would ride with the cousins in the back of my uncle Bo's pickup truck when he drove us up into the foothills where we could picnic and the men could go shooting. I remember standing up behind the cab, watching the tree branches filter the bright Carolina sunshine, letting the wind push my hair behind me, and then wrestling with my cousin, Butch, until my aunt yelled at us to stop.

"Ya'll are gonna fall out," she was always screaming, but we never did.

Every stop sign we passed was pocked with bullet holes.

"Fast flying bees," Uncle Jack told us with a perfectly serious expression.

"Hornets with lead in their tails," Bo laughed.

My mama's youngest brother, Bo, kept his guns, an ought-seven rifle and a lovingly restored old Parker shotgun, wrapped in a worn green army blanket. A fold of the blanket was loosely stitched down a third of its length to make a cloth bag, the only sewing Bo ever did in his life. He kept his cleaning kit—a little bag of patches and a plastic bottle of gun oil—in the blanket pouch with the guns. Some evenings he would spread the blanket out in front of the couch and sit there happily cleaning his guns slowly and thoroughly. All the while he would sip cold beer and talk about what a fine time a man could have with his weapons out in the great outdoors. "You got to sit still, perfectly still," he'd say, nod, and sip again, then dab a little more gun oil on the patch he was running through the rifle barrel.

"Oh, you're good at that," someone would always joke.

"The man an't never shot an animal once in his life," Bo's wife, Nessa, told us. "Shot lots of bottles, whiskey bottles, beer bottles, coke-cola bottles. The man's one of the great all-time bottle destroyers."

I grinned. Stop signs and bottles, paper targets and wooden fences. My uncles loved to shoot, it was true, but the only deer they ever brought home was one found drowned in a creek and another that Uncle Jack hit head-on one night when he was driving his Pontiac convertible with the busted headlights.

"Let me help you," I begged my uncle Bo one night when he had pulled out his blanket kit and started the ritual of cleaning his gun. I was eleven, shy but fearless. Bo just looked at me over the angle of the cigarette jutting out of the corner of his mouth. He shook his head.

"I'd be careful," I blurted.

"Nessa, you hear this child?" Bo yelled in the direction of the kitchen and then turned back to me. "An't no such thing as careful where girls and guns are concerned." He took the cigarette out of his mouth and gave me another of those cool, distant looks. "You an't got no business thinking about guns."

"But I want to learn to shoot."

He laughed a deep throaty laugh, coughed a little, then laughed again. "Girls don't shoot," he told me with a smile. "You can do lots of things, girl, but not shooting. That just an't gonna happen."

I glared at him and said, "I bet Uncle Jack will teach me. He knows how careful I can be."

Bo shook his head and tucked the cigarette back in the corner of his mouth. "It an't about careful, it's about you're a girl. You can whine and wiggle all you wont. An't nobody in this family gonna teach you to shoot." His face was stern, his smile completely gone. "That just an't gonna happen."

When I was in high school my best girlfriend was Anne, whose mama worked in the records division at the local children's hospital. One Sunday Anne invited me to go over to the woods out behind the mental hospital, to a hollow there where we could do some plinking.

"Plinking?"

"You know, plinking. Shooting bottles and cans." She pushed her hair back off her face and smiled at me. "If there's any water we'll fill the bottles up and watch it shoot up when the glass breaks. That's my favorite thing."

"You got a gun?" My mouth was hanging open.

"Sure. Mama gave me a rifle for my birthday. Didn't I tell you?"

"I don't think so." I looked away, so she wouldn't see how envious I felt. Her mama had given her a gun for her sixteenth birthday! I had always thought Anne's mama was something special, but that idea was simply amazing.

Anne's mama refused to cook, smoked Marlboros continuously, left the room any time any of her three children mentioned their dead father, and drank cocktails every evening while leaning back in her Lazy-Boy lounge chair and wearing dark eyeshades. "Don't talk to me," she'd hiss between yellow stained teeth. "I got crazy people and drunken orderlies talking at me all day long. I come home, I want some peace and quiet."

"My mama thinks a woman should be able to take care of herself," Anne told me.

"Right," I agreed. "She's right." Inside, I was seething with envy and excitement. Outside, I kept my face smooth and noncommittal. I wanted to shoot, wanted to shoot a shotgun like all my uncles, pepper stop signs and scare dogs. But I'd settle for a rifle, the kind of rifle a woman like Anne's mama would give her sixteen-year-old daughter.

That Sunday I watched closely as Anne slid a bullet into the chamber of her rifle and sighted down the gully to the paper target we had set up thirty feet away. Anne looked like Jane Fonda in *Cat Ballou*[1] after she lost her temper— fierce, blonde, and competent. I swallowed convulsively and wiped sweaty palms on my jeans. I would have given both my big toes to have been able to stand like that, legs apart, feet planted, arms up, and the big rifle perfectly steady as the center circle target was fissured with little bullet holes.

Anne was myopic, skinny, completely obsessed with T. E. Lawrence,[2] and neurotically self-conscious with boys, but holding that rifle tight to her shoulder and peppering the target, she looked different—older and far more interesting. She looked sexy, or maybe the gun looked sexy, I wasn't sure. But I wanted that look. Not Anne, but the power. I wanted to hold a rifle steady, the stock butting my shoulder tightly while I hit the target dead center. My mouth went dry. Anne showed me how to aim the gun a little lower than the center of the target.

"It shoots a little high," she said. "You got to be careful not to let it jump up when it fires." She stood behind me and steadied the gun in my hands. I put the

---

[1]Actor (b. 1937) in 1965 American movie about a school teacher turned outlaw.
[2]British scholar and soldier (1888–1935), known as "Lawrence of Arabia."

little notch at the peak of the barrel just under the target, tightened my muscles, and pulled the trigger. The rifle still jerked up a little, but a small hole appeared at the outer edge of the second ring of the target.

"Goddamn!" Anne crowed. "You got it, girl." I let the barrel of the rifle drop down, the metal of the trigger guard smooth and warm under my hand.

You got to hold still, I thought. Perfectly still. I sighted along the barrel again, shifting the target notch to the right of the jars Anne had set up earlier. I concentrated, focused, felt my arm become rigid, stern and strong. I pulled back on the trigger slowly, squeezing steadily, the way in the movies they always said it was supposed to be done. The bottle exploded, water shooting out in a wide fine spray.

"Goddamn!" Anne shouted again. I looked over at her. Her glasses had slipped down on her nose and her hair had fallen forward over one eye. Sun shone on her sweaty nose and the polished whites of her teeth. She was staring at me like I had stared at her earlier, her whole face open with pride and delight.

Sexy, yeah. I pointed the barrel at the sky and let my mouth widen into a smile.

"Goddamn," I said, and meant it with all my heart.

Study and Discussion Questions

1. List some details Allison gives us to establish the physical and social setting of her narrative. What do we learn about her family, her locale, and her social class in the first few paragraphs?

2. What does the second short section, about Bo, tell us about the place and use of guns in the lives of Allison's people?

3. Why does the eleven-year-old first person narrator want to learn to shoot? How does her uncle respond to this yearning and why does he respond the way he does?

4. How is Anne's mama "something special"? Who is she set in contrast to? What are the two contrasting philosophies about girls and guns we see in "Gun Crazy"?

5. In the fifth section, seven years or so after the narrative begins, the narrator finally does get to shoot a rifle. List several details that demonstrate how she feels about this.

Suggestions for Writing

1. Allison deftly and succinctly builds the narrative through five short sections. Consider Allison's "Gun Crazy" as an argument as well as a story. Trace the development of her argument from section one through section five. What does she establish in each of the five sections?

2. a. Guns and learning to shoot or handle them become in this autobiographical story a "contested symbol." What function does knowing how to shoot and care for a gun have in Allison's Southern white working-class culture? What is skill with a gun symbolic of; who are the contestants in the story for this symbol; what is the contest about; how is it waged; what is the prize?

    b. Think of one other symbol in contemporary culture that you see as contested, and discuss.

3. In the fifth and last section of "Gun Crazy," Allison mentions Jane Fonda in the film *Cat Ballou* as well as T. E. Lawrence (Lawrence of Arabia). Why is she invoking these two figures and how is she using them? How are both of them cultural icons? Think of other figures in the popular imagination that you might evoke and discuss what meanings these have.

❋ ❋ ❋

Growing Up
and Growing Older

Courtesy of Smithsonian American Art Museum, Washington, DC / Art Resource, NY

Fiction

ALDOUS HUXLEY (1894–1963)

Grandson of renowned biologist T. H. Huxley, Aldous Huxley was born in Godalming, England, and studied at Eton and Oxford. Unlike his grandfather, Huxley chose not to study science and instead took to reading and analyzing English literature. Initially a poet, Huxley soon found his writing niche in satire and social criticism. By the early 1920s, Huxley was traveling extensively and writing essays, novels and plays critiquing the folly of human behavior. In 1932, Huxley published *Brave New World*—an innovative science fiction novel which explores the modernist notion of "dystopia" and a future society deluded by the promise of scientific progress. Among his many writings, other notable works include *Antic Hay* (1923), *Point Counter Point* (1928), *Eyeless in Gaza* (1936), and *Island* (1962). The excerpt below, from *Brave New World*, introduces the reader to "Bokanovsky's Process"—a supposed scientific breakthrough where human twins can be cloned by the thousands.

FROM *Brave New World* (1932)

A squat grey building of only thirty-four stories. Over the main entrance the words, CENTRAL LONDON HATCHERY AND CONDITIONING CENTRE, and, in a shield, the World State's motto, COMMUNITY, IDENTITY, STABILITY.

The enormous room on the ground floor faced towards the north. Cold for all the summer beyond the panes, for all the tropical heat of the room itself, a harsh thin light glared through the windows, hungrily seeking some draped lay figure, some pallid shape of academic goose-flesh, but finding only the glass and nickel and bleakly shining porcelain of a laboratory. Wintriness responded to wintriness. The overalls of the workers were white, their hands gloved with a pale corpse-coloured rubber. The light was frozen, dead, a ghost. Only from the yellow barrels of the microscopes did it borrow a certain rich and living substance, lying along the polished tubes like butter, streak after luscious streak in long recession down the work tables.

"And this," said the Director opening the door, "is the Fertilizing Room."

Bent over their instruments, three hundred Fertilizers were plunged, as the Director of Hatcheries and Conditioning entered the room, in the scarcely breathing silence, the absent-minded, soliloquizing hum or whistle, of absorbed concentration. A troop of newly arrived students, very young, pink and callow, followed nervously, rather abjectly, at the Director's heels. Each of them carried a notebook, in which, whenever the great man spoke, he desperately scribbled.

Straight from the horse's mouth. It was a rare privilege. The D.H.C. for Central London always made a point of personally conducting his new students round the various departments.

"Just to give you a general idea," he would explain to them. For of course some sort of general idea they must have, if they were to do their work intelligently—though as little of one, if they were to be good and happy members of society, as possible. For particulars, as every one knows, make for virtue and happiness; generalities are intellectually necessary evils. Not philosophers but fret-sawyers and stamp collectors compose the backbone of society.

"To-morrow," he would add, smiling at them with a slightly menacing geniality, "you'll be settling down to serious work. You won't have time for generalities. Meanwhile . . ."

Meanwhile, it was a privilege. Straight from the horse's mouth into the notebook. The boys scribbled like mad.

Tall and rather thin but upright, the Director advanced into the room. He had a long chin and big, rather prominent teeth, just covered, when he was not talking, by his full, floridly curved lips. Old, young? Thirty? Fifty? Fifty-five? It was hard to say. And anyhow the question didn't arise; in this year of stability, A.F. 632, it didn't occur to you to ask it.

"I shall begin at the beginning," said the D.H.C. and the more zealous students recorded his intention in their notebooks: *Begin at the beginning.* "These," he waved his hand, "are the incubators." And opening an insulated door he showed them racks upon racks of numbered test-tubes. "The week's supply of ova. Kept," he explained, "at blood heat; whereas the male gametes," and here he opened another door, "they have to be kept at thirty-five instead of thirty-seven. [1]Full blood heat sterilizes." Rams wrapped in theremogene beget no lambs.

Still leaning against the incubators he gave them, while the pencils scurried illegibly across the pages, a brief description of the modern fertilizing process; spoke first, of course, of its surgical introduction—"the operation undergone voluntarily for the good of Society, not to mention the fact that it carries a bonus amounting to six months' salary"; continued with some account of the technique for preserving the excised ovary alive and actively developing; passed on to a consideration of optimum temperature, salinity, viscosity; referred to the liquor in which the detached and ripened eggs were kept; and, leading his charges to the work tables, actually showed them how this liquor was drawn off from the test-tubes; how it was let out drop by drop onto the specially warmed slides of the microscopes; how the eggs which it contained were inspected for abnormalities, counted and transferred to a porous receptacle; how (and he now took them to watch the operation) this receptacle was immersed in a warm bouillon containing free-swimming spermatozoa—at a minimum concentration of one hundred thousand per cubic centimetre, he

---

[1]35 and 37 degrees Centigrade are 95 and 98.6 degrees Fahrenheit, respectively.

insisted; and how, after ten minutes, the container was lifted out of the liquor and its contents re-examined; how, if any of the eggs remained unfertilized, it was again immersed, and, if necessary, yet again; how the fertilized ova went back to the incubators; where the Alphas and Betas remained until definitely bottled; while the Gammas, Deltas and Epsilons were brought out again, after only thirty-six hours, to undergo Bokanovsky's Process.

"Bokanovsky's Process," repeated the Director, and the students underlined the words in their little notebooks.

One egg, one embryo, one adult—normality. But a bokanovskified egg will bud, will proliferate, will divide. From eight to ninety-six buds, and every bud will grow into a perfectly formed embryo, and every embryo into a full-sized adult. Making ninety-six human beings grow where only one grew before. Progress.

"Essentially," the D.H.C. concluded, "bokanovskification consists of a series of arrests of development. We check the normal growth and, paradoxically enough, the egg responds by budding."

Responds by budding. The pencils were busy.

He pointed. On a very slowly band a rack-full of test-tubes was entering a large metal box, another rack-full was emerging. Machinery faintly purred. It took eight minutes for the tubes to go through, he told them. Eight minutes of hard X-rays being about as much as an egg can stand. A few died; of the rest, the least susceptible divided into two; most put out four buds; some eight; all were returned to the incubators, where the buds began to develop; then, after two days, were suddenly chilled, chilled and checked. Two, four, eight, the buds in their turn budded; and having budded were dosed almost to death with alcohol; consequently burgeoned again and having budded—bud out of bud out of bud—were thereafter—further arrest being generally fatal—left to develop in peace. By which time the original egg was in a fair way to becoming anything from eight to ninety-six embryos—a prodigious improvement, you will agree, on nature. Identical twins—but not in piddling twos and threes as in the old viviparous days, when an egg would sometimes accidentally divide; actually by dozens, by scores at a time.

"Scores," the Director repeated and flung out his arms, as though he were distributing largesse. "Scores."

But one of the students was fool enough to ask where the advantage lay.

"My good boy!" The Director wheeled sharply round on him. "Can't you see? Can't you *see*?" He raised a hand; his expression was solemn. "Bokanovsky's Process is one of the major instruments of social stability!"

Major instruments of social stability.

Standard men and women; in uniform batches. The whole of a small factory staffed with the products of a single bokanovskified egg.

"Ninety-six identical twins working ninety-six identical machines!" The voice was almost tremulous with enthusiasm. "You really know where you are. For the first time in history." He quoted the planetary motto. "Community, Identity, Stability." Grand words. "If we could bokanovskify indefinitely the whole problem would be solved."

Solved by standard Gammas, unvarying Deltas, uniform Epsilons. Millions of identical twins. The principle of mass production at last applied to biology.

"But, alas," the Director shook his head, "we *can't* bokanovskify indefinitely."

Ninety-six seemed to be the limit; seventy-two a good average. From the same ovary and with gametes of the same male to manufacture as many batches of identical twins as possible—that was the best (sadly a second best) that they could do. And even that was difficult.

"For in nature it takes thirty years for two hundred eggs to reach maturity. But our business is to stabilize the population at this moment, here and now. Dribbling out twins over a quarter of a century—what would be the use of that?"

Obviously, no use at all. But Podsnap's Technique had immensely accelerated the process of ripening. They could make sure of at least a hundred and fifty mature eggs within two years. Fertilize and bokanovskify—in other words, multiply by seventy-two—and you get an average of nearly eleven thousand brothers and sisters in a hundred and fifty batches of identical twins, all within two years of the same age.

"And in exceptional cases we can make one ovary yield us over fifteen thousand adult individuals."

Beckoning to a fair-haired, ruddy young man who happened to be passing at the moment, "Mr. Foster," he called. The ruddy young man approached. "Can you tell us the record for a single ovary, Mr. Foster?"

"Sixteen thousand and twelve in this Centre," Mr. Foster replied without hesitation. He spoke very quickly, had a vivacious blue eye, and took an evident pleasure in quoting figures. "Sixteen thousand and twelve; in one hundred and eighty-nine batches of identicals. But of course they've done much better," he rattled on, "in some of the tropical Centres. Singapore has often produced over sixteen thousand five hundred; and Mombasa has actually touched the seventeen thousand mark. But then they have unfair advantages. You should see the way a negro ovary responds to pituitary! It's quite astonishing, when you're used to working with European material. Still," he added, with a laugh (but the light of combat was in his eyes and the lift of his chin was challenging), "still, we mean to beat them if we can. I'm working on a wonderful Delta-Minus ovary at this moment. Only just eighteen months old. Over twelve thousand seven hundred children already, either decanted or in embryo. And still going strong. We'll beat them yet."

"That's the spirit I like!" cried the Director, and clapped Mr. Foster on the shoulder. "Come along with us and give these boys the benefit of your expert knowledge."

Mr. Foster smiled modestly. "With pleasure." They went.

In the Bottling Room all was harmonious bustle and ordered activity. Flaps of fresh sow's peritoneum ready cut to the proper size came shooting up in little lifts from the Organ Store in the sub-basement. Whizz and then, click! the lift-hatches flew open; the bottle-liner had only to reach out a hand, take the flap, insert, smooth-down, and before the lined bottle had had time to travel out of reach along the endless band, whizz, click! another flap of peritoneum had shot up from the depths, ready to be slipped into yet another bottle, the next of that slow interminable procession on the band.

Next to the Liners stood the Matriculators. The procession advanced; one by one the eggs were transferred from their test-tubes to the larger containers; deftly the peritoneal lining was slit, the morula dropped into place, the saline solution poured in . . . and already the bottle had passed, and it was the turn of the labellers. Heredity, date of fertilization, membership of Bokanovsky Group—details were transferred from test-tube to bottle. No longer anonymous, but named, identified, the procession marched slowly on; on through an opening in the wall, slowly on into the Social Predestination Room.

"Eighty-eight cubic metres of card-index," said Mr. Foster with relish, as they entered.

"Containing *all* the relevant information," added the Director.

"Brought up to date every morning."

"And co-ordinated every afternoon."

"On the basis of which they make their calculations."

"So many individuals, of such and such quality," said Mr. Foster.

"Distributed in such and such quantities."

"The optimum Decanting Rate at any given moment."

"Unforeseen wastages promptly made good."

"Promptly," repeated Mr. Foster. "If you knew the amount of overtime I had to put in after the last Japanese earthquake!" He laughed good-humouredly and shook his head.

"The Predestinators send in their figures to the Fertilizers."

"Who give them the embryos they ask for."

"And the bottles come in here to be predestinated in detail."

"After which they are sent down to the Embryo Store."

"Where we now proceed ourselves."

And opening a door Mr. Foster led the way down a staircase into the basement.

The temperature was still tropical. They descended into a thickening twilight. Two doors and a passage with a double turn insured the cellar against any possible infiltration of the day.

"Embryos are like photograph film," said Mr. Foster waggishly, as he pushed open the second door. "They can only stand red light."

And in effect the sultry darkness into which the students now followed him was visible and crimson, like the darkness of closed eyes on a summer's afternoon. The bulging flanks of row on receding row and tier above tier of bottles glinted with innumerable rubies, and among the rubies moved the dim red spectres of men and women with purple eyes and all the symptoms of lupus. The hum and rattle of machinery faintly stirred the air.

"Give them a few figures, Mr. Foster," said the Director, who was tired of talking.

Mr. Foster was only too happy to give them a few figures.

Two hundred and twenty metres long, two hundred wide, ten high. He pointed upwards. Like chickens drinking, the students lifted their eyes towards the distant ceiling.

Three tiers of racks: ground floor level, first gallery, second gallery.

The spidery steel-work of gallery above gallery faded away in all directions into the dark. Near them three red ghosts were busily unloading demijohns from a moving staircase.

The escalator from the Social Predestination Room.

Each bottle could be placed on one of fifteen racks, each rack, though you couldn't see it, was a conveyor travelling at the rate of thirty-three and a third centimetres an hour. Two hundred and sixty-seven days at eight metres a day. Two thousand one hundred and thirty-six metres in all. One circuit of the cellar at ground level, one on the first gallery, half on the second, and on the two hundred and sixty-seventh morning, daylight in the Decanting Room. Independent existence—so called.

"But in the interval," Mr. Foster concluded, "we've managed to do a lot to them. Oh, a very great deal." His laugh was knowing and triumphant.

"That's the spirit I like," said the Director once more. "Let's walk round. You tell them everything, Mr. Foster."

Mr. Foster duly told them.

Told them of the growing embryo on its bed of peritoneum. Made them taste the rich blood surrogate on which it fed. Explained why it had to be stimulated with placentin and thyroxin. Told them of the *corpus luteum* extract. Showed them the jets through which at every twelfth metre from zero to 2040 it was automatically injected. Spoke of those gradually increasing doses of pituitary administered during the final ninety-six metres of their course. Described the artificial maternal circulation installed on every bottle at Metre 112; showed them the reservoir of blood-surrogate, the centrifugal pump that kept the liquid moving over the placenta and drove it through the synthetic lung and waste-product filter. Referred to the embryo's troublesome tendency to anæmia, to the massive doses of hog's stomach extract and foetal foal's liver with which, in consequence, it had to be supplied.

Showed them the simple mechanism by means of which, during the last two metres out of every eight, all the embryos were simultaneously shaken into familiarity with movement. Hinted at the gravity of the so-called "trauma of decanting," and enumerated the precautions taken to minimize, by a suitable training of the bottled embryo, that dangerous shock. Told them of the tests for sex carried out in the neighbourhood of metre 200. Explained the system of labelling—a T for the males, a circle for the females and for those who were destined to become freemartins a question mark, black on a white ground.

"For of course," said Mr. Foster, "in the vast majority of cases, fertility is merely a nuisance. One fertile ovary in twelve hundred—that would really be quite sufficient for our purposes. But we want to have a good choice. And of course one must always leave an enormous margin of safety. So we allow as many as thirty per cent. of the female embryos to develop normally. The others get a dose of male sex-hormone every twenty-four metres for the rest of the course. Result: they're decanted as freemartins—structurally quite normal (except," he had to admit, "that they *do* have just the slightest tendency to grow beards), but sterile. Guaranteed sterile. Which brings us at last," continued Mr. Foster, "out of the realm of mere slavish imitation of nature into the much more interesting world of human invention."

He rubbed his hands. For of course, they didn't content themselves with merely hatching out embryos: any cow could do that.

"We also predestine and condition. We decant our babies as socialized human beings, as Alphas or Epsilons, as future sewage workers or future . . ." He was going to say "future World controllers," but correcting himself, said "future Directors of Hatcheries," instead.

The D.H.C. acknowledged the compliment with a smile.

They were passing Metre 320 on rack II. A young Beta-Minus mechanic was busy with screwdriver and spanner on the blood-surrogate pump of a passing bottle. The hum of the electric motor deepened by fractions of a tone as he turned the nuts. Down, down . . . A final twist, a glance at the revolution counter, and he was done. He moved two paces down the line and began the same process on the next pump.

"Reducing the number of revolutions per minute," Mr. Foster explained. "The surrogate goes round slower; therefore passes through the lung at longer intervals; therefore gives the embryo less oxygen. Nothing like oxygen-shortage for keeping an embryo below par." Again he rubbed his hands.

"But why do you want to keep the embryo below par?" asked an ingenuous student.

"Ass!" said the Director, breaking a long silence. "Hasn't it occurred to you that an Epsilon embryo must have an Epsilon environment as well as an Epsilon heredity?"

It evidently hadn't occurred to him. He was covered with confusion.

"The lower the caste," said Mr. Foster, "the shorter the oxygen." The first organ affected was the brain. After that the skeleton. At seventy per cent. of normal oxygen you got dwarfs. At less than seventy eyeless monsters.

"Who are no use at all," concluded Mr. Foster.

Whereas (his voice became confidential and eager), if they could discover a technique for shortening the period of maturation what a triumph, what a benefaction to Society!

"Consider the horse."

They considered it.

Mature at six; the elephant at ten. While at thirteen a man is not yet sexually mature; and is only full-grown at twenty. Hence, of course, that fruit of delayed development, the human intelligence.

"But in Epsilons," said Mr. Foster very justly, "we don't need human intelligence."

Didn't need and didn't get it. But though the Epsilon mind was mature at ten, the Epsilon body was not fit to work till eighteen. Long years of superfluous and wasted immaturity. If the physical development could be speeded up till it was as quick, say, as a cow's, what an enormous saving to the Community!

"Enormous!" murmured the students. Mr. Foster's enthusiasm was infectious.

He became rather technical; spoke of the abnormal endocrine coordination which made men grow so slowly; postulated a germinal mutation to account for it. Could the effects of this germinal mutation be undone? Could the individual Epsilon embryo be made a revert, by a suitable technique, to the normality of dogs and cows? That was the problem. And it was all but solved.

Pilkington, at Mombasa, had produced individuals who were sexually mature at four and full-grown at six and a half. A scientific triumph. But socially useless. Six-year-old men and women were too stupid to do even Epsilon work. And the process was an all-or-nothing one; either you failed to modify at all, or else you modified the whole way. They were still trying to find the ideal compromise between adults of twenty and adults of six. So far without success. Mr. Foster sighed and shook his head.

Their wanderings through the crimson twilight had brought them to the neighbourhood of Metre 170 on Rack 9. From this point onwards Rack 9 was enclosed and the bottles performed the remainder of their journey in a kind of tunnel, interrupted here and there by openings two or three metres wide.

"Heat conditioning," said Mr. Foster.

Hot tunnels alternated with cool tunnels. Coolness was wedded to discomfort in the form of hard X-rays. By the time they were decanted the embryos had a horror of cold. They were predestined to emigrate to the tropics, to be miners and acetate silk spinners and steel workers. Later on their minds would be made to endorse the judgment of their bodies. "We condition them to thrive on heat," concluded Mr. Foster. "Our colleagues upstairs will teach them to love it."

"And that," put in the Director sententiously, "that is the secret of happiness and virtue—liking what you've *got* to do. All conditioning aims at that: making people like their unescapable social destiny."

In a gap between two tunnels, a nurse was delicately probing with a long fine syringe into the gelatinous contents of a passing bottle. The students and their guides stood watching her for a few moments in silence.

"Well, Lenina," said Mr. Foster, when at last she withdrew the syringe and straightened herself up.

The girl turned with a start. One could see that, for all the lupus and the purple eyes, she was uncommonly pretty.

"Henry!" Her smile flashed redly at him—a row of coral teeth.

"Charming, charming," murmured the Director and, giving her two or three little pats, received in exchange a rather deferential smile for himself.

"What are you giving them?" asked Mr. Foster, making his tone very professional.

"Oh, the usual typhoid and sleeping sickness."

"Tropical workers start being inoculated at Metre 150," Mr. Foster explained to the students. "The embryos still have gills. We immunize the fish against the future man's diseases." Then, turning back to Lenina, "Ten to five on the roof this afternoon," he said, "as usual."

"Charming," said the Director once more, and, with a final pat, moved away after the others.

On Rack 10 rows of next generation's chemical workers were being trained in the toleration of lead, caustic soda, tar, chlorine. The first of a batch of two hundred and fifty embryonic rocket-plane engineers was just passing the eleven hundred metre mark on Rack 3. A special mechanism kept their containers in constant rotation. "To improve their sense of balance," Mr. Foster explained. "Doing repairs on the outside of a rocket in mid-air is a ticklish job. We slacken off the circulation when they're right way up, so that they're half starved, and double the flow of surrogate when they're upside down. They learn to associate topsy-turvydom with well-being; in fact, they're only truly happy when they're standing on their heads.

"And now," Mr. Foster went on, "I'd like to show you some very interesting conditioning for Alpha Plus Intellectuals. We have a big batch of them on Rack 5. First Gallery level," he called to two boys who had started to go down to the ground floor.

"They're round about Metre 900," he explained. "You can't really do any useful intellectual conditioning till the foetuses have lost their tails. Follow me."

But the Director had looked at his watch. "Ten to three," he said. "No time for the intellectual embryos, I'm afraid. We must go up to the Nurseries before the children have finished their afternoon sleep."

Mr. Foster was disappointed. "At least one glance at the Decanting Room," he pleaded.

"Very well then." The Director smiled indulgently. "Just one glance."

II

Mr. Foster was left in the Decanting Room. The D.H.C. and his students stepped into the nearest lift and were carried up to the fifth floor.

INFANT NURSERIES. NEO-PAVLOVIAN CONDITIONING ROOMS, announced the notice board.

The Director opened a door. They were in a large bare room, very bright and sunny; for the whole of the southern wall was a single window. Half a dozen nurses, trousered and jacketed in the regulation white viscose-linen uniform, their hair aseptically hidden under white caps, were engaged in setting out bowls of roses in a long row across the floor. Big bowls, packed tight with blossom. Thousands of petals, ripe-blown and silkily smooth, like the cheeks of innumerable little cherubs, but of cherubs, in that bright light, not exclusively pink and Aryan, but also luminously Chinese, also Mexican, also apoplectic with too much blowing of celestial trumpets, also pale as death, pale with the posthumous whiteness of marble.

The nurses stiffened to attention as the D.H.C. came in.

"Set out the books," he said curtly.

In silence the nurses obeyed his command. Between the rose bowls the books were duly set out—a row of nursery quartos opened invitingly each at some gaily coloured image of beast or fish or bird.

"Now bring in the children."

They hurried out of the room and returned in a minute or two, each pushing a kind of tall dumbwaiter laden, on all its four wire-netted shelves, with eight-month-old babies, all exactly alike (a Bokanovsky Group, it was evident) and all (since their caste was Delta) dressed in khaki.

"Put them down on the floor."

The infants were unloaded.

"Now turn them so that they can see the flowers and books."

Turned, the babies at once fell silent, then began to crawl towards those clusters of sleek colours, those shapes so gay and brilliant on the white pages. As they approached, the sun came out of a momentary eclipse behind a cloud. The roses flamed up as though with a sudden passion from within; a new and profound significance seemed to suffuse the shining pages of the books. From the ranks of the crawling babies came little squeals of excitement, gurgles and twitterings of pleasure.

The Director rubbed his hands. "Excellent!" he said. "It might almost have been done on purpose."

The swiftest crawlers were already at their goal. Small hands reached out uncertainly, touched, grasped, unpetaling the transfigured roses, crumpling the illuminated pages of the books. The Director waited until all were happily busy. Then, "Watch carefully," he said. And, lifting his hand, he gave the signal.

The Head Nurse, who was standing by a switchboard at the other end of the room, pressed down a little lever.

There was a violent explosion. Shriller and ever shriller, a siren shrieked. Alarm bells maddeningly sounded.

The children started, screamed; their faces were distorted with terror.

"And now," the Director shouted (for the noise was deafening), "now we proceed to rub in the lesson with a mild electric shock."

He waved his hand again, and the Head Nurse pressed a second lever. The screaming of the babies suddenly changed its tone. There was something desperate, almost insane, about the sharp spasmodic yelps to which they now gave utterance. Their little bodies twitched and stiffened; their limbs moved jerkily as if to the tug of unseen wires.

"We can electrify that whole strip of floor," bawled the Director in explanation. "But that's enough," he signalled to the nurse.

The explosions ceased, the bells stopped ringing, the shriek of the siren died down from tone to tone into silence. The stiffly twitching bodies relaxed, and what had become the sob and yelp of infant maniacs broadened out once more into a normal howl of ordinary terror.

"Offer them the flowers and the books again."

The nurses obeyed; but at the approach of the roses, at the mere sight of those gaily-coloured images of pussy and cock-a-doodle-doo and baa-baa black sheep, the infants shrank away in horror; the volume of their howling suddenly increased.

"Observe," said the Director triumphantly, "observe."

Books and loud noises, flowers and electric shocks—already in the infant mind these couples were compromisingly linked; and after two hundred repetitions of the same or a similar lesson would be wedded indissolubly. What man has joined, nature is powerless to put asunder.

"They'll grow up with what the psychologists used to call an 'instinctive' hatred of books and flowers. Reflexes unalterably conditioned. They'll be safe from books and botany all their lives." The Director turned to his nurses. "Take them away again."

Still yelling, the khaki babies were loaded on to their dumb-waiters and wheeled out, leaving behind them the smell of sour milk and a most welcome silence.

One of the students held up his hand; and though he could see quite well why you couldn't have lower-caste people wasting the Community's time over books, and that there was always the risk of their reading something which might undesirably decondition one of their reflexes, yet . . . well, he couldn't understand about the flowers. Why go to the trouble of making it psychologically impossible for Deltas to like flowers?

Patiently the D.H.C. explained. If the children were made to scream at the sight of a rose, that was on grounds of high economic policy. Not so very long ago (a century or thereabouts), Gammas, Deltas, even Epsilons, had been conditioned to like flowers—flowers in particular and wild nature in general. The idea was to make them want to be going out into the country at every available opportunity, and so compel them to consume transport.

"And didn't they consume transport?" asked the student.

"Quite a lot," the D.H.C. replied. "But nothing else."

Primroses and landscapes, he pointed out, have one grave defect: they are gratuitous. A love of nature keeps no factories busy. It was decided to abolish the love of nature, at any rate among the lower classes; to abolish the love of nature, but *not* the tendency to consume transport. For of course it was essential that they should keep on going to the country, even though they hated it. The problem was to find an economically sounder reason for consuming transport than a mere affection for primroses and landscapes. It was duly found.

"We condition the masses to hate the country," concluded the Director. "But simultaneously we condition them to love all country sports. At the same time, we see to it that all country sports shall entail the use of elaborate apparatus.

So that they consume manufactured articles as well as transport. Hence those electric shocks."

"I see," said the student, and was silent, lost in admiration.

There was a silence; then, clearing his throat, "Once upon a time," the Director began, "while our Ford was still on earth, there was a little boy called Reuben Rabinovitch. Reuben was the child of Polish-speaking parents." The Director interrupted himself. "You know what Polish is, I suppose?"

"A dead language."

"Like French and German," added another student, officiously showing off his learning.

"And 'parent'?" questioned the D.H.C.

There was an uneasy silence. Several of the boys blushed. They had not yet learned to draw the significant but often very fine distinction between smut and pure science. One, at last, had the courage to raise a hand.

"Human beings used to be . . ." he hesitated; the blood rushed to his cheeks. "Well, they used to be viviparous."

"Quite right." The Director nodded approvingly.

"And when the babies were decanted . . ."

"'Born'," came the correction.

"Well, then they were the parents—I mean, not the babies, of course; the other ones." The poor boy was overwhelmed with confusion.

"In brief," the Director summed up, "the parents were the father and the mother." The smut that was really science fell with a crash into the boys' eye-avoiding silence. "Mother," he repeated loudly rubbing in the science; and, leaning back in his chair, "These," he said gravely, "are unpleasant facts; I know it. But then most historical facts *are* unpleasant."

He returned to Little Reuben—to Little Reuben, in whose room, one evening, by an oversight, his father and mother (crash, crash!) happened to leave the radio turned on.

("For you must remember that in those days of gross viviparous reproduction, children were always brought up by their parents and not in State Conditioning Centres.")

While the child was asleep, a broadcast programme from London suddenly started to come through; and the next morning, to the astonishment of his crash and crash (the more daring of the boys ventured to grin at one another), Little Reuben woke up repeating word for word a long lecture by that curious old writer ("one of the very few whose works have been permitted to come down to us"), George Bernard Shaw,[2] who was speaking, according to a well-authenticated tradition, about his own genius. To Little Reuben's wink and snigger, this lecture was, of course, perfectly incomprehensible and, imagining that their child had suddenly gone mad, they sent for a doctor. He, fortunately, understood English, recognized the discourse as that which Shaw had

---

[2](1856–1960), British playwright

broadcasted the previous evening, realized the significance of what had happened, and sent a letter to the medical press about it.

"The principle of sleep-teaching, or hypnopædia, had been discovered." The D.H.C. made an impressive pause.

The principle had been discovered; but many, many years were to elapse before that principle was usefully applied.

"The case of Little Reuben occurred only twenty-three years after Our Ford's first T-Model was put on the market." (Here the Director made a sign of the T on his stomach and all the students reverently followed suit.) "And yet . . ."

Furiously the students scribbled. "*Hypnopædia, first used officially in A.F. 214. Why not before? Two reasons. (a) . . .*"

"These early experimenters," the D.H.C. was saying, "were on the wrong track. They thought that hypnopædia could be made an instrument of intellectual education . . ."

(A small boy asleep on his right side, the right arm stuck out, the right hand hanging limp over the edge of the bed. Through a round grating in the side of a box a voice speaks softly.

"The Nile is the longest river in Africa and the second in length of all the rivers of the globe. Although falling short of the length of the Mississippi-Missouri, the Nile is at the head of all rivers as regards the length of its basin, which extends through 35 degrees of latitude . . ."

At breakfast the next morning, "Tommy," some one says, "do you know which is the longest river in Africa?" A shaking of the head. "But don't you remember something that begins: The Nile is the . . ."

"The-Nile-is-the-longest-river-in-Africa-and-the-second-in-length-of-all-the-rivers-of-the-globe . . ." The words come rushing out. "Although-falling-short-of . . ."

"Well now, which is the longest river in Africa?"

The eyes are blank. "I don't know."

"But the Nile, Tommy."

"The-Nile-is-the-longest-river-in-Africa-and-second . . ."

"Then which river is the longest, Tommy?"

Tommy bursts into tears. "I don't know," he howls.)

That howl, the Director made it plain, discouraged the earliest investigators. The experiments were abandoned. No further attempt was made to teach children the length of the Nile in their sleep. Quite rightly. You can't learn a science unless you know what it's all about.

"Whereas, if they'd only started on *moral* education," said the Director, leading the way towards the door. The students followed him, desperately scribbling as they walked and all the way up in the lift. "Moral education, which ought never, in any circumstances, to be rational."

"Silence, silence," whispered a loud speaker as they stepped out at the fourteenth floor, and "Silence, silence," the trumpet mouths indefatigably repeated at intervals down every corridor. The students and even the Director himself rose automatically to the tips of their toes. They were Alphas, of course; but even Alphas have been well conditioned. "Silence, silence." All the air of the fourteenth floor was sibilant with the categorical imperative.

Fifty yards of tiptoeing brought them to a door which the Director cautiously opened. They stepped over the threshold into the twilight of a shuttered dormitory. Eighty cots stood in a row against the wall. There was a sound of light regular breathing and a continuous murmur, as of very faint voices remotely whispering.

A nurse rose as they entered and came to attention before the Director.

"What's the lesson this afternoon?" he asked.

"We had Elementary Sex for the first forty minutes," she answered. "But now it's switched over to Elementary Class Consciousness."

The Director walked slowly down the long line of cots. Rosy and relaxed with sleep, eighty little boys and girls lay softly breathing. There was a whisper under every pillow. The D.H.C. halted and, bending over one of the little beds, listened attentively.

"Elementary Class Consciousness, did you say? Let's have it repeated a little louder by the trumpet."

At the end of the room a loud speaker projected from the wall. The Director walked up to it and pressed a switch.

"... all wear green," said a soft but very distinct voice, beginning in the middle of a sentence, "and Delta Children wear khaki. Oh no, I don't want to play with Delta children. And Epsilons are still worse. They're too stupid to be able to read or write. Besides they wear black, which is such a beastly colour. I'm *so* glad I'm a Beta."

There was a pause; then the voice began again.

"Alpha children wear grey. They work much harder than we do, because they're so frightfully clever. I'm really awfully glad I'm a Beta, because I don't work so hard. And then we are much better than the Gammas and Deltas. Gammas are stupid. They all wear green, and Delta children wear khaki. Oh no, I *don't* want to play with Delta children. And Epsilons are still worse. They're too stupid to be able . . ."

The Director pushed back the switch. The voice was silent. Only its thin ghost continued to mutter from beneath the eighty pillows.

"They'll have that repeated forty or fifty times more before they wake; then again on Thursday, and again on Saturday. A hundred and twenty times three times a week for thirty months. After which they go on to a more advanced lesson."

Roses and electric shocks, the khaki of Deltas and a whiff of asafœtida— wedded indissolubly before the child can speak. But wordless conditioning is crude and wholesale; cannot bring home the finer distinctions, cannot inculcate the more complex courses of behaviour. For that there must be words, but words without reason. In brief, hypnopædia.

"The greatest moralizing and socializing force of all time."

The students took it down in their little books. Straight from the horse's mouth.

Once more the Director touched the switch.

". . . so frightfully clever," the soft, insinuating, indefatigable voice was saying. "I'm really awfully glad I'm a Beta, because . . ."

Not so much like drops of water, though water, it is true, can wear holes in the hardest granite; rather, drops of liquid sealing-wax, drops that adhere, incrust, incorporate themselves with what they fall on, till finally the rock is all one scarlet blob.

"Till at last the child's mind *is* these suggestions, and the sum of the suggestions *is* the child's mind. And not the child's mind only. The adult's mind too—all his life long. The mind that judges and desires and decides—made up of these suggestions. But all these suggestions are *our* suggestions!" The Director almost shouted in his triumph. "Suggestions from the State." He banged the nearest table. "It therefore follows . . ."

A noise made him turn around.

"Oh, Ford!" he said in another tone, "I've gone and woken the children."

Study and Discussion Questions

1. Why, in the world of *Brave New World,* are babies manufactured rather than born? Why are they conditioned so thoroughly once they've been made?
2. Who is "Our Ford" and why is the present year called "A.F. 632"? Why does the Director (when he is explaining the discovery of hypnopaedia) make "a sign of the T on his stomach" when he mentions "Our Ford"?
3. Why does Huxley repeatedly emphasize the diligence with which the students copy down the Director's every word?
4. What are some of the ways Huxley shapes our attitude toward the society he describes? Begin by looking at the imagery in the second paragraph.
5. What can we infer, from these first two chapters, about the political and economic structure of the society depicted in *Brave New World?*

Suggestions for Writing

1. Critics often discuss science fiction and utopian or dystopian literature in terms of "extrapolation," that is, a projection of current social trends into a distant future. What aspects of twentieth-century society are illuminated (and satirized) in this extrapolation?
2. The society of *Brave New World,* we learn later, provides its inhabitants with material abundance, unlimited physical pleasure, and freedom from unhappiness. Then what exactly is wrong with this society?
3. Is social conditioning always bad? What criteria could you suggest for deciding when it is good and when it is not? And how it should be accomplished?

❀ ❀ ❀

JAMAICA KINCAID (b. 1950)

Elaine Potter Richardson (Kincaid's original name) was born in St. John's, Antigua, in the Caribbean. The only daughter in a family of four children, Richardson left Antigua for the United States in 1966 at the age of 17 and entered the New School for Social Research in New York City to study photography and began to write. In 1973, Richardson changed her name to Jamaica Kincaid so she could write anonymously and in 1976 landed a job as a staff writer at *The New Yorker*, a job she held until 1995. While at *The New Yorker*, Kincaid published a collection of short stories, *At the Bottom of the River* (1983), as well as the novels *Annie John* (1985), *Lucy* (1990), and *A Small Place* (1988)—a book-length essay on the British legacy in Antigua after independence in 1981. Since 1995, Kincaid's works include *Autobiography of My Mother* (1996), *My Brother* (1997), *My Favorite Plant* (1988), and *My Garden Book* (1999). She currently teaches and lives in Bennington, Vermont. "Girl" is an early example of a recurring theme in Kincaid's work: the complex relationship between mothers and daughters.

Girl   (1983)

Wash the white clothes on Monday and put them on the stone heap; wash the color clothes on Tuesday and put them on the clothesline to dry; don't walk barehead in the hot sun; cook pumpkin fritters in very hot sweet oil; soak your little cloths right after you take them off; when buying cotton to make yourself a nice blouse, be sure that it doesn't have gum on it, because that way it won't hold up well after a wash; soak salt fish overnight before you cook it; is it true that you sing benna[1] in Sunday school?; always eat your food in such a way that it won't turn someone else's stomach; on Sundays try to walk like a lady and not like the slut you are so bent on becoming; don't sing benna in Sunday school; you mustn't speak to wharf-rat boys, not even to give directions; don't eat fruits on the street—flies will follow you; *but I don't sing benna on Sundays at all and never in Sunday school;* this is how to sew on a button; this is how to make a buttonhole for the button you have just sewed on; this is how to hem a dress when you see the hem coming down and so to prevent yourself from looking like the slut I know you are so bent on becoming; this is how you iron your father's khaki shirt so that it doesn't have a crease; this is how you iron your father's khaki pants so that they don't have a crease; this is how you grow okra—far from the house, because okra tree harbors red ants; when you are growing dasheen, make sure it gets plenty of water or else it

---

[1]Calypso or rock and roll.

makes your throat itch when you are eating it; this is how you sweep a corner; this is how you sweep a whole house; this is how you sweep a yard; this is how you smile to someone you don't like too much; this is how you smile to someone you don't like at all; this is how to smile to someone you like completely; this is how you set a table for tea; this is how you set a table for dinner; this is how you set a table for dinner with an important guest; this is how you set a table for lunch; this is how you set a table for breakfast, this is how to behave in the presence of men who don't know you very well, and this way they won't recognize immediately the slut I have warned you against becoming; be sure to wash every day, even if it is with your own spit: don't squat down to play marbles—you are not a boy, you know; don't pick people's flowers—you might catch something; don't throw stones at blackbirds, because it might not be a blackbird at all; this is how to make a bread pudding; this is how to make doukona; this is how to make pepper pot; this is how to make a good medicine for a cold; this is how to make a good medicine to throw away a child before it even becomes a child; this is how to catch a fish; this is how to throw back a fish you don't like, and that way something bad won't fall on you; this is how to bully a man; this is how a man bullies you; this is how to love a man, and if this doesn't work there are other ways, and if they don't work don't feel too bad about giving up; this is how to spit up in the air if you feel like it, and this is how to move quick so that it doesn't fall on you; this is how to make ends meet; always squeeze bread to make sure it's fresh; *but what if the baker won't let me feel the bread?;* you mean to say that after all you are really going to be the kind of woman who the baker won't let near the bread?

Study and Discussion Questions

1. Who is speaking? To whom? How old do you think the girl being addressed is?
2. Categorize and characterize the advice given.
3. What seems to be the speaker's main concern? What evidence is there that she has it in mind even when she's not talking about it directly?
4. Analyze the impact of the narrator's stringing so many words of advice together. What else makes the story funny?

Suggestions for Writing

1. What would the girl grow up to be like if the followed all the advice given? Discuss the story as a comment on women's roles in society.
2. Choose someone—a parent, older sibling, employer, teacher—who gives too much advice and write a short piece modeled on "Girl."

❋ ❋ ❋

TONI MORRISON (B. 1931)

Born in Lorain, Ohio, Toni Morrison received a B.A. in English from Howard University and her M.A. in English at Cornell. Yet it was her early life experiences in Ohio that would become a cornerstone of her writing: "No matter what I write, I begin there . . . Ohio offers an escape from the stereotyped black settings. It is neither plantation or ghetto" (*Black Women Writers at Work*, 1986). From such a vantage point, Morrison has sought to offer a more complicated version of the African American experience—one infused with myth and folklore, race and identity. After teaching for a few years, Morrison accepted a position as a book editor at Random House in New York in 1964. In 1969, Morrison published her first book, *The Bluest Eye*, at the age of 38. She spent the next 25 years at Random House, helping raise public awareness of other black writers as well as publishing her own work: *Sula* (1973); *Song of Solomon* (1977); *Tar Baby* (1981); *Beloved* (1987), which won the Pulitzer Prize for Fiction; *Jazz* (1992); *Paradise* (1998); and her most recent novel, *Love* (2003). In addition to her novels Morrison has written and edited several critical works, including *Playing in the Dark: Whiteness and the Literary Imagination* (1992), and coauthored several children's books with her son Slade Morrison. In 1993, Morrison became the first African American to win the Nobel Prize for literature. The excerpt below, taken from *The Bluest Eye*, looks at a young black girl's reaction to the "blue-eyed, yellow-haired, pink-skinned doll" given to her for Christmas.

FROM *The Bluest Eye*   (1970)

It had begun with Christmas and the gift of dolls. The big, the special, the loving gift was always a big, blue-eyed Baby Doll. From the clucking sounds of adults I knew that the doll represented what they thought was my fondest wish. I was bemused with the thing itself, and the way it looked. What was I supposed to do with it? Pretend I was its mother? I had no interest in babies or the concept of motherhood. I was interested only in humans my own age and size, and could not generate any enthusiasm at the prospect of being a mother. Motherhood was old age, and other remote possibilities. I learned quickly, however, what I was expected to do with the doll: rock it, fabricate storied situations around it, even sleep with it. Picture books were full of little girls sleeping with their dolls. Raggedy Ann dolls usually, but they were out of the question. I was physically revolted by and secretly frightened of those round moronic eyes, the pancake face, and orangeworms hair.

The other dolls, which were supposed to bring me great pleasure, succeeded in doing quite the opposite. When I took it to bed, its hard unyielding limbs resisted my flesh—the tapered fingertips on those dimpled hands scratched. If, in sleep, I turned, the bone-cold head collided with my own. It was a most uncomfortable, patently aggressive sleeping companion. To hold it was no more rewarding. The starched gauze or lace on the cotton dress irritated any embrace. I had only one desire: to dismember it. To see of what it was made, to discover the dearness, to find the beauty, the desirability that had escaped me, but apparently only me. Adults, older girls, shops, magazines, newspapers, window signs—all the world had agreed that a blue-eyed, yellow-haired, pink-skinned doll was what every girl child treasured. "Here," they said, "this is beautiful, and if you are on this day 'worthy' you may have it." I fingered the face, wondering at the single-stroke eyebrows; picked at the pearly teeth stuck like two piano keys between red bowline lips. Traced the turned-up nose, poked the glassy blue eyeballs, twisted the yellow hair. I could not love it. But I could examine it to see what it was that all the world said was lovable. Break off the tiny fingers, bend the flat feet, loosen the hair, twist the head around, and the thing made one sound—a sound they said was the sweet and plaintive cry "Mama," but which sounded to me like the bleat of a dying lamb, or, more precisely, our icebox door opening on rusty hinges in July. Remove the cold and stupid eyeball, it would bleat still, "Ahhhhhh," take off the head, shake out the sawdust, crack the back against the brass bed rail, it would bleat still. The gauze back would split, and I could see the disk with six holes, the secret of the sound. A mere metal roundness.

Grown people frowned and fussed: "You-don't-know-how-to-take-care-of-nothing. I-never-had-a-baby-doll-in-my-whole-life-and-used-to-cry-my-eyes-out-for-them. Now-you-got-one-a-beautiful-one-and-you-tear-it-up-what's-the-matter-with-you?"

How strong was their outrage. Tears threatened to erase the aloofness of their authority. The emotion of years of unfulfilled longing preened in their voices. I did not know why I destroyed those dolls. But I did know that nobody ever asked me what I wanted for Christmas. Had any adult with the power to fulfill my desires taken me seriously and asked me what I wanted, they would have known that I did not want to have anything to own, or to possess any object. I wanted rather to feel something on Christmas day. The real question would have been, "Dear Claudia, what experience would you like on Christmas?" I could have spoken up, "I want to sit on the low stool in Big Mama's kitchen with my lap full of lilacs and listen to Big Papa play his violin for me alone." The lowness of the stool made for my body, the security and warmth of Big Mama's kitchen, the smell of the lilacs, the sound of the music, and, since it would be good to have all of my senses engaged, the taste of a peach, perhaps, afterward.

Instead I tasted and smelled the acridness of tin plates and cups designed for tea parties that bored me. Instead I looked with loathing on new dresses that required a hateful bath in a galvanized zinc tub before wearing. Slipping around on the zinc, no time to play or soak, for the water chilled too fast, no time to enjoy one's nakedness, only time to make curtains of soapy water careen down between the legs. Then the scratchy towels and the dreadful and humiliating absence of dirt. The irritable, unimaginative cleanliness. Gone the ink marks from legs and face, all my creations and accumulations of the day gone, and replaced by goose pimples.

I destroyed white baby dolls.

But the dismembering of dolls was not the true horror. The truly horrifying thing was the transference of the same impulses to little white girls. The indifference with which I could have axed them was shaken only by my desire to do so. To discover what eluded me: the secret of the magic they weaved on others. What made people look at them and say, "Awwwww," but not for me? The eye slide of black women as they approached them on the street, and the possessive gentleness of their touch as they handled them.

If I pinched them, their eyes—unlike the crazed glint of the baby doll's eyes—would fold in pain, and their cry would not be the sound of an icebox door, but a fascinating cry of pain. When I learned how repulsive this disinterested violence was, that it was repulsive because it was disinterested, my shame floundered about for refuge. The best hiding place was love. Thus the conversion from pristine sadism to fabricated hatred, to fraudulent love. It was a small step to Shirley Temple. I learned much later to worship her, just as I learned to delight in cleanliness, knowing, even as I learned, that the change was adjustment without improvement.

Study and Discussion Questions

1. Why do adults give dolls to little girls?
2. Why does Claudia hate Shirley Temple?
3. What's wrong with the Christmas baby doll Claudia is given?
4. What would Claudia really like for Christmas?
5. How does Claudia's description of the doll undermine its purported beauty? What words and images does Morrison use?
6. What does the paragraph about taking a bath have to do with the subject of baby dolls?
7. Claudia says she transferred her destructive impulses toward dolls "to little white girls." How do you think this happens? Is she justified in feeling this way?
8. Why is love the best hiding place for shame?

Suggestions for Writing

1. Select one of the substantial paragraphs in this excerpt and analyze Morrison's imagery, her language, and how she makes a small unified episode out of the paragraph.
2. Were you given a Christmas or birthday present you hated when you were a child? Write a letter to the giver saying how and why you hated the present.

3. Make an argument for or against giving children toys that socialize them into gender-specific roles as adults. You might pick a particular toy to use as an example.

4. What is "adjustment without improvement" in the context of this piece of writing? What do you think Morrison is saying about how children are socialized—and particularly about how black children are socialized into a white world?

SANDRA CISNEROS (b. 1954)

Sandra Cisneros spent much of her young life moving with her family back and forth between Chicago, where she was born, and Mexico City. In an often repeated quote, she describes her independent feminine self as the "daughter of a Mexican father and a Mexican-American mother . . . sister to six brothers . . . nobody's mother and nobody's wife" (Introduction, *The House on Mango Street*, 1991). Cisneros draws frequently on her adolescent experience as a Latina in a working-class household of boys to explore issues of gender and race in both her poetry and prose. Her writings include the poetry collections *Bad Boys* (1980), *My Wicked, Wicked Ways* (1987), and *Loose Woman* (1994); the award-winning *The House on Mango Street* (1984) and *Woman Hollering Creek and Other Stories* (1991); the bilingual juvenile novel *Hairs/Pelitos* (1994); and her most recent prose work, *Caramelo* (2002). The short piece "The Family of Little Feet" is taken from *The House on Mango Street*.

The Family of Little Feet   (1984)

There was a family. All were little. Their arms were little, and their hands were little, and their height was not tall, and their feet very small.

The grandpa slept on the living room couch and snored through his teeth. His feet were fat and doughy like thick tamales, and these he powdered and stuffed into white socks and brown leather shoes.

The grandma's feet were lovely as pink pearls and dressed in velvety high heels that made her walk with a wobble, but she wore them anyway because they were pretty.

The baby's feet had ten tiny toes, pale and see-through like a salamander's, and these he popped into his mouth whenever he was hungry.

The mother's feet, plump and polite, descended like white pigeons from the sea of pillow, across the linoleum roses, down down the wooden stairs, over the chalk hopscotch squares. 5, 6, 7, blue sky.

Do you want this? And gave us a paper bag with one pair of lemon shoes and one red and one pair of dancing shoes that used to be white but were now pale blue. Here, and we said thank you and waited until she went upstairs.

Hurray! Today we are Cinderella because our feet fit exactly, and we laugh at Rachel's one foot with a girl's grey sock and a lady's high heel. Do you like these shoes? But the truth is it is scary to look down at your foot that is no longer yours and see attached a long long leg.

Everybody wants to trade. The lemon shoes for the red shoes, the red for the pair that were once white but are now pale blue, the pale blue for the lemon, and take them off and put them back on and keep on like this a long time until we are tired.

Then Lucy screams to take our socks off and yes, it's true. We have legs. Skinny and spotted with satin scars where scabs were picked, but legs, all our own, good to look at, and long.

It's Rachel who learns to walk the best all strutted in those magic high heels. She teaches us to cross and uncross our legs, and to run like a double-dutch rope, and how to walk down to the corner so that the shoes talk back to you with every step. Lucy, Rachel, me tee-tottering like so. Down to the corner where the men can't take their eyes off us. We must be Christmas.

Mr. Benny at the corner grocery puts down his important cigar: Your mother know you got shoes like that? Who give you those?

Nobody.

Them are dangerous, he says. You girls too young to be wearing shoes like that. Take them shoes off before I call the cops, but we just run.

On the avenue a boy on a home-made bicycle calls out: Ladies, lead me to heaven.

But there is nobody around but us.

Do you like these shoes? Rachel says yes, and Lucy says yes, and yes I say, these are the best shoes. We will never go back to wearing the other kind again. Do you like these shoes?

In front of the laundromat six girls with the same fat face pretend we are invisible. They are the cousins, Lucy says, and always jealous. We just keep strutting.

Across the street in front of the tavern a bum man on the stoop.

Do you like these shoes?

Bum man says, Yes, little girl. Your little lemon shoes are so beautiful. But come closer. I can't see very well. Come closer. Please.

You are a pretty girl, bum man continues. What's your name, pretty girl?

And Rachel says Rachel, just like that.

Now you know to talk to drunks is crazy and to tell them your name is worse, but who can blame her. She is young and dizzy to hear so many sweet things in one day, even if it is a bum man's whiskey words saying them.

Rachel, you are prettier than a yellow taxi cab. You know that.

But we don't like it. We got to go, Lucy says.

If I give you a dollar will you kiss me? How about a dollar. I give you a dollar, and he looks in his pocket for wrinkled money.

We have to go right now, Lucy says taking Rachel's hand because she looks like she's thinking about that dollar.

Bum man is yelling something to the air but by now we are running fast and far away, our high heel shoes taking us all the way down the avenue and around the block, past the ugly cousins, past Mr. Benny's, up Mango Street, the back way, just in case.

We are tired of being beautiful. Lucy hides the lemon shoes and the red shoes and the shoes that used to be white but are now pale blue under a powerful bushel basket on the back porch, until one Tuesday her mother, who is very clean, throws them away. But no one complains.

Study and Discussion Questions

1. About how old do you think Lucy, Rachel, and the speaker of this first-person plural story, Esperanza, are? What clues lead you to think this?
2. How are the high heels "magic"? Discuss the journey of these talismans through the girls' day—how they arrive, how they depart, and what the nature of their magic is.
3. Give examples of Cisneros's use of imagery, literal or figurative, in this story. What effect do these images have?
4. In one sense, this is a children's game of "dress up." What are the girls playing at?
5. How are the three girls seen differently by others after they take off their socks and put on the high heels? Give some examples.
6. Mr. Benny at the corner grocery comments that the shoes "are dangerous." Is he correct? How are the shoes dangerous?
7. "We are tired of being beautiful," begins the last paragraph of the story. What do you think the three girls learned from the high-heels game? What does the experience Lucy, Rachel, and Esperanza have with the high heels suggest about the passage from girlhood to womanhood?

Suggestions for Writing

1. Cisneros could have chosen to tell this story in the past tense and in the voice of an adult remembering an incident from her childhood. Instead, she gives us a young girl's voice and present tense. Do you find this perspective effective? What does Cisneros gain from choosing the child's voice? What might she be losing?
2. Write about an experience from your own childhood/youth when you got a glimpse, whether welcome or not, into the adult world or into your own future as a grown-up.

❀ ❀ ❀

JAMES BALDWIN (1924–1987)

Son of a Harlem preacher, Baldwin himself began preaching at age 14; this experience and his early religious training would have an enduring effect on his writing style. Throughout the 1950s and 1960s, Baldwin was a voice for civil rights, speaking and writing in protest of racial hatred. In both his essays and novels, he seeks to understand the social and psychological effects of racism and the role of love in combating such forces. He is perhaps best known for his nonfiction essays, collected in *Notes of a Native Son* (1955), *Nobody Knows My Name* (1961), and *The Fire Next Time* (1963), and for his fiction *Go Tell It On The Mountain* (1953), a coming-of-age story about a young black man in Harlem; *Giovanni's* Room (1956), a novel about gay life in Paris; and *Going to Meet the Man* (1965), a collection of short stories. He has also won acclaim as a dramatist, with *The Amen Corner* (1955) and *Blues for Mister Charlie* (1964). "Sonny's Blues," published in 1957, is demonstrative of the emotional, lyrical prose found in much of Baldwin's work.

Sonny's Blues   (1957)

I read about it in the paper, in the subway, on my way to work. I read it, and I couldn't believe it, and I read it again. Then perhaps I just stared at it, at the newsprint spelling out his name, spelling out the story. I stared at it in the swinging lights of the subway car, and in the faces and bodies of the people, and in my own face, trapped in the darkness which roared outside.

It was not to be believed and I kept telling myself that, as I walked from the subway station to the high school. And at the same time I couldn't doubt it. I was scared, scared for Sonny. He became real to me again. A great block of ice got settled in my belly and kept melting there slowly all day long, while I taught my classes algebra. It was a special kind of ice. It kept melting, sending trickles of ice water all up and down my veins, but it never got less. Sometimes it hardened and seemed to expand until I felt my guts were going to come spilling out or that I was going to choke or scream. This would always be at a moment when I was remembering some specific thing Sonny had once said or done.

When he was about as old as the boys in my classes his face had been bright and open, there was a lot of copper in it; and he'd had wonderfully direct brown eyes, and great gentleness and privacy. I wondered what he looked like now. He had been picked up, the evening before, in a raid on an apartment downtown, for peddling and using heroin.

I couldn't believe it: but what I mean by that is that I couldn't find any room for it anywhere inside me. I had kept it outside me for a long time. I hadn't wanted to know. I had had suspicions, but I didn't name them, I kept putting them away. I told myself that Sonny was wild, but he wasn't crazy. And he'd always been a good boy, he hadn't ever turned hard or evil or disrespectful, the way kids can, so quick, so quick, especially in Harlem. I didn't want to believe that I'd ever see my brother going down, coming to nothing, all that light in his face gone out, in the condition I'd already seen so many others. Yet it had happened and here I was, talking about algebra to a lot of boys who might, every one of them for all I knew, be popping off needles every time they went to the head. Maybe it did more for them than algebra could.

I was sure that the first time Sonny had ever had horse, he couldn't have been much older than these boys were now. These boys, now, were living as we'd been living then, they were growing up with a rush and their heads bumped abruptly against the low ceiling of their actual possibilities. They were filled with rage. All they really knew were two darknesses, the darkness of their lives, which was now closing in on them, and the darkness of the movies, which had blinded them to that other darkness, and in which they now, vindictively, dreamed, at once more together than they were at any other time, and more alone.

When the last bell rang, the last class ended, I let out my breath. It seemed I'd been holding it for all that time. My clothes were wet—I may have looked as though I'd been sitting in a steam bath, all dressed up, all afternoon. I sat alone in the classroom a long time. I listened to the boys outside, downstairs, shouting and cursing and laughing. Their laughter struck me for perhaps the first time. It was not the joyous laughter which—God knows why—one associates with children. It was mocking and insular, its intent was to denigrate. It was disenchanted, and in this, also, lay the authority of their curses. Perhaps I was listening to them because I was thinking about my brother and in them I heard my brother. And myself.

One boy was whistling a tune, at once very complicated and very simple, it seemed to be pouring out of him as though he were a bird, and it sounded very cool and moving through all that harsh, bright air, only just holding its own through all those other sounds.

I stood up and walked over to the window and looked down into the courtyard. It was the beginning of the spring and the sap was rising in the boys. A teacher passed through them every now and again, quickly, as though he or she couldn't wait to get out of that courtyard, to get those boys out of their sight and off their minds. I started collecting my stuff. I thought I'd better get home and talk to Isabel.

The courtyard was almost deserted by the time I got downstairs. I saw this boy standing in the shadow of a doorway, looking just like Sonny. I almost called his name. Then I saw that it wasn't Sonny, but somebody we used to know, a boy from around our block. He'd been Sonny's friend. He'd never been mine, having been too young for me, and, anyway, I'd never liked him. And now, even though he was a grown-up man, he still hung around that block, still spent hours on the street corners, was always high and raggy. I used to run into him from time to time and he'd often work around to asking me for a quarter or fifty cents. He always had some real good excuse, too, and I always gave it to him, I don't know why.

But now, abruptly, I hated him. I couldn't stand the way he looked at me, partly like a dog, partly like a cunning child. I wanted to ask him what the hell he was doing in the school courtyard.

He sort of shuffled over to me, and he said, "I see you got the papers. So you already know about it."

"You mean about Sonny? Yes, I already know about it. How come they didn't get you?"

He grinned. It made him repulsive and it also brought to mind what he'd looked like as a kid. "I wasn't there. I stay away from them people."

"Good for you." I offered him a cigarette and I watched him through the smoke. "You come all the way down here just to tell me about Sonny?"

"That's right." He was sort of shaking his head and his eyes looked strange, as though they were about to cross. The bright sun deadened his damp dark brown skin and it made his eyes look yellow and showed up the dirt in his kinked hair. He smelled funky. I moved a little away from him and I said, "Well, thanks. But I already know about it and I got to get home."

"I'll walk you a little ways," he said. We started walking. There were a couple of kids still loitering in the courtyard and one of them said goodnight to me and looked strangely at the boy beside me.

"What're you going to do?" he asked me. "I mean, about Sonny?"

"Look. I haven't seen Sonny for over a year, I'm not sure I'm going to do anything. Anyway, what the hell *can* I do?"

"That's right," he said quickly, "ain't nothing you can do. Can't much help old Sonny no more, I guess."

It was what I was thinking and so it seemed to me he had no right to say it.

"I'm surprised at Sonny, though," he went on—he had a funny way of talking, he looked straight ahead as though he were talking to himself—"I thought Sonny was a smart boy, I thought he was too smart to get hung."

"I guess he thought so too," I said sharply, "and that's how he got hung. And how about you? You're pretty goddamn smart, I bet."

Then he looked directly at me, just for a minute. "I ain't smart," he said. "If I was smart, I'd have reached for a pistol a long time ago."

"Look. Don't tell *me* your sad story, if it was up to me, I'd give you one." Then I felt guilty—guilty, probably, for never having supposed that the poor bastard *had* a story of his own, much less a sad one, and I asked, quickly, "What's going to happen to him now?"

He didn't answer this. He was off by himself some place. "Funny thing," he said, and from his tone we might have been discussing the quickest way to get to Brooklyn, "when I saw the papers this morning, the first thing I asked myself was if I had anything to do with it. I felt sort of responsible."

I began to listen more carefully. The subway station was on the corner, just before us, and I stopped. He stopped, too. We were in front of a bar and he ducked slightly, peering in, but whoever he was looking for didn't seem to be there. The juke box was blasting away with something black and bouncy and

I half watched the barmaid as she danced her way from the juke box to her place behind the bar. And I watched her face as she laughingly responded to something someone said to her, still keeping time to the music. When she smiled one saw the little girl, one sensed the doomed, still-struggling woman beneath the battered face of the semiwhore.

"I never *give* Sonny nothing," the boy said finally, "but a long time ago I come to school high and Sonny asked me how it felt." He paused, I couldn't bear to watch him, I watched the barmaid, and I listened to the music which seemed to be causing the pavement to shake. "I told him it felt great." The music stopped, the barmaid paused and watched the juke box until the music began again. "It did."

All this was carrying me some place I didn't want to go. I certainly didn't want to know how it felt. It filled everything, the people, the houses, the music, the dark, quicksilver barmaid, with menace; and this menace was their reality.

"What's going to happen to him now?" I asked again.

"They'll send him away some place and they'll try to cure him." He shook his head. "Maybe he'll even think he's kicked the habit. Then they'll let him loose"—he gestured, throwing his cigarette into the gutter. "That's all."

"What do you mean, that's *all?*"

But I knew what he meant.

"I *mean,* that's *all.*" He turned his head and looked at me, pulling down the corners of his mouth. "Don't you know what I mean?" he asked, softly.

"How the hell *would* I know what you mean?" I almost whispered it, I don't know why.

"That's right," he said to the air, "how would *he* know what I mean?" He turned toward me again, patient and calm, and yet I somehow felt him shaking, shaking as though he were going to fall apart. I felt that ice in my guts again, the dread I'd felt all afternoon; and again I watched the barmaid, moving about the bar, washing glasses, and singing. "Listen. They'll let him out and then it'll just start all over again. That's what I mean."

"You mean—they'll let him out. And then he'll just start working his way back in again. You mean he'll never kick the habit. Is that what you mean?"

"That's right," he said, cheerfully. "*You* see what I mean."

"Tell me," I said at last, "why does he want to die? He must want to die, he's killing himself, why does he want to die?"

He looked at me in surprise. He licked his lips. "He don't want to die. He wants to live. Don't nobody want to die, ever."

Then I wanted to ask him—too many things. He could not have answered, or if he had, I could not have borne the answers. I started walking. "Well, I guess it's none of my business."

"It's going to be rough on old Sonny," he said. We reached the subway station. "This is your station?" he asked. I nodded. I took one step down. "Damn!" he said, suddenly. I looked up at him. He grinned again. "Damn it if I didn't leave all my money home. You ain't got a dollar on you, have you? Just for a couple of days, is all."

All at once something inside gave and threatened to come pouring out of me. I didn't hate him any more. I felt that in another moment I'd start crying like a child.

"Sure," I said. "Don't sweat." I looked in my wallet and didn't have a dollar, I only had a five. "Here," I said. "That hold you?"

He didn't look at it—he didn't want to look at it. A terrible, closed look came over his face, as though he were keeping the number on the bill a secret from him and me. "Thanks," he said, and now he was dying to see me go. "Don't worry about Sonny. Maybe I'll write him or something."

"Sure," I said. "You do that. So long."

"Be seeing you," he said. I went on down the steps.

And I didn't write Sonny or send him anything for a long time. When I finally did, it was just after my little girl died, he wrote me back a letter which made me feel like a bastard.

Here's what he said:

Dear brother,

You don't know how much I needed to hear from you. I wanted to write you many a time but I dug how much I must have hurt you and so I didn't write. But now I feel like a man who's been trying to climb up out of some deep, real deep and funky hole and just saw the sun up there, outside. I got to get outside.

I can't tell you much about how I got here. I mean I don't know how to tell you. I guess I was afraid of something or I was trying to escape from something and you know I have never been very strong in the head (smile). I'm glad Mama and Daddy are dead and can't see what's happened to their son and I swear if I'd known what I was doing I would never have hurt you so, you and a lot of other fine people who were nice to me and who believed in me.

I don't want you to think it had anything to do with me being a musician. It's more than that. Or maybe less than that. I can't get anything straight in my head down here and I try not to think about what's going to happen to me when I get outside again. Sometime I think I'm going to flip and *never* get outside and sometime I think I'll come straight back. I tell you one thing, though, I'd rather blow my brains out than go through this again. But that's what they all say, so they tell me. If I tell you when I'm coming to New York and if you could meet me, I sure would appreciate it. Give my love to Isabel and the kids and I was sure sorry to hear about little Gracie. I wish I could be like Mama and say the Lord's will be done, but I don't know it seems to me that trouble is the one thing that never does get stopped and I don't know what good it does to blame it on the Lord. But maybe it does some good if you believe it.

Your brother,
Sonny

Then I kept in constant touch with him and I sent him whatever I could and I went to meet him when he came back to New York. When I saw him many things I thought I had forgotten came flooding back to me. This was because I had begun, finally, to wonder about Sonny, about the life that Sonny lived inside. This life, whatever it was, had made him older and thinner and it had deepened the distant stillness in which he had always moved. He looked very unlike my baby brother. Yet, when he smiled, when we shook hands, the baby brother I'd never known looked out from the depths of his private life, like an animal waiting to be coaxed into the light.

"How you been keeping?" he asked me.

"All right. And you?"

"Just fine." He was smiling all over his face. "It's good to see you again."

"It's good to see you."

The seven years' difference in our ages lay between us like a chasm: I wondered if these years would ever operate between us as a bridge. I was remembering, and it made it hard to catch my breath, that I had been there when he was born; and I had heard the first words he had ever spoken. When he started to walk, he walked from our mother straight to me. I caught him just before he fell when he took the first steps he ever took in this world.

"How's Isabel?"

"Just fine. She's dying to see you."

"And the boys?"

"They're fine, too. They're anxious to see their uncle."

"Oh, come on. You know they don't remember me."

"Are you kidding? Of course they remember you."

He grinned again. We got into a taxi. We had a lot to say to each other, far too much to know how to begin.

As the taxi began to move, I asked, "You still want to go to India?"

He laughed. "You still remember that. Hell, no. This place is Indian enough for me."

"It used to belong to them," I said.

And he laughed again. "They damn sure knew what they were doing when they got rid of it."

Years ago, when he was around fourteen, he'd been all hipped on the idea of going to India. He read books about people sitting on rocks, naked, in all kinds of weather, but mostly bad, naturally, and walking barefoot through hot coals and arriving at wisdom. I used to say that it sounded to me as though they were getting away from wisdom as fast as they could. I think he sort of looked down on me for that.

"Do you mind," he asked, "if we have the driver drive alongside the park? On the west side—I haven't seen the city in so long."

"Of course not," I said. I was afraid that I might sound as though I were humoring him, but I hoped he wouldn't take it that way.

So we drove along, between the green of the park and the stony, lifeless elegance of hotels and apartment buildings, toward the vivid, killing streets of our childhood. These streets hadn't changed, though housing projects jutted up out of them now like rocks in the middle of a boiling sea. Most of the houses in which we had grown up had vanished, as had the stores from which we had stolen, the basements in which we had first tried sex, the rooftops from which we had hurled tin cans and bricks. But houses exactly like the houses of our past yet dominated the landscape, boys exactly like the boys we once had been found themselves smothering in these houses, came down into the streets for light and air and found themselves encircled by disaster. Some escaped the trap, most didn't. Those who got out always left something of themselves behind, as some animals amputate a leg and leave it in the trap. It might be said, perhaps, that I had escaped, after all, I was a school teacher; or that Sonny had, he hadn't lived in Harlem for years. Yet, as the cab moved uptown through streets which seemed, with a rush, to darken with dark people, and as I covertly studied Sonny's face, it came to me that what we both were seeking through our separate cab windows was that part of ourselves which had been left behind. It's always at the hour of trouble and confrontation that the missing member aches.

We hit 110th Street and started rolling up Lenox Avenue. And I'd known this avenue all my life, but it seemed to me again, as it had seemed on the day I'd first heard about Sonny's trouble, filled with a hidden menace which was its very breath of life.

"We almost there," said Sonny.

"Almost." We were both too nervous to say anything more.

We live in a housing project. It hasn't been up long. A few days after it was up it seemed uninhabitably new, now, of course, it's already rundown. It looks like a parody of the good, clean, faceless life—God knows the people who live in it do their best to make it a parody. The beat-looking grass lying around isn't enough to make their lives green, the hedges will never hold out the streets, and they know it. The big windows fool no one, they aren't big enough to make space out of no space. They don't bother with the windows, they watch the TV screen instead. The playground is most popular with the children who don't play at jacks, or skip rope, or roller skate, or swing, and they can be found in it after dark. We moved in partly because it's not too far from where I teach, and partly for the kids; but it's really just like the houses in which Sonny and I grew up. The same things happen, they'll have the same things to remember. The moment Sonny and I started into the house I had the feeling that I was simply bringing him back into the danger he had almost died trying to escape.

Sonny has never been talkative. So I don't know why I was sure he'd be dying to talk to me when supper was over the first night. Everything went fine, the oldest boy remembered him, and the youngest boy liked him, and Sonny had remembered to bring something for each of them; and Isabel, who is really much nicer than I am, more open and giving, had gone to a lot of trouble about dinner and was genuinely glad to see him. And she's always been able to tease Sonny in a way that I haven't. It was nice to see her face so vivid again and to hear her laugh and watch her make Sonny laugh. She wasn't, or, anyway, she didn't seem to be, at all uneasy or embarrassed. She chatted as though there were no subject which had to be avoided and she got Sonny past his first, faint stiffness. And thank God she was there, for I was filled with that icy dread again. Everything I did seemed awkward to me, and everything I said sounded freighted with hidden meaning. I was trying to remember everything I'd heard about dope addiction and I couldn't help watching Sonny for signs. I wasn't doing it out of malice. I was trying to find out something about my brother. I was dying to hear him tell me he was safe.

"Safe!" my father grunted, whenever Mama suggested trying to move to a neighborhood which might be safer for children. "Safe, hell! Ain't no place safe for kids, nor nobody."

He always went on like this, but he wasn't, ever, really as bad as he sounded, not even on weekends, when he got drunk. As a matter of fact, he was always on the lookout for "something a little better," but he died before he found it. He died suddenly, during a drunken weekend in the middle of the war, when Sonny was fifteen. He and Sonny hadn't ever got on too well. And this was partly because Sonny was the apple of his father's eye. It was because he loved Sonny so much and was frightened for him, that he was always fighting with him. It doesn't do any good to fight with Sonny. Sonny just moves back, inside himself, where he can't be reached. But the principal reason that they never hit it off is that they were so much alike. Daddy was big and rough and loud-talking, just the opposite of Sonny, but they both had—that same privacy.

Mama tried to tell me something about this, just after Daddy died. I was home on leave from the army.

This was the last time I ever saw my mother alive. Just the same, this picture gets all mixed up in my mind with pictures I had of her when she was younger. The way I always see her is the way she used to be on a Sunday afternoon, say, when the old folks were talking after the big Sunday dinner. I always see her wearing pale blue. She'd be sitting on the sofa. And my father would be sitting in the easy chair, not far from her. And the living room would be full of church folks and relatives. There they sit, in chairs all around the living room, and the night is creeping up outside, but nobody knows it yet. You can see the darkness growing against the windowpanes and you hear the street noises every now and again, or maybe the jangling beat of a tambourine from one of the churches close by, but it's real quiet in the room. For a moment nobody's talking, but every face looks darkening, like the sky outside. And my mother rocks a little from the waist, and my father's eyes are closed. Everyone is looking at something a child can't see. For a minute they've forgotten the children. Maybe a kid is lying on the rug, half asleep. Maybe somebody's got a kid in his lap and is absent-mindedly stroking the kid's head. Maybe there's a kid, quiet and big-eyed, curled up in a big chair in the corner. The silence, the darkness coming, and the darkness in the faces frightens the child obscurely. He hopes that the hand which strokes his forehead will never stop—will never die. He hopes that there will never come a time when the old folks won't be sitting around the living room, talking about where they've come from, and what they've seen, and what's happened to them and their kinfolk.

But something deep and watchful in the child knows that this is bound to end, is already ending. In a moment someone will get up and turn on the light. Then the old folks will remember the children and they won't talk any more that day. And when the light fills the room, the child is filled with darkness. He knows that every time this happens he's moved just a little closer to that darkness outside. The darkness outside is what the old folks have been talking about. It's what they've come from. It's what they endure. The child knows that they won't talk any more because if he knows too much about what's happened to *them,* he'll know too much too soon, about what's going to happen to *him.*

The last time I talked to my mother, I remember I was restless. I wanted to get out and see Isabel. We weren't married then and we had a lot to straighten out between us.

There Mama sat, in black, by the window. She was humming an old church song, *Lord, you brought me from a long ways off.* Sonny was out somewhere. Mama kept watching the streets.

"I don't know," she said, "if I'll ever see you again, after you go off from here. But I hope you'll remember the things I tried to teach you."

"Don't talk like that," I said, and smiled. "You'll be here a long time yet."

She smiled, too, but she said nothing. She was quiet for a long time. And I said, "Mama, don't you worry about nothing. I'll be writing all the time, and you be getting the checks. . . ."

"I want to talk to you about your brother," she said, suddenly. "If anything happens to me he ain't going to have nobody to look out for him."

"Mama," I said, "ain't nothing going to happen to you *or* Sonny. Sonny's all right. He's a good boy and he's got good sense."

"It ain't a question of his being a good boy," Mama said, "nor of his having good sense. It ain't only the bad ones, nor yet the dumb ones that gets sucked under." She stopped, looking at me. "Your Daddy once had a brother," she said, and she smiled in a way that made me feel she was in pain. "You didn't never know that, did you?"

"No," I said, "I never knew that," and I watched her face.

"Oh, yes," she said, "your Daddy had a brother." She looked out of the window again. "I know you never saw your Daddy cry. But *I* did—many a time, through all these years."

I asked her, "What happened to his brother? How come nobody's ever talked about him?"

This was the first time I ever saw my mother look old.

"His brother got killed," she said, "when he was just a little younger than you are now. I knew him. He was a fine boy. He was maybe a little full of the devil, but he didn't mean nobody no harm."

Then she stopped and the room was silent, exactly as it had sometimes been on those Sunday afternoons. Mama kept looking out into the streets.

"He used to have a job in the mill," she said, "and, like all young folks, he just liked to perform on Saturday nights. Saturday nights, him and your father would drift around to different places, go to dances and things like that, or just sit around with people they knew, and your father's brother would sing, he had a fine voice, and play along with himself on his guitar. Well, this particular Saturday night, him and your father was coming home from some place, and they were both a little drunk and there was a moon that night, it was bright like day. Your father's brother was feeling kind of good, and he was whistling to himself, and he had his guitar slung over his shoulder. They was coming down a hill and beneath them was a road that turned off from the highway. Well, your father's brother, being always kind of frisky, decided to run down this hill, and he did, with that guitar banging and clanging behind him, and he ran across the road, and he was making water behind a tree. And your father was sort of amused at him and he was still coming down the hill, kind of slow. Then he heard a car motor and that same minute his brother stepped from behind the tree, into the road, in the moonlight. And he started to cross the road. And your father started to run down the hill, he says he don't know why. This car was full of white men. They was all drunk, and when they seen your father's brother they let out a great whoop and holler and they aimed the car straight at him. They was having fun, they just wanted to scare him, the way they do sometimes, you know. But they was drunk. And I guess the boy, being drunk, too, and scared, kind of lost his head. By the time he jumped it was too late. Your father says he heard his brother scream when the car rolled over him, and he heard the wood of that guitar when it give, and he heard them strings go flying, and he heard them white men shouting, and the car kept on a-going and it ain't stopped till this day. And, time your father got down the hill, his brother weren't nothing but blood and pulp."

Tears were gleaming on my mother's face. There wasn't anything I could say.

"He never mentioned it," she said, "because I never let him mention it before you children. Your Daddy was like a crazy man that night and for many a night thereafter. He says he never in his life seen anything as dark as that road after the lights of that car had gone away. Weren't nothing, weren't nobody on that road, just your Daddy and his brother and that busted guitar. Oh, yes. Your Daddy never did really get right again. Till the day he died he weren't sure but that every white man he saw was the man that killed his brother."

She stopped and took out her handkerchief and dried her eyes and looked at me.

"I ain't telling you all this," she said, "to make you scared or bitter or to make you hate nobody. I'm telling you this because you got a brother. And the world ain't changed."

I guess I didn't want to believe this. I guess she saw this in my face. She turned away from me, toward the window again, searching those streets.

"But I praise my Redeemer," she said at last, "that He called your Daddy home before me. I ain't saying it to throw no flowers at myself, but, I declare, it keeps me from feeling too cast down to know I helped your father get safely through this world. Your father always acted like he was the roughest, strongest man on earth. And everybody took him to be like that. But if he hadn't had *me* there—to see his tears!"

She was crying again. Still, I couldn't move. I said, "Lord, Lord, Mama, I didn't know it was like that."

"Oh, honey," she said, "there's a lot that you don't know. But you are going to find it out." She stood up from the window and came over to me. "You got to hold on to your brother," she said, "and don't let him fall, no matter what it looks like is happening to him and no matter how evil you gets with him. You going to be evil with him many a time. But don't you forget what I told you, you hear?"

"I won't forget," I said. "Don't you worry, I won't forget. I won't let nothing happen to Sonny."

My mother smiled as though she were amused at something she saw in my face. Then, "You may not be able to stop nothing from happening. But you got to let him know you's *there.*"

Two days later I was married, and then I was gone. And I had a lot of things on my mind and I pretty well forgot my promise to Mama until I got shipped home on a special furlough for her funeral.

And, after the funeral, with just Sonny and me alone in the empty kitchen, I tried to find out something about him.

"What do you want to do?" I asked him.

"I'm going to be a musician," he said.

For he had graduated, in the time I had been away, from dancing to the juke box to finding out who was playing what, and what they were doing with it, and he had bought himself a set of drums.

"You mean, you want to be a drummer?" I somehow had the feeling that being a drummer might be all right for other people but not for my brother Sonny.

"I don't think," he said, looking at me very gravely, "that I'll ever be a good drummer. But I think I can play a piano."

I frowned. I'd never played the role of the older brother quite so seriously before, had scarcely ever, in fact, *asked* Sonny a damn thing. I sensed myself in the presence of something I didn't really know how to handle, didn't understand. So I made my frown a little deeper as I asked: "What kind of musician do you want to be?"

He grinned, "How many kinds do you think there are?"

"Be *serious,*" I said.

He laughed, throwing his head back, and then looked at me. "I *am* serious."

"Well, then, for Christ's sake, stop kidding around and answer a serious question. I mean, do you want to be a concert pianist, you want to play classical music and all that, or—or what?" Long before I finished he was laughing again. "For Christ's *sake,* Sonny!"

He sobered, but with difficulty. "I'm sorry, But you sound so—*scared!*" and he was off again.

"Well, you may think it's funny now, baby, but's not going to be so funny when you have to make your living at it, let me tell you *that.*" I was furious because I knew he was laughing at me and I didn't know why.

"No," he said, very sober now, and afraid, perhaps, that he'd hurt me, "I don't want to be a classical pianist. That isn't what interests me. I mean"—he paused, looking hard at me, as though his eyes would help me to understand, and then gestured helplessly, as though perhaps his hand would help—"I mean, I'll have a lot of studying to do, and I'll have to study *everything*, but, I mean, I want to play *with*—jazz musicians." He stopped. "I want to play jazz," he said.

Well, the word had never before sounded as heavy, as real, as it sounded that afternoon in Sonny's mouth. I just looked at him and I was probably frowning a real frown by this time. I simply couldn't see why on earth he'd want to spend his time hanging around nightclubs, clowning around on bandstands, while people pushed each other around a dance floor. It seemed—beneath him, somehow. I had never thought about it before, had never been forced to, but I suppose I had always put jazz musicians in a class with what Daddy called "good-time people."

"Are you *serious?*"

"Hell, *yes,* I'm serious."

He looked more helpless than ever, and annoyed, and deeply hurt.

I suggested, helpfully: "You mean—like Louis Armstrong?"

His face closed as though I'd struck him. "No. I'm not talking about none of that old-time, down home crap."

"Well, look, Sonny, I'm sorry, don't get mad. I just don't altogether get it, that's all. Name somebody—you know, a jazz musician you admire."

"Bird."

"Who?"

"Bird! Charlie Parker! Don't they teach you nothing in the goddamn army?"

I lit a cigarette. I was surprised and then a little amused to discover that I was trembling. "I've been out of touch," I said. "You'll have to be patient with me. Now. Who's this Parker character?"

"He's just one of the greatest jazz musicians alive," said Sonny, sullenly, his hands in his pockets, his back to me. "Maybe *the* greatest," he added, bitterly, "that's probably why *you* never heard of him."

"All right," I said, "I'm ignorant. I'm sorry. I'll go out and buy all the cat's records right away, all right?"

"It don't," said Sonny, with dignity, "make any difference to me. I don't care what you listen to. Don't do me no favors."

I was beginning to realize that I'd never seen him so upset before. With another part of my mind I was thinking that this would probably turn out to be one of those things kids go through and that I shouldn't make it seem important by pushing it too hard. Still, I didn't think it would do any harm to ask: "Doesn't all this take a lot of time? Can you make a living at it?"

He turned back to me and half leaned, half sat, on the kitchen table. "Everything takes time," he said, "and—well, yes, sure, I can make a living at it. But what I don't seem to be able to make you understand is that it's the only thing I want to do."

"Well, Sonny," I said, gently, "you know people can't always do exactly what they *want* to do—"

"*No,* I don't know that," said Sonny, surprising me. "I think people *ought* to do what they want to do, what else are they alive for?"

"You getting to be a big boy," I said desperately, "it's time you started thinking about your future."

"I'm thinking about my future," said Sonny, grimly. "I think about it all the time."

I gave up. I decided, if he didn't change his mind, that we could always talk about it later. "In the meantime," I said, "you got to finish school." We had already decided that he'd have to move in with Isabel and her folks. I knew this wasn't the ideal arrangement because Isabel's folks are inclined to be dicty[1] and they hadn't especially wanted Isabel to marry me. But I didn't know what else to do. "And we have to get you fixed up at Isabel's."

There was a long silence. He moved from the kitchen table to the window. "That's a terrible idea. You know it yourself."

"Do you have a *better* idea?"

He just walked up and down the kitchen for a minute. He was as tall as I was. He had started to shave. I suddenly had the feeling that I didn't know him at all.

He stopped at the kitchen table and picked up my cigarettes. Looking at me with a kind of mocking, amused defiance, he put one between his lips. "You mind?"

"You smoking already?"

He lit the cigarette and nodded, watching me through the smoke. "I just wanted to see if I'd have the courage to smoke in front of you." He grinned and blew a great cloud of smoke to the ceiling. "It was easy." He looked at my face. "Come on, now. I bet you was smoking at my age, tell the truth."

I didn't say anything but the truth was on my face, and he laughed. But now there was something very strained in his laugh. "Sure. And I bet that ain't all you was doing."

He was frightening me a little. "Cut the crap," I said. "We already decided that you was going to go and live at Isabel's. Now what's got into you all of a sudden?"

"*You* decided it," he pointed out. "*I* didn't decide nothing." He stopped in front of me, leaning against the stove, arms loosely folded. "Look, brother. I don't want to stay in Harlem no more, I really don't." He was very earnest. He looked at me, then over toward the kitchen window. There was something in his eyes I'd never seen before, some thoughtfulness, some worry all his own. He rubbed the muscle of one arm. "It's time I was getting out of here."

"Where do you want to *go,* Sonny?"

"I want to join the army. Or the navy, I don't care. If I say I'm old enough, they'll believe me."

Then I got mad. It was because I was so scared. "You must be crazy. You goddamn fool, what the hell do you want to go and join the *army* for?"

---

[1]Having upper-class pretensions.

"I just told you. To get out of Harlem."

"Sonny, you haven't even finished *school.* And if you really want to be a musician, how do you expect to study if you're in the *army?*"

He looked at me, trapped, and in anguish. "There's ways. I might be able to work out some kind of deal. Anyway, I'll have the G.I. Bill when I come out."

"*If* you come out." We stared at each other. "Sonny, please. Be reasonable. I know the setup is far from perfect. But we got to do the best we can."

"I ain't learning nothing in school," he said. "Even when I go." He turned away from me and opened the window and threw his cigarette out into the narrow alley. I watched his back. "At least, I ain't learning nothing you'd want me to learn." He slammed the window so hard I thought the glass would fly out, and turned back to me. "And I'm sick of the stink of these garbage cans!"

"Sonny," I said, "I know how you feel. But if you don't finish school now, you're going to be sorry later that you didn't." I grabbed him by the shoulders. "And you only got another year. It ain't so bad. And I'll come back and I swear I'll help you do *whatever* you want to do. Just try to put up with it till I come back. Will you please do that? For me?"

He didn't answer and he wouldn't look at me.

"Sonny. You hear me?"

He pulled away. "I hear you. But you never hear anything *I* say."

I didn't know what to say to that. He looked out of the window and then back at me. "OK," he said, and sighed. "I'll try."

Then I said, trying to cheer him up a little, "They got a piano at Isabel's. You can practice on it."

And as a matter of fact, it did cheer him up for a minute. "That's right," he said to himself. "I forgot that." His face relaxed a little. But the worry, the thoughtfulness, played on it still, the way shadows play on a face which is staring into the fire.

But I thought I'd never hear the end of that piano. At first, Isabel would write me, saying how nice it was that Sonny was so serious about his music and how, as soon as he came in from school, or wherever he had been when he was supposed to be at school, he went straight to that piano and stayed there until suppertime. And, after supper, he went back to that piano and stayed there until everybody went to bed. He was at the piano all day Saturday and all day Sunday. Then he bought a record player and started playing records. He'd play one record over and over again, all day long sometimes, and he'd improvise along with it on the piano. Or he'd play one section of the record, one chord, one change, one progression, then he'd do it on the piano. Then back to the record. Then back to the piano.

Well, I really don't know how they stood it. Isabel finally confessed that it wasn't like living with a person at all, it was like living with sound. And the sound didn't make any sense to her, didn't make any sense to any of them— naturally. They began, in a way, to be afflicted by this presence that was living in their home. It was as though Sonny were some sort of god, or monster.

He moved in an atmosphere which wasn't like theirs at all. They fed him and he ate, he washed himself, he walked in and out of their door; he certainly wasn't nasty or unpleasant or rude, Sonny isn't any of those things; but it was as though he were all wrapped up in some cloud, some fire, some vision all his own; and there wasn't any way to reach him.

At the same time, he wasn't really a man yet, he was still a child, and they had to watch out for him in all kinds of ways. They certainly couldn't throw him out. Neither did they dare to make a great scene about that piano because even they dimly sensed, as I sensed, from so many thousands of miles away, that Sonny was at that piano playing for his life.

But he hadn't been going to school. One day a letter came from the school board and Isabel's mother got it—there had, apparently, been other letters but Sonny had torn them up. This day, when Sonny came in, Isabel's mother showed him the letter and asked where he'd been spending his time. And she finally got it out of him that he'd been down in Greenwich Village, with musicians and other characters, in a white girl's apartment. And this scared her and she started to scream at him and what came up, once she began—though she denies it to this day—was what sacrifices they were making to give Sonny a decent home and how little he appreciated it.

Sonny didn't play the piano that day. By evening, Isabel's mother had calmed down but then there was the old man to deal with, and Isabel herself. Isabel says she did her best to be calm but she broke down and started crying. She says she just watched Sonny's face. She could tell, by watching him, what was happening with him. And what was happening was that they penetrated his cloud, they had reached him. Even if their fingers had been a thousand times more gentle than human fingers ever are, he could hardly help feeling that they had stripped him naked and were spitting on that nakedness. For he also had to see that his presence, that music, which was life or death to him, had been torture for them and that they had endured it, not at all for his sake, but only for mine. And Sonny couldn't take that. He can take it a little better today than he could then but he's still not very good at it and, frankly, I don't know anybody who is.

The silence of the next few days must have been louder than the sound of all the music ever played since time began. One morning, before she went to work, Isabel was in his room for something and she suddenly realized that all of his records were gone. And she knew for certain that he was gone. And he was. He went as far as the navy would carry him. He finally sent me a postcard from some place in Greece and that was the first I knew that Sonny was still alive. I didn't see him any more until we were both back in New York and the war had long been over.

He was a man by then, of course, but I wasn't willing to see it. He came by the house from time to time, but we fought almost every time we met. I didn't like the way he carried himself, loose and dreamlike all the time, and I didn't like his friends, and his music seemed to be merely an excuse for the life he led. It sounded just that weird and disordered.

Then we had a fight, a pretty awful fight, and I didn't see him for months. By and by I looked him up, where he was living, in a furnished room in the Village, and I tried to make it up. But there were lots of other people in the room and Sonny just lay on his bed, and he wouldn't come downstairs with me, and he treated these other people as though they were his family and I weren't. So I got mad and then he got mad, and then I told him that he might just as well be dead as live the way he was living. Then he stood up and he told me not to worry about him any more in life, that he *was* dead as far as I was concerned. Then he pushed me to the door and the other people looked on as though nothing were happening, and he slammed the door behind me. I stood in the hallway, staring at the door. I heard somebody laugh in the room and then the tears came to my eyes. I started down the steps, whistling to keep from crying. I kept whistling to myself, *You going to need me, baby, one of these cold, rainy days.*

I read about Sonny's trouble in the spring. Little Grace died in the fall. She was a beautiful little girl. But she only lived a little over two years. She died of polio and she suffered. She had a slight fever for a couple of days, but it didn't seem like anything and we just kept her in bed. And we would certainly have called the doctor, but the fever dropped, she seemed to be all right. So we thought it had just been a cold. Then, one day, she was up, playing, Isabel was in the kitchen fixing lunch for the two boys when they'd come in from school, and she heard Grace fall down in the living room. When you have a lot of children you don't always start running when one of them falls, unless they start screaming or something. And, this time, Grace was quiet. Yet, Isabel says that when she heard that *thump* and then that silence, something happened in her to make her afraid. And she ran to the living room and there was little Grace on the floor, all twisted up, and the reason she hadn't screamed was that she couldn't get her breath. And when she did scream, it was the worst sound, Isabel says, that she'd ever heard in all her life, and she still hears it sometimes in her dreams. Isabel will sometimes wake me up with a low, moaning, strangled sound and I have to be quick to awaken her and hold her to me and where Isabel is weeping against me seems a mortal wound.

I think I may have written Sonny the very day that little Grace was buried. I was sitting in the living room in the dark, by myself, and I suddenly thought of Sonny. My trouble made his real.

One Saturday afternoon, when Sonny had been living with us, or, anyway, been in our house, for nearly two weeks, I found myself wandering aimlessly about the living room, drinking from a can of beer, and trying to work up the courage to search Sonny's room. He was out, he was usually out whenever I was home, and Isabel had taken the children to see their grandparents. Suddenly I was standing still in front of the living room window, watching Seventh Avenue. The idea of searching Sonny's room made me still. I scarcely dared to admit to myself what I'd be searching for. I didn't know what I'd do if I found it. Or if I didn't.

On the sidewalk across from me, near the entrance to a barbecue joint, some people were holding an old-fashioned revival meeting. The barbecue cook, wearing a dirty white apron, his conked[2] hair reddish and metallic in the pale sun, and a cigarette between his lips, stood in the doorway, watching them. Kids and older people paused in their errands and stood there, along with some older men and a couple of very tough-looking women who watched everything that happened on the avenue, as though they owned it, or were maybe owned by it. Well, they were watching this, too. The revival was being carried on by three sisters in black, and a brother. All they had were their voices and their Bibles and a tambourine. The brother was testifying and while he testified two of the sisters stood together, seeming to say, amen, and the third sister walked around with the tambourine outstretched and a couple of people dropped coins into it. Then the brother's testimony ended and the sister who had been taking up the collection dumped the coins into her palm and transferred them to the pocket of her long black robe. Then she raised both hands, striking the tambourine against the air, and then against one hand, and she started to sing. And the two other sisters and the brother joined in.

It was strange, suddenly, to watch, though I had been seeing these street meetings all my life. So, of course, had everybody else down there. Yet, they paused and watched and listened and I stood still at the window. "*Tis the old ship of Zion,*" they sang, and the sister with the tambourine kept a steady, jangling beat, "*it has rescued many a thousand!*" Not a soul under the sound of their voices was hearing this song for the first time, not one of them had been rescued. Nor had they seen much in the way of rescue work being done around them. Neither did they especially believe in the holiness of the three sisters and the brother, they knew too much about them, knew where they lived, and how. The woman with the tambourine, whose voice dominated the air, whose face was bright with joy, was divided by very little from the woman who stood watching her, a cigarette between her heavy, chapped lips, her hair a cuckoo's nest, her face scarred and swollen from many beatings, and her black eyes glittering like coal. Perhaps they both knew this, which was why, when, as rarely, they addressed each other, they addressed each other as Sister. As the singing filled the air the watching, listening faces underwent a change, the eyes focusing on something within; the music seemed to soothe a poison out of them; and time seemed, nearly, to fall away from the sullen, belligerent, battered faces, as though they were fleeing back to their first condition, while dreaming of their last. The barbecue cook half shook his head and smiled, and dropped his cigarette and disappeared into his joint. A man fumbled in his pockets for change and stood holding it in his hand impatiently, as though he had just remembered a pressing appointment further up the avenue. He looked furious. Then I saw Sonny, standing on the edge of the crowd. He was carrying a wide, flat notebook with a green cover, and it made him look, from where I was standing, almost like a schoolboy. The coppery sun brought out the copper in his skin, he was very faintly smiling, standing very still. Then the singing stopped, the tambourine turned into a collection plate again. The furious

---

[2]Straightened.

man dropped in his coins and vanished, so did a couple of the women, and Sonny dropped some change in the plate, looking directly at the woman with a little smile. He started across the avenue, toward the house. He has a slow, loping walk, something like the way Harlem hipsters walk, only he's imposed on this his own half-beat. I had never really noticed it before.

I stayed at the window, both relieved and apprehensive. As Sonny disappeared from my sight, they began singing again. And they were still singing when his key turned in the lock.

"Hey," he said.

"Hey, yourself. You want some beer?"

"No. Well, maybe." But he came up to the window and stood beside me, looking out. "What a warm voice," he said.

They were singing *If I could only hear my mother pray again!*

"Yes," I said, "and she can sure beat that tambourine."

"But what a terrible song," he said, and laughed. He dropped his notebook on the sofa and disappeared into the kitchen. "Where's Isabel and the kids?"

"I think they went to see their grandparents. You hungry?"

"No." He came back into the living room with his can of beer. "You want to come some place with me tonight?"

I sensed, I don't know how, that I couldn't possibly say no. "Sure. Where?"

He sat down on the sofa and picked up his notebook and started leafing through it. "I'm going to sit in with some fellows in a joint in the Village."

"You mean, you're going to play, tonight?"

"That's right." He took a swallow of his beer and moved back to the window. He gave me a sidelong look. "If you can stand it."

"I'll try," I said.

He smiled to himself and we both watched as the meeting across the way broke up. The three sisters and the brother, heads bowed, were singing *God be with you till we meet again.* The faces around them were very quiet. Then the song ended. The small crowd dispersed. We watched the three women and the lone man walk slowly up the avenue.

"When she was singing before," said Sonny, abruptly, "her voice reminded me for a minute of what heroin feels like sometimes—when it's in your veins. It makes you feel sort of warm and cool at the same time. And distant. And—and sure." He sipped his beer, very deliberately not looking at me. I watched his face. "It makes you feel—in control. Sometimes you've got to have that feeling."

"Do you?" I sat down slowly in the easy chair.

"Sometimes." He went to the sofa and picked up his notebook again. "Some people do."

"In order," I asked, "to play?" And my voice was very ugly, full of contempt and anger.

"Well"—he looked at me with great, troubled eyes, as though, in fact, he hoped his eyes would tell me things he could never otherwise say—"they *think* so. And *if* they think so—!"

"And what do *you* think?" I asked.

He sat on the sofa and put his can of beer on the floor. "I don't know," he said, and I couldn't be sure if he were answering my question or pursuing his thoughts. His face didn't tell me. "It's not so much to *play.* It's to *stand* it, to be able to make it at all. On any level." He frowned and smiled: "In order to keep from shaking to pieces."

"But these friends of yours," I said, "they seem to shake themselves to pieces pretty goddamn fast."

"Maybe." He played with the notebook. And something told me that I should curb my tongue, that Sonny was doing his best to talk, that I should listen. "But of course you only know the ones that've gone to pieces. Some don't—or at least they haven't *yet* and that's just about all *any* of us can say." He paused. "And then there are some who just live, really, in hell, and they know it and they see what's happening and they go right on. I don't know." He sighed, dropped the notebook, folded his arms. "Some guys, you can tell from the way they play, they on something *all* the time. And you can see that, well, it makes something real for them. But of course," he picked up his beer from the floor and sipped it and put the can down again, "they *want* to, too, you've got to see that. Even some of them that say they don't—*some,* not all."

"And what about you?" I asked—I couldn't help it. "What about you? Do *you* want to?"

He stood up and walked to the window and remained silent for a long time. Then he sighed. "Me," he said. Then: "While I was downstairs before, on my way here, listening to that woman sing, it struck me all of a sudden how much suffering she must have had to go through—to sing like that. It's *repulsive* to think you have to suffer that much."

I said: "But there's no way not to suffer—is there, Sonny?"

"I believe not," he said and smiled, "but that's never stopped anyone from trying." He looked at me. "Has it?" I realized, with this mocking look, that there stood between us, forever, beyond the power of time or forgiveness, the fact that I had held silence—so long!—when he had needed human speech to help him. He turned back to the window. "No, there's no way not to suffer. But you try all kinds of ways to keep from drowning in it, to keep on top of it, and to make it seem—well, like *you.* Like you did something, all right, and now you're suffering for it. You know?" I said nothing. "Well you know," he said, impatiently, "why *do* people suffer? Maybe it's better to do something to give it a reason, *any* reason."

"But we just agreed," I said, "that there's no way not to suffer. Isn't it better, then, just to—take it?"

"But nobody just takes it," Sonny cried, "that's what I'm telling you! *Everybody* tries not to. You're just hung up on the *way* some people try—it's not *your* way!"

The hair on my face began to itch, my face felt wet. "That's not true," I said, "that's not true. I don't give a damn what other people do, I don't even care how they suffer. I just care how *you* suffer." And he looked at me. "Please believe me," I said, "I don't want to see you—die—trying not to suffer."

"I won't," he said, flatly, "die trying not to suffer. At least, not any faster than anybody else."

"But there's no need," I said, trying to laugh, "is there? in killing yourself."

I wanted to say more, but I couldn't. I wanted to talk about will power and how life could be—well, beautiful. I wanted to say that it was all within; but was it? or, rather, wasn't that exactly the trouble? And I wanted to promise that I would never fail him again. But it would all have sounded—empty words and lies.

So I made the promise to myself and prayed that I would keep it.

"It's terrible sometimes, inside," he said, "that's what's the trouble. You walk these streets, black and funky and cold, and there's not really a living ass to talk to, and there's nothing shaking, and there's no way of getting it out—that storm inside. You can't talk it and you can't make love with it, and when you finally try to get with it and play it, you realize *nobody's* listening. So *you've* got to listen. You got to find a way to listen."

And then he walked away from the window and sat on the sofa again, as though all the wind had suddenly been knocked out of him. "Sometimes you'll do *anything* to play, even cut your mother's throat." He laughed and looked at me. "Or your brother's." Then he sobered. "Or your own." Then: "Don't worry. I'm all right now and I think I'll *be* all right. But I can't forget—where I've been. I don't mean just the physical place I've been, I mean where I've *been*. And *what* I've been."

"What have you been, Sonny?" I asked.

He smiled—but sat sideways on the sofa, his elbow resting on the back, his fingers playing with his mouth and chin, not looking at me. "I've been something I didn't recognize, didn't know I could be. Didn't know anybody could be." He stopped, looking inward, looking helplessly young, looking old. "I'm not talking about it now because I feel *guilty* or anything like that—maybe it would be better if I did, I don't know. Anyway, I can't really talk about it. Not to you, not to anybody," and now he turned and faced me. "Sometimes, you know, and it was actually when I was most *out* of the world, I felt that I was in it, that I was *with* it, really, and I could play or I didn't really have to *play*, it just came out of me, it was there. And I don't know how I played, thinking about it now, but I know I did awful things, those times, sometimes, to people. Or it wasn't that I *did* anything to them—it was that they weren't real." He picked up the beer can; it was empty; he rolled it between his palms: "And other times—well, I needed a fix, I needed to find a place to lean, I needed to clear a space to *listen*—and I couldn't find it, and I—went crazy, I did terrible things to *me*, I was terrible *for* me." He began pressing the beer can between his hands, I watched the metal begin to give. It glittered, as he played with it, like a knife, and I was afraid he would cut himself, but I said nothing. "Oh well. I can never tell you. I was all by myself at the bottom of something, stinking and sweating and crying and shaking, and I smelled it, you know? *my* stink, and I thought I'd die if I couldn't get away from it and yet, all the same, I knew that everything I was doing was just locking me in with it. And I didn't know," he paused, still flattening the beer can, "I didn't know, I still *don't* know, something kept telling me that maybe it was good to smell your own stink, but I didn't think that *that* was what I'd been trying to do—and—who can stand it?" and he abruptly dropped the ruined beer can, looking at me with a small, still smile, and then rose, walking to the window as though it were the lodestone rock. I watched his face, he watched the avenue. "I couldn't tell you when Mama died—but the reason I wanted to leave Harlem so bad was to get away from drugs. And then, when I ran away, that's what I was running from—really. When I came back, nothing had changed, *I* hadn't changed, I was just—older." And he stopped, drumming with his fingers on the windowpane. The sun had vanished, soon darkness would fall. I watched his face. "It can come again," he said, almost as though speaking to himself. Then he turned to me. "It can come again," he repeated. "I just want you to know that."

"All right," I said, at last. "So it can come again, All right."

He smiled, but the smile was sorrowful. "I had to try to tell you," he said.

"Yes," I said. "I understand that."

"You're my brother," he said, looking straight at me, and not smiling at all.

"Yes," I repeated, "yes. I understand that."

He turned back to the window, looking out. "All that hatred down there," he said, "all that hatred and misery and love. It's a wonder it doesn't blow the avenue apart."

We went to the only nightclub on a short, dark street, downtown. We squeezed through the narrow, chattering, jampacked bar to the entrance of the big room, where the bandstand was. And we stood there for a moment, for the lights were very dim in this room and we couldn't see. Then, "Hello, boy," said a voice and an enormous black man, much older than Sonny or myself, erupted out of all that atmospheric lighting and put an arm around Sonny's shoulder. "I been sitting right here," he said, "waiting for you."

He had a big voice, too, and heads in the darkness turned toward us.

Sonny grinned and pulled a little away, and said, "Creole, this is my brother. I told you about him."

Creole shook my hand. "I'm glad to meet you, son," he said, and it was clear that he was glad to meet me *there,* for Sonny's sake. And he smiled, "You got a real musician in *your* family," and he took his arm from Sonny's shoulder and slapped him, lightly, affectionately, with the back of his hand.

"Well. Now I've heard it all," said a voice behind us. This was another musician, and a friend of Sonny's, a coal-black, cheerful-looking man, built close to the ground. He immediately began confiding to me, at the top of his lungs, the most terrible things about Sonny, his teeth gleaming like a lighthouse and his laugh coming up out of him like the beginning of an earthquake. And it turned out that everyone at the bar knew Sonny, or almost everyone; some were musicians, working there, or nearby, or not working, some were simply hangers-on, and some were there to hear Sonny play. I was introduced to all of them and they were all very polite to me. Yet, it was clear that, for them, I was only Sonny's brother. Here, I was in Sonny's world. Or, rather: his kingdom. Here, it was not even a question that his veins bore royal blood.

They were going to play soon and Creole installed me, by myself, at a table in a dark corner. Then I watched them, Creole, and the little black man, and Sonny, and the others, while they horsed around, standing just below the bandstand. The light from the bandstand spilled just a little short of them and, watching them laughing and gesturing and moving about, I had the feeling that they, nevertheless, were being most careful not to step into that circle of light too suddenly: that if they moved into the light too suddenly, without thinking, they would perish in flame. Then, while I watched, one of them, the small, black man, moved into the light and crossed the bandstand and started fooling around with his drums. Then—being funny and being, also, extremely ceremonious—Creole took Sonny by the arm and led him to the piano. A woman's voice called Sonny's name and a few hands started clapping. And Sonny, also being funny and being ceremonious, and so touched, I think, that he could have cried, but neither hiding it nor showing it, riding it like a man, grinned, and put both hands to his heart and bowed from the waist.

Creole then went to the bass fiddle and a lean, very bright-skinned brown man jumped up on the bandstand and picked up his horn. So there they were, and the atmosphere on the bandstand and in the room began to change and tighten. Someone stepped up to the microphone and announced them. Then there were all kinds of murmurs. Some people at the bar shushed others. The waitress ran around, frantically getting in the last orders, guys and chicks got closer to each other, and the lights on the bandstand, on the quartet, turned to a kind of indigo. Then they all looked different there. Creole looked about him for the last time, as though he were making certain that all his chickens were in the coop, and then he—jumped and struck the fiddle. And there they were.

All I know about music is that not many people ever really hear it. And even then, on the rare occasions when something opens within, and the music enters, what we mainly hear, or hear corroborated, are personal, private, vanishing evocations. But the man who creates the music is hearing something else, is dealing with the roar rising from the void and imposing order on it as it hits the air. What is evoked in him, then, is of another order, more terrible because it has no words, and triumphant, too, for that same reason. And his triumph, when he triumphs, is ours. I just watched Sonny's face. His face was troubled, he was working hard, but he wasn't with it. And I had the feeling that, in a way, everyone on the bandstand was waiting for him, both waiting for him and pushing him along. But as I began to watch Creole, I realized that it was Creole who held them all back. He had them on a short rein. Up there, keeping the beat with his whole body, wailing on the fiddle, with his eyes half closed, he was listening to everything, but he was listening to Sonny. He was having a dialogue with Sonny. He wanted Sonny to leave the shoreline and strike out for the deep water. He was Sonny's witness that deep water and drowning were not the same thing—he had been there, and he knew. And he wanted Sonny to know. He was waiting for Sonny to do the things on the keys which would let Creole know that Sonny was in the water.

And, while Creole listened, Sonny moved, deep within, exactly like someone in torment. I had never before thought of how awful the relationship must be between the musician and his instrument. He has to fill it, this instrument, with the breath of life, his own. He has to make it do what he wants it to do. And a piano is just a piano. It's made out of so much wood and wires and little hammers and big ones, and ivory. While there's only so much you can do with it, the only way to find this out is to try; to try and make it do everything.

And Sonny hadn't been near a piano for over a year. And he wasn't on much better terms with his life, not the life that stretched before him now. He and the piano stammered, started one way, got scared, stopped; started another way, panicked, marked time, started again; then seemed to have found a direction, panicked again, got stuck. And the face I saw on Sonny I'd never seen before. Everything had been burned out of it, and, at the same time, things usually hidden were being burned in, by the fire and fury of the battle which was occurring in him up there.

Yet, watching Creole's face as they neared the end of the first set, I had the feeling that something had happened, something I hadn't heard. Then they finished, there was scattered applause, and then, without an instant's warning, Creole started into something else, it was almost sardonic, it was *Am I Blue*. And, as though he commanded, Sonny began to play. Something began to happen. And Creole let out the reins. The dry, low, black man said something awful on the drums, Creole answered, and the drums talked back. Then the horn insisted, sweet and high, slightly detached perhaps, and Creole listened, commenting now and then, dry, and driving, beautiful and calm and old. Then they all came together again, and Sonny was part of the family again. I could tell this from his face. He seemed to have found, right there beneath his fingers, a damn brand-new piano. It seemed that he couldn't get over it. Then, for awhile, just being happy with Sonny, they seemed to be agreeing with him that brand-new pianos certainly were a gas.

Then Creole stepped forward to remind them that what they were playing was the blues. He hit something in all of them, he hit something in me, myself, and the music tightened and deepened, apprehension began to beat the air. Creole began to tell us what the blues were all about. They were not about anything very new. He and his boys up there were keeping it new, at the risk of ruin, destruction, madness, and death, in order to find new ways to make us listen. For, while the tale of how we suffer, and how we are delighted, and how we may triumph is never new, it always must be heard. There isn't any other tale to tell, it's the only light we've got in all this darkness.

And this tale, according to that face, that body, those strong hands on those strings, has another aspect in every country, and a new depth in every generation. Listen, Creole seemed to be saying, listen. Now these are Sonny's blues. He made the little black man on the drums know it, and the bright, brown man on the horn. Creole wasn't trying any longer to get Sonny in the water. He was wishing him Godspeed. Then he stepped back, very slowly, filling the air with the immense suggestion that Sonny speak for himself.

Then they all gathered around Sonny and Sonny played. Every now and again one of them seemed to say, amen. Sonny's fingers filled the air with life, his life. But that life contained so many others. And Sonny went all the way back, he really began with the spare, flat statement of the opening phrase of the song. Then he began to make it his. It was very beautiful because it wasn't hurried and it was no longer a lament. I seemed to hear with what burning he had made it his, with what burning we had yet to make it ours, how we could cease lamenting. Freedom lurked around us and I understood, at last, that he could help us to be free if we would listen, that he would never be free until we did. Yet, there was no battle in his face now. I heard what he had gone through, and would continue to go through until he came to rest in earth. He had made it his: that long line, of which we knew only Mama and Daddy. And he was giving it back, as everything must be given back, so that, passing through death, it can live forever. I saw my mother's face again, and felt, for the first time, how the stones of the road she had walked on must have bruised her feet. I saw the moonlit road where my father's brother died. And it brought something else back to me, and carried me past it, I saw my little girl again and felt Isabel's tears again, and I felt my own tears begin to rise. And I was yet aware that this was only a moment, that the world waited outside, as hungry as a tiger, and that trouble stretched above us, longer than the sky.

Then it was over. Creole and Sonny let out their breath, both soaking wet, and grinning. There was a lot of applause and some of it was real. In the dark, the girl came by and I asked her to take drinks to the bandstand. There was a long pause, while they talked up there in the indigo light and after awhile I saw the girl put a Scotch and milk on top of the piano for Sonny. He didn't seem to notice it, but just before they started playing again, he sipped from it and looked toward me, and nodded. Then he put it back on top of the piano. For me, then, as they began to play again, it glowed and shook above my brother's head like the very cup of trembling.

Study and Discussion Questions

1. In what ways are Sonny and his brother different? How, for example, do their relationships to the Harlem community differ? What might account for these differences?
2. Why does Baldwin begin the story with the narrator reading about Sonny in the newspaper? Why does the narrator have so little interest in his brother at first? What is he afraid of? Why does he feel guilty?
3. How were the narrator and Sonny able to grow up together and yet remain such strangers?
4. What experiences bring the narrator closer to Sonny and help him understand his brother better?
5. Why does Sonny use heroin? Why does his music mean so much to him? Why the blues?
6. What has the narrator learned by the end of the story?
7. Events in the story are narrated out of chronological order. What is the effect of the story's structure?

Suggestions for Writing

1. What do you think Sonny's future might be? Write a brief narrative of the next five or ten years.
2. Listen to some instrumental music and try to put into words what is going on in it, in the way Baldwin does at the end of the story.
3. Imagine that, at the end of Sonny's performance, the narrator were, for some reason, swept off to another country, never to see or talk to his brother again. Write the letter he might have written, telling Sonny how he now feels about him.

NATHANIEL HAWTHORNE (1804–1864)

Nathaniel Hawthorne was born into an established Puritan family in Salem, Massachusetts. After graduating from Bowdoin College in 1825, Hawthorne aspired to literary fame and returned to Salem to begin writing stories. For the next decade, he irregularly sold his work to literary magazines. Finally, in 1837, Hawthorne published his first collection of short stories (then called "romances") *Twice-Told Tales*, which would bring him the literary acknowledgment he was seeking, but not the income necessary to support his new family. To supplement his income, Hawthorne was forced to take on other work, serving as a customs inspector in Boston for a few years, then as the American consul to Liverpool, appointed by his close friend President Franklin Pierce. Throughout these years, he continued to write, crafting short stories and novels that probed the individual's struggle with conscience and the weight of Puritan guilt. In a lush prose style, and with the frequent use of allegory, his works tend to move in and out of ambiguity, creating multiple levels of meaning. His other works include *Mosses from an Old Manse* (1846), *The Scarlet Letter* (1850), *The House of the Seven Gables* (1851), *The Blithedale Romance* (1852), and *The Marble Faun* (1860). "Young Goodman Brown," first published in *Mosses from an Old Manse*, is a prime example of the gothic and Puritan influences in Hawthorne's writing and "has provoked perhaps more discussion than any other short story in American fiction" (*Nathaniel Hawthorne*, Introduction, 1979).

Young Goodman Brown (1846)

Young Goodman[1] Brown came forth at sunset into the street at Salem village; but put his head back, after crossing the threshold, to exchange a parting

---

[1]Goodman and Goody (used later) were respectful terms of address for men and women not of the upper classes.

kiss with his young wife. And Faith, as the wife was aptly named, thrust her own pretty head into the street, letting the wind play with the pink ribbons of her cap while she called to Goodman Brown.

"Dearest heart," whispered she, softly and rather sadly, when her lips were close to his ear, "prithee put off your journey until sunrise and sleep in your own bed to-night. A lone woman is troubled with such dreams and such thoughts that she's afeard of herself sometimes. Pray tarry with me this night, dear husband, of all nights in the year."

"My love and my Faith," replied young Goodman Brown, "of all nights in the year, this one night must I tarry away from thee. My journey, as thou callest it, forth and back again, must needs be done 'twixt now and sunrise. What, my sweet, pretty wife, dost thou doubt me already, and we but three months married?"

"Then God bless you!" said Faith, with the pink ribbons; "and may you find all well when you come back."

"Amen!" cried Goodman Brown. "Say thy prayers, dear Faith, and go to bed at dusk, and no harm will come to thee."

So they parted; and the young man pursued his way until, being about to turn the corner by the meeting-house, he looked back and saw the head of Faith still peeping after him with a melancholy air, in spite of her pink ribbons.

"Poor little Faith!" thought he, for his heart smote him. "What a wretch am I to leave her on such an errand! She talks of dreams, too. Methought as she spoke there was trouble in her face, as if a dream had warned her what work is to be done to-night. But no, no; 'twould kill her to think it. Well, she's a blessed angel on earth; and after this one night I'll cling to her skirts and follow her to heaven."

With this excellent resolve for the future, Goodman Brown felt himself justified in making more haste on his present evil purpose. He had taken a dreary road, darkened by all the gloomiest trees of the forest, which barely stood aside to let the narrow path creep through, and closed immediately behind. It was all as lonely as could be; and there is this peculiarity in such a solitude, that the traveller knows not who may be concealed by the innumerable trunks and the thick boughs overhead; so that with lonely footsteps he may yet be passing through an unseen multitude.

"There may be a devilish Indian behind every tree," said Goodman Brown to himself; and he glanced fearfully behind him as he added, "What if the devil himself should be at my very elbow!"

His head being turned back, he passed a crook of the road, and, looking forward again, beheld the figure of a man, in grave and decent attire, seated at the foot of an old tree. He arose at Goodman Brown's approach and walked onward side by side with him.

"You are late, Goodman Brown," said he. "The clock of the Old South was striking as I came through Boston, and that is full fifteen minutes agone."

"Faith kept me back a while," replied the young man, with a tremor in his voice, caused by the sudden appearance of his companion, though not wholly unexpected.

It was now deep dusk in the forest, and deepest in that part of it where these two were journeying. As nearly as could be discerned, the second traveller was about fifty years old, apparently in the same rank of life as Goodman Brown, and bearing a considerable resemblance to him, though perhaps more in expression than features. Still they might have been taken for father and son. And yet, though the elder person was as simply clad as the younger, and as simple in manner too, he had an indescribable air of one who knew the world, and who would not have felt abashed at the governor's dinner table or in King William's court, were it possible that his affairs should call him thither. But the only thing about him that could be fixed upon as remarkable was his staff, which bore the likeness of a great black snake, so curiously wrought that it might almost be seen to twist and wriggle itself like a living serpent. This, of course, must have been an ocular deception, assisted by the uncertain light.

"Come, Goodman Brown," cried his fellow-traveller, "this is a dull pace for the beginning of a journey. Take my staff, if you are so soon weary."

"Friend," said the other, exchanging his slow pace for a full stop, "having kept covenant by meeting thee here, it is my purpose now to return whence I came. I have scruples touching the matter thou wot'st of."

"Sayest thou so?" replied he of the serpent, smiling apart. "Let us walk on, nevertheless, reasoning as we go; and if I convince thee not thou shalt turn back. We are but a little way in the forest yet."

"Too far! too far!" exclaimed the goodman, unconsciously resuming his walk. "My father never went into the woods on such an errand, nor his father before him. We have been a race of honest men and good Christians since the days of the martyrs; and shall I be the first of the name of Brown that ever took this path and kept"—

"Such company, thou wouldst say," observed the elder person, interpreting his pause. "Well said, Goodman Brown! I have been as well acquainted with your family as with ever a one among the Puritans; and that's no trifle to say. I helped your grandfather, the constable, when he lashed the Quaker woman so smartly through the streets of Salem; and it was I that brought your father a pitch-pine knot, kindled at my own hearth, to set fire to an Indian village, in King Philip's war.[2] They were my good friends, both; and many a pleasant walk have we had along this path, and returned merrily after midnight. I would fain be friends with you for their sake."

"If it be as thou sayest," replied Goodman Brown, "I marvel they never spoke of these matters; or, verily, I marvel not, seeing that the least rumor of the sort would have driven them from New England. We are a people of prayer, and good works to boot, and abide no such wickedness."

"Wickedness or not," said the traveller with the twisted staff, "I have a very general acquaintance here in New England. The deacons of many a church have drunk the communion wine with me; the selectmen of divers towns make me

---

[2]War between Indians and New England colonists, 1675–1676.

their chairman; and a majority of the Great and General Court are firm supporters of my interest. The governor and I, too—But these are state secrets."

"Can this be so?" cried Goodman Brown, with a stare of amazement at his undisturbed companion. "Howbeit, I have nothing to do with the governor and council; they have their own ways, and are no rule for a simple husbandman like me. But, were I to go on with thee, how should I meet the eye of that good old man, our minister, at Salem village? Oh, his voice would make me tremble both Sabbath day and lecture day."

Thus far the elder traveller had listened with due gravity; but now burst into a fit of irrepressible mirth, shaking himself so violently that his snake-like staff actually seemed to wriggle in sympathy.

"Ha! ha! ha!" shouted he again and again; then composing himself, "Well, go on, Goodman Brown, go on; but, prithee, don't kill me with laughing."

"Well, then, to end the matter at once," said Goodman Brown, considerably nettled, "there is my wife, Faith. It would break her dear little heart; and I'd rather break my own."

"Nay, if that be the case," answered the other, "e'en go thy ways, Goodman Brown. I would not for twenty old women like the one hobbling before us that Faith should come to any harm."

As he spoke he pointed his staff at a female figure on the path, in whom Goodman Brown recognized a very pious and exemplary dame, who had taught him his catechism in youth, and was still his moral and spiritual adviser, jointly with the minister and Deacon Gookin.

"A marvel, truly, that Goody Cloyse should be so far in the wilderness at nightfall," said he. "But with your leave, friend, I shall take a cut through the woods until we have left this Christian woman behind. Being a stranger to you she might ask whom I was consorting with and whither I was going."

"Be it so," said his fellow-traveller. "Betake you the woods, and let me keep the path."

Accordingly the young man turned aside, but took care to watch his companion, who advanced softly along the road until he had come within a staff's length of the old dame. She, meanwhile, was making the best of her way, with singular speed for so aged a woman, and mumbling some indistinct words—a prayer, doubtless—as she went. The traveller put forth his staff and touched her withered neck with what seemed the serpent's tail.

"The devil!" screamed the pious old lady.

"Then Goody Cloyse knows her old friend?" observed the traveller, confronting her and leaning on his writhing stick.

"Ah, forsooth, and is it your worship indeed?" cried the good dame. "Yea, truly is it, and in the very image of my old gossip, Goodman Brown, the grandfather of the silly fellow that now is. But—would your worship believe it?—my broomstick hath strangely disappeared, stolen, as I suspect, by that unhanged witch, Goody Cory, and that, too, when I was all anointed with the juice of smallage, and cinquefoil, and wolf's bane"—

"Mingled with fine wheat and the fat of a new-born babe," said the shape of old Goodman Brown.

"Ah, your worship knows the recipe," cried the old lady, cackling aloud. "So, as I was saying, being all ready for the meeting, and no horse to ride on, I made up my mind to foot it; for they tell me there is a nice young man to be taken into communion to-night. But now your good worship will lend me your arm, and we shall be there in a twinkling."

"That can hardly be," answered her friend. "I may not spare you my arm, Goody Cloyse; but here is my staff, if you will."

So saying, he threw it down at her feet, where, perhaps, it assumed life, being one of the rods which its owner had formerly lent to the Egyptian magi. Of this fact, however, Goodman Brown could not take cognizance. He had cast up his eyes in astonishment, and, looking down again, beheld neither Goody Cloyse nor the serpentine staff, but this fellow-traveller alone, who waited for him as calmly as if nothing had happened.

"That old woman taught me my catechism," said the young man; and there was a world of meaning in this simple comment.

They continued to walk onward, while the elder traveller exhorted his companion to make good speed and persevere in the path, discoursing so aptly that his arguments seemed rather to spring up in the bosom of his auditor than to be suggested by himself. As they went, he plucked a branch of maple to serve for a walking stick, and began to strip it of the twigs and little boughs, which were wet with evening dew. The moment his fingers touched them they became strangely withered and dried up as with a week's sunshine. Thus the pair proceeded, at a good free pace, until suddenly, in a gloomy hollow of the road, Goodman Brown sat himself down on the stump of a tree and refused to go any farther.

"Friend," said he, stubbornly, "my mind is made up. Not another step will I budge on this errand. What if a wretched old woman do choose to go to the devil when I thought she was going to heaven: is that any reason why I should quit my dear Faith and go after her?"

"You will think better of this by and by," said his acquaintance, composedly. "Sit here and rest yourself a while; and when you feel like moving again, there is my staff to help you along."

Without more words, he threw his companion the maple stick, and was as speedily out of sight as if he had vanished into the deepening gloom. The young man sat a few moments by the roadside, applauding himself greatly, and thinking with how clear a conscience he should meet the minister in his morning walk, nor shrink from the eye of good old Deacon Gookin. And what calm sleep would be his that very night, which was to have been spent so wickedly, but so purely and sweetly now, in the arms of Faith! Amidst these pleasant and praiseworthy meditations, Goodman Brown heard the tramp of horses along the road, and deemed it advisable to conceal himself within the verge of the forest, conscious of the guilty purpose that had brought him thither, though now so happily turned from it.

On came the hoof tramps and the voices of the riders, two grave old voices, conversing soberly as they drew near. These mingled sounds appeared to pass along the road, within a few yards of the young man's hiding-place; but, owing doubtless to the depth of the gloom at that particular spot, neither the travellers nor their steeds were visible. Though their figures brushed the small boughs by the wayside, it could not be seen that they intercepted, even for a moment, the faint gleam from the strip of bright sky athwart which they must have passed. Goodman Brown alternately crouched and stood on tiptoe, pulling aside the branches and thrusting forth his head as far as he durst without discerning so much as a shadow. It vexed him the more, because he could have sworn, were such a thing possible, that he recognized the voices of the minister and Deacon Gookin, jogging along quietly, as they were wont to do, when bound to some ordination or ecclesiastical council. While yet within hearing, one of the riders stopped to pluck a switch.

"Of the two, reverend sir," said the voice like the deacon's, "I had rather miss an ordination dinner than to-night's meeting. They tell me that some of our community are to be here from Falmouth and beyond, and others from Connecticut and Rhode Island, besides several of the Indian powwows, who, after their fashion, know almost as much deviltry as the best of us. Moreover, there is a goodly young woman to be taken into communion."

"Mighty well, Deacon Gookin!" replied the solemn old tones of the minister. "Spur up, or we shall be late. Nothing can be done, you know, until I get on the ground."

The hoofs clattered again; and the voices, talking so strangely in the empty air, passed on through the forest, where no church had ever been gathered or solitary Christian prayed. Wither, then, could these holy men be journeying so deep into the heathen wilderness? Young Goodman Brown caught hold of a tree for support, being ready to sink down on the ground, faint and overburdened with the heavy sickness of his heart. He looked up to the sky, doubting whether there really was a heaven above him. Yet there was the blue arch, and the stars brightening in it.

"With heaven above and Faith below, I will yet stand firm against the devil!" cried Goodman Brown.

While he still gazed upward into the deep arch of the firmament and had lifted his hands to pray, a cloud, though no wind was stirring, hurried across the zenith and hid the brightening stars. The blue sky was still visible, except directly overhead, where this black mass of cloud was sweeping swiftly northward. Aloft in the air, as if from the depths of the cloud, came a confused and doubtful sound of voices. Once the listener fancied that he could distinguish the accents of towns-people of his own, men and women, both pious and ungodly, many of whom he had met at the communion table, and had seen others rioting at the tavern. The next moment, so indistinct were the sounds, he doubted whether he had heard aught but the murmur of the old forest, whispering without a wind. Then came a stronger swell of those familiar tones, heard daily in the sunshine at Salem village, but never until now from a cloud of night. There was one voice, of a young woman, uttering lamentations, yet with an uncertain sorrow, and entreating for some favor, which, perhaps, it would grieve her to obtain; and all the unseen multitude, both saints and sinners, seemed to encourage her onward.

"Faith!" shouted Goodman Brown, in a voice of agony and desperation; and the echoes of the forest mocked him, crying, "Faith! Faith!" as if bewildered wretches were seeking her all through the wilderness.

The cry of grief, rage, and terror was yet piercing the night, when the unhappy husband held his breath for a response. There was a scream, drowned immediately in a louder murmur of voices, fading into far-off laughter, as the dark cloud swept away, leaving the clear and silent sky above Goodman Brown. But something fluttered lightly down through the air and caught on the branch of a tree. The young man seized it, and beheld a pink ribbon.

"My Faith is gone!" cried he, after one stupefied moment. "There is no good on earth; and sin is but a name. Come, devil; for to thee is this world given."

And, maddened with despair, so that he laughed loud and long, did Goodman Brown grasp his staff and set forth again, at such a rate that he seemed to fly along the forest path rather than to walk or run. The road grew wilder and drearier and more faintly traced, and vanished at length, leaving him in the heart of the dark wilderness, still rushing onward with the instinct that guides mortal man to evil. The whole forest was peopled with frightful sounds—the creaking of the trees, the howling of wild beasts, and the yell of Indians; while sometimes the wind tolled like a distant church bell, and sometimes gave a broad roar around the traveller, as if all Nature were laughing him to scorn. But he was himself the chief horror of the scene, and shrank not from its other horrors.

"Ha! ha! ha!" roared Goodman Brown when the wind laughed at him. "Let us hear which will laugh loudest. Think not to frighten me with your deviltry. Come witch, come wizard, come Indian powwow, come devil himself, and here comes Goodman Brown. You may as well fear him as he fear you."

In truth, all through the haunted forest there could be nothing more frightful than the figure of Goodman Brown. On he flew among the black Pines, brandishing his staff with frenzied gestures, now giving vent to an inspiration of horrid blasphemy, and now shouting forth such laughter as set all the echoes of the forest laughing like demons around him. The fiend in his own shape is less hideous than when he rages in the breast of man. Thus sped the demoniac on his course, until, quivering among the trees, he saw a red light before him, as when the felled trunks and branches of a clearing have been set on fire, and throw up their lurid blaze against the sky, at the hour of midnight. He paused, in a lull of the tempest that had driven him onward, and heard the swell of what seemed a hymn, rolling solemnly from a distance with the weight of many voices. He knew the tune; it was a familiar one in the choir of the village meeting-house. The verse died heavily away, and was lengthened by a chorus, not of human voices, but of all the sounds of the benighted wilderness pealing in awful harmony together. Goodman Brown cried out, and his cry was lost to his own ear by its unison with the cry of the desert.

In the interval of silence he stole forward until the light glared full upon his eyes. At one extremity of an open space, hemmed in by the dark wall of the forest, arose a rock, bearing some rude, natural resemblance either to an altar or a pulpit, and surrounded by four blazing pines, their tops aflame, their stems untouched, like candles at an evening meeting. The mass of foliage that had overgrown the summit of the rock was all on fire, blazing high into the night and fitfully illuminating the whole field. Each pendent twig and leafy festoon was in a blaze. As the red light arose and fell, a numerous congregation alternately shone forth, then disappeared in shadow, and again grew, as it were, out of the darkness, peopling the heart of the solitary woods at once.

"A grave and dark-clad company," quoth Goodman Brown.

In truth they were such. Among them, quivering to and fro between gloom and splendor, appeared faces that would be seen next day at the council board of the province, and others which, Sabbath after Sabbath, looked devoutly heavenward, and benignantly over the crowded pews, from the holiest pulpits in the land. Some affirm that the lady of the governor was there. At least there were high dames well known to her, and wives of honored husbands, and widows, a great multitude, and ancient maidens, all of excellent repute, and fair young girls, who trembled lest their mothers should espy them. Either the sudden gleams of light flashing over the obscure field bedazzled Goodman Brown, or he recognized a score of the church members of Salem village famous for their especial sanctity. Good old Deacon Gookin had arrived, and waited at the skirts of that venerable saint, his revered pastor. But, irreverently consorting with these grave, reputable, and pious people, these elders of the church, these chaste dames and dewy virgins, there were men of dissolute lives and women of spotted fame, wretches given over to all mean and filthy vice, and suspected even of horrid crimes. It was strange to see that the good shrank not from the wicked, nor were the sinners abashed by the saints. Scattered also among their pale-faced enemies were the Indian priests, or powwows, who had often scared their native forest with more hideous incantations than any known to English witchcraft.

"But where is Faith?" thought Goodman Brown; and as hope came into his heart, he trembled.

Another verse of the hymn arose, a slow and mournful strain, such as the pious love, but joined to words which expressed all that our nature can conceive of sin, and darkly hinted at far more. Unfathomable to mere mortals is the lore of fiends. Verse after verse was sung; and still the chorus of the desert swelled between like the deepest tone of a mighty organ; and with the final peal of that dreadful anthem there came a sound, as if the roaring wind, the rushing streams, the howling beasts, and every other voice of the unconcerted wilderness were mingling and according with the voice of guilty man in homage to the prince of all. The four blazing pines threw up a loftier flame, and obscurely discovered shapes and visages of horror on the smoke wreaths above the impious assembly. At the same moment the fire on the rock shot redly forth and formed a glowing arch above its base, where now appeared a figure. With reverence be it spoken, the figure bore no slight similitude, both in garb and manner, to some grave divine of the New England churches.

"Bring forth the converts!" cried a voice that echoed through the field and rolled into the forest.

At the word, Goodman Brown stepped forth from the shadow of the trees and approached the congregation, with whom he felt a loathful brotherhood by the sympathy of all that was wicked in his heart. He could have well-nigh sworn that the shape of his own dead father beckoned him to advance, looking downward from a smoke wreath, while a woman, with dim features of despair, threw out her hand to warn him back. Was it his mother? But he had no power to retreat one step, nor to resist, even in thought, when the minister and good old Deacon Gookin seized his arms and led him to the blazing rock. Thither came also the slender form of a veiled female, led between Goody Cloyse, that pious teacher of the catechism, and Martha Carrier, who had received the devil's promise to be queen of hell. A rampant hag was she. And there stood the proselytes beneath the canopy of fire.

"Welcome, my children," said the dark figure, "to the communion of your race. Ye have found thus young your nature and your destiny. My children, look behind you!"

They turned; and flashing forth, as it were, in a sheet of flame, the fiend worshippers were seen; the smile of welcome gleamed darkly on every visage.

"There," resumed the sable form, "are all whom ye have reverenced from youth. Ye deemed them holier than yourselves, and shrank from your own sin, contrasting it with their lives of righteousness and prayerful aspirations heavenward. Yet here are they all in my worshipping assembly. This night it shall be granted you to know their secret deeds: how hoary-bearded elders of the church have whispered wanton words to the young maids of their households; how many a woman, eager for widows' weeds, has given her husband a drink at bedtime and let him sleep his last sleep in her bosom; how beardless youths have made haste to inherit their fathers' wealth; and how fair damsels—blush not, sweet ones—have dug little graves in the garden, and bidden me, the sole guest, to an infant's funeral. By the sympathy of your human hearts for sin ye shall scent out all the places—whether in church, bed-chamber, street, field, or forest—where crime has been committed, and shall exult to behold the whole earth one stain of guilt, one mighty blood spot. Far more than this. It shall be yours to penetrate, in every bosom, the deep mystery of sin, the fountain of all wicked arts, and which inexhaustibly supplies more evil impulses than human power—than my power at its utmost—can make manifest in deeds. And now, my children, look upon each other."

They did so; and, by the blaze of the hell-kindled torches, the wretched man beheld his Faith, and the wife her husband, trembling before that unhallowed altar.

"Lo, there ye stand, my children," said the figure, in a deep and solemn tone, almost sad with its despairing awfulness, as if his once angelic nature could yet mourn for our miserable race. "Depending upon one another's hearts, ye had still hoped that virtue were not all a dream. Now are ye undeceived. Evil is the nature of mankind. Evil must be your only happiness. Welcome again, my children, to the communion of your race."

"Welcome," repeated the fiend worshippers, in one cry of despair and triumph.

And there they stood, the only pair, as it seemed, who were yet hesitating on the verge of wickedness in this dark world. A basin was hollowed, naturally, in the rock. Did it contain water, reddened by the lurid light? or was it blood? or, perchance, a liquid flame? Herein did the shape of evil dip his hand and prepare to lay the mark of baptism upon their foreheads, that they might be partakers of the mystery of sin, more conscious of the secret guilt of others, both in deed and thought, than they could now be of their own. The husband cast one look at his pale wife, and Faith at him. What polluted wretches would the next glance show them to each other, shuddering alike at what they disclosed and what they saw.

"Faith! Faith!" cried the husband, "look up to heaven, and resist the wicked one."

Whether Faith obeyed he knew not. Hardly had he spoken when he found himself amid calm night and solitude, listening to a roar of the wind which died heavily away through the forest. He staggered against the rock, and felt it chill and damp; while a hanging twig, that had been all on fire, besprinkled his cheek with the coldest dew.

The next morning young Goodman Brown came slowly into the street of Salem village, staring around him like a bewildered man. The good old minister was taking a walk along the graveyard to get an appetite for breakfast and meditate his sermon, and bestowed a blessing, as he passed, on Goodman Brown. He shrank from the venerable saint as if to avoid an anathema. Old Deacon Gookin was at domestic worship, and the holy words of his prayer were heard through the open window. "What God doth the wizard pray to?" quoth Goodman Brown. Goody Cloyse, that excellent old Christian, stood in the early sunshine at her own lattice, catechizing a little girl who had brought her a pint of morning's milk. Goodman Brown snatched away the child as from the grasp of the fiend himself. Turning the corner by the meeting-house, he spied the head of Faith, with the pink ribbons, gazing anxiously forth, and bursting into such joy at sight of him that she skipped along the street and almost kissed her husband before the whole village. But Goodman Brown looked sternly and sadly into her face, and passed on without a greeting.

Had Goodman Brown fallen asleep in the forest and only dreamed a wild dream of a witch-meeting?

Be it so if you will; but, alas! it was a dream of evil omen for young Goodman Brown. A stern, a sad, a darkly meditative, a distrustful, if not a desperate man did he become from the night of that fearful dream. On the Sabbath day, when the congregation were singing a holy psalm, he could not listen because an anthem of sin rushed loudly upon his ear and drowned all the blessed strain. When the minister spoke from the pulpit with power and fervid eloquence, and, with his hand on the open Bible, of the sacred truths of our religion, and of saint-like lives and triumphant deaths, and of future bliss or misery unutterable, then did Goodman Brown turn pale, dreading lest the roof should thunder down upon the gray blasphemer and his hearers. Often, awaking suddenly at midnight, he shrank from the bosom of Faith; and at morning or eventide, when the family knelt down at prayer, he scowled and muttered to himself, and gazed sternly at his wife, and turned away. And when he had lived long, and was borne to his grave a hoary corpse, followed by Faith, an aged woman, and children and grandchildren, a goodly procession, besides neighbors not a few, they carved no hopeful verse upon his tombstone, for his dying hour was gloom.

Study and Discussion Questions

1. Think about the names of the characters. What is the significance of these names?
2. Who is the person young Goodman Brown meets in the forest? Why does Hawthorne mention that the two resemble each other?
3. What is young Goodman Brown's errand this night? Why doesn't he tell his wife what it is?
4. What are the travelling companion's means of persuasion?
5. What finally causes Goodman Brown to go on with his journey?
6. Who is at the meeting in the woods? In what ways does that community differ from the one Goodman Brown (a) comes from and (b) expected to find there?
7. What does this story suggest is the "real" nature of human beings?

Suggestions for Writing

1. Write about a time you discovered something (or thought you discovered something) that caused a major shift in the way you saw the world.
2. How would the story and your response to it have been changed if Hawthorne had left out the suggestion that all this might have been a dream?

SHERMAN ALEXIE (b. 1966)

Sherman Alexie was born on the Spokane Indian Reservation in the state of Washington. Learning to read by the age of three, Alexie excelled at the BIA (Bureau of Indian Affairs) reservation school, but decided to attend Reardon High School, 32 miles from the reservation because he thought he would receive a stronger education there. Alexie, "The only Indian . . . except for the school mascot" (shermanalexie.com), graduated with honors. After receiving his B.A. in American Studies, Alexie was granted a National Endowment for

the Arts Poetry Fellowship in 1992. Whether in poetry, prose or drama, Alexie
has sought to bring the realities of modern reservation life to the public. His
work is laden with dark humor—a humor full of irony that is both critical of
the dominant culture and hopeful of a better future for all Native Americans.
Alexie has also gained notoriety as a slam poet and screenplay writer. His writings include the poetry collections *The Business of Fancydancing* (1991), *I
Would Steal Horses* (1993), and *The Man Who Loves Salmon* (1998); the short
story collection *The Lone Ranger and Tonto Fistfight in Heaven* (1993); the
novels *Reservation Blues* (1995) and *Indian Killer* (1996); and the screenplays
Smoke Signals (1998) and *The Business of Fancydancing* (2003). His latest
work is the collection of short stories *Ten Little Indians* (2003). The following
piece is taken from *The Lone Ranger and Tonto Fistfight in Heaven*.

Jesus Christ's Half-Brother Is Alive and Well on the Spokane Indian Reservation　　　　　　　　　(1993)

1966

Rosemary MorningDove gave birth to a boy today and seeing as how it was
nearly Christmas and she kept telling everyone she was still a virgin even
though Frank Many Horses said it was his we all just figured it was an accident.
Anyhow she gave birth to him but he came out all blue and they couldn't get
him to breathe for a long time but he finally did and Rosemary MorningDove
named him —————— which is unpronounceable in Indian and English but it
means: *He Who Crawls Silently Through the Grass with a Small Bow and One
Bad Arrow Hunting for Enough Deer to Feed the Whole Tribe.*
　We just call him James.

1967

Frank Many Horses and Lester FallsApart and I were drinking beers in the
Breakaway Bar playing pool and talking stories when we heard the sirens. Indians
get all excited when we hear sirens because it means fires and it means they need
firefighters to put out the fires and it means we get to be firefighters and it means
we get paid to be firefighters. Hell somebody always starts a fire down at the Indian
burial grounds and it was about time for the Thirteenth Annual All-Indian Burial
Grounds Fire so Frank and Lester and I ran down to the fire station expecting to
get hired but we see smoke coming from Commodity Village where all the really
poor Indians live so we run down there instead and it was Rosemary Morning-
Dove's house that was on fire. Indians got buckets of water but this fire was way

too big and we could hear a baby crying and Frank Many Horses gets all excited even though it's Lillian Many's baby right next to us. But Frank knows James is in the house so he goes running in before any of us can stop him and pretty soon I see Frank leaning out the upstairs window holding James and they're both a little on fire and Frank throws James out the window and I'm running my ass over to catch him before he hits the ground making like a high school football hero again but I miss him just barely slipping through my fingers and James hits the ground hard and I pick him up right away and slap the flames out with my hands all the while expecting James to be dead but he's just looking at me almost normal except the top of his head looks all dented in like a beer can.

He wasn't crying.

1967

I went down to the reservation hospital to see how James and Frank and Rosemary were doing and I got drunk just before I went so I wouldn't be scared of all the white walls and the sound of arms and legs getting sawed off down in the basement. But I heard the screams anyway and they were Indian screams and those can travel forever like all around the world and sometimes from a hundred years ago so I close my ears and hide my eyes and just look down at the clean clean floors. Oh Jesus I'm so drunk I want to pray but I don't and before I can change my mind about coming here Moses MorningDove pulls me aside to tell me Frank and Rosemary have died and since I saved James's life I should be the one who raises him. Moses says it's Indian tradi-tion but somehow since Moses is going on about two hundred years old and still drinking and screwing like he was twenty I figure he's just trying to get out of his grandfatherly duties. I don't really want any of it and I'm sick and the hospital is making me sicker and my heart is shaking and confused like when the nurse wakes you up in the middle of the night to give you a sleeping pill but I know James will end up some Indian kid at a welfare house making bas-kets and wearing itchy clothes and I'm only twenty myself but I take one look at James all lumpy and potato looking and I look in the mirror and see myself holding him and I take him home.

Tonight the mirror will forgive my face.

1967

All dark tonight and James couldn't sleep and just kept looking at the ceiling so I walk on down to the football field carrying James so we can both watch the stars looking down at the reservation. I put James down on the fifty-yard line and I run and run across the frozen grass wishing there was snow enough to make a trail and let the world know I was there in the morning. Thinking I could spell out my name or James's name or every name I could think of until I stepped on every piece of snow on the field like it was every piece of the world or at least every piece of this reservation that has so many pieces it might just be the world. I want to walk circles around James getting closer and closer to him in a new dance and a better kind of healing which could make James talk and walk before he learns to cry. But he's not crying and he's not walking and he's not talking and I see him sometimes like an old man passed out in the back of a reservation van with shit in his pants and a battered watch in his pocket that always shows the same damn time. So I pick James up from the cold and the grass that waits for spring and the sun to change its world but I can only walk home through the cold with another future on my back and James's future tucked in my pocket like an empty wallet or a newspaper that feeds the fire and never gets read.

Sometimes all of this is home.

1968

The world changing the world changing the world. I don't watch the TV any-more since it exploded and left a hole in the wall. The woodpile don't dream of me no more. It sits there by the ax and they talk about the cold that waits in cor-ners and surprises you on a warm almost spring day. Today I stood at the win-dow for hours and then I took the basketball from inside the wood stove and shot baskets at the hoop nailed to a pine tree in the yard. I shot and shot until the cold meant I was protected because my skin was too warm to feel any of it. I shot and shot until my fingertips bled and my feet ached and my hair stuck to the skin of my bare back. James waited by the porch with his hands in the dirt and his feet stuck into leather shoes I found in the dump under a washing machine. I can't believe the details I am forced to remember with each day that James comes closer to talking. I change his clothes and his dirty pants and I wash his face and the crevices of his little body until he shines like a new check.

This is my religion.

1968

Seems like the cold would never go away and winter would be like the bottom of my feet but then it is gone in one night and in its place comes the sun so large and laughable. James sitting up in his chair so young and he won't talk and the doctors at the Indian clinic say it's way too early for him to be talking anyhow but I see in his eyes something and I see in his eyes a voice and I see in his eyes a whole new set of words. It ain't Indian or English and it ain't cash register and it ain't traffic light or speed bump and it ain't window or door. Late one day James and I watch the sun fly across the sky like a basketball on fire until it falls down completely and lands in Benjamin Lake with a splash and shakes the ground and even wakes up Lester Falls-Apart who thought it was his father come back to slap his face again.

Summer coming like a car from down the highway.

1968

James must know how to cry because he hasn't cried yet and I know he's waiting for that one moment to cry like it was five hundred years of tears. He ain't walked anywhere and there are no blisters on his soles but there are dreams worn clean into his rib cage and it shakes and shakes with each breath and I see he's trying to talk when he grabs at the air behind his head or stares up at the sky so hard. All of this temperature rising hot and I set James down in the shade by the basketball court and I play and I play until the sweat of my body makes it rain everywhere on the reservation. I play and I play until the music of my shoes against pavement sounds like every drum. Then I'm home alone and I watch the cockroaches live their complicated lives.

I hold James with one arm and my basketball with the other arm and I hold everything else inside my whole body.

1969

I take James to the Indian clinic because he ain't crying yet and because all he does sometimes is stare and stare and sometimes he'll wrap his arms around the stray dogs and let them carry him around the yard. He's strong enough to hold his body off the ground but he ain't strong enough to lift his tongue from the bottom of his mouth to use the words for love or anger or hunger or good morning. Maybe he's only a few years old but he's got eyes that are ancient and old and dark like a castle or a lake where the turtles go to die and sometimes even to live. Maybe he's going to howl out the words when I least expect it or want it and he'll yell out a cuss word in church or a prayer in the middle of a grocery store. Today I moved through town and walked and walked past the people who hadn't seen me in so long maybe for months and they asked questions about me and James and no one bothered to knock on the door and look for the answers. It's just me and James walking and walking except he's on my back and his eyes are looking past the people who are looking past us for the coyote of our soul and the wolverine of our heart and the crazy crazy man that touches every Indian who spends too much time alone. I stand in the Trading Post touching the canned goods and hoping for a vision of all the miles until Seymour comes in with a twenty-dollar bill and buys a couple cases of beer and we drink and drink all night long. James gets handed from woman to woman and from man to man and a few children hold this child of mine who doesn't cry or recognize the human being in his own body. All the drunks happy to see me drunk again and back from the wagon and I fell off that wagon and broke my ass and dreams and I wake up the next morning in a field watching a cow watch me. With piss in my pants I make the long walk home past the HUD houses and abandoned cars and past the powwow grounds and the Assembly of God where the sinless sing like they could forgive us all. I get home and James is there with Suzy Song feeding him and rocking him like a boat or a three-legged chair.

I say no and I take James away and put him in his crib and I move into Suzy's arms and let her rock and rock me away from my stomach and thin skin.

1969

Long days and nights mean the sky looks the same all the time and James has no words yet but he dreams and kicks in his sleep and sometimes kicks his body against my body as he sleeps in my arms. Nobody dreams all the time because it would hurt too much but James keeps dreaming and sleeping through a summer rainstorm and heat lightning reaching down a hand and then a fist to tear a tree in half and then to tear my eyes in half with the light. We had venison for dinner. We ate deer and its wild taste shook me up and down my spine. James spit his mouthful out on the floor and the dogs came to finish it up and I ate and ate and the dogs ate and ate what they could find and the deer grew in my stomach. The deer grew horns and hooves and skin and eyes that pushed at my rib cage and I ate and ate until I could not feel anything but my stomach expanding and stretched full.

All my life the days I remember most with every detail sharp and clear are the days when my stomach was full.

1969

We played our first basketball game of the season tonight in the community center and I had Suzy Song watch James while I played and all of us warriors roaring against the air and the nets and the clock that didn't work and our memories and our dreams and the twentieth-century horses we called our legs. We played some Nez Percé team and they ran like they were still running from the cavalry and they were kicking the shit out of us again when I suddenly steal the ball from their half-white point guard and drive all the way to the bucket. I jump in the air planning to dunk it when the half-white point guard runs under me knocking my ass to the floor and when I land I hear a crunch and my leg bends in half the wrong way. They take me to the reservation hospital and later on they tell me my leg has exploded and I can't play ball for a long time or maybe forever and when Suzy comes by with James and they ask me if this is my wife and son and I tell them yes and James still doesn't make a noise and so they ask me how old he is. I tell them he's almost four years old and they say his physical development is slow but that's normal for an Indian child. Anyhow I have to have an operation and all but since I don't have the money or the strength or the memory and it's not covered by Indian Health I just get up and walk home almost crying because my leg and life hurt so bad. Suzy stays with me that night and in the dark she touches my knee and asks me how much it hurts and I tell her it hurts more than I can talk about so she kisses all my scars and she huddles up close to me and she's warm and she talks into my ear close. She isn't always asking questions and sometimes she has the answers. In the morning I wake up before her and I hobble into the kitchen and make some coffee and fix a couple of bowls of cornflakes and we sit in bed eating together while James lies still in his crib watching the ceiling so Suzy and I watch the ceiling too.

The ordinary can be like medicine.

1970

Early snow this year and James and I sit at home by the stove because I can't walk anywhere with my bad knee and since it is snowing so hard outside nobody could drive out to get us but I know somebody must be thinking about us because if they weren't we'd just disappear just like those Indians who used to climb the pueblos. Those Indians disappeared with food still cooking in the pot and air waiting to be breathed and they turned into birds or dust or the blue of the sky or the yellow of the sun.

There they were and suddenly they were forgotten for just a second and for just a second nobody thought about them and then they were gone.

1970

I took James down to the reservation hospital again because he was almost five years old and still hadn't bothered to talk yet or crawl or cry or even move when I put him on the floor and once I even dropped him and his head was bleeding and he didn't make a sound. They looked him over and said there was nothing wrong with him and that he's just a little slow developing and that's what the doctors always say and they've been saying that about Indians for five hundred years. Jesus I say don't you know that James wants to dance and to sing and to pound a drum so hard it hurts your ears and he ain't ever going to drop an eagle feather and he's always going to be respectful to elders at least the Indian elders and he's going to change the world. He's going to dynamite Mount Rushmore or hijack a plane and make it land on the reservation highway. He's going to be a father and a mother and a son and a daughter and a dog that will pull you from a raging river.

He'll make gold out of commodity cheese.

1970

Happy birthday James and I'm in the Breakaway Bar drinking too many beers when the Vietnam war comes on television. The white people always want to fight someone and they always get the dark-skinned people to do the fighting. All I know about this war is what Seymour told me when he came back from his tour of duty over there and he said all the gooks he killed looked like us and Seymour said every single gook he killed looked exactly like someone he knew on the reservation. Anyhow I go to a Christmas party over at Jana Wind's house and leave James with my auntie so I could get really drunk and not have to worry about coming home for a few days or maybe for the rest of my life. We all get really drunk and Jana's old man Ray challenges me to a game of one-on-one since he says I'm for shit now and was never any good anyway but I tell him I can't since my knee is screwed up and besides there's two feet of snow on the ground and where are we going to play anyhow? Ray says I'm chickenshit so I tell him come on and we drive over to the high school to the outside court and there's two feet of snow on the court and we can't play but Ray smiles and pulls out a bottle of kerosene and pours it all over the court and lights it up and pretty soon the snow is all melted down along with most of Lester FallsApart's pants since he was standing too close to the court when Ray lit the fire. Anyhow the court is clear and Ray and I go at it and my knee only hurts a little and everyone was cheering us on and I can't remember who won since I was too drunk and so was everyone else. Later I hear how Ray and Joseph got arrested for beating some white guy half to death and I say that Ray and Joseph are just kids but Suzy says nobody on the reservation is ever a kid and that we're all born grown up anyway. I look at James and I think maybe Suzy is wrong about Indian kids being born adults and that maybe James was born this way and wants to stay this way like a baby because he doesn't want to grow up and see and do everything we all do?

There are all kinds of wars.

1971

So much time alone with a bottle of one kind or another and James and I remember nothing except the last drink and a drunk Indian is like the thinker statue except nobody puts a drunk Indian in a special place in front of a library. For most Indians the only special place in front of a library might be a heating grate or a piece of sun-warmed cement but that's an old joke and I used to sleep with my books in piles all over my bed and sometimes they were the only thing keeping me warm and always the only thing keeping me alive.

Books and beer are the best and worst defense.

1971

Jesse WildShoe died last night and today was the funeral and usually there's a wake but none of us had the patience or energy to mourn for days so we buried Jesse right away and dug the hole deep because Jesse could fancydance like God had touched his feet. Anyhow we dug the hole all day and since the ground was still a little frozen we kept doing the kerosene trick and melting the ice and frost and when we threw a match into the bottom of the grave it looked like I suppose hell must look and it was scary. There we were ten little Indians making a hell on earth for a fancydancer who already had enough of that shit and probably wouldn't want to have any more of it and I kept wondering if maybe we should just take his body high up in the mountains and bury him in the snow that never goes away. Maybe we just sort of freeze him so he doesn't have to feel anything anymore and especially not some crazy ideas of heaven or hell. I don't know anything about religion and I don't confess my sins to anybody except the walls and the wood stove and James who forgives everything like a rock. He ain't talking or crying at all and sometimes I shake him a little too hard or yell at him or leave him in his crib for hours all alone but he never makes a sound. One night I get so drunk I leave him at somebody's house and forget all about him and can you blame me? The tribal police drag me into the cell for abandonment and I'm asking them who they're going to arrest for abandoning me but the world is spinning and turning back on itself like a snake eating its own tail. Like a snake my TV dinner rises from the table the next day and snaps at my eyes and wrists and I ask the tribal cop how long I've been drunk and he tells me for most of a year and I don't remember any of it. I've got the DT's so bad and the walls are Nazis making lampshades out of my skin and the toilet is a white man in a white hood riding me down on horseback and the floor is a skinny man who wants to teach me a trick he's learned to do with a knife and my shoes squeal and kick and pull me down into the dead pig pit of my imagination. Oh Jesus I wake up on the bottom of that mass grave with the bones of generations of slaughter and I crawl and dig my way up through layers and years of the lunch special. I dig for hours through the skin and eyes and the fresh blood soon enough and pull myself through the eye of a sow and pluck the maggots from my hair and I want to scream but I don't want to open my mouth and taste and taste and taste.

Like the heroin addict said I just want to be pure.

1971

Been in A.A. for a month because that was the only way to keep James with me and my auntie and Suzy Song both moved into the house with me to make sure I don't drink and to help take care of James. They show the same old movies in A.A. and it's always the same white guy who almost destroys his life and his wife and his children and his job but finally realizes the alcohol is killing him and he quits overnight and spends the rest of the movie and the rest of his whole life at a picnic with his family and friends and boss all laughing and saying we didn't even recognize you back then Bob and we're glad to have you back Daddy and we'll hire you back at twice the salary you old dog you. Yesterday I get this postcard from Pine Ridge and my cousin says all the Indians there are gone and do I know where they went? I write back and tell him to look in the A.A. meeting and then I ask him if there are more birds with eyes that look like his and I ask him if the sky is more blue and the sun more yellow because those are the colors we all become when we die. I tell him to search his dreams for a man dressed in red with a red tie and red shoes and a hawk head. I tell him that man is fear and will eat you like a sandwich and will eat you like an ice cream cone and will never be full and he'll come for you in your dreams like he was a bad movie. I tell him to turn his television toward the wall and to study the walls for imperfections and those could be his mother and father and the stain on the ceiling could be his sisters and maybe the warped floorboard squeaking and squeaking is his grandfather talking stories.

Maybe they're all hiding on a ship in a bottle.

1972

Been sober so long it's like a dream but I feel better somehow and Auntie was so proud of me she took James and me into the city for James's checkup and James still wasn't talking but Auntie and James and I ate a great lunch at Woolworth's before we headed back to the reservation. I got to drive and Auntie's uranium money Cadillac is a hell of a car and it was raining a little and hot so there were rainbows rainbows rainbows and the pine trees looked like wise men with wet beards or at least I thought they did. That's how I do this life sometimes by making the ordinary just like magic and just like a card trick and just like a mirror and just like the disappearing. Every Indian learns how to be a magician and learns how to misdirect attention and the dark hand is always quicker than the white eye and no matter how close you get to my heart you will never find out my secrets and I'll never tell you and I'll never show you the same trick twice.

I'm traveling heavy with illusions.

1972

Every day I'm trying not to drink and I pray but I don't know who I'm praying to and if it's the basketball gathering ash on the shelf or the blank walls crushing me into the house or the television that only picks up public channels. I've seen only painters and fishermen and I think they're both the same kind of men who made a different choice one time in their lives. The fisherman held a rod in his hand and said yes and the painter held a brush in his hand and said yes and sometimes I hold a beer in my hand and say yes. At those moments I want to drink so bad that it aches and I cry which is a strange noise in our house because James refuses tears and he refuses words but sometimes he holds a hand up above his head like he's reaching for something. Yesterday I neatly trip over Lester FallsApart lying drunk as a skunk in front of the Trading Post and I pick him up and he staggers and trembles and falls back down. Lester I say you got to stand up on your own and I pick him up and he falls down again.

Only a saint would have tried to pick him up the third time.

1972

The streetlight outside my house shines on tonight and I'm watching it like it could give me vision. James ain't talked ever and he looks at that streetlight like it was a word and maybe like it was a verb. James wanted to streetlight me and make me bright and beautiful so all the moths and bats would circle me like I was the center of the world and held secrets. Like Joy said that everything but humans keeps secrets. Today I get my mail and there's a light bill and a postcard from an old love from Seattle who asks me if I still love her like I used to and would I come to visit?

I send her my light bill and tell her I don't ever want to see her again.

1973

James talked today but I had my back turned and I couldn't be sure it was real. He said potato like any good Indian would because that's all we eat. But maybe he said I love you because that's what I wanted him to say or maybe he said geology or mathematics or college basketball. I pick him up and ask him again and again what did you say? He just smiles and I take him to the clinic and the doctors say it's about time but are you sure you didn't imagine his voice? I said James's voice sounded like a beautiful glass falling off the shelf and landing safely on a thick shag carpet.

The doctor said I had a very good imagination.

1973

I'm shooting hoops again with the younger Indian boys and even some Indian girls who never miss a shot. They call me old man and elder and give me a little bit of respect like not running too fast or hard and even letting me shoot a few more than I should. It's been a long time since I played but the old feelings and old moves are there in my heart and in my fingers. I see these Indian kids and I know that basketball was invented by an Indian long before that Naismith guy ever thought about it. When I play I don't feel like drinking so I wish I could play twenty-four hours a day seven days a week and then I wouldn't wake up shaking and quaking and needing just one more beer before I stop for good.

James knows it too and he sits on the sideline clapping when my team scores and clapping when the other team scores too. He's got a good heart. He always talks whenever I'm not in the room or I'm not looking at him but never when anybody else might hear so they all think I'm crazy. I am crazy. He says things like I can't believe. He says $E = MC^2$ and that's why all my cousins drink themselves to death. He says the earth is an oval marble that nobody can win. He says the sky is not blue and the grass is not green.

He says everything is a matter of perception.

1973

Christmas and James gets his presents and he gives me the best present of all when he talks right at me. He says so many things and the only thing that matters is that he says he and I don't have the right to die for each other and that we should be living for each other instead. He says the world hurts. He says the first thing he wanted after he was born was a shot of whiskey. He says all that and more. He tells me to get a job and to grow my braids. He says I better learn how to shoot left-handed if I'm going to keep playing basketball. He says to open a fireworks stand.

Every day now there are little explosions all over the reservation.

1974

Today is the World's Fair in Spokane and James and I drive to Spokane with a few cousins of mine. All the countries have exhibitions like art from Japan and pottery from Mexico and mean-looking people talking about Germany. In one little corner there's a statue of an Indian who's supposed to be some chief or another. I press a little button and the statue talks and moves its arms over and over in the same motion. The statue tells the crowd we have to take care of the earth because it is our mother. I know that and James says he knows more. He says the earth is our grandmother and that technology has become our mother and that they both hate each other. James tells the crowd that the river just a few yards from where we stand is all we ever need to believe in. One white woman asks me how old James is and I tell her he's seven and she tells me that he's so smart for an Indian boy. James hears this and tells the white woman that she's pretty smart for an old white woman. I know this is how it will all begin and how the rest of my life will be. I know when I am old and sick and ready to die that James will wash my body and take care of my wastes. He'll carry me from HUD house to sweathouse and he will clean my wounds. And he will talk and teach me something new every day.

But all that is so far ahead.

Study and Discussion Questions

1. Discuss the title of Alexie's story. (*Note:* Jesus did have a brother or cousin named James.) What possibilities for redemption exist in the story?
2. Consider the child's two names.
3. How does Alexie's narrator become a (single) parent? How does this change his life? How does he change in response? Note several examples of the narrator's development throughout the story.
4. What do we learn about life on the Reservation from this story? List at least five points, citing evidence from the text.
5. Discuss the structure of the story. Why do you think Alexie chose to narrate the story in short, date-headed sections? Why the pattern of the substantial paragraph followed by a short one-sentence paragraph? Do you find this an effective way of telling this particular story?
6. Choose a few *images* (literal or figurative) that particularly strike you and discuss each. What does each image evoke for you? How and why are they effective?
7. Alexie said in a 1996 talk, (November 9, 1996, University of Massachusetts/Boston) "The most revolutionary thing I can do is raise a kid that loves him or her self." Discuss Alexie's statement in relation to this story.
8. How is Alexie's narrator as a parent? List positive and negative qualities, citing examples for each.
9. If it takes a village to raise a child, how is the Spokane Indian community as parenting support for the narrator?
10. Discuss both the religious (in the sense of allusions to the story of Christ) and the spiritual (e.g., the circumstances of the adoption, James's "strangeness," the language Alexie uses) implications of "Jesus Christ's Half-Brother Is Alive and Well on the Spokane Indian Reservation."
11. Does James finally talk? Give evidence from the story to support your opinion.
12. As it happens, 1966, the year the story of James begins, is also the year Sherman Alexie was born. How might this biographical fact add to your interpretation of the story?

Suggestions for Writing

1. Do some reading and research on life on Indian reservations in the United States. Then discuss this story along with the three Sherman Alexie poems "Futures," "The Reservation Cab Driver," and "The Powwow at the End of the World".
2. In the Bible (the King James translation, if possible), read the Epistle of James in the New Testament. Also read Acts XV, where James makes an important speech to the Apostles. How do some of the issues and themes connected with the Biblical James resonate with the story of James and his adoptive father in Alexie's story?

❈ ❈ ❈

MARY E. WILKINS FREEMAN (1852–1930)

Mary Eleanor Wilkins was born and lived much of her life in Randolph, Massachusetts. After high school, she spent a year at Mount Holyoke Female Seminary and soon began earning a living writing. She married Dr. Charles Freeman in 1902, when she was almost fifty, and moved with him to New Jersey, but their marriage fell apart due to his growing alcoholism. Freeman was widely read during her lifetime, but her work fell into obscurity after her death. Although she wrote children's books, poetry, novels, and plays, it is her short fiction that brought a revaluation of her work in the 1980s. Working within a realist mode, Freeman was a protofeminist voice from the nineteenth century—questioning the sentimental fiction of her day as well as the limited roles available to women. Her most well-known story collections are *A Humble Romance* (1887) and *A New England Nun* (1891). "A Mistaken Charity" looks at the struggle of two aging women and their desire to be independent.

A Mistaken Charity   (1887)

There were in a green field a little, low, weather-stained cottage, with a footpath leading to it from the highway several rods distant, and two old women—one with a tin pan and old knife searching for dandelion greens among the short young grass, and the other sitting on the doorstep watching her, or, rather, having the appearance of watching her.

"Air there enough for a mess, Harriét?" asked the old woman on the doorstep. She accented oddly the last syllable of the Harriet, and there was a curious quality in her feeble, cracked old voice. Besides the question denoted by the arrangement of her words and the rising inflection, there was another, broader and subtler, the very essence of all questioning, in the tone of her voice itself; the cracked, quavering notes that she used reached out of themselves, and asked, and groped like fingers in the dark. One would have known by the voice that the old woman was blind.

The old woman on her knees in the grass searching for dandelions did not reply; she evidently had not heard the question. So the old woman on the doorstep, after waiting a few minutes with her head turned expectantly, asked again, varying her question slightly, and speaking louder:

"Air there enough for a mess, do ye s'pose, Harriét?"

The old woman in the grass heard this time. She rose slowly and laboriously; the effort of straightening out the rheumatic old muscles was evidently a painful one; then she eyed the greens heaped up in the tin pan, and pressed them down with her hand.

"Wa'al, I don't know, Charlotte," she replied, hoarsely. "There's plenty on 'em here, but I 'ain't got near enough for a mess; they do bile down so when you get 'em in the pot; an' it's all I can do to bend my j'ints enough to dig 'em."

"I'd give consider'ble to help ye, Harriét," said the old woman on the door-step.

But the other did not hear her; she was down on her knees in the grass again, anxiously spying out the dandelions.

So the old woman on the door-step crossed her little shrivelled hands over her calico knees, and sat quite still, with the soft spring wind blowing over her.

The old wooden door-step was sunk low down among the grasses, and the whole house to which it belonged had an air of settling down and mouldering into the grass as into its own grave.

When Harriet Shattuck grew deaf and rheumatic, and had to give up her work as tailoress, and Charlotte Shattuck lost her eyesight, and was unable to do any more sewing for her livelihood, it was a small and trifling charity for the rich man who held a mortgage on the little house in which they had been born and lived all their lives to give them the use of it, rent and interest free. He might as well have taken credit to himself for not charging a squirrel for his tenement in some old decaying tree in his woods.

So ancient was the little habitation, so wavering and mouldering, the hands that had fashioned it had lain still so long in their graves, that it almost seemed to have fallen below its distinctive rank as a house. Rain and snow had filtered through its roof, mosses had grown over it, worms had eaten it, and birds built their nests under its eaves; nature had almost completely overrun and obliterated the work of man, and taken her own to herself again, till the house seemed as much a natural ruin as an old treestump.

The Shattucks had always been poor people and common people; no especial grace and refinement or fine ambition had ever characterized any of them; they had always been poor and coarse and common. The father and his father before him had simply lived in the poor little house, grubbed for their living, and then unquestioningly died. The mother had been of no rarer stamp, and the two daughters were cast in the same mould.

After their parents' death Harriet and Charlotte had lived along in the old place from youth to old age, with the one hope of ability to keep a roof over their heads, covering on their backs, and victuals in their mouths—an all-sufficient one with them.

Neither of them had ever had a lover; they had always seemed to repel rather than attract the opposite sex. It was not merely because they were poor, ordinary, and homely; there were plenty of men in the place who would have matched them well in that respect; the fault lay deeper—in their characters. Harriet, even in her girlhood, had a blunt, defiant manner that almost amounted to surliness, and was well calculated to alarm timid adorers, and Charlotte had always had the reputation of not being any too strong in her mind.

Harriet had gone about from house to house doing tailorwork after the primitive country fashion, and Charlotte had done plain sewing and mending for the neighbors. They had been, in the main, except when pressed by some temporary anxiety about their work or the payment thereof, happy and contented, with that negative kind of happiness and contentment which comes not from gratified ambition, but a lack of ambition itself. All that they cared for they had had in tolerable abundance, for Harriet at least had been swift and capable about her work. The patched, mossy old roof had been kept over their heads, the coarse, hearty food that they loved had been set on their table, and their cheap clothes had been warm and strong.

After Charlotte's eyes failed her, and Harriet had the rheumatic fever, and the little hoard of earnings went to the doctors, times were harder with them, though still it could not be said that they actually suffered.

When they could not pay the interest on the mortgage they were allowed to keep the place interest free; there was as much fitness in a mortgage on the little house, anyway, as there would have been on a rotten old apple-tree; and the people about, who were mostly farmers, and good friendly folk, helped them out with their living. One would donate a barrel of apples from his abundant harvest to the two poor old women, one a barrel of potatoes, another a load of wood for the winter fuel, and many a farmer's wife had bustled up the narrow foot-path with a pound of butter, or a dozen fresh eggs, or a nice bit of pork. Besides all this, there was a tiny garden patch behind the house, with a straggling row of currant bushes in it, and one of gooseberries, where Harriet contrived every year to raise a few pumpkins, which were the pride of her life. On the right of the garden were two old apple-trees, a Baldwin and a Porter, both yet in a tolerably good fruit-bearing state.

The delight which the two poor old souls took in their own pumpkins, their apples and currants, was indescribable. It was not merely that they contributed largely towards their living; they were their own, their private share of the great wealth of nature, the little taste set apart for them alone out of her bounty, and worth more to them on that account, though they were not conscious of it, than all the richer fruits which they received from their neighbors' gardens.

This morning the two apple-trees were brave with flowers, the currant bushes looked alive, and the pumpkin seeds were in the ground. Harriet cast complacent glances in their direction from time to time, as she painfully dug her dandelion greens. She was a short, stoutly built old woman, with a large face coarsely wrinkled, with a suspicion of a stubble of beard on the square chin.

When her tin pan was filled to her satisfaction with the sprawling, spidery greens, and she was hobbling stiffly towards her sister on the door-step, she saw another woman standing before her with a basket in her hand.

"Good-morning, Harriet," she said, in a loud, strident voice, as she drew near. "I've been frying some doughnuts, and I brought you over some warm."

"I've been tellin' her it was real good in her," piped Charlotte from the door-step, with an anxious turn of her sightless face towards the sound of her sister's footstep.

Harriet said nothing but a hoarse "Good-mornin', Mis' Simonds." Then she took the basket in her hand, lifted the towel off the top, selected a doughnut, and deliberately tasted it.

"Tough," said she. "I s'posed so. If there is anything I 'spise on this airth it's a tough doughnut."

"Oh, Harriét!" said Charlotte, with a frightened look.

"They air tough," said Harriet, with hoarse defiance, "and if there is anything I 'spise on this airth it's a tough doughnut."

The woman whose benevolence and cookery were being thus ungratefully received only laughed. She was quite fleshy, and had a round, rosy, determined face.

"Well, Harriet," said she, "I am sorry they are tough, but perhaps you had better take them out on a plate, and give me my basket. You may be able to eat two or three of them if they are tough."

"They air tough—turrible tough," said Harriet, stubbornly; but she took the basket into the house and emptied it of its contents nevertheless.

"I suppose your roof leaked as bad as ever in that heavy rain day before yesterday?" said the visitor to Harriet, with an inquiring squint towards the mossy shingles, as she was about to leave with her empty basket.

"It was turrible," replied Harriet, with crusty acquiescence—"turrible. We had to set pails an' pans everywheres, an' move the bed out."

"Mr. Upton ought to fix it."

"There ain't any fix to it; the old ruff ain't fit to nail new shingles on to; the hammerin' would bring the whole thing down on our heads," said Harriet, grimly.

"Well, I don't know as it can be fixed, it's so old. I suppose the wind comes in bad around the windows and doors too?"

"It's like livin' with a piece of paper, or mebbe a sieve, 'twixt you an' the wind an' the rain," quoth Harriet, with a jerk of her head.

"You ought to have a more comfortable home in your old age," said the visitor, thoughtfully.

"Oh, it's well enough," cried Harriet, in quick alarm, and with a complete change of tone; the woman's remark had brought an old dread over her. "The old house'll last as long as Charlotte an' me do. The rain ain't so bad, nuther is the wind; there's room enough for us in the dry places, an' out of the way of the doors an' windows. It's enough sight better than goin' on the town." Her square, defiant old face actually looked pale as she uttered the last words and stared apprehensively at the woman.

"Oh, I did not think of your doing that," she said, hastily and kindly. "We all know how you feel about that, Harriet, and not one of us neighbors will see you and Charlotte go to the poorhouse while we've got a crust of bread to share with you."

Harriet's face brightened. "Thank ye, Mis' Simonds," she said, with reluctant courtesy. "I'm much obleeged to you an' the neighbors. I think mebbe we'll be able to eat some of them doughnuts if they air tough," she added, mollifyingly, as her caller turned down the foot-path.

"My, Harriét," said Charlotte, lifting up a weakly, wondering, peaked old face, "what did you tell her them doughnuts was tough fur?"

"Charlotte, do you want everybody to look down on us, an' think we ain't no account at all, just like any beggars, 'cause they bring us in vittles?" said Harriet, with a grim glance at her sister's meek, unconscious face.

"No, Harriét," she whispered.

"Do you want *to go to the poor-house?*"

"No, Harriét." The poor little old woman on the door-step fairly cowered before her aggressive old sister.

"Then don't hender me agin when I tell folks their doughnuts is tough an' their pertaters is poor. If I don't kinder keep up an' show some sperrit, I sha'n't think nothing of myself, an' other folks won't nuther, and fust thing we know they'll kerry us to the poorhouse. You'd 'a been there before now if it hadn't been for me, Charlotte."

Charlotte looked meekly convinced, and her sister sat down on a chair in the doorway to scrape her dandelions.

"Did you git a good mess, Harriét?" asked Charlotte, in a humble tone.

"Toler'ble."

"They'll be proper relishin' with that piece of pork Mis' Mann brought in yesterday. O Lord, Harriét, it's a chink!"

Harriet sniffed.

Her sister caught with her sensitive ear the little contemptuous sound. "I guess," she said, querulously, and with more pertinacity than she had shown in the matter of the doughnuts, "that if you was in the dark, as I am, Harriét, you wouldn't make fun an' turn up your nose at chinks. If you had seen the light streamin' in all of a sudden through some little hole that you hadn't known of before when you set down on the doorstep this mornin', and the wind with the smell of the apple blows in it came in your face, an' when Mis' Simonds brought them hot doughnuts, an' when I thought of the pork an' greens jest now— O Lord, how it did shine in! An' it does now. If you was me, Harriét, you would know there was chinks."

Tears began starting from the sightless eyes, and streaming pitifully down the pale old cheeks.

Harriet looked at her sister, and her grim face softened.

"Why, Charlotte, hev it that thar *is* chinks if you want to. Who cares?"

"Thar *is* chinks, Harriét."

"Wa'al, thar *is* chinks, then. If I don't hurry, I sha'n't get these greens in in time for dinner."

When the two old women sat down complacently to their meal of pork and dandelion greens in their little kitchen they did not dream how destiny slowly and surely was introducing some new colors into their web of life, even when it was almost completed, and that this was one of the last meals they would eat in their old home for many a day. In about a week from that day they were established in the "Old Ladies' Home" in a neighboring city. It came about in this wise: Mrs. Simonds, the woman who had brought the gift of hot dough-nuts, was a smart, energetic person, bent on doing good, and she did a great deal. To be sure, she always did it in her own way. If she chose to give hot doughnuts, she gave hot doughnuts; it made not the slightest difference to her if the recipients of her charity would infinitely have preferred ginger cookies. Still, a great many would like hot doughnuts, and she did unquestionably a great deal of good.

She had a worthy coadjutor in the person of a rich and childless elderly widow in the place. They had fairly entered into a partnership in good works, with about an equal capital on both sides, the widow furnishing the money, and Mrs. Simonds, who had much the better head of the two, furnishing the active schemes of benevolence.

The afternoon after the doughnut episode she had gone to the widow with a new project, and the result was that entrance fees had been paid, and old Harriet and Charlotte made sure of a comfortable home for the rest of their lives. The widow was hand in glove with officers of missionary boards and trustees of charitable institutions. There had been an unusual mortality among the inmates of the "Home" this spring, there were several vacancies, and the matter of the admission of Harriet and Charlotte was very quickly and easily arranged. But the matter which would have seemed the least difficult—inducing the two old women to accept the bounty which Providence, the widow, and Mrs. Simonds were ready to bestow on them—proved the most so. The struggle to persuade them to abandon their tottering old home for a better was a terrible one. The widow had pleaded with mild surprise, and Mrs. Simonds with benevolent determination; the counsel and reverend eloquence of the minister had been called in; and when they yielded at last it was with a sad grace for the recipients of a worthy charity.

It had been hard to convince them that the "Home" was not an almshouse under another name, and their yielding at length to anything short of actual force was only due probably to the plea, which was advanced most eloquently to Harriet, that Charlotte would be so much more comfortable.

The morning they came away, Charlotte cried pitifully, and trembled all over her little shrivelled body. Harriet did not cry. But when her sister had passed out the low, sagging door she turned the key in the lock, then took it out and thrust it slyly into her pocket, shaking her head to herself with an air of fierce determination.

Mrs. Simonds's husband, who was to take them to the depot, said to himself, with disloyal defiance of his wife's active charity, that it was a shame, as he helped the two distressed old souls into his light wagon, and put the poor little box, with their homely clothes in it, in behind.

Mrs. Simonds, the widow, the minister, and the gentleman from the "Home" who was to take charge of them, were all at the depot, their faces beaming with the delight of successful benevolence. But the two poor old women looked like two forlorn prisoners in their midst. It was an impressive illustration of the truth of the saying "that it is more blessed to give than to receive."

Well, Harriet and Charlotte Shattuck went to the "Old Ladies' Home" with reluctance and distress. They stayed two months, and then—they ran away.

The "Home" was comfortable, and in some respects even luxurious; but nothing suited those two unhappy, unreasonable old women.

The fare was of a finer, more delicately served variety than they had been accustomed to; those finely flavored nourishing soups for which the "Home" took great credit to itself failed to please palates used to common, coarser food.

"O Lord, Harriét, when I set down to the table here there ain't no chinks," Charlotte used to say. "If we could hev some cabbage, or some pork an' greens, how the light would stream in!"

Then they had to be more particular about their dress. They had always been tidy enough, but now it had to be something more; the widow, in the kindness of her heart, had made it possible, and the good folks in charge of the "Home," in the kindness of their hearts, tried to carry out the widow's designs.

But nothing could transform these two unpolished old women into two nice old ladies. They did not take kindly to white lace caps and delicate neckerchiefs. They liked their new black cashmere dresses well enough, but they felt as if they broke a commandment when they put them on every afternoon. They had always worn calico with long aprons at home, and they wanted to now; and they wanted to twist up their scanty gray locks into little knots at the back of their heads, and go without caps, just as they always had done.

Charlotte in a dainty white cap was pitiful, but Harriet was both pitiful and comical. They were totally at variance with their surroundings, and they felt it keenly, as people of their stamp always do. No amount of kindness and attention—and they had enough of both—sufficed to reconcile them to their new abode. Charlotte pleaded continually with her sister to go back to their old home.

"O Lord, Harriét," she would exclaim (by the way, Charlotte's "O Lord," which, as she used it, was innocent enough, had been heard with much disfavor in the "Home," and she, not knowing at all why, had been remonstrated with concerning it), "let us go home. I can't stay here no ways in this world. I don't like their vittles, an' I don't like to wear a cap; I want to go home and do different. The currants will be ripe, Harriét. O Lord, thar was almost a chink, thinking about 'em. I want some of 'em; an' the Porter apples will be gettin' ripe, an' we could have some apple-pie. This here ain't good; I want merlasses fur sweeting. Can't we get back no ways, Harriét? It ain't far, an' we could walk, an' they don't lock us in, nor nothin'. I don't want to die here; it ain't so straight up to heaven from here. O Lord, I've felt as if I was slantendicular from heaven ever since I've been here, an' it's been so awful dark. I ain't had any chinks. I want to go home, Harriét."

"We'll go to-morrow mornin'," said Harriet, finally; "we'll pack up our things an' go; we'll put on our old dresses, an' we'll do up the new ones in bundles, an' we'll jest shy out the back way to-morrow mornin'; an' we'll go. I kin find the way, an' I reckon we kin git thar, if it is fourteen mile. Mebbe somebody will give us a lift."

And they went. With a grim humor Harriet hung the new white lace caps with which she and Charlotte had been so pestered, one on each post at the head of the bedstead, so they would meet the eyes of the first person who opened the door. Then they took their bundles, stole slyly out, and were soon on the high-road, hobbling along, holding each other's hands, as jubilant as two children, and chuckling to themselves over their escape, and the probable astonishment there would be in the "Home" over it.

"O Lord, Harriét, what do you s'pose they will say to them caps?" cried Charlotte, with a gleeful cackle.

"I guess they'll see as folks ain't goin' to be made to wear caps agin their will in a free kentry," returned Harriet, with an echoing cackle, as they sped feebly and bravely along.

The "Home" stood on the very outskirts of the city, luckily for them. They would have found it a difficult undertaking to traverse the crowded streets. As it was, a short walk brought them into the free country road—free comparatively, for even here at ten o'clock in the morning there was considerable traveling to and from the city on business or pleasure.

People whom they met on the road did not stare at them as curiously as might have been expected. Harriet held her bristling chin high in air, and hobbled along with an appearance of being well aware of what she was about, that led folks to doubt their own first opinion that there was something unusual about the two old women.

Still their evident feebleness now and then occasioned from one and another more particular scrutiny. When they had been on the road a half-hour or so, a man in a covered wagon drove up behind them. After he had passed them, he poked his head around the front of the vehicle and looked back. Finally he stopped, and waited for them to come up to him.

"Like a ride, ma'am?" said he, looking at once bewildered and compassionate.

"Thankee," said Harriet, "we'd be much obleeged."

After the man had lifted the old women into the wagon, and established them on the back seat, he turned around, as he drove slowly along, and gazed at them curiously.

"Seems to me you look pretty feeble to be walking far," said he. "Where were you going?"

Harriet told him with an air of defiance.

"Why," he exclaimed, "it is fourteen miles out. You could never walk it in the world. Well, I am going within three miles of there, and I can go on a little farther as well as not. But I don't see—Have you been in the city?"

"I have been visitin' my married darter in the city," said Harriet, calmly.

Charlotte started, and swallowed convulsively.

Harriet had never told a deliberate falsehood before in her life, but this seemed to her one of the tremendous exigencies of life which justify a lie. She felt desperate. If she could not contrive to deceive him in some way, the man might turn directly around and carry Charlotte and her back to the "Home" and the white caps.

"I should not have thought your daughter would have let you start for such a walk as that," said the man. "Is this lady your sister? She is blind, isn't she? She does not look fit to walk a mile."

"Yes, she's my sister," replied Harriet, stubbornly: "an' she's blind; an' my darter didn't want us to walk. She felt reel bad about it. But she couldn't help it. She's poor, and her husband's dead, an' she's got four leetle children."

Harriet recounted the hardships of her imaginary daughter with a glibness that was astonishing. Charlotte swallowed again.

"Well," said the man, "I am glad I overtook you, for I don't think you would ever have reached home alive."

About six miles from the city an open buggy passed them swiftly. In it were seated the matron and one of the gentlemen in charge of the "Home." They never thought of looking into the covered wagon—and indeed one can travel in one of those vehicles, so popular in some parts of New England, with as much privacy as he could in his tomb. The two in the buggy were seriously alarmed, and anxious for the safety of the old women, who were chuckling maliciously in the wagon they soon left far behind. Harriet had watched them breathlessly until they disappeared on a curve of the road; then she whispered to Charlotte.

A little after noon the two old women crept slowly up the foot-path across the field to their old home.

"The clover is up to our knees," said Harriet; "an' the sorrel and the white-weed; an' there's lots of yaller butterflies."

"O Lord, Harriét, thar's a chink, an' I do believe I saw one of them yaller butterflies go past it," cried Charlotte, trembling all over, and nodding her gray head violently.

Harriet stood on the old sunken door-step and fitted the key, which she drew triumphantly from her pocket, in the lock, while Charlotte stood waiting and shaking behind her.

Then they went in. Everything was there just as they had left it. Charlotte sank down on a chair and began to cry. Harriet hurried across to the window that looked out on the garden.

"The currants air ripe," said she; "*an'* them pumpkins hev run all over every-thing."

"O Lord, Harriét," sobbed Charlotte, "thar is so many chinks that they air all runnin' together!"

Study and Discussion Questions

1. Look at the paragraphs that describe the Shattuck sisters' house and yard. How does the setting of this story mirror the characters?
2. What are the "chinks" referred to in the story? Why does Charlotte say at the end: "thar is so many chinks that they air all runnin' together"?
3. List the different kinds of charity in the story. Which ones are "mistaken" and which are not?
4. Why are Charlotte and Harriet uncomfortable in the Old Ladies' Home?
5. Describe the relationship between the two sisters.
6. What do you think is the author's attitude toward the Shattuck sisters?

7. Why does Harriet tell Mrs. Simonds that her doughnuts are "turrible tough"?
8. "It is more blessed to give than to receive." Is there any irony in Freeman's use of this maxim?

Suggestions for Writing

1. This story was published in 1887. What are some of the issues it raises that are still very much with us today?
2. Have you ever been either a recipient or a giver of charity? (Being taken to the movies by a friend when you couldn't afford it and volunteering your time and labor to help someone in need are examples.) Describe the situation and how you felt in it.
3. Define *charity*. Give some examples from your own experience or knowledge. Which of these are "mistaken" and which are not? Why?

❋ ❋ ❋

POETRY

WALT WHITMAN (1819–1892)

Walt Whitman was born in West Hills, New York. At an early age, his family moved to Brooklyn, where he attended grammar school until, at the age of 12, he was apprenticed to a printer to help meet the financial needs of his family. This early experience in the world of printing inevitably exposed the young Whitman to journalism and to a life of writing and publishing. In 1855, Whitman anonymously published *Leaves of Grass*, a book of poetry that he continued to revise, expand, and republish throughout his life. At the time, Whitman's effusive free verse radically challenged traditional notions of democracy, race, and religion. In like manner, his explicit treatment of sexuality, both heterosexual and homosexual, also engendered controversy, prompting several areas of the country to ban the book on grounds of obscenity. As Whitman evolved as a poet, so did later versions of *Leaves of Grass*, most notably the poems he wrote as a volunteer nurse during the Civil War that demonstrate a turn toward a more simplified, realist verse. Often referred to as the father of modern American poetry, Whitman's pioneering break from conventional poetic forms and themes has inspired generations of subsequent writers. His prose works include *Democratic Vistas* (1871).

A child said, What is the grass?

A child said, What is the grass? fetching it to me with full
hands;
How could I answer the child? . . . . I do not know what it
is any more than he.

I guess it must be the flag of my disposition, out of hopeful
green stuff woven.

Or I guess it is the handkerchief of the Lord,
A scented gift and remembrancer designedly dropped,
Bearing the owner's name someway in the corners, that we
may see and remark, and say Whose?

Or I guess the grass is itself a child. . . . the produced babe
of the vegetation.

Or I guess it is a uniform hieroglyphic,
And it means, Sprouting alike in broad zones and narrow
zones,
Growing among black folks as among white,
Kanuck, Tuckahoe, Congressman, Cuff, I give them the
same, I receive them the same.

And now it seems to me the beautiful uncut hair of graves.

Tenderly will I use you curling grass,
It may be you transpire from the breasts of young men,
It may be if I had known them I would have loved them;
It may be you are from old people and from women, and
from offspring taken soon out of their mother's laps,
And here you are the mother's laps.

This grass is very dark to be from the white heads of old
mothers,
Darker than the colorless beards of old men,
Dark to come from under the faint red roofs of mouths.

O I perceive after all so many uttering tongues!
And I perceive they do not come from the roofs of mouths
for nothing.

I wish I could translate the hints about the dead young men
and women,
And the hints about old men and mothers, and the offspring
taken soon out of their laps.

What do you think has become of the young and old men?
What do you think has become of the women and
children?

They are alive and well somewhere;
The smallest sprouts show there is really no death,
And if ever there was it led forward life, and does not wait
at the end to arrest it,
And ceased the moment life appeared.

All goes onward and outward.... and nothing collapses,
And to die is different from what any one supposed, and
luckier.

Study and Discussion Questions

1. When asked "what is the grass," the speaker claims not to know any more than the child; however, the rest of the poem is devoted to what he "guesses" and "supposes" it "may be." How effective is this structure in answering the child's question?
2. Considering all the images and suggestions offered by the speaker, what *is* the grass?
3. How is the child's "fetching . . . full hands" of grass ironically an illustration of what the grass is?
4. What does the last line of the poem mean?

Suggestion for Writing

1. Though this poem addresses a seemingly simple and innocent question, discuss how Whitman implies that the grass is more complex as it unifies humanity.

✸ ✸ ✸

CHRISTINA ROSSETTI (1830–1894)

Christina Georgina Rossetti was born in London on December 5, 1830, to Gabriele Rossetti, an Italian poet and political exile, and Frances Rossetti nee Polidori, the sister of the famous doctor and friend of Lord Byron, John William Polidori. She was raised among brilliant artists and poets amidst high society, and she and her siblings Dante, William, and Maria all became successful writers. Her father was a Roman Catholic, but Rossetti was raised by her mother in the Church of England. She began writing poetry at the age of twelve, mostly in the style of her favorite poets, John Keats, Sir Walter Scott, and Ann Radcliffe, and was first published at the age of eighteen. She was involved, along with her brothers, in the Pre-Raphaelite artistic movement, and was for a time engaged to James Collinson, a member of the Pre-Raphaelite Brotherhood, breaking off the engagement due to his reversion to Catholicism. Her most famous collection, *Goblin Market and Other Poems*, was published in 1862. This garnered her acclaim among the most influential poets of the time, and following the death of Elizabeth Barrett Browning the previous year, Rossetti was recognized as the most prominent female poet of the English language. Most of Rossetti's poetry engages in the tradition of the Romantic poets, and often focuses on religious and feminist themes. She passed away in 1894 from breast cancer, only a few weeks after her 64th birthday. Her published collections of poetry include *Goblin Market and Other Poems* (1862), *The Prince's Progress and Other Poems* (1866), *Sing-Song: A Nursery Rhyme Book* (1872), *A Pageant and Other Poems* (1881), *Verses* (1893), and *New Poems* (1895).

Goblin Market

composed in 1859, published in 1862

MORNING and evening
Maids heard the goblins cry:
"Come buy our orchard fruits,
Come buy, come buy:
Apples and quinces,
Lemons and oranges,
Plump unpecked cherries-
Melons and raspberries,
Bloom-down-cheeked peaches,
Swart-headed mulberries,
Wild free-born cranberries,
Crab-apples, dewberries,
Pine-apples, blackberries,
Apricots, strawberries—
All ripe together
In summer weather—
Morns that pass by,
Fair eves that fly;
Come buy, come buy;
Our grapes fresh from the vine,
Pomegranates full and fine,
Dates and sharp bullaces,
Rare pears and greengages,
Damsons and bilberries,
Taste them and try:
Currants and gooseberries,
Bright-fire-like barberries,
Figs to fill your mouth,
Citrons from the South,
Sweet to tongue and sound to eye,
Come buy, come buy."

Evening by evening
Among the brookside rushes,
Laura bowed her head to hear,
Lizzie veiled her blushes:
Crouching close together
In the cooling weather,
With clasping arms and cautioning lips,
With tingling cheeks and finger-tips.
"Lie close," Laura said,

Pricking up her golden head:
We must not look at goblin men,
We must not buy their fruits:
Who knows upon what soil they fed
Their hungry thirsty roots?"
"Come buy," call the goblins
Hobbling down the glen.
"O! cried Lizzie, Laura, Laura,
You should not peep at goblin men."
Lizzie covered up her eyes
Covered close lest they should look;
Laura reared her glossy head,
And whispered like the restless brook:
"Look, Lizzie, look, Lizzie,
Down the glen tramp little men.
One hauls a basket,
One bears a plate,
One lugs a golden dish
Of many pounds' weight.
How fair the vine must grow
Whose grapes are so luscious;
How warm the wind must blow
Through those fruit bushes."
"No," said Lizzie, "no, no, no;
Their offers should not charm us,
Their evil gifts would harm us."
She thrust a dimpled finger
In each ear, shut eyes and ran:
Curious Laura chose to linger
Wondering at each merchant man.
One had a cat's face,
One whisked a tail,
One tramped at a rat's pace,
One crawled like a snail,
One like a wombat prowled obtuse and furry,
One like a ratel tumbled hurry-scurry.
Lizzie heard a voice like voice of doves
Cooing all together:
They sounded kind and full of loves
In the pleasant weather.

Laura stretched her gleaming neck
Like a rush-imbedded swan,

Like a lily from the beck,
Like a moonlit poplar branch,
Like a vessel at the launch
When its last restraint is gone.

Backwards up the mossy glen
Turned and trooped the goblin men,
With their shrill repeated cry,
"Come buy, come buy."
When they reached where Laura was
They stood stock still upon the moss,
Leering at each other,
Brother with queer brother;
Signalling each other,
Brother with sly brother.
One set his basket down,
One reared his plate;
One began to weave a crown
Of tendrils, leaves, and rough nuts brown
(Men sell not such in any town);
One heaved the golden weight
Of dish and fruit to offer her:
"Come buy, come buy," was still their cry.
Laura stared but did not stir,
Longed but had no money:
The whisk-tailed merchant bade her taste
In tones as smooth as honey,
The cat-faced purr'd,
The rat-paced spoke a word
Of welcome, and the snail-paced even was heard;
One parrot-voiced and jolly
Cried "Pretty Goblin" still for "Pretty Polly";
One whistled like a bird.

But sweet-tooth Laura spoke in haste:
"Good folk, I have no coin;
To take were to purloin:
I have no copper in my purse,
I have no silver either,
And all my gold is on the furze
That shakes in windy weather
Above the rusty heather."
"You have much gold upon your head,"

They answered altogether:
"Buy from us with a golden curl."
She clipped a precious golden lock,
She dropped a tear more rare than pearl,
Then sucked their fruit globes fair or red:
Sweeter than honey from the rock,
Stronger than man-rejoicing wine,
Clearer than water flowed that juice;
She never tasted such before,
How should it cloy with length of use?
She sucked and sucked and sucked the more
Fruits which that unknown orchard bore,
She sucked until her lips were sore;
Then flung the emptied rinds away,
But gathered up one kernel stone,
And knew not was it night or day
As she turned home alone.

Lizzie met her at the gate
Full of wise upbraidings:
"Dear, you should not stay so late,
Twilight is not good for maidens;
Should not loiter in the glen
In the haunts of goblin men.
Do you not remember Jeanie,
How she met them in the moonlight,
Took their gifts both choice and many,
Ate their fruits and wore their flowers
Plucked from bowers
Where summer ripens at all hours?
But ever in the moonlight
She pined and pined away;
Sought them by night and day,
Found them no more, but dwindled and grew gray;
Then fell with the first snow,
While to this day no grass will grow
Where she lies low:
I planted daisies there a year ago
That never blow.
You should not loiter so."
"Nay hush," said Laura.
"Nay hush, my sister:
I ate and ate my fill,
Yet my mouth waters still;

To-morrow night I will
Buy more," and kissed her.
"Have done with sorrow;
I'll bring you plums to-morrow
Fresh on their mother twigs,
Cherries worth getting;
You cannot think what figs
My teeth have met in,
What melons, icy-cold
Piled on a dish of gold
Too huge for me to hold,
What peaches with a velvet nap,
Pellucid grapes without one seed:
Odorous indeed must be the mead
Whereon they grow, and pure the wave they drink,
With lilies at the brink,
And sugar-sweet their sap."

Golden head by golden head,
Like two pigeons in one nest
Folded in each other's wings,
They lay down, in their curtained bed:
Like two blossoms on one stem,
Like two flakes of new-fallen snow,
Like two wands of ivory
Tipped with gold for awful kings.
Moon and stars beamed in at them,
Wind sang to them lullaby,
Lumbering owls forbore to fly,
Not a bat flapped to and fro
Round their rest:
Cheek to cheek and breast to breast
Locked together in one nest.

Early in the morning
When the first cock crowed his warning,
Neat like bees, as sweet and busy,
Laura rose with Lizzie:
Fetched in honey, milked the cows,
Aired and set to rights the house,
Kneaded cakes of whitest wheat,
Cakes for dainty mouths to eat,
Next churned butter, whipped up cream,
Fed their poultry, sat and sewed;

Talked as modest maidens should
Lizzie with an open heart,
Laura in an absent dream,
One content, one sick in part;
One warbling for the mere bright day's delight,
One longing for the night.

At length slow evening came—
They went with pitchers to the reedy brook;
Lizzie most placid in her look,
Laura most like a leaping flame.
They drew the gurgling water from its deep
Lizzie plucked purple and rich golden flags,
Then turning homeward said: "The sunset flushes
Those furthest loftiest crags;
Come, Laura, not another maiden lags,
No wilful squirrel wags,
The beasts and birds are fast asleep."
But Laura loitered still among the rushes
And said the bank was steep.

And said the hour was early still,
The dew not fallen, the wind not chill:
Listening ever, but not catching
The customary cry,
"Come buy, come buy,"
With its iterated jingle
Of sugar-baited words:
Not for all her watching
Once discerning even one goblin
Racing, whisking, tumbling, hobbling;
Let alone the herds
That used to tramp along the glen,
In groups or single,
Of brisk fruit-merchant men.

Till Lizzie urged, "O Laura, come,
I hear the fruit-call, but I dare not look:
You should not loiter longer at this brook:
Come with me home.
The stars rise, the moon bends her arc,
Each glow-worm winks her spark,
Let us get home before the night grows dark;
For clouds may gather even
Though this is summer weather,

Put out the lights and drench us through;
Then if we lost our way what should we do?"

Laura turned cold as stone
To find her sister heard that cry alone,
That goblin cry,
"Come buy our fruits, come buy."
Must she then buy no more such dainty fruit?
Must she no more such succous pasture find,
Gone deaf and blind?
Her tree of life drooped from the root:
She said not one word in her heart's sore ache;
But peering thro' the dimness, naught discerning,
Trudged home, her pitcher dripping all the way;
So crept to bed, and lay
Silent 'til Lizzie slept;
Then sat up in a passionate yearning,
And gnashed her teeth for balked desire, and wept
As if her heart would break.

Day after day, night after night,
Laura kept watch in vain,
In sullen silence of exceeding pain.
She never caught again the goblin cry:
"Come buy, come buy,"
She never spied the goblin men
Hawking their fruits along the glen:
But when the noon waxed bright
Her hair grew thin and gray;
She dwindled, as the fair full moon doth turn
To swift decay, and burn
Her fire away.

One day remembering her kernel-stone
She set it by a wall that faced the south;
Dewed it with tears, hoped for a root,
Watched for a waxing shoot,
But there came none;
It never saw the sun,
It never felt the trickling moisture run:
While with sunk eyes and faded mouth
She dreamed of melons, as a traveller sees
False waves in desert drouth
With shade of leaf-crowned trees,
And burns the thirstier in the sandful breeze.

She no more swept the house,
Tended the fowls or cows,
Fetched honey, kneaded cakes of wheat,
Brought water from the brook:
But sat down listless in the chimney-nook
And would not eat.

Tender Lizzie could not bear
To watch her sister's cankerous care,
Yet not to share.
She night and morning
Caught the goblins' cry:
"Come buy our orchard fruits,
Come buy, come buy."
Beside the brook, along the glen
She heard the tramp of goblin men,
The voice and stir
Poor Laura could not hear;
Longed to buy fruit to comfort her,
But feared to pay too dear,

She thought of Jeanie in her grave,
Who should have been a bride;
But who for joys brides hope to have
Fell sick and died
In her gay prime,
In earliest winter-time,
With the first glazing rime,
With the first snow-fall of crisp winter-time.

Till Laura, dwindling,
Seemed knocking at Death's door:
Then Lizzie weighed no more
Better and worse,
But put a silver penny in her purse,
Kissed Laura, crossed the heath with clumps of furze
At twilight, halted by the brook,
And for the first time in her life
Began to listen and look.

Laughed every goblin
When they spied her peeping:
Came towards her hobbling,
Flying, running, leaping,
Puffing and blowing,
Chuckling, clapping, crowing,

Clucking and gobbling,
Mopping and mowing,
Full of airs and graces,
Pulling wry faces,
Demure grimaces,
Cat-like and rat-like,
Ratel and wombat-like,
Snail-paced in a hurry,
Parrot-voiced and whistler,
Helter-skelter, hurry-skurry,
Chattering like magpies,
Fluttering like pigeons,
Gliding like fishes,—
Hugged her and kissed her;
Squeezed and caressed her;
Stretched up their dishes,
Panniers and plates:
"Look at our apples
Russet and dun,
Bob at our cherries
Bite at our peaches,
Citrons and dates,
Grapes for the asking,
Pears red with basking
Out in the sun,
Plums on their twigs;
Pluck them and suck them,
Pomegranates, figs."

"Good folk," said Lizzie,
Mindful of Jeanie,
"Give me much and many";—
Held out her apron,
Tossed them her penny.
"Nay, take a seat with us,
Honor and eat with us,"
They answered grinning;
"Our feast is but beginning.
Night yet is early,
Warm and dew-pearly,
Wakeful and starry:
Such fruits as these
No man can carry;
Half their bloom would fly,
Half their dew would dry,
Half their flavor would pass by.

Sit down and feast with us,
Be welcome guest with us,
Cheer you and rest with us."
"Thank you," said Lizzie; "but one waits
At home alone for me:
So, without further parleying,
If you will not sell me any
Of your fruits though much and many,
Give me back my silver penny
I tossed you for a fee."
They began to scratch their pates,
No longer wagging, purring,
But visibly demurring,
Grunting and snarling.
One called her proud,
Cross-grained, uncivil;
Their tones waxed loud,
Their looks were evil.
Lashing their tails
They trod and hustled her,
Elbowed and jostled her,
Clawed with their nails,
Barking, mewing, hissing, mocking,
Tore her gown and soiled her stocking,
Twitched her hair out by the roots,
Stamped upon her tender feet,
Held her hands and squeezed their fruits
Against her mouth to make her eat.

White and golden Lizzie stood,
Like a lily in a flood,
Like a rock of blue-veined stone
Lashed by tides obstreperously, —
Like a beacon left alone
In a hoary roaring sea,
Sending up a golden fire, —
Like a fruit-crowned orange-tree
White with blossoms honey-sweet
Sore beset by wasp and bee, —
Like a royal virgin town
Topped with gilded dome and spire
Close beleaguered by a fleet
Mad to tear her standard down.

One may lead a horse to water,
Twenty cannot make him drink.

Though the goblins cuffed and caught her,
Coaxed and fought her,
Bullied and besought her,
Scratched her, pinched her black as ink,
Kicked and knocked her,
Mauled and mocked her,
Lizzie uttered not a word;
Would not open lip from lip
Lest they should cram a mouthful in;
But laughed in heart to feel the drip
Of juice that syruped all her face,
And lodged in dimples of her chin,
And streaked her neck which quaked like curd.
At last the evil people,
Worn out by her resistance,
Flung back her penny, kicked their fruit
Along whichever road they took,
Not leaving root or stone or shoot.
Some writhed into the ground,
Some dived into the brook
With ring and ripple.
Some scudded on the gale without a sound,
Some vanished in the distance.

In a smart, ache, tingle,
Lizzie went her way;
Knew not was it night or day;
Sprang up the bank, tore through the furze,
Threaded copse and dingle,
And heard her penny jingle
Bouncing in her purse, —
Its bounce was music to her ear.
She ran and ran
As if she feared some goblin man
Dogged her with gibe or curse
Or something worse:
But not one goblin skurried after,
Nor was she pricked by fear;
The kind heart made her windy-paced
That urged her home quite out of breath with haste
And inward laughter.

She cried "Laura," up the garden,
"Did you miss me?
Come and kiss me.
Never mind my bruises,

Hug me, kiss me, suck my juices
Squeezed from goblin fruits for you,
Goblin pulp and goblin dew.
Eat me, drink me, love me;
Laura, make much of me:
For your sake I have braved the glen
And had to do with goblin merchant men."

Laura started from her chair,
Flung her arms up in the air,
Clutched her hair:
"Lizzie, Lizzie, have you tasted
For my sake the fruit forbidden?
Must your light like mine be hidden,
Your young life like mine be wasted,
Undone in mine undoing,
And ruined in my ruin;
Thirsty, cankered, goblin-ridden?"
She clung about her sister,
Kissed and kissed and kissed her:
Tears once again
Refreshed her shrunken eyes,
Dropping like rain
After long sultry drouth;
Shaking with aguish fear, and pain,
She kissed and kissed her with a hungry mouth.

Her lips began to scorch,
That juice was wormwood to her tongue,
She loathed the feast:
Writhing as one possessed she leaped and sung,
Rent all her robe, and wrung
Her hands in lamentable haste,
And beat her breast.
Her locks streamed like the torch
Borne by a racer at full speed,
Or like the mane of horses in their flight,
Or like an eagle when she stems the light
Straight toward the sun,
Or like a caged thing freed,
Or like a flying flag when armies run.

Swift fire spread through her veins, knocked at her heart,
Met the fire smouldering there

And overbore its lesser flame,
She gorged on bitterness without a name:
Ah! fool, to choose such part
Of soul-consuming care!
Sense failed in the mortal strife:
Like the watch-tower of a town
Which an earthquake shatters down,
Like a lightning-stricken mast,
Like a wind-uprooted tree
Spun about,
Like a foam-topped water-spout
Cast down headlong in the sea,
She fell at last;
Pleasure past and anguish past,
Is it death or is it life?

Life out of death.
That night long Lizzie watched by her,
Counted her pulse's flagging stir,
Felt for her breath,
Held water to her lips, and cooled her face
With tears and fanning leaves:
But when the first birds chirped about their eaves,
And early reapers plodded to the place
Of golden sheaves,
And dew-wet grass
Bowed in the morning winds so brisk to pass,
And new buds with new day
Opened of cup-like lilies on the stream,
Laura awoke as from a dream,
Laughed in the innocent old way,
Hugged Lizzie but not twice or thrice;
Her gleaming locks showed not one thread of gray,
Her breath was sweet as May,
And light danced in her eyes.

Days, weeks, months, years
Afterwards, when both were wives
With children of their own;
Their mother-hearts beset with fears,
Their lives bound up in tender lives;
Laura would call the little ones
And tell them of her early prime,
Those pleasant days long gone

Of not-returning time:
Would talk about the haunted glen,
The wicked, quaint fruit-merchant men,
Their fruits like honey to the throat,
But poison in the blood;
(Men sell not such in any town;)
Would tell them how her sister stood
In deadly peril to do her good,
And win the fiery antidote:
Then joining hands to little hands
Would bid them cling together,
"For there is no friend like a sister,
In calm or stormy weather,
To cheer one on the tedious way,
To fetch one if one goes astray,
To lift one if one totters down,
To strengthen whilst one stands."

Study and Discussion Questions:

1. What is the effect of Rossetti's consistent use of animal imagery throughout the poem?
2. Why do you think Rossetti uses fruit to bring about Laura's downfall?
3. Both Laura and Lizzie make some sort of personal sacrifice to the goblin
   men. What is the significance of these sacrifices, and how does this relate
   to the poem's theme?
4. What is the effect of the poem's irregular meter and rhyme scheme?
5. Rossetti makes her intended message clear in the final lines of the
   poem, but how specifically do the events in the poem relate this
   message?
6. Why does Rossetti include the mention of the character Jeanie in the
   poem, and why is this character important?

Suggestions for Writing

1. "Goblin Market" focuses on the idea of the "fallen woman." Discuss
   Rossetti's approach to this concept, and explain whether or not modern
   society still holds similar beliefs.
2. To some degree, "Goblin Market" reads much like a fable or folktale, as
   it contains many fantasy elements and conveys a moral at the end.
   Compare and contrast the poem with other popular fables or folktales,
   addressing both narrative elements and moral lessons.

WILLIAM BLAKE (1757–1827)

William Blake was born in London to a middle class family, but his bent toward seeing the world in terms of visions quickly appeared. Blake saw more than the dirty world of a big city; rather he saw angels and other spiritual beings as he walked through life. He considered the world he lived in to be corrupted by its lack of imagination, and he set about creating his own Golden Age of art and poetry. Showing great artistic talent early in life, by age ten he began drawing in school and later became an engraver and design artist. He did not earn great sums as an artist, because his work was strange in an era that loved landscapes and careful representations of classic events such as Bible stories and historic battles. Blake's art illustrated more that could not be seen than that which could be seen.

He married his wife, Catherine, in 1782. She was devoted to him though the story goes that she nearly fainted when she first saw him due to his fiery eyes and passionate presence. From that early era came his first collection of poetry, *Poetical Sketches* (1783). When his younger brother Robert died, Blake's sense of connection to the spiritual world was strengthened. He wrote the *Songs of Experience* (1789) during this time of elation and spiritual growth, and these poems express his sense of the heavenly and spiritual. This bliss, however, was short-lived as Blake first followed and then rejected the Swedish theologian, Emanuel Swendenborg.Blake rejected Swendenborg's ideas about predestination, and wrote *The Marriage of Heaven and Hell* (1790–1793) as an attack on any such doctrine.

Blake then became connected with the champions of the French Revolution, including William Godwin, Tom Paine, and the Romantic poets, William Wordsworth, Samuel Coleridge, Robert Southey, and William Hazlitt. His protest against those who interfere with the rights of their fellow humans expressed itself in the most famous of his collections, *Songs of Experience* (1798–1794), and in *The French Revolution, America*, and the *Visions of the Daughters of Albion*. The last poem attacks marriage, which Blake disapproved of while he continued to be a faithful and devoted husband. The *Book of Thel* (1783) followed, a tale of a soul that refuses to be born into this wicked world. His mythology was elaborated and illustrated in *The Book* of *Urizen, The Song of Los, The Book of Ahania*, and *The Book of Los*.

From 1800 to 1803, the Blakes lived in a small town called Felpham, supported by a patron and poet friend named William Hayley, but Blake and Hayley differed in the nature of the poetry the two wrote, Hayley's being simple and sentimental, Blake's being mystical and complex. While at Felpham, Blake finished *The Four Zoas* and *Milton*; upon returning to London, he wrote the third of his "prophetic"works, *Jerusalem*. After that he spent many years in poverty, even painting dishes for Wedgwood, but was finally rediscovered in 1818 by a younger generation of painters, John Linnell, Samuel Palmer, John Varley, and George Richmond. He began to illustrate Dante and the book of Job, but these remained unfinished at the time of his death in 1827.

The Chimney Sweeper[1]   (1789)

When my mother died I was very young,
And my father sold me while yet my tongue
Could scarcely cry "'weep! 'weep! 'weep! 'weep!"
So your chimneys I sweep, and in soot I sleep.

There's little Tom Dacre, who cried when his head,   5
That curled like a lamb's back, was shaved: so I said
"Hush, Tom! never mind it, for when your head's bare
You know that the soot cannot spoil your white hair."

And so he was quiet, and that very night,
As Tom was a-sleeping, he had such a sight!   10
That thousands of sweepers, Dick, Joe, Ned, and Jack,
Were all of them locked up in coffins of black.

And by came an Angel who had a bright key,
And he opened the coffins and set them all free;
Then down a green plain leaping, laughing, they run,   15
And wash in a river, and shine in the sun.

Then naked and white, all their bags left behind,
They rise upon clouds and sport in the wind;
And the Angel told Tom, if he'd be a good boy,   20
He'd have God for his father, and never want joy.

And so Tom awoke; and we rose in the dark,
And got with our bags and our brushes to work.
Though the morning was cold, Tom was happy and warm;
So if all do their duty they need not fear harm.   25

Study and Discussion Questions

1. Who is the speaker of the poem? What experience is he describing?
2. What is significant about the speaker's repetition of the word " 'weep!"
   in line 3?

---

[1]Small boys had to go through the city crying out "Chimneys swept," but also cried
because they were forced to do dirty and dangerous work because they were small
enough to go up (or down) chimneys.

First published in *Songs of Innocence* in 1789.

3. Discuss the function of imagery in the poem. More specifically, consider how images of light and darkness highlight the speaker's perception of self and his job.
4. In line 24, the speaker concludes, "So if all do their duty they need not fear harm." How does he reach this conclusion? Additionally, do the speaker's final words generate hopefulness or desperation? Explain your answer.
5. Tom Dacre's hair is compared to "a lamb's back" in line 6. Discuss the symbolism of this line and relate this symbol to the function of Tom's dream.

The Chimney Sweeper   (1794)

A little black thing among the snow:
Crying weep, weep, in notes of woe!
Where are thy father & mother! say!
They are both gone up to the church to pray.

Because I was happy upon the heath,
And smil'd among the winters snow:
They clothed me in the clothes of death,
And taught me to sing the notes of woe.

And because I am happy, & dance & sing,
They think they have done me no injury:
And are gone to praise God & his Priest & King
Who make up a heaven of our misery.

Study and Discussion Questions

1. Who is the speaker of the poem? Explain the difference between this speaker and the speaker from the *Songs of Innocence* poem. Why is the shift in speakers important?
2. The poem begins, "A little black thing among the snow." What is the significance of this juxtaposition of light and darkness?
3. Explain the meaning of the final two lines in which the speaker notes that his parents "are gone to praise God and His priest and king, / Who made up a heaven of our misery." How is this paradoxical statement used to emphasize the thematic elements of the poem?
4. Is the tone in this poem different from the tone in *Songs of Innocence*? Use evidence from the poem to support your answer.
5. How does the poet conceptualize the church in this poem? Is this conception ironic? Why or why not?
6. Focusing on "The Chimney Sweeper" poems from Blake's *Songs of Innocence* and *Songs of Experience*, discuss how each poem complicates and modifies a reading of the other.

First published in *Songs of Experience* in 1794.

7. What is the significance of the number of stanzas in each poem? How does the deletion of stanzas in *Songs of Experience* underscore the thematic difference between the poems?
8. How do both poems conceptualize the child labor practices of eighteenth-century England? Specifically, consider how the poet's tone fosters this perception.

ROBERT FROST (1874–1963)

The son of a journalist who died when Robert Frost was only eleven, the now well-known poet lived with his mother in Lawrence, Massachusetts, where he worked at many jobs while finishing high school, where he was co-valedictorian of his class. While in school, he wrote for the *Lawrence High School Bulletin*. He married his co-valedictorian, Elinor White, and began his college career. Frost attended Dartmouth and Harvard, but dropped out of both shortly before the deaths of his three-year-old son and his mother. In search of financial stability, Frost bought a farm in Derry, New Hampshire, where he and Elinor had four more children while he wrote poetry and taught at the Pinkerton Academy. His first book, *A Boy's Will* appeared in 1913. Frost then sold the farm and moved his family to London where he met Ezra Pound who viewed Frost as a follower and composer of "Imagist"poems—poems of vivid pictoral language and minimal sentiment. However, Frost developed his own theory of the sound of poetry, that is, catching the word as it is heard and spoken. His *North of Boston* (1914) poems characterize his particular view of the purpose and practice of poetry. These poems use dramatic monologues to capture the realities of human life and words.

Frost returned to the United States in 1915 and bought another farm in New Hampshire, but this time he was not dependent on farm income and minimal teaching. While in Europe, Frost had become friends with powerful editors and publishers, including Ellery Sedgwick editor of the *Atlantic Monthly* and Henry Holt of the *New Republic*. He also became friends with the powerful poet and critic Louis Untermeyer. Frost taught at Amherst College and published his third book, *Mountain Interval* (1916). His fourth book, *New Hampshire*, won the Pulitzer Prize, followed by *West-Running Brook* in 1928, and *Collected Poems* in 1930, which won a second Pulitzer. Frost refused to join the political literary movements of the thirties but chose to write another personal and individual book, *A Further Range* (1936), which the critics attacked for lack of social relevance. In spite of its critics, the book also won a Pulitzer. In the late thirties, he suffered the deaths of two children and his wife, and he collapsed for a time. By 1942, however, he completed *A Witness Tree*, winner of yet another Pulitzer. This book was followed by *The Steeple Bush* in 1947 and *In the Clearing* in 1962. Frost spoke to the nation by reading "The Gift Outright" at President Kennedy's inauguration in 1961. He died two years later, a poet whose characters questioned their own comfortable assumptions about the world. With many well-wrought poems that demonstrate effective revisions of years of working and reworking, Frost was above all a craftsman.

The Road Not Taken   (1915)

Two roads diverged in a yellow wood,
And sorry I could not travel both
And be one traveler, long I stood
And looked down one as far as I could
To where it bent in the undergrowth;   5

Then took the other, as just as fair,
And having perhaps the better claim,
Because it was grassy and wanted wear;
Though as for that the passing there
Had worn them really about the same,   10

And both that morning equally lay
In leaves no step had trodden black.
Oh, I kept the first for another day!
Yet knowing how way leads on to way,
I doubted if I should ever come back.   15

I shall be telling this with a sigh
Somewhere ages and ages hence:
Two roads diverged in a wood, and I—
I took the one less traveled by,
And that has made all the difference.   20

Study and Discussion Questions

1. What is implicit in the poem's title?
2. After a first reading, and based on what many have been taught, what is the most obvious interpretation of this poem?

First appeared in the *Atlantic Monthly*, August 1915. First collected in *Mountain Interval* in 1916.

3. After closely rereading, is the meaning of this poem as obvious as it may have initially seemed? What could be an alternative interpretation of the poem?
4. How do the phrases "just as fair," "both that morning equally lay," and "I shall be telling this with a sigh" reveal more about the choice the speaker makes? How do these phrases further the tone of the poem?
5. What does the last line of the poem mean?

Suggestions for Writing

1. Many readers interpret this as a poem about individuality and making choices in life; however, Frost suggests that this poem is "tricky" and is merely a jest toward his friend Edward Thomas who was oftentimes indecisive about which path to take during their walks in the woods. Using a current issue or event, discuss what can happen when a person's initial intentions or situation is misinterpreted.
2. Think about this poem using the more commonly suggested theme of the *inescapable necessity to make a choice*. Using this theme, discuss the greater implications these inescapable choices can impose on society. Possible contexts for consideration are religion, politics, education, and humanitarian aid.
3. Discuss how Lyon's title "Neither Road Taken" (page 517) initially complicates the idea of choice illustrated in Frost's title "The Road Not Taken." How do the poems' situations complement one another?

❋ ❋ ❋

ROBERT HAYDEN (1913–1980)

Placed in a foster home as an infant, Robert Hayden grew up in a Detroit ghetto ironically called "Paradise Valley" by its residents. He attended Wayne State University for a short time but left in 1936 to work for the Federal Writer's Project, researching African American history and folklore that had been neglected by conventional history books. This experience with alternative historical narratives would have a profound impact on his poetry. In 1941, he entered Michigan University and studied under the poet W. H Auden, honing the technical aspects of his writing. In 1946, Hayden began teaching at Fisk University and would remain there for the next 23 years. Although he published his first poetry collection, *Heart-Shape in the Dust* in 1940, it wasn't until *Selected Poems* (1966) that Hayden was recognized as a skilled poet with his own poetic vision. In 1976, he was appointed as Consultant in Poetry to the Library of Congress (later retitled Poet Laureate). His other works include *Figure of Time: Poems* (1955), *A Ballad of Remembrance* (1962), *Words of Mourning Time* (1970), *The Night-Blooming Cereus* (1972), and *Angel of Ascent* (1975). "Those Winter Sundays," first published in *Selected Poems*, takes on the appearance of a loose sonnet, exploring the hard realizations of childhood.

Those Winter Sundays (1962)

Sundays too my father got up early
and put his clothes on in the blueblack cold,
then with cracked hands that ached
from labor in the weekday weather made
banked fires blaze. No one ever thanked him.   5

I'd wake and hear the cold splintering, breaking.
When the rooms were warm, he'd call,
and slowly I would rise and dress,
fearing the chronic angers of that house,

Speaking indifferently to him,   10
who had driven out the cold
and polished my good shoes as well.
What did I know, what did I know
of love's austere and lonely offices?

Study and Discussion Questions

1. Is the contrast in the poem between coldness and warmth only physical?
2. What is the significance of "and polished my good shoes as well"?
3. What, besides simply growing up, seems to have happened to change the speaker's attitude toward his father?
4. What does the last word of the poem mean? Why does Hayden use that word? Explain the last two lines.

Suggestion for Writing

1. Given the subject of the poem, how does Hayden avoid sentimentality?

SYLVIA PLATH (1932–1963)

In the barely 30 years of her life, Sylvia Plath created a body of poetry that broke through the mannerly conventions of post World War II American verse into intense, personal, passionately imaged lyrics that helped to revolutionize poetry in England and the United States. Born in Boston, she published her first poem at age eight; by the time she was 17, she was regularly sending poems and stories out to magazines. Her autographical novel, *The Bell Jar* (1963), is based on the year she both won a *Seventeen* magazine student editor contest and made her first suicide attempt. Plath graduated from

Smith College and then went to England to study at Cambridge University. There she met and married British poet Ted Hughes, whose poems were as intense and convention breaking as her own. Before their marriage shattered, Plath and Hughes had two children. She committed suicide on February 11, 1963. Plath published one volume of poetry before her death, *The Colossus* (1960), the title poem of which is included here. "The Colossus" seems to refer to her relation to her father, Otto Plath, an entomologist who published a book on bumblebees and who died when Sylvia was a child. Her famous poem "Daddy" references her father as well as Ted Hughes. *Ariel* (1965), containing poems written in the last two or three years of her life, established Sylvia Plath's reputation in what critics were then calling the "confessional" school of poetry, which also included Robert Lowell and Anne Sexton. In 1962, Plath's radio play in verse, *Three Women*, was broadcast on the BBC in London. Other books by Sylvia Plath published posthumously include a prose collection, *Johnny Panic and the Bible of Dreams*, *The Journals of Sylvia Plath*, *Letters Home*, a children's story in verse, *The Bed Book*, and three volumes of poetry—*Ariel*, *Crossing the Water*, and *Winter Trees*, all now included in *The Collected Poems of Sylvia Plath*.

The Colossus   (1960)

I shall never get you put together entirely,
Pieced, glued, and properly jointed.
Mule-bray, pig-grunt and bawdy cackles
Proceed from your great lips.
It's worse than a barnyard.   5

Perhaps you consider yourself an oracle,
Mouthpiece of the dead, or of some god or other.
Thirty years now I have laboured
To dredge the silt from your throat.
I am none the wiser.   10

Scaling little ladders with gluepots and pails of lysol
I crawl like an ant in mourning
Over the weedy acres of your brow
To mend the immense skull-plates and clear
The bald, white tumuli of your eyes.   15

A blue sky out of the Oresteia
Arches above us. O father, all by yourself
You are pithy and historical as the Roman Forum.
I open my lunch on a hill of black cypress.
Your fluted bones and acanthine hair are littered   20

In their old anarchy to the horizon-line.
It would take more than a lightning-stroke
To create such a ruin.
Nights, I squat in the cornucopia
Of your left ear, out of the wind,   25

Counting the red stars and those of plum-colour.
The sun rises under the pillar of your tongue.
My hours are married to shadow.
No longer do I listen for the scrape of a keel
On the blank stones of the landing.   30

Study and Discussion Questions

1. Look up "colossus" and "The Colossus of Rhodes" in a dictionary/
   encyclopedia. In this poem, who is the Colossus? What is the narrator's
   relation to him?
2. Look up all other allusions and words you don't know all the meanings
   of (e.g., "tumuli")—don't guess at what a word means in a poem.
3. What, literally, is happening in this poem? What is the setting? Who is the
   speaker of the poem and what is she spending her time doing?
4. List the images in the poem. Which of the five senses is Plath evoking?
5. "Mule-bray, pig-grunt and bawdy cackles/ Proceed from your great lips./
   It's worse than a barnyard." Discuss these lines from the first stanza.
   What does this poem say to us about language and creativity?
6. What is the particular tension in this poem between the "characters"?
7. What is the speaker of the poem's quest? Why does she need to do this?
8. Is she succeeding? Pick two images from the poem that suggest her
   success or failure.
9. What does "The Colossus" say about family and its effects on us? What
   does it say in particular about developing our creative potential?

Suggestion for Writing

1. Compare/contrast "The Colossus" with "Daddy". How far has the
   speaker of the poem traveled in three years in terms of her relation with
   the memory of her father? (Plath's father actually died close to her ninth
   birthday.) How far has the poet traveled in terms of her art? Discuss the
   language, images, structure, and rhythms of each poem as well as the
   story or quest of each poem.

❋ ❋ ❋

PHILIP LEVINE (b. 1928)

Philip Levine was born the son of Russian-Jewish immigrants in Detroit,
Michigan, and grew up in the industrial world of the auto factories. From the
time he was 14 and on through his 20s, Levine worked on the assembly lines as

he made his way through college. It was during this time that he began reading poetry and aspired to give a poetic voice to the blue-collar experience. In 1957, he received his M.F.A. from the University of Iowa and began a teaching career. Six years later he published his first volume of poetry, *On the Edge*, and has since published over 20 collections in 4 decades. Levine has made his reputation on verse that resists extravagant language and traditional poetic devices and is concentrated on the essence of the sincere, unadorned image. While some critics have questioned his lack of rhyme and meter, Levine has forged his own style of free-verse poetry—a "narrative poetry" that attempts to tell the stories of working people and to render this experience in a vernacular that is both common and perceptive. He was awarded the Pulitzer Prize for *The Simple Truth* in 1994. Other notable poetry collections include *Not This Pig* (1968), *5 Detroits* (1970), *They Feed They Lion* (1972), *7 Years From Somewhere* (1979), *Sweet Will* (1985), *A Walk With Tom Jefferson* (1988), *What Work Is* (1991, National Book Award), and his latest collection, *Breath: Poems* (2004).

Among Children   1991

I walk among the rows of bowed heads—
the children are sleeping through fourth grade
so as to be ready for what is ahead,
the monumental boredom of junior high
and the rush forward tearing their wings   5
loose and turning their eyes forever inward.
These are the children of Flint, their fathers
work at the spark plug factory or truck
bottled water in 5 gallon sea-blue jugs
to the widows of the suburbs. You can see   10
already how their backs have thickened,
how their small hands, soiled by pig iron,
leap and stutter even in dreams. I would like
to sit down among them and read slowly
from *The Book of Job* until the windows   15
pale and the teacher rises out of a milky sea
of industrial scum, her gowns streaming
with light, her foolish words transformed
into song, I would like to arm each one
with a quiver of arrows so that they might   20

rush like wind there where no battle rages
shouting among the trumpets, Ha! Ha!
How dear the gift of laughter in the face
of the 8 hour day, the cold winter mornings
without coffee and oranges, the long lines   25
of mothers in old coats waiting silently
where the gates have closed. Ten years ago
I went among these same children, just born,
in the bright ward of the Sacred Heart and leaned
down to hear their breaths delivered that day,   30
burning with joy. There was such wonder
in their sleep, such purpose in their eyes
closed against autumn, in their damp heads
blurred with the hair of ponds, and not one
turned against me or the light, not one   35
said, I am sick, I am tired, I will go home,
not one complained or drifted alone
unloved, on the hardest day of their lives.
Eleven years from now they will become
the men and women of Flint or Paradise,   40
the majors of a minor town, and I
will be gone into smoke or memory,
so I bow to them here and whisper
all I know, all I will never know.

Study and Discussion Questions

1. What has been, is, and will be the lives of these children, according to Philip Levine? List details.
2. What is Levine saying about being working class in the United States?
3. List and discuss the *images* Levine uses to literally and figuratively present the children.
4. Why does the poet want to read to the fourth-grade children "from *The Book of Job*"?
5. What is the relation of the poet/speaker of the poem to these children?
6. Industrial life has often been depicted in opposition to nature. Note where and how Levine uses images of nature in this poem.
7. Analyze the structure of "Among Children." Outline the stages of Levine's argument. Why do you think he chooses to begin the poem when the children are 9 or 10 years old?
8. Why do you think Levine wrote this poem in one long stanza instead of breaking it up into shorter stanzas? Note the length of his lines. Note also his use of enjambment, how and where he chooses to break his lines.

Suggestions for Writing

1. Choose an image or passage that is particularly moving or powerful for you in "Among Children" and write a paragraph discussing it—both your own individual response and an analysis of the sounds and connotations of words, the mood created, the people evoked, and whatever else seems important to you.

2. Find a copy of W. B. Yeats's poem "Among School Children." How has Levine used Yeats's famous poem as a starting point for his own? How and where do the two poems differ? Give specific examples from the poems. How is Levine's poem a political, spiritual, human, and poetic response to Yeats's poem? How is Levine's focus different from Yeats's? *Note:* Levine was 60 years old when his poem was published.

❋ ❋ ❋

JOHN UPDIKE (1932–2009)

John Updike was born in Shilington, Pennsylvania. He graduated from Harvard in 1954 and then moved to Oxford, England, to study art for a year. He later returned to the United States to work for the *New Yorker* magazine, which began publishing his work. Updike eventually settled in Ipswich, Massachusetts. Updike's subjects are the values and problems of middle-class America. In this fiction, Updike seeks to problematize this seemingly mundane world, addressing such themes as family, religion, morality, sports, and the dynamics of intimate relationships. His novels include *Rabbit, Run*, (1960), *Couples* (1968), *Rabbit Redux* (1971), *Rabbit Is Rich* (1981), *The Witches of Eastwick* (1984), *Roger's Version* (1986), *Rabbit at Rest* (1990), *In the Beauty of the Lilies* (1996) and *Gertrude and Cladius* (2000).

Ex-Basketball Player   (1957)

Pearl Avenue runs past the high-school lot,
Bends with the trolley tracks, and stops, cut off
Before it has a chance to go two blocks,
At Colonel McComsky Plaza. Berth's Garage
Is on the corner facing west, and there,   5
Most days, you'll find Flick Webb, who helps Berth out

Flick stands tall among the idiot pumps—
Five on a side, the old bubble-head style,
Their rubber elbows hanging loose and low
One's nostrils are two S's, and his eyes   10

An E and O. And one is squat, without
A head at all—more of a football type.

Once Flick played for the high-school team, the Wizards.
He was good: in fact, the best. In '46
He bucketed three hundred ninety points,   15
A county record still. The ball loved Flick.
I saw him rack up thirty-eight or forty
In one home game. His hands were like wild birds.

He never learned a trade, he just sells gas,
Checks oil, and changes flats. Once in a while,   20
As a gag, he dribbles an inner tube,
But most of us remember anyway.
His hands are fine and nervous on the lug wrench.
It makes no difference to the lug wrench, though.

Off work, he hangs around Mae's luncheonette   25
Grease-gray and kind of coiled, he plays pinball,
Smokes those thin cigars, nurses lemon phosphates.
Flick seldom says a word to Mae, just nods
Beyond her face toward bright applauding tiers
Of Necco Wafers, Nibs, and JuJu Beads.   30

Study and Discussion Questions

1. What are the various indications that Flick is diminished in the present?
2. What is the significance of the first four lines?
3. Analyze the imagery of the second stanza.
4. What is the meaning of the last line of the fourth stanza?

Suggestions for Writing

1. Is Flick unhappy now?
2. Describe someone you knew in high school whom you think is or soon
   will be somehow less than he or she then was. Is social class a factor?

T. S. ELIOT (1888–1965)

Thomas Stearns Eliot was born in St. Louis into a well-to-do family with roots
in New England. At a young age, Eliot was encouraged to write poetry by his
mother. He received both his B.A. and M.A. at Harvard and spent time studying at Oxford and at the Sorbonne in Paris. Eliot is considered a key figure in

modernist poetry and criticism. His major work, *The Waste Land* (1922), is considered one of the most important poems of the twentieth century, influencing and influenced by both the symbolist and imagist schools of poetry which sought to create layers of meaning through simplified language and concrete images. Eliot's other major volumes of poetry are *Prufrock and Other Observations* (1917) and *Four Quartets* (1943). Eliot's early, influential critical essays are collected in *The Sacred Wood* (1920), and he wrote several verse plays, including *Murder in the Cathedral* (1935) and *The Cocktail Party* (1949). He received the Nobel Prize for literature in 1948. "The Love Song of J. Alfred Prufrock" is an example of Eliot's early style and the beginnings of modernist poetry.

The Love Song of J. Alfred Prufrock   (1917)

S'io credesse che mia risposta fosse
A persona che mai tornasse al mondo,
Questa fiamma staria senza piu scosse.
Ma perciocche giammai di questo fondo
Non torno vivo alcun, s'i'odo il vero,
Senza tema d'infamia ti rispondo.[1]

Let us go then, you and I,
When the evening is spread out against the sky
Like a patient etherised upon a table;
Let us go, through certain half-deserted streets,
The muttering retreats   5
Of restless nights in one-night cheap hotels
And sawdust restaurants with oyster-shells:
Streets that follow like a tedious argument
Of insidious intent
To lead you to an overwhelming question . . .   10
Oh, do not ask, "What is it?"
Let us go and make our visit.
In the room the women come and go
Talking of Michelangelo.
The yellow fog that rubs its back upon the window-panes,   15
The yellow smoke that rubs its muzzle on the window-panes
Licked its tongue into the corners of the evening,

---

[1]From Dante's *Inferno,* spoken to Dante by Guido da Montelfeltro, who is wrapped in flame: "If I thought that my reply were to someone who could ever return to the world, this flame would shake no more. But since no one has ever returned alive from this place, if what I hear is true, without fear of infamy I answer you."

Lingered upon the pools that stand in drains,
Let fall upon its back the soot that falls from chimneys,
Slipped by the terrace, made a sudden leap,   20
And seeing that it was a soft October night,
Curled once about the house, and fell asleep.

And indeed there will be time
For the yellow smoke that slides along the street,
Rubbing its back upon the window-panes;   25
There will be time, there will be time
To prepare a face to meet the faces that you meet;
There will be time to murder and create,
And time for all the works and days of hands
That lift and drop a question on your plate;   30
Time for you and time for me,
And time yet for a hundred indecisions,
And for a hundred visions and revisions,
Before the taking of a toast and tea.

In the room the women come and go   35
Talking of Michelangelo.

And indeed there will be time
To wonder, "Do I dare?" and, "Do I dare?"
Time to turn back and descend the stair,
With a bald spot in the middle of my hair—   40
[They will say: "How his hair is growing thin!"]
My morning coat, my collar mounting firmly to the chin,
My necktie rich and modest, but asserted by a simple pin—
[They will say: "But how his arms and legs are thin!"]
Do I dare   45
Disturb the universe?
In a minute there is time
For decisions and revisions which a minute will reverse.

For I have known them all already, known them all:—
Have known the evenings, mornings, afternoons,   50
I have measured out my life with coffee spoons;
I know the voices dying with a dying fall
Beneath the music from a farther room.
      So how should I presume?
And I have known the eyes already, known them all—   55
The eyes that fix you in a formulated phrase,
And when I am formulated, sprawling on a pin,

When I am pinned and wriggling on the wall,
Then how should I begin
To spit out all the butt-ends of my days and ways?   60
    And how should I presume?

And I have known the arms already, known them all—
Arms that are braceleted and white and bare
[But in the lamplight, downed with light brown hair!]
Is it perfume from a dress   65
That makes me so digress?
Arms that lie along a table, or wrap about a shawl.
    And should I then presume?
    And how should I begin?

                    . . . . .

Shall I say, I have gone at dusk through narrow streets   70
And watched the smoke that rises from the pipes
Of lonely men in shirt-sleeves, leaning out of windows? . . .

I should have been a pair of ragged claws
Scuttling across the floors of silent seas.

                    . . . . .

And the afternoon, the evening, sleeps so peacefully!   75
Smoothed by long fingers,
Asleep . . . tired . . . or it malingers,
Stretched on the floor, here beside you and me.
Should I, after tea and cakes and ices,
Have the strength to force the moment to its crisis?   80
But though I have wept and fasted, wept and prayed,
Though I have seen my head [grown slightly bald] brought in upon a
            platter,
I am no prophet—and here's no great matter;
I have seen the moment of my greatness flicker,   85
And I have seen the eternal Footman hold my coat, and snicker,
And in short, I was afraid.

And would it have been worth it, after all,
After the cups, the marmalade, the tea,
Among the porcelain, among some talk of you and me,   90
Would it have been worth while,
To have bitten off the matter with a smile,
To have squeezed the universe into a ball
To roll it toward some overwhelming question,

To say: "I am Lazarus, come from the dead,   95
Come back to tell you all, I shall tell you all"—
If one, settling a pillow by her head,
    Should say: "That is not what I meant at all.
    That is not it, at all."

And would it have been worth it, after all,   100
Would it have been worth while,
After the sunsets and the dooryards and the sprinkled streets,
After the novels, after the teacups, after the skirts that trail along the floor—
And this, and so much more?—   105
It is impossible to say just what I mean!
But as if a magic lantern threw the nerves in patterns on a screen:
Would it have been worth while
If one, settling a pillow or throwing off a shawl,
And turning toward the window, should say: 110
    "That is not it at all,
    That is not what I meant, at all."

             . . . . .

No! I am not Prince Hamlet, nor was meant to be;
Am an attendant lord, one that will do
To swell a progress, start a scene or two,   115
Advise the prince; no doubt, an easy tool,
Deferential, glad to be of use,
Politic, cautious, and meticulous;
Full of high sentence, but a bit obtuse;
At times, indeed, almost ridiculous—   120
Almost, at times, the Fool.

I grow old . . . I grow old . . .
I shall wear the bottoms of my trousers rolled.

Shall I part my hair behind? Do I dare to eat a peach?
I shall wear white flannel trousers, and walk upon the beach.   125
I have heard the mermaids singing, each to each.

I do not think that they will sing to me.

I have seen them riding seaward on the waves
Combing the white hair of the waves blown back
When the wind blows the water white and black.   130
We have lingered in the chambers of the sea
By sea-girls wreathed with seaweed red and brown
Till human voices wake us, and we drown.

Study and Discussion Questions

1. Who are the "you and I" in line 1? What are they doing?
2. How does what Prufrock comments on in the first 69 lines reveal his state of mind? What different emotions do you see him feeling throughout the poem?
3. Characterize Prufrock. What is his self-image? What are his fears?
4. What kind of world does Prufrock live in? Describe the setting(s) of Prufrock's journey.
5. Prufrock is concerned with the past and future. He says, "For I have known them all already," and, though he says he is no prophet, he does look into the future and speculate about what will happen to him. How do what Prufrock sees in the past and fears in the future affect his present behavior?
6. Is this poem about love?
7. How does the allusion to Dante's *Inferno* help in understanding the poem? The allusion to John the Baptist? to Lazarus? to Hamlet?
8. How does Eliot use repetition in the poem? Note slight changes in some of the repeated phrases.

Suggestions for Writing

1. List every question Prufrock asks in the poem. Do they have anything in common?
2. Choose one image from the poem and explain what it adds to your knowledge of Prufrock.
3. What advice would you give Prufrock?

WILLIAM BUTLER YEATS (1865–1939)

William Butler Yeats was born in Dublin, Ireland, and studied art in college until he turned to writing. It is often said that Yeats was the greatest poet of the twentieth century, even though he preferred to work within more traditional poetics of rhyme and form in contrast to the modernist poets (such as Eliot) who were bringing such traditions into question. Yeats's marriage to Georgie Hyde-Lees, and her "automatic writing," "... in which [the] hand and pen presumably serve as unconscious instruments for the spirit world to send information" (Artists and Authors for Young Adults), helped him codify his interest in the occult and mysticism. He was active in Irish nationalist causes, helped found an Irish national theater, and served as a senator of the new Irish Free State. In 1933, he carefully shaped his many volumes of poetry into the definitive *Collected Poems* (1933). He received the Nobel Prize for literature in 1923. "Sailing to Byzantium" is one of several Yeats poems in this anthology.

Sailing to Byzantium[1]   (1927)

I

That is no country for old men. The young
In one another's arms, birds in the trees
—Those dying generations—at their song,
The salmon-falls, the mackerel-crowded seas,
Fish, flesh, or fowl, commend all summer long   5
Whatever is begotten, born, and dies.
Caught in that sensual music all neglect
Monuments of unageing intellect.

II

An aged man is but a paltry thing,
A tattered coat upon a stick, unless   10
Soul clap its hands and sing, and louder sing
For every tatter in its mortal dress,
Nor is there singing school but studying
Monuments of its own magnificence;
And therefore I have sailed the seas and come   15
To the holy city of Byzantium.

III

O sages standing in God's holy fire
As in the gold mosaic of a wall,
Come from the holy fire, perne in a gyre,[2]
And be the singing-masters of my soul.   20
Consume my heart away; sick with desire
And fastened to a dying animal
It knows not what it is; and gather me
Into the artifice of eternity.

---

[1]Now called Istanbul, Byzantium was the capital and cultural center of the Byzantine Empire.
[2]Unwind down a spiral.

IV

Once out of nature I shall never take   25
My bodily form from any natural thing,
But such a form as Grecian goldsmiths make
Of hammered gold and gold enamelling
To keep a drowsy Emperor awake;
Or set upon a golden bough to sing   30
To lords and ladies of Byzantium
Of what is past, or passing, or to come.

Study and Discussion Questions

1. *What* is "no country for old men"? Why?
2. What about Byzantium appeals to the speaker?
3. How does the speaker of the poem feel about aging?
4. How do people spend their time in the country of the young? How do they spend their time in Byzantium?
5. What constitutes immortality in this poem? What does the speaker mean when he asks to be gathered "into the artifice of eternity"?
6. Why, having left the world, will he sing "of what is past, or passing, or to come"?

Suggestions for Writing

1. Contrast Byzantium and the world the speaker of the poem has left in terms of the images used to describe each.
2. Write a sentence stating the main point of each stanza.

WILLIAM SHAKESPEARE (1564–1616)

Born in Stratford-on-Avon in England, William Shakespeare attended the free grammar school there, married Anne Hathaway when he was eighteen, and soon after went to live in London. Once there, Shakespeare began working as an actor and playwright, his first plays being presented in 1589. As a member of the acting company Lord Chamberlain's Men. Shakespeare established himself as the most popular playwright in London. Eventually the company had the resources to build The Globe Theater and, with Shakespeare as the principal playwright, established themselves as the leading troupe in London. While Shakespeare is considered the most important dramatist in the English language, his sonnets, published in 1609, have acquired renown based on their own literary merit. Patterned after the traditional Petrarchan sonnet and arranged as a dialogue between the poet and two central figures (a "friend" and the "Dark Lady"), Shakespeare's sonnets explore notions of beauty, friendship, and the uncertainty of human feelings. Sonnet 73, "That time of year thou mayst in me behold," utilizes stark images and precise metaphors to create a palpable sense of time.

That time of year thou mayst in me behold (1609)

LXXIII

That time of year thou mayst in me behold
When yellow leaves, or none, or few, do hang
Upon those boughs which shake against the cold,
Bare ruined choirs where late the sweet birds sang:
In me thou see'st the twilight of such day   5
As after sunset fadeth in the west,
Which by and by black night doth take away,
Death's second self that seals up all in rest:
In me thou see'st the glowing of such fire
That on the ashes of his youth doth lie   10
As the death-bed whereon it must expire,
Consumed with that which it was nourished by:
   This thou perceivest, which makes thy love more strong
   To love that well which thou must leave ere long.

Study and Discussion Questions

1. Who is speaking, and to whom? What are the relative ages of the two?
2. Explain line 12.
3. Explain in detail each of the three metaphors for growing old. How are they similar and how do they differ? What is the meaning of the order in which they appear?
4. How confident does the speaker seem in the assertion the final couplet makes?

Suggestions for Writing

1. Write a prose paragraph or two describing the speaker's attitude toward growing older.
2. What other metaphors might one use to describe aging? What are the associations and implications of each?

❀ ❀ ❀

WILLIAM CARLOS WILLIAMS (1883–1963)

Born of an English father and a Puerto Rican mother, William Carlos Williams grew up in Rutherford, New Jersey. Although his father introduced him to Shakespeare and Dante, the young Williams was more interested in math and science. While a medical student at the University of Pennsylvania, Williams began reading the poetry of John Keats and Walt Whitman; however, it was his friendship with Ezra Pound and other Imagist poets that helped him break from traditional, structured poetry and move toward a more precise, compact verse that sought to render images as they are perceived by the poet. With the publication of Eliot's "Wasteland" in 1922, Williams began to dislike the shape contemporary poetry was taking. In contrast to the angst of modernism, he was more concerned with creating a distinctively American poetry—a poetry that was intimately connected to locale. As a doctor in a small town (Paterson, New Jersey), he was privy to a side of ordinary life not traditionally seen as poetic. The real, human experience of his patients and townspeople were what Williams believed poetry should communicate. Although not widely known during his lifetime, Williams's work has had a considerable influence on American poetry. The more than 20 volumes of poetry he wrote during his lifetime have been gathered in the two-volume *The Collected Poems of William Carlos Williams* (1986), edited by A. Walton Litz and Christopher MacGowan. He was also a prolific writer of nonfiction essays and fiction (novels and short stories). For a complete bibliography, see the *Guide to the Poetry of William Carlos Williams* (1995). "To a Poor Old Woman" was published in *The Earlier Poems* (1951).

To a Poor Old Woman

munching a plum on
the street a paper bag
of them in her hand

They taste good to her
They taste good   5
to her. They taste
good to her

You can see it by
the way she gives herself
to the one half   10
sucked out in her hand

Comforted
a solace of ripe plums
seeming to fill the air
They taste good to her   15

Study and Discussion Questions

1. Discuss the sounds in and the sound of the poem. List the repeated consonant sounds (consonance). What effect do these sounds have?
2. In stanza two the same sentence is used three times. Why? How is the sentence changed by breaking the lines in different places?
3. If this four-stanza poem were a four-paragraph essay, what would be the main point of each paragraph? How does Williams gradually develop our understanding of the experience he is describing?
4. Is the first stanza really only three lines?
5. Discuss the dynamic tension between the title "To a Poor Old Woman" and the experience the poem presents. What images does the title conjure up for you? What images and sensations does the poem actually present? Is there any irony here and, if so, who is it directed at?
6. Why do you think Williams titles his poem "To A Poor Old Woman" rather than "A Poor Old Woman"?

Suggestion for Writing

1. Characterize someone through **images** of his or her relation to a particular food. This could end up as a poem in lines or as a short vivid prose piece. It could be serious, funny, or in any mood you choose.

PATRICIA SMITH (b. 1955)

Born on the West Side of Chicago, Patricia Smith would go to sleep at night listening to her father, a factory worker, read stories from the local newspaper. After graduating from high school, Smith entered Southern Illinois University in hopes of studying journalism, but soon left and took a job as a typist at the *Chicago Daily News*. Over time, Smith began writing entertainment reviews for the paper and in 1978 was hired at the *Chicago Sun-Times* as an entertainment writer. Smith would eventually become the first African American woman to write a weekly column at the *Boston Globe*. During these years as a journalist, Smith was also busy writing and performing poetry in both Chicago's and Boston's rising "slam" scene, of which she would become one of its central figures, winning the National Poetry Slam four times. Slam poetry has since taken hold throughout the country as one of our most vibrant and contemporary poetic forms. Smith has published three books of poetry, *Life According to Motown* (1991), *Big Towns, Big Talk* (1992), and *Close to Death* (1993). After her falling out with the *Boston Globe*, Smith coauthored with novelist Charles Johnson *Africans in America: America's Journey Through Slavery* (1998). Smith's live performance of "Undertaker" (dir. Angelica Brisk, Tied to the Tracks Films) was the subject of an award-winning short film on slam poetry.

Undertaker   (1993)

For Floyd Williams

When a bullet enters the brain, the head explodes.
I can think of no softer warning for the mothers
who sit doubled before my desk,
knotting their smooth brown hands,
and begging, fix my boy, fix my boy.   5
Here's his high school picture.
And the smirking, mildly mustachioed player
in the crinkled snapshot
looks nothing like the plastic bag of boy
stored and dated in the cold room downstairs.   10
In the picture, he is cocky and chiseled,
clutching the world by the balls. I know the look.
Now he is flaps of cheek,
slivers of jawbone, a surprised eye,
assorted teeth, bloody tufts of napped hair.   15
The building blocks of my business.
So I swallow hard, turn the photo face down
and talk numbers instead. The high price
of miracles startles the still-young woman,
but she is prepared. I know that she has sold   20
everything she owns, that cousins and uncles
have emptied their empty bank accounts,
that she dreams of her baby
in tuxedoed satin, flawless in an open casket,
a cross or blood red rose tacked to his fingers,   25
his halo set at a cocky angle.
I write a figure on a piece of paper
and push it across to her
while her chest heaves with hoping.
She stares at the number, pulls in   30
a slow weepy breath: "*Jesus.*"

But Jesus isn't on this payroll. I work alone
until the dim insistence of morning,
bent over my grisly puzzle pieces, gluing,
stitching, creating a chin with a brushstroke.   35
I plop glass eyes into rigid sockets,
then carve eyelids from a forearm, an inner thigh.

I plump shattered skulls, and paint the skin
to suggest warmth, an impending breath.
I reach into collapsed cavities to rescue   40
a tongue, an ear. Lips are never easy to recreate.

And I try not to remember the stories,
the tales the mothers must bring me
to ease their own hearts. *Oh,* they cry,
my Ronnie, my Willie, my Michael, my Chico.   45
It was self-defense. He was on his way home,
a dark car slowed down, they must have thought
he was someone else. He stepped between
two warring gang members at a party.
Really, he was trying to get off the streets,   50
trying to pull away from the crowd.
He was just trying to help a friend.
He was in the wrong place at the wrong time.
Fix my boy; he was a good boy. Make him the way he was.

But I have explored the jagged gaps   55
in the boy's body, smoothed the angry edges
of bulletholes. I have touched him in places
no mother knows, and I have birthed
his new face. I know he believed himself
invincible, that he most likely hissed   60
"Fuck you, man" before the bullets lifted him
off his feet. I try not to imagine
his swagger, his lizard-lidded gaze,
his young mother screaming into the phone.

She says she will find the money, and I know   65
this is the truth that fuels her, forces her
to place one foot in front of the other.
Suddenly, I want to take her down
to the chilly room, open the bag
and shake its terrible bounty onto the   70
gleaming steel table. I want her to see him,
to touch him, to press her lips to the flap of cheek.
The woman needs to wither, finally, and move on.

We both jump as the phone rattles in its hook.
I pray it's my wife, a bill collector, a wrong number.   75
But the wide, questioning silence on the other end
is too familiar. Another mother needing a miracle.
Another homeboy coming home.

Study and Discussion Questions

1. How is "Undertaker" a *dramatic* poem (look up the definition of dramatic poetry in "How Poetry Works"), both (a) technically and (b) emotionally?
2. How many "characters" are there in this poem? Who are they? What do we know about each one?
3. How does money come into the story this poem presents? Discuss "the high price of miracles."
4. What does the mother want? What does the undertaker want? Discuss the dramatic tension between the two characters.
5. Look up the word *irony* in an unabridged dictionary and in a dictionary of literary terms. Then discuss at least three ironies in Smith's poem.
6. The speaker of this poem is the undertaker himself. What do we see him doing in the poem? How does he feel about his job? What is the speaker's *tone?*

Suggestions for Writing

1. Imagine this dramatic poem being performed. How would you stage "Undertaker"?
2. Write a paragraph discussing what you think Smith means by the undertaker's last line: "Another homeboy coming home."
3. What figures from myth, fiction, history, and/or popular culture does the undertaker remind you of? How do these associations add to the poem's resonance?

❀ ❀ ❀

WOMEN AND MEN

FICTION

CHARLOTTE PERKINS GILMAN (1860–1935)

Soon after Charlotte Perkins Gilman's birth in Hartford, Connecticut, her father abandoned his wife and two children, leaving them in poverty. In need, Gilman's mother sought the help of relatives, in particular, Harriet Beecher Stowe and her sisters, all prominent writers and feminists during the era. In such an environment, Gilman developed a strong and independent sense of her self-worth as a woman. Early on in her career she worked as a teacher and a commercial artist. After becoming deeply depressed after the birth of her first child, a famous neurologist ordered complete bed rest, which made matters worse. Eventually, Gilman left her husband, moved to California, and began writing and speaking on economics and feminism. She edited *The Forerunner*, a feminist journal, from 1909 until 1916. Among Gilman's writings are *Women and Economics* (1898); *Herland* (1915), a utopian novel; and *The Living of Charlotte Perkins Gilman* (1935), her autobiography. The short story "The Yellow Wallpaper," considered one of Gilman's finest works, was written out of her encounter with the late-nineteenth-century medical profession's misdiagnosis of women's physiology and psychology.

The Yellow Wallpaper (1892)

It is very seldom that mere ordinary people like John and myself secure ancestral halls for the summer.

A colonial mansion, a hereditary estate, I would say a haunted house and reach the height of romantic felicity—but that would be asking too much of fate!

Still I will proudly declare that there is something queer about it.

Else, why should it be let so cheaply? And why have stood so long untenanted?

John laughs at me, of course, but one expects that.

John is practical in the extreme. He has no patience with faith, an intense horror of superstition, and he scoffs openly at any talk of things not to be felt and seen and put down in figures.

John is a physician, and *perhaps*—(I would not say it to a living soul, of course, but this is dead paper and a great relief to my mind)—*perhaps* that is one reason I do not get well faster.

You see, he does not believe I am sick! And what can one do?

If a physician of high standing, and one's own husband, assures friends and relatives that there is really nothing the matter with one but temporary nervous depression—a slight hysterical tendency—what is one to do?

My brother is also a physician, and also of high standing, and he says the same thing.

So I take phosphates or phosphites—whichever it is—and tonics, and air and exercise, and journeys, and am absolutely forbidden to "work" until I am well again.

Personally, I disagree with their ideas.

Personally, I believe that congenial work, with excitement and change, would do me good.

But what is one to do?

I did write for a while in spite of them; but it *does* exhaust me a good deal—having to be so sly about it, or else meet with heavy opposition.

I sometimes fancy that in my condition, if I had less opposition and more society and stimulus—but John says the very worst thing I can do is to think about my condition, and I confess it always makes me feel bad.

So I will let it alone and talk about the house.

The most beautiful place! It is quite alone, standing well back from the road, quite three miles from the village. It makes me think of English places that you read about, for there are hedges and walls and gates that lock, and lots of separate little houses for the gardeners and people.

There is a *delicious* garden! I never saw such a garden—large and shady, full of box-bordered paths, and lined with long grape-covered arbors with seats under them.

There were greenhouses, but they are all broken now.

There was some legal trouble, I believe, something about the heirs and coheirs; anyhow, the place has been empty for years.

That spoils my ghostliness, I am afraid, but I don't care—there is something strange about the house—I can feel it.

I even said so to John one moonlight evening, but he said what I felt was a draught, and shut the window.

I get unreasonably angry with John sometimes. I'm sure I never used to be so sensitive. I think it is due to this nervous condition.

But John says if I feel so I shall neglect proper self-control; so I take pains to control myself—before him, at least, and that makes me very tired.

I don't like our room a bit. I wanted one downstairs that opened onto the piazza and had roses all over the window, and such pretty old-fashioned chintz hangings! But John would not hear of it.

He said there was only one window and not room for two beds, and no near room for him if he took another.

He is very careful and loving, and hardly lets me stir without special direction.

I have a schedule prescription for each hour in the day; he takes all care from me, and so I feel basely ungrateful not to value it more.

He said he came here solely on my account, that I was to have perfect rest and all the air I could get. "Your exercise depends on your strength, my dear," said he, "and your food somewhat on your appetite; but air you can absorb all the time." So we took the nursery at the top of the house.

It is a big, airy room, the whole floor nearly, with windows that look all ways, and air and sunshine galore. It was nursery first, and then playroom and gymnasium, I should judge, for the windows are barred for little children, and there are rings and things in the walls.

The paint and paper look as if a boys' school had used it. It is stripped off— the paper—in great patches all around the head of my bed, about as far as I can reach, and in a great place on the other side of the room low down. I never saw a worse paper in my life. One of those sprawling, flamboyant patterns committing every artistic sin.

It is dull enough to confuse the eye in following, pronounced enough constantly to irritate and provoke study, and when you follow the lame uncertain curves for a little distance they suddenly commit suicide—plunge off at outrageous angles, destroy themselves in unheard-of contradictions.

The color is repellent, almost revolting: a smouldering unclean yellow, strangely faded by the slow-turning sunlight. It is a dull yet lurid orange in some places, a sickly sulphur tint in others.

No wonder the children hated it! I should hate it myself if I had to live in this room long.

There comes John, and I must put this away—he hates to have me write a word.

We have been here two weeks, and I haven't felt like writing before, since that first day.

I am sitting by the window now, up in this atrocious nursery, and there is nothing to hinder my writing as much as I please, save lack of strength.

John is away all day, and even some nights when his cases are serious.

I am glad my case is not serious!

But these nervous troubles are dreadfully depressing.

John does not know how much I really suffer. He knows there is no reason to suffer, and that satisfies him.

Of course it is only nervousness. It does weigh on me so not to do my duty in any way!

I meant to be such a help to John, such a real rest and comfort, and here I am a comparative burden already!

Nobody would believe what an effort it is to do what little I am able—to dress and entertain, and order things.

It is fortunate Mary is so good with the baby. Such a dear baby!

And yet I *cannot* be with him, it makes me so nervous.

I suppose John never was nervous in his life. He laughs at me so about this wallpaper!

At first he meant to repaper the room, but afterward he said that I was letting it get the better of me, and that nothing was worse for a nervous patient than to give way to such fancies.

He said that after the wallpaper was changed it would be the heavy bedstead, and then the barred windows, and then that gate at the head of the stairs, and so on.

"You know the place is doing you good," he said, "and really, dear, I don't care to renovate the house just for a three months' rental."

"Then do let us go downstairs," I said. "There are such pretty rooms there."

Then he took me in his arms and called me a blessed little goose, and said he would go down cellar, if I wished, and have it whitewashed into the bargain.

But he is right enough about the beds and windows and things.

It is as airy and comfortable a room as anyone need wish, and, of course, I would not be so silly as to make him uncomfortable just for a whim.

I'm really getting quite fond of the big room, all but that horrid paper.

Out of one window I can see the garden—those mysterious deep-shaded arbors, the riotous old-fashioned flowers, and bushes and gnarly trees.

Out of another I get a lovely view of the bay and a little private wharf belonging to the estate. There is a beautiful shaded lane that runs down there from the house. I always fancy I see people walking in these numerous paths and arbors, but John has cautioned me not to give way to fancy in the least. He says that with my imaginative power and habit of story-making, a nervous weakness like mine is sure to lead to all manner of excited fancies, and that I ought to use my will and good sense to check the tendency. So I try.

I think sometimes that if I were only well enough to write a little it would relieve the press of ideas and rest me.

But I find I get pretty tired when I try.

It is so discouraging not to have any advice and companionship about my work. When I get really well, John says we will ask Cousin Henry and Julia down for a long visit; but he says he would as soon put fireworks in my pillow-case as to let me have those stimulating people about now.

I wish I could get well faster.

But I must not think about that. This paper looks to me as if it *knew* what a vicious influence it had!

There is a recurrent spot where the pattern lolls like a broken neck and two bulbous eyes stare at you upside down.

I get positively angry with the impertinence of it and the everlastingness. Up and down and sideways they crawl, and those absurd unblinking eyes are every-where. There is one place where two breadths didn't match, and the eyes go all up and down the line, one a little higher than the other.

I never saw so much expression in an inanimate thing before, and we all know how much expression they have! I used to lie awake as a child and get more entertainment and terror out of blank walls and plain furniture than most children could find in a toy-store.

I remember what a kindly wink the knobs of our big old bureau used to have, and there was one chair that always seemed like a strong friend.

I used to feel that if any of the other things looked too fierce I could always hop into that chair and be safe.

The furniture in this room is no worse than inharmonious, however, for we had to bring it all from downstairs. I suppose when this was used as a playroom they had to take the nursery things out, and no wonder! I never saw such ravages as the children have made here.

The wallpaper, as I said before, is torn off in spots, and it sticketh closer than a brother—they must have had perseverance as well as hatred.

Then the floor is scratched and gouged and splintered, the plaster itself is dug out here and there, and this great heavy bed, which is all we found in the room, looks as if it had been through the wars.

But I don't mind it a bit—only the paper.

There comes John's sister. Such a dear girl as she is, and so careful of me! I must not let her find me writing.

She is a perfect and enthusiastic housekeeper, and hopes for no better profession. I verily believe she thinks it is the writing which made me sick!

But I can write when she is out, and see her a long way off from these windows.

There is one that commands the road, a lovely shaded winding road, and one that just looks off over the country. A lovely country, too, full of great elms and velvet meadows.

This wallpaper has a kind of sub-pattern in a different shade, a particularly irritating one, for you can only see it in certain lights, and not clearly then.

But in the places where it isn't faded and where the sun is just so—I can see a strange, provoking, formless sort of figure that seems to skulk about behind that silly and conspicuous front design.

There's sister on the stairs!

Well, the Fourth of July is over! The people are all gone, and I am tired out. John thought it might do me good to see a little company, so we just had Mother and Nellie and the children down for a week.

Of course I didn't do a thing. Jennie sees to everything now.

But it tired me all the same.

John says if I don't pick up faster he shall send me to Weir Mitchell[1] in the fall.

But I don't want to go there at all. I had a friend who was in his hands once, and she says he is just like John and my brother, only more so!

Besides, it is such an undertaking to go so far.

I don't feel as if it was worthwhile to turn my hand over for anything, and I'm getting dreadfully fretful and querulous.

I cry at nothing, and cry most of the time.

Of course I don't when John is here, or anybody else, but when I am alone.

And I am alone a good deal just now. John is kept in town very often by serious cases, and Jennie is good and lets me alone when I want her to.

So I walk a little in the garden or down that lovely lane, sit on the porch under the roses, and lie down up here a good deal.

I'm getting really fond of the room in spite of the wallpaper. Perhaps *because* of the wallpaper.

It dwells in my mind so!

---

[1]American neurologist (1829–1914) who treated Gilman.

I lie here on this great immovable bed—it is nailed down, I believe—and follow that pattern about by the hour. It is as good as gymnastics, I assure you. I start, we'll say, at the bottom, down in the corner over there where it has not been touched, and I determine for the thousandth time that I *will* follow that pointless pattern to some sort of a conclusion.

I know a little of the principle of design, and I know this thing was not arranged on any laws of radiation, or alternation, or repetition, or symmetry, or anything else that I ever heard of.

It is repeated, of course, by the breadths, but not otherwise.

Looked at in one way, each breadth stands alone; the bloated curves and flourishes—a kind of "debased Romanesque" with delirium tremens—go waddling up and down in isolated columns of fatuity.

But, on the other hand, they connect diagonally, and the sprawling outlines run off in great slanting waves of optic horror, like a lot of wallowing sea-weeds in full chase.

The whole thing goes horizontally, too, at least it seems so, and I exhaust myself trying to distinguish the order of its going in that direction.

They have used a horizontal breadth for a frieze, and that adds wonderfully to the confusion.

There is one end of the room where it is almost intact, and there, when the crosslights fade and the low sun shines directly upon it, I can almost fancy radiation after all—the interminable grotesque seems to form around a common center and rush off in headlong plunges of equal distraction.

It makes me tired to follow it. I will take a nap, I guess.

I don't know why I should write this.

I don't want to.

I don't feel able.

And I know John would think it absurd. But I *must* say what I feel and think in some way—it is such a relief!

But the effort is getting to be greater than the relief.

Half the time now I am awfully lazy, and lie down ever so much. John says I mustn't lose my strength, and has me take cod liver oil and lots of tonics and things, to say nothing of ale and wine and rare meat.

Dear John! He loves me very dearly, and hates to have me sick. I tried to have a real earnest reasonable talk with him the other day, and tell him how I wish he would let me go and make a visit to Cousin Henry and Julia.

But he said I wasn't able to go, nor able to stand it after I got there; and I did not make out a very good case for myself, for I was crying before I had finished.

It is getting to be a great effort for me to think straight. Just this nervous weakness, I suppose.

And dear John gathered me up in his arms, and just carried me upstairs and laid me on the bed, and sat by me and read to me till it tired my head.

He said I was his darling and his comfort and all he had, and that I must take care of myself for his sake, and keep well.

He says no one but myself can help me out of it, that I must use my will and self-control and not let any silly fancies run away with me.

There's one comfort—the baby is well and happy, and does not have to occupy this nursery with the horrid wallpaper.

If we had not used it, that blessed child would have! What a fortunate escape! Why, I wouldn't have a child of mine, an impressionable little thing, live in such a room for worlds.

I never thought of it before, but it is lucky that John kept me here after all; I can stand it so much easier than a baby, you see.

Of course I never mention it to them any more—I am too wise—but I keep watch for it all the same.

There are things in that wallpaper that nobody knows about but me, or ever will.

Behind that outside pattern the dim shapes get clearer every day.

It is always the same shape, only very numerous.

And it is like a woman stooping down and creeping about behind that pattern. I don't like it a bit. I wonder—I begin to think—I wish John would take me away from here!

It is so hard to talk with John about my case, because he is so wise, and because he loves me so.

But I tried it last night.

It was moonlight. The moon shines in all around just as the sun does.

I hate to see it sometimes, it creeps so slowly, and always comes in by one window or another.

John was asleep and I hated to waken him, so I kept still and watched the moonlight on that undulating wallpaper till I felt creepy.

The faint figure behind seemed to shake the pattern, just as if she wanted to get out.

I got up softly and went to feel and see if the paper *did* move, and when I came back John was awake.

"What is it, little girl?" he said. "Don't go walking about like that—you'll get cold."

I thought it was a good time to talk, so I told him that I really was not gaining here, and that I wished he would take me away.

"Why, darling!" said he. "Our lease will be up in three weeks, and I can't see how to leave before.

"The repairs are not done at home, and I cannot possibly leave town just now. Of course, if you were in any danger, I could and would, but you really are better, dear, whether you can see it or not. I am a doctor, dear, and I know. You are gaining flesh and color, your appetite is better, I feel really much easier about you."

"I don't weigh a bit more," said I, "nor as much; and my appetite may be better in the evening when you are here but it is worse in the morning when you are away!"

"Bless her little heart!" said he with a big hug. "She shall be as sick as she pleases! But now let's improve the shining hours by going to sleep, and talk about it in the morning!"

"And you won't go away?" I asked gloomily.

"Why, how can I, dear? It is only three weeks more and then we'll take a nice little trip of a few days while Jennie is getting the house ready. Really, dear, you are better!"

"Better in body perhaps—" I began, and stopped short, for he sat up straight and looked at me with such a stern, reproachful look that I could not say another word.

"My darling," said he, "I beg of you, for my sake and for our child's sake, as well as for your own, that you will never for one instant let that idea enter your mind! There is nothing so dangerous, so fascinating, to a temperament like yours. It is a false and foolish fancy. Can you not trust me as a physician when I tell you so?"

So of course I said no more on that score, and we went to sleep before long. He thought I was asleep first, but I wasn't, and lay there for hours trying to decide whether that front pattern and the back pattern really did move together or separately.

On a pattern like this, by daylight, there is a lack of sequence, a defiance of law, that is a constant irritant to a normal mind.

The color is hideous enough, and unreliable enough, and infuriating enough, but the pattern is torturing.

You think you have mastered it, but just as you get well under way in following, it turns a back-somersault and there you are. It slaps you in the face, knocks you down, and tramples upon you. It is like a bad dream.

The outside pattern is a florid arabesque, reminding one of a fungus. If you can imagine a toadstool in joints, an interminable string of toadstools, budding and sprouting in endless convolutions—why, that is something like it.

That is, sometimes!

There is one marked peculiarity about this paper, a thing nobody seems to notice but myself, and that is that it changes as the light changes.

When the sun shoots in through the east window—I always watch for that first long, straight ray—it changes so quickly that I never can quite believe it.

That is why I watch it always.

By moonlight—the moon shines in all night when there is a moon—I wouldn't know it was the same paper.

At night in any kind of light, in twilight, candlelight, lamplight, and worst of all by moonlight, it becomes bars! The outside pattern, I mean, and the woman behind it is as plain as can be.

I didn't realize for a long time what the thing was that showed behind, that dim sub-pattern, but now I am quite sure it is a woman.

By daylight she is subdued, quiet. I fancy it is the pattern that keeps her so still. It is so puzzling. It keeps me quiet by the hour.

I lie down ever so much now. John says it is good for me, and to sleep all I can.

Indeed he started the habit by making me lie down for an hour after each meal.

It is a very bad habit, I am convinced, for you see, I don't sleep.

And that cultivates deceit, for I don't tell them I'm awake—oh, no!

The fact is I am getting a little afraid of John.

He seems very queer sometimes, and even Jennie has an inexplicable look.

It strikes me occasionally, just as a scientific hypothesis, that perhaps it is the paper!

I have watched John when he did not know I was looking, and come into the room suddenly on the most innocent excuses, and I've caught him several times *looking at the paper!* And Jennie too. I caught Jennie with her hand on it once.

She didn't know I was in the room, and when I asked her in a quiet, a very quiet voice, with the most restrained manner possible, what she was doing with the paper, she turned around as if she had been caught stealing, and looked quite angry—asked me why I should frighten her so!

Then she said that the paper stained everything it touched, that she had found yellow smooches on all my clothes and John's and she wished we would be more careful!

Did not that sound innocent? But I know she was studying that pattern, and I am determined that nobody shall find it out but myself.

Life is very much more exciting now than it used to be. You see, I have something more to expect, to look forward to, to watch. I really do eat better, and am more quiet than I was.

John is so pleased to see me improve! He laughed a little the other day, and said I seemed to be flourishing in spite of my wallpaper.

I turned it off with a laugh. I had no intention of telling him it was *because* of the wallpaper—he would make fun of me. He might even want to take me away.

I don't want to leave now until I have found it out. There is a week more, and I think that will be enough.

I'm feeling so much better!

I don't sleep much at night, for it is so interesting to watch developments; but I sleep a good deal during the daytime.

In the daytime it is tiresome and perplexing.

There are always new shoots on the fungus, and new shades of yellow all over it. I cannot keep count of them, though I have tried conscientiously.

It is the strangest yellow, that wallpaper! It makes me think of all the yellow things I ever saw—not beautiful ones like buttercups, but old, foul, bad yellow things.

But there is something else about that paper—the smell! I noticed it the moment we came into the room, but with so much air and sun it was not bad. Now we have had a week of fog and rain, and whether the windows are open or not, the smell is here.

It creeps all over the house.

I find it hovering in the dining-room, skulking in the parlor, hiding in the hall, lying in wait for me on the stairs.

It gets into my hair.

Even when I go to ride, if I turn my head suddenly and surprise it—there is that smell!

Such a peculiar odor, too! I have spent hours in trying to analyze it, to find what it smelled like.

It is not bad—at first—and very gentle, but quite the subtlest, most enduring odor I ever met.

In this damp weather it is awful. I wake up in the night and find it hanging over me.

It used to disturb me at first. I thought seriously of burning the house—to reach the smell.

But now I am used to it. The only thing I can think of that it is like is the *color* of the paper! A yellow smell.

There is a very funny mark on this wall, low down, near the mopboard. A streak that runs round the room. It goes behind every piece of furniture, except the bed, a long, straight, even *smooch,* as if it had been rubbed over and over.

I wonder how it was done and who did it, and what they did it for. Round and round and round—round and round and round—it makes me dizzy!

I really have discovered something at last.

Through watching so much at night, when it changes so, I have finally found out.

The front pattern *does* move—and no wonder! The woman behind shakes it!

Sometimes I think there are a great many women behind, and sometimes only one, and she crawls around fast, and her crawling shakes it all over.

Then in the very bright spots she keeps still, and in the very shady spots she just takes hold of the bars and shakes them hard.

And she is all the time trying to climb through. But nobody could climb through that pattern—it strangles so; I think that is why it has so many heads.

They get through, and then the pattern strangles them off and turns them upside down, and makes their eyes white!

If those heads were covered or taken off it would not be half so bad.

I think that woman gets out in the daytime!

And I'll tell you why—privately—I've seen her!

I can see her out of every one of my windows!

It is the same woman, I know, for she is always creeping, and most women do not creep by daylight.

I see her in that long shaded lane, creeping up and down. I see her in those dark grape arbors, creeping all around the garden.

I see her on that long road under the trees, creeping along, and when a carriage comes she hides under the blackberry vines.

I don't blame her a bit. It must be very humiliating to be caught creeping by daylight!

I always lock the door when I creep by daylight. I can't do it at night, for I know John would suspect something at once.

And John is so queer now that I don't want to irritate him. I wish he would take another room! Besides, I don't want anybody to get that woman out at night but myself.

I often wonder if I could see her out of all the windows at once.

But, turn as fast as I can, I can only see out of one at one time.

And though I always see her, she *may* be able to creep faster than I can turn! I have watched her sometimes away off in the open country, creeping as fast as a cloud shadow in a wind.

If only that top pattern could be gotten off from the under one! I mean to try it, little by little.

I have found out another funny thing, but I shan't tell it this time! It does not do to trust people too much.

There are only two more days to get this paper off, and I believe John is beginning to notice. I don't like the look in his eyes.

And I heard him ask Jennie a lot of professional questions about me. She had a very good report to give.

She said I slept a good deal in the daytime.

John knows I don't sleep very well at night, for all I'm so quiet!

He asked me all sorts of questions, too, and pretended to be very loving and kind.

As if I couldn't see through him!

Still, I don't wonder he acts so, sleeping under this paper for three months.

It only interests me, but I feel sure John and Jennie are affected by it. Hurrah! This is the last day, but it is enough. John is to stay in town over night, and won't be out until this evening.

Jennie wanted to sleep with me—the sly thing; but I told her I should undoubtedly rest better for a night all alone.

That was clever, for really I wasn't alone a bit! As soon as it was moonlight and that poor thing began to crawl and shake the pattern, I got up and ran to help her.

I pulled and she shook. I shook and she pulled, and before morning we had peeled off yards of that paper.

A strip about as high as my head and half around the room.

And then when the sun came and that awful pattern began to laugh at me, I declared I would finish it today!

We go away tomorrow, and they are moving all my furniture down again to leave things as they were before.

Jennie looked at the wall in amazement, but I told her merrily that I did it out of pure spite at the vicious thing.

She laughed and said she wouldn't mind doing it herself, but I must not get tired.

How she betrayed herself that time!

But I am here, and no person touches this paper but Me—not *alive!*

She tried to get me out of the room—it was too patent! But I said it was so quiet and empty and clean now that I believed I would lie down again and sleep all I could, and not to wake me even for dinner—I would call when I woke.

So now she is gone, and the servants are gone, and the things are gone, and there is nothing left but that great bedstead nailed down, with the canvas mattress we found on it.

We shall sleep downstairs tonight, and take the boat home tomorrow.

I quite enjoy the room, now it is bare again.

How those children did tear about here!

This bedstead is fairly gnawed!

But I must get to work.

I have locked the door and thrown the key down into the front path.

I don't want to go out, and I don't want to have anybody come in, till John comes.

I want to astonish him.

I've got a rope up here that even Jennie did not find. If that woman does get out, and tries to get away, I can tie her!

But I forgot I could not reach far without anything to stand on!

This bed will *not* move!

I tried to lift and push it until I was lame, and then I got so angry I bit off a little piece at one corner—but it hurt my teeth.

Then I peeled off all the paper I could reach standing on the floor. It sticks horribly and the pattern just enjoys it! All those strangled heads and bulbous eyes and waddling fungus growths just shriek with derision!

I am getting angry enough to do something desperate. To jump out of the window would be admirable exercise, but the bars are too strong even to try.

Besides I wouldn't do it. Of course not. I know well enough that a step like that is improper and might be misconstrued.

I don't like to *look* out of the windows even—there are so many of those creeping women, and they creep so fast.

I wonder if they all come out of that wallpaper as I did?

But I am securely fastened now by my well-hidden rope—you don't get *me* out in the road there!

I suppose I shall have to get back behind the pattern when it comes night, and that is hard!

It is so pleasant to be out in this great room and creep around as I please!

I don't want to go outside. I won't, even if Jennie asks me to.

For outside you have to creep on the ground, and everything is green instead of yellow.

But here I can creep smoothly on the floor, and my shoulder just fits in that long smooch around the wall, so I cannot lose my way.

Why, there's John at the door!

It is no use, young man, you can't open it!

How he does call and pound!

Now he's crying to Jennie for an axe.

It would be a shame to break down that beautiful door!

"John, dear!" said I in the gentlest voice. "The key is down by the front steps, under a plantain leaf!"

That silenced him for a few moments.

Then he said, very quietly indeed, "Open the door, my darling!"

"I can't," said I. "The key is down by the front door under a plantain leaf!" And then I said it again, several times, very gently and slowly, and said it so often that he had to go and see, and he got it of course, and came in. He stopped short by the door.

"What is the matter?" he cried. "For God's sake, what are you doing!"

I kept on creeping just the same, but I looked at him over my shoulder.

"I've got out at last," said I, "in spite of you and Jane. And I've pulled off most of the paper, so you can't put me back!"

Now why should that man have fainted? But he did, and right across my path by the wall, so that I had to creep over him every time!

Study and Discussion Questions

1. What do the narrator and the woman in the wallpaper have in common?
2. Is the narrator right to be suspicious of her husband or is her suspicion simply a manifestation of her nervous ailment?
3. Why is the narrator so tired?
4. What kind of person does John want his wife to be? How does he try to maneuver her into being that?
5. What is the significance of the fact that the narrator's room was originally a nursery?
6. "There comes John, and I must put this away—he hates to have me write a word." Why doesn't John want her to write? Why does she disagree with him?
7. How does the way the narrator sees and feels about the yellow wallpaper change during the story?

Suggestions for Writing

1. Who is John? List the words that describe him. Write a brief character sketch.
2. Gilman wrote this story in 1890 as a warning about a treatment for nervous depression fashionable then. Gilman herself was told to "live as domestic a life as possible," to "have but two hours' intellectual life a day" and "never to touch pen, brush, or pencil again." Discuss the way in which the treatment which is supposed to cure the narrator worsens her condition, and speculate about the reasons.

❀ ❀ ❀

ERNEST HEMINGWAY (1899–1961)

Ernest Hemingway was born in Oak Park, Illinois. As a boy he went on frequent hunting and fishing trips in northern Michigan with his father, a doctor. He boxed and played football in high school and, after graduating, worked as a newspaper reporter. Near the end of World War I, Hemingway was a volunteer ambulance driver and then a soldier in Italy, where he was wounded. He spent much of the 1920s in Paris and the 1930s in Key West, Florida. He was an active supporter of the Republican Revolutionary Cause in the Spanish Civil War and worked as a war correspondent during World War II. His writings include the novels *The Sun Also Rises* (1926), *A Farewell to Arms* (1929), and *The Old Man and The Sea* (1952); the collections *In Our Time* (1925) and *The Fifth Column and the First Forty-Nine Stories* (1938); and the memoir *A Moveable Feast* (1964, posthumously). In 1954, he received the Nobel Prize for literature. "Hills Like White Elephants," taken from the short story collection *Men Without Women* (1927), demonstrates Hemingway's concise use of dialogue.

Hills Like White Elephants   (1927)

The hills across the valley of the Ebro were long and white. On this side there was no shade and no trees and the station was between two lines of rails in the sun. Close against the side of the station there was the warm shadow of the building and a curtain, made of strings of bamboo beads, hung across the open door into the bar, to keep out flies. The American and the girl with him sat at a table in the shade, outside the building. It was very hot and the express from Barcelona would come in forty minutes. It stopped at this junction for two minutes and went on to Madrid.

"What should we drink?" the girl asked. She had taken off her hat and put it on the table.

"It's pretty hot," the man said.

"Let's drink beer."

"*Dos cervezas,*" the man said into the curtain.

"Big ones?" a woman asked from the doorway.

"Yes. Two big ones."

The woman brought two glasses of beer and two felt pads. She put the felt pads and the beer glasses on the table and looked at the man and the girl. The girl was looking off at the line of hills. They were white in the sun and the country was brown and dry.

"They look like white elephants," she said.

"I've never seen one," the man drank his beer.

"No, you wouldn't have."

"I might have," the man said. "Just because you say I wouldn't have doesn't prove anything."

The girl looked at the bead curtain. "They've painted something on it," she said. "What does it say?"

"Anis del Toro. It's a drink."

"Could we try it?"

The man called "Listen" through the curtain. The woman came out from the bar.

"Four reales."

"We want two Anis del Toro."

"With water?"

"Do you want it with water?"

"I don't know," the girl said. "Is it good with water?"

"It's all right."

"You want them with water?" asked the woman.

"Yes, with water."

"It tastes like licorice," the girl said and put the glass down.

"That's the way with everything."

"Yes," said the girl. "Everything tastes of licorice. Especially all the things you've waited so long for, like absinthe."

"Oh, cut it out."

"You started it," the girl said. "I was being amused. I was having a fine time."

"Well, let's try and have a fine time."

"All right. I was trying. I said the mountains looked like white elephants. Wasn't that bright?"

"That was bright."

"I wanted to try this new drink. That's all we do, isn't it—look at things and try new drinks?"

"I guess so."

The girl looked across at the hills.

"They're lovely hills," she said. "They don't really look like white elephants. I just meant the coloring of their skin through the trees."

"Should we have another drink?"

"All right."

The warm wind blew the bead curtain against the table.

"The beer's nice and cool," the man said.

"It's lovely," the girl said.

"It's really an awfully simple operation, Jig," the man said. "It's not really an operation at all."

The girl looked at the ground the table legs rested on.

"I know you wouldn't mind it, Jig. It's really not anything. It's just to let the air in."

The girl did not say anything.

"I'll go with you and I'll stay with you all the time. They just let the air in and then it's all perfectly natural."

"Then what will we do afterward?"

"We'll be fine afterward. Just like we were before."

"What makes you think so?"

"That's the only thing that bothers us. It's the only thing that's made us unhappy."

The girl looked at the bead curtain, put her hand out and took hold of two of the strings of beads.

"And you think then we'll be all right and be happy."

"I know we will. You don't have to be afraid. I've known lots of people that have done it."

"So have I," said the girl. "And afterward they were all so happy."

"Well," the man said, "if you don't want to you don't have to. I wouldn't have you do it if you don't want to. But I know it's perfectly simple."

"And you really want to?"

"I think it's the best thing to do. But I don't want you to do it if you don't really want to."

"And if I do it you'll be happy and things will be like they were and you'll love me?"

"I love you now. You know I love you."

"I know. But if I do it, then it will be nice again if I say things are like white elephants, and you'll like it?"

"I'll love it. I love it now but I just can't think about it. You know how I get when I worry."

"If I do it you won't ever worry?"

"I won't worry about that because it's perfectly simple."

"Then I'll do it. Because I don't care about me."

"What do you mean?"

"I don't care about me."

"Well, I care about you."

"Oh, yes. But I don't care about me. And I'll do it and then everything will be fine."

"I don't want you to do it if you feel that way."

The girl stood up and walked to the end of the station. Across, on the other side, were fields of grain and trees along the banks of the Ebro. Far away, beyond the river, were mountains. The shadow of a cloud moved across the field of grain and she saw the river through the trees.

"And we could have all this," she said. "And we could have everything and every day we make it more impossible."

"What did you say?"

"I said we could have everything."

"We can have everything."

"No, we can't."

"We can have the whole world."

"No, we can't."

"We can go everywhere."

"No, we can't. It isn't ours any more."

"It's ours."

"No, it isn't. And once they take it away, you never get it back."

"But they haven't taken it away."

"We'll wait and see."

"Come on back in the shade," he said. "You mustn't feel that way."

"I don't feel any way," the girl said. "I just know things."

"I don't want you to do anything that you don't want to do—"

"Nor that isn't good for me," she said. "I know. Could we have another beer?"

"All right. But you've got to realize—"

"I realize," the girl said. "Can't we maybe stop talking?"

They sat down at the table and the girl looked across at the hills on the dry side of the valley and the man looked at her and at the table.

"You've got to realize," he said, "that I don't want you to do it if you don't want to. I'm perfectly willing to go through with it if it means anything to you."

"Doesn't it mean anything to you? We could get along."

"Of course it does. But I don't want anybody but you. I don't want any one else. And I know it's perfectly simple."

"Yes, you know it's perfectly simple."

"It's all right for you to say that, but I do know it."

"Would you do something for me now?"

"I'd do anything for you."

"Would you please please please please please please please stop talking?"

He did not say anything but looked at the bags against the wall of the station. There were labels on them from all the hotels where they had spent nights.

"But I don't want you to," he said, "I don't care anything about it."

"I'll scream," the girl said.

The woman came out through the curtains with two glasses of beer and put them down on the damp felt pads. "The train comes in five minutes," she said.

"What did she say?" asked the girl.

"That the train is coming in five minutes."

The girl smiled brightly at the woman, to thank her.

"I'd better take the bags over to the other side of the station," the man said. She smiled at him.

"All right. Then come back and we'll finish the beer."

He picked up the two heavy bags and carried them around the station to the other tracks. He looked up the tracks but could not see the train. Coming back, he walked through the barroom, where people waiting for the train were drinking. He drank an Anis at the bar and looked at the people. They were all waiting reasonably for the train. He went out through the bead curtain. She was sitting at the table and smiled at him.

"Do you feel better?" he asked.

"I feel fine," she said. "There's nothing wrong with me. I feel fine."

Study and Discussion Questions

1. What is this couple arguing about? What clues let you know? Why do you think Hemingway doesn't allow his characters to say directly what they are talking about?
2. What is the balance of power between the man and the woman in this story? How does Hemingway construct this balance of power? What factors are involved in the situation? What factors are involved in Hemingway's stylistic choices, including how the two characters are referred to?
3. What effects do the descriptions of the setting have in the midst of this couple's argument?
4. Why this particular title—"Hills Like White Elephants"? What does that mean to you? How does it fit the story?
5. The "girl" says: "That's all we do, isn't it—look at things and try new drinks?" Describe the life they seem to be leading. When do you think this story is set?
6. What is the man's argument? What does he want? Is he conflicted? How is he trying to get his way?
7. What is the woman's argument, or defense? What does she want—Is it possible that she wants more than one thing?
8. How does the lack of attribution in the dialogue affect the story and the way you perceive the characters?

Suggestions for Writing:

1. Write about communication and miscommunication between men and women, or between couples, from your own experience. How is communication and miscommunication happening in "Hills Like White Elephants"?
2. Jump to six months later and write a scene between the two characters in this story.

CRISTINA GARCIA (b. 1958)

Born in Havana in 1958, during the Cuban Revolution, Cristina Garcia was taken to the United States by her parents at the age of two. Garcia grew up in Brooklyn and would receive her B.A. in political science from Barnard College in 1979, followed by a degree in Latin American Studies from John Hopkins in 1981. After spending several years as a reporter and researcher for *Time* magazine, Garcia resigned her position to write fiction full time. In 1993 she published her first novel, *Dreaming in Cuban*, which became a finalist for the National Book Award and established her as a respected contemporary novelist. *Dreaming in Cuban* was followed by *The Aguero Sisters* (1997) and *Monkey Hunting* (2003). These generational epics explore Cuban

American identity (with a focus on the feminine) and are characterized by dramatic shifts from realism to magical realism. Garcia's poetic prose style eloquently shows the connections between history and character. "Inés in the Kitchen," one of her few short stories, was first published in *Little Havana Blues: A Cuban-American Literature Anthology* (1996).

Inés in the Kitchen   (1996)

Inés Maidique is twelve weeks pregnant and nauseous. Her back hurts, her breasts are swollen, and her feet no longer fit into her dressy shoes. Although she is barely showing, she walks around in sneakers to ease the soreness that has settled in every corner of her body. The eleven pounds she's gained feel like fifty.

When her husband returns home he'll expect her trussed up in a silk dress and pearls and wearing make-up and high heels. It's Friday and Richard likes for her to make a fuss over him at the end of the week. He'll be home in two hours so Inés busies herself preparing their dinner—a poached loin of lamb with mint chutney, cumin rice, ratatouille, and spiced bananas for dessert.

Richard will question her closely about what she's eaten that day. Inés will avoid telling him about the fudge cookies she devoured that morning in the supermarket parking lot. She hadn't wanted to eat the whole box, but bringing it home was unthinkable. Richard scoured the kitchen cabinets for what he called "illegal foods" and she was in no mood for his usual harangue.

With a long length of string Inés ties together the eye of loin and tenderloin at one inch intervals, leaving enough string at the ends to suspend the meat from the handles of the kettle. She slits the lamb in several places and inserts slivers of garlic. Then she sets about preparing the stock, skimming the froth as it simmers. Inés thinks about the initial excitement she'd felt when the blood test came back positive. She always knew, or thought she knew, she wanted a child, but now she is less certain.

The mint leaves give off a tart scent that clears her head with each pulse of the food processor. She adds fresh coriander, minced garlic, ginger root, honey, and a little lemon until the chutney congeals. Then she whisks it together with plain yogurt in a stainless steel bowl. Inés remembers the abortion she'd had the month before her college graduation. She was twenty-one and, like now, twelve weeks pregnant. The baby's father was Cuban, like her, a hematology resident at the hospital where Inés was finishing her practicum. Manolo Espada was not opposed to having the baby, only against getting married. This was unacceptable to Inés. After the abortion, she bled for five days and cramped so hard she passed out. Inés spent the summer working a double shift at an emergency room in Yonkers. Her child would have been eight years old by now. Inés thinks of this often.

Shortly before she was to marry Richard, Inés tracked down her old lover to San Francisco, where he'd been doing AIDS research with an eminent name in the field. Over the phone, Manolo told her he was leaving for Africa the following month on a two-year grant from the Department of Health. Inés abruptly forgot everything she had planned to say. Even if she'd wanted him again, it was too late. She'd already sent out her wedding invitations and Richard had put a down payment on the colonial house across from the riding stables. Manolo was going to Africa. It would have never worked out.

Ratatouille is one of Inés's favorite dishes. It's easy to prepare and she cooks big batches of it at a time then freezes it. The red peppers give the ratatouille a slightly sweetish taste. Inés heats the olive oil in a skillet then tosses in the garlic and chopped onion. She adds the cubed egg-plants and stirs in the remaining ingredients one at a time. On another burner she prepares the rice with chicken broth, cuminseed, and fresh parsley. If she times it right, dinner will be ready just as Richard walks through the door.

Her husband doesn't know about Inés's abortion, and only superficially about Manolo Espada. It is better this way. Richard doesn't like it when Inés's attention is diverted from him in any significant way. How, she wonders, will he get used to having a baby around? Richard was the only boy in a family of older sisters, and accustomed to getting his way. His father died when Richard was eight and his three sisters had worked as secretaries to put him through medical school. Richard had been the great hope of the Roth family. When he told them he was marrying a Catholic, his mother and sisters were devastated. Janice, the oldest, told him point-blank that Inés would ruin his life. Perhaps, Inés thinks, his sister was right.

Inés strains the stock through a fine sieve into an enormous ceramic bowl, discarding the bones and scraps. She pours the liquid back into the kettle and turns on the burner to moderately high. Carefully, she lowers the lamb into the stock without letting it touch the sides or the bottom of the kettle, then she ties the string to the handles, and sets the timer for twelve minutes.

Other things concern Inés. She's heard about men running off when their wives become pregnant and she's afraid that Richard, who places such a premium on her looks, will be repelled by her bloating body. As it is, Inés feels that Richard scrutinizes her for nascent imperfections. He abhors cellulite and varicose veins, the corporal trademarks of his mother and sisters, and so Inés works hard to stay fit. She swims, plays tennis, takes aerobics classes, and works out twice a week on the Nautilus machines at her gym. Her major weakness is a fondness for sweets. Inés loves chocolate, but Richard glares at her in restaurants if she so much as asks to see the dessert menu. To him a lack of self-discipline on such small matters is indicative of more serious character flaws.

What of her husband's good qualities? Richard takes her to the Bahamas every winter, although he spends most of the time scuba-diving, a sport which Inés does not share. And he is intelligent and well-informed and she believes he is faithful. Also, he isn't a tightwad like so many of her friends' husbands, watching every penny, and he doesn't hang out with the boys or play poker or anything like that. Richard is an adequate lover, too, although he lacks imagination. He likes what he likes, which does not include many of the things that Inés likes. Once, in bed, she asked Richard to pretend he was Henry Kissinger. The request offended him deeply. If Richard rejected so harmless a game, what would he say to the darker, more elaborate rituals she'd engaged in with Manolo?

The loin of lamb is medium rare, just the way Richard likes it. Inés lets it cool off on the cutting board for a few minutes before slicing it diagonally into thick, juicy slabs. She sets the table with their wedding linen and china and wedges two white candles into squat crystal holders. Inés thinks back on the five years she worked as a nurse. She was good at what she did and was sought after for the most important cardiology cases. More than one surgeon had jokingly proposed to her after she'd made a life-saving suggestion in the operating room. But like most men, they assumed she was unavailable. Someone so pretty, so self-contained, they thought, must already be spoken for.

When Richard first started working at the hospital, Inés felt drawn to him. There was something about his manner, about his nervous energy that appealed to her. It certainly wasn't his looks. Richard was skinny and tall with fleecy colorless hair, not at all like the mesomorphic Manolo whose skin seemed more of a pelt. For three months she and Richard worked side by side on coronary bypasses, ventricular aneurysm resections, mitral valve replacements. Their manner was always cordial and efficient, with none of the macabre bantering one often hears in operating rooms. One day, Richard looked up at her from a triple bypass and said, "Marry me, Inés." And so she did.

When Inés was a child, her father had predicted wistfully that she would never marry, while her mother seemed to gear her for little else. Inés remembers the beauty pageants she was forced to enter from an early age, the banana curls that hung from her skull like so many sausages. She'd won the "Little Miss Latin New York" pageant in 1964, when she was seven years old. Her mother still considers this to be Inés's greatest achievement. Inés had sung and played the piano to "Putting on the Ritz," which she'd translated to Spanish herself. Gerardo complained to his wife about sharing Inés with an auditorium full of leering strangers, but Haydée would not budge. "This is better than a dowry, Gerardo." But Gerardo preferred to have his daughter, dolled up in her starched Sunday dress and ruffled anklets, all to himself.

Gerardo expected Inés to drop everything to play the piano for him, and for many years she complied. This became more and more difficult as she got older. Her parents separated and her father would call at all hours on the private phone line he'd installed in Inés's bedroom, pleading with her to come play the white baby grand he had rented just for her. Sometimes he would stroke her hair or tickle her spine as she played, tease her about her tiny new breasts or affectionately pat her behind. Inés remembers how the air seemed different during those times, charged and hard to swallow. Now her father is dead. And what, she asks herself, does she really know about him?

Inés turns off all the burners and pours herself a glass of whole milk. She is doing all the right things to keep the life inside her thriving. But she accomplishes this without anticipation, only a sense of obligation. Sometimes she has a terrible urge to pour herself a glass of rum, although she hates the taste, and she knows what it would do to the baby, or to burn holes in the creamy calfskin upholstery of her husband's sports car. Other times, mostly in the early afternoons, she feels like setting fire to the damask curtains that keep their living room in a perpetual dusk. She dreams about blowing up her herb garden with its fragrant basil leaves, then stealing a thoroughbred from the stable across the street and riding it as fast as she can.

Inés finishes the last of her milk. She rinses the glass and leans against the kitchen sink. There is a jingling of keys at the front door. Richard is home.

Study and Discussion Questions

1. What do we suspect about Inés's state of mind from the title and the opening sentence of the story?
2. List four or five significant *facts* we learn about Inés during the course of the story.
3. Who are the men in Inés's life that we hear about? Characterize her relation with each one.
4. How and why does being pregnant become a crisis point for Inés?
5. Garcia intersperses Inés's musings with vivid detailed paragraphs on what she is cooking for dinner. Why? What is the function of these paragraphs in the story? What effect do they have on the reader?
6. How does Inés feel about her pregnancy? Locate and discuss three passages in the story that may bear on her attitude toward being pregnant.
7. Discuss Inés's fantasies of escape in the second to last paragraph.
8. How might ethnicity be a factor in this story? Locate passages where Inés's Cuban identity (or her husband's Anglo identity) is explicitly or implicitly part of the story's tension.
9. Does Inés develop and change, however subtly, as the story progresses? Has she come to some realization by the end of the story?

Suggestions for Writing

1. Is Inés feeling trapped in her life? What evidence do you have either way? What do you think she will do next?
2. Write a postscript to "Inés in the Kitchen" set sometime later—you choose the time.
3. Write a couple of paragraphs from Richard's point of view.
4. Why and how do you think pregnancy is an important transitional event, perhaps even a rite of passage, in the lives of women? If you haven't been pregnant or had children yourself, talk to a few women who have gone through that experience and discuss with them any ponderings about or crises of identity they had during their pregnancy or any significant realizations they came to.

5. Is there a comparably significant "rite of passage" event in the lives of men? (This rite of passage doesn't have to be biological.) Discuss its components and compare to pregnancy as a rite of passage.

JOHN UPDIKE (1932–2009)

John Updike was born in Shilington, Pennsylvania. He graduated from Harvard in 1954 and then moved to Oxford, England, to study art for a year. He later returned to the United States to work for the *New Yorker* magazine, which began publishing his work. Updike eventually settled in Ipswich, Massachusetts. Updike's subjects are the values and problems of middle-class America. In this fiction, Updike seeks to problematize this seemingly mundane world, addressing such themes as family, religion, morality, sports, and the dynamics of intimate relationships. His novels include *Rabbit, Run* (1960), *Couples* (1968), *Rabbit Redux* (1971), *Rabbit Is Rich* (1981), *The Witches of Eastwick* (1984), *Roger's Version* (1986) and *Rabbit at Rest* (1990), *In the Beauty of the Lilies* (1996), and *Gertrude and Claudius* (2000). In "A & P," first published in *Pigeon Feathers and Other Stories* (1962), Updike's rare use of humor adds to the ambiguity of the story's meaning.

A & P   (1962)

In walks these three girls in nothing but bathing suits. I'm in the third checkout slot, with my back to the door, so I don't see them until they're over by the bread. The one that caught my eye first was the one in the plaid green two-piece. She was a chunky kid, with a good tan and a sweet broad soft-looking can with those two crescents of white just under it, where the sun never seems to hit, at the top of the backs of her legs. I stood there with my hand on a box of HiHo crackers trying to remember if I rang it up or not. I ring it up again and the customer starts giving me hell. She's one of these cash-register-watchers, a witch about fifty with rouge on her cheekbones and no eyebrows, and I know it made her day to trip me up. She'd been watching cash registers for fifty years and probably never seen a mistake before.

By the time I got her feathers smoothed and her goodies into a bag—she gives me a little snort in passing, if she'd been born at the right time they would have burned her over in Salem—by the time I get her on her way the girls had circled around the bread and were coming back, without a pushcart, back my way along the counters, in the aisle between the checkouts and the Special bins. They didn't even have shoes on. There was this chunky one, with the two-piece—it was bright green and the seams on the bra were still sharp and her belly was still pretty pale so I guessed she just got it (the suit)—there was this one, with one of those chubby berry-faces, the lips all bunched together under her nose, this one, and a tall one, with black hair that hadn't quite frizzed right, and one of these sunburns right across under the eyes, and a chin that was too long—you know, the kind of girl other girls think is very "striking" and "attractive" but never quite makes it, as they very well know, which is why they like her so much—and then the third one, that wasn't quite so tall. She was the queen. She kind of led them, the other two peeking around and making their shoulders round. She didn't look around, not this queen, she just walked straight on slowly, on these long white primadonna legs. She came down a little hard on her heels, as if she didn't walk in her bare feet that much, putting down her heels and then letting the weight move along to her toes as if she was testing the floor with every step, putting a little deliberate extra action into it. You never know for sure how girls' minds work (do you really think it's a mind in there or just a little buzz like a bee in a glass jar?) but you got the idea she had talked the other two into coming in here with her, and now she was showing them how to do it, walk slow and hold yourself straight.

She had on a kind of dirty-pink—beige maybe, I don't know—bathing suit with a little nubble all over it and, what got me, the straps were down. They were off her shoulders looped loose around the cool tops of her arms, and I guess as a result the suit had slipped a little on her, so all around the top of the cloth there was this shining rim. If it hadn't been there you wouldn't have known there could have been anything whiter than those shoulders. With the straps pushed off, there was nothing between the top of the suit and the top of her head except just *her,* this clean bare plane of the top of her chest down from the shoulder bones like a dented sheet of metal tilted in the light. I mean, it was more than pretty.

She had sort of oaky hair that the sun and salt had bleached, done up in a bun that was unravelling, and a kind of prim face. Walking into the A & P with your straps down, I suppose it's the only kind of face you *can* have. She held her head so high her neck, coming up out of those white shoulders, looked kind of stretched, but I didn't mind. The longer her neck was, the more of her there was.

She must have felt in the corner of her eye me and over my shoulder Stokesie in the second slot watching, but she didn't tip. Not this queen. She kept her eyes moving across the racks, and stopped, and turned so slow it made my stomach rub the inside of my apron, and buzzed to the other two, who kind of huddled against her for relief, and then they all three of them went up the cat-and-dog-food-breakfast-cereal-macaroni-rice-raisins-season-ings-spreads-spaghetti-soft-drinks-crackers-and-cookies aisle. From the third slot I look straight up this aisle to the meat counter, and I watched them all the way. The fat one with the tan sort of fumbled with the cookies, but on second thought she put the package back. The sheep pushing their carts down the aisle—the girls were walking against the usual traffic (not that we have one-way signs or anything)—were pretty hilarious. You could see them, when Queenie's white shoulders dawned on them, kind of jerk, or hop, or hiccup, but their eyes snapped back to their own baskets and on they pushed. I bet you could set off dynamite in an A & P and the people would by and large keep reaching and checking oatmeal off their lists and muttering "Let me see, there was a third thing, began with A, asparagus, no, ah, yes, applesauce!" or whatever it is they do mutter. But there was no doubt, this jiggled them. A few houseslaves in pin curlers even looked around after pushing their carts past to make sure what they had seen was correct.

You know, it's one thing to have a girl in a bathing suit down on the beach, where what with the glare nobody can look at each other much anyway, and another thing in the cool of the A & P, under the fluorescent lights, against all those stacked packages, with her feet paddling along naked over our checkerboard green-and-cream rubber-tile floor.

"Oh Daddy," Stokesie said beside me. "I feel so faint."

"Darling," I said. "Hold me tight." Stokesie's married, with two babies chalked up on his fuselage already, but as far as I can tell that's the only difference. He's twenty-two, and I was nineteen this April.

"Is it done?" he asks, the responsible married man finding his voice. I forgot to say he thinks he's going to be manager some sunny day, maybe in 1990 when it's called the Great Alexandrov and Petrooshki Tea Company or something.

What he meant was, our town is five miles from a beach, with a big summer colony out on the point, but we're right in the middle of town, and the women generally put on a shirt or shorts or something before they get out of the car into the street. And anyway these are usually women with six children and varicose veins mapping their legs and nobody, including them, could care less. As I say, we're right in the middle of town, and if you stand at our front doors you can see two banks and the Congregational church and the newspaper store and three real-estate offices and about twenty-seven old freeloaders tearing up Central Street because the sewer broke again. It's not as if we're on the Cape; we're north of Boston and there's people in this town haven't seen the ocean for twenty years.

The girls had reached the meat counter and were asking McMahon something. He pointed, they pointed, and they shuffled out of sight behind a pyramid of Diet Delight peaches. All that was left for us to see was old McMahon patting his mouth and looking after them sizing up their joints. Poor kids, I began to feel sorry for them, they couldn't help it.

Now here comes the sad part of the story, at least my family says it's sad, but I don't think it's so sad myself. The store's pretty empty, it being Thursday afternoon, so there was nothing much to do except lean on the register and wait for the girls to show up again. The whole store was like a pinball machine and I didn't know which tunnel they'd come out of. After a while they come around out of the far aisle, around the light bulbs, records at discount of the Caribbean Six or Tony Martin Sings or some such gunk you wonder they waste the wax on, sixpacks of candy bars, and plastic toys done up in cellophane that fall apart when a kid looks at them anyway. Around they come, Queenie still leading the way, and holding a little gray jar in her hands. Slots Three through Seven are unmanned and I could see her wondering between Stokes and me, but Stokesie with his usual luck draws an old party in baggy gray pants who stumbles up with four giant cans of pineapple juice (what do these bums *do* with all that pineapple juice? I've often asked myself) so the girls come to me. Queenie puts down the jar and I take it into my fingers icy cold. Kingfish Fancy Herring Snacks in Pure Sour Cream: 49¢. Now her hands are empty, not a ring or a bracelet, bare as God made them, and I wonder where the money's coming from. Still with that prim look she lifts a folded dollar bill out of the hollow at the center of her nubbled pink top. The jar went heavy in my hand. Really, I thought that was so cute.

Then everybody's luck begins to run out. Lengel comes in from haggling with a truck full of cabbages on the lot and is about to scuttle into that door marked MANAGER behind which he hides all day when the girls touch his eye. Lengel's pretty dreary, teaches Sunday school and the rest, but he doesn't miss that much. He comes over and says, "Girls, this isn't the beach."

Queenie blushes, though maybe it's just a brush of sunburn I was noticing for the first time, now that she was so close. "My mother asked me to pick up a jar of herring snacks." Her voice kind of startled me, the way voices do when you see the people first, coming out so flat and dumb yet kind of tony, too, the way it ticked over "pick up" and "snacks." All of a sudden I slid right down her voice into her living room. Her father and the other men were standing around in icecream coats and bow ties and the women were in sandals picking up herring snacks on toothpicks off a big glass plate and they were all holding drinks the color of water with olives and sprigs of mint in them. When my parents have somebody over they get lemonade and if it's a real racy affair Schlitz in tall glasses with "They'll Do It Every Time" cartoons stencilled on.

"That's all right," Lengel said. "But this isn't the beach." His repeating this struck me as funny, as if it had just occurred to him, and he had been thinking all these years the A & P was a great big dune and he was the head lifeguard. He didn't like my smiling—as I say he doesn't miss much—but he concentrates on giving the girls that sad Sunday-school-superintendent stare.

Queenie's blush is no sunburn now, and the plump one in plaid, that I liked better from the back—a really sweet can—pipes up. "We weren't doing any shopping. We just came in for the one thing."

"That makes no difference," Lengel tells her, and I could see from the way his eyes went that he hadn't noticed she was wearing a two-piece before. "We want you decently dressed when you come in here."

"We *are* decent," Queenie says suddenly, her lower lip pushing, getting sore now that she remembers her place, a place from which the crowd that runs the A & P must look pretty crummy. Fancy Herring Snacks flashed in her very blue eyes.

"Girls, I don't want to argue with you. After this come in here with your shoulders covered. It's our policy." He turns his back. That's policy for you. Policy is what the kingpins want. What the others want is juvenile delinquency.

All this while, the customers had been showing up with their carts but, you know, sheep, seeing a scene, they had all bunched up on Stokesie, who shook open a paper bag as gently as peeling a peach, not wanting to miss a word. I could feel in the silence everybody getting nervous, most of all Lengel, who asks me, "Sammy, have you rung up their purchase?"

I thought and said "No" but it wasn't about that I was thinking. I go through the punches, 4, 9, GROC, TOT—it's more complicated than you think, and after you do it often enough, it begins to make a little song, that you hear words to, in my case "Hello (bing) there, you (gung) happy pee-pul (splat)!"—the splat being the drawer flying out. I uncrease the bill, tenderly as you may imagine, it just having come from between the two smoothest scoops of vanilla I had ever known there were, and pass a half and a penny into her narrow pink palm, and nestle the herrings in a bag and twist its neck and hand it over, all the time thinking.

The girls, and who'd blame them, are in a hurry to get out, so I say "I quit" to Lengel quick enough for them to hear, hoping they'll stop and watch me, their unsuspected hero. They keep right on going, into the electric eye; the door flies open and they flicker across the lot to their car, Queenie and Plaid and Big Tall Goony-Goony (not that as raw material she was so bad), leaving me with Lengel and a kink in his eyebrow.

"Did you say something, Sammy?"

"I said I quit."

"I thought you did."

"You didn't have to embarrass them."

"It was they who were embarrassing us."

I started to say something that came out "Fiddle-de-doo." It's a saying of my grandmother's, and I know she would have been pleased.

"I don't think you know what you're saying," Lengel said.

"I know you don't," I said. "But I do." I pull the bow at the back of my apron and start shrugging it off my shoulders. A couple customers that had been heading for my slot begin to knock against each other, like scared pigs in a chute.

Lengel sighs and begins to look very patient and old and gray. He's been a friend of my parents for years. "Sammy, you don't want to do this to your Mom and Dad," he tells me. It's true, I don't. But it seems to me that once you begin a gesture it's fatal not to go through with it. I fold the apron, "Sammy" stitched in red on the pocket, and put it on the counter, and drop the bow tie on top of it. The bow tie is theirs, if you've ever wondered. "You'll feel this for the rest of your life," Lengel says, and I know that's true, too, but remembering how he made that pretty girl blush makes me so scrunchy inside I punch the No Sale tab and the machine whirs "pee-pul" and the drawer splats out. One advantage to this scene taking place in summer, I can follow this up with a clean exit, there's no fumbling around getting your coat and galoshes, I just saunter into the electric eye in my white shirt that my mother ironed the night before, and the door heaves itself open, and outside the sunshine is skating around on the asphalt.

I look around for my girls, but they're gone, of course. There wasn't anybody but some young married screaming with her children about some candy they didn't get by the door of a powder-blue Falcon station wagon. Looking back in the big windows, over the bags of peat moss and aluminum lawn furniture stacked on the pavement, I could see Lengel in my place in the slot, checking the sheep through. His face was dark gray and his back stiff, as if he'd just had an injection of iron, and my stomach kind of fell as I felt how hard the world was going to be to me hereafter.

Study and Discussion Questions

1. What does the story gain from being narrated by Sammy rather than, say, by Stokesie, or even by an omniscient narrator?
2. Characterize Sammy's attitude toward "girls" and toward women. Does the way he views Queenie change?
3. What evidence is there of a difference in social class between Sammy and the three young women? Does this difference in any way help explain his quitting?
4. Aside from his desire to impress Queenie and her friends, why *does* Sammy quit? Explain the significance of his last words in the story: "I felt how hard the world was going to be to me hereafter."

Suggestions for Writing

1. Briefly retell of the story from Queenie's point of view.
2. "A & P" was published in 1962 and, presumably, takes place around then, before the women's liberation movement that began in the late 1960s. What, if anything, would likely be different if the story took place today?

JUDY GRAHN (b. 1940)

Judy Grahn grew up in a working-class family in New Mexico. She began writing poetry at the age of 10, but it didn't occur to her to become a full-time writer until the age of 25. She joined the Air Force when she was 19, but was discharged for being a lesbian. Grahn became an important figure in the lesbian/feminist movements of the late 1960s and helped found the Women's Press Collective—an independent press that gave women authors and women's issues an outlet for publication. In addition to raising the public awareness of feminism, Grahn has endeavored in her writing to redefine perceptions of gay and lesbian life, researching the histories of gay culture and its unacknowledged influence on modern society. Her works include the poetry collections *A Woman Is Talking to Death* (1974), *The Work of a Common Woman* (1978), and *The Queen of Wands* (1982); the nonfiction *Another Mother Tongue: Gay Words, Gay Worlds* (1984), *The Highest Apple: Sappho and the Lesbian Poetic*

Tradition (1985), *Blood and Bread and Roses* (1986), and *Really Reading Gertrude Stein* (1989); and the novel *Mundane's World* (1988). She has also coauthored *Inanna, Lady of Largest Heart: Poems of the Sumerian High Priestess Enheduanna* (2001). "Boys at the Rodeo" first appeared in *True-to-Life Adventure Stories* (1978).

Boys at the Rodeo   (1978)

A lot of people have spent time on some women's farm this summer of 1972 and one day six of us decide to go to the rodeo. We are all mature and mostly in our early thirties. We wear levis and shirts and short hair. Susan has shaved her head.

The man at the gate, who looks like a cousin of the sheriff, is certain we are trying to get in for free. It must have been something in the way we are walking. He stares into Susan's face. "I know you're at least fourteen," he says. He slaps her shoulder, in that comradely way men have with each other. That's when we know he thinks we are boys.

"You're over thirteen," he says to Wendy.

"You're over thirteen," he says to me. He examines each of us closely, and sees only that we have been outdoors, are muscled, and look him directly in the eye. Since we are too short to be men, we must be boys. Everyone else at the rodeo are girls.

We decide to play it straight, so to speak. We make up boys' names for each other. Since Wendy has missed the episode with Susan at the gate, I slap her on the shoulder to demonstrate. "This is what he did." Slam. She never missed a step. It didn't feel bad to me at all. We laugh uneasily. We have achieved the status of fourteen year old boys, what a disguise for travelling through the world. I split into two pieces for the rest of the evening, and have never decided if it is worse to be 31 years old and called a boy or to be 31 years old and called a girl.

Irregardless, we are starved so we decide to eat, and here we have the status of boys for real. It seems to us that all the men and all the women attached to the men and most of the children are eating steak dinner plates; and we are the only women not attached to men. We eat hot dogs, which cost one tenth as much. A man who has taken a woman to the rodeo on this particular day has to have at least $12.00 to spend. So he has charge of all of her money and some of our money too, for we average $3.00 apiece and have taken each other to the rodeo.

Hot dogs in hand we escort ourselves to the wooden stands, and first is the standing up ceremony. We are pledging allegiance for the way of life—the competition, the supposed masculinity and pretty girls. I stand up, cursing, pretending I'm in some other country. One which has not been rediscovered. The loudspeaker plays Anchors Aweigh, that's what I like about rodeos, always something unexpected. At the last one I attended in another state the men on horses threw candy and nuts to the kids, chipping their teeth and breaking their noses. Who is it, I wonder, that has put these guys in charge. Even quiet mothers raged over that episode.

Now it is time for the rodeo queen contest, and a display of four very young women on horses. They are judged for queen 30% on their horse*man*ship and 70% on the number of queen tickets which people bought on their behalf to 'elect' them. Talk about stuffed ballot boxes. I notice the winner as usual is the one on the registered thoroughbred whose daddy owns tracts and tracts of something—lumber, minerals, animals. His family name is all over the county.

The last loser sits well on a scrubby little pony and lives with her aunt and uncle. I pick her for the dyke even though it is speculation without clues. I can't help it, it's a pleasant habit. I wish I could give her a ribbon. Not for being a dyke, but for sitting on her horse well. For believing there ever was a contest, for not being the daughter of anyone who owns thousands of acres of anything.

Now the loudspeaker announces the girls' barrel races, which is the only grown women's event. It goes first because it is not really a part of the rodeo, but more like a mildly athletic variation of a parade by women to introduce the real thing. Like us boys in the stand, the girls are simply bearing witness to someone else's act.

The voice is booming that barrel racing is a new, modern event, that these young women are the wives and daughters of cowboys, and barrel racing is a way for them to participate in their own right. How generous of these northern cowboys to have resurrected barrel racing for women and to have forgotten the hard roping and riding which women always used to do in rodeos when I was younger. Even though I was a town child, I heard thrilling rumors of the all-women's rodeo in Texas, including that the finest brahma bull rider in all of Texas was a forty year old woman who weighed a hundred pounds.

Indeed, my first lover's first lover was a big heavy woman who was normally slow as a cold python, but she was just hell when she got up on a horse. She could rope and tie a calf faster than any cowboy within 500 miles of Sweetwater, Texas. That's what the West Texas dykes said, and they never lied about anything as important to them as calf roping, or the differences between women and men. And what about that news story I had heard recently on the radio, about a bull rider who was eight months pregnant? The newsman just had apoplectic fits over her, but not me. I was proud of her. She makes me think of all of us who have had our insides so overly protected from jarring we cannot possibly get through childbirth without an anesthetic.

While I have been grumbling these thoughts to myself, three barrels have been set up in a big triangle on the field, and the women one by one have raced their horses around each one and back to start. The trick is to turn your horse as sharply as possible without overthrowing the barrel.

After this moderate display, the main bulk of the rodeo begins, with calf roping, bronco riding, bull riding. It's a very male show during which the men demonstrate their various abilities at immobilizing, cornering, maneuvering and conquering cattle of every age.

A rodeo is an interminable number of roped and tied calves, ridden and unridden broncoes. The repetition is broken by a few antics from the agile, necessary clown. His long legs nearly envelope the little jackass he is riding for the satire of it.

After a number of hours they produce an event I have never seen before—goat tying. This is for the girls eleven and twelve. They use one goat for fourteen participants. The goat is supposed to be held in place on a rope by a large man on horseback. Each girl rushes out in a long run half way across the field, grabs the animal, knocks it down, ties its legs together. Sometimes the man lets his horse drift so the goat pulls six or eight feet away from her, something no one would allow to happen in a male event. Many of the girls take over a full minute just to do their tying, and the fact that only one goat has been used makes everybody say, 'poor goat, poor goat,' and start laughing. This has become the real comedy event of the evening, and the purpose clearly is to show how badly girls do in the rodeo.

Only one has broken through this purpose to the other side. One small girl is not disheartened by the years of bad training, the ridiculous crossfield run, the laughing superior man on his horse, or the shape-shifting goat. She downs it in a beautiful flying tackle. This makes me whisper, as usual, 'that's the dyke,' but for the rest of it we watch the girls look ludicrous, awkward, outclassed and totally dominated by the large handsome man on horse. In the stands we six boys drink beer in disgust, groan and hug our breasts, hold our heads and twist our faces at each other in embarrassment.

As the calf roping starts up again, we decide to use our disguises to walk around the grounds. Making our way around to the cowboy side of the arena, we pass the intricate mazes of rail where the stock is stored, to the chutes where they are loading the bull riders onto the bulls.

I wish to report that although we pass by dozens of men, and although we have pressed against wild horses and have climbed on rails overlooking thousands of pounds of angry animal flesh, though we touch ropes and halters, we are never once warned away, never told that this is not the proper place for us, that we had better get back for our own good, are not safe, etc., none of the dozens of warnings and threats we would have gotten if we had been recognized as thirty one year old girls instead of fourteen year old boys. It is a most interesting way to wander around the world for the day.

We examine everything closely. The brahma bulls are in the chutes, ready to be released into the ring. They are bulky, kindly looking creatures with rolling eyes; they resemble overgrown pigs. One of us whispers, "Aren't those the same kind of cattle that walk around all over the streets in India and never hurt anybody?"

Here in the chutes made exactly their size, they are converted into wild antagonistic beasts by means of a nasty belt around their loins, squeezed tight to mash their most tender testicles just before they are released into the ring. This torture is supplemented by a jolt of electricity from an electric cattle prod to make sure they come out bucking. So much for the rodeo as a great drama between man and nature.

A pale, nervous cowboy sits on the bull's back with one hand in a glove hooked under a strap around the bull's midsection. He gains points by using his spurs during the ride. He has to remain on top until the timing buzzer buzzes a few seconds after he and the bull plunge out of the gate. I had always considered it the most exciting event.

Around the fence sit many eager young men watching, helping, and getting in the way. We are easily accepted among them. How depressing this can be.

Out in the arena a dismounted cowboy reaches over and slaps his horse fiercely on the mouth because it has turned its head the wrong way.

I squat down peering through the rails where I see the neat, tight-fitting pants of two young men standing provocatively chest to chest.

"Don't you think Henry's a queer," one says with contempt.

"Hell, I *know* he's a queer," the other says. They hold an informal spitting contest for the punctuation. Meantime their eyes have brightened and their fronts are moving toward each other in their clean, smooth shirts. I realize they are flirting with each other, using Henry to bring up the dangerous subject of themselves. I am remembering all the gay cowboys I ever knew. This is one of the things I like about cowboys. They don't wear those beautiful pearl button shirts and tight levis for nothing.

As the events inside the arena subside, we walk down to a roped off pavillion where there is a dance. The band consists of one portly, bouncing enthusiastic man of middle age who is singing with great spirit into the microphone. The rest of the band are three grim, lean young men over fourteen. The drummer drums angrily, while jerking his head behind himself as though searching the air for someone who is already two hours late and had seriously promised to take him away from here. The two guitar players are sleepwalking from the feet up with their eyes so glassy you could read by them.

A redhaired man appears, surrounded by redhaired children who ask, "Are you drunk, Daddy?"

"No, I am not drunk," Daddy says.

"Can we have some money?"

"No," Daddy says, "I am not drunk enough to give you any money."

During a break in the music the redhaired man asks the bandleader where he got his band.

"Where did I get this band?" the bandleader puffs up, "I raised this band myself. These are all my sons—I raised this band myself." The redhaired man is so very impressed he is nearly bowing and kissing the hand of the bandleader, as they repeat this conversation two or three times. "This is *my* band," the bandleader says, and the two guitar players exchange grim and glassy looks.

Next the bandleader has announced "Okie From Muskogee," a song intended to portray the white country morality of cowboys. The crowd does not respond but he sings enthusiastically anyway. Two of his more alert sons drag themselves to the microphone to wail that they don't smoke marijuana in Muskogee—as those hippies down in San Francisco do, and they certainly don't. From the look of it they shoot hard drugs and pop pills.

In the middle of the song a very drunk thirteen year old boy has staggered up to Wendy, pounding her on the shoulder and exclaiming, "Can you dig it, brother?" Later she tells me she has never been called brother before, and she likes it. Her first real identification as one of the brothers, in the brotherhood of man.

We boys begin to walk back to our truck, past a cowboy vomiting on his own pretty boots, past another lying completely under a car. Near our truck, a young man has calf-roped a young woman. She shrieks for him to stop, hopping weakly along behind him. This is the first bid for public attention I have seen from any woman here since the barrel race. I understand that this little scene is a re-enactment of the true meaning of the rodeo, and of the conquest of the west. And oh how much I do not want to be her; I do not want to be the conquest of the west.

I am remembering how the clown always seems to be tall and riding on an ass, that must be a way of poking fun at the small and usually dark people who tried to raise sheep or goats or were sod farmers and rode burros instead of tall handsome blond horses, and who were driven under by the beef raisers. And so today we went to a display of cattle handling instead of a sheep shearing or a goat milking contest—or to go into even older ghost territory, a corn dance, or acorn gathering. . . .

As we reach the truck, the tall man passes with the rodeo queen, who must surely be his niece, or something. All this non-contest, if it is for anyone, must certainly be for him. As a boy, I look at him. He is his own spitting image, of what is manly and white and masterly, so tall in his high heels, so *well horsed*. His manner portrays his theory of life as the survival of the fittest against wild beasts, and all the mythical rest of us who are too female or dark, not straight, or much too native to the earth to now be trusted as more than witnesses, flags, cheerleaders and unwilling stock.

As he passes, we step out of the way and I am glad we are in our disguise. I hate to step out of his way as a full grown woman, one who hasn't enough class status to warrant his thinly polite chivalry. He has knocked me off the sidewalk of too many towns, too often.

Yet somewhere in me I know I have always wanted to be manly, what I mean is having that expression of courage, control, coordination, ability I associate with men. To *provide*.

But here I am in this truck, not a man at all, a fourteen year old boy only. Tomorrow is my thirty second birthday. We six snuggle together in the bed of this rickety truck which is our world for the time being. We are headed back to the bold and shakey adventures of our all-women's farm, our all-women's households and companies, our expanding minds, ambitions and bodies, we who are neither male nor female at this moment in the pageant world, who are not the rancher's wife, mother earth, Virgin Mary or the rodeo queen—we who are really the one who took her self seriously, who once took an all out dive at the goat believing that the odds were square and that she was truly in the contest.

And now that we know it is not a contest, just a play—we have run off with the goat ourselves to try another way of life.

Because I certainly do not want to be a 32 year old girl, or calf either, and I certainly also do always remember Gertrude Stein's[1] beautiful dykely voice saying, what is the use of being a boy if you grow up to be a man.

Study and Discussion Questions

1. Why does the man at the gate decide the women are boys?
2. What kind of freedom does being seen as 14-year-old boys give to these women in their thirties?
3. By providing a narrator who is an outsider to the scene, Grahn is able to penetrate the mystique of the rodeo. Discuss how this works in the section on the brahma bull riding.
4. Is Grahn only talking about the rodeo in this story or are there larger implications?
5. Why does the narrator award the word *dyke* to one of the losers of the queen contest and to the one girl who takes the goat-tying event seriously?
6. What is the tone of "Boys at the Rodeo"?

Suggestions for Writing

1. What does Grahn suggest about the rodeo as a male ritual?
2. If these six women had been seen as "girls," what would their day at the rodeo have been like?
3. Discuss the depiction of the goat-tying event as an example of social criticism.

LEWIS NORDAN

Born in August, 1939 in Forest, MS, Lewis Nordan has dedicated much of his writing to exploring the strange beauty of his home state. Nordan's formal education came from local sources like Millsaps College, Mississippi State University, and Auburn University, but he taught at the University of Pittsburgh during much of his professional career. His fiction is often noted for incorporating elements of magic realism and for finding the comedy in tragic moments.

---

[1]American writer (1874–1946).

Of his four novels, three collections of short stories, and memoir, his most celebrated contribution is the novel *Wolf Whistle*. The following selection is set in the fictitious Arrow Catcher, MS which is loosely based on Itta Bena, MS where he was raised.

The All-Girl Football Team   (1986)

Dressing in drag was not new to me. I had never worn a dress myself, but my father had.

My father was all man. His maleness defined him to me. Evenings, when he came home from work, I loved to hug him and to feel the rasp of a day's growth of beard against my face and neck. I loved to smell him, a fragrance of wool and leather and whiskey and shoepolish and aftershave.

Drag was not a frequent thing, only twice a year. Halloween, of course. Kids in costume would come to our house and ring the bell and Father would answer it in women's clothes. "Trick or treat, Gilbert," the children would say, and my father would try to guess who was behind each mask. He would drop candy into the plastic pumpkins or paper sacks and send the children on to the next house.

The other time was the Womanless Wedding. It was an annual affair, a minstrel show in rouge instead of blackface. The Rotary and the Lions—all the solid male citizens of Arrow Catcher, Mississippi—would put on a raucous play in drag and donate the money to charity. One year Mr. Rant got drunk and fell off the stage in a floor-length gown.

My father loved the Womanless Wedding. He took a different part each year: bride, mother of the bride, flower girl, maid of honor, whatever was available. He shaved his legs and Naired his chest and bleached the hair on his arms and plucked his eyebrows and rouged his lips and mascaraed his lashes and he was ready. He owned wigs. With a pedicure and a close shave, my father was a pretty good looking woman for his age.

So dressing in drag was not new.

In my junior year of high school, my class got the idea of putting on an all-girl football game. We were raising money for some worthwhile project or other—a new scoreboard for the gym, I think. The idea was for the junior and senior girls to put on uniforms and helmets and to play football against each other. The school principal agreed to let us use the stadium. We would charge admission and sell hot dogs and Cokes at the concession stand.

It seemed like a good idea.

The idea seemed even better when I first saw the girls in uniform. They were beautiful. Hulda Raby had long legs and boyish hips and large breasts, and when she was dressed in our school colors and was wearing pads and cleats and a rubber mouthpiece, I thought no one on earth had ever had such a good idea as the all-girl football team.

The girls were enthusiastic. They found a senior boy who agreed to coach them, Tony Pirelli, whose father owned the Arrow Cafe.

Positions were tried out for and assigned. Plays were drawn up and mimeographed and passed out to the players and carried around in notebooks and memorized. A wide-hipped girl named Tootie Nell Hightower learned to snap the ball, and Nadine Johnson learned to take the snap from center.

I stood on the sidelines and watched Nadine hunker into position behind the center's upturned rear-end and put her hands into position. *Green forty-two . . .* My heart jumped out of my chest.

Pads began to clash, helmets to clatter. Nadine was a natural at quarterback and could throw the bomb. Ednita Gillespie could get open. I saw these girls through new eyes. I feared them and I loved them.

The days passed. No one except the players was allowed inside the locker room, of course, not even Tony Pirelli, the kid who coached them. But each day after practice I hung outside in the parking lot and imagined them in there. I saw them unlace their cleats and fling them into a corner. I saw them strip dirty tape from their ankles and remove the Tuff-skin with alcohol. I smelled the pungency of their skin. I watched them walk through the locker room wearing only their shoulderpads, nothing else, the padding stained with sweat. I watched them soap up in the shower and play grabass and snap each other with towels. I saw them stand under the shower and let the water pour into their upturned faces and I watched one or another of them relax her bladder and allow the urine to run down her leg and swirl away in the drain.

Never before in the history of the whole wide world had anyone ever had such a good idea as the all-girl football team.

I wanted to be near the girls. I hung around the parking lot to watch them. At first a few other boys did the same, and we punched each other's arms and made jokes, but my interest outlasted theirs and soon I was the only boy in the parking lot.

My favorite part of the day was when the girls came out of the locker rooms after practice, after their showers.

Nadine Johnson came out, the quarterback. She had short hair and it was still wet and slicked back like a man's. Hulda Raby had blonde hair that hung down to her hips. One day she stepped out of the gym into the late afternoon sun and bent over and allowed her wet hair to hang down over her face, almost to the ground. She toweled it roughly with a white locker room towel and then flung her hair back over her head so that it hung down her back again. She dropped the towel behind her, arrogant, and she seemed to know that someone would pick it up for her. It was my joy to rush across the lot and place the towel into a bin of soiled linens.

Hulda Raby did not notice me, of course. My reward was to be close to the locker room door when the others came out.

Tootie Nell Hightower, the center—I could not look at her without seeing her bent over the ball, its leather nap gripped in her certain hands. Lynn Koontz—I heard the beauty of her name for the first time. It was a football player's name. You could play tight end for the Steelers with a name like Lynn Koontz. The twins, Exie Lee and Nora Lee Prestridge. The Sewell girls, Marty and Ruby. Ednita Gillespie, the wide receiver. I heard Nadine say to her, "Nita, honey, you got a great pair of hands."

I envied them their womanhood.

I watched them on the practice field each day after school. Tony Pirelli, their coach, seemed to me the luckiest boy in the world.

I insinuated myself into their midst. I volunteered to act as a flunky for the team. I helped line the field. I asked parents to act as referees and scorekeepers, and I made sure everyone had clean socks. I carried equipment and water bottles and the first aid kit. I saddlesoaped footballs and replaced broken elastic. I dealt with the high school principal, who was worried about the light bill, since the game was to be held at night.

It was springtime and the Mississippi Delta was Eden to me. I saw it as I had never seen it before, the whippoorwills and coons and owls and little bobwhites. Mornings the pecan trees outside my window were heavy with dew and smelled like big wet flowers.

In my dreams I listened to the music of *green forty-two hut hut hut* . . . It floated on the air like a fragrance of wisteria. I knew why men married, as my father had, and were true to the same woman over a lifetime. I thought of my father's mortality.

I went into my father's room and found his revolver and broke it open and poured its cartridges onto the chenille bedspread. I thought of my own mortality. I understood for the first time the difficulty of ever knowing who I am. I longed to be held as a lover by a woman in a football suit.

The all-girl football team idea got out of hand. It became elaborate.

Somebody suggested that we should have boy cheerleaders, dressed up in girls' cheerleading costumes. It would be hilarious, everybody said. What fun. Somebody else thought it would be just great if we made it homecoming as well. You know, with a homecoming court. Everyone agreed, Sure! Oh boy! It would be like the Womanless Wedding, only better. We'll hold the ceremony at halftime. We'll crown a homecoming queen!

I didn't like the idea. I said, "I'm against it. It's a silly idea. I vote no."

Everybody else said, "It'll be hilarious. Let's do it, sure it's great."

I wanted to say, Are you insane? We have discovered what makes women beautiful. The girl-children who were our classmates three weeks ago are now women—they are constellations! Do you want a constellation walking in a parade with some goon in a dress?

Instead I said, "No way. I'm not doing it. I've got to line the field. I've got to pump up the balls. Count me out, brother."

I did it anyway. I was elected cheerleader. That's small-town high school for you. It was a big joke. I didn't want to do it, so everybody voted on me. No try-outs, nothing. One day I get the news and a box with a cheerleader costume in it. I said, "Forget it."

Everybody said, "Be a sport."

Right up until the night of the big game I still wasn't going to do it. I wasn't even going to the game. Why should I? Nobody was taking the game seriously—nobody but me and the girls who were knocking their heads together.

Maybe this will explain it: One day after practice I saw Ednita Gillespie get into her father's pickup alone. She yanked open the door and, as she did, she put her fingers to one side of her nose and blew snot into the gravel driveway of the schoolhouse parking lot. The door banged shut behind her and she drove away.

Do you understand what I mean? It was not Ednita I loved. Not Tootie Nell or Lynn Koontz or Nadine Johnson. It was Woman. I had never known her before. She was a presence as essential and dangerous as geology. Somehow she held the magic that could make me whole and give me life.

That's why I wasn't going to the all-girl football game.

I said all this to my father in his room at the back of our house. In this room I could say anything. I could smell my father's whole life in this room, the guns in the closet, the feathers of birds he had killed, the blood of mammals, the mutton that greased the line of his fly-casting equipment.

I said, "It would take a fool. To dress up like a girl, when there are women—women, Daddy, not girls—dressed in pads and cleats."

What do you suppose my father said to me? Can you guess? Do you think he said, "Don't be silly, it's a school project. I want you to participate." Do you think he said, "It's up to you, of course, but I just want to tell you, you're going to be missing out on a whole lot of fun."

My father was a housepainter. He went to sixth grade and no further. He said, "I will dress you in a skirt and a sweater and nice underwear and you will feel beautiful."

I said, "Uh . . ."

He said, "You have never felt beautiful."

I said, "Well. . ."

It was near dark. The fall air had turned cold. In two hours the all-girl football game would begin. My mother was still at work.

Father drew my bath and put almond oil into the water and swished the water back and forth with his hand until it foamed up. He hung a green silk bathrobe on a hook on the bathroom door. He set out bathpowder and a powder puff he had bought new for me. He showed me how to shave my legs and underarms. It didn't matter that no one else would be able to see.

When I was clean and sweet-smelling, I came into his room wearing the robe. He gave me the clothes I would dress in.

I said, "Dad, is this queer?"

He did not answer.

I took the box with the uniform in it, and a small bag with new underwear.

I slipped into the lacy underpants, and then into the pantyhose.

I let him show me how to hook the bra, which he did not stuff with Kleenex. He gave me tiny false breasts, cups made of foam rubber, with perfect nipples on the ends. When I slipped on my sweater with the big AC on the front, you could see my nipples showing through.

I put on a half-slip and the skirt. He showed me how to apply my makeup. I could choose any wig I wanted. He spritzed me with Windsong.

I did not feel beautiful. I felt like a fool. I looked at myself in the mirror and saw that I looked like a fool as well. I stood like a boy, I walked like a boy, I scratched myself like a boy. I had a dumb boy-look on my face. My hands were boy-hands. My dick, for no good reason, was stiff and aching.

The masculine smells of my father's room-the rubber raingear and gun oil and fish scales stuck to his tacklebox—reached me through my false femininity and mocked me.

My father said, "How do you feel?"

I said, "Like a fucking fool."

I said, "I've got a hard on."

He said, "Do you know any cheers? Can you do one cheer for me before you go?"

I said, "I don't think so, Dad."

He said, "Well, I'll have my eyes on you the whole game. I'll be watching you from the stadium."

I said, "I wish there was a Book of Life, with all the right answers in the back."

He said, "Do 'Satisfied.' Just once, before you go. 'Satisfied' is my favorite cheer."

There was something about that football field: the brilliant natural carpet of green grass, the incredible lights, the strong straight lines of chalkdust, the serviceable steel bleachers filled with cheering people and the little Arrow Catcher High School marching band in uniform—there was something in all that scene that told me who I was. I did not feel beautiful, as my father had predicted. I was the same person I had always been, and yet the bass drum, with its flaking bow-and-arrow design and the words ARROW CATCHER, MISSISSIPPI, printed in faded letters around the perimeter of the drumhead, told me that the worst things about myself were not my enemies and that the Womanless Wedding held meaning for my father that I might never understand and did not need to understand.

I had come to the game late. The referees in their striped suits had already taken the field. The opposing teams, in black and gold uniforms, had finished warm-up calisthenics. Steel whistles sounded and drew the players from their final huddle and prayers.

The captains walked like warriors to the middle of the field. They watched the toss of the coin.

I watched it also, from the sidelines. The coin went up and up. It seemed suspended in the air beneath those blazing lights, above the green table of Delta land. The coin seemed forged of pure silver and big as a discus. It turned over and over, as if in slow motion. It hung for a century.

I jumped up and down in my wool skirt and saddle oxfords. I was a cheerleader at the center of the universe. I waved my pom-poms and clapped my hands and kicked my heels up behind me. I tossed my hair and fluttered my lashes without knowing I knew how to do these things. The coin that I was watching was a message of hope and goodness throughout the land.

It was a land I loved, this fine ellipse in a crook of the Yazoo River—its alligators and mallards and beaver dams, its rice paddies and soybeans and catfish farms.

Suddenly I knew that my father was right, that I did feel beautiful, except that now beauty had a different meaning for me. It meant that I was who I was, the core of me, the perfect center, and that the world was who it was and that those two facts were unchangeable. Grief had no sting, the future was not a thing to fear, all things were possible and personal and pure.

I watched the opening kickoff. It was a short grounder that scooted between the legs of the front line of girls in uniform.

By the time someone in the backfield picked it up, my small breasts had become a part of me, not rubber but flesh. My cock, beneath the lacy underpants, was what it had always been, this odd hard unpredictable equipment I had been born with, and yet it was also a moist opening into the hidden fragrance of another self that was me as well. My arms were woman-arms, my feet woman-feet, my voice, my lips, my fingers. I stood on the sweet sad brink of womanhood, and somehow I shared this newness with my father.

The game had begun, and I was the cheeriest cheerleader on the sidelines. One team scored a touchdown. Hulda Raby sustained a serious knee injury. Nadine threw the bomb to Ednita but had it intercepted. The band played the fight song, and we went through all the cheers.

My father and mother were in the bleachers, far up, and I could see the pride in their faces. I was a wonderful cheerleader, and they knew that I was.

We did "Satisfied," and in my heart I dedicated the cheer to my father.

I went to the principal, we cheerleaders called out, with our hands on our hips, sashaying as we pretended to walk haughtily into the principal's office.

Satisfied, came the refrain back from the cheering section, including my father and mother.

And the principal said, we called out, shaking our finger, as if the principal were giving us a stern talking-to.

And again the loud refrain, *Satisfied*.

That we couldn't lose...

Satisfied...

With the stuff we use...

Satisfied...

You take-a one step back . . . Here we put our hands behind our backs and jumped one step backward, cute and coy, as if we were obeying the principal's stern order.

Satisfied . . .

You take-a two steps up . . . Here we put on a look of mock surprise, as if we just could not understand what the principal was getting at with all his complicated instructions, but we put our hands on our hips and took two cute steps forward anyway.

The principal's final line is: *And then you strut your stuff, And then you strut your stuff, And then you strut your stuff.* Which we did, by wagging our sexy hips and prankishly twirling our index fingers in the air.

Sat-isss-fied!

The Mississippi Delta air was the Garden of Eden, filled with innocence and ripe apples. The blue of the skies shone through the darkness of the night and through the glare of the stadium lights. I smelled fig trees and a fragrance of weevil poison and sweet fishy water from the swamp.

The game went on. The huddles and the time-outs, the sweat and the bloody noses and the fourth-down punts.

And then halftime. I had literally forgotten all about halftime.

My whole world exploded into ceremony and beautiful ritual. The band was on the field in full uniform. The goalposts, were wrapped in black and gold crepe paper, and streamers were blowing in the autumn breeze. Boys with shaven legs strutted past the bleachers wearing majorette costumes. They carried bright banners on long poles. The band marched in formation, and then it formed a huge heart in the center of the field. It played "Let Me Call You Sweetheart," and I felt tears of joy and the fullness of nature well up in me. I knew that the world was a place of safety and hope and that my father was a great man. I knew that I was a beautiful woman and that because of this I had a chance of growing up to be as fine a man as my father. *Let me call you sweetheart I'm in love with you, Let me hear you whisper that you love me too*, I loved the girls in uniform; I would always love them. They were lined up under the home-team goalposts with the maids of the homecoming court. *Keep the love-light burning in your eyes so true . . .*

Nadine Johnson was the captain. She led the beautiful slow processional of players and maids toward the center of the field. The band played. There was a sweetness of Mowdown in the air from the rice paddies nearby.

I knew the meaning of love. I thought of my father, the way he had looked on the day of his wedding, the first of his weddings that I was old enough to attend. He had been the bride and had worn a high-bodice floor-length gown, antique white, with a train and veil. He carried a nosegay at his waist. When the minister asked whether any person here present could show just cause why this couple should not be joined in holy matrimony, a drunken pharmacist named H. L. Berryman, wearing a print dress and heels, jumped up out of the audience and fired a pistol in the air. My father fell into a swoon.

It was all part of the show, of course—and although I knew it was only a play and that my father was only an actor in it, I wanted to leap from my seat in the audience and make known to all the world that he was my father and that without him my own life was without meaning.

On the football field Nadine Johnson turned to a tiny boy child, three or four years old, who was a part of the homecoming ceremonies. He was wearing a ruffled dress with stiff petticoats and was standing beside Nadine with a satin pillow in his hands. There was a silvery crown on the pillow. The homecoming court was assembled around them, arms hooked in arms, smiles bright.

Nadine took the crown from the pillow, as flashbulbs went off.

A boy named Jeep Bennett was standing beside Nadine. He was wearing a yellow evening gown and had only three fingers on one hand. He had been in a hunting accident the year before and this year had been elected homecoming queen.

Nadine placed the crown on his proud head, and the flashbulbs went off again. The bleachers roared with applause and cheers and approval. Nadine kissed Jeep, and Jeep was demure and embarrassed.

I had wanted—dreamed!—of this moment, dreaded it in a way, because I had believed I would envy Jeep this perfection, this public kiss of a woman in a football suit, which I had believed for three weeks was the completion of love and sex and holy need.

And yet now that it was here, it was oddly meaningless to me. There was no jealousy in my heart, no lust for Nadine in all her sweaty beauty.

And yet there was lust in my heart, sweet romance. My breath caught in my throat, my tiny breasts rose and my nipples hardened. (Seemed to harden, I swear!)

I looked down the line of suited-up women and their male maids. Tootie Nell, wide-hipped and solid; Hulda, with a damaged knee; Lynn Koontz, her magical name. I looked at the drag-dressed boys who clung violet-like to the certain arms of these beautiful women.

And yes there was lust and even love in my heart, but not for the women in black-and-gold. The person I loved was wearing a business suit with a back-pleat in the skirt, so that when he walked you could see a triangle of his gray satin slip and the back of his beautiful knee. Tony Pirelli, the kid who coached the team, was an Italian boy with dark skin and dark eyes and a nut-brown wig that caressed his shoulders. He wore a soft gray silk blouse with ruffled sleeves and, at his throat, a ruffled ascot. His shoes were patent leather slingback pumps with two-inch heels, and the girls had given him a corsage, which he wore on his breast.

I hated my thoughts and my feelings. I was certain my father could read them all the way to the top of the bleachers.

I had never seen anyone so beautiful as Tony Pirelli. He never smiled, and now his sadness called out to me, it made me want to hold him and protect him from all harm, to kiss his lips and neck, to close his brown eyes with my kisses, to hold his small breasts in my hands and to have him touch my own breasts.

I believed I was a lesbian. What else could I call myself? I felt like a fool for not having noticed before. I was a fool for having strutted my stuff during the cheers, for having loved the Mississippi Delta and the sentimental songs played by the band.

I didn't see the rest of the game. The band played and the crepe paper rattled and the banners whipped and the crowds cheered, and I ran away from the side-lines and through the gate and away from the football field and the school grounds.

This happened in the autumn I was sixteen years old. Now I am forty-five years old, and all of it seems too fantastic to be true. Maybe my memory has exaggerated the facts, somehow.

I remember what happened afterward very accurately, though.

I ran through the little town of Arrow Catcher, Mississippi, toward my par-ents' home. I don't know what I wanted there, the safety of my father's room, I think, the fishing rods and reels with names like Shakespeare and Garcia, the suits of camouflage and the rubber hip-waders. I was still wearing my cheer-leader costume and my makeup and false breasts and even the wig.

And then something happened, by magic I suppose, that stopped me. The Southern sky seemed to fill with light—no, not light, but with something like light, with meaning, I want to say.

I stood in the street where I had stopped and I listened to the distant brass of the Arrow Catcher High School marching band. It sounded like the blare of circus horns. I took deep breaths and exhaled them into the frosty air.

I took from my skirt pocket the lace handkerchief my father had put there for me, and I dabbed at my eyes, careful not to smear the mascara more than it was already smeared.

I began walking back toward the football field. I was not a woman. I did not feel like a woman. I was not in love with a boy. I was a boy in costume for one night of the year, and I was my father's child and the child of this strange south-ern geography. I was beautiful, and also wise and sad and somehow doomed with joy.

The gymnasium was decorated in black and gold. There was a table with a big crystal punch bowl, and other tables with ironed white tablecloths and trays of sandwiches and cookies. Around the walls of the gym our parents had placed potted plants and baskets of flowers. The girls had changed to their party dresses, the boys had put on the trousers and sport jackets our parents had brought for us. We were proper boys and girls, and our costumes were stuffed into bags in the locker rooms where we changed.

A phonograph blared out the music we loved.

I danced close to Nadine Johnson and imagined, as I felt her cool check against mine, that I could see the future. I imagined I would marry-not Nadine but some woman like Nadine, some beautiful woman, faceless for now—and that together we would have sons and that we would love them and teach them to be gentle and to love the music we were dancing to and to wear dresses and that, in doing this, we would somehow never grow old and that love would last forever.

Study and Discussion Questions

1. What might dressing in drag symbolize for the narrator throughout the story? Apply the same question to the girls dressed in football gear and the narrator's father.
2. What is the transformation the girls have gone through and why is the narrator so obsessed with their transformation?
3. Make a list of different actions performed by the girls and the narrator throughout the story. Which actions are traditionally classified as masculine and which actions are classified as feminine?
4. This story is set in the Mississippi Delta. How does the setting influence the reading of the story, and how does it influence the narrator's questions concerning his sexual identity?
5. Considering the narrator's struggle with conventional gender roles, can a man be beautiful?

Suggestions for Writing

1. Though the narrator obsesses over the girls' transformation throughout much of the story, he undergoes a transformation of his own. Describe his transformation and development throughout the story.
2. The narrator says that dressing in drag holds special significance for his father. Considering what the narrator tells us about the father and his actions, write a short essay or paragraph discussing the impact of this knowledge on the narrator.
3. Starting with the narrator's arrival at the football game, reread the football game scene and the halftime pageantry. Explain what the coin toss and cheering teach the narrator about himself.
4. Compare this story with another work that questions gender roles, such as "Boys at the Rodeo" (page 323).

EDGAR ALLAN POE (1809–1849)

The son of traveling actors, Edgar Allan Poe was probably abandoned by his father shortly after his birth. In any case, his father died in 1810, and his mother continued to act, moving frequently with her children until 1811, when she too died, leaving Poe and his siblings destitute. Poe was adopted by the family of John and Frances Allan, and at his baptism assumed his benefactor's name. Despite this early gesture of connectedness, Poe's relationship with the Allans was fractious, especially after Poe began attending the University of Virginia in 1836. Here Poe was known both for his writing and also for his gambling and drinking. His repeated, abusive pleas for money caused John Allan to cut him off periodically. After one such incident Poe left the university and joined the army. During his service he published his first book of poetry, *Tamerlane and Other Poems* (1827). His second, *Al Aaraaf*, was published in 1829. In 1830, through Allan's influence, Poe was awarded an appointment to West Point, but he was soon expelled. Among cadets the legend still circulates that he forced this himself by showing up naked for morning formation, but it is more likely that drinking and gambling lay at the heart of the matter. In any event, this disgrace seems to have been fortuitous, because at this time Poe began to devote himself to writing, publishing several stories and winning a fiction contest in 1832.

In 1833 he became editor of the *Southern Literary Messenger*, one of several important literary posts he would fill in his life. In 1839 he became editor of *Burton's Gentleman's Magazine*; in 1840 editor of Graham's; and in 1845 editor of the *Broadway Journal*. He published a great deal of his own poetry and fiction in these journals, as well as numerous reviews (many of them quite strident), and in this way had a significant impact on literary trends and tastes. However, despite the fact that he continued to be awarded editorial positions, the same kind of behavior that resulted in his dismissal from West Point— drinking, gambling, and a disinclination to bow to authority—led him regularly into conflict with his employers. And although he published his work regularly, he was never far from poverty. He also had a tendency to pick literary fights, and was most famously dismissive of the New England transcendentalists. Some speculate that this kind of controversy may have been a ploy to sell magazines.

Although his writing career was relatively brief and his habits were self-destructive, Poe managed to amass an impressive canon before his death in 1849. In addition to such works as "Ligeia"(1838); "The Fall of the House of Usher" (1839); *Tales of the Grotesque and Arabesque* (1840); and the popular "The Raven" (1844); Poe is credited with the invention of the detective story. His character C. Auguste Dupin from "The Murders in the Rue Morgue"; "The Mystery of Marie Roget"; and "The Purloined Letter"served as type for Sherlock Holmes and countless other detectives. In these and other stories Poe demonstrates an obsession with the dark side of human psychology. Many of his tales explore a concept he labeled "the spirit of perverseness . . . the unfathomable longing of the soul to vex itself." This phenomenon can be seen in stories such as "The Black Cat" and "The Tell-Tale Heart," in which seemingly rational characters are drawn to commit ghastly crimes for reasons they cannot explain. While his last years were clouded by the death of his wife from tuberculosis in 1846, he seemed on the road to recovery when, in 1849, he stopped in Baltimore on his way to Philadelphia and was found on the street four days later, unconscious and near death. The exact cause of his death on October 7 remains a mystery.

—David L. G. Arnold, *University of Wisconsin, Stevens Point*

Hop-Frog   (1849)

I never knew any one so keenly alive to a joke as the king was. He seemed to live only for joking. To tell a good story of the joke kind, and to tell it well, was the surest road to his favour. Thus it happened that his seven ministers were all noted for their accomplishments as jokers. They all took after the king, too, in being large, corpulent, oily men, as well as inimitable jokers. Whether people grow fat by joking, or whether there is something in fat itself which predisposes to a joke, I have never been quite able to determine; but certain it is that a lean joker is a rara avis in terris.

About the refinements, or, as he called them, the 'ghosts' of wit, the king troubled himself very little. He had an especial admiration for breadth in a jest, and would often put up with length, for the sake of it. Over-niceties wearied him. He would have preferred Rabelais's Gargantua to the Zadig of Voltaire; and, upon the whole, practical jokes suited his taste far better than verbal ones.

At the date of my narrative, professing jesters had not altogether gone out of fashion at court. Several of the great continental 'powers' still retained their 'fools', who wore motley, with caps and bells, and who were expected to be always ready with sharp witticisms, at a moment's notice, in consideration of the crumbs that fell from the royal table.

Our king, as a matter of course, retained his 'fool'. The fact is, he required something in the way of folly—if only to counterbalance the heavy wisdom of the seven wise men who were his ministers—not to mention himself.

His fool, or professional jester, was not only a fool, however. His value was trebled in the eyes of the king by the fact of his being also a dwarf and a cripple. Dwarfs were as common at court, in those days, as fools; and many monarchs would have found it difficult to get through their days (days are rather longer at court than elsewhere) without both a jester to laugh with, and a dwarf to laugh at. But, as I have already observed, your jesters, in ninety-nine cases out of a hundred, are fat, round, and unwieldy—so that it was no small source of self-gratulation with our king that, in Hop-Frog (this was the fool's name) he possessed a triplicate treasure in one person.

I believe the name 'Hop-Frog' was not given to the dwarf by his sponsors at baptism, but it was conferred upon him, by general consent of the seven ministers, on account of his inability to walk as other men do. In fact, Hop-Frog could only get along by a sort of interjectional gait—something between a leap and a wriggle—a movement that afforded illimitable amusement, and of course consolation, to the king, for (notwithstanding the protuberance of his stomach and a constitutional swelling of the head) the king, by his whole court, was accounted a capital figure.

But although Hop-Frog, through the distortion of his legs, could move only with great pain and difficulty along a road or floor, the prodigious muscular power which nature seemed to have bestowed upon his arms, by way of compensation for deficiency in the lower limbs, enabled him to perform many feats of wonderful dexterity, where trees or ropes were in question, or anything else to climb. At such exercises he certainly much more resembled a squirrel, or a small monkey, than a frog.

I am not able to say, with precision, from what country Hop-Frog originally came. It was from some barbarous region, however, that no person ever heard of—a vast distance from the court of our king. Hop-Frog, and a young girl very little less dwarfish than himself (although of exquisite proportions, and a marvellous dancer), had been forcibly carried off from their respective homes in adjoining provinces, and sent as presents to the king, by one of his ever-victorious generals.

Under these circumstances, it is not to be wondered at that a close intimacy arose between the two little captives. Indeed, they soon became sworn friends. Hop-Frog, who, although he made a great deal of sport, was by no means popular, had it not in his power to render Trippetta many services; but she, on account of her grace and exquisite beauty (although a dwarf), was universally admired and petted: so she possessed much influence; and never failed to use it, whenever she could, for the benefit of Hop-Frog.

On some grand state occasion—I forget what—the king determined to have a masquerade; and whenever a masquerade, or anything of that kind, occurred at our court, then the talents both of Hop-Frog and Trippetta were sure to be called in play. Hop-Frog, in especial, was so inventive in the way of getting up pageants, suggesting novel characters and arranging costume for masked balls, that nothing could be done, it seems, without his assistance.

The night appointed for the fete had arrived. A gorgeous hall had been fitted up, under Trippetta's eye, with every kind of device which could possibly give eclat to a masquerade. The whole court was in a fever of expectation. As for costumes and characters, it might well be supposed that everybody had come to a decision on such points. Many had made up their minds as to what roles they should assume, a week, or even a month, in advance; and, in fact, there was not a particle of indecision anywhere—except in the case of the king and his seven ministers. Why they hesitated I never could tell, unless they did it by way of a joke. More probably, they found it difficult, on account of being so fat, to make up their minds. At all events, time flew; and, as a last resource, they sent for Trippetta and Hop-Frog.

When the two little friends obeyed the summons of the king, they found him sitting at his wine with the seven members of his cabinet council; but the monarch appeared to be in a very ill humour. He knew that Hop-Frog was not fond of wine; for it excited the poor cripple almost to madness; and madness is no comfortable thing. But the king loved his practical jokes, and took pleasure in forcing Hop-Frog to drink and (as the king called it) 'to be merry'.

'Come here, Hop-Frog,' said he, as the jester and his friend entered the room: 'swallow this bumper to the health of your absent friends' (here Hop-Frog sighed), 'and then let us have the benefit of your invention. We want characters—characters, man—something novel—out of the way. We are wearied with this everlasting sameness. Come, drink! the wine will brighten your wits.'

Hop-Frog endeavoured, as usual, to get up a jest in reply to these advances from the king; but the effort was too much. It happened to be the poor dwarf's birthday, and the command to drink to his 'absent friends' forced the tears to his eyes. Many large, bitter drops fell into the goblet as he took it, humbly, from the hand of the tyrant.

'Ah! ha! ha! ha!' roared the latter, as the dwarf reluctantly drained the beaker. 'See what a glass of good wine can do! Why, your eyes are shining already!'

Poor fellow! his large eyes gleamed rather than shone, for the effect of wine on his excitable brain was not more powerful than instantaneous. He placed the goblet nervously on the table, and looked round upon the company with a half-insane stare. They all seemed highly amused at the success of the king's 'joke'.

'And now to business,' said the prime minister, a very fat man.

'Yes,' said the king; 'come, Hop-Frog, lend us your assistance. Characters, my fine fellow; we stand in need of characters—all of us—ha! ha! ha!' and as this was seriously meant for a joke, his laugh was chorused by the seven.

Hop-Frog also laughed, although feebly and somewhat vacantly.

'Come, come,' said the king, impatiently, 'have you nothing to suggest?'

'I am endeavouring to think of something novel,' replied the dwarf, abstractedly, for he was quite bewildered by the wine.

'Endeavouring!' cried the tyrant, fiercely; 'what do you mean by that? Ah, I perceive. You are sulky, and want more wine. Here, drink this!' and he poured out another gobletful and offered it to the cripple, who merely gazed at it, gasping for breath.

'Drink, I say!' shouted the monster, 'or by the fiends—'

The dwarf hesitated. The king grew purple with rage. The courtiers smirked. Trippetta, pale as a corpse, advanced to the monarch's seat, and, falling to her knees before him, implored him to spare her friend.

The tyrant regarded her, for some moments, in evident wonder at her audacity. He seemed quite at a loss what to do or say—how most becomingly to express his indignation. At last, without uttering a syllable, he pushed her violently from him, and threw the contents of the brimming goblet in her face.

The poor girl got up as best she could, and, not daring even to sigh, resumed her position at the foot of the table.

There was a dead silence for about half a minute, during which the falling of a leaf, or of a feather, might have been heard. It was interrupted by a low, but harsh and protracted grating sound which seemed to come at once from every corner of the room.

'What—what—what are you making that noise for?' demanded the king, turning furiously to the dwarf.

The latter seemed to have recovered, in great measure, from his intoxication, and looking fixedly but quietly into the tyrant's face, merely ejaculated:

'I—I? How could it have been me?'

'The sound appeared to come from without,' observed one of the courtiers. 'I fancy it was the parrot at the window, whetting his bill upon his cage-wires.'

'True,' replied the monarch, as if much relieved by the suggestion; 'but, on the honour of a knight, I could have sworn that it was the gritting of this vagabond's teeth.'

Hereupon the dwarf laughed (the king was too confirmed a joker to object to any one's laughing), and displayed a set of large, powerful, and very repulsive teeth. Moreover, he avowed his perfect willingness to swallow as much wine as desired. The monarch was pacified; and having drained another bumper with no very perceptible ill effect, Hop-Frog entered at once, and with spirit, into the plans for the masquerade.

'I cannot tell what was the association of idea,' observed he, very tranquilly, and as if he had never tasted wine in his life, 'but just after your majesty had struck the girl and thrown the wine in her face—just after your majesty had done this, and while the parrot was making that odd noise outside the window, there came into my mind a capital diversion—one of my own country frolics—often enacted among us, at our masquerades: but here it will be new altogether. Unfortunately, however, it requires a company of eight persons, and—'

'Here we are!' cried the king, laughing at his acute discovery of the coincidence; 'eight to a fraction—I and my seven ministers. Come! what is the diversion?'

'We call it,' replied the cripple, 'the Eight Chained Ourang-Outangs, and it really is excellent sport if well enacted.'

'We will enact it,' remarked the king, drawing himself up, and lowering his eyelids.

'The beauty of the game,' continued Hop-Frog, 'lies in the fright it occasions among the women.'

'Capital!' roared in chorus the monarch and his ministry.

'I will equip you as ourang-outangs,' proceeded the dwarf; 'leave all that to me. The resemblance shall be so striking that the company of masqueraders will take you for real beasts—and, of course, they will be as much terrified as astonished.'

'Oh, this is exquisite!' exclaimed the king. 'Hop-Frog! I will make a man of you.'

'The chains are for the purpose of increasing the confusion by their jangling. You are supposed to have escaped, en masse, from your keepers. Your majesty cannot conceive the effect produced, at a masquerade, by eight chained ourang-outangs, imagined to be real ones by most of the company, and rushing in with savage cries among the crowd of delicately and gorgeously habited men and women. The contrast is inimitable.'

'It must be,' said the king: and the council arose hurriedly (as it was growing late), to put in execution the scheme of Hop-Frog.

His mode of equipping the party as ourang-outangs was very simple, but effective enough for his purposes. The animals in question had, at the epoch of my story, very rarely been seen in any part of the civilized world; and as the imitations made by the dwarf were sufficiently beast-like and more than sufficiently hideous, their truthfulness to nature was thus thought to be secured.

The king and his ministers were first encased in tight-fitting stockinette shirts and drawers. They were then saturated with tar. At this stage of the process, some one of the party suggested feathers; but the suggestion was at once overruled by the dwarf, who soon convinced the eight, by ocular demonstration, that the hair of such a brute as the ourang-outang was much more efficiently represented by flax. A thick coating of the latter was accordingly plastered upon the coating of tar. A long chain was now procured. First, it was passed about the waist of the king, and tied; then about another of the party, and also tied, then about all successively, and in the same manner. When this chaining arrangement was complete, and the party stood as far apart from each other as possible, they formed a circle; and to make all things appear natural, Hop-Frog passed the residue of the chain, in two diameters, at right angles, across the circle, after the fashion adopted, at the present day, by those who capture Chimpanzees, or other large apes, in Borneo.

The grand saloon in which the masquerade was to take place, was a circular room, very lofty, and receiving the light of the sun only through a single window at top. At night (the season for which the apartment was especially designed), it was illuminated principally by a large chandelier, depending by a chain from the centre of the sky-light, and lowered, or elevated, by means of a counterbalance as usual; but (in order not to look unsightly) this latter passed outside the cupola and over the roof.

The arrangements of the room had been left to Trippetta's superintendence; but, in some particulars, it seems, she had been guided by the calmer judgment of her friend the dwarf. At his suggestion it was that, on this occasion, the chandelier was removed. Its waxen drippings (which, in weather so warm, it was quite impossible to prevent) would have been seriously detrimental to the rich dresses of the guests, who, on account of the crowded state of the saloon, could not all be expected to keep from out its centre—that is to say, from under the chandelier. Additional sconces were set in various parts of the hall, out of the way; and a flambeau, emitting sweet odour, was placed in the right hand of each of the Caryatides that stood against the wall—some fifty or sixty altogether.

The eight ourang-outangs, taking Hop-Frog's advice, waited patiently until midnight (when the room was thoroughly filled with masqueraders) before making their appearance. No sooner had the clock ceased striking,

however, than they rushed, or rather rolled in, all together—for the impedi-
ment of their chains caused most of the party to fall, and all to stumble as
they entered.

The excitement among the masqueraders was prodigious, and filled the
heart of the king with glee. As had been anticipated, there were not a few of
the guests who supposed the ferocious-looking creatures to be beasts of some
kind in reality, if not precisely ourang-outangs. Many of the women swooned
with affright; and had not the king taken the precaution to exclude all weapons
from the saloon, his party might soon have expiated their frolic in their blood.
As it was, a general rush was made for the doors; but the king had ordered
them to be locked immediately upon his entrance; and, at the dwarf's
suggestion, the keys had been deposited with him.

While the tumult was at its height, and each masquerader attentive only to
his own safety (for, in fact, there was much real danger from the pressure of
the excited crowd), the chain by which the chandelier ordinarily hung, and
which had been drawn up on its removal, might have been seen very gradually
to descend, until its hooked extremity came within three feet of the floor.

Soon after this, the king and his seven friends, having reeled about the hall
in all directions, found themselves, at length, in its centre, and, of course, in
immediate contact with the chain. While they were thus situated, the dwarf,
who had followed closely at their heels, inciting them to keep up the commotion, took hold of their own chain at the intersection of the two portions which
crossed the circle diametrically and at right angles. Here, with the rapidity of
thought, he inserted the hook from which the chandelier had been wont to
depend; and, in an instant, by some unseen agency, the chandelier-chain was
drawn so far upward as to take the hook out of reach, and, as an inevitable
consequence, to drag the ourang-outangs together in close connection, and
face to face.

The masqueraders, by this time, had recovered, in some measure, from their
alarm; and, beginning to regard the whole matter as a well-contrived pleas-
antry, set up a loud shout of laughter at the predicament of the apes.

'Leave them to me!' now screamed Hop-Frog, his shrill voice making itself
easily heard through all the din. 'Leave them to me. I fancy I know them. If
I can only get a good look at them, I can soon tell who they are.'

Here, scrambling over the heads of the crowd, he managed to get to the wall;
when, seizing a flambeau from one of the Caryatides, he returned, as he went,
to the centre of the room—leaped, with the agility of a monkey, upon the king's
head—and thence clambered a few feet up the chain—holding down the torch
to examine the group of ourang-outangs, and still screaming, 'I shall soon find
out who they are!'

And now, while the whole assembly (the apes included) were convulsed
with laughter, the jester suddenly uttered a shrill whistle; when the chain flew
violently up for about thirty feet—dragging with it the dismayed and struggling
ourang-outangs, and leaving them suspended in mid-air between the sky-light
and the floor. Hop-Frog, clinging to the chain as it rose, still maintained his

relative position in respect to the eight maskers, and still (as if nothing were the matter) continued to thrust his torch down towards them, as though endeavouring to discover who they were.

So thoroughly astonished were the whole company at this ascent, that a dead silence, of about a minute's duration, ensued. It was broken by just such a low, harsh, grating sound, as had before attracted the attention of the king and his councillors, when the former threw the wine in the face of Trippetta. But, on the present occasion, there could be no question as to whence the sound issued. It came from the fang-like teeth of the dwarf, who ground them and gnashed them as he foamed at the mouth, and glared, with an expression of maniacal rage, into the upturned countenances of the king and his seven companions.

'Ah, ha!' said at length the infuriated jester. 'Ah, ha! I begin to see who these people are, now!' Here, pretending to scrutinize the king more closely, he held the flambeau to the flaxen coat which enveloped him, and which instantly burst into a sheet of vivid flame. In less than half a minute the whole eight ourang-outangs were blazing fiercely, amid the shrieks of the multitude who gazed at them from below, horror-stricken, and without the power to render them the slightest assistance.

At length the flames, suddenly increasing in virulence, forced the jester to climb higher up the chain, to be out of their reach; and as he made this movement, the crowd again sank, for a brief instant, into silence. The dwarf seized his opportunity, and once more spoke:

'I now see distinctly,' he said, 'what manner of people these maskers are. They are a great king and his seven privy-councillors—a king who does not scruple to strike a defenceless girl, and his seven councillors who abet him in the outrage. As for myself, I am simply Hop-Frog, the jester—and this is my last jest.'

Owing to the high combustibility of both the flax and the tar to which it adhered, the dwarf had scarcely made an end of his brief speech before the work of vengeance was complete. The eight corpses swung in their chains, a fetid, blackened, hideous, and indistinguishable mass. The cripple hurled his torch at them, clambered leisurely to the ceiling, and disappeared through the sky-light.

It is supposed that Trippetta, stationed on the roof of the saloon, had been the accomplice of her friend in his fiery revenge, and that, together, they effected their escape to their own country: for neither was seen again.

Study and Discussion Questions

1. What point of view did Poe employ in this story? What do you know about the narrator? Why is this significant?
2. What physical characteristic do the king and his seven ministers share? Why is this important?

3. Describe Hop-Frog; how does his appearance connect to the nature of his "final jest"? To develop this fully, consider Poe's use of animal imagery.

4. Consider Hog-Frog's motive(s) for revenge; list as many as you can, then rank them in order of importance.

5. This is a revenge story, one in which the protagonist fights back after being bullied and humiliated, in part due to physical and social inequality. Relate this situation to an incident from your own life or from the experience of someone you know.

6. What qualities of Hop-Frog make him a non-traditional protagonist? Is he a sympathetic character? Why or why not?

7. How is this story ironic?

Suggestions for Writing

1. Study the life of Edgar Allan Poe and compare it to this story.

2. Consider an act of revenge that occurred in recent history; how does it relate to this story?

3. Make a case for the behavior of the king and his ministers; in doing so, focus on the standards of an earlier time.

4. Research the impact of bullying on young people or other groups who lack power and autonomy.

5. Compare the acts of gallantry that you see in "Hop-Frog" and "A&P" (page 318). Think about the motivation of both protagonists and their execution of purpose.

❂ ❂ ❂

POETRY

JOHN DONNE (1572–1631)

John Donne was born in London into a prominent Roman Catholic family. Because of his religion, he was prevented from taking a degree at Oxford; he became an Anglican convert soon after. He participated in naval expeditions and upon return to England studied law and was appointed secretary to Sir Thomas Egerton. But his secret marriage to Egerton's niece cost him his position and led to brief imprisonment. Donne struggled to earn a living for a number of years, but eventually found a patron to support his writing. In 1615, he was ordained an Anglican priest and his sermons became immensely popular. Only after his death did he gain a reputation as the leading "metaphysical" poet. His *Poems* were published by his son in 1633.

The Flea (1633)

Mark but this flea, and mark in this,
How little that which thou deny'st me is;
It sucked me first, and now sucks thee,
And in this flea, our two bloods mingled be;
Thou know'st that this cannot be said   5
A sin, or shame, or loss of maidenhead,
   Yet this enjoys before it woo,
    And pampered swells with one blood made of two,
   And this, alas, is more than we would do.

Oh stay, three lives in one flea spare,   10
Where we almost, yea more than married are.
This flea is you and I, and this
Our marriage bed, and marriage temple is;
Though parents grudge, and you, we are met,
And cloistered in these living walls of jet.   15
   Though use make you apt to kill me,
    Let not to this, self murder added be,
   And sacrilege, three sins in killing three.

Cruel and sudden, hast thou since
Purpled thy nail, in blood of innocence?   20

Wherein could this flea guilty be,
Except in that drop which it sucked from thee?
Yet thou triumph'st, and say'st that thou
Find'st not thyself, nor me the weaker now;
   'Tis true, then learn how false, fears be;   25
   Just so much honour, when thou yield'st to me,
   Will waste, as this flea's death took life from thee.

Study and Discussion Questions

1. To whom is the poem addressed?
2. "The Flea" is an example of a *conceit,* an ingenious metaphor. What does the speaker of the poem mean when he says: "This flea is you and I, and this/ Our marriage bed, and marriage temple is"?
3. What literally is happening in this poem?
4. What is the tone of the poem?

Suggestions for Writing

1. Write a description of how you imagine the setting and characters in this poem.
2. What is happening in each stanza of "The Flea"? That is, what are the stages of the speaker's argument?
3. Write an answer to the speaker of the poem from the point of view of the person to whom the poem is addressed.

WILLIAM BLAKE (1757–1827)

William Blake was born in London. Although he didn't receive a formal education, he did study art and drawing as a young boy. At fourteen, he was apprenticed to an engraver and earned a meager living engraving for the rest of his life. Blake self-published his poems, often surrounding the verse with his own elaborate illustrations. For many, understanding a Blake poem in its entirety means seeing the original combination of words and images. Although Blake lived during the same period as such Romantic poets as Wordsworth and Shelly, his distinctive focus on the inner life of the individual, religious symbolism, and mystical themes varies greatly from the idealization of nature in Romantic poetry. For this reason, his visionary poetics were little appreciated during his time. Since his rediscovery in the 1920s, the work of Blake, like that of John Donne before him, is considered a cornerstone that defines "metaphysical" poetry. His major works include *Songs of Innocence* (1789), *The*

Marriage of Heaven and Hell (1790), and *Songs of Experience* (1794). In the poem "The Garden of Love," first published in *Songs of Experience*, a questioning speaker walks into a speculative, gothic-like realm where religiosity takes on a darker tint.

The Garden of Love

(1794)

I went to the Garden of Love,
And saw what I never had seen:
A Chapel was built in the midst,
Where I used to play on the green.

And the gates of this Chapel were shut, 5
And "Thou shalt not" writ over the door;
So I turn'd to the Garden of Love
That so many sweet flowers bore;

And I saw it was filled with graves,
And tomb-stones where flowers should be; 10
And Priests in black gowns were walking their rounds,
And binding with briars my joys & desires.

Study and Discussion Questions

1. What contrast runs through the poem?
2. What does "Thou shalt not" allude to?
3. Why a *garden* of love?
4. Why are the gates of the chapel shut?
5. Discuss the importance of the rhythm and internal rhymes of the last two lines.

Suggestion for Writing

1. What is the poem saying about organized religion? What do you think of what it is saying?

EDNA ST. VINCENT MILLAY (1892–1950)

Raised in Camden, Maine, Millay published her first poem at the age of fourteen. Under the guidance of a dedicated mother, Millay underwent an intensive study program of music and literature, always encouraged to be strong-willed and independent. Her poem "Renascence," published in *Lyric Year* in 1912, was met with critical praise and helped secure a scholarship for Millay at Vasser College. After graduating, she moved to New York's Greenwich Village—a "bohemian" community of actors, painters and writers—and began to write poetry and plays. In 1923, she became the first woman to win the Pulitzer Prize for poetry for her collection *The Ballad of the Harp-Weaver* (1923). Although Millay was an active and popular poet during the modernist movement of the first half of the twentieth century, her conservative and formal techniques (she is best known for her sonnets) set her apart from the free-verse developments of the era. While her form remained traditional, her content did not. Like the work of the Greek poet Sappho, many of Millay's precise and lyric poems explore the physical and mental aspects of female sexuality and sexual autonomy. Select works from her 15 volumes of poetry, several plays, essays, and short fiction include the poetry works *Renascence and Other Poems* (1912), *A Few Figs from Thistles: Poems and Sonnets* (1921), *Fatal Interview* (1931), *Wine from These Grapes* (1934), *Make Bright the Arrows* (1940), and the drama collection *Three Plays* (1926). In "An Ancient Gesture," Millay's distinct lyricism enhances the poem's subtle play of meanings.

An Ancient Gesture   (1954)

I thought, as I wiped my eyes on the corner of my apron:
Penelope did this too.
And more than once: you can't keep weaving all day
And undoing it all through the night;
Your arms get tired, and the back of your neck gets tight   5
And along towards morning, when you think it will never be light,
And your husband has been gone, and you don't know where, for years,
Suddenly you burst into tears;
There is simply nothing else to do.

And I thought, as I wiped my eyes on the corner of my apron: 10
This is an ancient gesture, authentic, antique,
In the very best tradition, classic, Greek;
Ulysses did this too.
But only as a gesture,—a gesture which implied

To the assembled throng that he was much too moved to speak.   15
He learned it from Penelope ...
Penelope,[1] who really cried.

Study and Discussion Questions

1. What are the two senses of the word *gesture* which emerge in the poem? Note the references to *gesture.* Look up the word in an unabridged dictionary.
2. Compare/contrast the characters of Penelope and of Ulysses (Odysseus) as they are presented in Millay's poem.
3. Who is the third character in the poem? What does it appear her situation is? How does she feel about it?
4. Trace the rhyme scheme of this poem using the method where each subsequent letter in the alphabet identifies a new rhyme.
5. Look at the first line of each stanza. Why do you think Millay did this? What effect does it have?

Suggestion for Writing

1. Write a paragraph exploring the tone of "An Ancient Gesture." How does the speaker of the poem feel about her own situation and how does this develop through the poem? Why do you think she chose to foreground the story of Penelope while only implying her own? What emotion are you feeling by the end of "An Ancient Gesture" and how might that be connected to choices of word and structure the poet made?

ROBERT BROWNING (1812–1889)

Robert Browning was born to a wealthy banker whose library became the playground for the eager young scholar. Browning's schooling consisted of a few years at Peckham and some lectures at London University in 1830. Otherwise he was educated by private tutors and by himself, reading his father's vast collection of books. His father had his son's first small volume of verses privately printed as *Incondita*, while Browning was still a child. Browning's first real publication was *Pauline* in 1833. Shortly after the publication of this poem, he left on the first of his many travels to Europe. While in Italy, he wrote *Paracelsus*,

---

[1]Penelope: Wife of Odysseus (Ulysses) in Homer's *Odyssey,* who waited years for her husband, thought dead, to return from the Trojan War. She promised to marry one of her numerous suitors when she had finished her weaving, but each night she unwove what she had done that day.

a poem about a sorcerer's experiences and motivations. This poem was published in 1835. His next two works did not enhance his reputation, a play called *Strafford* that closed after five nights and a dense poem *Sordello* (1840) that was so learned and complex that it gave Browning the reputation of being unintelligible to the reading public. In 1846 he met, fell in love with, and married the much more successful poet Elizabeth Barrett. They moved to Florence and had one son. They lived in Florence until her death in 1861. There he wrote *Christmas Eve and Easter Day* (1850) and *Men and Women* (1855). Browning had begun the writing that would build the reputation which he now holds. He was not much appreciated by the Victorians, who admired sentiment and feeling, while his poetry took a tactile view of the human psyche, often letting his speakers reveal damaging information about themselves while apparently boasting or reporting events. He is considered one of the great psychological poets.

After Barrett Browning's death, he moved to London where he withdrew for a short time but then began to travel and give presentations widely. He published *Dramatis Personae* (1864) and *The Ring and the Book* four years later. The latter is one of the longest and most complex poems in English. It deals with a trial for a murder of a young woman, but the real content of the poem includes dramatic monologues of everyone involved in the crime. Each speaker has seen and experienced something different, making the poem a testimony to modern psychological research into the unreliability of eyewitnesses. The poem never resolves the truth of the murder, for there is not truth, only the many perspectives of those involved, truly a postmodern perspective on reality. After completing this poem Browning began to write mysterious and grotesque poems and also began to translate Greek tragedies, but none of these was successful. At the end of his life he moved to Venice to live, dying at his son's palazzo. He is buried in poet's corner in Westminster Abbey. He remains one of the brilliant thinkers and philosophers of his era, as well as a great poet.

My Last Duchess   (1842)

Ferrara[1]

That's my last Duchess painted on the wall,
Looking as if she were alive. I call
That piece a wonder, now; Frà Pandolf's hands
Worked busily a day, and there she stands.
Will't please you sit and look at her? I said   5
"Frà Pandolf" by design, for never read
Strangers like you that pictured countenance,

---

[1]Ferrara, a city in northern Italy, is the scene.

The depth and passion of its earnest glance,
But to myself they turned (since none puts by
The curtain I have drawn for you, but I)   10
And seemed as they would ask me, if they durst,
How such a glance came there; so, not the first
Are you to turn and ask thus. Sir, 't was not
Her husband's presence only, called that spot
Of joy into the Duchess' cheek; perhaps   15
Frà Pandolf chanced to say, "Her mantle laps
Over my lady's wrist too much," or "Paint
Must never hope to reproduce the faint
Half-flush that dies along her throat." Such stuff
Was courtesy, she thought, and cause enough   20
For calling up that spot of joy. She had
A heart—how shall I say?—too soon made glad,
Too easily impressed; she liked whate'er
She looked on, and her looks went everywhere.
Sir, 't was all one! My favor at her breast,   25
The dropping of the daylight in the West,
The bough of cherries some officious fool
Broke in the orchard for her, the white mule
She rode with round the terrace—all and each
Would draw from her alike the approving speech,   30
Or blush, at least. She thanked men,—good! but thanked
Somehow—I know not how—as if she ranked
My gift of a nine-hundred-years-old name
With anybody's gift. Who'd stoop to blame
This sort of trifling? Even had you skill   35
In speech—which I have not—to make your will
Quite clear to such an one, and say "Just this
Or that in you disgusts me; here you miss,
Or there exceed the mark"—and if she let
Herself be lessoned so, nor plainly set   40
Her wits to yours, forsooth, and made excuse—
E'en then would be some stooping; and I choose
Never to stoop. Oh, sir, she smiled, no doubt,
Whene'er I passed her; but who passed without
Much the same smile? This grew; I gave commands;   45
Then all smiles stopped together. There she stands
As if alive. Will 't please you rise? We'll meet
The company below, then. I repeat,
The Count your master's known munificence

First published in *Dramatic Lyrics* 1842 and retitled as printed in the 1849 *Dramatic Romances and Lyrics*.

Is ample warrant that no just pretense   50
Of mine for dowry will be disallowed;
Though his fair daughter's self, as I avowed
At starting, is my object. Nay, we'll go
Together down, sir. Notice Neptune, though,
Taming a sea-horse, thought a rarity,   55
Which Claus of Innsbruck cast in bronze for me!

Study and Discussion Questions

1. What does the Duke reveal about his personality throughout the poem?
2. How does the Duke present his former Duchess? Is his description reliable? Why or why not?
3. Browning's poem is an example of an "ekphrasis," which is a piece of literature that discusses a visual work of art. What is the significance of Browning's use of this literary device?
4. What is the effect of the prevalent use of enjambment in this poem?
5. To whom is the Duke speaking and why?
6. What is the significance of the statue of Neptune mentioned in the final lines?

Suggestions for Writing

1. Write a response to this poem from the point of view of the Duchess giving an account of the events the Duke describes as well as a description of the Duke himself.
2. Browning's poem deals squarely with the issue of power struggles between men and women in romantic relationships. Pinpoint some of these instances of conflict present in the poem and discuss whether modern day couples experience such conflicts.

ALFRED, LORD TENNYSON (1809–1892)

Alfred Tennyson's life spanned most of the years of Queen Victoria's reign. He was born in a Lincolnshire rectory into a talented and literate family, the fourth child and one of eight sons and four daughters. All the children were brought up as intellectuals. Tennyson's publication of poetry included the works of his two brothers, Frederick and Charles (*Poems by Two Brothers*, 1827). Tennyson looked the part of a poet, tall and slender with an elegant head, and he was quickly adopted by the artistic circle at school. At Trinity College, Cambridge, he became a member of the poets' club, The Apostles, where he met Arthur Henry Hallam, whose early death was to shape both Tennyson's temperament and his poetry. Before that event, however, Tennyson won the Chancellor's prize for a poem titled "Timbuctoo" and saw his first volume of poetry published in 1830, *Poems, Chiefly Lyrical*. His second volume appeared in 1832.

In 1833, Hallam, by then engaged to Tennyson's sister, Emily, died in Vienna. Tennyson began his poem on faith and doubt, *In Memoriam*, that was eventually to make him famous. He worked on the poem for seventeen years. At the same time, he worked on *Idylls of the King*, a long work retelling the tales of King Arthur from Malory but molded into the Victorian mindset. In 1842, he published Poems, which included *Ulysses* and *Morte D'Arthur*. In 1847, his popular satire on women's place in the world, *Princess*, appeared. These were difficult times for Tennyson, despite the success of the latest poems. Then in 1850 he married Emily Sellwood and finally published *In Memoriam*. That year he was chosen to succeed Wordsworth as Poet Laureate. A long formal poem, *Ode on the Death of the Duke of Wellington* (1852) preceded *Maud* (1855), a romantic tale of love and death, followed by *Enoch Arden* and *Northern Farmer* (1964). He dedicated a new edition of *Idylls* to the memory of Queen Victoria's beloved husband Prince Albert, who had died in 1861, and became a great favorite of the queen. In 1884, he became Lord Tennyson and published *Becket*, a successful drama. In his last years, he wrote apace, publishing *Tiresias and Other Poems* in 1885, *Locksley Hall Sixty Years After* in 1886, *Demeter and Other Poems* in 1889, and *The Death of Oenone* in 1892, published just after his death. Assessments of Tennyson's work was, in turn, criticized and then praised in the past century. During most of the twentieth century, he was thought to be too ornate for most readers, but in time his poetic talent and his ability to bring sound and light to life were honored. Those who love a talented wordsmith and those who love a mythic vision of ancient England love Tennyson.

The Lady of Shalott   (1832)

Part I

On either side the river lie
Long fields of barley and of rye,
That clothe the wold and meet the sky;
And thro' the field the road runs by
        To many-tower'd Camelot;
And up and down the people go,
Gazing where the lilies blow
Round an island there below,
        The island of Shalott.

Willows whiten, aspens quiver,
Little breezes dusk and shiver
Thro' the wave that runs for ever
By the island in the river
        Flowing down to Camelot.
Four gray walls, and four gray towers,
Overlook a space of flowers,

And the silent isle imbowers
    The Lady of Shalott.

By the margin, willow-veil'd
Slide the heavy barges trail'd
By slow horses; and unhail'd
The shallop flitteth silken-sail'd
    Skimming down to Camelot:
But who hath seen her wave her hand?
Or at the casement seen her stand?
Or is she known in all the land,
    The Lady of Shalott?

Only reapers, reaping early
In among the bearded barley,
Hear a song that echoes cheerly
From the river winding clearly,
    Down to tower'd Camelot:
And by the moon the reaper weary,
Piling sheaves in uplands airy,
Listening, whispers "'Tis the fairy
    Lady of Shalott."

Part II

There she weaves by night and day
A magic web with colours gay.
She has heard a whisper say,
A curse is on her if she stay
    To look down to Camelot.
She knows not what the curse may be,
And so she weaveth steadily,
And little other care hath she,
    The Lady of Shalott.

And moving thro' a mirror clear
That hangs before her all the year,
Shadows of the world appear.
There she sees the highway near
    Winding down to Camelot:
There the river eddy whirls,
And there the surly village-churls,
And the red cloaks of market girls,
    Pass onward from Shalott.

Sometimes a troop of damsels glad,
An abbot on an ambling pad,
Sometimes a curly shepherd-lad,
Or long-hair'd page in crimson clad,
      Goes by to tower'd Camelot;
And sometimes thro' the mirror blue
The knights come riding two and two:
She hath no loyal knight and true,
      The Lady of Shalott.

But in her web she still delights
To weave the mirror's magic sights,
For often thro' the silent nights
A funeral, with plumes and lights
      And music, went to Camelot:
Or when the moon was overhead,
Came two young lovers lately wed;
"I am half-sick of shadows," said
      The Lady of Shalott.

Part III

A bow-shot from her bower-eaves,
He rode between the barley-sheaves,
The sun came dazzling thro' the leaves,
And flamed upon the brazen greaves
      Of bold Sir Lancelot.
A redcross knight for ever kneel'd
To a lady in his shield,
That sparkled on the yellow field,
      Beside remote Shalott.

The gemmy bridle glitter'd free,
Like to some branch of stars we see
Hung in the golden Galaxy.
The bridle-bells rang merrily
      As he rode down to Camelot:
And from his blazon'd baldric slung
A mighty silver bugle hung,
And as he rode his armour rung,
      Beside remote Shalott.

All in the blue unclouded weather
Thick-jewell'd shone the saddle-leather,

The helmet and the helmet-feather
Burn'd like one burning flame together,
      As he rode down to Camelot.
As often thro' the purple night,
Below the starry clusters bright,
Some bearded meteor, trailing light,
      Moves over still Shalott.

His broad clear brow in sunlight glow'd;
On burnish'd hooves his war-horse trode;
From underneath his helmet flow'd
His coal-black curls as on he rode,
      As he rode down to Camelot.
From the bank and from the river
He flash'd into the crystal mirror,
"Tirra lirra," by the river
      Sang Sir Lancelot.

She left the web, she left the loom,
She made three paces thro' the room,
She saw the water-lily bloom,
She saw the helmet and the plume,
      She look'd down to Camelot.
Out flew the web and floated wide;
The mirror crack'd from side to side;
"The curse is come upon me," cried
      The Lady of Shalott.

Part IV

In the stormy east-wind straining,
The pale-yellow woods were waning,
The broad stream in his banks complaining,
Heavily the low sky raining
      Over tower'd Camelot;
Down she came and found a boat
Beneath a willow left afloat,
And round about the prow she wrote
      The Lady of Shalott.

And down the river's dim expanse—
Like some bold seër in a trance,
Seeing all his own mischance—
With a glassy countenance

Did she look to Camelot.
And at the closing of the day
She loosed the chain, and down she lay;
The broad stream bore her far away,
        The Lady of Shalott.

Lying, robed in snowy white
That loosely flew to left and right—
The leaves upon her falling light—
Thro' the noises of the night
        She floated down to Camelot:
And as the boat-head wound along
The willowy hills and fields among,
They heard her singing her last song,
        The Lady of Shalott.

Heard a carol, mournful, holy,
Chanted loudly, chanted lowly,
Till her blood was frozen slowly,
And her eyes were darken'd wholly,
        Turn'd to tower'd Camelot;
For ere she reach'd upon the tide
The first house by the water-side,
Singing in her song she died,
        The Lady of Shalott.

Under tower and balcony,
By garden-wall and gallery,
A gleaming shape she floated by,
A corse between the houses high,
        Silent into Camelot.
Out upon the wharfs they came,
Knight and burgher, lord and dame,
And round the prow they read her name,
        The Lady of Shalott.

Who is this? and what is here?
And in the lighted palace near
Died the sound of royal cheer;
And they cross'd themselves for fear,
        All the knights at Camelot:
But Lancelot mused a little space;
He said, "She has a lovely face;
God in his mercy lend her grace,
        The Lady of Shalott."

Study and Discussion Questions

1. How does Tennyson's use of the ballad format affect the poem?
2. What is significant about the detailed descriptions of the activity beyond the Lady's tower room?
3. What role does Lancelot play in this poem?
4. How are the Lady's mirror and her weaving symbolic?
5. What exactly is the Lady's curse, and what do you think Tennyson is metaphorically trying to convey with it?
6. Why do you think Tennyson incorporates so much sound imagery throughout the poem, and what is its effect?

Suggestions for Writing

1. "The Lady of Shalott" has often been the subject of many pieces of art, particularly paintings. Discuss why you think artists are so drawn to this poem, and examine some of these artworks, determining different artists' approach to the poem.
2. The obvious setting of this poem is Arthurian England. Discuss what effect this gives the poem and whether the poem would have the same effect if it were set in a different time and place.

D. H. LAWRENCE (1885–1939)

David Herber Lawrence was born into a lower-middle-class family from Nottinghampshire, England. His father was a coal miner and his mother was a schoolteacher. He attended the University College of Nottingham and then taught school for four years. The publication of his first poems and the short story "The White Peacock" in 1911 convinced him he could pursue writing full-time. Although more known for his novels and short stories, Lawrence's poetry has garnered its own critical recognition. Influenced by Imagism and other modernist forms, Lawrence's poems often utilize images in nature (flowers, the sun, the moon) to symbolize aspects of humanness. And like his prose, many of his poems explore the psychological and erotic undertones of heterosexual desire—motifs that were deemed "indecent" by the reading public of his day but are now seen as pioneering aspects of his work. In addition to his novels and poetry, the prolific Lawrence wrote essays, literary criticism, and travel journals, many of them detailing his expatriate life while living in various countries outside his native England. Such works include the poetry collections *Love Poems and Others* (1913), *Look! We Have Come Through!* (1917), *Tortoises* (1921), *Birds, Beasts and Flowers* (1923), and *Pansies* (1929) and the novels *Sons and Lovers* (1913), *The Rainbow* (1915), *Women in Love* (1920), *Kangaroo*

(1923), and *Lady Chatterley's Lover* (1928). "Gloire de Dijon" was published in *Look! We Have Come Through!.*

Gloire de Dijon[1]   (1917)

When she rises in the morning
I linger to watch her;
She spreads the bath-cloth underneath the window
Glistening white on the shoulders,
While down her sides the mellow   5
Golden shadow glows as
She stoops to the sponge, and her swung breasts
Sway like full-blown yellow
Gloire de Dijon roses.

She drips herself with water, and her shoulders   10
Glisten as silver, they crumple up
Like wet and falling roses, and I listen
For the sluicing of their rain-disheveled petals,
In the window full of sunlight
Concentrates her golden shadow   15
Fold on fold, until it glows as
Mellow as the glory roses.

Study and Discussion Questions

1. What is the literal and the implied "story" of this poem? Who is the "I," the speaker of the poem? What is his relation to the woman? What is she doing?
2. By the end of the first stanza, we know the woman is being compared to a particular kind of rose. Why didn't Lawrence simply call the poem "yellow rose"? Why "Gloire de Dijon"?
3. List the images which compare the rose and the woman bathing. List color images. List kinetic images (images of movement). Are there images of sound, smell, or touch?
4. Note sound patterns in the poem: (a) repeated consonant sounds (consonance), inside a word as well as at its beginning, and (b) repeated vowel sounds (assonance). What effect does each of the patterns you note have? What kind of mood do they collectively develop?

---

[1]*Gloire de Dijon* ("Glory of Dijon"): a yellow hybrid tea rose.

Suggestion for Writing

1. Compare/contrast "Gloire de Dijon" with one or more of the following love poems: Pablo Neruda, "Every Day You Play," Leopold Sedar Senghor, "You Held the Black Face," Edna St. Vincent Millay, "Love is not all: It is not meat nor drink."

ELIZABETH BISHOP (1911–1979)

Elizabeth Bishop was born in Worcester, Massachusetts. Her father died while she was still an infant, and, when Elizabeth was five her mother was hospitalized for mental illness, leaving her to be raised by her grandparents and other relatives. She studied at Vassar College (1930–1934), where she developed a friendship with poet Marianne Moore, who encouraged her to pursue poetry instead of medicine. The two became life-long friends. After graduating, Bishop led a transient, traveling life, living in New York City, France, and Key West, and eventually settled in Brazil, though she spent her last few years in Boston. Her experiences traveling and living as an exile would become central themes in her poetry. During her life, Bishop composed only 101 poems. Despite this relatively small number, her work was recognized by her contemporaries (like her good friend Robert Lowell) as some of the most evocative, crafted verse in American poetry, and in 1956 she was awarded the Pulitzer Prize for her collection *North and South—A Cold Spring*. Known for her astute observation and subtle irony, Bishop's poetry often details human relationships and human interaction with the natural world in a language noted for its rhythm and meter. Other poetry collections include *Questions of Travel* (1965), *The Complete Poems* (1969), and *Geography III* (1976). "One Art," published in *Geography III*, is written in the form of a villanelle, composed of five tercets and a final quatrain.

One Art (1976)

The art of losing isn't hard to master;
so many things seem filled with the intent
to be lost that their loss is no disaster.

Lose something every day. Accept the fluster
of lost door keys, the hour badly spent.   5
The art of losing isn't hard to master.

Then practice losing farther, losing faster:
places, and names, and where it was you meant
to travel. None of these will bring disaster.

I lost my mother's watch. And look! my last, or   10
next-to-last, of three loved houses went.
The art of losing isn't hard to master.

I lost two cities, lovely ones. And, vaster,
some realms I owned, two rivers, a continent.
I miss them, but it wasn't a disaster.   15
—Even losing you (the joking voice, a gesture
I love) I shan't have lied. It's evident
the art of losing's not too hard to master
though it may look like (*Write* it!) like disaster.

Study and Discussion Questions

1. Bishop's "One Art" is a type of poem called a villanelle. Figure out the rhyme scheme of the poem, labeling the first rhyme "A" and marking those throughout the poem and the second rhyme "B" and marking those throughout the poem. Note that the rhymes do not have to be exact.
2. The first line—"The art of losing isn't hard to master"—becomes a refrain, repeated throughout the poem. Does the line change its meaning or carry a different emotional resonance as the poem goes on? Discuss.
3. There is a second and partial refrain in the poem, built on the lines that end with the word *disaster*. How do the two refrains together create a tension in the poem?
3. What are the "things" lost in this poem? How do the losses change as the poem develops?
4. What does the speaker of the poem keep telling herself she feels or should be feeling about these losses?
5. How would you describe the tone of "One Art"? Does it change in the course of the poem?
6. "It's evident" in the last stanza of "One Art" that the poet has been working up to mentioning a very serious loss. What is it? How might a) writing about such a loss, and b) using a very strict form in which to do so, be of help in such a situation?

Suggestion for Writing

1. If you were to write a poem (not necessarily a villanelle) titled "One Art," what would your poem be about? What is the "one art" *you* would write about? Give it a try.

ANNE SEXTON (1928–1974)

Anne Sexton was born in Newton, Massachusetts, attended Garland Junior College for a year, and married at twenty. After one of many nervous break-downs she was to suffer throughout her life, a psychiatrist urged her to try writ-ing, which she did with immediate success. Often labeled as "confessional" poetry, much of Sexton's work explores deep and intimate aspects of her life, especially the torment of her mental illness. Yet to characterize all her work in this way obscures her work as a whole. Similar to the poetry of Sharon Olds, some of Sexton's work embraces physical desire and its ambivalent coupling with love and relationships. In *Transformations* (1971), Sexton again broke from the confessional mode to rewrite in poetry several Brothers Grimm fairy tales—including Sleeping Beauty, Hansel and Gretel, and Snow White—from a feminist perspective. Her poetry collections include *To Bedlam and Part Way Back* (1960), *Live or Die* (1966, winner of the Pulitzer Prize), *Love Poems* (1969), and *The Death Notebooks* (1974). At the age of forty-five, she took her own life. "Her Kind" is from Sexton's collection *To Bedlam and Part Way Back*.

Her Kind   (1960)

I have gone out, a possessed witch,
haunting the black air, braver at night;
dreaming evil, I have done my hitch
over the plain houses, light by light:
lonely thing, twelve-fingered, out of mind.   5
A woman like that is not a woman, quite.
I have been her kind.

I have found the warm caves in the woods,
filled them with skillets, carvings, shelves,
closets, silks, innumerable goods;   10
fixed the suppers for the worms and the elves:
whining, rearranging the disaligned.
A woman like that is misunderstood.
I have been her kind.

I have ridden in your cart, driver,   15
waved my nude arms at villages going by,
learning the last bright routes, survivor
where your flames still bite my thigh
and my ribs crack where your wheels wind.
A woman like that is not ashamed to die.   20
I have been her kind.

Study and Discussion Questions

1. List the three different repetitions in the poem. How do these hold the poem together and deepen your understanding of the speaker as the poem goes on?
2. What are the details Sexton's narrator gives you about her witch self in the first stanza?
3. How does the second stanza complicate or make more complex the primary witch image?
4. What is literally happening in stanza three? What historical fact is Sexton evoking?
5. Given what seems to be happening in stanza three, why does the speaker of the poem call herself a "survivor"?
6. Describe the structure of the poem: the rhyme scheme, the number of lines in each stanza, the number of syllables in each line.
7. What do you think the speaker of the poem means by "her kind"?

Suggestion for Writing

1. What *historical* self images are available to women? To men? List as many as you can for each gender. Why might a woman choose a self-image as a witch?
2. Compare/contrast Anne Sexton's "Her Kind" to Sylvia Plath's "Daddy": the use of mythology and history, the relation between men and women in a patriarchal society, the self-image of the speaker of each poem, images in each poem, sound and structure of each poem, the story each poem tells.

AMIRI BARAKA (b. 1934)

Amiri Baraka was born LeRoi Jones in Newark, New Jersey, into an African-American, middle-class family. After high school, he received an academic scholarship to Rutgers, but he transferred to the all-black Howard University to be in contact with more African Americans. Jones left without a degree, entered the Air Force, but was discharged after three years for possessing communist literature; he moved to New York's bohemian Lower East Side shortly thereafter. It is here that Jones began his artistic career as poet and dramatist at the height of the Beat Movement. His friendship with Beat poet Allen Ginsburg helped him develop his early poetry. By the 1960s, though, Jones became disenchanted with the apolitical nature of this environment and became increasingly involved with black nationalist politics, taking the Muslim name Amiri Baraka. His play *Dutchman* (1964), winner of the Obie Award for best American play, with its overt critique of racism and obvious

social commentary, marked a new shift in Baraka's writing. He would spend
the decade living in Harlem and writing more consciously about black experience in white America. Today, Baraka, a self-proclaimed Marxist and
activist, continues to write socially aware but often controversial poetry. His
poem "Somebody Blew Up America" (2002), written and recited after
September 11, 2001, incurred public criticism for its scathing attack on American history and culture. In almost 50 years of writing, Baraka has composed
over twenty plays and screenplays, dozens of poetry collections, and nonfiction essays. Selected works include the plays *The Toilet* (1964), *J-E-L-L-O*
(1970), and *Primitive World* (1984) and the poetry collections *April 13* (1959),
Preface to a Twenty Volume Suicide Note (1961), *Black Magic* (1969), *Spirit
Reach* (1972), and *Funk Lore: New Poems* (1996). His latest nonfiction is *Jesse
Jackson & Black People* (2003) and *Jubilee* (2003). "Beautiful *Black Women* …,"
published in *Black Magic*, is demonstrative of Baraka's intense focus on black
life in the 1960s.

Beautiful Black Women . . .   (1969)

Beautiful black women, fail, they act. Stop them, raining.
They are so beautiful, we want them with us. Stop them, raining.
Beautiful, stop raining, they fail. We fail them and their lips
stick out perpetually, at our weakness. Raining. Stop them. Black
queens. Ruby Dee[1] weeps at the window, raining, being lost in her   5
life, being what we all will be, sentimental bitter frustrated
deprived of her fullest light. Beautiful black women, it is
still raining in this terrible land. We need you. We flex our
muscles, turn to stare at our tormentor, we need you. Raining.
We need you, reigning, black queen. This/terrible black ladies   10
wander, Ruby Dee weeps, the window, raining, she calls, and her voice
is left to hurt us slowly. It hangs against the same wet glass, her
sadness and age, and the trip, and the lost heat, and the gray cold
buildings of our entrapment. Ladies. Women. We need you. We are still
trapped and weak, but we build and grow heavy with our knowledge.   15
    Women.
Come to us. Help us get back what was always ours. Help us. women.
    Where
are you, women, where, and who, and where, and who, and will
    you help   20
us, will you open your bodysouls, will you lift me up mother, will you
let me help you, daughter, wife/lover, will you

---

[1]American actor (b. 1924).

Study and Discussion Questions

1. Line 2 reads, in part, "we want them with us." Who does "we" refer to? And where are the black women, if not "with us"?
2. Who is "our tormentor"? Does "our" refer to the same group of people as "we"? If so, what does this suggest about the speaker?
3. Why does Baraka repeat "raining" so often?
4. "Help us get back what was always ours." What does this mean?

Suggestions for Writing

1. What does the speaker want black women to be and do?
2. How might a black woman reply to this poem?

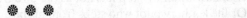

KARL SHAPIRO (1913–2000)

Carl Shapiro was raised in a middle-class Jewish family in Baltimore, Maryland. He attended the University of Maryland for a short time, but left after feeling alienated by the largely Anglo-Saxon student body and by the German Jewish students who seemed to look down upon his Russian-Jewish ancestry. This experience prompted him to change his first name to the German "Karl." His self-published *Poems* won him a scholarship to Johns Hopkins University in 1937. In 1941, his studies were cut short after being drafted to fight in World War II. The war would be the inspiration for his Pulitzer Prize–winning *V-Letter and Other Poems* (1944). Shapiro's work spans 5 decades, and, while it shows considerable variation throughout this time, the satirical and imagistic nature of his verse has remained consistent—moving between formal and free-verse structures, with one eye on the local and the other on society at large. He taught at a number of universities and was editor of *Poetry* magazine. His other publications include *Essays on Rime* (1945), *Poems of a Jew* (1958), *The Bourgeois Poet* (1964), *Adult Bookstore* (1976), and *New and Selected Poems, 1940–1986* (1987). "Buick" was published in *Poems: 1940–1953* (1953).

Buick   (1953)

As a sloop with a sweep of immaculate wing on her delicate spine
And a keel as steel as a root that holds in the sea as she leans,
Leaning and laughing, my warm-hearted beauty, you ride, you ride,
You tack on the curves with parabola speed and a kiss of goodbye,
Like a thoroughbred sloop, my new high-spirited spirit, my kiss.   5

As my foot suggests that you leap in the air with your hips of a girl,
My finger that praises your wheel and announces your voices of song,
Flouncing your skirts, you blueness of joy, you flirt of politeness,
You leap, you intelligence, essence of wheelness with silvery nose,
And your platinum clocks of excitement stir like the hairs of a fern.   10

But how alien you are from the booming belts of your birth and the smoke
Where you turned on the stinging lathes of Detroit and Lansing at night
And shrieked at the torch in your secret parts and the amorous tests,
But now with your eyes that enter the future of roads you forget;
You are all instinct with your phosphorous glow and your streaking hair.   15

And now when we stop it is not as the bird from the shell that I leave
Or the leathery pilot who steps from his bird with a sneer of delight,
And not as the ignorant beast do you squat and watch me depart,
But with exquisite breathing you smile, with satisfaction of love,
And I touch you again as you tick in the silence and settle in sleep.   20

Study and Discussion Questions

1. Who is speaking in the poem? Why can you assume the speaker is male? What else can you say about him?
2. Go through the poem and list the ways in which the speaker compares his car to a woman. The poem is ostensibly about the speaker's feelings for his car. But what does it suggest about how he perceives women?
3. How do sound and rhythm in the first stanza help convey the speaker's experience as he drives? How and why is the first line of the third stanza different from what comes before? What new emotion does the third stanza reveal?
4. What is the function of the negative comparisons ("it is not as . . .") in the last stanza? How is the speaker feeling at the end of the poem?
5. What is the poet's attitude toward the speaker, towards the *persona* he has created? How can you tell?

Suggestions for Writing

1. To what extent is "Buick" an accurate portrayal of male feelings rather than just a parody of them?
2. Why are cars in our culture usually seen as female? What other kinds of objects or machines are viewed in gendered terms? Why are they so often seen as female?
3. Which line or phrase from the poem stands out most in your mind? Try to explain why.
4. Try writing a poem or prose passage in which the speaker dramatizes his or her intense emotional relationship with an object other than an automobile. Think carefully before ascribing a gender to this object.

OLGA BROUMAS (b. 1949)

Olga Broumas was born in Greece and moved to the United States at age ten. She obtained her B.A. in architecture from the University of Pennsylvania and her M.F.A. at the University of Oregon, where she helped found the women's studies program. Although English is Broumas's second language, her poetic skill won her the Yale Younger Poets Award in 1977 for *Beginning with O*— a mixed collection of poems on female relationships and love, erotic desire and myth. While many of these themes surface again and again in her poetry, what makes them uniquely Broumas's is the compact syntax and rhythmic quality of her verse. Other poetry collections include *Soie Sauvage* (1980), *Pastoral Jazz* (1983), *Perpetua* (1989), and *All of the Above* (1991); four works with classical scholar T. Begley (including *Sappho's Gymnasium*, [1994] and *Rave: Poems, 1975–1999* [1999]). She has also translated the work of Greek poet Odysseus Elytis. Broumas's propensity for feminist revision of myth appears in the poem "Cinderella," first published in *Beginning with O*.

Cinderella (1977)

> *. . . the joy that isn't shared*
> *I heard, dies young.*
> Anne Sexton, 1928–1974

Apart from my sisters, estranged
from my mother, I am a woman alone
in a house of men
who secretly
call themselves princes, alone   5
with me usually, under cover of dark. I am the one allowed in

to the royal chambers, whose small foot conveniently
fills the slipper of glass. The woman writer, the lady
umpire, the madam chairman, anyone's wife.
I know what I know.   10
And I once was glad

of the chance to use it, even alone
in a strange castle, doing overtime on my own, cracking
the royal code. The princes spoke
in their fathers' language, were eager to praise me   15
my nimble tongue. I am a woman in a state of siege, alone

as one piece of laundry, strung on a windy clothesline a
mile long. A woman co-opted by promises: the lure

of a job, the ruse of a choice, a woman forced
to bear witness, falsely   20
against my kind, as each
other sister was judged inadequate, bitchy, incompetent,
jealous, too thin, too fat. I know what I know.
What sweet bread I make

for myself in this prosperous house   25
is dirty, what good soup I boil turns
in my mouth to mud. Give
me my ashes. A cold stove, a cinder-block pillow, wet
canvas shoes in my sisters', my sisters' hut. Or I swear

I'll die young   30
like those favored before me, hand-picked each one
for her joyful heart.

Study and Discussion Questions

1. What price has the speaker of the poem had to pay for success?
2. List specific images of loneliness in the poem.
3. What is the speaker's relation to other women? What is her relation
   to men?

Suggestion for Writing

1. How has Broumas rewritten the Cinderella fairy tale for modern readers? What changes has she made in the story? (Remember, there is more
   than one version of the fairy tale.) How do the changes serve her
   purpose?

❀ ❀ ❀

Money and Work

FICTION

TILLIE OLSEN (1913?–2007)

Tillie Lerner was born in Omaha, Nebraska, the daughter of social activist Jewish-Russian immigrants. During the Great Depression she had to quit high school to work; she also began work as a labor activist and writer. She joined the Communist Party at the age of seventeen and was arrested and jailed for her part in several Depression-era strikes. She then married Jack Olsen and raised four children while continuing to work as a waitress and secretary, writing little until the 1950s. Those twenty years of raising children and making ends meet have served as the foundation of much of her writing. Although Olsen hasn't published much in her lifetime, she has gained acclaim for the emotional intensity of her prose and her ability to make apparent the heroic in common people. As the title of her book *Silences* (1978) suggests, Olsen's work, steeped in issues of class, race, and gender, seeks to give an authentic voice to the silent and stifled worlds of the oppressed. Her other works include the short story collection *Tell Me a Riddle* (1961) and the novel *Yonnondio* (1974). In "I Stand Here Ironing," first published in *Tell Me a Riddle*, Olsen shifts narration from present to past as a mother takes inventory of her daughter's life and her own role as a working-class parent.

I Stand Here Ironing (1954)

I stand here ironing, and what you asked me moves tormented back and forth with the iron.

"I wish you would manage the time to come in and talk with me about your daughter. I'm sure you can help me understand her. She's a youngster who needs help and whom I'm deeply interested in helping."

"Who needs help." . . . Even if I came, what good would it do? You think because I am her mother I have a key, or that in some way you could use me as a key? She has lived for nineteen years. There is all that life that has happened outside of me, beyond me.

And when is there time to remember, to sift, to weigh, to estimate, to total? I will start and there will be an interruption and I will have to gather it all together again. Or I will become engulfed with all I did or did not do, with what should have been and what cannot be helped.

She was a beautiful baby. The first and only one of our five that was beautiful at birth. You do not guess how new and uneasy her tenancy in her now-loveliness. You did not know her all those years she was thought homely, or see her poring over her baby pictures, making me tell her over and over how beautiful she had been—and would be, I would tell her—and was now, to the seeing eye. But the seeing eyes were few or nonexistent. Including mine.

I nursed her. They feel that's important nowadays. I nursed all the children, but with her, with all the fierce rigidity of first motherhood, I did like the books then said. Though her cries battered me to trembling and my breasts ached with swollenness, I waited till the clock decreed.

Why do I put that first? I do not even know if it matters, or if it explains anything.

She was a beautiful baby. She blew shining bubbles of sound. She loved motion, loved light, loved color and music and textures. She would lie on the floor in her blue overalls patting the surface so hard in ecstasy her hands and feet would blur. She was a miracle to me, but when she was eight months old I had to leave her daytimes with the woman downstairs to whom she was no miracle at all, for I worked or looked for work and for Emily's father, who "could no longer endure" (he wrote in his good-bye note) "sharing want with us."

I was nineteen. It was the pre-relief, pre-WPA world of the depression. I would start running as soon as I got off the streetcar, running up the stairs, the place smelling sour, and awake or asleep to startle awake, when she saw me she would break into a clogged weeping that could not be comforted, a weeping I can hear yet.

After a while I found a job hashing at night so I could be with her days, and it was better. But it came to where I had to bring her to his family and leave her.

It took a long time to raise the money for her fare back. Then she got chicken pox and I had to wait longer. When she finally came, I hardly knew her, walking quick and nervous like her father, looking like her father, thin, and dressed in a shoddy red that yellowed her skin and glared at the pockmarks. All the baby loveliness gone.

She was two. Old enough for nursery school they said, and I did not know then what I know now—the fatigue of the long day, and the lacerations of group life in the kinds of nurseries that are only parking places for children.

Except that it would have made no difference if I had known. It was the only place there was. It was the only way we could be together, the only way I could hold a job.

And even without knowing, I knew. I knew the teacher that was evil because all these years it has curdled into my memory, the little boy hunched in the corner, her rasp, "why aren't you outside, because Alvin hits you? that's no reason, go out, scaredy." I knew Emily hated it even if she did not clutch and implore "don't go Mommy" like the other children, mornings.

She always had a reason why we should stay home. Momma, you look sick. Momma, I feel sick. Momma, the teachers aren't there today, they're sick. Momma, we can't go, there was a fire there last night. Momma, it's a holiday today, no school, they told me.

But never a direct protest, never rebellion. I think of our others in their three-, four-year-oldness—the explosions, the tempers, the denunciations, the demands—and I feel suddenly ill. I put the iron down. What in me demanded that goodness in her? And what was the cost, the cost to her of such goodness?

The old man living in the back once said in his gentle way: "You should smile at Emily more when you look at her." What *was* in my face when I looked at her? I loved her. There were all the acts of love.

It was only with the others I remembered what he said, and it was the face of joy, and not of care or tightness or worry I turned to them—too late for Emily. She does not smile easily, let alone almost always as her brothers and sisters do. Her face is closed and sombre, but when she wants, how fluid. You must have seen it in her pantomimes, you spoke of her rare gift for comedy on the stage that rouses a laughter out of the audience so dear they applaud and applaud and do not want to let her go.

Where does it come from, that comedy? There was none of it in her when she came back to me that second time, after I had had to send her away again. She had a new daddy now to learn to love, and I think perhaps it was a better time.

Except when we left her alone nights, telling ourselves she was old enough.

"Can't you go some other time, Mommy, like tomorrow?" she would ask. "Will it be just a little while you'll be gone? Do you promise?"

The time we came back, the front door open, the clock on the floor in the hall. She rigid awake. "It wasn't just a little while. I didn't cry. Three times I called you, just three times, and then I ran downstairs to open the door so you could come faster. The clock talked loud. I threw it away, it scared me what it talked."

She said the clock talked loud again that night I went to the hospital to have Susan. She was delirious with the fever that comes before red measles, but she was fully conscious all the week I was gone and the week after we were home when she could not come near the new baby or me.

She did not get well. She stayed skeleton thin, not wanting to eat, and night after night she had nightmares. She would call for me, and I would rouse from exhaustion to sleepily call back: "You're all right, darling, go to sleep, it's just a dream," and if she still called, in a sterner voice, "now go to sleep, Emily, there's nothing to hurt you." Twice, only twice, when I had to get up for Susan anyhow, I went in to sit with her.

Now when it is too late (as if she would let me hold and comfort her like I do the others) I get up and go to her at once at her moan or restless stirring. "Are you awake, Emily? Can I get you something?" And the answer is always the same: "No, I'm all right, go back to sleep, Mother."

They persuaded me at the clinic to send her away to a convalescent home in the country where "she can have the kind of food and care you can't manage for her, and you'll be free to concentrate on the new baby." They still send children to that place. I see pictures on the society page of sleek young women planning affairs to raise money for it, or dancing at the affairs, or decorating Easter eggs or filling Christmas stockings for the children.

They never have a picture of the children so I do not know if the girls still wear those gigantic red bows and the ravaged looks on the every other Sunday when parents can come to visit "unless otherwise notified"—as we were notified the first six weeks.

Oh it is a handsome place, green lawns and tall trees and fluted flower beds. High up on the balconies of each cottage the children stand, the girls in their red bows and white dresses, the boys in white suits and giant red ties. The parents stand below shrieking up to be heard and the children shriek down to be heard, and between them the invisible wall "Not To Be Contaminated by Parental Germs or Physical Affection."

There was a tiny girl who always stood hand in hand with Emily. Her parents never came. One visit she was gone. "They moved her to Rose Cottage" Emily shouted in explanation. "They don't like you to love anybody here."

She wrote once a week, the labored writing of a seven-year-old. "I am fine. How is the baby. If I write my leter nicly I will have a star. Love." There never was a star. We wrote every other day, letters she could never hold or keep but only hear read—once. "We simply not have room for children to keep any personal possessions," they patiently explained when we pieced one Sunday's shrieking together to plead how much it would mean to Emily, who loved so to keep things, to be allowed to keep her letters and cards.

Each visit she looked frailer. "She isn't eating," they told us.

(They had runny eggs for breakfast or mush with lumps, Emily said later, I'd hold it in my mouth and not swallow. Nothing ever tasted good, just when they had chicken.)

It took us eight months to get her released home, and only the fact that she gained back so little of her seven lost pounds convinced the social worker.

I used to try to hold and love her after she came back, but her body would stay stiff, and after a while she'd push away. She ate little. Food sickened her, and I think much of life too. Oh she had physical lightness and brightness, twinkling by on skates, bouncing like a ball up and down up and down over the jump rope, skimming over the hill; but these were momentary.

She fretted about her appearance, thin and dark and foreign-looking at a time when every little girl was supposed to look or thought she should look a chubby blonde replica of Shirley Temple. The doorbell sometimes rang for her, but no one seemed to come and play in the house or be a best friend. Maybe because we moved so much.

There was a boy she loved painfully through two school semesters. Months later she told me how she had taken pennies from my purse to buy him candy. "Licorice was his favorite and I brought him some every day, but he still liked Jennifer better'n me. Why, Mommy?" The kind of question for which there is no answer.

School was a worry to her. She was not glib or quick in a world where glibness and quickness were easily confused with ability to learn. To her overworked and exasperated teachers she was an overconscientious "slow learner" who kept trying to catch up and was absent entirely too often.

I let her be absent, though sometimes the illness was imaginary. How different from my now-strictness about attendance with the others. I wasn't working. We had a new baby, I was home anyhow. Sometimes, after Susan grew old enough, I would keep her home from school, too, to have them all together.

Mostly Emily had asthma, and her breathing, harsh and labored, would fill the house with a curiously tranquil sound. I would bring the two old dresser mirrors and her boxes of collections to her bed. She would select beads and single earrings, bottle tops and shells, dried flowers and pebbles, old postcards and scraps, all sorts of oddments; then she and Susan would play Kingdom, setting up landscapes and furniture, peopling them with action.

Those were the only times of peaceful companionship between her and Susan. I have edged away from it, that poisonous feeling between them, that terrible balancing of hurts and needs I had to do between the two, and did so badly, those earlier years.

Oh there are conflicts between the others too, each one human, needing, demanding, hurting, taking—but only between Emily and Susan, no, Emily toward Susan that corroding resentment. It seems so obvious on the surface, yet it is not obvious. Susan, the second child, Susan, golden- and curly-haired and chubby, quick and articulate and assured, everything in appearance and manner Emily was not; Susan, not able to resist Emily's precious things, losing or sometimes clumsily breaking them; Susan telling jokes and riddles to company for applause while Emily sat silent (to say to me later: that was *my* riddle, Mother, I told it to Susan); Susan, who for all the five years' difference in age was just a year behind Emily in developing physically.

I am glad for that slow physical development that widened the difference between her and her contemporaries, though she suffered over it. She was too vulnerable for that terrible world of youthful competition, of preening and parading, of constant measuring of yourself against every other, of envy, "If I had that copper hair," "If I had that skin. . . ." She tormented herself enough about not looking like the others, there was enough of the unsureness, the having to be conscious of words before you speak, the constant caring—what are they thinking of me? without having it all magnified by the merciless physical drives.

Ronnie is calling. He is wet and I change him. It is rare there is such a cry now. That time of motherhood is almost behind me when the ear is not one's own but must always be racked and listening for the child cry, the child call. We sit for a while and I hold him, looking out over the city spread in charcoal with its soft aisles of light. "*Shoogily,*" he breathes and curls closer. I carry him back to bed, asleep. *Shoogily.* A funny word, a family word, inherited from Emily, invented by her to say: *comfort.*

In this and other ways she leaves her seal, I say aloud. And startle at my saying it. What do I mean? What did I start to gather together, to try and make coherent? I was at the terrible, growing years. War years. I do not remember them well. I was working, there were four smaller ones now, there was not time for her. She had to help be a mother, and housekeeper, and shopper. She had to set her seal. Mornings of crisis and near hysteria trying to get lunches packed, hair combed, coats and shoes found, everyone to school or Child Care on time, the baby ready for transportation. And always the paper scribbled on by a smaller one, the book looked at by Susan then mislaid, the homework not done. Running out to that huge school where she was one, she was lost, she was a drop; suffering over the unpreparedness, stammering and unsure in her classes.

There was so little time left at night after the kids were bedded down. She would struggle over books, always eating (it was in those years she developed her enormous appetite that is legendary in our family) and I would be ironing, or preparing food for the next day, or writing V-mail to Bill, or tending the baby. Sometimes, to make me laugh, or out of her despair, she would imitate happenings or types at school.

I think I said once: "Why don't you do something like this in the school amateur show?" One morning she phoned me at work, hardly understandable through the weeping: "Mother, I did it. I won, I won; they gave me first prize; they clapped and clapped and wouldn't let me go."

Now suddenly she was Somebody, and as imprisoned in her difference as she had been in anonymity.

She began to be asked to perform at other high schools, even in colleges, then at city and statewide affairs. The first one we went to, I only recognized her that first moment when thin, shy, she almost drowned herself into the curtains. Then: Was this Emily? The control, the command, the convulsing and deadly clowning, the spell, then the roaring, stamping audience, unwilling to let this rare and precious laughter out of their lives.

Afterwards: You ought to do something about her with a gift like that—but without money or knowing how, what does one do? We have left it all to her, and the gift has as often eddied inside, clogged and clotted, as been used and growing.

She is coming. She runs up the stairs two at a time with her light graceful step, and I know she is happy tonight. Whatever it was that occasioned your call did not happen today.

"Aren't you ever going to finish the ironing, Mother? Whistler painted his mother in a rocker. I'd have to paint mine standing over an ironing board." This is one of her communicative nights and she tells me everything and nothing as she fixes herself a plate of food out of the icebox.

She is so lovely. Why did you want me to come in at all? Why were you concerned? She will find her way.

She starts up the stairs to bed. "Don't get me up with the rest in the morning." "But I thought you were having midterms." "Oh, those," she comes back in, kisses me, and says quite lightly, "in a couple of years when we'll all be atom-dead they won't matter a bit."

She has said it before. She *believes* it. But because I have been dredging the past, and all that compounds a human being is so heavily and meaningful in me, I cannot endure it tonight.

I will never total it all. I will never come in to say: She was a child seldom smiled at. Her father left me before she was a year old. I had to work her first six years when there was work, or I sent her home and to his relatives. There were years she had care she hated. She was dark and thin and foreign-looking in a world where the prestige went to blondeness and curly hair and dimples, she was slow where glibness was prized. She was a child of anxious, not proud, love. We were poor and could not afford for her the soil of easy growth. I was a young mother, I was a distracted mother. There were the other children pushing up, demanding. Her younger sister seemed all that she was not. There were years she did not want me to touch her. She kept too much in herself, her life was such she had to keep too much in herself. My wisdom came too late. She has much to her and probably little will come of it. She is a child of her age, of depression, of war, of fear.

Let her be. So all that is in her will not bloom—but in how many does it? There is still enough left to live by. Only help her to know—help make it so there is cause for her to know—that she is more than this dress on the ironing board, helpless before the iron.

Study and Discussion Questions

1. How does ironing function as a symbol in this story?
2. How does the narrator feel about herself as a mother?
3. What regrets does the mother have about Emily's childhood?
4. "And when is there time . . . ," the mother says. How does the paragraph that begins this way anticipate what happens in the story?
5. What forms did the narrator's love for her daughter take?
6. What connections can you make between Emily's gift for comedy and her early life?

Suggestions for Writing

1. How did economic factors affect the narrator's relationship with her daughter?
2. Who is the narrator's imagined audience, the "you" of the opening sentence? What is the narrator's tone?
3. If Emily were to write an account of these same years, what might she say?

WILLIAM FAULKNER (1897–1962)

William Faulkner grew up in Oxford, Mississippi. His ancestors included a great-grandfather who was a famous Civil War colonel and popular novelist. Little interested in high school, Faulkner dropped out and, because he was too short for the U.S. Army, enlisted in the Canadian Royal Air Force. He studied briefly at the University of Mississippi, held odd jobs in New York City, and in 1924 published a volume of poetry. He then turned to fiction and published the novel *Soldier's Pay* in 1926. *Sartoris* (1929) was the first of his many novels set in the fictional Yoknapatawpha County in Mississippi and *The Sound and the Fury*

(1929) and *As I Lay Dying* (1930) followed soon after. One distinguishing aspect of much of Faulkner's work is his use of the literary device called "stream of consciousness," where the author attempts to describe the continuous flow of thought as it passes through a character's mind. Among Faulkner's major novels are *Sanctuary* (1931), *Light in August* (1932), *Absalom, Absalom!* (1936), and the three novels that comprise the Snopes Trilogy: *The Hamlet* (1940), *The Town* (1957), and *The Mansion* (1959). He received the Nobel Prize for literature in 1950. The short story "Spotted Horses" was originally published in 1931. Faulkner would later rework the story and incorporate it into *The Hamlet.*

Spotted Horses (1931)

I

Yes, sir. Flem Snopes has filled that whole country full of spotted horses. You can hear folks running them all day and all night, whooping and hollering, and the horses running back and forth across them little wooden bridges ever now and then kind of like thunder. Here I was this morning pretty near half way to town, with the team ambling along and me setting in the buckboard about half asleep, when all of a sudden something come swurging up outen the bushes and jumped the road clean, without touching hoof to it. It flew right over my team, big as a billboard and flying through the air like a hawk. It taken me thirty minutes to stop my team and untangle the harness and the buckboard and hitch them up again.

That Flem Snopes. I be dog if he ain't a case, now. One morning about ten years ago, the boys was just getting settled down on Varner's porch for a little talk and tobacco, when here come Flem out from behind the counter, with his coat off and his hair all parted, like he might have been clerking for Varner for ten years already. Folks all knowed him; it was a big family of them about five miles down the bottom. That year, at least. Share-cropping. They never stayed on any place over a year. Then they would move on to another place, with the chap or maybe the twins of that year's litter. It was a regular nest of them. But Flem. The rest of them stayed tenant farmers, moving ever year, but here come Flem one day, walking out from behind Jody Varner's counter like he owned it. And he wasn't there but a year or two before folks knowed that, if him and Jody was both still in that store in ten years more, it would be Jody clerking for Flem Snopes. Why, that fellow could make a nickel where it wasn't but four cents to begin with. He skun me in two trades, myself, and the fellow that can do that, I just hope he'll get rich before I do; that's all.

All right. So here Flem was, clerking at Varner's, making a nickel here and there and not telling nobody about it. No, sir. Folks never knowed when Flem got the better of somebody lessen the fellow he beat told it. He'd just set there in the storechair, chewing his tobacco and keeping his own business to hisself, until about a week later we'd find out it was somebody else's business he was keeping to hisself—provided the fellow he trimmed was mad enough to tell it. That's Flem.

We give him ten years to own ever thing Jody Varner had. But he never waited no ten years. I reckon you-all know that gal of Uncle Billy Varner's, the youngest one; Eula. Jody's sister. Ever Sunday ever yellow-wheeled buggy and curried riding horse in that country would be hitched to Bill Varner's fence, and the young bucks setting on the porch, swarming around Eula like bees around a honey pot. One of these here kind of big, soft-looking gals that could giggle richer than plowed new-ground. Wouldn't none of them leave before the others, and so they would set there on the porch until time to go home, with some of them with nine and ten miles to ride and then get up tomorrow and go back to the field. So they would all leave together and they would ride in a clump down to the creek ford and hitch them curried horses and yellow-wheeled buggies and get out and fight one another. Then they would get in the buggies again and go on home.

Well, one day about a year ago, one of them yellow-wheeled buggies and one of them curried saddle-horses quit this country. We heard they was heading for Texas. The next day Uncle Billy and Eula and Flem come in to town in Uncle Bill's surrey, and when they come back, Flem and Eula was married. And on the next day we heard that two more of them yellow-wheeled buggies had left the country. They mought have gone to Texas, too. It's a big place.

Anyway, about a month after the wedding, Flem and Eula went to Texas, too. They was gone pretty near a year. Then one day last month, Eula come back, with a baby. We figured up, and we decided that it was as well-growed a three-months-old baby as we ever see. It can already pull up on a chair. I reckon Texas makes big men quick, being a big place. Anyway, if it keeps on like it started, it'll be chewing tobacco and voting time it's eight years old.

And so last Friday here come Flem himself. He was on a wagon with another fellow. The other fellow had one of these two-gallon hats and a ivory-handled pistol and a box of gingersnaps sticking out of his hind pocket, and tied to the tail-gate of the wagon was about two dozen of them Texas ponies, hitched to one another with barbed wire. They was colored like parrots and they was quiet as doves, and ere a one of them would kill you quick as a rattlesnake. Nere a one of them had two eyes the same color, and nere a one of them had ever see a bridle, I reckon; and when that Texas man got down offen the wagon and walked up to them to show how gentle they was, one of them cut his vest clean offen him, same as with a razor.

Flem had done already disappeared; he had went on to see his wife, I reckon, and to see if that ere baby had done gone on to the field to help Uncle Billy plow maybe. It was the Texas man that taken the horses on to Mrs. Littlejohn's lot. He had a little trouble at first, when they come to the gate, because they hadn't never see a fence before, and when he finally got them in and taken a pair of wire cutters and unhitched them and got them into the barn and poured some shell corn into the trough, they durn nigh tore down the barn. I reckon they thought that shell corn was bugs, maybe. So he left them in the lot and he announced that the auction would begin at sunup to-morrow.

That night we was setting on Mrs. Littlejohn's porch. You-all mind the moon was nigh full that night, and we could watch them spotted varmints swirling along the fence and back and forth across the lot same as minnows in a pond. And then now and then they would all kind of huddle up against the barn and rest themselves by biting and kicking one another. We would hear a squeal, and then a set of hoofs would go Bam! against the barn, like a pistol. It sounded just like a fellow with a pistol, in a nest of cattymounts,[1] taking his time.

II

It wasn't ere a man knowed yet if Flem owned them things or not. They just knowed one thing: that they wasn't never going to know for sho if Flem did or not, or if maybe he didn't just get on that wagon at the edge of town, for the ride or not. Even Eck Snopes didn't know, Flem's own cousin. But wasn't nobody surprised at that. We knowed that Flem would skin Eck quick as he would ere a one of us.

They was there by sunup next morning, some of them come twelve and sixteen miles, with seed-money tied up in tobacco sacks in their overalls, standing along the fence, when the Texas man come out of Mrs. Littlejohn's after breakfast and clumb onto the gate post with that ere white pistol butt sticking outen his hind pocket. He taken a new box of gingersnaps outen his pocket and bit the end offen it like a cigar and spit out the paper, and said the auction was open. And still they was coming up in wagons and a horse- and mule-back and hitching the teams across the road and coming to the fence. Flem wasn't nowhere in sight.

But he couldn't get them started. He begun to work on Eck, because Eck holp him last night to get them into the barn and feed them that shell corn. Eck got out just in time. He come outen that barn like a chip on the crest of a busted dam of water, and clumb into the wagon just in time.

He was working on Eck when Henry Armstid come up in his wagon. Eck was saying he was skeered to bid on one of them, because he might get it, and the Texas man says, "Them ponies? Them little horses?" He clumb down offen the gate post and went toward the horses. They broke and run, and him following them, kind of chirping to them, with his hand out like he was fixing to catch a fly, until he got three or four of them cornered. Then he jumped into them, and then we couldn't see nothing for a while because of the dust. It was a big cloud of it, and them blare-eyed, spotted things swoaring outen it twenty foot to a jump, in forty directions without counting up. Then the dust settled and there they was, that Texas man and the horse. He had its head twisted clean around like a owl's head. Its legs was braced and it was trembling like a new bride and groaning like a saw mill, and him holding its

---

[1]Wildcats.

head wrung clean around on its neck so it was snuffing sky. "Look it over," he says, with his heels dug too and that white pistol sticking outen his pocket and his neck swole up like a spreading adder's until you could just tell what he was saying, cussing the horse and talking to us all at once: "Look him over, the fiddle-headed son of fourteen fathers. Try him, buy him; you will get the best—" Then it was all dust again, and we couldn't see nothing but spotted hide and mane, and that ere Texas man's boot-heels like a couple of walnuts on two strings, and after a while that two-gallon hat come sailing out like a fat old hen crossing a fence.

When the dust settled again, he was just getting outen the far fence corner, brushing himself off. He come and got his hat and brushed it off and come and clumb onto the gate post again. He was breathing hard. He taken the ginger-snap box outen his pocket and et one, breathing hard. The hammer-head horse was still running round and round the lot like a merry-go-round at a fair. That was when Henry Armstid come shoving up to the gate in them patched overalls and one of them dangle-armed shirts of hisn. Hadn't nobody noticed him until then. We was all watching the Texas man and the horses. Even Mrs. Littlejohn; she had done come out and built a fire under the wash-pot in her back yard, and she would stand at the fence a while and then go back into the house and come out again with a arm full of wash and stand at the fence again. Well, here come Henry shoving up, and then we see Mrs. Armstid right behind him, in that ere faded wrapper and sunbonnet and them tennis shoes. "Git on back to that wagon," Henry says.

"Henry," she says.

"Here, boys," the Texas man says; "make room for missus to git up and see. Come on, Henry," he says; "here's your chance to buy that saddle-horse missus has been wanting. What about ten dollars, Henry?"

"Henry," Mrs. Armstid says. She put her hand on Henry's arm. Henry knocked her hand down.

"Git on back to that wagon, like I told you," he says.

Mrs. Armstid never moved. She stood behind Henry, with her hands rolled into her dress, not looking at nothing. "He hain't no more despair than to buy one of them things," she says. "And us not five dollars ahead of the pore house, he hain't no more despair." It was the truth, too. They ain't never made more than a bare living offen that place of theirs, and them with four chaps and the very clothes they wears she earns by weaving by the firelight at night while Henry's asleep.

"Shut your mouth and git on back to that wagon," Henry says. "Do you want I taken a wagon stake to you here in the big road?"

Well, that Texas man taken one look at her. Then he begun on Eck again, like Henry wasn't even there. But Eck was skeered. "I can git me a snapping turtle or a water moccasin for nothing. I ain't going to buy none."

So the Texas man said he would give Eck a horse. "To start the auction, and because you holp me last night. If you'll start the bidding on the next horse," he says, "I'll give you that fiddle-head horse."

I wish you could have seen them, standing there with their seed-money in their pockets, watching that Texas man give Eck Snopes a live horse, all fixed to call him a fool if he taken it or not. Finally Eck says he'll take it. "Only I just starts the bidding," he says. "I don't have to buy the next one lessen I ain't overtopped." The Texas man said all right, and Eck bid a dollar on the next one, with Henry Armstid standing there with his mouth already open, watching Eck and the Texas man like a mad-dog or something. "A dollar," Eck says.

The Texas man looked at Eck. His mouth was already open too, like he had started to say something and what he was going to say had up and died on him. "A dollar?" he says. "One dollar? You mean, *one* dollar, Eck?"

"Durn it," Eck says; "two dollars, then."

Well, sir, I wish you could a seen that Texas man. He taken out that ginger-snap box and held it up and looked into it, careful, like it might have been a diamond ring in it, or a spider. Then he throwed it away and wiped his face with a bandanna. "Well," he says. "Well, Two dollars. Two dollars. Is your pulse all right, Eck?" he says. "Do you have agersweats[2] at night, maybe?" he says. "Well," he says, "I got to take it. But are you boys going to stand there and see Eck get two horses at a dollar a head?"

That done it. I be dog if he wasn't nigh as smart as Flem Snopes. He hadn't no more than got the words outen his mouth before here was Henry Armstid, waving his hand. "Three dollars," Henry says. Mrs. Armstid tried to hold him again. He knocked her hand off, shoving up to the gate post.

"Mister," Mrs. Armstid says, "we got chaps in the house and not corn to feed the stock. We got five dollars I earned my chaps a-weaving after dark, and him snoring in the bed. And he hain't no more despair."

"Henry bids three dollars," the Texas man says. "Raise him a dollar, Eck, and the horse is yours."

"Henry," Mrs. Armstid says.

"Raise him, Eck," the Texas man says.

"Four dollars," Eck says.

"Five dollars," Henry says, shaking his fist. He shoved up right under the gate post. Mrs. Armstid was looking at the Texas man too.

"Mister," she says, "if you take that five dollars I earned my chaps a-weaving for one of them things, it'll be a curse onto you and yourn during all the time of man."

But it wasn't no stopping Henry. He had shoved up, waving his fist at the Texas man. He opened it; the money was in nickels and quarters, and one dollar bill that looked like a cow's cud. "Five dollars," he says. "And the man that raises it'll have to beat my head off, or I'll beat hisn."

"All right," the Texas man says. "Five dollars is bid. But don't you shake your hand at me."

---

[2]Ague, cold sweats.

III

It taken till nigh sundown before the last one was sold. He got them hotted up once and the bidding got up to seven dollars and a quarter, but most of them went around three or four dollars, him setting on the gate post and picking the horses out one at a time by mouth-word, and Mrs. Littlejohn pumping up and down at the tub and stopping and coming to the fence for a while and going back to the tub again. She had done got done too, and the wash was hung on the line in the back yard, and we could smell supper cooking. Finally they was all sold; he swapped the last two and the wagon for a buckboard.

We was all kind of tired, but Henry Armstid looked more like a maddog than ever. When he bought, Mrs. Armstid had went back to the wagon, setting in it behind them two rabbit-sized, bone-pore mules, and the wagon itself looking like it would fall all to pieces soon as the mules moved. Henry hadn't even waited to pull it outen the road; it was still in the middle of the road and her setting in it, not looking at nothing, ever since this morning.

Henry was right up against the gate. He went up to the Texas man. "I bought a horse and I paid cash," Henry says. "And yet you expect me to stand around here until they are all sold before I can get my horse. I'm going to take my horse outen that lot."

The Texas man looked at Henry. He talked like he might have been asking for a cup of coffee at the table. "Take your horse," he says.

Then Henry quit looking at the Texas man. He begun to swallow, holding onto the gate. "Ain't you going to help me?" he says.

"It ain't my horse," the Texas man says.

Henry never looked at the Texas man again, he never looked at nobody. "Who'll help me catch my horse?" he says. Never nobody said nothing. "Bring the plowline," Henry says. Mrs. Armstid got outen the wagon and brought the plowline. The Texas man got down offen the post. The woman made to pass him, carrying the rope.

"Don't you go in there, missus," the Texas man says.

Henry opened the gate. He didn't look back. "Come on here," he says.

"Don't you go in there, missus," the Texas man says.

Mrs. Armstid wasn't looking at nobody, neither, with her hands across her middle, holding the rope. "I reckon I better," she says. Her and Henry went into the lot. The horses broke and run. Henry and Mrs. Armstid followed.

"Get him into the corner," Henry says. They got Henry's horse cornered finally, and Henry taken the rope, but Mrs. Armstid let the horse get out. They hemmed it up again, but Mrs. Armstid let it get out again, and Henry turned and hit her with the rope. "Why didn't you head him back?" Henry says. He hit her again. "Why didn't you?" It was about that time I looked around and see Flem Snopes standing there.

It was the Texas man that done something. He moved fast for a big man. He caught the rope before Henry could hit the third time, and Henry whirled and made like he would jump at the Texas man. But he never jumped. The Texas man went and taken Henry's arm and led him outen the lot. Mrs. Armstid come behind them and the Texas man taken some money outen his pocket and he give it into Mrs. Armstid's hand. "Get him into the wagon and take him on home," the Texas man says, like he might have been telling them he enjoyed his supper.

Then here come Flem. "What's that for, Buck?" Flem says.

"Thinks he bought one of them ponies," the Texas man says. "Get him on away, missus."

But Henry wouldn't go. "Give him back that money," he says. "I bought that horse and I aim to have him if I have to shoot him."

And there was Flem, standing there with his hands in his pockets, chewing, like he had just happened to be passing.

"You take your money and I take my horse," Henry says. "Give it back to him," he says to Mrs. Armstid.

"You don't own no horse of mine," the Texas man says. "Get him on home, missus."

Then Henry seen Flem. "You got something to do with these horses," he says. "I bought one. Here's the money for it." He taken the bill outen Mrs. Armstid's hand. He offered it to Flem. "I bought one. Ask him. Here. Here's the money," he says, giving the bill to Flem.

When Flem taken the money, the Texas man dropped the rope he had snatched outen Henry's hand. He had done sent Eck Snopes's boy up to the store for another box of gingersnaps, and he taken the box outen his pocket and looked into it. It was empty and he dropped it on the ground. "Mr. Snopes will have your money for you to-morrow," he says to Mrs. Armstid. "You can get it from him to-morrow. He don't own no horse. You get him into the wagon and get him on home." Mrs. Armstid went back to the wagon and got in. "Where's that ere buckboard I bought?" the Texas man says. It was after sundown then. And then Mrs. Littlejohn come out on the porch and rung the supper bell.

IV

I come on in and et supper. Mrs. Littlejohn would bring in a pan of bread or something, then she would go out to the porch a minute and come back and tell us. The Texas man had hitched his team to the buckboard he had swapped them last two horses for, and him and Flem had gone, and then she told that the rest of them that never had ropes had went back to the store with I.O. Snopes to get some ropes, and wasn't nobody at the gate but Henry Armstid, and Mrs. Armstid setting in the wagon in the road, and Eck Snopes and that boy of hisn. "I don't care how many of them fool men gets killed by them thing," Mrs. Littlejohn says, "but I ain't going to let Eck Snopes take that boy into that lot again." So she went down to the gate, but she come back without the boy or Eck neither.

"It ain't no need to worry about that boy," I says. "He's charmed." He was right behind Eck last night when Eck went to help feed them. The whole drove of them jumped clean over that boy's head and never touched him. It was Eck that touched him. Eck snatched him into the wagon and taken a rope and frailed the tar outen him.

So I had done et and went to my room and was undressing, long as I had a long trip to make next day; I was trying to sell a machine to Mrs. Bundren up past Whiteleaf; when Henry Armstid opened that gate and went in by hisself. They couldn't make him wait for the balance of them to get back with their ropes. Eck Snopes said he tried to make Henry wait, but Henry wouldn't do it. Eck said Henry walked right up to them and that when they broke, they run clean over Henry like a haymow breaking down. Eck said he snatched that boy of hisn out of the way just in time and that them things went through that gate like a creek flood and into the wagons and teams hitched side the road, busting wagon tongues and snapping harness like it was fishing-line, with Mrs. Armstid still setting in their wagon in the middle of it like something carved outen wood. Then they scattered, wild horses and tame mules with pieces of harness and single trees dangling offen them, both ways up and down the road.

"There goes ourn, paw!" Eck says his boy said. "There it goes, into Mrs. Littlejohn's house." Eck says it run right up the steps and into the house like a boarder late for supper. I reckon so. Anyway, I was in my room, in my underclothes, with one sock on and one sock in my hand, leaning out the window when the commotion busted out, when I heard something run into the melodeon in the hall; it sounded like a railroad engine. Then the door to my room come sailing in like when you throw a tin bucket top into the wind and I looked over my shoulder and see something that looked like a fourteen-foot pinwheel a-blaring its eyes at me. It had to blare them fast, because I was already done jumped out the window.

I reckon it was anxious, too. I reckon it hadn't never seen barbed wire or shell corn before, but I know it hadn't never seen underclothes before, or maybe it was a sewing-machine agent it hadn't never seen. Anyway, it swirled and turned to run back up the hall and outen the house, when it met Eck Snopes and that boy just coming in, carrying a rope. It swirled again and run down the hall and out the back door just in time to meet Mrs. Littlejohn. She had just gathered up the clothes she had washed, and she was coming onto the back porch with a armful of washing in one hand and a scrubbing-board in the other, when the horse skidded up to her, trying to stop and swirl again. It never taken Mrs. Littlejohn no time a-tall.

"Git outen here, you son," she says. She hit it across the face with the scrubbing-board; that ere scrubbing-board split as neat as ere a axe could have done it, and when the horse swirled to run back up the hall, she hit it again with what was left of the scrubbing-board, not on the head this time. "And stay out," she says.

Eck and that boy was half-way down the hall by this time. I reckon that horse looked like a pinwheel to Eck too. "Git to hell outen here, Ad!" Eck says. Only there wasn't time. Eck dropped flat on his face, but the boy never moved. The boy was about a yard tall maybe, in overhalls just like Eck's; that horse swoared over his head without touching a hair. I saw that, because I was just coming back up the front steps, still carrying that ere sock and still in my underclothes, when the horse come onto the porch again. It taken one look at me and swirled again and run to the end of the porch and jumped the banisters and the lot fence like a hen-hawk and lit in the lot running and went out the gate again and jumped eight or ten upside-down wagons and went on down the road. It was a full moon then. Mrs. Armstid was still setting in the wagon like she had done been carved outen wood and left there and forgot.

That horse. It ain't never missed a lick. It was going about forty miles a hour when it come to the bridge over the creek. It would have had a clear road, but it so happened that Vernon Tull was already using the bridge when it got there. He was coming back from town; he hadn't heard about the auction; him and his wife and three daughters and Mrs. Tull's aunt, all setting in chairs in the wagon bed, and all asleep, including the mules. They waked up when the horse hit the bridge one time, but Tull said the first he knew was when the mules tried to turn the wagon around in the middle of the bridge and he seen that spotted varmint run right twixt the mules and run up the wagon tongue like a squirrel. He said he just had time to hit it across the face with his whip-stock, because about that time the mules turned the wagon around on that ere one-way bridge and that horse clumb across one of the mules and jumped down onto the bridge again and went on, with Vernon standing up in the wagon and kicking at it.

Tull said the mules turned in the harness and clumb back into the wagon too, with Tull trying to beat them out again, with the reins wrapped around his wrist. After that he says all he seen was overturned chairs and womenfolks' legs and white drawers shining in the moonlight, and his mules and that spotted horse going on up the road like a ghost.

The mules jerked Tull outen the wagon and drug him a spell on the bridge before the reins broke. They thought at first that he was dead, and while they was kneeling around him, picking the bridge splinters outen him, here come Eck and that boy, still carrying the rope. They was running and breathing a little hard. "Where'd he go?" Eck says.

V

I went back and got my pants and shirt and shoes on just in time to go and help get Henry Armstid outen the trash in the lot. I be dog if he didn't look like he was dead, with his head hanging back and his teeth showing in the moonlight, and a little rim of white under his eyelids. We could still hear them horses, here and there; hadn't none of them got more than four-five miles away yet, not knowing the country, I reckon. So we could hear them and folks yelling now and then: "Whooey. Head him!"

We toted Henry into Mrs. Littlejohn's. She was in the hall; she hadn't put down the armful of clothes. She taken one look at us, and she laid down the busted scrubbing-board and taken up the lamp and opened a empty door. "Bring him in here," she says.

We toted him in and laid him on the bed. Mrs. Littlejohn set the lamp on the dresser, still carrying the clothes. "I'll declare, you men," she says. Our shadows was way up the wall, tiptoeing too; we could hear ourselves breathing. "Better get his wife," Mrs. Littlejohn says. She went out, carrying the clothes.

"I reckon we had," Quick says. "Go get her, somebody."

"Whyn't you go?" Winterbottom says.

"Let Ernest git her," Durley says. "He lives neighbors with them."

Ernest went to fetch her. I be dog if Henry didn't look like he was dead. Mrs. Littlejohn come back, with a kettle and some towels. She went to work on Henry, and then Mrs. Armstid and Ernest come in. Mrs. Armstid come to the foot of the bed and stood there, with her hands rolled into her apron, watching what Mrs. Littlejohn was doing, I reckon.

"You men git outen the way," Mrs. Littlejohn says. "Git outside," she says. "See if you can't find something else to play with that will kill some more of you."

"Is he dead?" Winterbottom says.

"It ain't your fault if he ain't," Mrs. Littlejohn says. "Go tell Will Varner to come up here. I reckon a man ain't so different from a mule, come long come short. Except maybe a mule's got more sense."

We went to get Uncle Billy. It was a full moon. We could hear them, now and then, four mile away: "Whooey. Head him." The country was full of them, one on ever wooden bridge in the land, running across it like thunder: "Whooey. There he goes. Head him."

We hadn't got far before Henry begun to scream. I reckon Mrs. Littlejohn's water had brung him to; anyway, he wasn't dead. We went on to Uncle Billy's. The house was dark. We called to him, and after a while the window opened and Uncle Billy put his head out, peart as a peckerwood,[3] listening. "Are they still trying to catch them durn rabbits?" he says.

He come down, with his britches on over his night-shirt and his suspenders dangling, carrying his horse-doctoring grip. "Yes, sir," he says, cocking his head like a woodpecker, "They're still a-trying."

We could hear Henry before we reached Mrs. Littlejohn's. He was going Ah-Ah-Ah. We stopped in the yard. Uncle Billy went on in. We could hear Henry. We stood in the yard, hearing them on the bridges, this-a-way and that: "Whooey. Whooey."

"Eck Snopes ought to caught hisn," Ernest says.

"Looks like he ought," Winterbottom said.

Henry was going Ah-Ah-Ah steady in the house; then he begun to scream. "Uncle Billy's started," Quick says. We looked into the hall. We could see the light where the door was. Then Mrs. Littlejohn come out.

"Will needs some help," she says. "You, Ernest. You'll do." Ernest went into the house.

---

[3]Woodpecker.

"Hear them?" Quick said. "That one was on Four Mile bridge." We could hear them; it sounded like thunder a long way off; it didn't last long:

"Whooey."

We could hear Henry: "Ah-Ah-Ah-Ah-Ah."

"They are both started now," Winterbottom says. "Ernest too."

That was early in the night. Which was a good thing, because it taken a long night for folks to chase them things right and for Henry to lay there and holler, being as Uncle Billy never had none of this here chloryfoam to set Henry's leg with. So it was considerate of Flem to get them started early. And what do you reckon Flem's com-ment was?

That's right. Nothing. Because he wasn't there. Hadn't nobody see him since that Texas man left.

VI

That was Saturday night. I reckon Mrs. Armstid got home about daylight, to see about the chaps. I don't know where they thought her and Henry was. But lucky the oldest one was a gal, about twelve, big enough to take care of the little ones. Which she did for the next two days. Mrs. Armstid would nurse Henry all night and work in the kitchen for hern and Henry's keep, and in the afternoon she would drive home (it was about four miles) to see to the chaps. She would cook up a pot of victuals and leave it on the stove, and the gal would bar the house and keep the little ones quiet. I would hear Mrs. Littlejohn and Mrs. Armstid talking in the kitchen. "How are the chaps making out?" Mrs. Littlejohn says.

"All right," Mrs. Armstid says.

"Don't they git skeered at night?" Mrs. Littlejohn says.

"Ina May bars the door when I leave," Mrs. Armstid says. "She's got the axe in bed with her. I reckon she can make out."

I reckon they did. And I reckon Mrs. Armstid was waiting for Flem to come back to town; hadn't nobody seen him until this morning; to get her money the Texas man said Flem was keeping for her. Sho. I reckon she was.

Anyway, I heard Mrs. Armstid and Mrs. Littlejohn talking in the kitchen this morning while I was eating breakfast. Mrs. Littlejohn had just told Mrs. Armstid that Flem was in town. "You can ask him for that five dollars," Mrs. Littlejohn says.

"You reckon he'll give it to me?" Mrs. Armstid says.

Mrs. Littlejohn was washing dishes, washing them like a man, like they was made out of iron. "No," she says. "But asking him won't do no hurt. It might shame him. I don't reckon it will, but it might."

"If he wouldn't give it back, it ain't no use to ask," Mrs. Armstid says.

"Suit yourself," Mrs. Littlejohn says. "It's your money."

I could hear the dishes.

"Do you reckon he might give it back to me?" Mrs. Armstid says. "That Texas man said he would. He said I could get it from Mr. Snopes later."

"Then go and ask him for it," Mrs. Littlejohn says.

I could hear the dishes.

"He won't give it back to me," Mrs. Armstid says.

"All right," Mrs. Littlejohn says. "Don't ask him for it, then."

I could hear the dishes; Mrs. Armstid was helping. "You don't reckon he would, do you?" she says. Mrs. Littlejohn never said nothing. It sounded like she was throwing the dishes at one another. "Maybe I better go and talk to Henry about it," Mrs. Armstid says.

"I would," Mrs. Littlejohn says. I be dog if it didn't sound like she had two plates in her hands, beating them together. "Then Henry can buy another five-dollar horse with it. Maybe he'll buy one next time that will out and out kill him. If I thought that, I'd give you back the money, myself."

"I reckon I better talk to him first," Mrs. Armstid said. Then it sounded like Mrs. Littlejohn taken up all the dishes and throwed them at the cookstove, and I come away.

That was this morning. I had been up to Bundren's and back, and I thought that things would have kind of settled down. So after breakfast, I went up to the store. And there was Flem, setting in the store-chair and whittling, like he might not have ever moved since he come to clerk for Jody Varner. I. O. was leaning in the door, in his shirt sleeves and with his hair parted too, same as Flem was before he turned the clerking job over to I. O. It's a funny thing about them Snopes: they all looks alike, yet there ain't ere a two of them that claims brothers. They're always just cousins, like Flem and Eck and Flem and I. O. Eck was there too, squatting against the wall, him and that boy, eating cheese and crackers outen a sack; they told me that Eck hadn't been home a-tall. And that Lon Quick hadn't got back to town, even. He followed his horse clean down to Samson's Bridge, with a wagon and a camp outfit. Eck finally caught one of hisn. It run into a blind lane at Freeman's and Eck and the boy taken and tied their rope across the end of the lane, about three foot high. The horse come to the end of the lane and whirled and run back without ever stopping. Eck says it never seen the rope a-tall. He says it looked just like one of these here Christmas pinwheels. "Didn't it try to run again?" I says.

"No," Eck says, eating a bite of cheese offen his knife blade. "Just kicked some."

"Kicked some?" I says.

"It broke its neck," Eck says.

Well, they was squatting there, about six of them, talking, talking at Flem; never nobody knowed yet if Flem had ere a interest in them horses or not. So finally I come right out and asked him. "Flem's done skun all of us so much," I says, "that we're proud of him. Come on, Flem," I says, "how much did you and that Texas man make offen them horses? You can tell us. Ain't nobody here but Eck that bought one of them; the others ain't got back to town yet, and Eck's your own cousin; he'll be proud to hear, too. How much did you-all make?"

They was all whittling, not looking at Flem, making like they was studying. But you could a heard a pin drop. And I. O. He had been rubbing his back up and down on the door, but he stopped now, watching Flem like a pointing dog. Flem finished cutting the sliver offen his stick. He spit across the porch, into the road. "'Twarn't none of my horses," he says.

I. O. cackled, like a hen, slapping his legs with both hands. "You boys might just as well quit trying to get ahead of Flem," he said.

Well, about that time I see Mrs. Armstid come outen Mrs. Littlejohn's gate, coming up the road. I never said nothing. I says, "Well, if a man can't take care of himself in a trade, he can't blame the man that trims him."

Flem never said nothing, trimming at the stick. He hadn't seen Mrs. Armstid. "Yes, sir," I says. "A fellow like Henry Armstid ain't got nobody but hisself to blame."

"Course he ain't," I. O. says. He ain't seen her, neither. "Henry Armstid's a born fool. Always is been. If Flem hadn't a got his money, somebody else would."

We looked at Flem. He never moved. Mrs. Armstid come on up the road.

"That's right," I says. "But, come to think of it, Henry never bought no horse." We looked at Flem; you could a heard a match drop. "That Texas man told her to get that five dollars back from Flem next day. I reckon Flem's done already taken that money to Mrs. Littlejohn's and give it to Mrs. Armstid."

We watched Flem. I. O. quit rubbing his back against the door again. After a while Flem raised his head and spit across the porch, into the dust. I. O. cackled, just like a hen. "Ain't he a beating fellow, now?" I. O. says.

Mrs. Armstid was getting closer, so I kept on talking, watching to see if Flem would look up and see her. But he never looked up. I went on talking about Tull, about how he was going to sue Flem, and Flem setting there, whittling his stick, not saying nothing else after he said they wasn't none of his horses.

Then I. O. happened to look around. He seen Mrs. Armstid. "Psssst!" he says. Flem looked up. "Here she comes!" I. O. says. "Go out the back. I'll tell her you done went in to town to-day."

But Flem never moved. He just set there, whittling, and we watched Mrs. Armstid come up onto the porch, in that ere faded sunbonnet and wrapper and them tennis shoes that made a kind of hissing noise on the porch. She come onto the porch and stopped, her hands rolled into her dress in front, not looking at nothing.

"He said Saturday," she says, "that he wouldn't sell Henry no horse. He said I could get the money from you."

Flem looked up. The knife never stopped. It went on trimming off a sliver same as if he was watching it. "He taken that money off with him when he left," Flem says.

Mrs. Armstid never looked at nothing. We never looked at her, neither, except that boy of Eck's. He had a half-et cracker in his hand, watching her, chewing.

"He said Henry hadn't bought no horse," Mrs. Armstid says. "He said for me to get the money from you today."

"I reckon he forgot about it," Flem said. "He taken that money off with him Saturday." He whittled again. I. O. kept on rubbing his back, slow. He licked his lips. After a while the woman looked up the road, where it went on up the hill, toward the graveyard. She looked up that way for a while, with that boy of Eck's watching her and I. O. rubbing his back slow against the door. Then she turned back toward the steps.

"I reckon it's time to get dinner started," she says.

"How's Henry this morning, Mrs. Armstid?" Winterbottom says.

She looked at Winterbottom; she almost stopped. "He's resting, I thank you kindly," she says.

Flem got up, outen the chair, putting his knife away. He spit across the porch. "Wait a minute, Mrs. Armstid," he says. She stopped again. She didn't look at him. Flem went on into the store, with I. O. done quit rubbing his back now, with his head craned after Flem, and Mrs. Armstid standing there with her hands rolled into her dress, not looking at nothing. A wagon come up the road and passed; it was Freeman, on the way to town. Then Flem come out again, with I. O. still watching him. Flem had one of these little striped sacks of Jody Varner's candy; I bet he still owes Jody that nickel, too. He put the sack into Mrs. Armstid's hand, like he would have put it into a hollow stump. He spit again across the porch. "A little sweetening for the chaps," he says.

"You're right kind," Mrs. Armstid says. She held the sack of candy in her hand, not looking at nothing. Eck's boy was watching the sack, the half-et cracker in his hand; he wasn't chewing now. He watched Mrs. Armstid roll the sack into her apron. "I reckon I better get on back and help with dinner," she says. She turned and went back across the porch. Flem set down in the chair again and opened his knife. He spit across the porch again, past Mrs. Armstid where she hadn't went down the steps yet. Then she went on, in that ere sunbonnet and wrapper all the same color, back down the road toward Mrs. Littlejohn's. You couldn't see her dress move, like a natural woman walking. She looked like a old snag still standing up and moving along on a high water. We watched her turn in at Mrs. Littlejohn's and go outen sight. Flem was whittling. I. O. begun to rub his back on the door. Then he begun to cackle, just like a durn hen.

"You boys might just as well quit trying," I. O. says. "You can't git ahead of Flem. You can't touch him. Ain't he a sight, now?"

I be dog if he ain't. If I had brung a herd of wild cattymounts into town and sold them to my neighbors and kinfolks, they would have lynched me. Yes, sir.

Study and Discussion Questions

1. List or sum up the characteristics of each of the following characters in the story: the Texan, Flem, Mrs. Littlejohn, Mrs. Armstid, Henry Armstid.
2. Who is the narrator of "Spotted Horses"? What is his relation to the events of the story?
3. Who owns the horses?
4. What words are used to describe the horses? What are the horses compared to?
5. What do Flem and the spotted horses have in common?
6. What is Mrs. Littlejohn's opinion of the situation? Give examples of her expressing her opinion.

Suggestions for Writing

1. Find a passage that made you smile or laugh and analyze Faulkner's use of humor.
2. Though he is the focus of much of the story, Flem Snopes rarely speaks and is not even present for much of the action. How is it, then, that Flem has so much power? Why is it, as I. O. says, that "you can't touch him"?
3. What do the horses represent or mean to the community? How do they operate as a symbol in the story? That is, what do they come to mean for the reader?
4. Consider Henry Armstid's purchase of a horse and how the Texas man handles that situation. Can you state the unwritten code of ethics out of which the Texas man is acting? What is Flem Snope's relation to that same code of ethics?

❀ ❀ ❀

TONI CADE BAMBARA (1939–1995)

Toni Cade Bambara was born in New York City. In 1959, she obtained her B.A. in Theater Arts at Queens College and her M.A. from City College of the City University of New York in 1964. During this time, and throughout the 1960s, Bambara worked persistently as a social activist in Harlem and Brooklyn and published a few short stories in magazines. Her experiences as a "cultural worker" (a phrase she often used) inevitably found their way into her stories— stories with radical plots, lively street dialogue, and resilient characters: "I work to celebrate, to applaud the tradition of struggle in our community, to bring together all those characters, just ordinary folks on the block who've been waiting in the wings, characters we thought we had to ignore because they weren't pimp-flashy or hustler-slick . . ." (*Notable Black American Women*, 2002). The publication of *The Black Woman: An Anthology* (1970), edited by Bambara, was one of the first anthologies specifically about the black female experience. In 1972, with Toni Morrison as her editor, Bambara published her first collection of short stories, *Gorilla My Love*. In addition to her writing, Bambara was also active in the theater and wrote several screenplays. Her other works include *Tales and Stories for Black Folks* (1971, editor and contributor); the short story collection *The Sea Birds Are Still Alive* (1977); and the novels *The Salt Eaters* (1980), *If Blessing Comes* (1987), and *These Bones Are Not My Child* (1999). "The Lesson" first appeared in *Gorilla My Love*.

The Lesson   (1972)

Back in the days when everyone was old and stupid or young and foolish and me and Sugar were the only ones just right, this lady moved on our block with nappy hair and proper speech and no makeup. And quite naturally we laughed at her, laughed the way we did at the junk man who went about his business like he was some big-time president and his sorry-ass horse his secretary. And we kinda hated her too, hated the way we did the winos who cluttered up our parks and pissed on our handball walls and stank up our hallways and stairs so you couldn't halfway play hide-and-seek without a goddamn gas mask. Miss Moore was her name. The only woman on the block with no first name. And she was black as hell, cept for her feet, which were fish-white and spooky. And she was always planning these boring-ass things for us to do, us being my cousin, mostly, who lived on the block cause we all moved North the same time and to the same apartment then spread out gradual to breathe. And our parents would yank our heads into some kinda shape and crisp up our clothes so we'd be presentable for travel with Miss Moore, who always looked like she was going to church, though she never did. Which is just one of things the grownups talked about when they talked behind her back like a dog. But when she came calling with some sachet she'd sewed up or some gingerbread she'd made or some book, why then they'd all be too embarrassed to turn her down and we'd get handed over all spruced up. She'd been to college and said it was only right that she should take responsibility for the young ones' education, and she not even related by marriage or blood. So they'd go for it. Specially Aunt Gretchen. She was the main gofer in the family. You got some ole dumb shit foolishness you want somebody to go for, you send for Aunt Gretchen. She been screwed into the go-along for so long, it's a blood-deep natural thing with her. Which is how she got saddled with me and Sugar and Junior in the first place while our mothers were in a la-de-da apartment up the block having a good ole time.

So this one day Miss Moore rounds us all up at the mailbox and it's puredee hot and she's knockin herself out about arithmetic. And school suppose to let up in summer I heard, but she don't never let up. And the starch in my pinafore scratching the shit outta me and I'm really hating this nappy-head bitch and her goddamn college degree. I'd much rather go to the pool or to the show where it's cool. So me and Sugar leaning on the mailbox being surly, which is a Miss Moore word. And Flyboy checking out what everybody brought for lunch. And Fat Butt already wasting his peanut-butter-and-jelly sandwich like the pig he is. And Junebug punchin on Q.T.'s arm for potato chips. And Rosie Giraffe shifting from one hip to the other waiting for somebody to step on her foot or ask her if she from Georgia so she can kick ass, preferably Mercedes'. And Miss Moore asking us do we know what money is, like we a bunch of retards. I mean real money, she say, like it's only poker chips or monopoly papers we lay on the grocer. So right away I'm tired of this and say so. And would much rather snatch Sugar and go to the Sunset and terrorize the West Indian kids and take their hair ribbons and their money too. And Miss Moore files that remark away for next week's lesson on brotherhood, I can tell. And finally I say we oughta get to the subway cause it's cooler and besides we might meet some cute boys. Sugar done swiped her mama's lipstick, so we ready.

So we heading down the street and she's boring us silly about what things cost and what our parents make and how much goes for rent and how money ain't divided up right in this country. And then she gets to the part about we all poor and live in the slums, which I don't feature. And I'm ready to speak on that, but she steps out in the street and hails two cabs just like that. Then she hustles half the crew in with her and hands me a five-dollar bill and tells me to calculate 10 percent tip for the driver. And we're off. Me and Sugar and Junebug and Flyboy hangin out the window and hollering to everybody, putting lipstick on each other cause Flyboy a faggot anyway, and making farts with our sweaty armpits. But I'm mostly trying to figure how to spend this money. But they all fascinated with the meter ticking and Junebug starts laying bets as to how much it'll read when Flyboy can't hold his breath no more. Then Sugar lays bets as to how much it'll be when we get there. So I'm stuck. Don't nobody want to go for my plan, which is to jump out at the next light and run off to the first bar-b-que we can find. Then the driver tells us to get the hell out cause we there already. And the meter reads eighty-five cents. And I'm stalling to figure out the tip and Sugar say give him a dime. And I decide he don't need it bad as I do, so later for him. But then he tries to take off with Junebug foot still in the door so we talk about his mama something ferocious. Then we check out that we on Fifth Avenue and everybody dressed up in stockings. One lady in a fur coat, hot as it is. White folks crazy.

"This is the place," Miss Moore say, presenting it to us in the voice she uses at the museum. "Let's look in the windows before we go in."

"Can we steal?" Sugar asks very serious like she's getting the ground rules squared away before she plays. "I beg your pardon," say Miss Moore, and we fall out. So she leads us around the windows of the toy store and me and Sugar screamin, "This is mine, that's mine, I gotta have that, that was made for me, I was born for that," till Big Butt drowns us out.

"Hey, I'm goin to buy that there."

"That there? You don't even know what it is, stupid."

"I do so," he say punchin on Rosie Giraffe. "It's a microscope."

"Whatcha gonna do with a microscope, fool?"

"Look at things."

"Like what, Ronald?" ask Miss Moore. And Big Butt ain't got the first notion. So here go Miss Moore gabbing about the thousands of bacteria in a drop of water and the somethinorother in a speck of blood and the million and one living things in the air around us is invisible to the naked eye. And what she say that for? Junebug go to town on that "naked" and we rolling. Then Miss Moore ask what it cost. So we all jam into the window smudgin it up and the price tag say $300. So then she ask how long'd take for Big Butt and Junebug to save up their allowances. "Too long," I say. "Yeh," adds Sugar, "outgrown it by that time." And Miss Moore say no, you never outgrow learning instruments. "Why, even medical students and interns and," blah, blah, blah. And we ready to choke Big Butt for bringing it up in the first damn place.

"This here costs four hundred eighty dollars," say Rosie Giraffe. So we pile up all over her to see what she pointin out. My eyes tell me it's a chunk of glass cracked with something heavy, and different-color inks dripped into the splits, then the whole thing put into a oven or something. But for $480 it don't make sense.

"That's a paperweight made of semi-precious stones fused together under tremendous pressure," she explains slowly, with her hands doing the mining and all the factory work.

"So what's a paperweight?" asks Rosie Giraffe.

"To weigh paper with, dumbbell," say Flyboy, the wise man from the East.

"Not exactly," say Miss Moore, which is what she say when you warm or way off too. "It's to weigh paper down so it won't scatter and make your desk untidy." So right away me and Sugar curtsy to each other and then to Mercedes who is more the tidy type.

"We don't keep paper on top of the desk in my class," say Junebug, figuring Miss Moore crazy or lyin one.

"At home, then," she say. "Don't you have a calendar and a pencil case and a blotter and a letter-opener on your desk at home where you do your home-work?" And she know damn well what our homes look like cause she nosys around in them every chance she gets.

"I don't even have a desk," say Junebug. "Do we?"

"No. And I don't get no homework neither," say Big Butt.

"And I don't even have a home," say Flyboy like he do at school to keep the white folks off his back and sorry for him. Send this poor kid to camp posters, is his specialty.

"I do," says Mercedes. "I have a box of stationery on my desk and a picture of my cat. My godmother bought the stationery and the desk. There's a big rose on each sheet and the envelopes smell like roses."

"Who wants to know about your smelly-ass stationery," say Rosie Giraffe fore I can get my two cents in.

"It's important to have a work area all your own so that . . ."

"Will you look at this sailboat, please," say Flyboy, cuttin her off and pointin to the thing like it was his. So once again we tumble all over each other to gaze at this magnificent thing in the toy store which is just big enough to maybe sail two kittens across the pond if you strap them to the posts tight. We all start recit-ing the price tag like we in assembly. "Handcrafted sailboat of fiberglass at one thousand one hundred ninety-five dollars."

"Unbelievable," I hear myself say and am really stunned. I read it again for myself just in case the group recitation put me in a trance. Same thing. For some reason this pisses me off. We look at Miss Moore and she lookin at us, waiting for I dunno what.

"Who'd pay all that when you can buy a sailboat set for a quarter at Pop's, a tube of glue for a dime, and a ball of string for eight cents? It must have a motor and a whole lot else besides," I say. "My sailboat cost me about fifty cents."

"But will it take water?" say Mercedes with her smart ass.

"Took mine to Alley Pond Park once," say Flyboy. "String broke, Lost it. Pity."

"Sailed mine in Central Park and it keeled over and sank. Had to ask my father for another dollar."

"And you got the strap," laugh Big Butt. "The jerk didn't even have a string on it. My old man wailed on his behind."

Little Q.T. was staring hard at the sailboat and you could see he wanted it bad. But he too little and somebody'd just take it from him. So what the hell. "This boat for kids, Miss Moore?"

"Parents silly to buy something like that just to get all broke up," say Rosie Giraffe.

"That much money it should last forever," I figure.

"My father'd buy it for me if I wanted it."

"Your father, my ass," say Rosie Giraffe getting a chance to finally push Mercedes.

"Must be rich people shop here," say Q.T.

"You are a very bright boy," say Flyboy. "What was your first clue?" And he rap him on the head with the back of his knuckles, since Q. T. the only one he could get away with. Though Q. T. liable to come up behind you years later and get his licks in when you half expect it.

"What I want to know is," I says to Miss Moore though I never talk to her, I wouldn't give the bitch that satisfaction, "is how much a real boat costs? I figure a thousand'd get you a yacht any day."

"Why don't you check that out," she says, "and report back to the group?" Which really pains my ass. If you gonna mess up a perfectly good swim day least you could do is have some answers. "Let's go in," she say like she got something up her sleeve. Only she don't lead the way. So me and Sugar turn the corner to where the entrance is, but when we get there I kinda hang back. Not that I'm scared, what's there to be afraid of, just a toy store. But I feel funny, shame. But what I got to be shamed about? Got as much right to go in as anybody. But somehow I can't seem to get hold of the door, so I step away for Sugar to lead. But she hangs back too. And I look at her and she looks at me and this is ridiculous. I mean, damn, I have never ever been shy about doing nothing or going nowhere. But then Mercedes steps up and then Rosie Giraffe and Big Butt crowd in behind and shove, and next thing we all stuffed into the doorway with only Mercedes squeezing past us, smoothing out her jumper and walking right down the aisle. Then the rest of us tumble in like a glued-together jigsaw done all wrong. And people lookin at us. And it's like the time me and Sugar crashed into the Catholic church on a dare. But once we got in there and everything so hushed and holy and the candles and the bowin and the handkerchiefs on all the drooping heads, I just couldn't go through with the plan. Which was for me to run up to the altar and do a tap dance while Sugar played the nose flute and messed around in the holy water. And Sugar kept givin me the elbow. Then later teased me so bad I tied her up in the shower and turned it on and locked her in. And she'd be there till this day if Aunt Gretchen hadn't finally figured I was lyin about the boarder takin a shower.

Same thing in the store. We all walkin on tiptoe and hardly touchin the games and puzzles and things. And I watched Miss Moore who is steady watchin us like she waitin for a sign. Like Mama Drewery watches the sky and sniffs the air and takes note of just how much slant is in the bird formation.

Then me and Sugar bump smack into each other, so busy gazing at the toys, 'specially the sailboat. But we don't laugh and go into our fat-lady bump-stomach routine. We just stare at that price tag. Then Sugar run a finger over the whole boat. And I'm jealous and want to hit her. Maybe not her, but I sure want to punch somebody in the mouth.

"Watcha bring us here for, Miss Moore?"

"You sound angry, Sylvia. Are you mad about something?" Givin me one of them grins like she tellin a grown-up joke that never turns out to be funny. And she's lookin very closely at me like maybe she plannin to do my portrait from memory. I'm mad, but I won't give her that satisfaction. So I slouch around the store bein very bored and say, "Let's go."

Me and Sugar at the back of the train watchin the tracks whizzin by large then small then gettin gobbled up in the dark. I'm thinkin about this tricky toy I saw in the store. A clown that somersaults on a bar then does chin-ups just cause you yank lightly at his leg. Cost $35. I could see me askin my mother for a $35 birthday clown. "You wanna who that costs what?" she'd say, cocking her head to the side to get a better view of the hole in my head. Thirty-five dollars could buy new bunk beds for Junior and Gretchen's boy. Thirty-five dollars and the whole household could go visit Granddaddy Nelson in the country. Thirty-five dollars would pay for the rent and the piano bill too. Who are these people that spend that much for performing clowns and $1,000 for toy sailboats? What kinda work they do and how they live and how come we ain't in on it? Where we are is who we are, Miss Moore always pointin out. But it don't necessarily have to be that way, she always adds then waits for somebody to say that poor people have to wake up and demand their share of the pie and don't none of us know what kind of pie she talkin about in the first damn place. But she ain't so smart cause I still got her four dollars from the taxi and she sure ain't gettin it. Messin up my day with this shit. Sugar nudges me in my pocket and winks.

Miss Moore lines us up in front of the mailbox where we started from, seem like years ago, and I got a headache for thinkin so hard. And we lean all over each other so we can hold up under the draggy-ass lecture she always finishes us off with at the end before we thank her for borin us to tears. But she just looks at us like she readin tea leaves. Finally she say, "Well, what did you think of F. A. O. Schwartz?"

Rosie Giraffe mumbles, "White folks crazy."

"I'd like to go there again when I get my birthday money," says Mercedes, and we shove her out the pack so she has to lean on the mailbox by herself.

"I'd like a shower. Tiring day," say Flyboy.

Then Sugar surprises me by sayin, "You know, Miss Moore, I don't think all of us here put together eat in a year what that sailboat costs." And Miss Moore lights up like somebody goosed her. "And?" she say, urging Sugar on. Only I'm standin on her foot so she don't continue.

"Imagine for a minute what kind of society it is in which some people can spend on a toy what it would cost to feed a family of six or seven. What do you think?"

"I think," say Sugar pushing me off her feet like she never done before, cause I whip her ass in a minute, "that this is not much of a democracy if you ask me. Equal chance to pursue happiness means an equal crack at the dough, don't it?" Miss Moore is besides herself and I am disgusted with Sugar's treachery. So I stand on her foot one more time to see if she'll shove me. She shuts up, and Miss Moore looks at me, sorrowfully I'm thinkin. And somethin weird is goin on, I can feel it in my chest.

"Anybody else learn anything today?" lookin dead at me. I walk away and Sugar has to run to catch up and don't even seem to notice when I shrug her arm off my shoulder.

"Well, we got four dollars anyway," she says.

"Uh hunh."

"We could go to Hascombs and get half a chocolate layer and then go to the Sunset and still have plenty money for potato chips and ice-cream sodas."

"Uh hunh."

"Race you to Hascombs," she say.

We start down the block and she gets ahead which is O.K. by me cause I'm goin to the West End and then over to the Drive to think this day through. She can run if she want to and even run faster. But ain't nobody gonna beat me at nuthin.

Study and Discussion Questions

1. What exactly is the lesson Miss Moore is trying to teach? To what extent does the narrator, Sylvia, learn it? What are the sources of her resistance to it?
2. Why does Sylvia feel ashamed entering the toy store? What does this reveal about her?
3. What is the significance of the last sentence of the story?
4. Why does Miss Moore feel the need to teach Sylvia and her friends a lesson now that they would no doubt eventually learn on their own?
5. What does Bambara gain by using Sylvia as a first-person narrator?
6. Who is Miss Moore? What is her role in the neighborhood? Why is she taking the children on these "field trips"?
7. Discuss the interactions between Miss Moore and the children in the toy store. Discuss the interactions between the children while they are in the store.

Suggestions for Writing

1. What kind of society is it, Miss Moore asks, "in which some people can spend on a toy what it would cost to feed a family of six or seven?" How would you answer?
2. Describe the first time you can remember being aware of social class differences.

❋ ❋ ❋

ALICE WALKER (b. 1944)

Alice Walker was born in Eatonton, Georgia. Her parents were sharecroppers who managed to raise eight children (Walker was the youngest) on minimal wages. At the age of eight, Walker's brother accidentally shot her in the eye with a BB gun, blinding her right eye. Due to the accident, Walker withdrew and became very shy. It was during this time that she began to develop an acute ability to observe people and to write. In 1961, she was awarded a scholarship to Spelman College. After graduating, she moved to Mississippi and became active in the civil rights movement. In 1967, she published her first essay, "The Civil Rights Movement: What Good Was It?" and her professional career as a writer began. While her reputation as a writer grew through the 1970s with the publication of the short story collection *In Love and Trouble* (1973) and the novel *Meridian* (1976), it was her novel *The Color Purple* (1983), winner of the Pulitzer Prize, that signaled Walker's recognition by a broader audience. Influenced by Zora Neale Hurston and Jean Toomer, Walker's work is imbued with the concept of the "womanist"—a phrase she penned as an alternative to "feminist." And indeed, Walker is best known for her powerful depictions of black women who persevere despite brutal oppression from men and society. Her other works include the short story collection *You Can't Keep a Good Woman Down* (1981); the novels *The Temple of My Familiar* (1989), *Possessing the Street of Joy* (1992), *By The Light of My Father's Smile* (1998), *The Way Forward Is With a Broken Heart* (2000), and *Now is the Time to Open Your Heart* (2004); the poetry collection *Revolutionary Petunias* (1973); and the essay collections *In Search of Our Mothers' Gardens: Womanist Prose* (1983) and *Anything We Love Can Be Saved: A Writer's Activism* (1997). "Everyday Use" was first published in *In Love and Trouble*.

Everyday Use (1973)

for your grandmama

I will wait for her in the yard that Maggie and I made so clean and wavy yesterday afternoon. A yard like this is more comfortable than most people know. It is not just a yard. It is like an extended living room. When the hard clay is swept clean as a floor and the fine sand around the edges lined with tiny, irregular grooves, anyone can come and sit and look up into the elm tree and wait for the breezes that never come inside the house.

Maggie will be nervous until after her sister goes: she will stand hopelessly in corners, homely and ashamed of the burn scars down her arms and legs, eying her sister with a mixture of envy and awe. She thinks her sister has held life always in the palm of one hand, that "no" is a word the world never learned to say to her.

You've no doubt seen those TV shows where the child who has "made it" is confronted, as a surprise, by her own mother and father, tottering in weakly from backstage. (A pleasant surprise, of course: What would they do if parent and child came on the show only to curse out and insult each other?) On TV mother and child embrace and smile into each other's faces. Sometimes the mother and father weep, the child wraps them in her arms and leans across the table to tell how she would not have made it without their help. I have seen these programs.

Sometimes I dream a dream in which Dee and I are suddenly brought together on a TV program of this sort. Out of a dark and soft-seated limousine I am ushered into a bright room filled with many people. There I meet a smiling, gray, sporty man like Johnny Carson who shakes my hand and tells me what a fine girl I have. Then we are on the stage and Dee is embracing me with tears in her eyes. She pins on my dress a large orchid, even though she has told me once that she thinks orchids are tacky flowers.

In real life I am a large, big-boned woman with rough, man-working hands. In the winter I wear flannel nightgowns to bed and overalls during the day. I can kill and clean a hog as mercilessly as a man. My fat keeps me hot in zero weather. I can work outside all day, breaking ice to get water for washing; I can eat pork liver cooked over the open fire minutes after it comes steaming from the hog. One winter I knocked a bull calf straight in the brain between the eyes with a sledge hammer and had the meat hung up to chill before nightfall. But of course all this does not show on television. I am the way my daughter would want me to be: a hundred pounds lighter, my skin like an uncooked barley pancake. My hair glistens in the hot bright lights. Johnny Carson has much to do to keep up with my quick and witty tongue.

But that is a mistake. I know even before I wake up. Who ever knew a Johnson with a quick tongue? Who can even imagine me looking a strange white man in the eye? It seems to me I have talked to them always with one foot raised in flight, with my head turned in whichever way is farthest from them. Dee, though. She would always look anyone in the eye. Hesitation was no part of her nature.

"How do I look, Mama?" Maggie says, showing just enough of her thin body enveloped in pink skirt and red blouse for me to know she's there, almost hidden by the door.

"Come out into the yard," I say.

Have you ever seen a lame animal, perhaps a dog run over by some careless person rich enough to own a car, sidle up to someone who is ignorant enough to be kind to him? That is the way my Maggie walks. She has been like this, chin on chest, eyes on ground, feet in shuffle, ever since the fire that burned the other house to the ground.

Dee is lighter than Maggie, with nicer hair and a fuller figure. She's a woman now, though sometimes I forget. How long ago was it that the other house burned? Ten, twelve years? Sometimes I can still hear the flames and feel Maggie's arms sticking to me, her hair smoking and her dress falling off her in little black papery flakes. Her eyes seemed stretched open, blazed open by the flames reflected in them. And Dee. I see her standing off under the sweet gum tree she used to dig gum out of; a look of concentration on her face as she watched the last dingy gray board of the house fall in toward the red-hot brick chimney. Why don't you do a dance around the ashes? I'd wanted to ask her. She had hated the house that much.

I used to think she hated Maggie, too. But that was before we raised the money, the church and me, to send her to Augusta to school. She used to read to us without pity; forcing words, lies, other folks' habits, whole lives upon us two, sitting trapped and ignorant underneath her voice. She washed us in a river of make-believe, burned us with a lot of knowledge we didn't necessarily need to know. Pressed us to her with the serious way she read, to shove us away at just the moment, like dimwits, we seemed about to understand.

Dee wanted nice things. A yellow organdy dress to wear to her graduation from high school; black pumps to match a green suit she'd made from an old suit somebody gave me. She was determined to stare down any disaster in her efforts. Her eyelids would not flicker for minutes at a time. Often I fought off the temptation to shake her. At sixteen she had a style of her own: and knew what style was.

I never had an education myself. After second grade the school was closed down. Don't ask me why: in 1927 colored asked fewer questions than they do now. Sometimes Maggie reads to me. She stumbles along good-naturedly but can't see well. She knows she is not bright. Like good looks and money, quickness passed her by. She will marry John Thomas (who has mossy teeth in an earnest face) and then I'll be free to sit here and I guess just sing church songs to myself. Although I never was a good singer. Never could carry a tune. I was always better at a man's job. I used to love to milk till I was hooked in the side in '49. Cows are soothing and slow and don't bother you, unless you try to milk them the wrong way.

I have deliberately turned my back on the house. It is three rooms, just like the one that burned, except the roof is tin; they don't make shingle roofs any more. There are no real windows, just some holes cut in the sides, like the portholes in a ship, but not round and not square, with rawhide holding the shutters up on the outside. This house is in a pasture, too, like the other one. No doubt when Dee sees it she will want to tear it down. She wrote me once that no matter where we "choose" to live, she will manage to come see us. But she will never bring her friends. Maggie and I thought about this and Maggie asked me, "Mama, when did Dee ever *have* any friends?"

She had a few. Furtive boys in pink shirts hanging about on washday after school. Nervous girls who never laughed. Impressed with her they worshiped the well-turned phrase, the cute shape, the scalding humor that erupted like bubbles in lye. She read to them.

When she was courting Jimmy T she didn't have much time to pay to us, but turned all her faultfinding power on him. He *flew* to marry a cheap city girl from a family of ignorant flashy people. She hardly had time to recompose herself.

When she comes I will meet—but there they are!

Maggie attempts to make a dash for the house; in her shuffling way, but I stay her with my hand. "Come back here," I say. And she stops and tries to dig a well in the sand with her toe.

It is hard to see them clearly through the strong sun. But even the first glimpse of leg out of the car tells me it is Dee. Her feet were always neat-looking, as if God himself had shaped them with a certain style. From the other side of the car comes a short, stocky man. Hair is all over his head a foot long and hanging from his chin like a kinky mule tail. I hear Maggie suck in her breath. "Uhnnnh," is what it sounds like. Like when you see the wriggling end of a snake just in front of your foot on the road. "Uhnnnh."

Dee next. A dress down to the ground, in this hot weather. A dress so loud it hurts my eyes. There are yellows and oranges enough to throw back the light of the sun. I feel my whole face warming from the heat waves it throws out. Earrings gold, too, and hanging down to her shoulders. Bracelets dangling and making noises when she moves her arm up to shake the folds of the dress out of her armpits. The dress is loose and flows, and as she walks closer, I like it. I hear Maggie go "Uhnnnh" again. It is her sister's hair. It stands straight up like the wool on a sheep. It is black as night and around the edges are two long pigtails that rope about like small lizards disappearing behind her ears.

"Wa-su-zo-Tean-o!"[1] she says, coming on in that gilding way the dress makes her move. The short stocky fellow with the hair to his navel is all grinning and he follows up with "Asalamalakim,[2] my mother and sister!" He moves to hug Maggie but she falls back, right up against the back of my chair. I feel her trembling there and when I look up I see the perspiration falling off her chin.

"Don't get up," says Dee. Since I am stout it takes something of a push. You can see me trying to move a second or two before I make it. She turns, showing white heels through her sandals, and goes back to the car. Out she peeks next with a Polaroid. She stoops down quickly and lines up picture after picture of me sitting there in front of the house with Maggie cowering behind me. She never takes a shot without making sure the house is included. When a cow comes nibbling around the edge of the yard she snaps it and me and Maggie *and* the house. Then she puts the Polaroid in the back seat of the car, and comes up and kisses me on the forehead.

Meanwhile Asalamalakim is going through motions with Maggie's hand. Maggie's hand is as limp as a fish, and probably as cold, despite the sweat, and she keeps trying to pull it back. It looks like Asalamalakim wants to shake hands but wants to do it fancy. Or maybe he don't know how people shake hands. Anyhow, he soon gives up on Maggie.

"Well," I say. "Dee."

"No, Mama," she says. "Not 'Dee,' Wangero Leewanika Kemanjo!"

"What happened to 'Dee'?" I wanted to know.

---

[1]Swahili greeting.
[2]Arabic greeting.

"She's dead," Wangero said. "I couldn't bear it any longer, being named after the people who oppress me."

"You know as well as me you was named after your aunt Dicie," I said. Dicie is my sister. She named Dee. We called her "Big Dee" after Dee was born.

"But who was *she* named after?" asked Wangero.

"I guess after Grandma Dee," I said.

"And who was she named after?" asked Wangero.

"Her mother," I said, and saw Wangero was getting tired. "That's about as far back as I can trace it," I said. Though, in fact, I probably could have carried it back beyond the Civil War through the branches.

"Well," said Asalamalakim, "there you are."

"Uhnnnh," I heard Maggie say.

"There I was not," I said, "before 'Dicie' cropped up in our family, so why should I try to trace it that far back?"

He just stood there grinning, looking down on me like somebody inspecting a Model A car. Every once in a while he and Wangero sent eye signals over my head.

"How do you pronounce this name?" I asked.

"You don't have to call me by it if you don't want to," said Wangero.

"Why shouldn't I?" I asked. "If that's what you want us to call you, we'll call you."

"I know it might sound awkward at first," said Wangero.

"I'll get used to it," I said. "Ream it out again."

Well, soon we got the name out of the way. Asalamalakim had a name twice as long and three times as hard. After I tripped over it two or three times he told me to just call him Hakim-a-barber. I wanted to ask him was he a barber, but I didn't really think he was, so I didn't ask.

"You must belong to those beef-cattle peoples down the road," I said. They said "Asalamalakim" when they met you, too, but they didn't shake hands. Always too busy: feeding the cattle, fixing the fences, putting up salt-lick shelters, throwing down hay. When the white folks poisoned some of the herd the men stayed up all night with rifles in their hands. I walked a mile and a half just to see the sight.

Hakim-a-barber said, "I accept some of their doctrines, but farming and raising cattle is not my style." (They didn't tell me, and I didn't ask, whether Wangero (Dee) had really gone and married him.)

We sat down to eat and right away he said he didn't eat collards and pork was unclean. Wangero, though, went on through the chitlins and corn bread, the greens and everything else. She talked a blue streak over the sweet potatoes. Everything delighted her. Even the fact that we still used the benches her daddy made for the table when we couldn't afford to buy chairs.

"Oh, Mama!" she cried. Then turned to Hakim-a-barber. "I never knew how lovely these benches are. You can feel the rump prints," she said, running her hands underneath her and along the bench. Then she gave a sigh and her hand closed over Grandma Dee's butter dish. "That's it!" she said. "I knew there was something I wanted to ask you if I could have." She jumped up from the table and went over in the corner where the churn stood, the milk in it clabber by now. She looked at the churn and looked at it.

"This churn top is what I need," she said. "Didn't Uncle Buddy whittle it out of a tree you all used to have?"

"Yes," I said.

"Uh huh," she said happily. "And I want the dasher, too."

"Uncle Buddy whittle that, too?" asked the barber.

Dee (Wangero) looked up at me.

"Aunt Dee's first husband whittled the dash," said Maggie so low you almost couldn't hear her. "His name was Henry, but they called him Stash."

"Maggie's brain is like an elephant's," Wangero said, laughing. "I can use the churn top as a centerpiece for the alcove table," she said, sliding a plate over the churn, "and I'll think of something artistic to do with the dasher."

When she finished wrapping the dasher the handle stuck out. I took it for a moment in my hands. You didn't even have to look close to see where hands pushing the dasher up and down to make butter had left a kind of sink in the wood. In fact, there were a lot of small sinks; you could see where thumbs and fingers had sunk into the wood. It was beautiful light yellow wood, from a tree that grew in the yard where Big Dee and Stash had lived.

After dinner Dee (Wangero) went to the trunk at the foot of my bed, and started rifling through it. Maggie hung back in the kitchen over the dishpan. Out came Wangero with two quilts. They had been pieced by Grandma Dee and then Big Dee and me had hung them on the quilt frames on the front porch and quilted them. One was in the Lone Star pattern. The other was Walk Around the Mountain. In both of them were scraps of dresses Grandma Dee had worn fifty and more years ago. Bits and pieces of Grandpa Jarrell's Paisley shirts. And one teeny faded blue piece, about the size of a penny matchbox, that was from Great Grandpa Ezra's uniform that he wore in the Civil War.

"Mama," Wangero said sweet as a bird. "Can I have these old quilts?"

I heard something fall in the kitchen, and a minute later the kitchen door slammed.

"Why don't you take one or two of the others?" I asked. "These old things was just done by me and Big Dee from some tops your grandma pieced before she died."

"No," said Wangero. "I don't want those. They are stitched around the borders by machine."

"That'll make them last better," I said.

"That's not the point," said Wangero. "These are all pieces of dresses Grandma used to wear. She did all this stitching by hand. Imagine!" She held the quilts securely in her arms, stroking them.

"Some of the pieces, like those lavender ones, come from old clothes her mother handed down to her," I said, moving up to touch the quilts. Dee (Wangero) moved back just enough so that I couldn't reach the quilts. They already belonged to her.

"Imagine!" she breathed again, clutching them closely to her bosom.

"The truth is," I said, "I promised to give them quilts to Maggie, for when she marries John Thomas."

She gasped like a bee had stung her.

"Maggie can't appreciate these quilts!" she said. "She'd probably be backward enough to put them to everyday use."

"I reckon she would," I said. "God knows I been saving 'em for long enough with nobody using 'em. I hope she will!" I didn't want to bring up how I had offered Dee (Wangero) a quilt when she went away to college. Then she had told me they were old-fashioned, out of style.

"But they're *priceless!*" she was saying now, furiously; for she has a temper. "Maggie would put them on the bed and in five years they'd be in rags. Less than that!"

"She can always make some more," I said. "Maggie knows how to quilt."

Dee (Wangero) looked at me with hatred. "You just will not understand. The point is these quilts, *these* quilts!"

"Well," I said, stumped. "What would *you* do with them?"

"Hang them," she said. As if that was the only thing you *could* do with quilts.

Maggie by now was standing in the door. I could almost hear the sound her feet made as they scraped over each other.

"She can have them, Mama," she said, like somebody used to never winning anything, or having anything reserved for her. "I can 'member Grandma Dee without the quilts."

I looked at her hard. She had filled her bottom lip with checkerberry snuff and it gave her face a kind of dopey, hangdog look. It was Grandma Dee and Big Dee who taught her how to quilt herself. She stood there with her scarred hands hidden in the folds of her skirt. She looked at her sister with something like fear but she wasn't mad at her. This was Maggie's portion. This was the way she knew God to work.

When I looked at her like that something hit me in the top of my head and ran down to the soles of my feet. Just like when I'm in church and the spirit of God touches me and I get happy and shout. I did something I never had done before: hugged Maggie to me, then dragged her on into the room, snatched the quilts out of Miss Wangero's hands and dumped them into Maggie's lap. Maggie just sat there on my bed with her mouth open.

"Take one or two of the others," I said to Dee.

But she turned without a word and went out to Hakim-a-barber.

"You just don't understand," she said, as Maggie and I came out to the car.

"What don't I understand?" I wanted to know.

"Your heritage," she said. And then she turned to Maggie, kissed her, and said, "You ought to try to make something of yourself, too, Maggie. It's really a new day for us. But from the way you and Mama still live you'd never know it."

She put on some sunglasses that hid everything above the tip of her nose and her chin.

Maggie smiled; maybe at the sunglasses. But a real smile, not scared. After we watched the car dust settle I asked Maggie to bring me a dip of snuff. And then the two of us sat there just enjoying, until it was time to go in the house and go to bed.

Study and Discussion Questions

1. Who is the first-person narrator of this story?
2. Why do you think the mother describes herself in terms of the work she does? What are the differences between the real mother and the TV version she sometimes dreams?
3. What are we told about Dee before we ever meet her?
4. What does the house-burning incident tell us about the three characters and their relation to each other?
5. What does the title of the story refer to?
6. How has Dee changed, according to her mother? What have social class and class mobility to do with this?
7. Why does Dee take pictures of the house and want the churn top and the quilts?
8. What does Dee plan to do with the quilts? What will Maggie do with them?

Suggestions for Writing

1. Contrast Maggie and Dee.
2. Do you have any sympathy for Dee? If so, on what grounds? If not, why not?
3. Discuss the importance in this story of education, what it is, and what one does with it.
4. What is the wealth this family possesses? How do Maggie, Dee, and the mother each see that wealth and themselves in relation to it?
5. What does "Everyday Use" suggest about one's relation to one's past, heritage, and tradition?
6. Discuss the importance of names in the story.
7. Write about an experience you've had going home, either from your own perspective or from the point of view of another family member.

HARVEY PEKAR (1939–2010)

Harvey Pekar was born in Cleveland, Ohio, and has lived there all his life. The town itself has been the setting for Pekar's autobiographical *American Splendor*—a literary comic-book series based on his life as a file clerk at a Veteran's Administration hospital. Pekar self-published the comic annually from 1976 to the early 1990s, employing various illustrators (Robert Crumb, Sue Cavey, Frank Stack, and Joe Zabel, among others) to do the drawings. In 1987, it won the American Book Award. A few years later, the comic's popularity caught the attention of Dark Horse Comics, who took over publication. Pekar calls himself a "working-class intellectual," and *American Splendor* focuses on Pekar's introspective and heroic search for meaning amidst the complexity of a modern working-class life. In addition to *American Splendor*, Pekar has written as a music critic and is currently a freelance writer for a radio station in Cleveland. His other works include Our Cancer Year (1994)—a graphic novel about his fight with cancer, and most recently, his book length graphic autobiography, *The Quitter* (2005).

STORY BY HARVEY PEKAR
ART BY R. CRUMB

SUNDAY MORNING

HMMM..., THAT WOMAN FROM THAT BIG PUBLISHER NEVER GOT BACK T'ME. GUESS SHE WASN'T SERIOUS; PROB'LY WANTED A FREE BOOK OR WAS TOO LAZY T'LOOK FOR MY STUFF ON THE STANDS OR SUMP'N'.

BUT WHAT IF SHE'D BEEN SERIOUS? WHAT IF THEY'D HAVE PUBLISHED MY STUFF AND IT'D SOLD WELL AND I'D HAVE MADE ENOUGH TO SUPPORT MYSELF AS A WRITER?

HOW IMPORTANT IS THAT TO ME?

IT'D BE NICE NOT TO HAVE TO GET UP EV'RY MORNING AND GO TO WORK, TO BE ABLE TO READ OR WORK ON STORIES AND ARTICLES WHENEVER I FELT LIKE IT.

BUT THEN I'D SORT OF BE OUT OF THE STRUGGLE, SORT OF IN AN IVORY TOWER WATCHING THE MAINSTREAM OF LIFE GO BY RATHER THAN PARTICIPATING IN IT...

I'D BE ALIENATED BUT I WOULDN'T THINK I HAD THE RIGHT TO FEEL BAD ABOUT IT. I MEAN, I'D BE A WELL-PAID, FAMOUS AUTHOR. WHAT RIGHT WOULD I HAVE TO COMPLAIN ABOUT ANYTHING?

MAYBE MY WRITING WOULD SUFFER. I'VE GOT A PRETTY UNIQUE VIEWPOINT NOW... I'M A WRITER BUT IN A LOTTA WAYS I'VE GOT A WORKING MAN'S OUTLOOK ON LIFE. I'D HAVE TO AS LONG AS I'VE WORKED AT REGULAR DAY JOBS.

A COUPLA THOSE, ANNA RYE BREAD...

STILL, MAYBE I'M MAKING TOO MUCH OF THIS. AS LONG AS I'M ALIVE I'LL BE FINDING INTERESTING THINGS TO WRITE ABOUT, MEETING INTERESTING PEOPLE...

IF I LIVED A DIFFERENT LIFE I COULD STILL WRITE ABOUT IT.

Study and Discussion Questions

1. What is a "hypothetical quandary"? Look up the words in a large dictionary. Give an example of a hypothetical quandary in your own life. What is Pekar's hypothetical quandary in this story?
2. Describe the setting of this story.
3. What literally happens in this story? Give a plot summary.
4. Is the ending of "Hypothetical Quandary" a satisfactory answer to the protagonist's dilemma? Say how or how not. Would it be for you?
5. What do we learn about the main character from the way he is presented visually?
6. In the introduction to the collection *American Splendor: The Life and Times of Harvey Pekar,* from which this piece comes, illustrator R. Crumb writes in 1985, "Pekar has proven once and for all that even the most seemingly dreary and monotonous of lives is filled with poignancy and heroic struggle. . . . What Pekar does is certainly new to the comic book medium. There's never been anything even approaching this kind of stark realism." If you have read other comic books or graphic novels, how were they similar to and different from "Hypothetical Quandary"?
7. Harvey Pekar has worked with several artists in the course of his career creating serious comics about his life and times. Characterize R. Crumb's art work in this particular story.
8. Why include a comic strip such as this in a literature anthology?

Suggestions for Writing

1. See the 2003 biographical film about Harvey Pekar, *American Splendor* and write about "Hypothetical Quandary" in the context of what you have learned about Pekar's life.
2. Select one panel or frame in "Hypothetical Quandary" and analyze it— in terms of mood or atmosphere, presentation of character and setting, relation of words to picture, use of black and white, use of space, and any other aspects you find interesting.

❀ ❀ ❀

POETRY

BERTOLT BRECHT (1898–1956)

Bertolt Brecht was born in Augsburg, Germany, studied medicine at Munich University, and worked as an orderly in a military hospital during World War I. Afterward, Brecht became a radical critic of war and nationalism and began to write. Though he also wrote poetry and prose, Brecht found his strongest artistic outlet in drama. Regardless of genre, as a Marxist, Brecht saw the vocation of writer as socially responsible for social education. His work, through the use of satire and unconventional forms, questioned his era's perceptions of literature and its cultural role. Brecht's "theater of alienation" (Adorno) or "epic theater" sought to dismantle traditional Aristotelian notions of catharsis by staging dramas that didn't allow an audience to escape from reality, but instead presented an unadorned, unsentimental exposition of human crises. His theatrical ideas have heavily influenced modern drama. His work was banned in Germany in the 1930s with the rise of Hitler, forcing Brecht to leave. He would eventually move to California in 1941, where he worked with Charlie Chaplin and others in the film industry. A prolific writer of plays, poetry, and prose, selected works include his major plays *The Three-Penny Opera* (1928), *The Life of Galileo* (1939), *Mother Courage and Her Children* (1941), *The Good Woman of Setzuan* (1943), and *The Caucasian Chalk Circle* (1954). The poem "A Worker Reads History" illustrates Brecht's concern for the working class, and his techniques of defamiliarization and reframing perspective on a subject.

A Worker Reads History   (1936)

Translated by H. R. Hays.

Who built the seven gates of Thebes?
The books are filled with names of kings.
Was it kings who hauled the craggy blocks of stone?
And Babylon, so many times destroyed,
Who built the city up each time? In which of Lima's houses,   5
That city glittering with gold, lived those who built it?
In the evening when the Chinese wall was finished
Where did the masons go? Imperial Rome
Is full of arcs of triumph. Who reared them up? Over whom
Did the Caesars triumph? Byzantium lives in song,   10
Were all her dwellings palaces? And even in Atlantis of the legend
The night the sea rushed in,
The drowning men still bellowed for their slaves.

Young Alexander conquered India.
He alone? 15
Caesar beat the Gauls.
Was there not even a cook in his army?
Philip of Spain wept as his fleet
Was sunk and destroyed. Were there no other tears?
Frederick the Great triumphed in the Seven Years War. Who 20
Triumphed with him?

Each page a victory,
At whose expense the victory ball?
Every ten years a great man,
Who paid the piper? 25

So many particulars.
So many questions.

Study and Discussion Questions

1. List the different roles in the poem (invisible in history books) that members of the working classes have played.
2. Why are so many sentences in the poem questions? Is this only a rhetorical device?
3. What are the meanings and the irony of "Each page a victory"?
4. Explain "Every ten years a great man, Who paid the piper?"

Suggestions for Writing

1. Where do women of the working classes appear in the poem? Why doesn't Brecht mention *their* work?
2. To what extent and how were the working classes represented in the history you learned in school?
3. Write a poem or paragraph about a woman or an African American or a member of another historically dispossessed group reading history.

JONATHAN SWIFT (1667–1745)

Jonathon Swift was born in Dublin, Ireland and educated at Trinity College there. Throughout a very active and political life, Swift held a variety of positions—secretary for essayist and diplomat Sir Williams Temple; vicar; political pamphleteer; journalist; and Dean of St. Patrick's Cathedral in Dublin. By 1720, he had become a passionate critic of British imperial exploitation of Ireland, writing caustic satire on behalf of Irish national interests. Swift is best known for his prose writings, including *Battle of the Books* (1704), *The Tale of a Tub*

(1704), *Gulliver's Travels* (1726), and *A Modest Proposal* (1729). "A Description of the Morning," written in rhymed couplets, was first published in the Tory journal *The Tattler*.

Description of the Morning   (1709)

Now hardly here and there a hackney-coach
Appearing, showed the ruddy morn's approach.
Now Betty from her master's bed had flown,
And softly stole to discompose her own;
The slip-shod 'prentice from his master's door   5
Had pared the dirt and sprinkled round the floor.
Now Moll had whirled her mop with dext'rous airs,
Prepared to scrub the entry and the stairs.
The youth with broomy stumps began to trace
The kennel-edge, where wheels had worn the place.[1]   10
The small-coal man was heard with cadence deep,
Till drowned in shriller notes of chimney-sweep:
Duns at his lordship's gate began to meet;
And brickdust Moll had screamed through half the street.
The turnkey now his flock returning sees,   15
Duly let out a-nights to steal for fees:[2]
The watchful bailiffs take their silent stands,
And schoolboys lag with satchels in their hands.

Study and Discussion Questions

1. Spell out what each person described is doing and why.
2. What is the speaker's attitude toward what is described?
3. What comment is the poem making on differences in social class?
4. What is the significance of the juxtaposition in the last two lines?
5. What is the rhyme scheme of this poem?
6. How does the use of couplets as a structure for Swift's description of a morning work with the content or meaning of the poem? How does what he does with the couplets change as the poem goes on?

Suggestions for Writing

1. There is a long tradition of poems describing the morning's beauty in *pastoral* terms, picturing glorious fields, idle shepherds, and so on. What relation does "A Description of the Morning" have to such poems?

---

[1] The youth is scavenging in the gutter.
[2] To pay their jailer.

2. Try capturing Swift's tone in a poem or a paragraph describing the morning at a place you are familiar with. Use whatever genre (prose or poetry) and whatever form within the genre (e.g., if poetry, line length, rhyme or not) are appropriate to the place you are describing and your feelings about it.

JUDY GRAHN (b. 1940)

Judy Grahn grew up in New Mexico and has worked as a waitress, typist, sandwich maker, and meat wrapper. She has also taught in women's writing programs in New York and Berkeley, and she cofounded the Gay and Lesbian Studies Program at the New College of California in San Francisco. Grahn was a cofounder of the Women's Press Collective in 1970 in northern California. Her writings include *The Work of a Common Woman* (1978) and *The Queen of Wands* (1982), poetry; *Another Mother Tongue: Gay Words, Gay Worlds* (1984) and *Blood and Bread and Roses* (1986), nonfiction; *Mundane's World* (1988) a novel; and *Really Reading Gertrude Stein* (1989). She has also edited two volumes of *True to Life Adventure Stories* (1978, 1980). Grahn has consistently brought a working-class perspective into feminist poetry. "Ella, in a square apron, along Highway 80," is one of seven portraits of working-class women in the sequence, *The Common Woman Poems* (1969).

Ella, in a square apron, along Highway 80   (1969)

She's a copperheaded waitress,
tired and sharp-worded, she hides
her bad brown tooth behind a wicked
smile, and flicks her ass
out of habit, to fend off the pass   5
that passes for affection.
She keeps her mind the way men
keep a knife—keen to strip the game
down to her size. She has a thin spine,
swallows her eggs cold, and tells lies.   10
She slaps a wet rag at the truck drivers
if they should complain. She understands
the necessity for pain, turns away
the smaller tips, out of pride, and
keeps a flask under the counter. Once,   15
she shot a lover who misused her child.

Before she got out of jail, the courts had pounced
and given the child away. Like some isolated lake,
her flat blue eyes take care of their own stark
bottoms. Her hands are nervous, curled, ready   20
to scrape.
The common woman is as common
as a rattlesnake.

Study and Discussion Questions

1. Describe Ella's character. What kind of person is she? What outside forces have helped shape who she is?
2. Would you call Ella a survivor? What are the means she uses to survive, psychologically and spiritually as well as physically?
3. The last line of this poem is "The common woman is as common/as a rattlesnake." How is Ella like a rattlesnake? List words and phrases in the poem that contribute to the rattlesnake image.
4. Grahn said in her preface to *The Common Woman Poems*, of which "Ella, in a square apron, along Highway 80" is the second in the sequence, that one of her goals in writing these poems was to change the stereotypes of the work that women do. How has your sense of the person who brings your coffee changed now that you've read Grahn's poem?
5. Read the poem out loud. Locate and list some of the sound patterns in the poem. These may include end rhyme, internal rhyme, off rhyme, consonance, assonance.

Suggestions for Writing

1. "Ella, in a square apron, along Highway 80" is the second in a sequence of seven poems Judy Grahn wrote about women and their lives. She called this sequence *The Common Woman Poems*. Freewrite for five or ten minutes on the word *common*, writing down all the meanings and associations of "common" that come to mind and any words you can think of that are related to the word "common." In what ways is Ella a "common woman"? How is Grahn redefining the concept of "common"?
2. Write a poetic portrait of a woman or man: (a) about their relation to their work and (b) using a controlling metaphor or image as Grahn does in "Ella . . ." with the rattlesnake image.

❋ ❋ ❋

CARL SANDBURG (1878–1967)

Born to Swedish immigrants in Galesburg, Illinois, Sandburg's imagistic poetry celebrated the vibrant and continuous flow of Midwestern America. Sandburg left school at thirteen to work odd jobs and to travel (sometimes in freight trains), experiencing first hand working-class life. He served as a war correspondent during the Spanish-American War and afterward enrolled in college in Galesburg, but left to continue his travels. Although he never obtained his degree, it was here that Sandburg began to write poetry. In addition to his vagabond lifestyle, Sandburg's participation in socialist politics in Milwaukee (1908–1914) and his subsequent job as a private secretary for the town's socialist mayor helped shape his humanistic view of the world. In 1916 he published his first book of poetry, *Chicago Poems*, establishing himself as an important figure in the literary scene of the Chicago Renaissance. Sandburg's rhythmic free verse is often compared to Walt Whitman's (whom he read in college), characterized by the colloquial patterns of everyday speech and a profound belief in the essential goodness of the common American. His *Complete Poems* was awarded the Pulitzer Prize for poetry in 1950. Other poetic works include *Cornhuskers* (1918), *Smoke and Steel* (1920), and *The People, Yes* (1936). Sandburg also won a Pulitzer for his six-volume biography of Abraham Lincoln, a work that took 15 years to complete. "Chicago" was first published in *Chicago Poems*.

Chicago (1916)

       Hog Butcher for the World,
       Tool Maker, Stacker of Wheat,
       Player with Railroads and the Nation's Freight Handler;
       Stormy, husky, brawling,
       City of the Big Shoulders: 5
They tell me you are wicked and I believe them, for I have seen your
    painted women under the gas lamps luring the farm boys.
And they tell me you are crooked and I answer: Yes, it is true I have
    seen the gunman kill and go free to kill again.
And they tell me you are brutal and my reply is: On the faces of 10
    women and children I have seen the marks of wanton hunger.
And having answered so I turn once more to those who sneer at this
    my city, and I give them back the sneer and say to them:
Come and show me another city with lifted head singing so proud
    to be alive and coarse and strong and cunning. 15
Flinging magnetic curses amid the toil of piling job on job, here is a tall
    bold slugger set vivid against the little soft cities;
Fierce as a dog with tongue lapping for action, cunning as a savage
    pitted against the wilderness,
       Bareheaded, 20
       Shoveling,
       Wrecking,
       Planning,
       Building, breaking, rebuilding,

Under the smoke, dust all over his mouth, laughing with white teeth,   25
Under the terrible burden of destiny laughing as a young man laughs,
Laughing even as an ignorant fighter laughs who has never lost a battle,
Bragging and laughing that under his wrist is the pulse,
    and under his ribs the heart of the people,
            Laughing!   30
Laughing the stormy, husky, brawling laughter of Youth, half-naked,
    sweating, proud to be Hog Butcher, Tool Maker, Stacker of Wheat,
    Player with Railroads and Freight Handler to the Nation.

Study and Discussion Questions

1. What criticisms of the city does the speaker accept? What is it about the city that the speaker celebrates nonetheless?
2. How does the style of the poem match the speaker's feelings about Chicago?
3. What do the way the city is personified and the dismissal of "the soft little cities" tell us about the speaker's values?

Suggestions for Writing

1. What do the treatment of the city's problems and the way physical labor is portrayed in the poem suggest about the social class of the speaker?
2. Write a poem or an image-filled prose piece about the city or town you live in. Like "Chicago," it might be a poem of praise. If you don't like where you live, you might consider writing a parody of Sandburg's style.

❋ ❋ ❋

JIMMY SANTIAGO BACA (b. 1952)

Of Chicano and Apache heritage, Jimmy Santiago Baca was born in Santa Fe, New Mexico, and spent much of his childhood in an orphanage, until he ran away at age eleven. He lived on the street and at twenty was convicted of drug possession and sentenced to a maximum security prison for 10 years, experiencing prison brutality (solitary confinement, shock treatments). During this time, Baca taught himself to read and began studying and writing poetry. Encouraged by another inmate, Baca sent a poem to *Mother Jones* magazine and the poem was published. In 1979, Baca published his first collection of poems (while still in prison) *Immigrants in Our Own Land*, which took a hard look at prison life and the individual's courage to persevere in such conditions. In a mixed and varied verse, Baca's poems at times utilize long, proselike lines, then abruptly shift to short, staccato rhythms. His other poetry collections include *Swords of Darkness* (1981), *Black Mesa Poems* (1989), *In The Way of the Sun* (1997), *Set This Book on Fire* (1999), *C-Train (Dream Boy's Story), and Thirteen Mexicans*

(2002); the memoir *A Place to Stand: The Making of a Poet* (2002); the essay collection *Working in the Dark: Reflections of a Poet of the Barrio* (1992); and his latest work, the short story collection *The Importance of a Piece of Paper* (2002). "So Mexicans are Taking Jobs From Americans" was published in *Immigrants in Our Own Land.*

So Mexicans Are Taking Jobs From Americans   (1979)

O Yes? Do they come on horses
with rifles, and say,
                    Ese gringo,[1] gimmee your job?
And do you, gringo, take off your ring,
drop your wallet into a blanket   5
spread over the ground, and walk away?

I hear Mexicans are taking your jobs away.
Do they sneak into town at night,
and as you're walking home with a whore,
do they mug you, a knife at your throat,   10
saying, I want your job?

Even on TV, an asthmatic leader
crawls turtle heavy, leaning on an assistant,
and from a nest of wrinkles on his face,
a tongue paddles through flashing waves   15
of lightbulbs, of cameramen, rasping
"They're taking our jobs away."

Well, I've gone about trying to find them,
asking just where the hell are these fighters.

The rifles I hear sound in the night   20
are white farmers shooting blacks and browns
whose ribs I see jutting out
and starving children,
I see the poor marching for a little work,
I see small white farmers selling out   25
to clean-suited farmers living in New York,
who've never been on a farm,
don't know the look of a hoof or the smell
of a woman's body bending all day long in fields.

---

[1]Hey, whitey.

I see this, and I hear only a few people   30
got all the money in this world, the rest
count their pennies to buy bread and butter.

Below that cool green sea of money,
millions and millions of people fight to live,
search for pearls in the darkest depths   35
of their dreams, hold their breath for years
trying to cross poverty to just having something.
The children are dead already. We are killing them,
that is what America should be saying;
on TV, in the streets, in offices, should be saying,   40
    "We aren't giving the children a chance to live."

Mexicans are taking our jobs, they say instead.
What they really say is, let them die,
and the children too.

Study and Discussion Questions

1. To whom is the poem addressed; who is Baca's imagined reader? How
    does Baca's portrait of the reader and the reader's culture make you feel?
2. How would you characterize Baca's tone in this poem? Does the tone
    change as the poem goes on?
3. How, according to the poem, do Americans characterize Mexicans? What
    emotions motivate these characterizations?
4. What, instead, does Baca say is the true picture of these Mexicans?
5. What does the situation Baca writes about in this poem have to do with
    money and social class? Give examples from the poem of behavior moti-
    vated by people wanting to hold on to their money or property and of
    people wanting to make a living.
6. The starving children appear in the middle of the poem and their image
    dominates by the poem's end. How does this image change the argument
    and the tone of the poem? Do you find it effective?

Suggestions for Writing

1. Analyze the extended image in the five-line stanza that begins, "Below
    that cool green sea of money."
2. Take a position on immigration into the United States. You might look
    up statistics on immigration patterns over the past hundred years. Does
    immigration help, hurt, or have little effect on the quality of life and the
    availability of work for most Americans? Has the rise of the global econ-
    omy over the past twenty or so years changed the immigration issue in
    any significant way? Baca's poem raises ethical as well as economic con-
    cerns; how in fact do we respond to the world's starving children?

GWENDOLYN BROOKS (1917–2000)

Gwendolyn Brooks grew up in Chicago. She began writing poetry at an early age, publishing her first poem at age thirteen. After receiving her BA in English from Wilson Junior College in 1936, Brooks worked for the NAACP Youth Council. During this time, Brooks was greatly influenced by poet Langston Hughes and other writers from the Harlem Renaissance who encouraged her to study the modernist poetry of Eliot and Pound. As is evident in much of her early work, Brooks combines the technical skill and form of modernist poetry with the imagery and rhythms of African American life and language. In 1950, she became the first African American to win the Pulitzer Prize for her poetry collection *Annie Allen* (1950). In 1967, Brook's visit to Fisk University was a transformative moment for her as a poet and African American. Impressed by the energy of young black poets like Leroi Jones, Brooks' penchant for formal structures (she was a master of the sonnet) and themes loosened. While her devotion to the African American experience remained, her poetry increasingly became more political, more contentious, as she became aware of her role as a black feminist in the Civil Rights Movement. In 1985, she was appointed poetry consultant to the Library of Congress (Poet Laureate). She has written several poetry collections, including *A Street in Bronzeville* (1945), *Annie Allen* (1950), *The Bean Eaters* (1960), *In the Mecca* (1968), *Beckonings* (1975), *Black Love* (1982), and *In Montgomery* (2001, posthumously); the novel *Maud Martha* (1953); and the autobiography *Report from Part One* (1972). "Bronzeville Woman in a Red Hat" appeared in Brooks's collection *The Bean Eaters.*

Bronzeville[1] Woman in a Red Hat   (1960)

hires out to Mrs. Miles

I

They had never had one in the house before.
     The strangeness of it all. Like unleashing
A lion, really. Poised
To pounce. A puma. A panther. A black
Bear.   5
There it stood in the door,
Under a red hat that was rash, but refreshing—
In a tasteless way, of course—across the dull dare,
The semi-assault of that extraordinary blackness.
The slackness   10
Of that light pink mouth told little. The eyes told of heavy care . . .

---

[1]African American neighborhood in Chicago.

But that was neither here nor there,
And nothing to a wage-paying mistress as should
Be getting her due whether life had been good
For her slave, or bad.   15
There it stood
in the door. They had never had
One in the house before.

But the Irishwoman had left!
A message had come.   20
Something about a murder at home.
A daughter's husband—"berserk," that was the phrase:
The dear man had "gone berserk"
And short work—
With a hammer—had been made   25
Of this daughter and her nights and days.
The Irishwoman (underpaid,
Mrs. Miles remembered with smiles),
Who was a perfect jewel, a red-faced trump,
A good old sort, a baker   30
Of rum cake, a maker
Of Mustard, would never return.
Mrs. Miles had begged the bewitched woman
To finish, at least, the biscuit blending,
To tarry till the curry was done,   35
To show some concern
For the burning soup, to attend to the tending
Of the tossed salad. "Inhuman,"
Pasty Houlihan had called Mrs. Miles.
"Inhuman." And "a fool."   40
And "a cool
One."

The Alert Agency had leafed through its files—
On short notice could offer
Only this dusky duffer   45
That now made its way to her kitchen and sat on her kitchen stool.

II

Her creamy child kissed by the black maid! square on the mouth!
World yelled, world writhed, world turned to light and rolled
Into her kitchen, nearly knocked her down.

Quotations, of course, from baby books were great   50
Ready armor; (but her animal distress
Wore, too and under, a subtler metal dress,
Inheritance of approximately hate).
Say baby shrieked to see his finger bleed,
Wished human humoring—there was a kind   55
Of unintimate love, a love more of the mind
To order the nebulousness of that need.
—This was the way to put it, this the relief.
This sprayed a honey upon marvelous grime.
This told it possible to postpone the reef.   60
Fashioned a huggable darling out of crime.
Made monster personable in personal sight
By cracking mirrors down the personal night.

Disgust crawled through her as she chased the theme.
She, quite supposing purity despoiled,   65
Committed to sourness, disordered, soiled,
Went in to pry the ordure from the cream.
Cooing, "Come." (Come out of the cannibal wilderness,
Dirt, dark, into the sun and bloomful air.
Return to freshness of your right world, wear   70
Sweetness again. Be done with beast, duress.)

Child with continuing cling issued his No in final fire,
                Kissed back the colored maid,
                Not wise enough to freeze or be afraid.
                Conscious of kindness, easy creature bond.   75
                Love had been handy and rapid to respond.

Heat at the hairline, heat between the bowels,
Examining seeming coarse unnatural scene,
She saw all things except herself serene:
Child, big black woman, pretty kitchen towels.   80

Study and Discussion Questions

1. Who is the speaker of this poem?
2. How is the Bronzeville woman described in part I? What is she compared to?
3. Why does Mrs. Miles refer to her as "it"?
4. What does the stanza about her previous domestic worker, the Irish woman, tell us about Mrs. Miles?
5. What is the crisis described in part II? Why is it a crisis for Mrs. Miles?

Suggestions for Writing

1. Gwendolyn Brooks, who is black, has created a white upper-middle-class persona, Mrs. Miles, through whose eyes we see the black woman who comes to work for her. How does this situation create intentional irony in the poem?
2. Are there any places where human sympathy and identification begin to break through the wall of Mrs. Miles's racism? What does she do when that happens?
3. What does Mrs. Miles's racism consist of? Give examples.

LANGSTON HUGHES (1902–1967)

Langston Hughes was born in Joplin, Missouri and raised primarily by his maternal grandmother in Lawrence, Kansas. He entered Columbia University in 1920, but left a year later, working odd jobs and traveling throughout Europe and Africa. During this time Hughes would publish his first poems and novels and establish himself as a central figure in the literary and artistic movement known as the Harlem Renaissance. Influenced by such writers as W.E.B. Dubois and the poet Walt Whitman, Hughes' work often expresses subtle political meaning in a style influenced by the rhythms of African American music (the blues) and language. Intentionally eschewing traditional poetic form, his poetry aspired to reach ordinary people, both black and white, by writing in an accessible way that spoke to and acknowledged their experiences. For this he became know as a "the bard of Harlem." His works include the poetry collections *The Weary Blues* (1926), *Fine Clothes to the Jew* (1927), *The Dream Keeper and Other Poems* (1932), *Freedom's Plow* (1943), *Fields of Wonder* (1947), *Montage of a Dream Deferred* (1951), *Ask Your Mama: Twelve Moods for Jazz* (1961) and *The Panther and the Lash* (1967); the novels *Not Without Laughter* (1930) and *Tambourines of Glory* (1958); the short story collections *The Ways of White Folks* (1934), *Simple Speaks His Mind* (1950), *Simple Takes a Wife* (1953) and *Something in Common and Other Stories* (1963); and the autobiography *I Wonder as I Wander* (1956). Hughes also published essays and children's books. "Ballad of the Landlord" comes from his book-length sequence *Montage of a Dream Deferred*, set in post World War II Harlem.

Ballad of the Landlord   (1951)

Landlord, landlord,
My roof has sprung a leak.
Don't you 'member I told you about it
Way last week?

Landlord, landlord,   5
These steps is broken down.
When you come up yourself
It's a wonder you don't fall down.

Ten Bucks you say I owe you?
Ten Bucks you say is due?   10
Well, that's Ten Bucks more'n I'll pay you
Till you fix this house up new.

What? You gonna get eviction orders?
You gonna cut off my heat?
You gonna take my furniture and   15
Throw it in the street?

Um-huh! You talking high and mighty.
Talk on—till you get through.
You ain't gonna be able to say a word
If I land my fist on you.   20

Police! Police!
Come and get this man!
He's trying to ruin the government
And overturn the land!

Copper's whistle!   25
Patrol bell!
Arrest.

Precinct Station.
Iron cell.
Headlines in press: 30

MAN THREATENS LANDLORD
          •
       •   •
TENANT HELD NO BAIL
          •
       •   •

JUDGE GIVES NEGRO 90 DAYS IN COUNTY JAIL

Study and Discussion Questions

1. Who is speaking in the first five stanzas? Who is speaking in stanza six?
2. Describe what is happening in the last 10 lines of the poem.

3. Why does Hughes call this poem a "ballad"? Look up the word, consider its form and themes, and discuss how this might be a ballad.
4. What happens in the opening five stanzas? What we hear is a monologue, yet we get the sense of a drama. How does Hughes accomplish this?
5. Make an outline of the events described in the poem from the opening stanza to the final line. How do events escalate?
6. What do race and social class have to do with the dynamics and the outcome of this ballad/story?

❀ ❀ ❀

PHILIP LEVINE (b. 1928)

Philip Levine was born the son of Russian-Jewish immigrants in Detroit, Michigan, and grew up in the industrial world of the auto factories. From the time he was 14 and on through his twenties, Levine worked on the assembly lines as he made his way through college. It was during this time that he began reading poetry and aspired to give a poetic voice to the blue-collar experience. In 1957, he received his M.F.A. from the University of Iowa and began a teaching career. Six years later he published his first volume of poetry *On the Edge* and has since published over 20 collections in 4 decades. Levine has forged his own style of free-verse poetry—a sometimes imaged, sometimes narrative poetry that attempts to tell the stories of working people and to render this experience in a vernacular that is both accessible and vivid. He was awarded the Pulitzer Prize for *The Simple Truth* in 1994. Other notable poetry collections include *Not This Pig* (1968), *5 Detroits* (1970), *They Feed They Lion* (1972), *7 Years From Somewhere* (1979), *Sweet Will* (1985), *A Walk With Tom Jefferson* (1988), *What Work Is* (1991, winner National Book Award), *Mercy* (2001), and his latest collection *Breath* (2004). He has also written a memoir, *The Bread of Time* (2001), and a nonfiction collection, *So Ask: Essays, Conversations, and Interviews* (2002).

You Can Have It   (1979)

My brother comes home from work
and climbs the stairs to our room.
I can hear the bed groan and his shoes drop
one by one. You can have it, he says.

The moonlight streams in the window   5
and his unshaven face is whitened

like the face of the moon. He will sleep
long after noon and waken to find me gone.

Thirty years will pass before I remember
that moment when suddenly I knew each man   10
has one brother who dies when he sleeps
and sleeps when he rises to face this life,

and that together they are only one man
sharing a heart that always labors, hands
yellowed and cracked, a mouth that gasps   15
for breath and asks, Am I gonna make it?

All night at the ice plant he had fed
the chute its silvery blocks, and then I
stacked cases of orange soda for the children
of Kentucky, one gray boxcar at a time   20

with always two more waiting. We were twenty
for such a short time and always in
the wrong clothes, crusted with dirt
and sweat. I think now we were never twenty.

In 1948 in the city of Detroit, founded   25
by de la Mothe Cadillac for the distant purposes
of Henry Ford, no one wakened or died,
no one walked the streets or stoked a furnace,

for there was no such year, and now
that year has fallen off all the old newspapers,   30
calendars, doctors' appointments, bonds,
wedding certificates, drivers licenses.

The city slept. The snow turned to ice.
The ice to standing pools or rivers
racing in the gutters. Then bright grass rose   35
between the thousands of cracked squares,

and that grass died. I give you back 1948.
I give you all the years from then
to the coming one. Give me back the moon
with its frail light falling across a face.   40

Give me back my young brother, hard
and furious, with wide shoulders and a curse

for God and burning eyes that look upon
all creation and say, You can have it.

Study and Discussion Questions

1. "You Can Have It" begins with a portrait of the speaker's brother. What do we learn about the brother in the first half of the poem?
2. Discuss the images of moon and water in the poem.
3. What is the work situation of the two brothers? How is that important to the tension between duality and identity in the poem? And, by the way, Philip Levine actually has a twin brother.
4. Discuss stanzas three and four where the poem metamorphoses from biography into philosophy. What is Levine saying here? And what is the effect of his using a working-class situation as the basis of this philosophical statement?
5. Why 1948? Why does Levine say, in stanza eight, that "there was no such year as 1948"?
6. Discuss Levine's images in stanzas seven to the end of the poem.
7. The poem ends as it began (in the title) with the words "You can have it." What does this sentence mean to you by the time you've reached the end of the poem?
8. What is Levine's attitude toward memory in this poem?
9. How does Levine use sound in "You Can Have It"? Look at any one stanza closely, read it aloud, and listen for sound patterns.

Suggestions for Writing

1. Choose a passage from the poem that you especially liked and discuss the images and word choices. Look up any words that you don't know, or that seem important, to check for fuller definitions.
2. Write a poem or a prose paragraph vividly capturing a memory at least 10 years in your past.

MARY FELL (b. 1947)

Mary Fell was born to working-class parents in Worcester, Massachusetts. In 1964, she enrolled at Worcester State College as an English major. It is here that Fell began writing poetry amidst the volatile political movements of the 1960s. After graduating, Fell did social work for the City of Worcester until returning to school to obtain her M.F.A. at the University of Massachusetts Amherst in 1981. She currently teaches at Indiana University. Much of Fell's work centers on how our lives relate to the human experiences of others. Fell's poetry endeavors to present working-class experience in very real, unsentimental ways through earthy, precise imagery. Her poetry collections include *Triangle Fire*

(1983), *The Persistence of Memory* (1984), and *Worcester in Sunlight and Darkness* (1991). "Triangle Fire" is a sequence of poems that revisit the tragic 1911 factory fire that took the lives of 146 immigrant women workers.

The Triangle Fire[1]

(1983)

1. Havdallah[2]

This is the great divide
by which God split
the world:
on the Sabbath side
he granted rest,   5
eternal toiling
on the workday side.

But even one
revolution of the world
is an empty promise   10
where bosses
where bills to pay
respect no heavenly bargains.
Until each day is ours

let us pour   15
darkness in a dish
and set it on fire,
bless those who labor
as we pray, praise God
his holy name,   20
strike for the rest.

2. Among the Dead

First a lace of smoke
decorated the air of the workroom,
the far wall unfolded
into fire. The elevator shaft   25
spun out flames like a bobbin,
the last car sank.

---

[1]On March 25, 1911, a fire started at the Triangle Shirtwaist Company, on the ninth floor of the Asch building. Hundreds of women workers, mostly Italian and Russian Jewish immigrants, had been locked in to keep out union organizers and therefore could not escape. Nearly one hundred fifty women, some as young as fourteen, died in the fire.
[2]Ceremony marking the end of the Jewish Sabbath.

I leaped for the cable,
my only chance. Woven steel
burned my hands as I wound   30
to the bottom.

I opened my eyes. I was lying
in the street. Water and blood
washed the cobbles, the sky
rained ash. A pair of shoes   35
lay beside me, in them
two blistered feet.
I saw the weave in the fabric
of a girl's good coat,
the wilted nosegay pinned to her collar.   40
Not flowers, what I breathed then,
awake among the dead.

3. Asch Building

In a window,
lovers embrace
haloed by light.   45
He kisses her, holds her
gently, lets her go
nine stories to the street.

Even the small ones
put on weight   50
as they fall:
eleven thousand pounds split
the fireman's net,
implode the deadlights

on the Greene Street side,   55
until the basement catches them
and holds. Here
two faceless ones are found
folded neatly over the steam pipes
like dropped rags.   60

I like the one
on that smoky ledge, taking stock
in the sky's deliberate mirror.
She gives her hat

to wind, noting its style,   65
spills her week's pay

from its envelope, a joke
on those who pretend
heaven provides, and chooses
where there is no choice   70
to marry air, to make
a disposition of her life.

4. Personal Effects
One lady's
handbag, containing
rosary beads, elevated   75
railroad ticket, small pin
with picture, pocket knife,
one small purse containing
$1.68 in cash,
handkerchiefs,   80
a small mirror, a pair of gloves,
two thimbles, a Spanish
comb, one yellow metal ring,
five keys, one
fancy glove button,   85
one lady's handbag containing
one gent's watch case
number of movement 6418593
and a $1 bill,
one half dozen postal cards,   90
a buttonhook, a man's photo,
a man's garter,
a razor strap,
one portion of limb and hair
of human being.   95

5. Industrialist's Dream
This one's
dependable won't
fall apart
under pressure doesn't
lie down on the job   100
doesn't leave early
come late

won't join unions
strike
ask for a raise   105
unlike one hundred
forty six
others I could name
who couldn't
take the heat this one's   110
still at her machine
and doubtless
of spotless moral
character you
can tell by the bones   115
pure white
this one
does what she's told
and you don't hear
her complaining.   120

6. The Witness

Woman, I might have watched you
sashay down Washington Street
some warm spring evening
when work let out,
your one thin dress   125
finally right for the weather,
an ankle pretty
as any flower's stem, full
breasts the moon's envy, eyes bold
or modest as you passed me by.   130

I might have thought, as heat
climbed from the pavement,
what soft work you'd make
for a man like me:
even the time clock, thief of hours,   135
kinder, and the long day
passing in a dream.
Cradled in that dream
I might have slept
forever, but today's nightmare   140
vision woke me:
your arms aflame, wings
of fire, and you a falling star,
a terrible lump of coal

in the burning street.   145
No dream, your hair of smoke,
your blackened face.
No dream the fist I make,
taking your hand
of ashes in my own.   150

7. Cortege

A cold rain comforts the sky.
Everything ash-colored under clouds.
I take my place in the crowd,

move without will as the procession moves,
a gray wave breaking against the street.   155
Up ahead, one hundred and forty seven

coffins float, wreckage of lives. I follow
the box without a name. In it
whose hand encloses whose heart? Whose mouth

presses the air toward a scream?   160
She is no one, the one I claim
as sister. When the familiar is tagged

and taken away, she remains.
I do not mourn her. I mourn no one.
I do not praise her. No one   165

is left to praise. Seventy years after
her death, I walk in March rain behind her.
She travels before me into the dark.

Study and Discussion Questions

1. "The Triangle Fire" is a poetic sequence of seven connected poems. Let's look first at the poems one by one. To understand the first poem, "Havdallah," you need to know that havdallah is from a word meaning "to separate." It is the ritual at the end of the Jewish Sabbath to mark the separation of the Sabbath from the days of work. A special candle, made out of three separate candles, is lighted at the moment you see three stars in the sky on Saturday evening. How does understanding this ritual help you decode the imagery of this opening poem in the sequence?
2. Given the meaning of "havdallah," how does the poem become ironic in stanza two?
3. In stanza three of "Havdallah," how does the speaker of the poem suggest how the secular and the sacred in our lives are separate but intertwined?

4. Read the footnote and any other research you've done about the Triangle Shirtwaist Company Fire in 1911. Poem 2, "Among the Dead," takes us into that event. Who is speaking here? What happens in this poem?

5. Poem 3, "Asch Building," is based on eyewitness accounts of workers trapped on the eighth and ninth floors who had to make the decision to jump or burn. (Think for a moment about having to make that decision.) List the separate stories in "Asch Building" about some of these people.

6. Discuss the irony in the story told in the last two stanzas of "Asch Building." How does it connect to the irony in "Havdallah"?

7. Who is speaking in "Asch Building"?

8. Poem 4, "Personal Effects," is in a new style. Describe how it differs from the first three poems. How is this style effective at this point in the poem?

9. Who is speaking in poem 5, "Industrialist's Dream"? What point of view is being represented here? Discuss the irony in the extended visual image of "this one."

10. Poem 6, "The Witness," shifts point of view again. Who is speaking here? Who is he speaking to?

11. Does the witness in poem 6 develop or change during the poem? What is his attitude toward the woman at the beginning? How does it change? Discuss the last three lines of the poem.

12. In the seventh and final poem of the sequence, "Cortege," the point of view shifts again. (Look up *cortege* in a dictionary.) Look at the last three lines of the poem. Who do you think is speaking here?

13. "She is no one, the one I claim/as sister." What is the speaker's relation to this woman and all the rest who died that day? The Triangle Fire is from Mary Fell's collection titled *The Persistence of Memory*. What does memory have to do with this poem?

Suggestions for Writing

1. Write a paper about how the seven poems in this poetic sequence work off of each other and work together. What does each of the poems provide for us as readers? How do our understanding of and feelings about this workers' tragedy develop through the seven poems? What is Fell doing through the style and structure of her sequence to make this happen?

2. Research the Triangle Shirtwaist Company Fire of March 25, 1911: the fire itself, the events leading up to it, and the political and social aftermath. Make a poster, a visual and graphic representation, that illuminates the event and provides context for Mary Fell's poetic sequence.

3. How is Fell's "The Triangle Fire" a poem of witness? Look up the several meanings of "witness" in the dictionary. In addition, what does the word "witness" suggest to you? Why might contemporary working-class poets write some 70 years later about an historical event like this one?

4. Lest you think that what happened to the workers at the Triangle Shirtwaist Company in 1911 could not happen today, do some research on current conditions in sweatshops and factories around the world and in the United States—places where a lot of the clothes we wear and the toys we played with as children or buy for our own children are made.

❋ ❋ ❋

Peace and War

Courtesy of the Estate of Pablo Picasso/Artists Rights Society (ARS), New York

FICTION

RAY BRADBURY (b. 1920)

Born in Waukegan, Illinois, Ray Bradbury grew up reading the "pulp" fiction of his era and began writing at an early age. During high school, his family moved to Los Angeles, where he further worked on his writing, publishing his first story in 1938 at the age of 18. He would begin his reputation as an author writing science fiction and fantasy stories for the same pulp magazines he read growing up. The publication of *The Martian Chronicles* in 1950 brought him new literary fame. While he is usually thought of as a science fiction writer, Bradbury's work cannot be classified into one genre. Often allegorical in nature, much of Bradbury's work serves as a warning to humanity about the ills and moral deprivations that may come from technological advance. He has published novels, essays, poetry, screenplays, and plays, including the novels *Fahrenheit 451* (1953, which was made into a film), *Dandelion Wine* (1957), and *Something Wicked This Way Comes* (1962); and the story collections *The Illustrated Man* (1951) and *I Sing The Body Electric* (1969). His most recent work is *One For the Road: A New Story Collection* (2002). "August 2026: There Will Come Soft Rains" is a story from *The Martian Chronicles*.

August 2026: There Will Come Soft Rains (1950)

In the living room the voice-clock sang, *Tick-tock, seven o'clock, time to get up, time to get up, seven o'clock!* as if it were afraid that nobody would. The morning house lay empty. The clock ticked on, repeating and repeating its sounds into the emptiness. *Seven-nine, breakfast time, seven-nine!*

In the kitchen the breakfast stove gave a hissing sigh and ejected from its warm interior eight pieces of perfectly browned toast, eight eggs sunnyside up, sixteen slices of bacon, two coffees, and two cool glasses of milk.

"Today is August 4, 2026," said a second voice from the kitchen ceiling, "in the city of Allendale, California." It repeated the date three times for memory's sake. "Today is Mr. Featherstone's birthday. Today is the anniversary of Tilita's marriage. Insurance is payable, as are the water, gas, and light bills."

Somewhere in the walls, relays clicked, memory tapes glided under electric eyes.

Eight-one, tick-tock, eight-one o'clock, off to school, off to work, run, run, eight-one! But no doors slammed, no carpets took the soft tread of rubber heels. It was raining outside. The weather box on the front door sang quietly: "Rain, rain, go away; rubbers, raincoats for today . . ." And the rain tapped on the empty house, echoing.

Outside, the garage chimed and lifted its door to reveal the waiting car. After a long wait the door swung down again.

At eight-thirty the eggs were shriveled and the toast was like stone. An aluminum wedge scraped them into the sink, where hot water whirled them down a metal throat which digested and flushed them away to the distant sea. The dirty dishes were dropped into a hot washer and emerged twinkling dry.

Nine-fifteen, sang the clock, *time to clean.*

Out of warrens in the wall, tiny robot mice darted. The rooms were acrawl with the small cleaning animals, all rubber and metal. They thudded against chairs, whirling their mustached runners, kneading the rug nap, sucking gently at hidden dust. Then, like mysterious invaders, they popped into their burrows. Their pink electric eyes faded. The house was clean.

Ten o'clock. The sun came out from behind the rain. The house stood alone in a city of rubble and ashes. This was the one house left standing. At night the ruined city gave off a radioactive glow which could be seen for miles.

Ten-fifteen. The garden sprinklers whirled up in golden founts, filling the soft morning air with scatterings of brightness. The water pelted window-panes, running down the charred west side where the house had been burned evenly free of its white paint. The entire west face of the house was black, save for five places. Here the silhouette in paint of a man mowing a lawn. Here, as in a photograph, a woman bent to pick flowers. Still farther over, their images burned on wood in one titanic instant, a small boy, hands flung into the air; higher up, the image of a thrown ball, and opposite him a girl, hands raised to catch a ball which never came down.

The five spots of paint—the man, the woman, the children, the ball—remained. The rest was a thin charcoaled layer.

The gentle sprinkler rain filled the garden with falling light.

Until this day, how well the house had kept its peace. How carefully it had inquired, "Who goes there? What's the password?" and, getting no answer from lonely foxes and whining cats, it had shut up its windows and drawn shades in an old-maidenly preoccupation with self-protection which bordered on a mechanical paranoia.

It quivered at each sound, the house did. If a sparrow brushed a window, the shade snapped up. The bird, startled, flew off! No, not even a bird must touch the house!

The house was an altar with ten thousand attendants, big, small, servicing, attending, in choirs. But the gods had gone away, and the ritual of the religion continued senselessly, uselessly.

Twelve noon.

A dog whined, shivering, on the front porch.

The front door recognized the dog voice and opened. The dog, once huge and fleshy, but now gone to bone and covered with sores, moved in and through the house, tracking mud. Behind it whirred angry mice, angry at having to pick up mud, angry at inconvenience.

For not a leaf fragment blew under the door but what the wall panels flipped open and the copper scrap rats flashed swiftly out. The offending dust, hair, or paper, seized in miniature steel jaws, was raced back to the burrows. There, down tubes which fed into the cellar, it was dropped into the sighing vent of an incinerator which sat like evil Baal in a dark corner.

The dog ran upstairs, hysterically yelping to each door, at last realizing, as the house realized, that only silence was here.

It sniffed the air and scratched the kitchen door. Behind the door, the stove was making pancakes which filled the house with a rich baked odor and the scent of maple syrup.

The dog frothed at the mouth, lying at the door, sniffing, its eyes turned to fire. It ran wildly in circles, biting at its tail, spun in a frenzy, and died. It lay in the parlor for an hour.

Two o'clock, sang a voice.

Delicately sensing decay at last, the regiments of mice hummed out as softly as blown gray leaves in an electrical wind.

Two-fifteen.

The dog was gone.

In the cellar, the incinerator glowed suddenly and a whirl of sparks leaped up the chimney.

Two thirty-five.

Bridge tables sprouted from patio walls. Playing cards fluttered onto pads in a shower of pips. Martinis manifested on an oaken bench with egg-salad sandwiches. Music played.

But the tables were silent and the cards untouched.

At four o'clock the tables folded like great butterflies back through the paneled walls.

Four-thirty.

The nursery walls glowed.

Animals took shape: yellow giraffes, blue lions, pink antelopes, lilac panthers cavorting in crystal substance. The walls were glass. They looked out upon color and fantasy. Hidden films clocked through well-oiled sprockets, and the walls lived. The nursery floor was woven to resemble a crisp, cereal meadow. Over this ran aluminum roaches and iron crickets, and in the hot still air butterflies of delicate red tissue wavered among the sharp aroma of animal spoors! There was the sound like a great matted yellow hive of bees within a dark bellows, the lazy bumble of a purring lion. And there was the patter of okapi feet and the murmur of a fresh jungle rain, like other hoofs, falling upon the summer-starched grass. Now the walls dissolved into distances of parched weed, mile on mile, and warm endless sky. The animals drew away into thorn brakes and water holes.

It was the children's hour.

Five o'clock. The bath filled with clear hot water.

Six, seven, eight o'clock. The dinner dishes manipulated like magic tricks, and in the study a click. In the metal stand opposite the hearth where a fire now blazed up warmly, a cigar popped out, half an inch of soft gray ash on it, smoking, waiting.

Nine o'clock. The beds warmed their hidden circuits, for nights were cool here.

Nine-five. A voice spoke from the study ceiling:

"Mrs. McClellan, which poem would you like this evening?"

The house was silent.

The voice said at last, "Since you express no preference, I shall select a poem at random." Quiet music rose to back the voice. "Sara Teasdale.[1] As I recall, your favorite. . . .

"There will come soft rains and the smell of the ground,
And swallows circling with their shimmering sound;

And frogs in the pools singing at night,
And wild plum trees in tremulous white;

Robins will wear their feathery fire,
Whistling their whims on a low fence-wire;

And not one will know of the war, not one
Will care at last when it is done.

Not one would mind, neither bird nor tree,
If mankind perished utterly;

And Spring herself, when she woke at dawn
Would scarcely know that we were gone."

The fire burned on the stone hearth and the cigar fell away into a mound of quiet ash on its tray. The empty chairs faced each other between the silent walls, and the music played.

At ten o'clock the house began to die.

The wind blew. A falling tree bough crashed through the kitchen window. Cleaning solvent, bottled, shattered over the stove. The room was ablaze in an instant!

"Fire!" screamed a voice. The house lights flashed, water pumps shot water from the ceilings. But the solvent spread on the linoleum, licking, eating, under the kitchen door, while the voices took it up in chorus: "Fire, fire, fire!"

The house tried to save itself. Doors sprang tightly shut, but the windows were broken by the heat and the wind blew and sucked upon the fire.

The house gave ground as the fire in ten billion angry sparks moved with flaming ease from room to room and then up the stairs. While scurrying water

---

[1]American poet (1884–1933).

rats squeaked from the walls, pistoled their water, and ran for more. And the wall sprays let down showers of mechanical rain.

But too late. Somewhere, sighing, a pump shrugged to a stop. The quenching rain ceased. The reserve water supply which had filled baths and washed dishes for many quiet days was gone.

The fire crackled up the stairs. It fed upon Picassos and Matisses in the upper halls, like delicacies, baking off the oily flesh, tenderly crisping the canvases into black shavings.

Now the fire lay in beds, stood in windows, changed the colors of drapes!

And then, reinforcements.

From attic trapdoors, blind robot faces peered down with faucet mouths gushing green chemical.

The fire backed off, as even an elephant must at the sight of a dead snake. Now there were twenty snakes whipping over the floor, killing the fire with a clear cold venom of green froth.

But the fire was clever. It had sent flame outside the house, up through the attic to the pumps there. An explosion! The attic brain which directed the pumps was shattered into bronze shrapnel on the beams.

The fire rushed back into every closet and felt of the clothes hung there.

The house shuddered, oak bone on bone, its bared skeleton cringing from the heat, its wire, its nerves revealed as if a surgeon had torn the skin off to let the red veins and capillaries quiver in the scalded air. Help, help! Fire! Run, run! Heat snapped mirrors like the first brittle winter ice. And the voices wailed Fire, fire, run, run, like a tragic nursery rhyme, a dozen voices, high, low, like children dying in a forest, alone, alone. And the voices fading as the wires popped their sheatings like hot chestnuts. One, two, three, four, five voices died.

In the nursery the jungle burned. Blue lions roared, purple giraffes bounded off. The panthers ran in circles, changing color, and ten million animals, running before the fire, vanished off toward a distant steaming river. . . .

Ten more voices died. In the last instant under the fire avalanche, other choruses, oblivious, could be heard announcing the time, playing music, cutting the lawn by remote-control mower, or setting an umbrella frantically out and in the slamming and opening front door, a thousand things happening, like a clock shop when each clock strikes the hour insanely before or after the other, a scene of maniac confusion, yet unity; singing, screaming, a few last cleaning mice darting bravely out to carry the horrid ashes away! And one voice, with sublime disregard for the situation, read poetry aloud in the fiery study, until all the film spools burned, until all the wires withered and the circuits cracked.

The fire burst the house and let it slam flat down, puffing out skirts of spark and smoke.

In the kitchen, an instant before the rain of fire and timber, the stove could be seen making breakfasts at a psychopathic rate, ten dozen eggs, six loaves of toast, twenty dozen bacon strips, which, eaten by fire, started the stove working again, hysterically hissing!

The crash. The attic smashing into kitchen and parlor. The parlor into cellar, cellar into sub-cellar. Deep freeze, armchair, film tapes, circuits, beds, and all like skeletons thrown in a cluttered mound deep under.

Smoke and silence. A great quantity of smoke.

Dawn showed faintly in the east. Among the ruins, one wall stood alone. Within the wall, a last voice said, over and over again and again, even as the sun rose to shine upon the heaped rubble and steam:

"Today is August 5, 2026, today is August 5, 2026, today is. . . ."

Study and Discussion Questions

1. Think about the Sara Teasdale poem that gives the story its title. How does it apply to the situation the story narrates?
2. Who is the main character of this story?
3. Summarize the story's plot. What does Bradbury use to move you from one event to the next?
4. Though there are no actual human beings in this story, list some of the traces or evidence of people.
5. What can this house do? What can't it do?
6. What is the mood or atmosphere of "August 2026: There Will Come Soft Rains"? What words and images create this mood?
7. Discuss the significance and the use of time in this story.

Suggestions for Writing

1. This is a rare example of a story without any human beings in it. How is that absence necessary to the meaning of this story?
2. Bradbury writes, "The house was an altar with ten thousand attendants, big, small, servicing, attending, in choirs. But the gods had gone away, and the ritual of the religion continued senselessly, uselessly." Discuss this passage as a comment on our current relation to science and technology.

AMBROSE BIERCE (1842–1914?)

Born in rural Meigs County, Ohio, Ambrose Bierce grew up working on the family farm. Despite not having any formal education, his father's library exposed him to a wide range of books. At 19, he joined the Union Army at the beginning of the Civil War and served four years. The experience of war would make a deep imprint on his view of the world. When the war ended, Bierce went to San Francisco and began to forge his reputation as "The Wickedest Man in San Francisco"—a title earned for his scathing and often misanthropic satires of people and human nature. His fiction carries a similar tone, cynical and full of dark humor. Following in the American gothic tradition of Edgar Allen Poe, Bierce's stories hover between reality and the supernatural where characters are faced with morbid twists of fate, vengeful ghosts, and irrationality. In 1913 he went to Mexico to cover the Mexican Civil War and disappeared; his death remains a mystery. Selected works include *Tales of Soldiers and Civilians* (1891), *Can Such Things Be?* (1893), *Fantastic Fables* (1899), and *The Cynic's Word Book* (1906), later retitled *The Devils Dictionary* (1911). "An Occurrence at Owl Creek Bridge," first published in *Tales of Soldiers and Civilians*, is one of Bierce's most famous stories.

An Occurrence at Owl Creek Bridge   (1892)

I

A man stood upon a railroad bridge in northern Alabama, looking down into the swift water twenty feet below. The man's hands were behind his back, the wrists bound with a cord. A rope closely encircled his neck. It was attached to a stout cross-timber above his head and the slack fell to the level of his knees. Some loose boards laid upon the sleepers supporting the metals of the railway supplied a footing for him and his executioners—two private soldiers of the Federal army, directed by a sergeant who in civil life may have been a deputy sheriff. At a short remove upon the same temporary platform was an officer in the uniform of his rank, armed. He was a captain. A sentinel at each end of the bridge stood with his rifle in the position known as "support," that is to say, vertical in front of the left shoulder, the hammer resting on the forearm thrown straight across the chest—a formal and unnatural position, enforcing an erect carriage of the body. It did not appear to be the duty of these two men to know what was occurring at the centre of the bridge; they merely blockaded the two ends of the foot planking that traversed it.

Beyond one of the sentinels nobody was in sight; the railroad ran straight away into a forest for a hundred yards, then, curving, was lost to view. Doubtless there was an outpost farther along. The other bank of the stream was open ground—a gentle acclivity topped with a stockade of vertical tree trunks, loopholed for rifles, with a single embrasure through which protruded the muzzle of a brass cannon commanding the bridge. Midway of the slope between bridge and fort were the spectators—a single company of infantry in line, at "parade rest," the butts of the rifles on the ground, the barrels inclining slightly backward against the right shoulder, the hands crossed upon the stock. A lieutenant stood at the right of the line, the point of his sword upon the ground, his left hand resting upon his right. Excepting the group of four at the centre of the bridge, not a man moved. The company faced the bridge, staring stonily, motionless. The sentinels, facing the banks of the stream, might have been statues to adorn the bridge. The captain stood with folded arms, silent, observing the work of his subordinates, but making no sign. Death is a dignitary who when he comes announced is to be received with formal manifestations of respect, even by those most familiar with him. In the code of military etiquette silence and fixity are forms of deference.

The man who was engaged in being hanged was apparently about thirty-five years of age. He was a civilian, if one might judge from his habit, which was that of a planter. His features were good—a straight nose, firm mouth, broad forehead, from which his long, dark hair was combed straight back, falling behind his ears to the collar of his well-fitting frock-coat. He wore a mustache and pointed beard, but no whiskers; his eyes were large and dark gray, and had a kindly expression which one would hardly have expected in one whose neck was in the hemp. Evidently this was no vulgar assassin. The liberal military code makes provision for hanging many kinds of persons, and gentlemen are not excluded.

The preparations being complete, the two private soldiers stepped aside and each drew away the plank upon which he had been standing. The sergeant turned to the captain, saluted and placed himself immediately behind that officer, who in turn moved apart one pace. These movements left the condemned man and the sergeant standing on the two ends of the same plank, which spanned three of the cross-ties of the bridge. The end upon which the civilian stood almost, but not quite, reached a fourth. This plank had been held in place by the weight of the captain; it was now held by that of the sergeant. At a signal from the former the latter would step aside, the plank would tilt and the condemned man go down between two ties. The arrangement commended itself to his judgment as simple and effective. His face had not been covered nor his eyes bandaged. He looked a moment at his "unsteadfast footing," then let his gaze wander to the swirling water of the stream racing madly beneath his feet. A piece of dancing driftwood caught his attention and his eyes followed it down the current. How slowly it appeared to move! What a sluggish stream!

He closed his eyes in order to fix his last thoughts upon his wife and children. The water, touched to gold by the early sun, the brooding mists under the banks at some distance down the stream, the fort, the soldiers, the piece of drift—all had distracted him. And now he became conscious of a new disturbance. Striking through the thought of his dear ones was a sound which he could neither ignore nor understand, a sharp, distinct, metallic percussion like the stroke of a blacksmith's hammer upon the anvil; it had the same ringing quality. He wondered what it was, and whether immeasurably distant or near by—it seemed both. Its recurrence was regular, but as slow as the tolling of a death knell. He awaited each stroke with impatience and—he knew not why—apprehension. The intervals of silence grew progressively longer; the delays became maddening. With their greater infrequency the sounds increased in strength and sharpness. They hurt his ear like the thrust of a knife; he feared he would shriek. What he heard was the ticking of his watch.

He unclosed his eyes and saw again the water below him. "If I could free my hands," he thought, "I might throw off the noose and spring into the stream. By diving I could evade the bullets and, swimming vigorously, reach the bank, take to the woods and get away home. My home, thank God, is as yet outside their lines; my wife and little ones are still beyond the invader's farthest advance."

As these thoughts, which have here to be set down in words, were flashed into the doomed man's brain rather than evolved from it, the captain nodded to the sergeant. The sergeant stepped aside.

II

Peyton Farquhar was a well-to-do planter, of an old and highly respected Alabama family. Being a slave owner and like other slave owners a politician he was naturally an original secessionist and ardently devoted to the Southern cause. Circumstances of an imperious nature, which it is unnecessary to relate here, had prevented him from taking service with the gallant army that had fought the disastrous campaigns ending with the fall of Corinth, and he chafed under the inglorious restraint, longing for the release of his energies, the larger life of the soldier, the opportunity for distinction. That opportunity, he felt, would come, as it comes to all in war time. Meanwhile he did what he could. No service was too humble for him to perform in aid of the South, no adventure too perilous for him to undertake if consistent with the character of a civilian who was at heart a soldier, and who in good faith and without too much qualification assented to at least a part of the frankly villainous dictum that all is fair in love and war.

One evening while Farquhar and his wife were sitting on a rustic bench near the entrance to his grounds, a gray-clad soldier rode up to the gate and asked for a drink of water. Mrs. Farquhar was only too happy to serve him with her own white hands. While she was fetching the water her husband approached the dusty horseman and inquired eagerly for news from the front.

"The Yanks are repairing the railroads," said the man, "and are getting ready for another advance. They have reached the Owl Creek bridge, put it in order and built a stockade on the north bank. The commandant has issued an order, which is posted everywhere, declaring that any civilian caught interfering with the railroad, its bridges, tunnels or trains will be summarily hanged. I saw the order."

"How far is it to the Owl Creek bridge?" Farquhar asked.

"About thirty miles."

"Is there no force on this side the creek?"

"Only a picket post half a mile out, on the railroad, and a single sentinel at this end of the bridge."

"Suppose a man—a civilian and student of hanging—should elude the picket post and perhaps get the better of the sentinel," said Farquhar, smiling, "what could he accomplish?"

The soldier reflected. "I was there a month ago," he replied. "I observed that the flood of last winter had lodged a great quantity of driftwood against the wooden pier at this end of the bridge. It is now dry and would burn like tow."

The lady had now brought the water, which the soldier drank. He thanked her ceremoniously, bowed to her husband and rode away. An hour later, after nightfall, he repassed the plantation, going northward in the direction from which he had come. He was a Federal scout.

III

As Peyton Farquhar fell straight downward through the bridge he lost consciousness and was as one already dead. From this state he was awakened—ages later, it seemed to him—by the pain of a sharp pressure upon his throat, followed by a sense of suffocation. Keen, poignant agonies seemed to shoot from his neck downward through every fibre of his body and limbs. These pains appeared to flash along well-defined lines of ramification and to beat with an inconceivably rapid periodicity. They seemed like streams of pulsating fire heating him to an intolerable temperature. As to his head, he was conscious of nothing but a feeling of fullness—of congestion. These sensations were unaccompanied by thought. The intellectual part of his nature was already effaced; he had power only to feel, and feeling was torment. He was conscious of motion. Encompassed in a luminous cloud, of which he was now merely the fiery heart, without material substance, he swung through unthinkable arcs of oscillation, like a vast pendulum. Then all at once, with terrible suddenness, the light about him shot upward with the noise of a loud plash; a frightful roaring was in his ears, and all was cold and dark. The power of thought was restored; he knew that the rope had broken and he had fallen into the stream. There was no additional strangulation; the noose about his neck was already suffocating him and kept the water from his lungs. To die of hanging at the bottom of a river!—the idea seemed to him ludicrous. He opened his eyes in the darkness and saw above him a gleam of light, but how distant, how inaccessible! He was still sinking, for the light became fainter and fainter until it was a mere glimmer. Then it began to grow and brighten, and he knew that he was rising toward the surface—knew it with reluctance, for he was now very comfortable. "To be hanged and drowned," he thought, "that is not so bad; but I do not wish to be shot. No; I will not be shot; that is not fair."

He was not conscious of an effort, but a sharp pain in his wrist apprised him that he was trying to free his hands. He gave the struggle his attention, as an idler might observe the feat of a juggler, without interest in the outcome. What splendid effort!—what magnificent, what superhuman strength! Ah, that was a fine endeavor! Bravo! The cord fell away; his arms parted and floated upward, the hands dimly seen on each side in the growing light. He watched them with a new interest as first one and then the other pounced upon the noose at his neck. They tore it away and thrust it fiercely aside, its undulations resembling those of a water-snake. "Put it back, put it back!" He thought he shouted these words to his hands, for the undoing of the noose had been succeeded by the direst pang that he had yet experienced. His neck ached horribly; his brain was on fire; his heart, which had been fluttering faintly, gave a great leap, trying to force itself out at his mouth. His whole body was racked and wrenched with an insupportable anguish! But his disobedient hands gave no heed to the command. They beat the water vigorously with quick, downward strokes, forcing him to the surface. He felt his head emerge; his eyes were blinded by the sunlight; his chest expanded convulsively, and with a supreme and crowning agony his lungs engulfed a great draught of air, which instantly he expelled in a shriek!

He was now in full possession of his physical senses. They were, indeed, preternaturally keen and alert. Something in the awful disturbance of his organic system had so exalted and refined them that they made record of things never before perceived. He felt the ripples upon his face and heard their separate sounds as they struck. He looked at the forest on the bank of the stream, saw the individual trees, the leaves and the veining of each leaf—saw the very insects upon them: the locusts, the brilliant-bodied flies, the gray spiders stretching their webs from twig to twig. He noted the prismatic colors in all the dewdrops upon a million blades of grass. The humming of the gnats that danced above the eddies of the stream, the beating of the dragon-flies' wings, the strokes of the water-spiders' legs, like oars which had lifted their boat—all these made audible music. A fish slid along beneath his eyes and he heard the rush of its body parting the water.

He had come to the surface facing down the stream; in a moment the visible world seemed to wheel slowly round, himself the pivotal point, and he saw the bridge, the fort, the soldiers upon the bridge, the captain, the sergeant, the two privates, his executioners. They were in silhouette against the blue sky. They shouted and gesticulated, pointing at him. The captain had drawn his pistol, but did not fire; the others were unarmed. Their movements were grotesque and horrible, their forms gigantic.

Suddenly he heard a sharp report and something struck the water smartly within a few inches of his head, spattering his face with spray. He heard a second report, and saw one of the sentinels with his rifle at his shoulder, a light cloud of blue smoke rising from the muzzle. The man in the water saw the eye of the man on the bridge gazing into his own through the sights of the rifle. He observed that it was a gray eye and remembered having read that gray eyes were keenest, and that all famous marksmen had them. Nevertheless, this one had missed.

A counter-swirl had caught Farquhar and turned him half round; he was again looking into the forest on the bank opposite the fort. The sound of a clear, high voice in a monotonous singsong now rang out behind him and came across the water with a distinctness that pierced and subdued all other sounds, even the beating of the ripples in his ears. Although no soldier, he had frequented camps enough to know the dread significance of that deliberate, drawling, aspirated chant; the lieutenant on shore was taking a part in the morning's work.

How coldly and pitilessly—with what an even, calm intonation, presaging, and enforcing tranquility in the men—with what accurately measured intervals fell those cruel words:

"Attention, company! . . . Shoulder arms! . . . Ready! . . . Aim! . . . Fire!"

Farquhar dived—dived as deeply as he could. The water roared in his ears like the voice of Niagara, yet he heard the dulled thunder of the volley and, rising again toward the surface, met shining bits of metal, singularly flattened, oscillating slowly downward. Some of them touched him on the face and hands, then fell away, continuing their descent. One lodged between his collar and neck; it was uncomfortably warm and he snatched it out.

As he rose to the surface, gasping for breath, he saw that he had been a long time under water; he was perceptibly farther down stream—nearer to safety. The soldiers had almost finished reloading; the metal ramrods flashed all at once in the sunshine as they were drawn from the barrels, turned in the air, and thrust into their sockets. The two sentinels fired again, independently and ineffectually.

The hunted man saw all this over his shoulder; he was now swimming vigorously with the current. His brain was as energetic as his arms and legs; he thought with the rapidity of lightning.

"The officer," he reasoned, "will not make that martinet's error a second time. It is as easy to dodge a volley as a single shot. He has probably already given the command to fire at will. God help me, I cannot dodge them all!"

An appalling plash within two yards of him was followed by a loud, rushing sound, *diminuendo,* which seemed to travel back through the air to the fort and died in an explosion which stirred the very river to its deeps! A rising sheet of water curved over him, fell down upon him, blinded him, strangled him! The cannon had taken a hand in the game. As he shook his head free from the commotion of the smitten water he heard the deflected shot humming through the air ahead, and in an instant it was cracking and smashing the branches in the forest beyond.

"They will not do that again," he thought; "the next time they will use a charge of grape. I must keep my eye upon the gun; the smoke will apprise me—the report arrives too late; it lags behind the missile. That is a good gun."

Suddenly he felt himself whirled round and round—spinning like a top. The water, the banks, the forests, the now distant bridge, fort and men—all were commingled and blurred. Objects were represented by their colors only; circular horizontal streaks of color—that was all he saw. He had been caught in a vortex and was being whirled on with a velocity of advance and gyration that made him giddy and sick. In a few moments he was flung upon the gravel at the foot of the left bank of the stream—the southern bank—and behind a projecting point which concealed him from his enemies. The sudden arrest of his motion, the abrasion of one of his hands on the gravel, restored him, and he wept with delight. He dug his fingers into the sand, threw it over himself in handfuls and audibly blessed it. It looked like diamonds, rubies, emeralds; he could think of nothing beautiful which it did not resemble. The trees upon the bank were giant garden plants; he noted a definite order in their arrangement, inhaled the fragrance of their blooms. A strange, roseate light shone through the spaces among their trunks and the wind made in their branches the music of æolian harps. He had no wish to perfect his escape—was content to remain in that enchanting spot until retaken.

A whiz and rattle of grapeshot among the branches high above his head roused him from his dream. The baffled cannoneer had fired him a random farewell. He sprang to his feet, rushed up the sloping bank, and plunged into the forest.

All that day he traveled, laying his course by the rounding sun. The forest seemed interminable; nowhere did he discover a break in it, not even a woodman's road. He had not known that he lived in so wild a region. There was something uncanny in the revelation.

By nightfall he was fatigued, footsore, famishing. The thought of his wife and children urged him on. At last he found a road which led him in what he knew to be the right direction. It was as wide and straight as a city street, yet it seemed untraveled. No fields bordered it, no dwelling anywhere. Not so much as the barking of a dog suggested human habitation. The black bodies of the trees formed a straight wall on both sides, terminating on the horizon in a point, like a diagram in a lesson in perspective. Overhead, as he looked up through this rift in the wood, shone great golden stars looking unfamiliar and grouped in strange constellations. He was sure they were arranged in some order which had a secret and malign significance. The wood on either side was full of singular noises, among which—once, twice, and again—he distinctly heard whispers in an unknown tongue.

His neck was in pain and lifting his hand to it he found it horribly swollen. He knew that it had a circle of black where the rope had bruised it. His eyes felt congested; he could no longer close them. His tongue was swollen with thirst; he relieved its fever by thrusting it forward from between his teeth into the cold air. How softly the turf had carpeted the untraveled avenue—he could no longer feel the roadway beneath his feet!

Doubtless, despite his suffering, he had fallen asleep while walking, for now he sees another scene—perhaps he has merely recovered from a delirium. He stands at the gate of his own home. All is as he left it, and all bright and beautiful in the morning sunshine. He must have traveled the entire night. As he pushes open the gate and passes up the wide white walk, he sees a flutter of female garments; his wife, looking fresh and cool and sweet, steps down from the veranda to meet him. At the bottom of the steps she stands waiting, with a smile of ineffable joy, an attitude of matchless grace and dignity. Ah, how beautiful she is! He springs forward with extended arms. As he is about to clasp her he feels a stunning blow upon the back of the neck; a blinding white light blazes all about him with a sound like the shock of a cannon—then all is darkness and silence!

Peyton Farquhar was dead; his body, with a broken neck, swung gently from side to side beneath the timbers of the Owl Creek bridge.

Study and Discussion Questions

1. How does Bierce work to make us think Farquhar's imagined escape is real? What hints are there along the way that it is in fact imaginary?
2. Trace Bierce's manipulation of point of view throughout the story. What does it accomplish? Why does Bierce narrate the events leading up to the hanging in a flashback in Part II rather than at the beginning of the story?
3. Characterize the way Bierce describes the hanging proceedings in the first two paragraphs. Compare it to the way he describes Farquhar's imaginary escape. What does this contrast in style suggest?
4. Why do you think Bierce, who himself volunteered to fight on the Union side in the Civil War, makes his hero a Southern planter, a slave owner, a supporter of the Confederates? How does this choice shape the kind of statement the story makes about war?

Suggestions for Writing

1. One critic has argued that the story makes fun of "the orthodox war yarn in which the hero's death or survival is noble and significant." Interpret the story taking this statement as your thesis. (You might begin by reexamining the characterization of Farquhar in Part II.)
2. How would you go about making a film of this story? How would you handle the shifts in point of view, the flashback, and the imaginary nature of Farquhar's escape? (If you've seen and remember a film version, discuss how well you think it does the job.)

LOUISE ERDRICH (b. 1954)

Louise Erdrich grew up in Wahpeton, North Dakota. Her father, a German immigrant, and her mother, an Ojibwa Indian, passed down to her a rich tradition of story telling. She would eventually obtain her B.A. at Dartmouth and her M.A. in writing from John Hopkins in 1979. In 1981, she married another writer, Mike Dorris. During the next decade, the two collaborated on several publications, working together and providing feedback for each other. For a short time they published under their penname "Milou North." When her poem "Indian Boarding School" won the 1983 Pushcart Prize, the public began to notice her work—both poetry and prose. Although she has written more prose in her career, her two volumes of poetry, *Jacklight* (1984) and *Baptism of Desire* (1989), have been highly acclaimed. In these two volumes, Erdrich uses her imaginative story-telling abilities to write a multifaceted poetry—wandering deftly through themes of family, love, history, Native American mythologizing, and the tension between Ojibwa reservation life and white America. These same story-telling techniques can be found in her prose. Among her novels are *The Beet Queen* (1986), *Tracks* (1988), *A Link With the River* (1989), *The Crown of Columbus* (1991), *The Antelope Wife* (1998), and her latest work *Four Souls* (2004). "The Red Convertible" is one of fourteen stories that comprise her first novel, *Love Medicine* (1984).

The Red Convertible   (1984)

I was the first one to drive a convertible on my reservation. And of course it was red, a red Olds. I owned that car along with my brother Henry Junior. We owned it together until his boots filled with water on a windy night and he bought out my share. Now Henry owns the whole car, and his younger brother Lyman (that's myself), Lyman walks everywhere he goes.

How did I earn enough money to buy my share in the first place? My one talent was I could always make money. I had a touch for it, unusual in a Chippewa. From the first I was different that way, and everyone recognized it. I was the only kid they let in the American Legion Hall to shine shoes, for example, and one Christmas I sold spiritual bouquets for the mission door to door. The nuns let me keep a percentage. Once I started, it seemed the more money I made the easier the money came. Everyone encouraged it. When I was fifteen I got a job washing dishes at the Joliet Café, and that was where my first big break happened.

It wasn't long before I was promoted to bussing tables, and then the short-order cook quit and I was hired to take her place. No sooner than you know it I was managing the Joliet. The rest is history. I went on managing. I soon become part owner, and of course there was no stopping me then. It wasn't long before the whole thing was mine.

After I'd owned the Joliet for one year, it blew over in the worst tornado ever seen around here. The whole operation was smashed to bits. A total loss. The fryalator was up in a tree, the grill torn in half like it was paper. I was only sixteen. I had it all in my mother's name, and I lost it quick, but before I lost it I had every one of my relatives, and their relatives, to dinner, and I also bought that red Olds I mentioned, along with Henry.

The first time we saw it! I'll tell you when we first saw it. We had gotten a ride up to Winnipeg, and both of us had money. Don't ask me why, because we never mentioned a car or anything, we just had all our money. Mine was cash, a big bankroll from the Joliet's insurance. Henry had two checks—a week's extra pay for being laid off, and his regular check from the Jewel Bearing Plant.

We were walking down Portage anyway, seeing the sights, when we saw it. There it was, parked, large as life. Really as *if* it was alive. I thought of the word *repose*, because the car wasn't simply stopped, parked, or whatever. That car reposed, calm and gleaming, a FOR SALE sign in its left front window. Then, before we had thought it over at all, the car belonged to us and our pockets were empty. We had just enough money for gas back home.

We went places in that car, me and Henry. We took off driving all one whole summer. We started off toward the Little Knife River and Mandaree in Fort Berthold and then we found ourselves down in Wakpala somehow, and then suddenly we were over in Montana on the Rocky Boys, and yet the summer was not even half over. Some people hang on to details when they travel, but we didn't let them bother us and just lived our everyday lives here to there.

I do remember this one place with willows. I remember I laid under those trees and it was comfortable. So comfortable. The branches bent down all around me like a tent or a stable. And quiet, it was quiet, even though there was a powwow close enough so I could see it going on. The air was not too still, not too windy either. When the dust rises up and hangs in the air around the dancers like that, I feel good. Henry was asleep with his arms thrown wide. Later on, he woke up and we started driving again. We were somewhere in Montana, or maybe on the Blood Reserve—it could have been anywhere. Anyway it was where we met the girl.

All her hair was in buns around her ears, that's the first thing I noticed about her. She was posed alongside the road with her arm out, so we stopped. That girl was short, so short her lumber shirt looked comical on her, like a nightgown. She had jeans on and fancy moccasins and she carried a little suitcase.

"Hop on in," says Henry. So she climbs in between us.

"We'll take you home," I says. "Where do you live?"

"Chicken," she says.

"Where the hell's that?" I ask her.

"Alaska."

"Okay," says Henry, and we drive.

We got up there and never wanted to leave. The sun doesn't truly set there in summer, and the night is more a soft dusk. You might doze off, sometimes, but before you know it you're up again, like an animal in nature. You never feel like you have to sleep hard or put away the world. And things would grow up there. One day just dirt or moss, the next day flowers and long grass. The girl's name was Susy. Her family really took to us. They fed us and put us up. We had our own tent to live in by their house, and the kids would be in and out of there all day and night. They couldn't get over me and Henry being brothers, we looked so different. We told them we knew we had the same mother, anyway.

One night Susy came in to visit us. We sat around in the tent talking of this thing and that. The season was changing. It was getting darker by that time, and the cold was even getting just a little mean. I told her it was time for us to go. She stood up on a chair.

"You never seen my hair," Susy said.

That was true. She was standing on a chair, but still, when she unclipped her buns the hair reached all the way to the ground. Our eyes opened. You couldn't tell how much hair she had when it was rolled up so neatly. Then my brother Henry did something funny. He went up to the chair and said, "Jump on my shoulders." So she did that, and her hair reached down past his waist, and he started twirling, this way and that, so her hair was flung out from side to side.

"I always wondered what it was like to have long pretty hair," Henry says. Well we laughed. It was a funny sight, the way he did it. The next morning we got up and took leave of those people.

On to greener pastures, as they say. It was down through Spokane and across Idaho then Montana and very soon we were racing the weather right along under the Canadian border through Columbus, Des Lacs, and then we were in Bottineau County and soon home. We'd made most of the trip, that summer, without putting up the car hood at all. We got home just in time, it turned out, for the army to remember Henry had signed up to join it.

I don't wonder that the army was so glad to get my brother that they turned him into a Marine. He was built like a brick outhouse anyway. We liked to tease him that they really wanted him for his Indian nose. He had a nose big and sharp as a hatchet, like the nose on Red Tomahawk, the Indian who killed Sitting Bull, whose profile is on signs all along the North Dakota highways. Henry went off to training camp, came home once during Christmas, then the next thing you know we got an overseas letter from him. It was 1970, and he said he was stationed up in the northern hill country. Whereabouts I did not know. He wasn't such a hot letter writer, and only got off two before the enemy caught him. I could never keep it straight, which direction those good Vietnam soldiers were from.

I wrote him back several times, even though I didn't know if those letters would get through. I kept him informed all about the car. Most of the time I had it up on blocks in the yard or half taken apart, because that long trip did a hard job on it under the hood.

I always had good luck with numbers, and never worried about the draft myself. I never even had to think about what my number was. But Henry was never lucky in the same way as me. It was at least three years before Henry came home. By then I guess the whole war was solved in the government's mind, but for him it would keep on going. In those years I'd put his car into almost perfect shape. I always thought of it as his car while he was gone, even though when he left he said, "Now it's yours," and threw me his key.

"Thanks for the extra key," I'd said. "I'll put it up in your drawer just in case I need it." He laughed.

When he came home, though, Henry was very different, and I'll say this: the change was no good. You could hardly expect him to change for the better, I know. But he was quiet, so quiet, and never comfortable sitting still anywhere but always up and moving around. I thought back to times we'd sat still for whole afternoons, never moving a muscle, just shifting our weight along the ground, talking to whoever sat with us, watching things. He'd always had a joke, then, too, and now you couldn't get him to laugh, or when he did it was more the sound of a man choking, a sound that stopped up the throats of other people around him. They got to leaving him alone most of the time, and I didn't blame them. It was a fact: Henry was jumpy and mean.

I'd bought a color TV set for my mom and the rest of us while Henry was away. Money still came very easy. I was sorry I'd ever bought it though, because of Henry. I was also sorry I'd bought color, because with black-and-white the pictures seem older and farther away. But what are you going to do? He sat in front of it, watching it, and that was the only time he was completely still. But it was the kind of stillness that you see in a rabbit when it freezes and before it will bolt. He was not easy. He sat in his chair gripping the armrests with all his might, as if the chair itself was moving at a high speed and if he let go at all he would rocket forward and maybe crash right through the set.

Once I was in the room watching TV with Henry and I heard his teeth click at something. I looked over, and he'd bitten through his lip. Blood was going down his chin. I tell you right then I wanted to smash that tube to pieces. I went over to it but Henry must have known what I was up to. He rushed from his chair and shoved me out of the way, against the wall. I told myself he didn't know what he was doing.

My mom came in, turned the set off real quiet, and told us she had made something for supper. So we went and sat down. There was still blood going down Henry's chin, but he didn't notice it and no one said anything, even though every time he took a bite of his bread his blood fell onto it until he was eating his own blood mixed in with the food.

While Henry was not around we talked about what was going to happen to him. There were no Indian doctors on the reservation, and my mom was afraid of trusting Old Man Pillager because he courted her long ago and was jealous of her husbands. He might take revenge through her son. We were afraid that if we brought Henry to a regular hospital they would keep him.

"They don't fix them in those places," Mom said; "they just give them drugs."

"We wouldn't get him there in the first place," I agreed, "so let's just forget about it."

Then I thought about the car.

Henry had not even looked at the car since he'd gotten home, though like I said, it was in tip-top condition and ready to drive. I thought the car might bring the old Henry back somehow. So I bided my time and waited for my chance to interest him in the vehicle.

One night Henry was off somewhere. I took myself a hammer. I went out to that car and I did a number on its underside. Whacked it up. Bent the tail pipe double. Ripped the muffler loose. By the time I was done with the car it looked worse than any typical Indian car that has been driven all its life on reservation roads, which they always say are like government promises—full of holes. It just about hurt me, I'll tell you that! I threw dirt in the carburetor and I ripped all the electric tape off the seats. I made it look just as beat up as I could. Then I sat back and waited for Henry to find it.

Still, it took him over a month. That was all right, because it was just getting warm enough, not melting, but warm enough to work outside.

"Lyman," he says, walking in one day, "that red car looks like shit."

'Well it's old," I says. "You got to expect that."

"No way!" says Henry. "That car's a classic! But you went and ran the piss right out of it, Lyman, and you know it don't deserve that. I kept that car in A-one shape. You don't remember. You're too young. But when I left, that car was running like a watch. Now I don't even know if I can get it to start again, let alone get it anywhere near its old condition."

"Well you try," I said, like I was getting mad, "but I say it's a piece of junk."

Then I walked out before he could realize I knew he'd strung together more than six words at once.

After that I thought he'd freeze himself to death working on that car. He was out there all day, and at night he rigged up a little lamp, ran a cord out the window, and had himself some light to see by while he worked. He was better than he had been before, but that's still not saying much. It was easier for him to do the things the rest of us did. He ate more slowly and didn't jump up and down during the meal to get this or that or look out the window. I put my hand in the back of the TV set, I admit, and fiddled around with it good, so that it was almost impossible now to get a clear picture. He didn't look at it very often anyway. He was always out with that car or going off to get parts for it. By the time it was really melting outside, he had it fixed.

I had been feeling down in the dumps about Henry around this time. We had always been together before. Henry and Lyman. But he was such a loner now that I didn't know how to take it. So I jumped at the chance one day when Henry seemed friendly. It's not that he smiled or anything. He just said, "Let's take that old shitbox for a spin." Just the way he said it made me think he could be coming around.

We went out to the car. It was spring. The sun was shining very bright. My only sister, Bonita, who was just eleven years old, came out and made us stand together for a picture. Henry leaned his elbow on the red car's windshield, and he took his other arm and put it over my shoulder, very carefully, as though it was heavy for him to lift and he didn't want to bring the weight down all at once.

"Smile," Bonita said, and he did.

That picture. I never look at it anymore. A few months ago, I don't know why, I got his picture out and tacked it on the wall. I felt good about Henry at the time, close to him. I felt good having his picture on the wall, until one night when I was looking at television. I was a little drunk and stoned. I looked up at the wall and Henry was staring at me. I don't know what it was, but his smile had changed, or maybe it was gone. All I know is I couldn't stay in the same room with that picture. I was shaking. I got up, closed the door, and went into the kitchen. A little later my friend Ray came over and we both went back into that room. We put the picture in a brown bag, folded the bag over and over tightly, then put it way back in a closet.

I still see that picture now, as if it tugs at me, whenever I pass that closet door. The picture is very clear in my mind. It was so sunny that day Henry had to squint against the glare. Or maybe the camera Bonita held flashed like a mirror, blinding him, before she snapped the picture. My face is right out in the sun, big and round. But he might have drawn back, because the shadows on his face are deep as holes. There are two shadows curved like little hooks around the ends of his smile, as if to frame it and try to keep it there—that one, first smile that looked like it might have hurt his face. He has his field jacket on and the worn-in clothes he'd come back in and kept wearing ever since. After Bonita took the picture, she went into the house and we got into the car. There was a full cooler in the trunk. We started off, east, toward Pembina and the Red River because Henry said he wanted to see the high water.

The trip over there was beautiful. When everything starts changing, drying up, clearing off, you feel like your whole life is starting. Henry felt it, too. The top was down and the car hummed like a top. He'd really put it back in shape, even the tape on the seats was very carefully put down and glued back in layers. It's not that he smiled again or even joked, but his face looked to me as if it was clear, more peaceful. It looked as though he wasn't thinking of anything in particular except the bare fields and windbreaks and houses we were passing.

The river was high and full of winter trash when we got there. The sun was still out, but it was colder by the river. There were still little clumps of dirty snow here and there on the banks. The water hadn't gone over the banks yet, but it would, you could tell. It was just at its limit, hard swollen, glossy like an old gray scar. We made ourselves a fire, and we sat down and watched the current go. As I watched it I felt something squeezing inside me and tightening and trying to let go all at the same time. I knew I was not just feeling it myself; I knew I was feeling what Henry was going through at that moment. Except that I couldn't stand it, the closing and opening. I jumped to my feet. I took Henry by the shoulders and I started shaking him. "Wake up," I says, "wake up, wake up, wake up!" I didn't know what had come over me. I sat down beside him again.

His face was totally white and hard. Then it broke, like stones break all of a sudden when water boils up inside them.

"I know it," he says. "I know it. I can't help it. It's no use."

We start talking. He said he knew what I'd done with the car. It was obvious it had been whacked out of shape and not just neglected. He said he wanted to give the car to me for good now, it was no use. He said he'd fixed it just to give it back and I should take it.

"No way," I says, "I don't want it."

"That's okay," he says, "you take it."

"I don't want it, though," I says back to him, and then to emphasize, just to emphasize, you understand, I touch his shoulder. He slaps my hand off.

"Take that car," he says.

"No," I say, "make me," I say, and then he grabs my jacket and rips the arm loose. That jacket is a class act, suede with tags and zippers. I push Henry backwards, off the log. He jumps up and bowls me over. We go down in a clinch and come up swinging hard, for all we're worth, with our fists. He socks my jaw so hard I feel like it swings loose. Then I'm at his ribcage and land a good one under his chin so his head snaps back. He's dazzled. He looks at me and I look at him and then his eyes are full of tears and blood and at first I think he's crying. But no, he's laughing. "Ha! Ha!" he says. "Ha! Ha! Take good care of it."

"Okay," I says, "okay, no problem. Ha! Ha!"

I can't help it, and I start laughing, too. My face feels fat and strange, and after a while I get a beer from the cooler in the trunk, and when I hand it to Henry he takes his shirt and wipes my germs off. "Hoof-and-mouth disease," he says. For some reason this cracks me up, and so we're really laughing for a while, and then we drink all the rest of the beers one by one and throw them in the river and see how far, how fast, the current takes them before they fill up and sink.

"You want to go on back?" I ask after a while. "Maybe we could snag a couple nice Kashpaw girls."

He says nothing. But I can tell his mood is turning again.

"They're all crazy, the girls up here, every damn one of them."

"You're crazy too," I say, to jolly him up. "Crazy Lamartine boys!"

He looks as though he will take this wrong at first. His face twists, then clears, and he jumps up on his feet. "That's right!" he says. "Crazier 'n hell. Crazy Indians!"

I think it's the old Henry again. He throws off his jacket and starts swinging his legs out from the knees like a fancy dancer. He's down doing something between a grouse dance and a bunny hop, no kind of dance I ever saw before, but neither has anyone else on all this green growing earth. He's wild. He wants to pitch whoopee! He's up and at me and all over. All this time I'm laughing so hard, so hard my belly is getting tied up in a knot.

"Got to cool me off!" he shouts all of a sudden. Then he runs over to the river and jumps in.

There's boards and other things in the current. It's so high. No sound comes from the river after the splash he makes, so I run right over. I look around. It's getting dark. I see he's halfway across the water already, and I know he didn't swim there but the current took him. It's far. I hear his voice, though, very clearly across it.

"My boots are filling," he says.

He says this in a normal voice, like he just noticed and he doesn't know what to think of it. Then he's gone. A branch comes by. Another branch. And I go in.

By the time I get out of the river, off the snag I pulled myself onto, the sun is down. I walk back to the car, turn on the high beams, and drive it up the bank.

I put it in first gear and then I take my foot off the clutch. I get out, close the door, and watch it plow softly into the water. The headlights reach in as they go down, searching, still lighted even after the water swirls over the back end. I wait. The wires short out. It is all finally dark. And then there is only the water, the sound of it going and running and going and running and running.

Study and Discussion Questions

1. How does the tone of the story shift when Henry returns from Vietnam?
2. How has Henry changed now that he's back from Vietnam?
3. List the various ways that Erdrich gives us clues throughout "The Red Convertible" about how it will end.
4. What are the phases the car goes through? How do these stand for what Lyman and Henry are going through?
5. What does the description of Henry's picture tell us about Henry? About the narrator Lyman? Why is the picture incident placed where it is in the story?
6. Why do Henry and Lyman fight down by the river?
7. How does the first paragraph of the story manage to tell us exactly what the end of the story will be and yet not give that ending away?

Suggestions for Writing

1. Discuss the image of the red convertible's "drowning." Why does Lyman send the car into the water? Why do you think the car's lights are left on?
2. Are there any ways in which Erdrich suggests that being Native Americans shapes Henry's and Lyman's experience?
3. Pick one incident in the story (e.g., the visit to long-haired Susy in Alaska, or Henry's watching TV and biting through his lip) and discuss why you think Erdrich included it.

❀ ❀ ❀

DONALD BARTHELME (1931–1989)

Donald Barthelme was born in Philadelphia but grew up in Houston, Texas. As a college student at the University of Houston, Barthelme was active as an editor and reporter for the school newspaper. After serving in the army for a couple of years, Barthelme returned to Houston and began writing in a variety of contexts, as well as taking a job as the director of the Contemporary Arts Museum. In 1962, he moved to New York and began writing short stories for *The New Yorker* magazine. His work was instantly recognized for its radical, unconventional uses of language—intentional misspellings, ambiguous meanings, and unusual form. Indeed, one of Barthelme's goals was to draw attention to the complexities of language while at the same maintaining the semblance of a narrative structure that supported his satirical critique of modern life. Yet his work tends to defy easy categorization into one set genre. Like Franz Kafka, Barthelme works in the world of the absurd and bizarre. Selected works include the short story collections *Unspeakable Practices, Unnatural Acts* (1968), *City Life* (1970), *Sadness* (1972), *Guilty Pleasures* (1974), and *Sixty Stories* (1981); and the novels *Snow White* (1967), *The Dead Father* (1975), *Paradise* (1986), and *The King* (1990, published posthumously). "Report" was first published in *Unspeakable Practices, Unnatural Acts*.

Report   (1968)

Our group is against the war. But the war goes on. I was sent to Cleveland to talk to the engineers. The engineers were meeting in Cleveland. I was supposed to persuade them not to do what they are going to do. I took United's 4:45 from LaGuardia arriving in Cleveland at 6:13. Cleveland is dark blue at that hour. I went directly to the motel, where the engineers were meeting. Hundreds of engineers attended the Cleveland meeting. I noticed many fractures among the engineers, bandages, traction. I noticed what appeared to be fracture of the carpal scaphoid in six examples. I notice numerous fractures of the humeral shaft, of the os calcis, of the pelvic girdle. I noticed a high incidence of clay-shoveller's fracture. I could not account for these fractures. The engineers were making calculations, taking measurements, sketching on the blackboard, drinking beer, throwing bread, buttonholing employers, hurling glasses into the fireplace. They were friendly.

They were friendly. They were full of love and information. The chief engineer wore shades. Patella in Monk's traction, clamshell fracture by the look of it. He was standing in a slum of beer bottles and microphone cable. "Have some of this chicken à la Isambard Kingdom Brunel[1] the Great Ingineer," he said. "And declare who you are and what we can do for you. What is your line, distinguished guest?"

"Software," I said. "In every sense. I am here representing a small group of interested parties. We are interested in your thing, which seems to be functioning in the midst of so much dysfunction, function is interesting. Other people's things don't seem to be working. The State Department's thing doesn't seem to be working. The U.N.'s thing doesn't seem to be working. The democratic left's thing doesn't seem to be working. Buddha's thing—"

"Ask us anything about our thing, which seems to be working," the chief engineer said. "We will open our hearts and heads to you, Software Man, because we want to be understood and loved by the great lay public, and have our marvels appreciated by that public, for which we daily unsung produce tons of new marvels each more life-enhancing than the last. Ask us anything.

---

[1]Nineteenth-century British engineer.

Do you want to know about evaporated thin-film metallurgy? Monolithic and hybrid integrated-circuit processes? The algebra of inequalities? Optimization theory? Complex high-speed micro-miniature closed and open loop systems? Fixed variable mathematical cost searches? Epitaxial deposition of semi-conductor materials? Gross interfaced space gropes? We also have specialists in the cuckooflower, the doctorfish, and the dumdum bullet as these relate to aspects of today's expanding technology, and they do in the damnedest ways."

I spoke to him then about the war. I said the same things people always say when they speak against the war. I said that the war was wrong. I said that large countries should not burn down small countries. I said that the government had made a series of errors. I said that these errors once small and forgivable were now immense and unforgivable. I said that the government was attempting to conceal its original errors under layers of new errors. I said that the government was sick with error, giddy with it. I said that ten thousand of our soldiers had already been killed in pursuit of the government's errors. I said that tens of thousands of the enemy's soldiers and civilians had been killed because of various errors, ours and theirs. I said that we are responsible for errors made in our name. I said that the government should not be allowed to make additional errors.

"Yes, yes," the chief engineer said, "there is doubtless much truth in what you say, but we can't possibly *lose* the war, can we? And stopping is losing, isn't it? The war regarded as a process, stopping regarded as an abort? We don't know *how* to lose a war. That skill is not among our skills. Our array smashes their array, that is what we know. That is the process. That is what is.

"But let's not have any more of this dispiriting downbeat counterproductive talk. I have a few new marvels here I'd like to discuss with you just briefly. A few new marvels that are just about ready to be gaped at by the admiring layman. Consider for instance the area of realtime online computer-controlled wish evaporation. Wish evaporation is going to be crucial in meeting the rising expectations of the world's peoples, which are as you know rising entirely too fast."

I noticed then distributed about the room a great many transverse fractures of the ulna. "The development of the pseudo-ruminant stomach for underdeveloped peoples," he went on, "is one of our interesting things you should be interested in. With the pseudo-ruminant stomach they can chew cuds, that is to say, eat grass. Blue is the most popular color worldwide and for that reason we are working with certain strains of your native Kentucky *Poa pratensis,* or bluegrass, as the staple input for the p/r stomach cycle, which would also give a shot in the arm to our balance-of-payments thing don't you know. . . ." I noticed about me then a great number of metatarsal fractures in banjo splints. "The kangaroo initiative . . . eight hundred thousand harvested last year . . . highest percentage of edible protein of any herbivore yet studied . . ."

"Have new kangaroos been planted?"

The engineer looked at me.

"I intuit your hatred and jealousy of our thing," he said. "The ineffectual always hate our thing and speak of it as anti-human, which is not at all a meaningful way to speak of our thing. Nothing mechanical is alien to me," he said (amber spots making bursts of light in his shades), "because I am human, in a sense, and if I think it up, then 'it' is human too, whatever 'it' may be. Let me tell you, Software Man, we have been damned forbearing in the matter of this little war you declare yourself to be interested in. Function is the cry, and our thing is functioning like crazy. There are things we could do that we have not done. Steps we could take that we have not taken. These steps are, regarded in a certain light, the light of our enlightened self-interest, quite justifiable steps. We could, of course, get irritated. We could, of course, *lose patience.*

"We could, of course, release thousands upon thousands of self-powered crawling-along-the-ground lengths of titanium wire eighteen inches long with a diameter of .0005 centimetres (that is to say, invisible) which, scenting an enemy, climb up his trouser leg and wrap themselves around his neck. We have developed those. They are within our capabilities. We could, of course, release in the arena of the upper air our new improved pufferfish toxin which precipi- tates an identity crisis. No special technical problems there. That is almost laughably easy. We could, of course, place up to two million maggots in their rice within twenty-four hours. The maggots are ready, massed in secret staging areas in Alabama. We have hypodermic darts capable of piebalding the enemy's pig- mentation. We have rots, blights, and rusts capable of attacking his alphabet. Those are dandies. We have a hut-shrinking chemical which penetrates the fibres of the bamboo, causing it, the hut, to strangle its occupants. This operates only after 10 P.M., when people are sleeping. Their mathematics are at the mercy of a suppurating surd we have invented. We have a family of fishes trained to attack their fishes. We have the deadly testicle-destroying telegram. The cable companies are coöperating. We have a green substance that, well, I'd rather not talk about. We have a secret word that, if pronounced, produces mul- tiple fractures in all living things in an area the size of four football fields."

"That's why—"

"Yes. Some damned fool couldn't keep his mouth shut. The point is that the whole structure of enemy life is within our power to *rend, vitiate, devour,* and *crush.* But that's not the interesting thing."

"You recount these possibilities with uncommon relish."

"Yes I realize that there is too much relish here. But *you* must realize that these capabilities represent in and of themselves highly technical and complex and interesting problems and hurdles on which our boys have expended many thousands of hours of hard work and brilliance. And that the effects are often grossly exaggerated by irresponsible victims. And that the whole thing repre- sents a fantastic series of triumphs for the multidisciplined problem-solving team concept."

"I appreciate that."

"We *could* unleash all this technology at once. You can imagine what would happen then. But that's not the interesting thing."

"What is the interesting thing?"

"The interesting thing is that we have a *moral sense*. It is on punched cards, perhaps the most advanced and sensitive moral sense the world has ever known."

"Because it is on punched cards?"

"It considers all considerations in endless and subtle detail," he said. "It even quibbles. With this great new moral tool, how can we go wrong? I confidently predict that, although we *could* employ all this splendid new weaponry I've been telling you about, *we're not going to do it.*"

"We're not going to do it?"

I took United's 5:44 from Cleveland arriving at Newark at 7:19. New Jersey is bright pink at that hour. Living things move about the surface of New Jersey at that hour molesting each other only in traditional ways. I made my report to the group. I stressed the friendliness of the engineers. I said, It's all right. I said, We have a moral sense. I said, *We're not going to do it.* They didn't believe me.

Study and Discussion Questions

1. Describe the chief engineer's attitude toward the war, toward technology, toward social problems, and toward morality.
2. What do the chief engineer's discussions of "wish evaporation" and the "pseudo-ruminant stomach" suggest about how he views the people of poor nations?
3. What kind of person is Software Man? What does he represent? What effect does his talk with the chief engineer have on him?
4. Reread the long paragraph in which the chief engineer describes the new weapons available. How are we supposed to react? What is the effect of the matter-of-fact tone in which these bizarre horrors are described?
5. "Report" was first published during the Vietnam War. What in the story points to that war in particular?
6. Compare/contrast the attitude toward weapons technology in this story with actual attitudes toward weapons technology in the military and government today.

Suggestions for Writing

1. Discuss a product of modern technology that you find frightening.
2. Speculate on how high-technology weaponry changes the nature of war.

❊ ❊ ❊

TIM O'BRIEN (b. 1946)

Tim O'Brien was born in Austin, Minnesota. After high school, he entered Macalester College in St. Paul to study political science. He graduated in 1968 summa cum laude. Any intentions of studying further, however, were dashed after being drafted into the army to fight in Vietnam. The traumatic experience of Vietnam had a deep impact on his life, and, after returning to the United States, he turned to writing as a way to cope with the insanity of war. In 1973, while studying at Harvard, O'Brien published *If I Die in a Combat Zone, Box Me Up and Ship Me Home*, a memoir of his experience in Vietnam—a work that compelled American culture to rethink the human costs of war and established him as the writerly conscience of Vietnam. In a terse, compact prose style (he is often compared to Ernest Hemingway in both theme and technique) O'Brien often disrupts standard narrative sequence by rearranging linear plot schemes through the blurring of reality and imagination. Within this mode, his protagonists grapple with false and romantic notions of courage, integrity, wisdom, and fear. While Vietnam serves as the backdrop for many of his works, O'Brien has explored other themes in more recent books yet still maintains a commitment to the human desire to find understanding in a chaotic world. Selected works include *Northern Lights* (1975), *Going After Cacciato* (1978, National Book Award), *The Nuclear Age* (1985), *The Things They Carried* (1990), *In the Lake of the Woods* (1994), *Tomcat in Love* (1998) and his latest novel *July, July,* (2002). "The Man I Killed" comes from *The Things They Carried*.

The Man I Killed   (1990)

His jaw was in his throat, his upper lip and teeth were gone, his one eye was shut, his other eye was a star-shaped hole, his eyebrows were thin and arched like a woman's, his nose was undamaged, there was a slight tear at the lobe of one ear, his clean black hair was swept upward into a cowlick at the rear of the skull, his forehead was lightly freckled, his fingernails were clean, the skin at his left cheek was peeled back in three ragged strips, his right cheek was smooth and hairless, there was a butterfly on his chin, his neck was open to the spinal cord and the blood there was thick and shiny and it was this wound that had killed him. He lay face-up in the center of the trail, a slim, dead, almost dainty young man. He had bony legs, a narrow waist, long shapely fingers. His chest was sunken and poorly muscled—a scholar, maybe. His wrists were the wrists of a child. He wore a black shirt, black pajama pants, a gray ammunition belt, a gold ring on the third finger of his right hand. His rubber sandals had been blown off. One lay beside him, the other a few meters up the trail. He had been born, maybe, in 1946 in the village of My Khe near the central coastline of Quang Ngai Province,[1] where his parents farmed, and where his family had lived for several centuries, and where, during the time of the French, his father and two uncles and many neighbors

---

[1]Province in central South Vietnam.

had joined in the struggle for independence. He was not a Communist. He was a citizen and a soldier. In the village of My Khe, as in all of Quang Ngai, patriotic resistance had the force of tradition, which was partly the force of legend, and from his earliest boyhood the man I killed would have listened to stories about the heroic Trung sisters and Tran Hung Dao's famous rout of the Mongols and Le Loi's final victory against the Chinese at Tot Dong.[2] He would have been taught that to defend the land was a man's highest duty and highest privilege. He had accepted this. It was never open to question. Secretly, though, it also frightened him. He was not a fighter. His health was poor, his body small and frail. He liked books. He wanted someday to be a teacher of mathematics. At night, lying on his mat, he could not picture himself doing the brave things his father had done, or his uncles, or the heroes of the stories. He hoped in his heart that he would never be tested. He hoped the Americans would go away. Soon, he hoped. He kept hoping and hoping, always, even when he was asleep.

"Oh, man, you fuckin' trashed the fucker," Azar said. "You scrambled his sorry self, look at that, you *did,* you laid him out like Shredded fuckin' Wheat."

"Go away," Kiowa said.

"I'm just saying the truth. Like oatmeal."

"Go," Kiowa said.

"Okay, then, I take it back," Azar said. He started to move away, then stopped and said, "Rice Krispies, you know? On the dead test, this particular individual gets A-Plus."

Smiling at this, he shrugged and walked up the trail toward the village behind the trees.

Kiowa kneeled down.

"Just forget that crud," he said. He opened up his canteen and held it out for a while and then sighed and pulled it away. "No sweat, man. What else could you do?"

Later, Kiowa said, "I'm serious. Nothing *anybody* could do. Come on, stop staring."

The trail junction was shaded by a row of trees and tall brush. The slim young man lay with his legs in the shade. His jaw was in his throat. His one eye was shut and the other was a star-shaped hole.

Kiowa glanced at the body.

"All right, let me ask a question," he said. "You want to trade places with him? Turn it all upside down—you *want* that? I mean, be honest."

The star-shaped hole was red and yellow. The yellow part seemed to be getting wider, spreading out at the center of the star. The upper lip and gum and teeth were gone. The man's head was cocked at a wrong angle, as if loose at the neck, and the neck was wet with blood.

"Think it over," Kiowa said.

---

[2]The Trung sisters led a Vietnamese rebellion against Chinese rule in A.D. 40; Tran Hung Dao repelled a Mongol attack in 1287; Le Loi defeated the Chinese in 1426.

Then later he said, "Tim, it's a *war*. The guy wasn't Heidi—he had a weapon, right? It's a tough thing, for sure, but you got to cut out that staring."

Then he said, "Maybe you better lie down a minute."

Then after a long empty time he said, "Take it slow. Just go wherever the spirit takes you."

The butterfly was making its way along the young man's forehead, which was spotted with small dark freckles. The nose was undamaged. The skin on the right cheek was smooth and fine-grained and hairless. Frail-looking, delicately boned, the young man would not have wanted to be a soldier and in his heart would have feared performing badly in battle. Even as a boy growing up in the village of My Khe, he had often worried about this. He imagined covering his head and lying in a deep hole and closing his eyes and not moving until the war was over. He had no stomach for violence. He loved mathematics. His eyebrows were thin and arched like a woman's, and at school the boys sometimes teased him about how pretty he was, the arched eyebrows and long shapely fingers, and on the playground they mimicked a woman's walk and made fun of his smooth skin and his love for mathematics. The young man could not make himself fight them. He often wanted to, but he was afraid, and this increased his shame. If he could not fight little boys, he thought, how could he ever become a soldier and fight the Americans with their airplanes and helicopters and bombs? It did not seem possible. In the presence of his father and uncles, he pretended to look forward to doing his patriotic duty, which was also a privilege, but at night he prayed with his mother that the war might end soon. Beyond anything else, he was afraid of disgracing himself, and therefore his family and village. But all he could do, he thought, was wait and pray and try not to grow up too fast.

"Listen to me," Kiowa said. "You feel terrible, I know that."

Then he said, "Okay, maybe I *don't* know."

Along the trail there were small blue flowers shaped like bells. The young man's head was wrenched sideways, not quite facing the flowers, and even in the shade a single blade of sunlight sparkled against the buckle of his ammunition belt. The left cheek was peeled back in three ragged strips. The wounds at his neck had not yet clotted, which made him seem animate even in death, the blood still spreading out across his shirt.

Kiowa shook his head.

There was some silence before he said, "Stop *staring.*"

The young man's fingernails were clean. There was a slight tear at the lobe of one ear, a sprinkling of blood on the forearm. He wore a gold ring on the third finger of his right hand. His chest was sunken and poorly muscled—a scholar, maybe. His life was now a constellation of possibilities. So, yes, maybe a scholar. And for years, despite his family's poverty, the man I killed would have been determined to continue his education in mathematics. The means for this were arranged, perhaps, through the village liberation cadres, and in

1964 the young man began attending classes at the university in Saigon, where he avoided politics and paid attention to the problems of calculus. He devoted himself to his studies. He spent his nights alone, wrote romantic poems in his journal, took pleasure in the grace and beauty of differential equations. The war, he knew, would finally take him, but for the time being he would not let himself think about it. He had stopped praying; instead, now, he waited. And as he waited, in his final year at the university, he fell in love with a classmate, a girl of seventeen, who one day told him that his wrists were like the wrists of a child, so small and delicate, and who admired his narrow waist and the cowlick that rose up like a bird's tail at the back of his head. She liked his quiet manner; she laughed at his freckles and bony legs. One evening, perhaps, they exchanged gold rings.

Now one eye was a star.

"You okay?" Kiowa said.

The body lay almost entirely in shade. There were gnats at the mouth, little flecks of pollen drifting above the nose. The butterfly was gone. The bleeding had stopped except for the neck wounds.

Kiowa picked up the rubber sandals, clapping off the dirt, then bent down to search the body. He found a pouch of rice, a comb, a fingernail clipper, a few soiled piasters, a snapshot of a young woman standing in front of a parked motorcycle. Kiowa placed these items in his rucksack along with the gray ammunition belt and rubber sandals.

Then he squatted down.

"I'll tell you the straight truth," he said. "The guy was dead the second he stepped on the trail. Understand me? We all had him zeroed. A good kill—weapon, ammunition, everything." Tiny beads of sweat glistened at Kiowa's forehead. His eyes moved from the sky to the dead man's body to the knuckles of his own hands. "So listen, you best pull your shit together. Can't just sit here all day."

Later he said, "Understand?"

Then he said, "Five minutes, Tim. Five more minutes and we're moving out."

The one eye did a funny twinkling trick, red to yellow. His head was wrenched sideways, as if loose at the neck, and the dead young man seemed to be staring at some distant object beyond the bell-shaped flowers along the trail. The blood at the neck had gone to a deep purplish black. Clean fingernails, clean hair—he had been a soldier for only a single day. After his years at the university, the man I killed returned with his new wife to the village of My Khe, where he enlisted as a common rifleman with the 48th Vietcong Battalion. He knew he would die quickly. He knew he would see a flash of light. He knew he would fall dead and wake up in the stories of his village and people.

Kiowa covered the body with a poncho.

"Hey, you're looking better," he said. "No doubt about it. All you needed was time—some mental R&R."

Then he said, "Man, I'm sorry."

Then later he said, "Why not talk about it?"

Then he said, "Come on, man, talk."

He was a slim, dead, almost dainty young man of about twenty. He lay with one leg bent beneath him, his jaw in his throat, his face neither expressive nor inexpressive. One eye was shut. The other was a star-shaped hole.

"Talk," Kiowa said.

Study and Discussion Questions

1. Why do you think the narrator describes the dead man's body in such detail?
2. Why does the narrator persist in imagining the life of the man he killed?
3. What's the significance of the narrator's guess that the dead man was born in a place "where his family had lived for several centuries"?
4. Why do you think the narrator imagines that the man he killed was a fearful and reluctant soldier?
5. Why does the narrator assert that the dead man "was not a Communist"?
6. What role does Azar play in the story? What do his reactions add to the story's condemnation of war? And what is Kiowa's role?

Suggestions for Writing

1. What can we infer about the narrator of "The Man I Killed"? Write a sketch of what you imagine him to be like.
2. In an effort to ease the narrator's guilt, Kiowa says: "Tim, it's a *war*. The guy wasn't Heidi—he had a weapon, right?" How might Tim reply? How might you?

✾ ✾ ✾

Poetry

WILFRED OWEN (1893–1918)

Wilfred Owen was born in Oswestry, England, and raised in a strict Calvinist home. His interest in poetry began at an early age, in particular the poetry of John Keats. Hoping to enroll at the University of London, Owen was unable to secure a scholarship that would have enabled him to pay the tuition. In 1913, he left to teach English in France, returning two years later to enlist in the British Army at the height of World War I. After many months fighting on the Western Front, Owen suffered shell shock and was hospitalized. It was during this convalescence that Owen met Siegfried Sassoon, another injured soldier and poet who encouraged and worked with Owen on his poetry. At the time, Owen had already published a few poems, but Sassoon's influence impelled Owen to develop the innovative poetry he would become known for. His brutal depictions of the realities of war helped to dismantle the era's popular and romanticized versions of valor and heroism. Owen's verse stood as the voice of the silent and unknown soldier. He was killed at the front in 1918, a week before the Armistice that ended World War I. His *Poems* appeared in 1920. "Dulce Et Decorum Est" is one of Owen's best-known poems.

Dulce Et Decorum Est[1] (1920)

Bent double, like old beggars under sacks,
Knock-kneed, coughing like hags, we cursed through sludge,
Till on the haunting flares we turned our backs
And towards our distant rest began to trudge.
Men marched asleep. Many had lost their boots   5
But limped on, blood-shod. All went lame; all blind;
Drunk with fatigue; deaf even to the hoots
Of tired, outstripped Five-Nines[2] that dropped behind.

Gas! Gas! Quick boys!—An ecstasy of fumbling,
Fitting the clumsy helmets just in time;   10
But someone still was yelling out and stumbling
And flound'ring like a man in fire or lime . . .

---

[1]See the last two lines for full quotation from Horace: "It is sweet and proper to die for one's country."
[2]Gas shells.

Dim, through the misty panes and thick green light,
As under a green sea, I saw him drowning.

In all my dreams, before my helpless sight,   15
He plunges at me, guttering, choking, drowning.

If in some smothering dreams you too could pace
Behind the wagon that we flung him in,
And watch the white eyes writhing in his face,
His hanging face, like a devil's sick of sin;   20
If you could hear, at every jolt, the blood
Come gargling from the froth-corrupted lungs,
Obscene as cancer, bitter as the cud
Of vile, incurable sores on innocent tongues,—
My friend, you would not tell with such high zest   25
To children ardent for some desperate glory,
The old Lie: Dulce et decorum est
Pro patria mori.

Study and Discussion Questions

1. Who is speaking in the poem? Where is he? What does he list in the first stanza about the conditions of himself and the other soldiers?
2. In terms of the "plot" of this poem, what happens, suddenly, in the second stanza?
3. Where is the speaker of the poem in the third, two-line, stanza?
4. Note the change in verb tense in the final stanza. How is this prepared for in the previous couplet?
5. To whom is the poem addressed? How does Owens involve the reader before the poem is done? And why does he want to do so?
6. Look at the images: What are the soldiers in general and the dying soldier in particular compared to?
7. Do some research on World War I weapons and modes of warfare. How does Owen's use of metaphor and simile capture the experience?

Suggestions for Writing

1. Which image in the poem strikes you most forcefully? Why?
2. Write your own critique (or defense) of the quote from Horace.
3. Compare World War I warfare and weapons with contemporary warfare and weapons.
4. Write a contemporary poem on the actual experience of battle. What is your theme? Choose the words and the images to convey that theme and mood.

EMILY DICKINSON (1830–1886)

Emily Dickinson was born in Amherst, Massachusetts in 1830. Raised in an intellectual and religious environment, Dickinson's exposure to both literature and Calvinism would play central roles in her poetry. While the common assumption has been that Dickinson made few attempts to publish her poetry in her lifetime, it is clear now, by evidence of the hundreds of letters she wrote, that she made an earnest effort to be recognized, submitting poetry quite often throughout the 1850s and 1860s. It was after these decades of rejection that Dickinson assumed the reclusive lifestyle she is now famous for. At the time of her death in 1886, Dickinson had written over 1500 poems, the majority of them found bundled in her dresser drawer. Due to her sister Lavinia's dedication and work, Dickinson's first volume of poems (titled *Poems*) was published in 1890. Even at this time, publishers were reluctant to publish Dickinson's verse, claiming it was unorthodox and amateur. But the public thought differently. *Poems* was an instant success and went through 16 editions in the next eight years. As is the case with many artists, Dickinson was an innovator ahead of her time. Her radical verse, eschewing traditional forms and meter, experimented with what was later called "slant" and internal rhymes—rhymes that did not necessarily fall at the end of a line, but were often embedded within lines. Moreover, her uneven line breaks, abrupt dashes, and terse, lyrical metaphors were techniques that wouldn't be accepted as valid poetic forms until the Imagist Movement of the early twentieth-century. Dickinson was a constant revisionist, reworking and polishing her poems and their meanings. Thus, when you read a Dickinson poem, you are presented with rich allegories, irony, and symbolism packed tightly in precise language. The 770-page *The Complete Poems of Emily Dickinson*, edited by Thomas Johnson, was published in 1970.

Flags vex a dying face   (1890)

The world feels dusty
When we stop to die;
We want the dew then,
Honors taste dry.

Flags vex a dying face,   5
But the least fan
Stirred by a friend's hand
Cools like the rain. . . .

Study and Discussion Questions

1. Since Emily Dickinson did not generally give her poems titles, "flags vex a dying face" was chosen by an editor. Usually when a poem is without a title, the first line of the poem serves that function. Why do you think whoever chose this title used the fifth line of the poem rather than the first?

2. This poem was written in the nineteenth century, after the Civil War, and though it can apply to any kind of death, what makes it pertinent to war-related deaths?

3. Discuss Dickinson's imagery in this poem. What are the two groups of images in tension here?

4. Look at Dickinson's end rhymes in this eight-line, two-stanza poem. Chart the rhyme pattern. Emily Dickinson uses slant rhyme frequently; which are the slant rhymes in this poem?

Suggestions for Writing

1. In Dickinson's view, what are the priorities when someone is close to death? Do you agree or disagree? How does she make her case in this poem?

2. Write about Emily Dickinson's word choices, especially her verbs, adjectives, and adverbs, in this poem. Try substituting another word for one of hers in several places and see whether it works and how it changes the meaning and the mood.

❀ ❀ ❀

MARGARET ATWOOD (b. 1939)

Margaret Atwood was born in Ottawa, Canada, and spent her early childhood in the rugged wilderness of northern Quebec until her family moved to Toronto in 1946. While attending the University of Toronto, Atwood took classes with the literary critic and scholar Northrop Frye and was introduced to the thought of Carl Jung and archetypal theory—ideas that would later have an impact on her writing. In 1962, she obtained her M.A. from Radcliffe College and continued on to do Ph.D. work at Harvard. The political ferment of the 1960s, and especially the rise of feminism (and her own active role in the movement), set the backdrop for her early poetry and fiction. In 1969 she published her first novel, *The Edible Woman*—a book that explores representations of women and female identity in a patriarchal society—themes that surface again and again in Atwood's work. While feminist concerns are at the base of Atwood's writing, it is her literary technique and experimentation that force readers to reassess the social implications of power. Through satire and the use of dystopian settings, Atwood "creates unease" in the reader, thus (ideally) instigating awareness. Selected works include the poetry collections *Double Persephone* (1961), *Power*

Politics (1973), *True Stories* (1981), and *The Journals of Susanna Moodie* (1997); the short story collections *Wilderness Tips* (1991), *Good Bones and Simple Murders* (1992); and the novels *Surfacing* (1972), *The Handmaid's Tale* (1985), *The Robber Bride* (1993), *Alias Grace* (1996), *The Blind Assassin* (2000), and *Oryx and Crack* (2003). In her poem "At first I was given centuries," Atwood moves through a history seen by women who, for centuries, have endured the loss of their lovers to war.

At first I was given centuries (1971)

At first I was given centuries
to wait in caves, in leather
tents, knowing you would never come back

Then it speeded up: only
several years between 5
the day you jangled off
into the mountains, and the day (it was
spring again) I rose from the embroidery
frame at the messenger's entrance.

That happened twice, or was it 10
more; and there was once, not so
long ago, you failed,
and came back in a wheelchair
with a moustache and a sunburn
and were insufferable. 15

Time before last though, I remember
I had a good eight months between
running alongside the train, skirts hitched, handing
you violets in at the window
and opening the letter; I watched 20
your snapshot fade for twenty years.

And last time (I drove to the airport
still dressed in my factory
overalls, the wrench
I had forgotten sticking out of the back 25
pocket; there you were,
zippered and helmeted, it was zero
hour, you said Be

Brave) it was at least three weeks before
I got the telegram and could start regretting.   30

But recently, the bad evenings
there are only seconds
between the warning on the radio and the
explosion; my hands
don't reach you   35

and on quieter nights
you jump up from
your chair without even touching your dinner
and I can scarcely kiss you goodbye
before you run out into the street and they shoot   40

Study and Discussion Questions

1. Who is speaking; who is the "I" of the poem? Who is the "you" of the poem?
2. In what ways does the speaker change and in what ways remain the same?
3. Describe the progression of situations from stanza to stanza.
4. Discuss how time is used in this poem.
4. Who are "they" in the last line?
5. Why do you think there is no period at the end of the poem?
6. Discuss the gender roles described in the poem.

Suggestions for Writing

1. Can you identify any particular wars the speaker has lived through? What are the clues?
2. What is the mood of the poem? What feelings does it evoke as you read it?
3. Compare/contrast "At first I was given centuries" to another Margaret Atwood poem about war, "The Loneliness of the Miliary Historian," on the issues of both war and gender.

e. e. cummings (1894–1962)

Edward Estlin Cummings was born in Cambridge, Massachusetts, the son of a well-known Harvard professor and congregational minister. After receiving his M.A. at Harvard in 1916, Cummings left for France to become a volunteer ambulance driver during World War I. His rebellious attitudes led to his internment for several months in a French prison camp as a suspected spy—an experience he described in his first published work *The Enormous*

Room (1922). Although this was a prose work, its experimental style (blending autobiography with symbolic poetry) was a precursor to the particular style of poetry cummings would subsequently develop. Infused with the transcendental thinking of Ralph Waldo Emerson and influenced by the English Romantic poets, cummings's work unsettles traditional poetic themes such as love and beauty through the intentional use of jumbled words, improper grammar, dislocated syntax, and a lack of capitalization (he wrote his name as *e. e. cummings*). While some critics have suggested such techniques are simple tricks and gimmicks, others contend that cummings's disregard for language conventions created original work that celebrates the importance and energy of play in poetry. His poetry includes *Tulips and Chimneys* (1923), *XLI Poems* (1925), *is 5* (1926), *ViVa* (1931), *1 × 1* (1944), and *Ninety-Five Poems* (1958). In "next to of course god america i," first published in 1926, cummings uses his brand of wordplay for a serious critique of American society.

"next to of course god america i (1926)

"next to of course god america i
love you land of the pilgrims' and so forth oh
say can you see by the dawn's early my
country 'tis of centuries come and go
and are no more what of it we should worry   5
in every language even deafanddumb
thy sons acclaim your glorious name by gorry
by jingo by gee by gosh by gum
why talk of beauty what could be more beautiful than these heroic happy dead   10
who rushed like lions to the roaring slaughter
they did not stop to think they died instead
then shall the voice of liberty be mute?"

He spoke. And drank rapidly a glass of water

Study and Discussion Questions

1. Who is speaking in lines 1 to 13? What is the setting?
2. Identify the original sources of as many of the familiar phrases used as you can. Why does Cummings run them together?
3. Why has Cummings written this as a (Petrarchan) sonnet? What is the function of the last line?
4. Discuss the phrase "these heroic happy dead." What is the poem saying about war?

Suggestions for Writing

1. Restate as an argument the point the poem is making.
2. Compare/contrast e. e. cummings's "next to of course god america i" with another post–World War I poem, Wilfred Owen's "Dulce Et Decorum Est." Look both at the rhetorical point each is making and at the poetic strategies each uses.

❋ ❋ ❋

CAROLYN FORCHÉ (b. 1950)

Forché's poetic skill was recognized early when she was awarded the Yale Younger Poets Award in 1975 for her collection *Gathering the Tribes*. That same year she received her M.F.A. from Bowling Green State University. Two years later she began working as a journalist for Amnesty International in El Salvador and lived there for several years. Forché was deeply affected by the human rights violations in the poverty-stricken country—disproportionate wealth, martial law, and inadequate health care. Her second volume of poetry, *The Country Between Us* (1981), published after her time in El Salvador, is marked by a change in tone and greater political awareness. While *Gathering the Tribes* explored Forché's girlhood growing up in the Midwestern city of Detroit, Michigan, *The Country Between Us* engages head-on with the atrocities Forché witnessed while living in El Salvador. Stylistically, Forché has been noted for the narrative quality or her poetry, her work in the prose poem form, and for her ability to blend the personal and the political to make larger claims about humanity. Like another Detroit poet, Philip Levine, Forché's poetry is built around the juxtaposition of precisely rendered images, weaving place, the senses, and language to create a verse that succeeds both lyrically and thematically. Her other works include the poetry collection *The Angel of History* (1994) and *Blue Hour* (2003). She has also published translations of Salvadorian poet Claribel Alegria and French poet Robert Desnos and edited the anthology *Against Forgetting: Twentieth-Century Poetry of Witness* (1993). "The Colonel," taken from *The Country Between Us*, is a prose poem.

The Colonel   (1978)

What you have heard is true. I was in his house. His wife carried a tray of coffee and sugar. His daughter filed her nails, his son went out for the night. There were daily papers, pet dogs, a pistol on the cushion beside him. The moon swung bare on its black cord over the house. On the television was a cop show. It was in English. Broken bottles were embedded in the walls around the house to scoop the kneecaps from a man's legs or cut his hands to lace. On the windows there were gratings like those in liquor stores. We had dinner, rack of lamb, good wine, a gold bell was on the table for calling the maid. The maid brought green mangoes, salt, a type of bread. I was asked how I enjoyed the country. There was a brief commercial in Spanish. His wife took everything away. There was some talk then of how difficult it had become to govern. The parrot said hello on the terrace. The colonel told it to shut up, and pushed himself from the table. My friend said to me with his eyes: say nothing. The colonel returned with a sack used to bring groceries home. He spilled many human ears on the table. They were like dried peach halves. There is no other way to say this. He took one of them in his hands, shook it in our faces, dropped it into a water glass. It came alive there. I am tired of fooling around he said. As for the rights of anyone, tell your people they can go fuck themselves. He swept the ears to the floor with his arm and held the last of his wine in the air. Something for your poetry, no? he said. Some of the ears on the floor caught this scrap of his voice. Some of the ears on the floor were pressed to the ground.

Study and Discussion Questions

1. What is going on in the poem? Who is the colonel? Why is the speaker visiting him?
2. Characterize the speaker's tone. What does it suggest?
3. Why does Forché mention such commonplace details as the daily papers, the pet dogs, the colonel's daughter's filing her nails?
4. Choose a section of this prose poem and look at and listen to the sound of the poem. How is Forché using assonance and consonance, repetition, and rhyme/slant rhyme? How does this create a mood and pull the observations together?
5. Why does the colonel have a sack of human ears? Why does he show them to the speaker?
6. What is the symbolic significance of the poem's final image?
7. Forché edited a large international collection of poetry entitled *Against Forgetting: The Poetry of Witness.* Look up the word *witness* for its various meanings. What do you think a "poetry of witness" is? How is "The Colonel" a poem of witness?

Suggestions for Writing

1. How is this "prose poem" like poetry and how is it like prose? Why do you think Forché chose this form instead of writing the poem in lines?
2. "On the television was a cop show. It was in English." What is the significance of this detail? Look into the history of El Salvador in the last few decades (Forché's subject) and discuss the poem in that context.

DENISE LEVERTOV (1923–1997)

Denise Levertov was born at Ilford, England. Her mother was Welsh and her father a Russian Jew who became an Anglican priest. After serving as a nurse during World War II, Levertov moved to the United States in 1948 and began establishing herself as a serious poet. While many critics associate her early work with the Black Mountain College poets of the 1950s such as Charles Olson and Robert Creeley, Levertov's work more precisely follows in the Imagist tradition of H. D. and William Carlos Williams. Her poetry is often noted for its balance between the material and spiritual worlds of existence. For Levertov, poetry was a mystical act: "To believe, as an artist, in inspiration or the intuitive, to know that without imagination . . . no amount of acquired scholarship or brilliant reasoning will suffice, is to live with the door of one's life open to the transcendent, the numinous" (241, *Levertov, New and Selected Essays*, 1992). Her writings include the poetry collections *The Jacob's Ladder* (1961), *The Sorrow Dance* (1968), *Relearning the Alphabet* (1970), *Freeing the Dust* (1975), *Candles in Babylon* (1982), *Breathing the Water* (1987), *A Door in the Hive* (1989), and *Sands of the Well* (1996); and several essay collections, including *The Poet in the World* (1973) and *Light Up the Cave* (1981). The poem "Life at War," written in 1968, is an example of Levertov's increasing preoccupation with the impact of the Vietnam War.

Life at War   (1968)

The disasters numb within us
caught in the chest, rolling
in the brain like pebbles. The feeling
resembles lumps of raw dough

weighing down a child's stomach on baking day.   5
Or Rilke said it, 'My heart . . .
Could I say of it, it overflows
with bitterness . . . but no, as though

its contents were simply balled into
formless lumps, thus   10
do I carry it about.'
The same war
continues.
We have breathed the grits of it in, all our lives,
our lungs are pocked with it,   15
the mucous membrane of our dreams

coated with it, the imagination
filmed over with the gray filth of it:

the knowledge that humankind,

delicate Man, whose flesh   20
responds to a caress, whose eyes
are flowers that perceive the stars,
whose music excels the music of birds,
whose laughter matches the laughter of dogs,
whose understanding manifests designs   25
fairer than the spider's most intricate web,

still turns without surprise, with mere regret
to the scheduled breaking open of breasts whose milk
runs out over the entrails of still-alive babies,
transformation of witnessing eyes to pulp-fragments,   30
implosion of skinned penises into carcass-gulleys.

We are the humans, men who can make;
whose language imagines *mercy,*
lovingkindness; we have believed one another
mirrored forms of a God we felt as good—   35

who do these acts, who convince ourselves
it is necessary; these acts are done
to our own flesh; burned human flesh
is smelling in Viet Nam as I write.

Yes, this is the knowledge that jostles for space   40
in our bodies along with all we
go on knowing of joy, of love;

our nerve filaments twitch with its presence
day and night,
nothing we say has not the husky phlegm of it in the saying,   45
nothing we do has the quickness, the sureness,
the deep intelligence living at peace would have.

Study and Discussion Questions

1. What images does Levertov use to describe what war does?
2. What images does she use to describe what human beings are and can be?
3. What does Levertov mean when she writes: "these acts are done/to our own flesh"?

Suggestions for Writing

1. Which one or more of the following best describes your initial response to this poem: despair, joy, nausea, pain, hope, disgust, shock, indifference? Why?
2. What does "living at peace" mean to you?
3. In a short paragraph, write what you see as the argument Levertov is making in this poem. That is, attempt to translate the poem into a brief, reasoned essay.

JAY PARINI (b. 1948)

Jay Parini grew up in Scranton, Pennsylvania, attended Lafayette College, and received his Ph.D. from the University of St. Andrews in Scotland in 1975. Parini is known for his diverse choice of genre, moving fluidly among poetry, prose, and biography. As he states in Contemporary Authors Online (2005), "Although my primary interest is writing poetry, I am now doing a lot of fiction and criticism . . . In a sense I use writing to pay attention to the world, to explain it to myself. The poems arise out of a strong wish to embody things: objects, emotions, ideas." Parini's poetry is often compared to that of Robert Frost's—introspective and searching, seeking to understand humankind's relationship to nature and the cosmos. Coincidentally, in 1999, Parini published the biography *Robert Frost: A Life*, a contemporary and sympathetic portrait of Frost and his complicated legacy. But Parini has created his own poetic style, one marked by craft and emotion and an innate sense of the malleability of language. He currently teaches at Middlebury College in Vermont. His writings include the poetry collections *Singing in Time* (1972), *Anthracite Country* (1982), *Town Life* (1988), and *House of Days* (1998); the novels *The Love Run* (1980), *The Patch Boys* (1986), *The Last Station* (1990), and *The Apprentice Lover* (2002); and the biographies *John Steinbeck: A Biography* (1995) and *One Matchless Time: The Life of William Faulkner* (2004). The poem "After the Terror" was written in response to the terrorist attacks of September 11, 2001.

After the Terror   (2003)

Everything has changed, though nothing has.
They've changed the locks on almost every door,
and windows have been bolted just in case:

It's business as usual, someone says.
Is anybody left to mind the store?   5
Everything has changed, though nothing has.

The same old buildings huddle in the haze,
with faces at the windows, floor by floor,
the windows they have bolted just in case.

No cause for panic, they maintain, because   10
the streets go places they have been before.
Everything has changed, though nothing has.

We're still a country that is ruled by laws.
The system's working, and it's quite a bore
that windows have been bolted just in case.   15

Believe in victory and all that jazz.
Believe we're better off, that less is more.
Everything has changed, though nothing has.
The windows have been bolted just in case.

Study and Discussion Questions

1. "After the Terror" is a villanelle, a type of poem which has a fixed form: five tercets, or three-line stanzas, plus one quatrain. What do you notice about the rhyme scheme of this poem and the use of repetition?
2. What does the title tell you about the subject of the poem?
3. The opening stanza sets the proposition for the poem; what is that proposition?
4. What kind of changes have been instituted, according to Parini? What hasn't changed?
5. What are the two images in the opening stanza?
6. Stanzas two, three, four, and five could be seen as stages in an argument Parini is making. What point does each stanza make? Through what image is each point made?
7. If we accept that Parini is making an argument here (and you may not), then the final quatrain is his conclusion. What is it?

Suggestions for Writing

1. Do you see "After the Terror" as a poem about fear and what we do with it? About the futility of changing the locks and bolting the windows after the disaster? About the political decisions that September 11, 2001, put in motion and their effect on the country? About . . . (add your own interpretation here)? Write a paper in dialogue with Parini's poem.

2. Compare/contrast "After the Terror" with another example of the villanelle form: "One Art" by Elizabeth Bishop.

ADRIENNE RICH (b. 1929)

Born in Baltimore, Maryland, Adrienne Rich grew up in an intellectual and artistic environment—her mother was a musician, her father a professor at Johns Hopkins University. Her poetic ability was first recognized by W. H. Auden when he selected *A Change of World* for the Yale Younger Poets Award in 1951 while Rich was attending Radcliffe College. Rich would marry two years later and have three children. The experience of motherhood would have a large impact on her perception of women in society (a topic she explores in *Of Woman Born: Motherhood as Experience and Institution*, 1976). While family responsibilities slowed her artistic output amidst the arrival of the 1960s, the Vietnam War, and the rise of feminism, Rich's work moved from its early formal structure to a more radical and political style, experimenting with line length, unorthodox spacing, dialogue, and longer sequencing. By the end of the 1960s, and into the 1970s, Rich produced some of her best-known work (poetry as well as essays)— writing that centers on acts of "transformation." For Rich, change is inevitable, but change and transformation are not synonymous: ". . . if the imagination is to transcend and transform experience, it has to question, to challenge, to conceive of alternatives, perhaps to the very life you are living at that moment" (from her essay, "When We Dead Awaken: Writing as Re-Vision"). This process often centers on questions of sexuality and what Rich sees as a patriarchal culture that has degraded the value of women. As exemplified throughout her career, Rich continues to assert the need for writers to participate actively in both the private and public well-being of a culture. Her other works include the poetry collections *Snapshots of a Daughter-in-Law: Poems 1954–1962* (1963), *Leaflets: Poems* (1969), The Will to Change: Poems, 1968–1970 (1971), *Diving into the Wreck: Poems, 1971–1972* (1973), *Twenty-One Love Poems* (1977), *The Fact of a Doorframe: Poems Selected and New, 1950–1984* (1984), *Dark Fields of the Republic, 1991–1995* (1995); and the essay collections *On Lies, Secrets, and Silence: Selected Prose, 1966–1978* (1979) and *What is Found There: Notebooks on Poetry and Politics* (1993). The following poem, the title poem of the collection, takes a critical look at the civilian consequences of war.

The School Among the Ruins   (2004)

Beirut. Baghdad. Sarajevo. Bethlehem. Kabul. Not of course here.

1.

Teaching the first lesson and the last
—great falling light of summer will you last
longer than schooltime?

When children flow
in columns at the doors   5
BOYS GIRLS and the busy teachers

open or close high windows
with hooked poles drawing darkgreen shades

closets unlocked, locked
questions unasked, asked, when   10

love of the fresh impeccable
sharp-pencilled yes
order without cruelty

a street on earth neither heaven nor hell
busy with commerce and worship   15
young teachers walking to school

fresh bread and early-open foodstalls

2.

When the offensive rocks the sky when nightglare
misconstrues day and night when lived-in

rooms from the upper city   20
tumble cratering lower streets

cornices of olden ornament human debris
when fear vacuums out the streets

When the whole town flinches
blood on the undersole thickening to glass   25

Whoever crosses hunched knees bent a contested zone
knows why she does this suicidal thing

School's now in session day and night
children sleep
in the classrooms teachers rolled close   30

3.

How the good teacher loved
his school the students
the lunchroom with fresh sandwiches

lemonade and milk
the classroom glass cages   35
of moss and turtles
teaching responsibility

A morning breaks without bread or fresh-poured milk
parents or lesson-plans
diarrhea first question of the day   40
children shivering it's September
Second question: where is my mother?

4.

One: I don't know where your mother
is Two: I don't know
why they are trying to hurt us   45
Three: or the latitude and longitude
of their hatred Four: I don't know if we
hate them as much I think there's more toilet paper
in the supply closet I'm going to break it open

Today this is your lesson: 50
write as clearly as you can
your name home street and number
down on this page
No you can't go home yet
but you aren't lost   55
this is our school

I'm not sure what we'll eat
we'll look for healthy roots and greens
searching for water though the pipes are broken

5.

There's a young cat sticking   60
her head through window bars
she's hungry like us
but can feed on mice
her bronze erupting fur
speaks of a life already wild   65

her golden eyes
don't give quarter She'll teach us Let's call her
Sister
when we get milk we'll give her some

6.

I've told you, let's try to sleep in this funny camp   70
All night pitiless pilotless things go shrieking
above us to somewhere

Don't let your faces turn to stone
Don't stop asking me why
Let's pay attention to our cat she needs us   75

Maybe tomorrow the bakers can fix their ovens

7.

"We sang them to naps told stories made
shadow-animals with our hands

washed human debris off boots and coats
sat learning by heart the names   80
some were too young to write
some had forgotten how"

Study and Discussion Questions

1. What function does the preface to the poem—"Beruit. Baghdad. Sarajevo. Bethlehem. Kabul. Not of course here."—serve?

2. There are seven sections to "The School Among the Ruins." What purpose does each section have? How does each section develop the overall image of the school among the ruins? As well as an image, is there a story being told here? What is it?
3. List at least four things that have changed for the students and teachers now that the school is in a war zone.
4. Discuss the images and the importance of food in the poem.
5. Discuss the appearance of the cat in section 5. How does the teacher turn this into a lesson? How is this lesson a measure of their changed circumstances?
6. In section 6 the teacher says to the students: "Don't let your faces turn to stone/ Don't stop asking me why." Discuss.
7. Section seven is in quotation marks. Who is speaking here and to whom? Identify the point of view in each of the seven sections of "The School Among the Ruins."
8. "The School Among the Ruins" gives us a vivid image of the situation of children in a time of war. Why do you think Adrienne Rich set this poem in a school instead of, say, in a refugee camp or some other location?

Suggestions for Writing

1. Do some research on the situation of children in a contemporary war zone.
2. Write a short poem or vivid prose piece from the point of view of one of the boys or girls in Rich's "The School Among the Ruins."

ADDITIONAL READINGS: SELECTIONS FROM MSU CREATIVE WRITERS

Courtesy of Megan Bean, MSU Photographer

FICTION

BECKY HAGENSTON

Becky Hagenston's second book of stories, *Strange Weather*, won the Spokane Prize for Short Fiction. Her first collection, *A Gram of Mars*, received the Mary McCarthy Prize. Her fiction has appeared in *The Southern Review, Crazyhorse, The Gettysburg Review, Mid-American Review, Shenandoah*, and many other journals, as well as the O. Henry anthology. Currently an Associate Professor of English at Mississippi State University, Hagenston earned her M.A. from New Mexico State University and her M.F.A. from the University of Arizona. "Vines" and "Anthony" appear in *Strange Weather*, published in 2010 by Press 53.

Vines

Their house sat on the beach, behind three palm trees, in a shade that came and went with the winds. Ronald flew an airplane and his wife Haley, who grew tomatoes, could look up and see the shadow of his plane flying over her garden. It wasn't easy growing a tomato garden right on the beach, but she had read a lot of books and taken some gardening classes at the community college, so she knew what she was doing. She used a very rare and special dirt that she made herself, and the winds blew enough that the palm trees provided just the right amount of shade.

Every day, Ronald got in his plane and scoured the seas for anyone who might be drowning, or for ships that were in trouble. It wasn't a job he got paid for—he had enough money from his late father's baked bean emporium—but it was one he took very seriously. Just last month, a cruise ship full of chefs sank, and if Ronald hadn't been flying his plane right then, they all would have drowned. The ocean was strewn with herbs and vegetables and chefs, bobbing frantically and screaming, waving spatulas and corkscrews. Ronald called the Coast Guard on his radio and flew around in circles until they arrived in boats to scoop up the chefs.

When he told his wife what he'd done, she insisted he invite the chefs over for dinner. They used up every last tomato on her vines, for their sauces and soups. They baked bread and made hors d'oeuvres with cheese sauces and tiny fish, and clapped each other on their backs and stuck their fingers in the pots while they cooked.

For the occasion, Ronald drove across the beach to the liquor store and bought wine, and Haley pulled out the folding chairs, and they all sat late into the night, talking—some of the chefs could speak English—and enjoying the food, most of which was tomato-based. Later, inside the house, Haley and Ronald made love, while the chefs slept on the beach, rolled in blankets. The next morning the chefs got in their van and drove away, tooting their horn, leaving behind their dirty pots and pans, and a garden full of empty vines.

Haley and Ronald met four years ago, in a dating class. Ronald was there because even though he was rich, he wasn't very attractive–he was ugly—and women dumped him after he'd bought them presents. They told him he didn't have enough personality to make up for his ugliness, so he was hoping this class would help him have more personality, at least on dates. At least on a first date.

Haley was there because even though she was very beautiful, she had a terrible, terrible secret: for three days every year, everything she touched turned to dirt. This had, of course, created problems in all of her relationships; as a child she had ruined her mother's necklaces, her father's shoes, her sister's prom dress. She'd been trying it on, six years old, and it turned to dirt right on her, crumbling away and leaving her standing naked in front of the mirror. Her sister had threatened to throw her out the window, then screamed nonstop until their mother took her to J.C. Penny for another, even more expensive, dress. It was kept locked in the armoire, along with the other things Haley was not allowed to touch. The one thing that didn't turn to dirt at her touch was human flesh. But only *human* flesh; she'd reduced five cats and two dogs to mulch by the time she was two.

For three days every year, Haley's mother and father kept her home from school, put her in a tent in the backyard where she couldn't do any damage. In the winter, they set up a heater for her. In the summer, she was instructed to play in the dirt that was already there, and when she was finished they used it on their garden.

There was, unfortunately, never any way of predicting when the three dirt days would happen.

When she was sixteen, she let a neighbor boy take her to McDonald's, and was just getting over her nervousness when her Big Mac crumbled into soil. The boy tried to ignore it—he was very polite—but she was afraid to touch his car so she walked home, and he thought that was rude.

She hadn't been on a date since, and she was twenty-five years old. She hoped to learn some skills in this class about how to meet men she could communicate with, men who would accept her for who she was and not think her rude when she refused to touch their cars.

In the first class, the instructor paired up the students and made them interview each other. She ended up with the ugliest man she'd ever seen, who told her he wanted to meet a woman who saw him for who he was on the inside; she told him about her Terrible Secret, and he took hold of her hands and kissed them. They didn't go to any of the other classes. They got married and moved to the beach, and Ronald bought an airplane with his late father's fortune, and Haley grew tomatoes, and for a while everything was perfect.

Two months after the chefs left, Haley realized she was pregnant. When she told her husband, they cried for happiness and for despair, because what if their baby had to suffer as they'd suffered? What if she turned her crib to dirt, what if no one liked her, what if she grew up ugly and afraid? Then they vowed that they would never keep her outside in a tent, and they would tell her she was beautiful even if she was not, even if it meant hiding mirrors from her.

But then the baby was born, a girl, and she *was* beautiful. They named her Stacy. A year passed, and she grew hair and teeth and learned how to say words, and nothing turned to dirt in her grasp. And better still, nothing turned to dirt in Haley's grasp, either. She thought maybe, somehow, she might have missed those three days, but the next year again nothing happened, and then the next, until she realized she was cured.

Stacy loved tomatoes; she'd crawl around outside in the summer and eat them off the vine. And when she was older, Haley told her the story of the chefs who came to their house the night she was conceived, and how they made tomato soup and tomato sauce and tomato and cheese dips, and fish with tomatoes. Stacy wanted to hear that story over and over. She listened rapt, her face and mouth covered with seeds and juice, her eyes as wild as the bobbing, soupy sea.

As the years went by, Ronald continued to fly his plane, and the beach became more and more crowded with tourists, some of whom came from far away to buy Haley's sauces. Stacy went to school, and when she was 18 she told her parents she wanted to move to Paris and become a chef.

Ronald and Haley were not happy. "Can't you go to the community college?" Haley asked her, knowing she was asking the impossible. Because Stacy needed to know more than Haley or the noncredit cooking classes could teach her, she needed to use spices Haley had never heard of, oils from exotic lands, leaves from trees that grew far away. She needed to learn about puddings and cakes, things that went beyond tomatoes, things tomatoes had no use for.

So she went. Her parents stood on the beach and watched the sliver of her jumbo jet vanish over the water, and five days later they got a post card of the Eiffel Tower.

Condos were going up all over the beach, and sometimes camera crews filmed tv shows there. Haley and Ronald were asked to sell their house, and they said no, so a construction crew cut down their palm trees instead, and built a Sno-Cone stand and parking lot. Next to that was a kiosk where you could get your picture made into a keychain.

When Stacy left, the tomatoes didn't grow as well, and when the palm trees came down they didn't grow at all. Haley bought Miracle Grow, but that didn't work. And even though they were rich, they felt starved, and even though they were together, they felt alone. Stacy called rarely, and her voice was sounding different, foreign and staticky and annoyed. She told her parents she couldn't see them anymore because they made her feel strange and unwell, and why couldn't they be like other parents? Why couldn't they go out to movies with friends? Why didn't they move to New York or someplace exciting?

Sometimes she sent them canned tomatoes, but they weren't the same, and they weren't enough.

There was something wrong with Haley. She felt old and tired and sad. Ronald asked, "What can I get you?" but she couldn't think of anything she wanted except her daughter and tomatoes, and since Stacy would not come home, Ronald flew over the countryside looking for the best tomatoes he could find. He'd bring them to her in her bed, on a golden plate. She'd take one weary bite and then shake her head and fall back against her pillows. But Ronald had noticed something: when he flew his plane across their garden, the tomatoes grew a little. He told this to Haley, and she struggled out of bed with a look on her face that made him want to weep.

"Would you?" she asked, and he would.

He flew and he flew, and because he loved her so much, cruise ships sank and children floated out to sea in their blow-up rafts. And finally Haley couldn't remember his face at all, and it was as if all she'd ever loved was the angel-shaped shadow that cast itself across her garden, and made it grow.

Anthony

The ghost had gotten inside her daughter like a tapeworm and refused to come out. How had it happened? Was it something Cindy ate? Something in the water? The water in Boardtown, Alabama was bad, everybody knew it; Nia usually bought bottled water at Wal-Mart but this week she'd been cheap, she'd been lazy, she hadn't wanted to haul all those bottles to the car. And now a ghost inhabited her child and wouldn't be budged.

Her husband Jake blamed it on Nia; *he* would never let something like this happen to their child; he would have beat the crap out of that ghost before it could get near his daughter. Nia didn't argue with him. She had been planning to leave him for months. He had a temper and she was almost positive he was screwing the waitress at Longshots, the bar where they'd met seven years ago and where he spent more and more of his time, sometimes not coming home until three-thirty in the morning. The bar closed at two, so what the hell was he doing until three-thirty? Not that she cared.

"It's because you don't make her take a bath every day," he said. "It's because you feed her macaroni and cheese from a box. That shit is horrible for a kid."

"How the hell do you know what I feed her? Since when are you around for any meals anyway?" Sometimes she argued with him just because she wanted to see how close he would get to hitting her. He'd done it once and she'd threatened to take Cindy and leave if he ever did it again, and now when he clenched his fists and got up in her face, she stared right back at him and said, "I dare you," and watched him use every ounce of his strength not to bash her in the nose. She wanted to laugh every time, because she was leaving him anyway.

It must have happened on Tuesday night, when—yes, she *had* forgotten to give Cindy a bath after her dinner of mac and cheese from a box. Nia had been on the computer finishing up her homework for Accounting 101, a ridiculously easy course taught by a man who looked like he was twelve. Still, it was hard to keep up when you had a child and a full-time job at Blockbuster. She wanted more for herself, and just when she thought she was getting somewhere— didn't it figure—something like this had to happen.

The kindergarten teacher, Miss Missy, had been the one to take Cindy to the nurse's office on Wednesday morning. Miss Missy had seen many things in her life: she'd seen a crop dusting plane fall out of the sky above the cotton fields behind her house; she'd woken up in the middle of the night to see her baby sister in the arms of a Skunk Ape (startled by Missy's cries, it had dropped the baby back in the crib and fled out the window); she'd seen the spirit of her lynched grandfather swinging from a tree.

So when tiny, blonde Cindy Morgan's stomach shouted, "Time to party!" in the voice of a young black male, Miss Missy kept her wits. The children were just down for their naps, and Miss Missy was in the process of cleaning up the Nilla wafer crumbs and milk cartons from snack time. She detested Nilla wafers, but the children loved them. Those, and Fig Newtons. Her own childhood in Tuscaloosa had been filled with chitlins—which stunk halfway down the street—and pork barbeque. She and her sister munched happily on fried pig snouts ("*Snoots*," her Mawmaw called them) after school, watching The *Munsters* and *Gilligan's Island* until their mother came home from work.

"Time to party!" said Cindy Morgan's belly, and the other children turned on their mats and yawned, and Cindy sat up and said, in her own baby-voice, "Miss Missy, I feel funny."

Miss Missy walked briskly across the room, knelt, and felt Cindy's forehead.

"I ain't sick, I'm dead," said the voice from Cindy's stomach. Or maybe it was more the solar plexis. It was hard to be sure.

Nurse would know.

Nurse felt dread when she saw Miss Missy marching Cindy Morgan into her office. She had noticed the girl earlier that month, being dropped off twenty minutes late in a rusty orange El Camino by a woman in a too-short skirt and too-high heels. Mothers like this were usually bad news; they usually had boyfriends with tattoos and motorcycles, boyfriends who didn't like little children. Or liked them too much.

Please, no bruises, Nurse prayed silently, and looked Miss Missy in the eye, as if daring her to say what Nurse least wanted to hear.

"Cindy here is having stomach . . . . difficulties," said Miss Missy. She put her hands on Cindy's shoulders and said, "Sweetheart, Nurse will take care of you, okay?"

"Okay," said Cindy Morgan, and then Miss Missy spun on a heel—Nurse admired Miss Missy's ability to wear heels—and was gone.

Nurse leaned down and looked into Cindy's pale blue eyes. "Does your tummy hurt?" she asked, smiling, relieved that her worst fears had not come to pass. Two weeks ago, she had lifted up Timmy Maxwell's Pooh Bear shirt to discover cigarette burns around his nipples. A woman from Social Services had arrived to lead a sobbing Timmy out to a big white car. Nurse hadn't seen him since.

She led Cindy into an examination room and helped the girl up to the paper-covered table. "Can you tell me where it hurts?"

"I feel like dancin'," said the voice of a young black man. Then he laughed, a joyful sound that made Nurse almost laugh, too.

Cindy frowned. "He wants to dance," she said. "But I don't."

"Well, now, let's just take a look." Nurse lifted up Cindy's pink Care Bears shirt and placed her stethoscope on her white stomach.

"It's cold," Cindy said, and then giggled.

"Breathe deeply," said Nurse. "That's a good girl. Will you lie down for me, sweetheart?"

Cindy lay her head back on the paper pillow and closed her eyes. Nurse touched around her belly button very gently, trying to locate the source of the strange male voice. She had never encountered anything like this before, had never read about it in nursing school or on any of the nursing blogs she looked at every evening while she ate a Lean Cuisine in front of her computer.

"Hello?" said Nurse. "Is anybody there?"

"*I'm* here," said the young male voice. "I'm here and I'm ready to party. Hell yeah!" He laughed again, and Nurse couldn't help smiling. Then he said, gently, "You're a damn good nurse," and Nurse felt herself blushing and had to turn away and clear her throat.

Nia was at work that Wednesday afternoon, scanning in new DVDs of some violent Mexican movie she couldn't pronounce, when she got the phone call from the nurse's office. Then she had to bribe Sherry to cover for her by offering to work the weekend shift. Sherry was a sorority girl and she worked at Blockbuster because, as the poorest girl in the sorority, she needed the money but only if she could work a job that wouldn't make her seem like too much of a loser. Before Blockbuster, she had worked at McDonalds, which was humiliating, absolutely mortifying, all that grease, all those miserable single mothers she had to work with! She lasted one day because at the start of her second shift, Tad from Psi Upsilon came in and ordered hashbrowns and then said, "Fuck, Sherry. What are you doing here?" and Sherry took off her paper cap and yelled, "I quit!" right there. She'd hoped Tad might be so impressed by this that he'd ask her out, but he'd just laughed and asked for ketchup.

Blockbuster was better because a) there was no grease and b) she could watch movies all day long and c) sometimes she could get Nia to take over the weekend shift for her, so she could go out with her friends, cruise the bars—there weren't many—and meet up with boys, though not Tad, because he'd date-raped this girl Racine and everybody knew it, even though she refused to go to campus police.

Nia always had a frazzled look about her, and her hair looked like it had been bleached too many times. Sometimes Sherry wished she could give Nia a make-over.

When Nia got Cindy home, she took her temperature (normal, just as the nurse had said) and tucked her into bed and brought her some chicken noodle soup.

"It's probably just a virus, sweetheart," she told Cindy, and she heard the young man sigh heavily and mutter something.

"Did you want to speak up?" Nia demanded, and the young man said, "No, ma'am," very politely. "Do you want to leave, then?" she said, and he didn't answer.

When Jake got home, Nia took him into the living room and explained, quietly, what the nurse had told her: Cindy had the ghost of a young black man living in her stomach, and he didn't seem dangerous, but they ought to keep an eye on her.

That's when Jake accused her of not feeding or bathing Cindy properly, and that's when Nia dared him to smack her.

Jake could be a good father when he put his mind to it, and he picked Cindy up from her bed and kissed her on the cheek and said, "What's this about feeling bad?"

"I'm okay now," she said.

"Who are you?" Jake demanded of Cindy's stomach. "What do you want from us?"

"Don't yell at him," said Nia. "His name is Anthony." She'd actually had a pleasant, though brief, conversation with the young man. He'd died in a car accident, but he wouldn't talk much about that except to say that people should wear their seatbelts.

"Anthony?" shouted Jake. "Make thyself known!"

"For God's sake, Jake," said Nia. "He's not a Shakespearan actor. He's just a teenaged boy."

"Can I have the television in my room?" Cindy wanted to know, and Anthony said, "Say please," and Cindy said, "Please?"

"Show some respect," Anthony said, and then didn't say anything else for the rest of the night, although he chuckled occasionally during the *Happy Days* reruns.

That night, Miss Missy told her new boyfriend Hank about Cindy Morgan.

"It must be so hard on the family," she said. "But people learn to live with things, you find ways to get by."

Hank, who taught third grade, thought Miss Missy (he just called her Missy) was the most graceful, beautiful, intelligent woman he had ever met. He loved the little gap in her teeth and he loved that she wore such sexy clothes to work, those tight pencil skirts and high heels. No jumpers and sneakers for her, like the other kindergarten teachers wore.

They had only been dating for two months but he was ready to ask her to marry him; he could picture their children playing in the swingset at his mother's house, could imagine calling, "Henry! Deanne! Time for dinner!"

Now was not the time to propose, however; Missy looked vexed. She paced the floor in her bare feet. She sat down on the sofa and put her head in her hands. The polish on her toenails was pink and the polish on her fingernails was silver. He felt his breath catch, and tried to focus.

Hank had never heard of this particular situation, but he admired Missy's ability to try to get to the bottom of things. "I think they'll be fine," he told her, and she leaned against him and closed her eyes. And even though he had transparencies to make and dioramas to grade, he stroked her head and said "There, there," until she was snoring.

Nurse was at home, eating a Lean Cuisine in front of her computer and Googling "child ghosts", which did not produce the result she was looking for. "Stomach ghost" she tried, and then "haunted stomach" but again, the results proved fruitless. Then she found herself tempted to type in the dating website that had gotten her here in the first place, living alone in a podunk Alabama town, so she turned the computer off. She told herself she wasn't that lonely, and if she was she should just go to sleep and not think about it.

Cindy's pediatrician said, "I can't vaccinate her for this, but I don't think she's in any danger."

"She's not," said Anthony.

"They're getting along pretty well," said Nia. "I hear them talking late at night sometimes."

"How long has this been going on?" the pediatrician asked, suddenly suspicious.

"Only about . . . less than a week?" Nia said. She was lying. It had been three weeks since Anthony made his appearance, but she told herself it wasn't as if Cindy was *ill*. Besides, Cindy hated the doctor. But the school Nurse was scaring Nia with stories of parasites and poltergeists and wanted Cindy to take antibiotics, so Nia thought she'd better get a second opinion.

And Cindy and Anthony *were* getting along; that part was true. Last night Nia had hovered outside Cindy's door—Cindy liked to keep it closed now, even though she used to be afraid of the dark—and heard Cindy giggling, and then Anthony laughing, and then Cindy talking, Anthony replying. More giggling from both of them. What on earth did they have to say to one another, a six-year-old and a dead fifteen-year-old? Nia was tempted to hide a tape recorder under Cindy's bed, but she wasn't entirely sure how to rig it so it wouldn't click loudly when it shut off.

"How's your husband handling this?" the pediatrician asked, in low tones.

Nia rolled her eyes. "Fine," she said.

The truth was, Jake had been mad because Anthony was black. He wanted a white ghost. He wanted, specifically, Marilyn Monroe. "Or James Dean!" he'd said. "How cool would that be?"

What could you do with a man like that?

"You feel all right, don't you, Cindy-girl?" said the pediatrician, producing a green lollipop from his coat, and Cindy said, "Yes, sir, I feel fine. Thank you for asking."

"Well, now!" laughed the pediatrician. "Aren't you polite."

Nia felt stung. It was Anthony who'd taught her that.

He still sometimes said "hell" and wistfully said he wanted to party, but only when Cindy was taking a nap or preoccupied with cartoons.

"What kind of party do you want, Anthony?" Nia asked once, when they were watching tv together on the sofa. (Cindy had fallen asleep during *Dateline*; Anthony enjoyed it, as he enjoyed most of the programs Nia watched.) All she could get out of him was a sigh. He did that a lot, and it made her sad for him. It made him seem older than his years.

Jake thought Anthony was a riot. At first, yes, he was pissed off, and not because he was a racist, either. He just figured that if his daughter was going to have a ghost in her stomach, it ought to be someone . . . . well, famous. Someone interesting. He wanted the tv news crews to come over and interview him, and interview the famous person, and maybe film the two of them together— Jake and James Dean—chatting about cars or something.

But Anthony was a cool little dude, and he cracked Jake up. One evening, when Nia was at her accounting class and Cindy was napping on the sofa (Cindy napped a lot lately), he had said, "You know how to make a hormone?"

"A what?" said Jake.

"Don't pay her."

When Jake stopped laughing he said, "Do you—did you play any sports when you were alive? Basketball, maybe?"

"Nah," said Anthony. "I had to take care of my little brothers after school, help out my mother and shit."

"What about your dad?"

"What about him?" Anthony said bitterly.

Anthony needed a father figure, someone to talk about guy stuff with, someone to guide him in the ways of women.

"You can talk to me," Jake said. "I'm here for you."

"'Preciate it," Anthony said.

One night, when Cindy was sound asleep, Nia tiptoed into her daughter's bedroom and whispered, "Anthony? Are you awake?"

"I'm awake," he said. "Don't need no sleep. Just lyin' here, collectin' my thoughts."

She pulled a chair next to the bed, stroked Cindy on her pale forehead. "I'm just wondering how long you were planning on staying? Not that it isn't nice having you."

"Nice bein' here!" he cried. "I mean it. I like you people. You all right."

Nia felt relieved, then remembered why she was there. "I was just thinking," she said, "that there might be something you want, or need . . . something to, I don't know, help you go toward the light? Somehow?"

He didn't say anything.

"Don't you have parents wondering where you are? I know that if I were dead and Cindy was also dead, and I didn't get to see her, I'd worry."

"Dunno," he said, and gave one of his sad little sighs.

Then, because she had spent lunch hour crying in the Blockbuster bathroom, and because she was failing her accounting class, and because here was this sad boy lost and far from home, she broke down and wept. "I'm sorry," she sniffled, "I'm sorry if it's my fault."

"It ain't," Anthony said gently. "Shit just happens."

"I'm thinking I should leave Jake," she admitted, and cried a little harder.

"Aw, man, that sucks," Anthony said. "Whaddya gonna do that for anyways?"

"He's a terrible husband," she said. "He's never home, and I know he's screwing some slut he met at Longshots! Sorry," she added, and blushed. Sometimes it was hard to remember that Anthony was barely more than a child himself.

"Seems like he's home all the time," Anthony said, and Nia realized it was true. Just last night, she had come home from class to find Jake, Cindy and Anthony playing Candyland on the kitchen table. "Where's the babysitter?" she had demanded, and Jake said, "I sent her home," and moved his marker toward Gumdrop Mountain.

And two nights ago, Jake had offered to help cook dinner.

"Because I'm such a terrible cook, is that right?" she'd snapped, and he'd kissed her on the cheek and said no, he just wanted to help out.

"I only married him because I was pregnant," she whispered. Anthony didn't say anything, and so after a moment she gave Cindy's tummy a pat and tiptoed from the room.

Miss Missy enjoyed having Anthony in the classroom. He was never disruptive, and the other students listened to him. If anyone got too rambunctious— if Gino pulled Caroline's hair, or Dana hit Rachel—Anthony would say, "Have some respect!" and they would stop.

You expected ghosts to be trouble, but Anthony was a joy, and this is what she wrote on his progress report. But it concerned her that he wasn't getting the kind of education he needed. *Anthony could go very far*, she wrote, *if he had the opportunity*.

On Cindy's report, she wrote: *Needs to speak up more in class*. Then, because she liked the girl, she added: *Cindy is a sweet child, and she knows most of her numbers*.

At the parent-teacher conference, she suggested to Cindy's parents that Anthony needed a tutor. Just because he was dead and stuck inside a six-year-old's body didn't mean he should be denied a good education. Everyone had things to overcome.

"We're all," she said, "differerently-abled, in our own way."

"We'll look into it," Cindy's father said. "We only want the best for him."

"You're good parents," Miss Missy said. "Anthony is lucky he found you."

Their usual babysitter was busy, so when Jake asked Nia on a date ("Remember dates?" he asked), they had to scramble to find someone else. Nia immediately thought of Sherry.

"He doesn't need a babysitter," Jake had insisted.

"No, but she does," said Nia.

Really, thank God she was the responsible parent around here. Thank God at least one of them was watching out for their daughter.

"Will you be nice to the babysitter?" Nia asked Cindy, and Cindy yawned and said, "Okay," in a tiny voice.

"That's my girl," Nia said.

Sherry was surprised by how neat Nia's house was; she'd been expecting something much dumpier and red-necky—maybe a Confederate flag and a beat-up pickup truck in the driveway—but it wasn't bad at all, certainly no trashier than some of the fraternity houses she'd been to. There were candles and potpourri in the living room and framed pictures of Cindy as a baby, Nia holding her and smiling at the camera, looking almost beautiful. Most surprising of all, Nia's husband was a hottie. How did someone like her end up with someone like him?

Nia had led Sherry through the house (she caught a glimpse of the master bedroom, of the neatly made bed and the big pillows), ending up in the kitchen and saying, "Here's all the emergency numbers, poison control, you know the drill. I'll have my cell phone with me. Help yourself to the Hot Pockets in the freezer. Cindy already had her dinner."

"Is there anybody else I should call if I can't get through? Cindy's grandparents or something?" Sherry didn't care about Cindy's grandparents, she was just nosy.

"Grandparents are dead," Nia said, and then frowned as if something had just occurred to her. "Actually, there is someone you could contact." That's when she told Sherry about Anthony. "He's been quiet the past few hours, but he'll probably be around later on. He likes to watch Dateline. He's really good with kids, and he's smarter than you'd think for someone so young. I just didn't feel comfortable leaving her alone, you know? Because they do share the same body, so if she fell down or something, there's nothing he could really do."

Sherry nodded. "Gotcha," she said. She couldn't wait to call up Tad—he wasn't her boyfriend, exactly, but he had started hanging around the store lately, and a couple of times they made out in the back room. She gave him DVDs from the sale rack—who was going to notice if they were gone anyway? But she didn't think that was the only reason he liked her. He told her Racine made up the date-rape stuff, and she believed him because it was exactly the sort of thing Racine would do.

Cindy was lying on the floor, coloring in a My Pretty Pony coloring book. Sherry sat down next to her. She was terrible with kids, but she needed the money, so what could she do? "Hey there," she said, in a fake-sounding voice. "Whatcha got there?"

"My Pretty Pony," Cindy said. "Do you want to color with me?"

The girl looked pale and her eyes were bleary.

"Um, not really," Sherry said. She'd read somewhere that it was important to be honest with kids. Was that in her Marriage and the Family class? She'd pretty much snoozed through that one. That class was full of brainless debutantes who wanted to be married by the time they were twenty.

"Okay," Cindy sighed, and went back to listlessly running a blue crayon over the page.

With Cindy occupied, Sherry made herself comfortable on the sofa and took out her cell phone.

"Who you callin?" It startled her, that voice coming out of Cindy's stomach.

"Tad," she said, and the voice laughed as if that was the funniest thing in the world.

"Tad! Tad ain't a name. *Tad*. Oh, *Tad*." He was imitating a British voice now. "I *say* now Tad, tally ho and all that."

"Cut that out. You don't even know him. He's in a fraternity and he's really cute and really cool."

"Yeah, he sounds like a real—" he lowered his voice. "A real dick weed, you know?"

"You don't know shit," she said. Then something occurred to her. "Do you? I mean, can you see what he's doing right now?"

"Jackin' off," he said. "But he sure ain't thinking of you."

Sherry didn't buy it. "You're just being a jerk."

Cindy gave a loud sigh and put her head down on her coloring book.

"That's right sweetie," said Sherry. "You take a nap now."

Sherry told Anthony about Tad, about how he came to the store and she gave him DVDs and how they kissed in the back room, and how he didn't date rape Racine after all.

"He's using you," Anthony said. "That is typical male behavior, is what that is. He ever take you on a date?"

"No," she said. "But so what?"

"You know so what," he said. "You can do better."

"I can?" said Sherry. She felt herself getting weepy. It was true, everything Anthony was saying. "I want him to like me!" she wailed. "I want him."

"Why?"

"Because," she said, and started crying again. Finally she managed to whisper, "Because he doesn't want me."

They talked and talked, and Anthony told her jokes, and she forgot all about the Hot Pockets and watching tv and she even forgot about calling Tad. When she heard the keys jingling in the lock a little before midnight, she quickly scooped up snoring Cindy and tucked her into bed. When Nia peeked her head in, Sherry was stroking Cindy's cheek and saying, "You're such a sweetheart, such a sweetheart."

Sometimes Nurse poked her head into Miss Missy's classroom and said, "Can I please speak to Cindy?" She felt it was important to keep close tabs on the girl, make sure she was doing all right.

Also, she enjoyed talking to Anthony. She even found herself telling him about Rick, the man she'd met online, the man she had moved to Alabama for and who had broken her heart. She'd met him in a chat room for certain personality types, and after chatting for a few months he bought a plane ticket to Boston. Nurse was 42 and Rick was 36, and—she didn't tell Anthony this part—the sex as the best she'd ever had. Her ex-husband Denny had been clumsy. Two months later she'd quit her job at Boston General and moved to Alabama for love. Or, more accurately, for sex—again, she didn't tell Anthony this, only that "I really thought I'd found my soul mate, the man I'd spend the rest of my life with."

But after supporting him for six months—paying his rent, buying dog food for his ridiculous Doberman—she'd had enough. Soon, she would make her way back east, but she had used up all her savings and she had to get her head on straight, "so here I am," she said, "and I have to tell myself I'm doing some good with my life, that I'm making some kind of difference, ortherwise I'll go nuts." Then she told him—because he was such a good listener—about the poverty and the abuse and the kids who came to her office twice a week for baths because they had no hot water at home. It almost broke her heart, she was almost ready to give up, and then—

"And then?" said Anthony.

"And then you came along," she said, and patted Cindy on the knee.

Miss Missy found Cindy hiding in the coat cubby, crying and pounding on her stomach.

"Cindy sweetheart, what is it?"

Cindy continued pummeling her stomach with her tiny fists. "I hate you!" she sobbed. "Go home."

Miss Missy took her by the hand and led her down the hall to the Nurse, who gave Cindy a red lollipop and told her she shouldn't hit people.

"Yes, ma'am," Cindy said weakly.

"I'm sure you didn't mean to hurt Anthony's feelings."

"Yes, ma'am," Cindy whispered.

The pediatrician said, "She'll eat when she's hungry."

"But it's been two whole days," Nia said. "Her teacher says she won't even drink her milk during snack time."

"You feeling all right, Cindy-girl?" said the pediatrician.

"She's fine," said Anthony.

"You're looking out for her, young man, aren't you?" said the pediatrician. "Keep it up. Maybe you-all should take her out for a cheeseburger. You feel like a cheeseburger, Cindy?"

Cindy shrugged.

"She doesn't have a fever," the pediatrician said. "But if she's feeling poorly, let her stay home from school a couple of days."

The tutor came for three hours in the morning and taught Anthony history, English, and math. Since Cindy couldn't stay awake long enough to read, the tutor read the text books out loud to Anthony and then asked him questions. The Socratic Method. The tutor was a twenty-nine-year-old named Mark who was majoring in Special Education and needed the money to pay tuition. Last year he'd tutored a blind girl, but she was kind of a bitch—he hated to admit it, but it was true—and so it was a pleasure to have a tutee as enthusiastic and intelligent as Anthony. He was lazy at times—but what fifteen-year-old wasn't?

Mark read him "A Good Man is Hard to Find" and Anthony laughed at the beginning, at the grandmother and the cat and the bratty kids, and then he got quiet and then he started saying, "Oh no way, man. No way." After Mark finished Anthony said, "I didn't see that coming. Man. That was a damn good story. What else you got?"

Sometimes Mark stayed for four hours instead of three, but he told Nia not to worry about paying him for the extra hour.

"Anthony honey," said Nia, spooning chicken noodle soup into Cindy's mouth. "You have to go." It broke her heart to say it.

"Got nowhere *to* go," he said. "I like you people."

"Well, Cindy's feeling bad and I hate to say it, but I think it's because of you."

"Maybe she has the flu," said Anthony, sulkily. "Ain't my fault if she has the flu."

"It *might* be the flu," Nia allowed. "But I don't think so."

Anthony didn't answer. He didn't say anything the rest of the day, or the next, or the day after that. Cindy got out of bed and lay on the floor in her nightgown, coloring.

One evening at dinner, Jake said, "Anthony, you want to watch *Die Hard* with me?" No response. "God damn it," said Jake. "I'm going out for a little while."

Alone in the house with Cindy, Nia felt a depth of emptiness she hadn't felt in months. When Cindy crawled into her lap with a Berenstein Bears book, Nia said, "Not now honey, Mommy's tired." Then, feeling guilty, she said, "Oh, okay." But she couldn't muster up much enthusiasm.

It wasn't that she was upset that Jake had left, that he had probably gone to Longshots to meet up with the waitress. She felt relieved. She had realized, over the past few months, with Jake always around—always wanting to spend time with her, always after her in bed—that not only did she not love him, she never could. His hands were rough; he had a dumb sense of humor. *He's a good man*, she told herself; *he's a good father*.

She had married him because she couldn't think of a better alternative. It was hard being a single mother; her own mother had raised her and they had nearly starved, had slept in the car for two weeks, had shoplifted milk and hot dogs.

She and Jake had hardly even known each other; they had slept together more than dated; she was missing her ex when he came along. She'd had too much too drink.

She used to tell herself that she could fall in love with him, if he'd give her the chance. But she couldn't. She never would.

Miss Missy noticed that Cindy Morgan was losing her blank, haunted look. Her eyes were no longer lined with black circles. She was drinking her milk, and she played patty cake.

But the class was in shambles.

Without Anthony in the classroom, Dana hit Rachel and Gregory pushed Benjamin off the swings and Wendall gave Marty a black eye. Veronica cried in the corner during story time and kicked anyone who got near her.

"Children need role models," Miss Missy said to Hank.

"Our children will be happy," he said, and Miss Missy was so surprised she couldn't think of a response.

Nurse treated the children's cuts and took their temperatures, and she called Social Services when a third grader named Reggie showed up in her office with welts on his back.

Sometimes she stayed awake until three a.m., emailing men and telling them she was thinner, blonder, and happier than she actually was. Sometimes she told them she would meet them, but she never did.

Jake started staying out until three-thirty every night, and when he got home he passed out on the sofa. One early morning Nia thought she heard him crying in his sleep, and she wished there was something she could do. But there wasn't.

She missed Anthony. She knew he was there—where else could he go?—but he refused to speak. Sometimes she could swear she heard him sniffling, just a little. It broke her heart.

And then one night when she was tucking Cindy in, Anthony said, "I missed talking to ya'll."

Nia was so happy she picked Cindy out of bed and kissed her on the stomach, which made her daughter shriek and kick and wail.

"Don't do that again," Nia said. "Do you promise?"

"I promise," said Anthony, but he had to say it twice, so Nia could hear him over Cindy's sobs.

It was Miss Missy who told Nurse that Cindy Morgan was no longer enrolled in school, that Cindy's mother had moved away, taking the child and leaving the father behind. He had come home from work and found them gone.

"That's too bad," said Nurse. She looked like she was about to cry. "I'll miss them."

"Yes," said Miss Missy. She was mulling over Hank's proposal and had been distracted for the past few days; there was so much risk involved, this tying of oneself to another. Things could get complicated.

Nurse was staring sullenly at the floor. Miss Missy thought of giving her a hug, of telling her everything would be fine. She wanted to reassure Nurse that she would find love someday, that she had to have faith that everything would work out for the best. She wanted to ask Nurse if she thought she was doing the right thing, marrying Hank, because things could go so wrong so fast, and you never knew what you were in for.

"They might be back," Nurse said, in a hoarse whisper. "They might."

"They might," said Miss Missy. She gave Nurse an awkward pat on the arm, then headed back to her classroom to dole out the Nilla wafers.

❀ ❀ ❀

MICHAEL KARDOS

Michael Kardos is the author of the story collection *One Last Good Time*. He received a degree in music from Princeton University, an M.F.A. in fiction from The Ohio State University, and a Ph.D. in English from the University of Missouri. His short stories have appeared in *The Southern Review, Crazyhorse, Prairie Schooner*, and many other magazines and anthologies, and were cited as Notable Stories in the 2009 and 2010 editions of *Best American Short Stories*. He co-directs the creative writing program at Mississippi State University. "Lures of Last Resort" and "Population 204" appear in *One Last Good Time*, published in 2011 by Press 53.

Lures of Last Resort

One July morning, three men came walking up to my dad and me while we fished off the public pier. This was back in my hometown, in Breakneck Beach, home of the Breakneck Beach Sea Devils and Rex's Italian Sausages. The particular rod I was fishing with, and the reel, too, I'd gotten that spring for doing nothing more than turning a year older. I had just dropped my line into the water when I saw the three men coming our way. They weren't fishermen. Their work pants were ironed smooth, and as they got close I could smell aftershave. Their faces didn't have the wrinkles you get from squinting into the sun. Didn't carry fishing rods either, these men. One of them held an expensive-looking camera. Another carried a small plastic box. The third man didn't carry anything; he just smiled dumbly.

"Take a look at this, gentlemen," the man carrying the box said to us. His voice sounded deep and resonant like the disc jockeys that my folks listened to on the radio. *Fat Billy spinning the oldies. Big Joey bringin' it to you.* This man wasn't big, though, just tall. And skinny like me. He unclasped the box. "You gentlemen won't believe what you see."

I wasn't any gentleman. What ten-year-old is? And the green plastic box, and those feathery lures that looked like little peacocks—I'd seen them before. They were Reel Catch lures, manufactured right here in Breakneck Beach, and my dad used to sell them. Until a month earlier, Dad had sold all sorts of Reel Catch gear to tackle shops and sporting-goods stores. He had spent his days driving up and down the Jersey Shore drumming up orders for reels and fillet knives and those portable toilets for boats with no johns. And lures, too, same as these.

"You'll catch your supper in no time flat," the man said. His v-neck shirt said Reel Catch in one corner and had a stitched-on logo that looked like the lures in the box.

Since mid-June we'd been fishing that pier, my dad and I, every sticky morning from sunrise to ten a.m. I'd wake to the sound of my bedroom door squeaking open. "Up and at 'em," my dad would say, then leave me in the dark to pull on some clothes while he went to the kitchen for coffee, which always smelled good even though, like beer, it was off-limits.

That summer you could have caught fish just by asking nicely. Flukes and snappers. Flounders. Bluefish. Didn't matter to me what we caught; I didn't eat fish, and Dad was allergic. (Mom would eat anything we put on her plate and pretend to like it.) At the end of the fishing pier, my dad would fillet our day's catch and separate the fillets into baggies, and when we came home we'd strut around the apartment complex like a couple of heroes, ringing doorbells and giving everybody free fish that'd stink up their apartments in about a minute. What we didn't give away my dad would put in the freezer, till the freezer had nothing but fish in it and my mother would say things like "We have enough fish, don't we?" or "Maybe tomorrow you two ought to take a rest." But we never did.

The man holding the box said, "These lures're made special like that, colorful, to attract—"

"I know exactly what they're meant to do," my dad said. "Who the hell do you think I am? Son, why don't you tell these men who I am."

So I told them. "My dad is Lee Gernipoethy."

The men looked at one another and then back at my dad. "Well, Jesus, we didn't . . . we were sent out here on a little promotional stint. That's all. Giving away some lures. We didn't know. . . ."

You say our last name like Gunnipuddy, and it's a name people don't forget. Especially when you're a big man like my dad, six-two and broad like the linebacker he'd been till senior year, when he quit high school for reasons that, though he never said so outright, had a lot to do with my being born. These men obviously had started working for Reel Catch after my dad got fired, because they hadn't recognized him. Though by now the name Gernipo-ethy must have already been legend. Dad had been chewed out for some minor infraction, the story goes, when he lifted his manager's desk right up in the air—and this wasn't some small desk, either—and threw it through the window. It fell two stories to the parking lot below. Then Dad spent the night in jail.

It's a story I learned years later, when I was fifteen. By then my mother had already been remarried a while. To Rodney. One night, Rodney got home from his job as customer service manager at the water company and found me in the parking lot setting free a daddy-longleg I'd caught in the bathroom sink. I'd scooped it up in my cupped hands and run outside with it tickling my palms. After I let it go, Rodney and I went inside, and Rodney got a bot-tle of Budweiser from the refrigerator and then told me the story of my dad's night in jail. Rodney liked to tell stories, and I didn't like the way he told this one—his eyes gleaming, hands in motion, voice animated, pausing every so often to take long swallows from his beer. It was exactly the way he told my mom and me the outrageous and sad excuses customers had for not paying their water bill. *But that's Lee*, he concluded. *That's old Lee for you. A real character, that one.*

Except he wasn't a character—he was my dad, even if I hadn't seen him in a few years—and I sat there at the kitchen table wondering what Rodney's point was in telling me a story that made my dad look foolish, till Rodney slapped me on the shoulder and said, as if we were old chums, *But you know something? You don't have one bit of your old man's mean streak in you.*

He went to the refrigerator again, I remember, and came back with two more bottles of Budweiser. *I'm going to give you a beer tonight, son*, he said, and I punched that man in the eye as hard as I could. In thirty minutes a brown shopping bag full of my clothes sat next to me on the curb where you wait for Greyhound busses to take you away to new places. Mom was still out, working the four-to-midnight shift at the Breakneck Beach Diner, and I knew she'd be heartbroken. But I went anyway. When you make up your mind to move on, you move on. And so that's what I did.

Back when I was ten, though, I didn't know the details of Dad's job or how he lost it. I knew that suddenly he had time for fishing, and that he expected me to come along. But once our lines were in the water, he had this way of forgetting I was even there, of looking off at the horizon for long periods, not answering my questions about why clouds went pink at sunrise, or whether fish felt pain when they bit the hook, or whether a tidal wave would demolish this whole town. *Dad?* I would say, trying to draw him back to me. Nothing. *Dad!* My dad was obviously involved in some heavy thinking. All the same, I'd have preferred that he answer my questions.

"Give my son some lures, then, if that's what you're here to do." Dad sure was paying attention now, watching the men hard. The man holding the box of lures handed me three of them. "Is that all you're planning to give my kid? Kid's a good fisherman, needs plenty of lures."

"It's okay, Dad," I said. "Three's enough." But my dad wasn't listening. He had taken a small step closer to the man with the lures, and the men were glancing down at the fishing knife that hung free in Dad's belt. They were taking that knife seriously. Dad spat off to the side, looked again at the man holding the lures, and raised his eyebrows as if waiting for an answer.

The man handed me the entire box. Must've been thirty lures in there, all peacock-looking and ready for action.

"Thanks," I said, taking the box.

"No thanks necessary, son," my dad said. "That's his job, giving out fishing tackle. Don't know what that other man's job is"—he nodded to the dumb-looking one—"I never heard of it taking two men to hand out lures. Big waste of money, you ask me."

"We're on the same sales team," the man said, the man who barely reached my dad's chin.

"Sales team!" My dad ran a hand through his hair. "Fellows are teammates? Like in baseball?" He shook his head in disbelief. "Salesmen have what're called territories," he explained to me. "If they start working in pairs, then they've got to start splitting commissions." He waited for them to dispute what he'd said, but they didn't. "And *that* man"—he nodded to the photographer—"it's that man's job to take pictures of the people who've gotten the lures. Action photos, preferably. Isn't that right? For next year's catalogue?"

The photographer said, "Or the local paper. Or both."

"Well, then," my dad said to me, "let's catch some fish." He pulled the knife from his belt, cut off the lure he'd been using, and dropped it into the little bucket where we kept our tackle. Then he removed one of the Reel Catch lures from its plastic package and tied it on. He did the same with my line, too, then tucked the knife back through his belt. This all took a few minutes. Some other fishermen were on the pier that morning, but I had all the giveaways. So the three men waited.

The fishing pier wasn't two blocks from the firehouse, and as Dad was slowly tying on the Reel Catch lures—deliberately slowly, I'm sure, because I'd seen him tie on lures before in two seconds—the firehouse started blaring its siren. Loudest thing you ever heard. Happened almost every day, far more often than there could be fires. I yelled from deep within my throat: "I love you Carla Van Sickle I love you Carla Van Sickle I love you Carla Van Sickle!" Over and over I yelled it, for maybe thirty seconds. What I knew was, as long as you matched your yelling to the pitch of the siren, nobody could hear you. It could be your own secret. Carla was the third-smartest and second-prettiest girl in my class, and I loved her with a wholeness that I had never loved anybody with before or probably ever would again. She was skinny, with eyes the color of a first-place ribbon and a voice like smooth paint. She wore cutoffs that her mom trimmed for her, and little white strands of denim were always draping down her legs. I walked into walls for her, literally missed doors on purpose, because when I did, she laughed, and her laugh was worth an army of bruises.

By the time the siren died down again, Dad had the Reel Catch lures on. I set down the plastic box at my feet and we both cast our lines into the water. Fluke, we were going for, so we stood there jiggling our rods, waiting for the fish to bite.

"Get yourself ready," Dad said to the photographer.

"Are we going to be in the newspaper?" I asked my dad, and the end of my rod bent over. I yanked the rod upward, and the reel made a metallic buzzing sound, an exhilarating sound, the sound of a big fish. Everything that had been said or thought only seconds before was now miles in the past.

"Dad!" My rod bent like crazy. "I got one!"

The three men came closer. The photographer raised his camera. I imagined Dad and me in the paper, the sports section, and we were smiling big newsprint teeth, and there was a caption that made us seem tough and outdoorsy. I could smell fish blood.

But my dad shook his head. "Nah—he's only caught the ground. Look." He took the rod from my hands and held it steady. The whirring stopped and the rod straightened. He yanked the rod again—more whirring. "See? It's just the ground."

The men exhaled. The photographer lowered his camera.

My dad pulled the knife from his belt and cut the line. "That's one Reel Catch lure we won't be seeing again."

Once the Reel Catch reps saw we weren't catching any fish with their tackle, they and the photographer started muttering to one another about having to get back to the showroom. Yet they waited, and at first Dad appeared to pay no notice, just kept jerking his fishing rod up and down. Finally, without turning toward them, he said, "I don't think you men are going to get what you're after today." Without another word, the men nodded and slunk away.

As soon as they were gone, Dad reeled in his line. "There's a reason I don't use these lures, son. See that hook?" He laid the Reel Catch lure on his palm. "Hook's too big for that lure. The design's all wrong."

I reeled in my line, and we rigged up our old lures again. Dad put the Reel Catch lures back into the plastic box and closed the clasp. "Those are lures of last resort," he said. "If I was stranded on a deserted island with no food, I'd rather try clubbing fish over the head than catching them with a Reel Catch lure."

I laughed, and cast my line into the water. Dad told me that it's more important for lures to reflect light off the sun than it is for them to look like actual fish. Better off using tin foil than some fancy colorful lure.

"I'd rather jump into the water and grab them myself," I said, "than catch them with a Reel Catch lure."

My dad cast his own line into the water. "I'd rather call them on the phone, invite them to dinner, than catch them with a Reel Catch lure."

"I'd rather shoot them with a gun," I said, looking up at my dad, "than catch them with a Reel Catch lure."

"Guns are dangerous," my dad said. "You keep away from guns."

We stood there for a while, not talking, just fishing, until my dad spat over the end of the pier, sized me up, and said, "Biggest animal on Earth's the blue whale, not some dinosaur." Then he said, "Whales eat a lot of plankton. Tons and tons of it."

My dad had been doing some heavy thinking on the pier, but now he was done with thinking. Now he was looking at me, telling me that love made you do crazy things, but that sometimes crazy things were called for. Saying that I'm likely to grow to his height if I eat and sleep enough. That the tide rises just over six feet during a full moon. He was answering every question I'd ever asked, and others I'd forgotten or never asked in the first place.

He said that fighting never got you anywhere, and that only lazy people fished past noon. That tidal waves didn't ever hit this coast. But yes, in theory the town would flood.

He didn't speak quickly, yet there was urgency in his voice as if what he was telling me was vitally important. I know now he believed he was talking with me, father to son, for the last time, and so he was making up for all the lost moments, and the lost moments to come. I have no idea what he had planned, specifically, beyond getting in his car and driving in some predetermined direction, but my hunch is that his destination was beside the point. After leaving Breakneck Beach myself at fifteen, I picked up and moved every year or two, and not once did the destination matter at all. It's more a feeling that if you stay, your bones will crush. Your gut will bleed. You'll behave in a way you can't live with.

A dull knife is more dangerous than a sharp one, he said. In lake fishing, you're better off along the shoreline than in the middle of the lake. He said that every mass has gravity—it's why the Earth revolves around the sun, and why the moon revolves around the Earth. An albacore fights like a fish twice its size. "Albacore's the best thing you'll ever catch," he said, and I imagined what a battle that must be.

"Do you know why the beach erodes?" my dad asked.

I said that I didn't.

So he told me. And then he told me some more.

The next morning at eight-thirty, I got out of bed and found Mom at the kitchen table staring at the wall, a half-eaten English muffin on her plate. The radio was on, the volume low, probably so that it wouldn't wake me. I was almost next to her before she seemed to notice me.

"Where's Dad?" I asked.

Mom pursed her lips, stood, and went to the refrigerator. "Which jelly do you want?" She opened the refrigerator door. "Strawberry?"

"Where is he?" I sat down in one of the kitchen chairs. But she didn't answer me. She'd begun moving things around in the refrigerator, slamming down jars on the shelves, rearranging everything. I started to feel seasick. "Mom?" I tried to sound calm, although I could feel my neck beating and the spit in my mouth going dry. "What's going on? Where is he?"

"*Where is he, where is he . . .*" She slammed the refrigerator door and spun to glare at me. I must have shrunk away, because then her face softened and she came over to the table. She stood over me for a few seconds, just looking. "Listen to me. Just be quiet and listen." She sat next to me at the table. Mom still had long hair then, and some strands had fallen over her face, but she didn't seem to notice. She was watching me closely. "You're ten years old and I'm not going to lie to you. You think your father's a great man, don't you? Your hero, probably. He isn't perfect, you know." She picked up her English muffin, examined it, and put it back in her plate.

I asked her for the millionth time, Where *was* he?

"How the hell should I know?" Mom scrunched up her face like she might sneeze, but she didn't. She stayed frozen that way while the clock over the stove clicked a few times. Then she said, "Sorry. Okay? I'm sorry. I'm just telling you how it is. He leaves sometimes, but he always comes home. The last time, you were too young for me to explain what was going on. You probably don't even remember."

But suddenly I did remember. Sort of. Actually, all I remembered was the seasick feeling, as if the apartment building were rolling in waves, same as I was feeling now. "How many times has he left?" I asked.

"Several times," she said. "But not for a few years."

"Where does he go?"

"That depends. It all depends."

"Why does he leave?" I asked. We were both calming down, now. We were just talking. I was asking questions, and my mother was answering them.

"Your father would say for love. He loves me, so he leaves. He loves me, so he returns. Love, love, love. So finally I said to him . . ." She shook her head. "Well, never mind what I said to him. But don't worry. He'll be back. I'm not going to lie to you. Your father's left, but he's coming back. He'll be back."

Either Dad's departures had lost their weight, or else Mom needed to act as if they had, because she spent the day doing ordinary things. Sweeping. Studying for a class she was taking in stenography. Humming along to the radio. Making me snacks: a plate of bologna and cheese, crackers, slices of carrots.

I couldn't eat. For two days I sat on the rug in the living room with one hand on the telephone, convincing myself that I could feel it preparing to ring. Convinced that if one hand *weren't* on the phone, then it wouldn't ring and it would be my fault.

"Go outside," my mother told me. "I'll let you know if anybody calls."

On the third day, I woke up early without even meaning to, before sunup, and decided to be a man. I got my fishing rod and tackle from behind the washing machine, and without waking Mom I went outside and walked the five blocks to the fishing pier. I didn't want to use the regular lures. They were my dad's, and I didn't want any help from him or his lures. And so I rigged up one of my own—the Reel Catch lures—but all morning long I didn't get a single hit. Dad had been right about one thing: these lures were no good.

A few of the usual fishermen were out, all grown men, everyone standing at a polite distance from one another and looking off to the horizon. Closest to me, a thin, silver-haired man wearing overalls and dirty sneakers uncapped a thermos and poured himself a steaming drink into the lid. He met my gaze while taking a sip and then saluted me with the lid. We were just two men, fishing. I laid down my rod and went over to him.

"Is that coffee?"

When he said that it was, I asked him for a sip. The man creased his forehead at me, he tilted his head, but then he offered the thermos lid and said to be careful, it's hot. I hadn't ever drunk coffee before, and it tasted as bitter as I imagined tar must, but I swallowed a big mouthful anyway, burning my throat some, said thank you, and went for my rod again.

The morning was cooler than usual, the ocean calm, and watching the horizon myself I started making plans. I would quit school and find a job earning money for Mom and me. I imagined starting my own newspaper where I would sell advertising space to companies like Reel Catch. I was ten, but I swear I thought of that idea and several others as well. I would become famous for having a successful newspaper and being so young. I decided to start my newspaper that afternoon, walking door-to-door in the apartment building and selling subscriptions.

When I got home, drunk from my own ideas, both my parents were sitting at the kitchen table, their pinkies interlocked. Mom's eyes were red, but she was smiling and seemed content. Proud almost, as if she'd won a bet with herself. Dad's hair was mussed, he was unshaven, but other than that it could have been any other summer morning.

"Son," my dad said, and nodded as if we were both men who understood something important.

But I understood nothing. Seeing him, all I knew was that I wouldn't get to prove myself after all. There would be no newspaper, no fame, because my dad had failed at something as easy as walking out on us. And feeling disappointed in him made me feel shameful for feeling disappointed, and that, you can imagine, led me to feeling angry, furious, for having been made to feel shame over how I was feeling, which isn't exactly something that a person had any control over. Not at ten. Not when we're talking about a person's dad leaving and then coming home again. I glared at him.

"Well?" he said, his eyes clear and wide and inviting. "Were they biting?"

For a moment I'd forgotten I was carrying a fishing rod. "Like crazy," I said, and went to put away the gear and pretend that he had never even come home. I made it as far as the doorway when my dad must have decided it wasn't time yet to be written off by his own damn son.

"What kind of fish did you catch?"

"Bluefish," I said. "Big ones. And an albacore." I turned around to face him. He was sitting back in his chair, his arms folded, his gaze on me. "Yeah, I did.

And you were right about albacore, it really . . ."—and then I realized too late that he had drawn me into the lie so that he could catch me in it and watch me thrash around.

Population 204

No customers were in the Wawa food mart when the thunderclap hit and the lights went out. At one a.m. there were just the three of us—me in the stockroom tagging cans, Jillian on the register, and Phillip behind the hoagie counter. I felt my way out of the stockroom and looked around the store. The emergency lights had come on and were casting long, weird shadows. And while normally the place is filled with buzzing and humming from the refrigeration unit, the cash register, the air-conditioning—now, nothing. Just the rain hitting the roof overhead and the pavement outside. Jillian and Phillip were looking at me for advice or maybe reassurance. I wasn't used to being looked at for those things. I wasn't even their boss. But after the manager and the assistant manager, I was next in the chain of command. So I told them, "Maybe it'll come back on real quick."

It didn't. We listened to the rain and waited. The rain got heavier, then heavier still. A few people went by on the sidewalk, hunched into themselves underneath their raincoats and umbrellas. Usually this time of night our customers were quiet, middle-aged guys like myself looking for milk and TV dinners. Or they're teenagers with the munchies. Business was slow even on clear nights, let alone a stormy one. I told Jillian and Phillip that they could go home if they wanted. It was summer in New Jersey, and without the air-conditioning the store was already getting stuffy. Customers weren't going to come in here with all the lights off, and the register wouldn't work even if they did. Phillip said thanks, but no thanks. He'd punched in already and needed the money. Standing around like this was easy work.

"You feel the same way, Jillian?" I asked.

She sniffled. "I could use the money."

"You crying?" I asked. She'd been very quiet since she got here. I mean she'd always been quiet, but tonight she was being extra quiet.

She sniffled again. "No, Joe, I'm all right." But I went to aisle three and got a box of tissues anyway.

"You should tell us what's the matter," Phillip said. "Tell us all about it." He came over and sat on Jillian's counter, on the conveyer belt that had stopped moving. I punched my thumb through the top of the tissue box to open it and handed it to Jillian. She pulled out a few tissues, set the box next to her at the register, and dried her eyes as one of the emergency lights back by the fruit flickered a few times and went out.

"So go ahead," Phillip said. "Spill your guts." Phillip studied communications at Jersey Central College, and customers seemed to like talking with him while he made their hoagies. He was very outgoing for a guy with so many pimples on his face. Jillian, on the other hand, kept to herself, rarely saying more to the customers than *Enjoy your day*, or more to Phillip than *Good morning* or *Is there cheese on this hoagie?* So Phillip must have been hoping that with the lights off and him sitting so close, Jillian might open up a little.

"I received a letter today," she said. "My grandmother fell and broke her hip."

"Well, that's too bad," I said. "She an old lady, your grandmother?"

"Eighty-three."

"That's too bad for her—when you break your hip at that age, isn't much chance you're going to walk again." I wasn't saying it to be mean, just stating a fact of life.

"How'd she fall?" Phillip asked. "Stairs?"

"She fell off a tightrope," Jillian said. Phillip looked at me, but I didn't know what to say to that.

Jillian came out from behind the register and opened up a beach chair with porpoises on it that we sold for $9.99. She set the box of tissues on the floor next to her and sighed. "When you drive to my hometown, there's a sign at the border saying Population 204." Phillip was looking at her skeptically. So was I. I'd never heard of a town that small. "This is in Missouri," she said. "A pretty little town in the Ozark Mountains."

So here was her life story, I thought. Unlike Phillip, I wasn't so determined to get quiet people to start talking. I figured that not talking was their right. I felt like not talking myself sometimes, and while Phillip wasn't a bad kid, I had no special urge to communicate with him. Sure, I was lonely, I could have told him. Hadn't seen a naked woman outside of a magazine for four years, not since Lilah's speech got muddy and her memories went haywire and the population of my apartment decreased by one. I could have told him about that. But I wasn't going to.

Jillian must have felt different from me, though, because here came her life story, just for the asking—even if the part about her grandmother walking a tightrope at eighty-three made no sense at all. And when she went on to say that everybody in her little town in the Ozarks was training to be circus performers, I knew she was pulling our leg. What I didn't know was why. I sat on the floor near the two of them, put my arms around my knees, and listened to Jillian talk about the town's children learning to guess people's weight and juggle flaming torches and ride unicycles and paint their faces. "And my best friend growing up," she said, "was a lion named Grouchy."

That old lion was a regular piece of work from the sound of it, rolling around on its back so that you'd scratch its belly and always on the lookout for apple butter. But that wasn't all. This town of hers had a tightrope—the one that led to her grandmother's busted hip—tied between an old sugar maple tree and the schoolhouse. Every day at lunchtime the children in town had to walk the length of the rope before heading home to eat their sandwiches.

"Sounds pretty difficult," I said.

"It wasn't so hard," she said. "Though some days we'd be blindfolded. Other days, we'd have to walk backwards. Anyone fell and the whole class had to start again." Each spring, she explained, the town put on a festival for all the neighboring towns, two whole weeks of circus acts, and part of it was showing off all of the children's new skills.

I wasn't too comfortable sitting on the ground, but I wasn't about to move. This was by far the most I'd heard out of Jillian since she'd applied for the job two years earlier.

"The problem," she said, "was that the town's population was 204. Like the sign said. You've seen signs like that, haven't you? When you drive into a town?"

"I've seen it," I said. "Never a town that small, though."

"Well, in Missouri, towns can get even smaller than that. But my town had 204, like the sign said. Whenever someone died, somebody new was needed in town so that the population would stay at 204. After a funeral, there'd be festive celebrations in the days that followed, so that people would go home and make love, and soon enough there would be a new child—"

When I laughed, Jillian narrowed her eyes as if I'd done something I shouldn't have, and I *felt* ashamed. Then her eyes widened again. "But sometimes a child would be born without someone having passed away first. Those times, people didn't like so much. It meant someone had to die."

"So that the population would stay at 204," I said soberly.

She nodded.

Men coming into the Wawa were always fascinated by Jillian. They'd linger at the register and say things too goofy to say in front of their girlfriends or wives. She wasn't pretty in the usual way—her teeth were crooked, for one, and her arms were thick, and her neck had moles on it—but she had grayish blue eyes that watched you more closely than most eyes did. I would sometimes get to thinking about Jillian when I was at home alone. I didn't run into many women in the course of a day. And of the three women who worked at this Wawa, Jillian was the prettiest. I hadn't ever taken much of a liking to her personally. Not that I didn't like her. I just never felt one way or the other. But that was before I knew she would sit here with the power out and spin tales like this one, touching her throat absently with the bony fingers of her left hand, and clenching her jaw a little when recalling a detail like the brassy *oom-pah* of her mother's tuba-playing.

"Guess my weight," I said to her. "Guess it right now." Not that I even knew my own weight. Probably 230, maybe more. I'd been eating junk for a long time.

"That isn't my skill," she said. "And anyway, I'm telling a story. I'm just about to get to the important part."

But her story got interrupted by two boys, high-school age, knocking on the glass door of the Wawa. They both wore baseball caps and smirks. They looked exactly like every boy I'd ever seen in my entire life. One of them leaned his head in. "You open or what?" Water dripped from the brim of his cap onto the floor.

"Look like we're open?" I didn't get up.

"We're dying for some Wa-dogs, man. Come on, we're starving."

Stoned, too. At night, kids coming in here were always drunk or stoned. I knew they didn't mean it as a personal insult, but I couldn't help thinking of it that way. As if we were people you couldn't come and visit sober.

"We're closed," I said.

After the kids had left, I said to Jillian and Phillip that we ought to eat some hotdogs. Over by the hoagie counter was a machine that rotated the dogs and kept them warm. But with the power off, they were just going to get cold. "What do you say?"

"Lay one on me, big guy," Phillip said. "Jillian?"

"I'm a little hungry," she said.

"Go on with your story," I said, but Jillian waited until I had gone behind the hoagie counter and gotten our dogs. I put mustard and kraut on them and carried them back. Then I went to the refrigerated section and got us each a soda. Jillian handed Phillip and me each a few tissues for napkins.

When I sat down again, we each took a bite of our hotdogs. I liked the idea of this, us all eating together. It felt like something we ought to be doing. Jillian chewed politely and then swallowed. She wiped her mouth with a tissue and explained that whenever there was a birth, one of the town's elders usually would volunteer to keep the town's population steady, but not always. "It could get thorny," she said. One day, the town needed someone to step forward and nobody would, until her favorite schoolteacher said, *I'll do it*. This teacher wasn't old; the only gray in her hair came from worrying about her students.

In a state of despair, early the next morning—and without telling anyone—Jillian did something nobody in her town had ever done: she went away, vowing never to return. All of her money bought her a used car that she drove east, farther and farther, until there were no more states to cross, no more towns. Just a studio apartment and a job as a cashier. She cut her hair short, and colored it brown, and changed her name, because she didn't want any reminders of the life she had left behind.

And after a few years, sometimes entire days went by without her thinking about life back in the Ozarks.

"But now your grandmother is ill," I said.

"Not just ill," she said. "*Old* and ill. And I just keep thinking about that sign."

"Population 204."

"That's right," she said. "So if I'm ever going to see her again—"

"Now wait just a minute," Phillip said. "How'd you find out about your grandmother's injury if nobody knows where you are?"

"My mother knows where I am," she said.

Phillip was missing the point, though, and I wanted to set him right. So what if Jillian was pulling our leg? Who cared, for that matter, why she was doing it? She was taking herself seriously, and so should we.

"Well, I sure am sorry about your situation," I said, and gave Phillip the hard look I gave him whenever he left the deli station a mess. "You must love your grandmother a lot."

"I do."

Phillip sighed. "Do you think . . . you'll go back there, to your circus town?" He glanced at me, and I nodded.

"I'm not sure," she said. "I'm thinking I might."

Jillian took a long draw from her soda. Phillip had already finished his, and asked Jillian for a sip. I felt like I should say something vague and uplifting. But how could I know what to say when I didn't know if her grandmother really was ill, or what sort of town she was raised in, or even if she'd ever been to Missouri? She didn't have a trace of an accent. I didn't even know if her real name was Jillian or not. I didn't know *what* to believe, or if Jillian knew for herself. But I'd have been grateful if the Wawa's lights never came on again. Later, when the sun rose and I was home again, I knew that I'd lie in bed and think about the three of us sitting together in the dark with our hotdogs and sodas. I could almost believe that we were beside a campfire, old friends telling stories from deep inside our hearts.

"I think that'd be the right thing, Jillian," I told her. "It's important to be with your family when they're sick." And before I could stop myself, I was telling them about Lilah. I didn't get emotional. I didn't need to borrow any of Jillian's tissues. But I told them things. How Lilah was exactly my height but wore heels so she'd look taller. How after she lost her sense of smell, she always overdid the perfume. I talked about headaches and seizures. I told the story of how, on one of the last good days, our car had skidded on black ice and nearly gone off a drawbridge, and how for the couple of seconds we were sliding toward the edge I had felt relieved because at least we'd go out together. And when the car had come to a stop up against the guardrail, and we knew we were alive and safe for the moment, I had felt a different sort of relief—a lot like what I was feeling right now, here in the Wawa. With the two of them. Which was probably more than I needed to say. Jillian touched her throat, and Phillip nodded, then wiped his sweaty forehead with his palm. It was getting very warm.

The rain was still hitting the roof, the sky still rumbling, and I had no reason to think the lights were coming on anytime soon. I coughed into my closed fist and suggested that we put all the fruit into shopping carts and wheel them back to the storeroom where there was a refrigerator that even without power would keep things cold for several hours.

"Right, chief," Phillip said, and hopped off the conveyer belt. He extended a hand to Jillian, helping her out of the chair.

The three of us went to the rear aisle, where the fruit was. Jillian started picking over the apples in the dark, lifting one, turning it over in her hand, setting it back down. Before long she had four small apples in her right hand and three in her left.

She threw them high in the air.

❀ ❀ ❀

POETRY

RICHARD LYONS

Richard Lyons is a graduate of the writing programs at the University of Arizona and the University of Houston. He is a recipient of a 1992 Lavan Award from the Academy of American Poets. His books are *These Modern Nights* (University of Missouri Press), *Hours of the Cardinal* (University of South Carolina Press), and *Fleur Carnivore* (The Word Works in Washington, D.C.). Prior to joining the English Department faculty at Mississippi State University in 1994, he taught at Rhodes College in Memphis, TN.

Symmetry

I remember erecting a screened-in porch
for a house I lived in, the staple gun
all afternoon like a giant mosquito

whirring above a sleeper's ear.
One month later, to the day, I found a hummingbird, dead,
and I thought *be careful*

as I turned it over with a long yellow pencil.

It was terrifyingly symmetrical, each wing an inch,
its torso, even its needle nose compass an inch.

Its neck an iridescent emerald.
Its underside a burnt sandalwood ash
coming off a bit with the pencil.

Neither Road Taken

A bright car pulled up where I was walking,
the driver leaning over. I didn't hear his questions,

my arms gesticulated some configuration of streets.

It was winter & ice hung in the branches like a thousand lost
sewing needles descending through the fabric of the afternoon.

It was spring & everything was imminence.
It was summer & the clouds swiftly passed over our heated element.

I told the man I was born beneath the wooden trestle of a train,
that loud noises captured my attention,

not the lefts & rights of destination.

Bearing the white needlepoint of a scar at the base of my neck,
I told him the road to the right was covered in hyacinth,

the one to the left dropped down along the aqueduct to hell.
Choose the oldest, I said to him, choose the oldest.

CATHERINE PIERCE

Catherine Pierce is the author of *Famous Last Words* (Saturnalia, 2008) and *The Girls of Peculiar* (Saturnalia, 2012). Her poems have appeared in *Slate, Boston Review, Ploughshares, The Best American Poetry 2011*, and elsewhere. She earned her B.A. from Susquehanna University, her M.F.A. from The Ohio State University, and her Ph.D. from the University of Missouri. She co-directs the creative writing program at Mississippi State University. The following poems appear in *Famous Last Words*.

Love Poem to Fear

Around you, my body is a wire
pulled taut, my jaw a bear-trap
waiting. You have such wicked timing—

arriving just before I drop
into sleep, or worse, when
the one I'm trying to love

is close enough to see me
waver. Then it's questions
and concern, and I feel only

your fingers on my lips, your teeth
against my neck, your smooth-
as-cyanide voice spinning

all your false promises.
Sometimes you vanish
for days. Then, I sleep

till morning, wake against
a shadowless body to clear sky,
green grass, perfect eggs

for breakfast. Those days
I almost forget you. But you're
no gentleman—no warning

and you're back, all bombast
and mystery. Everything
yours for the taking.

Why You Love the Annoyances in Your Dreams

You can't get your basketball shoes laced.
When you do, the game is nearly over
and you've just realized you're late

for a Spanish final. When you reach
the classroom, you remember you dropped
Spanish three months ago. You rush back

to the game, which is just wrapping up. Then
you're at a conference, but the conference
is in Schenectady and it's March. Also,

the hotel bathroom is covered in cat fur.
Gross, you say. You can't find
the number for your friend's room

and when you do he is that kid
from sixth grade who stole your copy
of *The Hobbit* and called you troll boy.

He wears a business suit and is marginally
successful. He busts you about old times
and on your way out you stub your toe.

In dreams, these annoyances are epic.
Your stomach twists; your teeth grind. And
you love them for this. Even in sleep, you know

that once you drop like a rock into waking,
everything will shift. In your daytime world,
when your car stalls on I-70, or you miss

the big deadline, or the cat runs out of food
during the county's biggest snowstorm
since '94, even as you pound your steering wheel,

even then, you'll know all too well
that these are your life's small highlights.
You're just biding time until the tragedies.

Soon, your wife will take the day off,
make the bed with perfect hospital
corners, and vanish for Cabo.

You'll feel a lump in some never-before-
considered spot. Your mother will fall
and shatter her hip and your sister

will call you, frantic and frightened, but
you'll be across the country
at a conference in Schenectady, New York,

with no one to shake you awake and say,
what a bummer of a night for you, but
it's morning now, wake up, it's morning.

In Which I Imagine Myself Into a Slasher Flick

The Jennies get it first.
The Trishes. The Ambers.
Never my silhouette through
shower steam. Never my red
mouth in close-up. I've got

straight As and no boyfriend.
I've got Friday nights
and sleeping neighbor children.
But worry. Because I've got
an unadorned name. Sharp
vision by moonlight.
My father's rusted hatchet
and a jetliner scream.

"Well, gentlemen, you are about to see a baked Appel."
—last words of gangster George Appel, before being put to death by
electric chair

Each time his girl visited, lips pressed
like stained tulips, cheeks pinched
into heat for the man behind the glass,
she left shaking her head, scuffing
her Sunday shoes against the pavement.

Why did she believe this time
might be different? That this morning
he might remember her breasts beneath
the winter coat, the nub of her earlobe
in his teeth? All he watched for now

was the expression of her mouth.
What about this, he'd say. *What's cooking?*
Or *How about you fry up something good?*
Then he'd grin and say *I'm on fire!*
Electric, even. At first, the girl wept,

chewed her nails—he was hysterical,
surely raped and maddened in that cell.
But each imagined rimshot carried her
further from her wedding,
her sand-white dress, solid hands

around her waist. She tried,
she told her mother. She brought
caramels, pinups, photographs of herself
naked, and he would say *I got a good one*
today. What do you call a fruit in a chair?

What do you get when you cross ...
She threatened to stop coming. But
each time he would beg, his face drooping
like a wet stocking. When the day came,
the girl was there, eyes swollen, hands nervous.

She heard the words, then silence broken
only by his choked laugh, the laugh
broken by the current. In bed that night
she would not tell him how the orderlies
wheeled the gurney in. How,

when they strapped him on, no one
made a sound. She would tell him instead
about the guards doubling over, the priest bowing
into his grin. The whole gray room vibrating
with the aftershock of his wit.